Infrastructure Sustainability
and Design

YOU'RE OVERSEEING A large-scale project, but you're not an engineering or construction specialist, and so you need an overview of the related sustainability concerns and processes. To introduce you to the main issues, experts from the fields of engineering, planning, public health, environmental design, architecture, and landscape architecture review current sustainable large-scale projects, the roles team members hold, and design approaches, including alternative development and financing structures. They also discuss the challenges and opportunities of sustainability within infrastructural systems, such as those for energy, water, and waste, so that you know what's possible. And best of all, they present here for the first time the Zofnass Environmental Evaluation Methodology guidelines, which will help you and your team improve infrastructure design, engineering, and construction.

Spiro N. Pollalis is Professor of Design, Technology and Management at the Harvard Design School, practices as urban planner, and is the Chairman of the public company for the redevelopment of the site of the old Athens Airport in Greece.

Andreas Georgoulias is Lecturer at the Harvard Design School, where he teaches and researches sustainable development.

Stephen J. Ramos is an Assistant Professor in the College of Environment and Design at the University of Georgia.

Daniel L. Schodek is the Kumagai Research Professor of Architectural Technology at the Harvard Design School, where he taught from 1969 until 2008.

Infrastructure Sustainability and Design

EDITED BY

Spiro Pollalis, Andreas Georgoulias, Stephen Ramos,
and Daniel Schodek

Routledge
Taylor & Francis Group

NEW YORK AND LONDON

First published 2012
by Routledge
711 Third Avenue, New York, NY 10017

Simultaneously published in the UK
by Routledge
2 Park Square, Milton Park, Abingdon, Oxon OX14 4RN

Routledge is an imprint of the Taylor & Francis Group, an informa business

Library of Congress Cataloging in Publication Data
Infrastructure sustainability and design / Spiro Pollalis ... [et al.].
     p. cm.
Includes index.
1. City planning--Environmental aspects. 2. Urban ecology (Sociology) 3. Sustainable development.
4. Ecological engineering. I. Pollalis, Spiro N., 1954-
NA9053.E58I54 2012
711'.12—dc23
2011019546

ISBN: 978-0-415-89316-9 (hbk)
ISBN: 978-0-203-12031-6 (ebk)

Designed and typeset by Alex Lazarou

Printed and bound in India by Replika Press Pvt Ltd

CONTENTS

FOREWORD

THE BEGINNING OF MY PASSION for the environment began where I grew up in Belmont, Massachusetts. It was a little house surrounded by woods on Belmont Hill, and it was through those woods that I first developed my appreciation for nature and the natural world. That is where this story really begins. After graduating from Harvard University I spent 15 years working on Wall Street at which point I made the decision to apply my sense of finance to the challenge of the environment. I started the Environmental Financial Consulting Group in 1990 and our purpose and mission was to help environmental engineering consulting firms operate more effectively, more efficiently, more profitably, and to help them grow and provide better services to their clients. In essence, we helped them perform their own environmental missions.

The difficulty when dealing with the environment is that it is not a single issue, problem, or challenge. We need the brain power, insight, and knowledge from various different fields if we are going to be able to solve some of the great environmental challenges of our time.

I, like many, have been very impressed recently with the sustainable rating systems for buildings: their ability to bring attention to sustainability, establish a set of metrics, and sensitize people to important issues. I had to ask the question, '*Could we do the equivalent for large infrastructure projects?*' What about the airports, the bridges, the roads, the parks, and the wastewater facilities? What about the numerous large infrastructure projects taking place all over the world? Could we come up with a way of measuring, analyzing, and evaluating the sustainability of infrastructure projects in a way that would encourage people to maximize that sustainability? That was the seed of this endeavor.

I recognized that if anyone could appreciate and understand the subtlety and issues of sustainable design it would be the engineering and design firms who were our clients. I also felt that Harvard University with its Center for the Environment and various pockets of genius in the field could also play a key role. It occurred to me that the engineers and designers who would be implementing this system, with their cumulative knowledge and practical experience, combined in a collaborative effort with the best of what Harvard had to offer through all of its different departments and schools might provide the answer we needed.

I feel there are three unique elements of this project. The first is the power of Harvard University: the strength of their research, and the convening power they bring to the table. The second is the fact that a majority of the leading engineering firms are committed to this effort. The 25 engineering firms who have been engaged since the project's inception represent $50 billion in engineering revenues, or 60–70 percent of all engineering revenues worldwide. The third is the opportunity to develop a set of metrics, a measurement of sustainable infrastructure that will have a significant impact on preserving our environment.

I wish to thank all who have provided their time, insights, knowledge, experience, and energy in developing a meaningful response to the great environmental questions we face, what I feel is a global mandate, in order to help us fulfill our responsibility as citizens of this wonderful world, to fulfill this critical mission; this global challenge.

Paul Zofnass
The Environmental Financial Consulting Group

ACKNOWLEDGMENTS

This book is the result of the first two years of the research of the Zofnass Program for Sustainable Infrastructure at Harvard University. The decision for the book to be produced was made at the very first meeting with the Harvard advisers in February 2009, as a joint effort of Harvard and the industry advisers of the Zofnass Program.

Paul Zofnass and his sister Joan Zofnass have provided their generous financial, emotional, and often administrative support to the Zofnass Program and have embraced enthusiastically the publication of this book. Spiro Pollalis, Andreas Georgoulias, and Dan Schodek, and many students, graduates, and faculty members at Harvard University have carried out the research. Industry advisers have financially supported the program, reviewed the produced material, and participated in quarterly meetings, ensuring that the research effort is linked to the frontiers of industry needs. Aimee Taberner and Brian Kenet, core members of the Zofnass Program team, have been instrumental in multiple ways towards the materialization of this effort. Anthony Kane, MDES '10, has reviewed this publication, and Richa Shukla, MAUD '10, has worked with the visual material.

Infrastructure Sustainability
and Design

Introduction:
Sustainability—A Broad Perspective

SPIRO POLLALIS AND DANIEL SCHODEK
HARVARD UNIVERSITY GRADUATE SCHOOL OF DESIGN

A FRAMEWORK FOR THE SUSTAINABILITY OF INFRASTRUCTURE

This book summarizes the first phase of the research on the environmental sustainability of infrastructure as part of the Zofnass Program at Harvard University. In the fall of 2008, when we started the Program, there was little available to meaningfully address and measure the impact on the environment of large infrastructure systems.

Our vast networks of energy, water, waste, transportation, landscapes, and communications are the fundamental means by which our society sustains life and well-being. These systems inherently impact on and interact with our environment and the natural processes that occur within it. In our society, climate change, energy use, clean water, and other environmental issues are commonly discussed and debated—yet surprisingly little attention is paid to the environmental roles of our great infrastructure systems. On the other hand, much attention has recently been paid to buildings as single, stand-alone units.

The usage and definition of the term "sustainability" vary widely. In its broadest connotation, sustainability encompasses interactive environmental, social, and economic issues that are present within local, regional, and global contexts and with a time dimension. Cultural, political, geographic and other factors are key dimensions; scale and scope are relevant as well. The idea of "meeting the reasonable needs of the current generation while enhancing the lives and systems of future generations," or at least not preventing future generations from meeting their needs, runs through most discussions of sustainability. Still, any specific meaning of the term remains elusive. The term can be construed to apply to everything from the continuance of life in the universe to impacts of land development in suburbia on food production. This scope is intellectually exciting, but less than useful in any attempt to systematically assess the degree to which sustainability is actually achieved within a specific context.

In the remainder of this book, we focus primarily on *environmental sustainability* and in treating it in a way that makes environmental evaluations and assessments on specific infrastructure projects feasible. Links and interactions with social and economic sustainability are identified and appreciated, but not systematically addressed.

THE FOUR AXES OF ENVIRONMENTAL SUSTAINABILITY

As part of the Zofnass research, we have defined the dimensions of environmental sustainability along four axes:

- allocation of resources
- impact on the natural world
- climate change
- quality of life.

These four dimensions address how we use the resources of the planet, what is the impact on habitats, what is the impact on the environment as a whole, and finally what is the impact on humans. The latter focuses on health and well-being, which may include socio-economic elements, constituting the framework for future expansion into social and economic sustainability. The stated dimensions are big and often controversial topics in themselves, with their own definitional problems. Nonetheless, they are useful in conveying the character of operationally useful measures for understanding the relative sustainability of diverse projects.

Resource allocation objectives aim for the optimal usage of resources that will have the least impact on the current environment and resource availability, and which will maximize the potential of future generations to have access to the resources they will need. Major subcategories include energy, materials, and water. The *natural world* is considered to be defined by measures that seek to preserve and enhance the ecological systems that sustain us, such as built infrastructure that seek to minimize disruptions to land of high biodiversity and high habitat quality, and that promote the rejuvenation and growth of degraded systems. Major subcategories include habitat and site selection. *Climate change* considerations aim to minimize long-term climate change, resulting from human activities and infrastructure, and to promote infrastructure projects that are adaptable and resilient to future conditions that may result from climate change. Major subcategories include carbon emissions and adaptability to climate change. *Quality of life* considerations aim to maximize the quality of life of those who are affected by infrastructure projects, both now and in the future. Within this framework, infrastructure is viewed as having a dual function: first to provide the required service, and second to provide this service at an acceptable quality level. Major subcategories include: social, economic, and political wellness; health and wellness; education; information and values. Later we will see that these categories and subcategories can be used to establish specific environmental evaluation measures.

Types of infrastructure

In its broadest sense, the term infrastructure can refer to the many fundamental facilities and services that support the functioning of an organization, community, or society; as such, it can have physical, social, political, and other dimensions. Physical infrastructure systems, for example, include transportation and communications systems, while institutions, including schools, hospitals, and post offices, are often classed as infrastructure when discussing how societies function. This book will focus on the set of fundamental *physical* systems, services, and networks that support the built environment and protect the natural world, and that are essential to sustaining a civilized and productive society. Major infrastructure categories within this characterization are energy, water, waste, transportation, landscape, and information. There are overlaps and synergies when it comes to characterizing specific systems, but the broad categories are a useful device for conceptualizing physical infrastructure as it relates to the built environment.

Energy systems are familiarly subcategorized in terms of their sources (oil, gas, nuclear, renewable, and other), their transformation to produce energy, and the energy distribution. *Water* systems consist primarily of water supply, stormwater removal and retention systems, and wastewater systems. *Waste* systems include solid waste and recycling systems. *Transportation* systems include familiar air, rail, and vehicular systems, but also waterways and ports. The *landscape* category addresses land use at large and includes both private and public realm spaces for *societal* needs. The *information* systems category addresses telecommunications and other artifacts of our modern age, including management and control of all infrastructure systems.

Most of these broad categorizations of infrastructure types can be further conceptualized as being either networks or nodes in greater systems. This distinction is useful in defining the target or scope of any sustainability study. Network components typically serve distribution or collection functions, while nodal points are often locations of different kinds of facilities for a variety of source, treatment, and control needs. Distribution and collection networks can be characterized in terms of their geometries and extents. In some cases, the "facility" characterization dominates a target of concern in a sustainability study, e.g., an airport within an air transportation system. In other cases the "network" characterization is dominant, e.g., transportation routes. Obviously, as one drills down, most major facilities are in turn composed of their own networks and nodes, depending on planning centralized or decentralized infrastructure systems. For example, airports have many network-oriented systems for baggage handling, people movement, refueling, etc., but also have major components that are subfacilities unto themselves, e.g., individual terminal buildings. In making an environmental valuation of a project, a clear definition of these networks and components is obviously necessary, since these components are what are ultimately built and that create the environmental impact.

Measuring sustainability

After defining the framework for both sustainability and infrastructure, the focus shifts on how the sustainability of infrastructure projects can be measured and evaluated. Methods for measurement and evaluation of performance are invariably a key component of any attempt to improve the planning and operation of complex systems. However, many individuals, organizations, and agencies are highly interested in using such a system. Airports, for example, have created their own sustainability guidelines, imposing financial penalties to older planes or even banning them. However, when most of the focus is on the sustainability of the buildings and the terminal, most of the impact of air traffic is lost. Other industries and large consulting firms have also sought to create sustainability guidelines to help them understand issues and guide their clients on infrastructure development. Nevertheless, the lack of a uniform and consistent approach invariably creates problems for all groups involved—from design and engineering firms to oversight agencies. Industry standards are needed to level the field and give credibility to the methods used to ensure sustainable projects, and the Zofnass Program aims to fill this gap.

Developing a consistent approach to measuring and evaluating infrastructure sustainability is not easy. What is the hierarchy of measures or metrics that can be used to characterize sustainability? Going beyond the high-level measures of climate change, the natural world, resource allocation, and the quality of life, what are the more specific evaluation metrics that should be used to think about design features for energy, water, waste, transportation, large landscape complexes, and information systems? Do we consider all components of the entire value chain of processes, products, and activities that surround the inception, design and development, use and decommissioning of an infrastructure system, or some selected aspect? What are the boundaries of the system evaluated? Any methodology for the environmental evaluation of a project is a tool that can be put to different purposes. Is it to provide an understanding of the environmental qualities and impact of a project, a form of guide? Is it to provide a basis for comparing competing project alternatives? Is it to be used as a decision-making tool for a group to decide whether to proceed or not proceed with actually building a project (a go/no-go decision-making tool)? Can it have any kind of legal mandate? Who makes these evaluations, and who judges results?

In other fields, too much attention is paid to reduce the consumption per unit, with little attention to the need and the resulting absolute numbers. An insulation-packed residence may be certified based on a metric on energy use per unit of floor area regardless if a closer look reveals that the house is occupied by a couple but comprised over 5000 square feet (464 square meters) of floor area. A metric based on energy use per capita would have captured the situation more accurately. Many metrics that are promulgated as efficiency measures and widely used in the engineering world, however, are based on some sort of unit basis and can be similarly misleading.

A confounding reality is that there are many different stakeholders—from government agencies to environmental advocates and the general public, from planers, designers, and engineers to contractors—involved with the lifetime of most infrastructure systems that often tend to have different sustainability objectives and related value systems. These many questions are briefly addressed in the chapters of this book.

As we look to the future, new cities are being planned throughout the world and the need to have clear design intentions *vis-à-vis* urban sustainability is becoming increasingly important, with a direct impact on the planning and design of their infrastructure systems. Furthermore, our existing cities and towns are in need of thoughtful changes. The chapters in Part 4 of this book deal with such planning opportunities in greater depth.

SHEDDING LIGHT ON SOME FUNDAMENTAL ISSUES OF THE ZOFNASS FRAMEWORK

Several issues and the related questions were raised by the research team, the Harvard Academic Advisors, and the Sustainability Industry Advisory Board in the process of exploring the vast territory of the sustainability of infrastructure. Answering some of these questions took a long time and had a positive impact on our research. Among those are:

The economics dimension

In this day and age it is almost impossible to divorce questions of project cost or economic and social impact. For truly large public infrastructure projects, questions of broad-scale economic and social impact as reflected in issues such as job creation are everyday newspaper concerns that in turn have strong political dimensions to them. Literal project costs and possible impacts on taxes or other societal services are likewise of intense concern.

From the viewpoint of structuring an environmental evaluation methodology, the question naturally arises as to whether economics and costs should be directly part of any assigned rating, or if the rating should be concerned only with describing environmental qualities. This is not an easy choice. Many stakeholders in a project, ranging from overseeing public agencies to many engineering companies engaged in project design, would very much welcome a formal decision-making tool that includes costs and economic considerations. It is generally argued that costs are too important to "leave out" and projects would be better designed with them included. Full accountability is also argued.

Conversely, the inclusion of costs or economic concerns in an environmental evaluation leads many to argue that the value of the methodology in really understanding the environmental consequences of a project is irrevocably compromised, even to the extent that a project with truly poor environmental qualities might be highly rated. Examples here abound. Recently, public leaders with strong community support in an economically depressed seacoast town in Greece moved to establish a power plant burning low-quality coal—normally a recipe for receiving low environmental ratings—primarily because of the economic benefits that might locally accrue, including job creation and independence from imported gas or oil.

This general problem is hardly a new one. Discussions related to costs and benefits have probably been part of every infrastructure project ever built anywhere, with "benefits" being as broadly construed as needed within the context of the society and the times. The term "costs" is also often similarly broadly or narrowly construed. To many economists, costs can refer to all sorts of impacts. To others, costs might refer to literal and immediate project expenses for design, construction, and operations. In this discussion, we will adopt the more literal meaning of costs and use the term "economics" to refer to broader issues.

A number of methodologies have evolved over the years to deal with how to incorporate both cost and economic concerns with the benefits or positive attributes of a project. Perhaps the most well known is "cost–benefit analysis," where explicit numerical values are assigned to all benefits—even seemingly intangible ones—as a way of expediting comparisons. "Life cycle cost analysis" looks at not only the initial costs of designing and constructing a project, but also at the costs of its operations over its lifetime. This involves making projections about not only initial expenses, but also cost (e.g., maintenance, renovation, modification) and revenue streams

over the expected lifetime of a project. There are relative advantages and disadvantages to these many different approaches. From an environmental evaluation point of view, any methodology that converts environmental assessment measures into some type of cost equivalent for decision-making purposes is problematic. Major understandings of the effects of a project on important measures related to the natural world, resource use and allocation, climate change, and the quality of life can easily get lost or subsumed in hard-to-understand hybrid figures.

Who pays for sustainable infrastructure?

Among the fundamental questions, as we address the sustainability of infrastructure, is the additional cost and who will assume that cost. Although some argue that sustainable infrastructure may not cost more, it is hard to support such an argument based only on design and construction costs, and without considering life cycle costing. When we consider life cycle costing, sustainable projects may cost less. Sustainable projects may become more cost-efficient when we consider and properly price externalities related to quality of life, the natural world, and climate change. However, not only are such externalities not part of the budget of the project, but also operating costs often come from different budgets. Looking at what happens with buildings offers little help. As a rule, sustainable buildings, based on the prevailing rating systems, cost almost the same as other buildings, have a higher market value, and bring higher rents, so market forces drive developers to build sustainable buildings.

According to politicians and marketers, sustainable infrastructure will succeed only when cost is properly addressed. The dilemma to build a less sustainable project that will cost less is real and taxpayers may not see benefits, especially when such benefits are outside their immediate reach, such as limiting climate change. Based on our analysis, market forces alone may not be sufficient and policy will be required to build sustainable infrastructure, at least initially and until the benefits will be well understood.

A single rating system for all infrastructure types?

Infrastructure types are quite diverse. How much is there in common between a power plant and an airport? How can a common rating system address the sustainability of such diverse projects? This has been an accepted challenge for the Zofnass Program. We did not want to create specialized systems for each type of infrastructure. On the contrary, our effort was to identify a broad net that could cover within reason the entire spectrum of infrastructure works.

What is the boundary of an infrastructure project regarding sustainability?

The operations of infrastructure projects, the primary focus for rating their sustainability, expand well beyond their physical boundaries. Airports serve as a typical example. Airports are part of the larger transportation network and they are nodes to its sustainability. So, what is the sustainability boundary of an airport? Is it the project site? Does it include the immediate air space? Does it include the ground transportation to the city? Does it include the entire air space until the plane lands at the destination airport? Depending on the definition, the boundary for rating the sustainability of the airport may be beyond reach.

Planning: assessing alternatives

One of the thorniest aspects of evaluating a project is that of whether it is needed at all in the first place. Then, what should be the right approach to address the problem? If the project is built, no matter what the need, then there will indeed be sustainability consequences. We would hope, of course, that the project would have positive features that would lead to an overall enhancement in some aspect of sustainability important to society. This is surely the case with many of our infrastructure developments that provide needed water, energy, or some other service vital to our well-being.

For large projects, the question of need is invariably played out within a larger socio-political platform involving many stakeholders.

This arena has its own rules, or lack thereof, and how consensus is reached is a topic largely outside of the scope of this book. Environmental sustainability evaluations can add value to this discussion, however, in helping all groups understand project implications. Nonetheless, these evaluations must usually be made on the basis of only very preliminary planning and design documents, and are thus inherently somewhat speculative. However, there is urgency in developing reliable evaluation approaches that aid in this stage of the process. In the methods suggested in this book, once a go decision is made for a project—even one with perhaps dubious need from the viewpoint of some stakeholders—the evaluation intent is to aid in making the resultant project as sustainable as possible.

Any form of evaluation methodology could potentially be used as an aid to making decisions that affect the design and construction of a project. Certainly a desired use is to decide whether a proposed project should be built at all (a go/no-go decision). Another desired use is to compare and select among alternative design proposals. Making any kind of decision on a major infrastructure project is, of course, an inherently intense project that attracts the interest of many different kinds of stakeholders. As already noted above, these stakeholders often have widely differing values *vis-à-vis* environmental concerns, which are intrinsically difficult to mediate.

Being true to promise: rate future stages

In any sustainability evaluation, it is necessary to define exactly *what* is being evaluated. In consumer goods, this is at first a seemingly trivial task—it is the object itself. In architecture, it is "the building." For infrastructure, a "water system" means the purification of water and the network for delivering water to the user.

In the definition of sustainability discussed in a previous section, the phrase "with a time dimension" was used. This refers to the basic question of when and how long sustainability issues are considered. In sharp contrast to most consumer goods whose production and use lifetimes are short, infrastructure systems invariably take a long time to design and construct, and then they can be in active use for a very long time. Decades are common, but even longer is not unusual for some types, during which time they may be significantly modified, renovated, or upgraded. Environmental impacts change throughout these stages. For major infrastructure projects, the project timeline can be usefully considered as a series of major delivery phases: planning, design, construction, operations, and decommissioning. Operation phases are normally the longest, although construction phases can last surprisingly long as well. What is relevant at the moment is that the kinds of sustainability issues present in each phase can be radically different. Not only are potential impacts different, but who and what is impacted can differ as well. Local community businesses near a construction site, for example, might be very negatively impacted during construction phases, but could positively benefit after the project is completed. As will be seen in Chapters 14 and 15, evaluation methodologies often differ in their focus or emphasis, depending on the project phases under consideration. The Zofnass methodology discussed in Chapter 16 assigns a separate value for each phase.

Extending the time notion, we should include much earlier stages of material extraction, production, and transportation when considering sustainability. There are potential environmental impacts at each stage. The sustainability impact notions need not be conceptualized in terms of value chains alone. Simple interconnected cause-and-effect analyses always remain useful. Uncontrolled emissions from a plant might well cause downwind air pollution and health sustainability consequences to populations far removed from the plant itself.

A rating system or design guidelines?

For determining the sustainability of a project, varying types of evaluation measures can be established, including goals, requirements, guidelines, metrics, standards, etc. In the Zofnass framework, these measures are based on the four broad sustainability categories: resource use and allocation, natural world, climate change, quality of life, but underlying criteria could be defined in other ways as well. *Goals* broadly define the aspired sustainability results. What are we trying to accomplish? *Requirements* define what

function a project or some component must minimally provide to achieve these goals. *Metrics* are used to quantify the performance, efficiency, or progress of a project towards meeting goals. Units of measurement are specified. *Standards* are established with acknowledged criteria for performance. Normally, standards are monitored for compliance by an overseeing organization or agency. Related code requirements and regulations are normally legally enforceable. *Guidelines*, by contrast, are by definition not mandatory, but do serve to provide recommended rules or procedures for determining best practice or a course of action. Some leeway, however, is provided. As discussed in Chapter 15, existing evaluation methodologies often make use of a mix of these approaches, but usually with one or another dominating.

In any evaluation methodology, clarity with regard to the use of the above measures is absolutely essential. Rigorously defined and quantitatively measurable criteria are attractive, but a methodology based solely on these kinds of measures may not only be costly and difficult to implement on a specific project, but also may fail to capture the essence of many important sustainability goals that are inherently hard to quantitatively represent. A quantitative metric cannot be established, for example, if the performance reflected cannot be measured in any reasonable and repeatable way. The question of whether the set of metrics does indeed capture a project's sustainability performance always remains pertinent. Actual standards, in turn, should be based on valid metrics. If standards are indeed to be monitored for compliance, then it is necessary to establish an appropriate and acknowledged oversight body; otherwise, the standards should rather be considered as non-mandatory goals or guidelines.

Many existing sustainability efforts have assumed the form of non-mandatory guidelines, often with a liberal mix of quantifiable metrics and qualitative recommendations for best practices.

Based on the principle that "what cannot be measured cannot be improved," our objective from the very beginning has been to establish a rating system, a system to measure the sustainability of infrastructure projects. However, the very same rating system can be transformed to a series of guidelines to navigate the decision makers towards a sustainable infrastructure project.

A single rating or four broad ratings?

All methodologies for assessing the environmental sustainability of a project, which have aimed at yielding a single-valued "result" or "rating," face problems in comparing and reflecting value for different sustainability dimensions. In terms of the four broad categories of sustainability described earlier, for example, how are impacts with regard to the "natural world" valued relative to those in the "quality of life"? Design approaches that might seek to reduce "climate change" impacts might adversely impact seemingly judicious approaches to "resource allocation." Similarly, when projects are evaluated with the intent of getting a single-valued "rating," relative judgments of this type must invariably be made, which in turn can be dependent on the goals and values of the evaluator; hence, they can be quite controversial. Nonetheless, such value judgments are implicitly or explicitly made in many existing evaluation schema.

Who certifies the rating?

The certification can be obtained in two ways. First, a dedicated organization monitors the compliance to the established set of metrics. This is a major consideration, as monitoring bodies require commitment and resources to maintain. As with the need for a group to maintain and monitor evaluation standards, there is also the need to clearly identify "who judges," what documentation is required and what is the timeframe for such certification. Alternatively, the client or a major shareholder can self-certify his or her facility, following detailed procedures in a transparent process. The latter is simpler, is less arbitrary, and can be equally effective if posted on the Internet and is accessible to all parties concerned.

How can we secure innovation?

Any rating system must reward innovation. A rating system based on multiple choices inherently limits innovation as all possible outcomes have been considered by the makers of the rating system in advance. In a rapidly changing field, such as sustainability, the rating system must allow open-ended responses, to provide the setting for innovative alternatives that may not have been considered earlier. Nevertheless, such new concepts must be evaluated by settings that allow open-minded, knowledgeable people to apply judgment in evaluating scientific evidence and prudent management. Such an example is the capturing of carbon emissions of power plants and storing them under the sea bedrock, an untested but highly promising technology to reduce emissions in the air while providing safe energy.

Part 1
Dimensions of Sustainability

PERHAPS THE GREATEST STEP the current generation has taken toward truly understanding sustainability is the recognition of the broad and interdisciplinary impacts it has. These can be grouped into the four categories of mitigating man-made impacts on the earth's climate, efficiently using our natural resources for generations to come, protecting and preserving the natural world, and maintaining a high quality of human life. For each, a unique set of challenges and questions must be addressed and the first step in finding solutions is understanding the issues. Within this section we begin by identifying the scope of the challenge that faces developing sustainable infrastructure.

1

Climate Change and Infrastructure

RICHARD JOHN

NATIONAL ENERGY FOUNDATION, UK

CLIMATE CHANGE is a major risk factor that long-term infrastructure developments need to address. The world has already warmed (see Figure 1.1) and the rate of change is likely to increase significantly. Climate change risks are both direct and indirect (see Figure 1.2). There is a need for infrastructure projects to adapt to a changing climate and, with the developments they serve, to mitigate the effects of climate change through the reduction of carbon emissions.

A key issue in designing and operating infrastructure projects to ensure that they are sufficiently resilient in the face of climate change is their long-term nature and the significant uncertainty associated with risk. It is likely that the indirect impacts of climate change—for example on the developments that the infrastructure serves—will on the whole be more significant than their direct impact on the infrastructure project.

As such, the most credible approach to ensuring that infrastructure development projects can live with, or adapt to, climate change is to undertake a comprehensive Life Cycle Assessment of risk to both the infrastructure project and developments that the infrastructure supports. An approach can then be adopted that aims to maximise the project's resilience in a way that does not incur undue economic costs.

Given the huge long-term impacts of climate change and the current uncertainty and unpredictability of attempts to correct climate change through so-called geo-engineering—an issue that may also have an impact on infrastructure—there is a compelling case to ensure that infrastructure and the developments it supports is designed and implemented to minimise life cycle carbon emissions.

Recognising its importance, given the timescale over which climate change operates, and its interactions with other sustainability issues, risk assessment associated with infrastructure development and operation should include a broad range of sustainability issues including climate change. Other key uncertainties that this chapter will cover are the impact of technological developments, the importance of developments associated with governance as well as technology and economics, and the role of infrastructure companies.

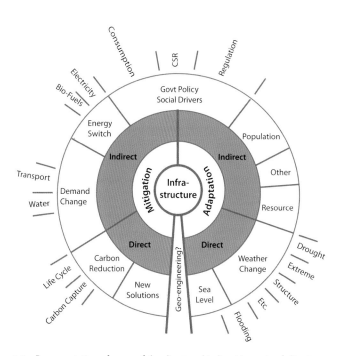

Temperature Anomaly (°C)

-2.5   -1.5   -0.5   0   +0.5   +1.5   +2.5

1.1 Mean surface temperature change for the period 2000 to 2009 relative to the average temperature from 1951 to 1980
Source: NASA

1.2 Representation of some of the direct and indirect impacts of climate change on infrastructure

CLIMATE CHANGE

Climate change has been cited as the most challenging environmental issue faced by mankind. The science of climate change at the global level is relatively mature,[1] and there is a strong scientific consensus that increasing greenhouse gas concentrations in the atmosphere will result in increased temperatures. Significant global warming has already been observed (see Figures 1.3, 1.4 and 1.5) over the last hundred years, and the scientific consensus is that this warming is associated with anthropogenic effects (i.e., caused by man). Projections for average global temperature rises by the end of the century vary depending on assumptions used regarding the growth of carbon emissions—largely linked to economic growth and the model used to project the degree of warming. By the end of the century, an additional temperature rise of between 2 to 4°C is fairly typical, but with significant regional effects. More extreme weather events, and a sea level rise that recent estimates place as a maximum of 2 meters, are expected. Acidification of the ocean and associated impact on marine life such as coral reefs are also projected.

Global temperature rise projections cannot be lightly dismissed when it comes to decisions regarding infrastructure developments, although the projected impacts on a particular development are less easy to consider because predicted temperature rises will have significant impacts for almost all human activities.[2]

At the same time climate change has two other attributes:

- It is long term in its impacts, and there is considerable uncertainty associated with the magnitude and timescale of climate variations at a local level.[3]
- There is considerable uncertainty as to how climate change will have indirect impacts on infrastructure development and its use, for example due to the disruption of the global energy supply.

As such, politics and uncertainty are as relevant to infrastructure development as the potential to reduce greenhouse gas emissions from a particular infrastructure development, or the design and engineering options available to allow it to be adapted to future climate change.

Embedding climate change for future infrastructure developments therefore requires an understanding of two key areas:

- The risks (political, economic, value, supply and demand changes, etc.) associated with climate change in terms of infrastructure and the developments it will serve over its projected lifetime.
- The potential to increase the resilience, and value, of a particular infrastructure development in the face of both the direct and indirect impacts of climate change.

RESPONSE TO CLIMATE CHANGE

It is broadly accepted[4] that solutions to climate change include a combination of measures including:

- ending deforestation, increasing reforestation
- renewable energy use
- fossil fuel power generation with carbon capture and storage
- nuclear energy
- energy efficiency
- low carbon transportation
- low carbon manufacturing/production
- use of materials for construction with low embodied energy (carbon) and a move to those that sequester carbon
- reducing the need to transport people and goods through appropriate spatial planning.

Whilst there is no legally binding international treaty to deal with climate change, the response to climate change by the European Union (EU)[5] and the UK specifically indicate the likely range of measures to both ensure mitigation and adaptation to climate change. For example, the Climate Change Act sets a legally binding target of an 80% reduction in greenhouse gas emissions by 2050 cf. 1990.[6]

1.3 Landslides associated with more extreme weather events will disrupt transport and other infrastructure projects. Risk assessment and cost–benefit analyses can be undertaken to protect key infrastructure assets
Source: FEMA

1.4 Wildfires are more likely in those areas that will become hotter and drier—steps will need to be taken to minimize disruption to infrastructure such as electricity grids
Source: US Marine Corps

1.5 Flooding, New Orleans, Hurricane Katrina. Rising sea levels and predicted increased incidence of extreme weather events will make many coastal communities more prone to flooding, so requiring a review of flood defence options globally
Source: Executive Office of the President

In the UK, senior government advisers have said that, in addition to strenuous efforts to reduce greenhouse gas emissions (mitigation), the UK should prepare itself to adapt to 4°C of climate change by the end of the century, and many infrastructure companies now have a compulsory requirement to report on the extent to which they are planning their infrastructure to be resilient in the face of climate change. The EU has developed its own views on what relatively modest rises in atmospheric emissions mean for Europe.[7]

In the UK the approach to a low carbon economy by 2050 will include the decarbonisation of the electricity supply system, and energy switching from fossil fuel use to electricity provided by low carbon sources.[8] This will be achieved through a supply side mix of:

- nuclear
- renewables
- fossil fuel with carbon capture and sequestration
- sustainable biofuels
- aggressive energy efficiency measures so as to address limitations associated with supply-side timetable, and rate of technological innovation
- use of waste heat.

Associated with the above is the use of embedded generation in new and refurbishment projects (renewables, and Combined Heat and Power (CHP) Systems), with the additional benefit of supporting a degree of resilience within the electricity network. The proposed generating mix, and extensive use of embedded generation and fuel switching, implies the need for smart grid systems.

Transportation systems that encourage modes that are inherently more carbon efficient have also been proposed.

Most of the measures listed above will affect new and existing infrastructure projects either directly or indirectly. The example also highlights the current situation, which is that governments sometimes need to use legislation, regulations, and price signals to encourage infrastructure companies to invest in low-carbon solutions that are resilient in the face of climate change.

CLIMATE CHANGE RISKS—DIRECT

Globally the world will warm, but the extent to which it will, how this global change will affect communities and infrastructure at a local level, and the timescale associated with changes are less certain. An assessment of the literature supports the hypothesis that, as our knowledge of climate change as a physical science improves, the projections of the rate at which the climate is changing, and the extent to which it will change, are becoming more extreme.

Figures 1.6a and 1.6b are examples of projections of rainfall and temperature across Europe towards the end of the century.[9] However, it should be recognised that different climate models and economic growth forecasts result in different projections, underlining that projections of climate change at a local level are subject to significant variation. Figures 1.6a and 1.6b also highlight the very significant changes that are predicted for Europe, with subsequent impacts on infrastructure and infrastructure requirements. Modelling work has shown that under a broad range of assumptions and models the impact for some parts of Europe are reasonably consistent—in the case of Spain, most, but not all, projections conclude that it will become significantly hotter and drier—whereas the outcomes for other areas are far less consistent. Although ongoing improvements in climate models mean that projections of climate change at a global level are likely to continue to improve, these models will continue to be affected by assumptions associated with future levels of greenhouse gas emissions. Climate modelling at the local level will also be less certain than that associated with global predictions.

The work in figures 1.6a and 1.6b illustrates the levels of climate change on a regional basis under a range of scenarios and models. Other, more recent, modelling work has shown that the level of climate change illustrated in Figures 1.6a and 1.6b in Europe might conceivably occur closer to 2060 than the end of the century.[10]

Studies associated with Figures 1.6a and 1.6b, and elsewhere[11] give some sense of the range of adaptation strategies that will be increasingly necessary with infrastructure projects, but which will clearly differ depending on geographic location and actual outcomes including:

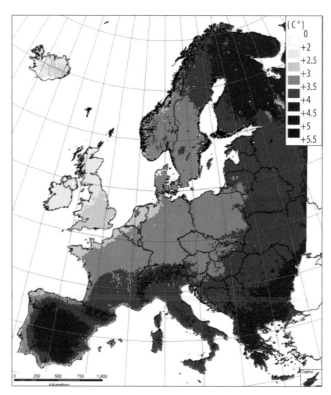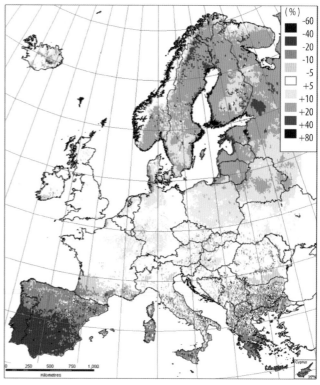

1.6a and b

Projections of climate change impacts in Europe towards the end of the century—temperature and rainfall

Source: European Commission

- flooding associated with increased rainfall, storm surges, and sea level rise
- drought and water shortage resulting in wildfires, structural subsidence, and domino effects such as power station closures
- permafrost reduction and its impact on structural stability
- more extreme weather events such as land slips and increased wind and other loading on structures.

In terms of direct impacts a key question for any infrastructure is what degree of climate change should be planned for over what period? Perhaps a second issue, addressed later in the section "Governance and Infrastructure," is what is the stimulus for infrastructure to accommodate likely changes in climate?

A set of projections for Australia (CSRIO) in the shorter term (2030) are given in Figure 1.7. They reflect the degree of uncertainty associated with different climate models and emission scenarios. The projections also highlight that even a relatively modest increase in annual temperature can have a profound effect on, for example, electricity transmission because of a significantly increased risk from wildfires. In part this is because of the sensitivity of the Australian bush to even small changes in temperature and rainfall. The impact of climate change on infrastructure needs (water and power generation) in such areas is already being felt.

In the instance of such direct climatic effects on infrastructure, engineers can provide solutions that, to an extent, allow projects to deal with climatic change, or at least allow for planning to be undertaken that:

- allows for an upgrade path to make a project more robust in the face of climate change
- provides an approach that allows the rapid reinstatement of projects in the face of disruption.

The key questions are therefore:

- How can a new, or the adaptation of an existing, infrastructure development be planned based on a changing climate where the magnitude and impacts of the change are inherently uncertain?
- How can infrastructure developments accommodate a diverse series of risks, many of which in their own right are exacerbated by the impacts of climate change?

A series of climate change issues arise which challenge behaviour. Take, for instance, a low-lying island in the Pacific. How does one plan for climate change for islands that lie only a few meters above sea level, and where current sea level rises have already begun to affect freshwater reservoirs? There are short-term adaptation

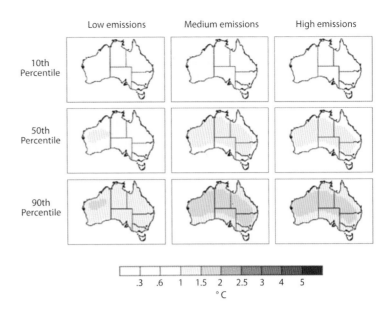

1.7 Projections for summer 2030 relative to the period 1980–99 based on a range of carbon emission scenarios. Note: the percentiles refer to consistency between climate models. The 50th percentile (the mid-point of the spread of model results) provides a best-estimate result

Source: CISRO

measures to improve freshwater provision. However, in these instances continuing to ensure a freshwater supply, and habitation of the islands, will become an ever-increasing challenge. The choice between incremental steps to adapt to climate change and encroaching sea levels, and to move the population to another location, is essentially a political one.

There have been a number of ways in which infrastructure developments have been planned based on projections of climate change, including:

- leaving standard setting to the regulator/government department/ professional body, where the body sets standards based on the criteria as it sees them
- risk assessment based on a costing of impacts and of adaptation measures associated with a range of climate change scenarios
- foresight approach—where an organisation looks at infrastructure development and risk associated with a wide range of issues, weighs these according to an overall risk assessment, and accommodates climate change in the context of other risks. Such approaches can be based on rigorous analysis or simply dictated by management belief.

Although it is possible to engineer solutions to climate change, there comes a point where indirect effects of climate change come to dominate. As a hypothetical example, if a new bridge is being planned, from an engineering perspective it is a relatively easy matter to design the bridge to cope with an increase in projected sea level rise and projected extreme weather events, recognizing the uncertainty associated with the prediction of such events, and the costs of accommodating that uncertainty. However, where is the greatest risk? Is it in the bridge, the approach roads, or the development that the bridge serves? If the community serviced by the bridge cannot adapt to changing climate then the function of the bridge is no longer relevant in the changed climate scenario because the community would not exist to require it. So why be overly concerned about adapting the bridge to long-term climate change? This takes us neatly to the next section.

CLIMATE CHANGE RISKS—INDIRECT

Many climate change reports identify the indirect impacts of climate change on infrastructure needs that have a potentially much greater impact on the viability of the infrastructure than direct effects. Such impacts could include:

- political risk—political, and subsequently regulatory, pressures are placed on infrastructure companies to either adapt to or mitigate a particular infrastructure as part of a climate adaptation/ mitigation strategy agreed at a regional, national, or global level. Such risks can affect infrastructure organisations in different ways—at one level by incurring costs in reducing carbon emissions or adapting infrastructure to the impacts of climate change, through to an ability to continue to trade
- energy and other resource constraints driven by climate change— extreme climate events, or a change in energy consumption patterns brought about by changes in population needs, will affect energy infrastructure, and that infrastructure is dependent on energy security
- social trends—people will inevitably respond in some way to climate change. How they do so will be linked to demographic, consumption, societal values, and other trends. Many have predicted significant population migrations associated with climate change and these will affect infrastructure needs
- technology changes– some solutions to climate change have major implications for energy infrastructure such as charging points and smart grids for electric vehicles

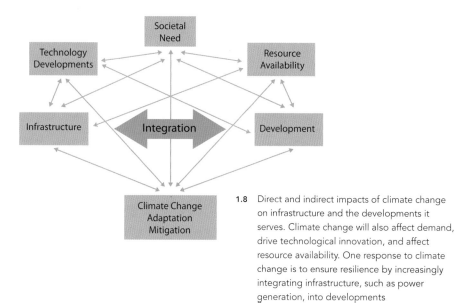

1.8 Direct and indirect impacts of climate change on infrastructure and the developments it serves. Climate change will also affect demand, drive technological innovation, and affect resource availability. One response to climate change is to ensure resilience by increasingly integrating infrastructure, such as power generation, into developments

- changes in regional economic viability, and hence affordability of remedial action, associated with both direct and indirect climate change issues (e.g., water)
- health effects associated with climate change
- conflicts sparked by direct or indirect impacts of climate change.

The challenge with the indirect consequences of climate change is that they are not always foreseeable and are often outside of the control of many who have an impact on infrastructure. However, given their potential impact, a risk assessment associated with climate change and infrastructure needs to accommodate both direct and indirect effects.

TECHNOLOGY CHANGES

Technology developments associated with energy, transportation, and water treatment will all affect infrastructure directly. Technologies such as carbon capture and storage will, if successful, create new infrastructure requirements.

However, other technologies may have profound effects on the need for infrastructure or allow solutions that are inherently more resilient to climate change.

Technology developments will continue to change the options available to shape future and current infrastructure, and the developments that are served by this infrastructure. Some believe that technology will resolve climate change issues either through improvements in energy efficiency or, alternatively, through enabling so-called geo-engineering approaches.

Although efficiency trends should result in reduced emissions, this is not always the case. For example, global population and consumption increases counter the gains of more efficient electrical appliances. This is illustrated in Figure 1.10.

1.9 Old and newer PC technologies. The continuing exponential growth in IT processing power, memory, and communication rates implies significant direct and indirect implications on future infrastructure needs due to change in capability and its impact on future demand

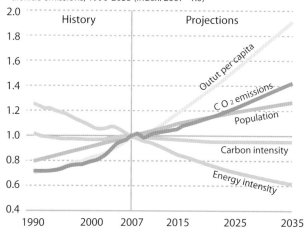

Impacts of four Kaya factors on world carbon dioxide emissions, 1990-2035 (Index: 2007=1.0)

1.10 Predicted impacts of so called "Kaya" factors on world carbon dioxide emissions. Consumption and population increases tend to outweigh the benefits of ongoing efficiency improvements. Ultimately the world's energy supply has to be decarbonised if targets to reduce greenhouse gas emissions by 80% in developed nations are to be achieved
Source: DoE—EIA (2010)

1.11a and b
Electric, fuel cell, and hydrogen vehicles offer a potential low-carbon solution to individual mobility that requires new infrastructure. Traffic congestion will limit this benefit, and often points to the need for low-carbon public transportation
Source: 1.11a, Tony Hisgett; 1.11b, Atwater Village

NEW, EXISTING INFRASTRUCTURE SOLUTIONS

The solutions to climate change are diverse and reflect the range of economies, societies, and geographies around the world. The opportunities to design and operate infrastructure for new developments—such as Masdar, where there are clear drivers to push for a sustainable approach that includes "zero carbon"—is very different from, say, a smaller-scale redevelopment of part of an established city where the constraints associated with development and infrastructure tend to be inherently more constrained.

As an example, London has recently required that 20% of a building's energy use be provided by renewable energy sources where it is practical to do so.[12] Some have commented that it would be more economic in terms of £/CO_2 emissions saved to put renewable energy sources outside of London rather than embedding renewable-energy schemes into new buildings. The ongoing costs and practicality of maintaining renewable-energy systems that are integrated in buildings (photovoltaic panels for example) may lead them to producing less power than predicted. Others take the line that such moves provide a powerful message to building occupants of the importance of energy and climate change, and point to grid security and job creation aspects of embedded generation. London has also pressed for the installation of district heating networks as part of new developments, with the assumption that this will facilitate the provision of low-grade heat energy from, for example, power stations.

Even if we look at infrastructure needs in 2050, for most of the developed world most developments with us now will be with us in 2050. Refurbishing and updating existing infrastructure tends to be more constrained than when starting with a new development.

THE ROLE OF INFRASTRUCTURE COMPANIES

So what can infrastructure companies do when it comes to tackling climate change? At a recent workshop led by the author for the Business Council for Sustainable Development in the UK, the following suggestions were made:

- Infrastructure companies need to consider climate change, security of supply, and other sustainability issues in their development of business strategies—in other words, how they identify new services, position themselves, and understand and deal with risk. Two key attributes of future infrastructure companies will therefore need to be "insight" in terms of foreseeing future infrastructure requirements, and "agility" in being able to adapt to changing requirements.
- Recognising the importance of government action in setting the climate change agenda. Infrastructure companies have a key role in informing government policy making about the practicality and impacts of proposed policies.
- Having a more joined-up approach between infrastructure development and operation, and the development it serves. An example on energy infrastructure would be the use of embedded generation within the development, including the use of waste heat to provide the low-grade heat necessary to meet building demand.
- Infrastructure companies need to encourage the maintenance and development of engineering research and training capability. Climate change requires very significant changes in the way we do things, and this implies innovative engineering solutions. Without a healthy research and training infrastructure it is unlikely that the necessary skills will be available to tackle climate change.
- Infrastructure companies need to maintain an awareness of what is a rapidly changing position in terms of our understanding

1.12 Future infrastructure requirements

1.13 Illustration of the integration of many "green" features already being introduced into developments. The illustration shows how it is possible to embed infrastructure into new and existing developments
Source: AECOM/UK Green Building Council

of, and response to, climate change. There is a huge need to identify and use "best practice" associated with climate change engineering practices and technological advances, whether it be, for example, in energy storage, traffic management, or water reduction and reuse.

- There are some key infrastructure technologies where a particularly rapid expansion in uptake and knowledge is required if we are to tackle climate change/security of supply issues—carbon capture and sequestration; renewable energy; electric/hydrogen transportation systems; demand-side management; and end-use energy efficiency being a small selection.
- Infrastructure companies should act as advocates to inform others on climate change issues and their impact on business, and to identify new solutions. As a minimum, infrastructure companies have to ensure compliance with legislation and regulations. At a higher level their role should be to understand how climate change solutions affect them and what is needed across a range of stakeholders to allow solutions.
- Although an infrastructure company's biggest sustainability impacts are likely to be through projects they work on, it is important that engineering companies "walk the talk" on climate change in their own business so as to set the tone internally and increasingly meet the demands of customers as well as legislation and regulators.

GOVERNANCE AND INFRASTRUCTURE

Experiences in Europe have shown that the implementation of low-carbon technologies and approaches in infrastructure and other developments require an appropriate governance structure associated with their development and use. As examples:

- The use of decentralised generation linked to district (sometimes called community) heating requires incentives or requirements placed on individuals or companies to take the supply if the scheme is to be viable.
- Enabling a carbon capture and storage regime requires enabling legislation and new regulations. These need to set out who is responsible for risks associated with such a new technology.
- In existing developments how might a series of existing contractual commitments be affected by requirements to develop and/or adopt new infrastructure, and who should take the risks and costs of these?

GEO-ENGINEERING?

Some publications[13] have identified the role of geo-engineering in moderating the climate. Although the role of infrastructure development is unclear in this context, it is possible that some future infrastructure projects will be associated with geo-engineering approaches. An example is the possible establishment of a network of devices aimed to sequester carbon dioxide from the atmosphere. At this stage the use of such approaches should be considered speculative, although there is some sentiment that climate change will require a mix of mitigation (measures to reduce greenhouse gas emissions), adaptation, and geo-engineering solutions.

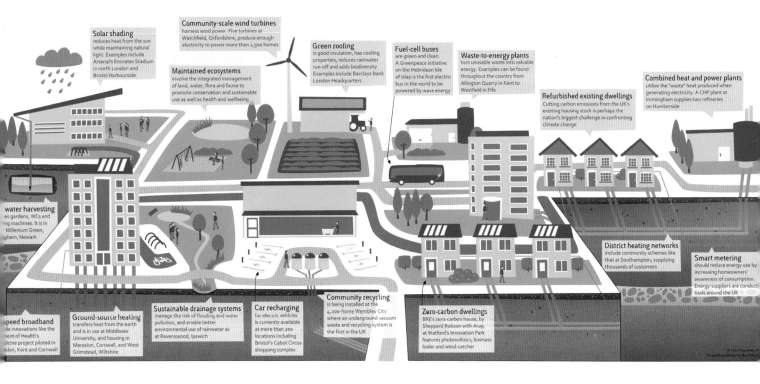

CONCLUSION

Future infrastructure requirements will be greatly affected by the need to both adapt to the climate and reduce emissions so as to reduce the future impact of climate change. Climate change cannot be considered solely in the context of infrastructure. Its impacts on the communities it serves are at least as important. The timescale, and uncertainties, associated with climate change, particularly at the local level, require that infrastructure companies need a sophisticated risk-based approach to accommodating climate change and other, often interlinked, sustainability issues.

NOTES

1   Intergovernmental Panel on Climate Change (IPCC), "2007 Assessment Reports" (2007), www.ipcc.org.ch.

2   N. Stern, *The Economics of Climate Change* (Cambridge: Cambridge University Press, 2006), www.hmtreasury.gov.uk/independent_reviews/stern_review_economics_climate_change/stern_review_report.cfm.

3   IPCC, "2007 Assessment Reports"; Stern, *The Economics of Climate Change.*

4   IPCC, "2007 Assessment Reports".

5   European Commission, "Adapting to Climate Change in Europe—Options for EU action", 2007, http://eur-lex.europa.eu/LexUriServ/LexUriServ.do?uri=CELEX.

6   DECC, "Climate Change Act", 2008, www.decc.gov.uk.

7   European Commission, "Adapting to Climate Change in Europe".

8   Committee on Climate Change, "Building a Low-Carbon Economy—the UK's Contribution to Tackling Climate Change", 2008, www.theccc.org.uk; Committee on Climate Change, "Meeting Carbon Budgets—the Need for a Step Change", 2009, www.theccc.org.uk; Committee on Climate Change, "Building a Low-Carbon Economy—the UK's Contribution to Tackling Climate Change", 2010, www.theccc.org.uk.

9   European Commission, "Adapting to Climate Change in Europe".

10 *Guardian*, "Met Office Warns of Catastrophic Climate Change in Our Lifetime", September 28th 2009, www.guardian.co.uk/environment/2009/sep/28/met-office-study-global-warming.

11 CSRIO, "Climate change in Australia", 2007, http://climatechangeinaustralia.com.au.

12 Mayor of London, *The London Plan* (London: Greater London Authority, 2008), www.london.gov.uk/thelondonplan/thelondonplan.jsp.

13 IMechE, "Geo-Engineering—Giving Us Time to Act?" 2009, www.imeche.org.uk; Royal Society, "Geoengineering the Climate: Science, Governance and Uncertainty", 2009, http://royalsociety.org/geoengineering-the-climate/.

2

Resource Allocation

GREGORY NORRIS

HARVARD SCHOOL OF PUBLIC HEALTH

THE ZOFNASS FRAMEWORK for infrastructure sustainability calls for optimum allocation of resources in the development and operation of infrastructure. To support the consideration of this goal, the present chapter addresses the following topics in turn:

- First, we briefly summarize resource allocation within the Zofnass Program.
- Next, we introduce the framework of Life Cycle Assessment (LCA) as a means for characterizing quantitatively the use of resources in infrastructure construction and operation.
- Third, we review the different types of resource use and consumption, and the metrics or indicators that have been developed to date within the field of LCA; we place particular emphasis on energy considerations in this vein.
- Fourth, we use the tools, databases, and framework of LCA to characterize some of the ways that the development and operation of infrastructure consume scarce resources.
- Finally, we turn to the goal of optimizing resource consumption, and we reflect on two complementary approaches to optimization. One is optimization from the vantage point of the infrastructure planning or design team, and a second is promotion of "bottom-up" or "distributed" optimization throughout the supply chains that enable the construction and operation of infrastructure. We conclude with brief discussion of a coming "informational infrastructure" that will increase the data resources available to designer optimization, and the scope of distributed optimization, in mutually reinforcing ways.

RESOURCE ALLOCATION WITHIN THE ZOFNASS PROGRAM

Together with natural world, climate change, and quality of life, the fourth major category within the Zofnass Program is resource allocation. The Program aims for "the optimal allocation of resources, which has the least impact on the current environment and resource availability, and maximizes the potential of future generations to have access to the resources they will need."[1]

Within the resource allocation category, three subcategories are identified:

- materials
- energy
- water.

Achieving the aim of resource allocation stated in these terms requires an ability to do two things, which we can call resource use *quantification*, and resource use *impact assessment*. For resource use quantification, we need accurate estimates of the quantity of each resource that will be consumed during each of the phases of the life cycle of an infrastructure project: design, construction, operations, and decommissioning. And for resource use impact assessment, we must be able to assess two types of impact, per unit of resource consumed, for each of the resource subcategories above:

- the impacts of resource use on the current environment
- the impacts of resource use on resource availability for present and future generations.

An ability to do both resource use quantification and resource use impact assessment is provided by the method, tools, and data sources of product LCA, which we summarize in the next section.

LIFE CYCLE ASSESSMENT

Product LCA was first introduced in the late 1960s, as a method for accounting for the energy and resource requirements of the life cycles of product systems.[2] It has been standardized under the ISO 14040 series of standards. ISO 14000 in general addresses environmental management, and the 14040 series address LCA in particular. ISO 14040 describes the principles and framework for LCA, while 14044, "Requirements and Guidelines," describes in detail the ways that a LCA needs to be conducted and documented, depending on the intended use, in order to be ISO-compliant.

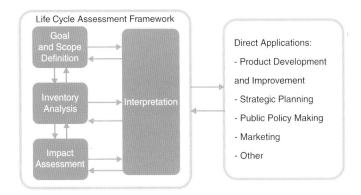

2.1 LCA Framework according to ISO 14040

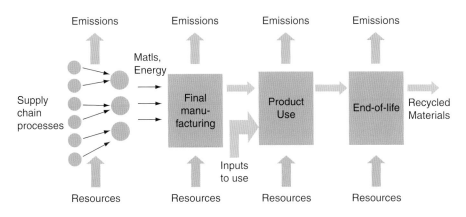

2.2 Scope of LCA

The main components of a LCA are represented in the following diagram, which is drawn from ISO 14040.

Goal and scope definition is the first stage of an LCA, and it governs the decisions that will be taken in the rest of an assessment. This first stage defines the intended use of the results, the audience, the alternatives, the metrics by which they will be evaluated, and the boundaries that will govern modeling, data gathering, and selection of appropriate pre-existing data resources.

Resource use quantification via life cycle inventory analysis

Next comes inventory analysis. This is the stage that generates what we called, in the introduction, the resource use quantification: estimates of the quantity of each resource that will be consumed during each of the phases of the life cycle of an infrastructure project. In LCA terminology, this information is contained in what is called a life cycle inventory, or LCI.

LCAs attempt to be comprehensive in two dimensions. First, they are supposed to include all *activities* that are linked to, or influenced by, any portion of the product life cycle. Second, they attempt to include the full set of pollution releases and resource consumption flows that may lead to impacts of concern, for the environment and for human health, which were identified as part of the assessment during the goal and scope phase.

A conceptual illustration of this comprehensiveness is provided in Figure 2.2.

The modeling activity supporting an LCI analysis actually tends to begin in the middle of the diagram in Figure 2.2, by identifying the quantity of final product needed to provide a given level of *function* to a user. An example for water supply infrastructure would be enabling the transmission and distribution of water over a specified distance, at a specified flow rate and pressure capacity, for a specified service life. An example for transportation infrastructure might be enabling the transport of people and/or goods from point A to point B, at a specified transport capacity, perhaps with specified maximum transport times, over a specified service life. The definition and quantification of the function provided by alternative "product systems" occurs during the goal and scope phase of a product LCA; the same would be true for an infrastructure system in an infrastructure LCA.

LCAs then seek to compare different alternatives that provide this same level of function. During the use of a product, there might be resources consumed (the green arrow up into the "product use" phase) and/or emissions released to the environment (the red arrow out of the "product use" phase). For infrastructure LCA, the "use phase" corresponds to the operations phase for the infrastructure system. This operations phase will generally require inputs of a variety of produced materials and energy. In studies of water supply system alternatives, for example, supply of pumping energy needs to be factored into the study—especially if there are differences in the energy requirements among the different alternatives, due to differences in factors such as inner diameter or surface smoothness.

Once the operational phase has been described, the LCA looks back "upstream": What does it take to manufacture and install the pipe that will span 100 yards for 40 years? If, for example, the pipe lasts an average of 20 years, then we will need 200 linear yards of pipe to provide the function, plus the energy and equipment and materials to install the pipe twice. The data gathered for the infrastructure construction stage is similar to the data gathered for the operations phase: required are quantities of natural resources consumed, quantities of emissions and wastes generated, and quantities of material and energy inputs to the infrastructure manufacturing processes.

Next, because of the material and energy inputs to infrastructure construction, an LCA requires data for the entirety of each of the supply chains that produce the material and energy inputs to construction and operation. This is the so-called "cradle-to-gate" portion of the life cycle model. Most studies by most analysts rely on existing and publicly available databases to provide the bulk of this information. The databases most widely used are those that are available in the LCA modeling software used by analysts. Currently, the two major LCA software tools in the world are SimaPro[3] and GaBi[4]; the major LCI database available for use in these and other related software tools is the ecoinvent database,[5] which contains data on the outputs and inputs to over 4000 different interconnected processes or activities in the supply chains and life cycles of thousands of goods and services.

In fact, there are two styles of LCI database: process-level, and input/output. Process-level LCI databases contain models that describe production supply chains as an interconnected system of unit processes, linked by material or energy flows. In process-level LCI, these unit processes are generally at the level of individual engineering unit processes, such as manufacturing operations, fuel-specific power plants generating electricity, individual transportation legs by a specific mode, and so on. Process-level LCI databases contain information generally derived from samples of a number of similar manufacturing operations of a specific type and within a specific geographic region. For each unit process in the database, the data include quantities of each pollutant released to air, water, or land; inflows of raw materials and intermediate materials; and the resulting products. Ecoinvent is a process-level database.

The other type of LCI database contains what is called input/output data. In these databases, the "unit processes" are whole sectors of the economy, rather than more precise engineering unit processes. In these databases, each sector purchases goods and services from other sectors; the flows between sectors are measured in dollar terms rather than physical and energy units. Each sector also has emissions coefficients (kg of each pollutant per dollar of product output) and may also have natural resource consumption coefficients. These databases are called "input/output" databases because they make use of economic input/output data tables. These are influential models, particularly in screening analyses. One example of an input/output database for LCA is the freely available "Open IO" database.[6]

Finally, a LCA typically addresses the product end-of-life phase. Modeling this step requires data on the end-of-life fates of the materials (how much is typically sent to landfill versus recycling versus incineration), and then we require data on the input requirements and emissions and resource flows associated with the end-of-life processes. For landfilling, recycling, and municipal incineration, the LCI databases described above contain data on the input requirements and the emissions and wastes from these processes. These data are examples of the sort that will be applied to model the decommissioning phase in an infrastructure LCA.

The LCI result of an LCA contains, as a subset, the data we described earlier as a resource use quantification: the quantity of each resource that will be consumed during each of the phases of the life cycle of an infrastructure project. In particular, a typical LCI will contain such estimates for more than 100 different natural resources that can be grouped into the categories of materials, energy, and water resources. If desired, an LCI model could be used to generate what we might call an "inventory of intermediate flows": a tabulation of all the produced inputs (not from nature) that are used by all the activities over the entire infrastructure system's life cycle.

Resource use impact assessment via Life Cycle Impact Assessment

The end result from LCI modeling that makes use of LCI databases as described in the previous section is a table of estimated total life cycle releases (in kg) for each of hundreds of different pollutants to air, and of others to water, and still others to land. This is a sum, over the entire system, of the orange arrows depicted in Figure 2.2. The life cycle inventory results also include estimates of the total kg of each resource extracted from the environment—a sum of the gray arrows in Figure 2.2. These inventory flows are estimated because of the different impacts that they can cause on human health and the environment. As a next step in the LCA, the methods of life cycle impact assessment (LCIA) are used to characterize each of these hundreds of different flows in terms of their relative and potential cumulative influence on impacts of concern.

LCI analysis and LCIA are combined in most LCA studies, but they are separate steps and they make use of different data sources and models. The LCI databases describe the process chains and the flows

into and out of each process. The LCIA models characterize the relative influence of different pollution flows—from whatever process they may originate—on environmental impact categories. They do the same for flows of resources—to whatever processes might use them.

For resource use impact assessment within the Zofnass Program, we need to assess two types of impact, per unit of resource consumed, for each of the more than 100 water, energy, or material resources extracted from the environment over the life cycle of infrastructure alternatives:

- the impacts of resource use on the current environment
- the impacts of resource use on resource availability for present and future generations.

In the next section we review leading impact assessment methods from within LCIA that are appropriate for application to resource use impact assessment of infrastructure alternatives.

RESOURCE CONSUMPTION CATEGORIES AND INDICATORS

The methods of LCIA have evolved over the past 40 years of LCA practice, and they continue to advance as a result of ongoing research by practitioners inside and outside the field of LCA. In this section we review the state-of-the-art metrics or indicators from LCIA that address three types of resource use impact, the first two of which are referred to explicitly within the resource allocation portion of the Zofnass Program:

- impacts of resource use on the environment
- impacts of resource use on availability of resources
- impacts of resource use on human health via environmental impact pathways.

Modern LCIA methods are comprehensive in the sense that they attempt to address the fullest possible set of impact categories. The methodology of LCIA has evolved since 2000 to a point of stability

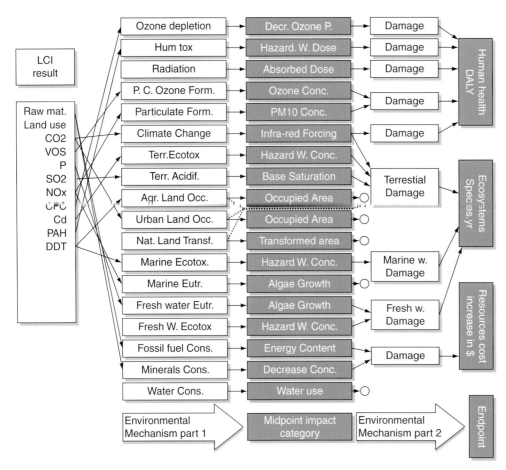

2.3 Schematic of the ReCiPe method for LCIA

around the concepts of "midpoint" and "endpoint" indicators. Midpoint indicators relate to specific categories, which generally number over 10 in a given method. These midpoint indicators are then related to the smallest possible number of so-called "damage categories" or "endpoints," which cannot be further combined except through value judgments. Endpoints are areas of concern in their own right. The endpoint categories that have been included in the most recent LCIA methods are:

- ecosystem quality
- resource depletion
- human health.

The most recent LCIA method published is the ReCiPe method.[7] This method has the three endpoint categories listed above. Note that they relate, in order, to the same three impact categories

named further above as deserving of attention within the Zofnass framework on resource allocation.

Impacts of resource use on the environment

From an LCA perspective, nearly every activity in the entire life cycle of a product, and thus of infrastructure systems as well, has a variety of impacts on the environment. The routes to such impacts begin, in LCA models, with what are called "elementary flows." Elementary flows include releases of substances (including pollutants) to air, to water, and to soil. Other elementary flows with explicit environmental impacts include the occupation of land, and the transformation of land from one usage state to another.

As shown in Figure 2.3, the midpoint categories that pertain to impacts of resource use on the environment include:

- climate change
- terrestrial ecotoxicity
- terrestrial acidification
- agricultural land occupation
- urban land occupation
- transformation of land from natural state
- marine ecotoxicity
- marine eutrophication
- freshwater eutrophication
- freshwater ecotoxicity.

These midpoint indicators in turn are influenced by hundreds of different elementary flows, which in turn are associated with virtually all of the activities in the life cycle of an infrastructure system. They all are related to a final endpoint indicator that measures ecosystem quality impacts in terms of the number of species impacted, and the duration of this impact. We will explore these impacts in greater depth in the next section.

Impacts of resource use on resource availability for present and future generations

The ReCiPe midpoint indicators that relate to the endpoint of resource depletion are:

- fossil fuel consumption
- mineral consumption
- water consumption.

The elementary flows that influence these midpoint indicators are less numerous than those leading to ecosystem impacts. Elementary flows relating to fossil fuel consumption are all extractions of fossil fuel resources (crude oil, natural gas, coal, and other minor fuels) from the earth. Elementary flows relating to water consumption are consumptive uses of freshwater resources. And elementary flows relating to mineral consumption are extractions of mineral resources that are scarce enough that consumption of an existing resource leaves remaining resources whose quality is lower, as

measured in terms of the cost of extracting the next unit of the mineral.

Impacts of resource use on human health via environmental impact pathways

As shown in Figure 2.3, the midpoint categories that pertain to impacts of resource use (and any other activity) on human health include:

- stratospheric ozone depletion
- human toxicity
- radiation
- photochemical ozone formation
- climate change.

These midpoint indicators in turn are influenced by hundreds of different elementary flows, which in turn are associated with virtually all of the activities in the life cycle of an infrastructure system. They all are related to a final endpoint indicator that measures human health impacts in terms of Disability-Adjusted Life-Years. We will explore these impacts, too, in greater depth in the next section.

RESOURCE CONSUMPTION IN INFRASTRUCTURE LIFE CYCLES

The Zofnass Program defines infrastructure as "The set of fundamental physical systems, services, and networks that support the built environment and protect the natural world and are essential to sustaining a civilized and productive society. Infrastructure broadly falls within six major categories: water, energy, waste, transportation, landscape, and information."[8] In this section, we use the tools, databases, and framework of LCA to illustrate how LCA translates the many ways that the construction and operation of infrastructure have impacts on resource scarcity (availability for future generations) and environmental quality. We do so in the context of alternative infrastructures for transportation.

GOAL, SCOPE, AND FUNCTIONAL UNIT

As we saw earlier, an LCA begins with defining the goal and scope of the assessment. In our case, we would like to explore the implications of resource utilization in the life cycles of alternative transportation infrastructures. In a formal or classical LCA comparison, we need to compare alternatives that deliver an equivalent function, measured via a "functional unit." As mentioned earlier, for transportation infrastructure, the function might be enabling the transport of goods from point A to point B, at a specified transport capacity, perhaps with specified maximum transport times, over a specified service life.

In the present example, we will examine (in a very quick, cursory, illustrative fashion) the infrastructure needed to transport 1 kg of freight from New York to Los Angeles. We will quickly compare the requirements for transport via road (truck), rail (train), and sea (ocean freighter).

It is advisable to precede a full LCA study with what is called a "scoping LCA." That is, before investing resources in a full-blown study, with primary data collection, it is advisable to conduct (or consult an existing example of) what amounts to a quick, "desktop" study, using data already available. The purpose of such a scoping assessment is to get a sense, ahead of time, of what are likely to be the major issues, the major environmental impact categories, the major life cycle phases, the major assumptions, and the major processes and parameters on which primary data will need to be gathered during the actual study. To illustrate the data and methods of LCA for sustainable resource allocation, we will outline a sort of hypothetical scoping assessment here.

The function of interest is freight transport from New York to Los Angeles. Let's say for the moment that shipping time is not paramount, so that rail, truck, and sea routes are all considered functionally equivalent alternatives. Let's also say that the temporal scope of this assessment is near-term, with a focus on existing technology.

For any LCA, including a scoping LCA, we must find LCI data—lots of it! In a scoping LCA, we make use of existing databases. It is important to use *comparable* data in all cases, so in our study we will draw data from the same database: the ecoinvent database

described earlier. We will make use of the Impact 2002 method for impact assessment, and we'll consider multiple damage categories (the endpoints of human health, ecosystem quality, climate change, and resource consumption), with a particular focus on resource consumption.

Transport of freight requires:

- production of a vehicle (truck, train, or ship)
- operation of the vehicle
- maintenance and repair of the vehicle
- disposal of the vehicle at its end of life
- construction of the supporting infrastructure
  - road network, in the case of truck transport
  - rail network, in the case of rail freight
  - port infrastructure, in the case of ocean freight
- operation, maintenance, and repair of the supporting infrastructure
- disposal of infrastructure at its end of life.

Each of the above seven components of the transport system life cycle entails the consumption of resources. For example, operation of the vehicles consumes fossil fuels. Production, maintenance, and repair of the vehicles require fossil fuels, the extraction of ores to produce metal vehicle parts, the use of water resources, etc. The construction, operation, and maintenance of the infrastructure consumes fossil, mineral, and water resources, it transforms land from one use to another, and it occupies land. Each of the above transport system components has a global supply chain with literally thousands of unit processes in it, each of which may not only consume resources but also release pollutants and wastes to air, water, and land. And all of these processes, and their potential impacts, are potentially within the scope of our LCA, given its broad goals summarized earlier.

The very simple function that each of the transport systems are to provide is the transport of 1 kg of freight from New York to Los Angeles. Note that, while the distance between these cities is fixed, the transport distance by mode will vary. Quick use of web-based transport distance calculators yield approximate distance assumptions of 2800 miles for truck, 3000 for rail, and 5600 for ship.

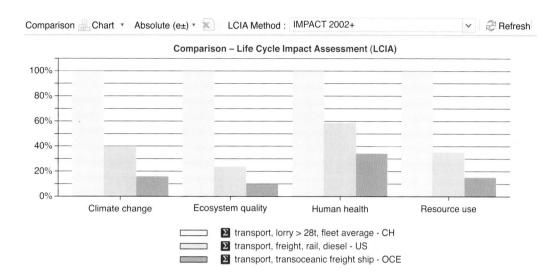

2.4

Comparison of LCIs of three freight transport modes

Table 2.1 Comparison of LCIs of three freight transport modes

P	Amount	Unit	Product	Loc.	Climate change (%)	Ecosystem quality (%)	Human health (%)	Resource use (%)
Σ	2800	t-km	Transport, lorry >2 …	CH	100	100	100	100
Σ	3000	t-km	Transport freight …	US	39.53	23.70	58.37	35.07
Σ	5600	t-km	Transport …	OCE	15.86	10.10	33.65	14.45

The transport processes readily available, the ecoinvent database allocates the burdens of transporting freight over 1 mile on a per-kg basis. This implies that the freight transport infrastructure is limited by weight capacity rather than volume, which is a safe assumption for the transport of heavy (e.g., primary) goods, but not for the transport of finished (consumer) goods. The latter are often limited by volume. We will assume that our focus is on the transport of heavy, primary goods, in order to simplify our work. The data in the ecoinvent database allocate the burdens of operating (and constructing, and maintaining) the vehicles via the infrastructure, on a per kg (or per ton) of freight basis.

In order to estimate the amount of each of the seven transport system life cycle components required to transport a ton of freight over a mile, the database includes assumptions about the:

• load capacity of vehicles
• lifetime mileage of the vehicles
• lifetime of the road, rail, and port infrastructure systems, and their annual utilization levels.

Based on these assumptions, we can estimate (that is, we can begin by using ecoinvent estimates of) the requirements, per ton of freight shipped, for:

• vehicle fuel use and emissions, per ton-mile
• vehicle construction, operation, maintenance, and disposal, per ton-mile
• infrastructure construction, operation, maintenance, and disposal, per ton-mile.

The above can then be multiplied by the mode-specific distances, and we can make our initial comparisons. Since all of the assumptions about vehicle and infrastructure capacity and lifetime are transparent in the ecoinvent database, we could later modify these assumptions if desired.

The top-level comparison of the three modes yields the results shown in Figure 2.4. In this figure, the results for each impact category are expressed in different units of impact, so the results have been normalized such that the mode with the highest impact in a given impact category has impacts of 100%. As we see here, the ocean freight system life cycle has the lowest impact on each of the damage categories, on a per ton-mile basis, while the truck transport system has the highest impact for all impact categories. Rail falls in between these two on all categories. The results from Figure 2.4 are also presented in tabular form in Table 2.1.

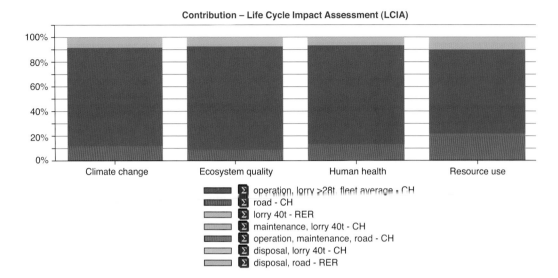

2.5
Relative impacts of each life cycle component, for truck freight, using data from ecoinvent, and using the Impact 2002 method for LCIA

Table 2.2   Relative impacts of each life cycle component, for truck freight, using data from ecoinvent, and using the Impact 2002 method for LCIA

Product	Loc.	Climate change (%)	Ecosystem quality ... (%)	Human health (%)	Resource use (%)
Operation, lorry >28 t, fleet average	CH	80.04	84.42	80.71	69.03
Road	CH	11.05	7.11	12.55	19.21
Lorry, 40 t	RER	5.20	5.16	4.44	4.74
Maintenance, lorry 40 t	CH	2.78	2.03	1.57	4.77
Operation, maintenance, road	CH	0.55	1.13	0.44	2.10
Disposal, lorry 40 t	CH	0.23	0.02	0.05	0.01
Disposal, road	RER	0.12	0.11	0.15	0.11

Next, we examine one mode at a time, to understand in more detail the relative importance of the life cycle components (vehicle operation, vehicle construction, vehicle maintenance and repair, infrastructure construction, and infrastructure maintenance and repair). We find that for each mode, the operation of the vehicle has a higher impact than each of the other components, for each impact category. We also find that the share of total life cycle impacts associated with each component varies by mode and by impact category.

Figure 2.5 and Table 2.2 present the results for truck transport; Figure 2.6 and Table 2.3 present the results for rail transport; and Figure 2.7 and Table 2.4 present the results for ocean freight transport.

Figure 2.5 and Table 2.2 show relative impacts of each life cycle component, for truck freight, using data from ecoinvent, and using the Impact 2002 method for LCIA.

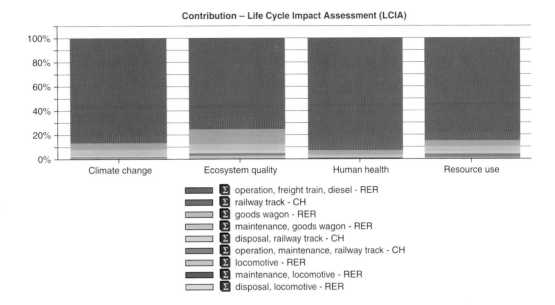

2.6
Relative impacts of each life cycle component, for US rail freight, using data from ecoinvent, and using the Impact 2002 method for LCIA

Table 2.3 Relative impacts of each life cycle component, for US rail freight, using data from ecoinvent, and using the Impact 2002 method for LCIA

Product	Loc.	Climate change (%)	Ecosystem quality ... (%)	Human health (%)	Resource use (%)
Operation, freight train, diesel	RER	79.59	66.30	89.31	79.10
Railway track	CH	7.77	9.75	4.13	6.54
Goods wagon	RER	5.14	12.16	3.64	4.89
Maintenance, goods wagon	RER	4.78	5.13	1.12	4.22
Disposal, railway track	CH	1.38	2.50	1.02	1.55
Operation, maintenance, railway track	CH	0.61	2.23	0.33	2.93
Locomotive	RER	0.53	1.68	0.36	0.58
Maintenance, locomotive	RER	0.14	0.21	0.06	0.15
Disposal, locomotive	RER	0.01	0.01	0.01	0.00

Figure 2.6 and Table 2.3 show relative impacts of each life cycle component, for US rail freight, using data from ecoinvent, and using the Impact 2002 method for LCIA.

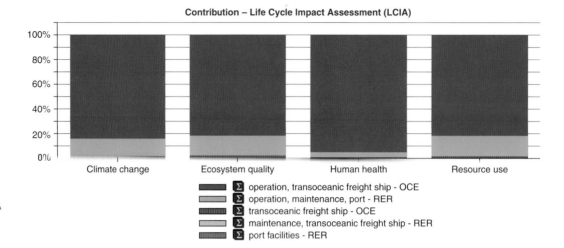

2.7
Relative impacts of each life cycle component, for ocean freight, using data from ecoinvent, and using the Impact 2002 method for LCIA

Table 2.4   Relative impacts of each life cycle component, for ocean freight, using data from ecoinvent, and using the Impact 2002 method for LCIA

Product	Loc.	Climate change (%)	Ecosystem quality ... (%)	Human health (%)	Resource use (%)
Operation, transoceanic freight ship	OCE	84.37	82.33	95.63	82.19
Operation, maintenance, port	RER	14.01	15.50	3.66	16.32
Transoceanic freight ship	OCE	1.57	2.11	0.67	1.42
Maintenance, transoceanic freight ship	RER	0.02	0.03	0.01	0.03
Port facilities	RER	0.01	0.01	0.01	0.01

Table 2.5   Relative impacts of each life cycle component, for each mode, relative to the impact category of resource depletion, using data from ecoinvent, and using the Impact 2002 method for LCIA

	Truck	Rail	Ocean
Vehicle operation	69%	79%	82%
Vehicle construction	4.7%	5.5%	1.4%
Vehicle maintenance and repair	4.8%	1.2%	<1%
Infrastructure construction (road, railway, port)	19.2%	6.5%	<1%
Infrastructure operation, maintenance, and repair (not counting vehicle operation)	2.1%	2.9%	16.3%
Disposal of vehicle and infrastructure	<1%	1.6%	<1%

Figure 2.7 and Table 2.4 show relative impacts of each life cycle component, for ocean freight, using data from ecoinvent, and using the Impact 2002 method for LCIA.

The impact category of "resource consumption" includes the depletion-related impacts of consuming both fossil fuels and mineral resources, as mentioned earlier. For this impact category, the relative importance of each life cycle component can be summarized as follows, drawing on the results presented in Tables 2.2, 2.3, and 2.4.

Table 2.5 shows relative impacts of each life cycle component, for each mode, relative to the impact category of resource depletion, using data from ecoinvent, and using the Impact 2002 method for LCIA

OPTIMIZING RESOURCE CONSUMPTION

In this final section, we turn to the goal of optimizing resource consumption, and we reflect on two complementary approaches to optimization. One is optimization from the vantage point of the infrastructure planning or design team, and a second is promotion of "bottom-up" or "distributed" optimization throughout the supply chains that enable the construction and operation of infrastructure. As it turns out, there is a major role to play for new forms of "informational infrastructure" that can increase the data resources available to designer optimization, and the scope of distributed optimization, in mutually reinforcing ways.

Planner/designer-driven
optimization of resource allocation

The most obvious application of the metrics, data, and tools offered by LCA to optimizing resource allocation for sustainable infrastructure would be done by planners and designers of new infrastructure projects. The planning and design teams can do this work on at least two levels.

First, the teams can begin by doing LCAs of alternative project designs, comparing them, and selecting the designs that minimize the impacts of interest, based on the metrics and data sources selected. As we have seen, this process begins with the goal and scope phase, which identifies the decision context, the functions to be provided by the alternatives, the impact categories of interest and how they will be modeled, and the scope of the modeling and assessment. The LCIA will then generate estimates of the quantities of each specific resource consumed, as well as the quantities of each pollutant release, from all (significant) activities induced by the entire life cycle of each proposed infrastructure system. They will do this by combining their own data on the bills of materials to construct each project, plus estimates of the maintenance and operation input requirements over the system life, together with extensive databases on the elementary flows associated with each activity in the supply chains of each of these inputs to construction and operation and decommissioning. The LCIA will translate the resulting data on hundreds of resource and pollution flows into a handful of summary metrics for consideration. And the planning and design team, perhaps with broader stakeholder input, will interpret the results, hopefully asking further questions of the modelers and analysts so that they do sensitivity analysis and uncertainty analysis on each of their models and all important underlying assumptions, to assess the robustness of the conclusions.

The above application scenario is an important and powerful one. It is being increasingly applied by leading architectural, engineering, and design teams on building and construction projects. The main factors limiting wider use are:

- The need for seamless integration of LCA information with the tools and databases that planners and designers currently use to establish bills of materials and input requirements during operation and decommissioning.
- The need to continue to advance the reliability and ensure the full scope of methods to estimate all the primary and secondary consequences of different infrastructure configurations during the operations phase. These include, for example, short-term and long-term influence of the transportation system on variables such as vehicle miles traveled by mode, automobile ownership and fleet efficiencies, and the responses of future settlement and land-use decisions and investment. Then, the output from

these models, too, needs to be linked to LCA information, although this is not a difficult step.

- The need for more comprehensive, up-to-date, and transparent LCI data on the full range of inputs to the construction, operation, and decommissioning of infrastructure projects. These databases require considerable investment by their owner/managers to be expanded and maintained, because the supply chains involved are global, continually evolving, and contain hundreds of activities that may make important contributions to the impacts of interest. The database owner/manager teams are small in relation to the scale of the data collection and maintenance job. Also, the funding required to support each of a few massive data collection and maintenance projects is major, and therefore rarely forthcoming from government agencies, even though the results of such projects are needed by a wide range of actors in society.

Our final section identifies a promising, complementary response to the third factor above—the need to find new ways to generate the LCI data needed to support sustainable resource allocation.

Bottom-up optimization of resource allocation – and data feedback loops

Up to the present moment, LCA tools are expensive (costing in the order of $10,000) and so are the databases, adding another $2,000–$20,000 in cost, depending on the scope of the database and the number of analysts at the purchasing firm who will have access to the tools and data. What's more, these tools are designed by and for LCA specialists; they are not something that a busy employee with a broad job description at an average firm, particularly at small or medium enterprises, can pick up and use readily. These are some of the reasons that the application of LCA has tended so far to remain within the context of the centralized planner–designer scenario outlined above.

However, there are both pressures, and opportunities, to change this. On the pressure side, companies like Walmart are actively seeking greater transparency into their supply chains, for business

reasons. And they are being asked by stakeholders to provide transparency about the environmental and social impacts in their supply chains as well. Finally, both Walmart and its stakeholders want to see clear and compelling progress in reducing costs and adverse environmental and social impacts in these same supply chains.

The challenge is that it tends to be only the actors in these supply chains who have the ability to generate information about their local impacts, and about the nature and location of their immediate suppliers. It is also these same actors, distributed across these vast supply chains, who are essential to engage in most efforts to reduce costs and improve impacts. And this brings us to the opportunity side of the story.

Work is underway to make LCA tools universally accessible to the actors across global supply chains, by driving down the cost to obtain and to use the tools and the data, and by driving up the local business benefits of doing so. And, work is also underway to make it possible for the actors at each node in these supply chains to share results with one another, while still keeping secure and confidential the business-sensitive information used to generate these results.

An open-source project[9] underway since 2005 has worked to enable and incentivize bottom-up collection of unit process data worldwide. It is doing this by developing and offering during 2011 two knowledge management components:

- downloadable free software for calculating cradle-to-gate LCA results (and visualizing and understanding their drivers)
- web-accessible free hosting of data that enables controlled sharing of product-specific cradle-to-gate LCA results. The server can accept data from, respond to queries from, and send data to any LCA-relevant software tools now in use, as well as the free downloadable software developed within the project itself. The server also hosts other "raw" data besides cradle-to-gate results.

The fact that such a system enables sharing of data across supply chains means that companies *could* use data from their suppliers in their calculations, if these suppliers created such data and uploaded

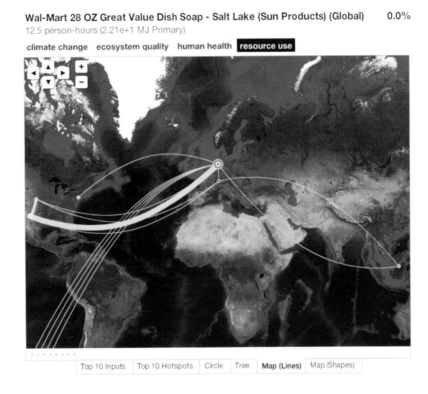

Wal-Mart 28 OZ Great Value Dish Soap - Salt Lake (Sun Products) (Global)   0.0%
12.5 person-hours (2.21e+1 MJ Primary)

climate change   ecosystem quality   human health   resource use

| Top 10 Inputs | Top 10 Hotspots | Circle | Tree | **Map (Lines)** | Map (Shapes) |

2.8
Supply chain visualization
in the open-source
Earthster tool

it to the server. If there is a demand for such data, companies will ask their suppliers to download, calculate, and publish cradle-to-gate results, and this request will propagate global supply chains, rapidly (exponentially) increasing the scope of the activity.

As mentioned above, companies must be capable *and incentivized* to collect on-site data in order for the system to work. This in turn requires that the benefits to companies for doing so exceed the costs of doing so, which can be brought about by lowering costs and increasing benefits.

Ways to lower the cost of bottom-up data collection include:

• making the software free to download and use
• designing the system to be very simple to use
• making the software code open source, meaning that programmers can do such things as:
  – make the user interface available in all languages
  – create user interfaces adapted to specific user groups, sectors, etc.
  – continually innovate the user interface to enhance usability.

Ways to increase the *benefits* of bottom-up data collection include:

• software that helps companies quickly understand the life cycle impacts of their products; understand relative contributions of each input to impacts; visually identify hot spots in the supply chain, etc.
• enabling the exchange of cradle-to-gate LCA results across companies (and software platforms) within supply chains, including:
  – sharing of cradle-to-gate results with actual and potential customers, while keeping unit process data confidential
  – user ability to manage access to the data, to update the data, and even to "de-publish" data
• making use of user input to present the user with opportunities for sustainable innovation. For example, the software could automatically query regionally-relevant databases that contain data on hundreds of different sustainable manufacturing resources, including technical assistance and financing for investments
• providing the ability to report progress over time, and to assess the impacts of progress in the supply chain upon the cradle-to-gate impacts of a company's own products.

The key to this scenario is that advances in software and in data-sharing services enable the *benefits* of unit process data

33

collection and on-site use to exceed the *costs* of doing so. Free software for on-site use of such data, and free services for sharing results within supply chains, may make the benefit/cost ratio greater than 1. Once this is true, the activity can become widespread, especially given the network dynamic of data demand within supply chains. As this new generation of tools becomes available at scale across supply chains, it will enable the sustainability of resource allocation to be optimized "from the bottom up," across global supply chains.

And, once the activity becomes widespread, current and new actors from inside and outside the existing LCA community can offer services for review and aggregation of the unit process data being generated by each of these thousands or millions of activities around the globe, so that it can be added to existing and new industry average databases, driving down their cost while dramatically increasing their scope and coverage.

NOTES

1   "Z simple: an overview of the Zofnass Program for Infrastructure Sustainability," www.gsd.harvard.edu/research/research_centers/ zofnass/.
2   R.G. Hunt, Franklin W.E., "LCA—how it came about—personal reflections on the origin and the development of LCA in the USA." *International Journal of Life Cycle Assessment* 1 (1996): 4–7.
3   www.pre.nl.
4   www.pe-international.com.
5   http://ecoinvent.ch.
6   www.open-io.org.
7   M. Goedkoop, Heijungs R., Huijbregts M., et al., ReCiPe 2008. *A Life Cycle Impact Assessment Method Which Comprises Harmonised Category Indicators at the Midpoint and the Endpoint Level* (The Hague, The Netherlands: VROM, 2009).
8   "Z simple."
9   www.earthster.org.

3

Infrastructure and Nature: Reciprocal Effects and Patterns for our Future

RICHARD T.T. FORMAN

HARVARD UNIVERSITY GRADUATE SCHOOL OF DESIGN

NATURE … the patterns and processes beyond human control … is the giant on earth, daily nurturing and periodically perturbing us. We in turn create an extensive infrastructure … the basic framework and facilities servicing people on the land … with linear features reaching almost everywhere. Nature affecting infrastructure, infrastructure affecting nature … titanic interactions not to be missed.

My objective in this chapter is to explore these reciprocal effects, highlighting the resulting spatial patterns, and pinpointing key principles to use for a better future on the land. Roadways, railways, pipelines, powerlines and other corridors underpin today's society. Fortunately, a rather robust literature has rapidly emerged in a mere 25 years to elucidate this huge topic (Figure 3.1).[1] "Landscape ecology" analyzes spatial patterns, functional flows and movements, and change over time for large land areas, such as seen from an airplane window or in a broad satellite image. "Road ecology" studies and catalyzes solutions for the interactions among vehicles, roads, plants, animals, earth, water, and air across the land. "Urban region ecology" analyzes the interactions among plants/animals and the physical environment for the city within its interdependent surrounding ring-around-the-city. Throughout this analysis key principles emerge for planning and policy.

WHAT TO LOOK FOR

In the USA the National Environmental Policy Act (NEPA) of 1969 established the principle of preparing environmental impact statements to minimize, and mitigate if necessary, the environmental impacts of major infrastructure projects.[2] Analogous environment impact statements are required in many nations, states, and provinces. Overall these have had a positive yet modest effect in protecting the natural environment. However, four decades of experience has shown that such statements vary enormously in content and quality, and too often are tailored to support a political decision.

So, let us first consider the seven major specific ecological attributes that should be evaluated for infrastructure, whether a new project or a system currently in use:

3.1 A literature of books on landscape ecology (top), road ecology (bottom left), and urban region ecology (bottom right)

1. *Natural habitat* or *natural community*. This denotes the assemblage of plants, animals, and microbes in an area unplanted and without intensive human management or use. Natural ecosystem, natural vegetation, and natural area are related terms. A semi-natural area is typically dominated by natural vegetation patterns with intensive human-use unbuilt spaces intermixed.

2. *Biodiversity*. This ecological attribute primarily refers to the number of native species, and usually focuses on the rare species present. Sometimes the number, rare examples, and representative examples of the natural communities or habitats present are included.

3. *Wildlife movement*. This refers to the movement of animals in their daily home-range foraging for food and access to water, dispersal of sub-adults to an appropriate new home-range area, and (in some cases) seasonal migration, as well as to the spatial patterns and routes on land that facilitate or inhibit species movement.

4. *Groundwater and surface water*. Shallow groundwater aquifers, subsurface water, and above-ground surface water are naturally distributed and flow according to weather, rock, soil, and vegetation patterns. These flows maintain water bodies, including aquifer, stream, river, lake, pond, wetland, and estuary. Weather patterns cause droughts and floods, while human activities commonly disrupt water flows.

5. *Soil erosion, nutrients, and chemicals*. Wind and water erode soil particles from bare areas and slopes. Meanwhile mineral nutrients (e.g., nitrogen and phosphorus) and oft-toxic chemicals are transported with the eroded particles, as well as in dissolved form, often underground.

6. *Aquatic ecosystems and water quality*. Natural aquatic ecosystems in stream, river, lake, pond, vernal pool, and estuary are sensitive to altered levels of physical (temperature, light), chemical (pH, phosphorus/nitrogen), and biological (algae density, non-native fish) conditions in the water. All can be rapidly degraded by human activities.

7. *Aquatic habitats and fish*. Virtually all natural water bodies have a considerable diversity of habitats, which together support a long, much-linked food web, as well as natural fish populations and their movement patterns. Human activities can rapidly cause habitat loss, food-web simplification, and disruption of fish patterns.

All of the above should be seriously addressed in an environmental impact statement for a major project, and additionally in evaluations of local activities.

In the search for deeper, longer-term answers and solutions, it helps to simply look in a mirror. We create similar underlying patterns and results in almost all of our projects and activities (Table 3.1). We simplify, linearize, attempt to control, consume nature, and much more. These basic mechanisms and patterns are grist for elucidating principles and designing solutions for human effects, including infrastructure, on nature. This frontier to explore awaits us.

Table 3.1 How do we affect nature?

We simplify
We linearize, geometricize
We attempt to control
We reduce variability, and thus adaptability
We multiply, and sprawl
We pollute, contaminate
We eliminate, impoverish
We degrade patterns
We disrupt processes
We perforate, and dissect
We fragment, and shrink
We consume, and over-consume

Table 3.2 Processes of powerful nature and powerful humans, with typical time frames

Nature's forces and processes

Eternal … seemingly	Our time scale (years to decades)	Quickly here and gone (weeks-to-years)	Instantaneous … seemingly (minutes to days)
Bacterial decomposition	Ecological succession	Disease, pest outbreak and spread	Earthquake
Fungal mold, rot	Seawater rise, saltwater intrusion	Plant colonization of surfaces	Hurricane, cyclone
Corrosion, rusting		Drought	Tornado
Consuming termites, ants, beetles			Flood
Weathering, freezing–thawing			Fire
Gradual sinking, subsiding			Tsunami
Extreme heat, cold events			Volcanic eruption
UV solar radiation			Sinkhole drops
Vibrations from trains, traffic, machines			

Human activities across the land

Decades to centuries	Years to decades	Years
Spread of cities, towns	Cropland landscape	Pipeline, powerline
Road network system	Ranchland with livestock	Airport
Railway network system	Mining, oil, gas area	Dam, reservoir, water supply
	Shipping port	War

BIG PICTURES

Such underlying perspectives lead inexorably to the big picture. Think of major projects or human activities that have affected a large area. Examples are: 1) draining Russia's Aral Sea; 2) transforming Louisiana's delta area; 3) creating the 1930s US Dust Bowl; 4) construction/care/explosion at Chernobyl; 5) draining/filling half of America's wetlands; 6) Australia swept by non-native species; 7) Florida's 100-mile Kissimmee River straightened to half its length; 8) one-fifth of the Amazon rainforest lost due to road construction; 9) China's Three Gorges Dam; and 10) 50 years of American sprawl. All were bad for the displaced residents, and almost all were good for certain distant economic interests. Most Brazilians applaud the rainforest development, whereas most Euro-Americans decry it. Florida's ranchers like the river straightening while conservationists try to reverse it. More to the point here, all the examples caused extensive habitat loss. Furthermore, all degraded habitat over a much larger area. These large-area effects were at the time frame of decades.

Yet, environmental successes have also resulted from large projects. Consider: 1) lead removal from gasoline, and consequent reduction in soil; 2) forest protection of water supplies for Boston and New York; 3) development of the US National Forest system; 4) 30-year restoration of Lake Washington in Seattle; 5) reduction of fluorocarbons and the resulting ozone hole; 6) natural and agricultural land sustained by an urban growth boundary around Portland, Oregon; 7) plummeting of DDT in the environment and in us; 8) restoration of Okefenokee, the largest eastern US national wildlife refuge; and 9) the amazing worldwide habitat protection (1965–2005) from 2 to 15 million km^2, i.e., to 10 percent of the world's land surface. In these cases habitat increased, and degraded habitat recovered. Natural wildlife populations increased. Benefits to aquatic ecosystems, to water quality, to reducing soil erosion, to air quality, and more occurred. Again, a few decades were usually the salient time frame for major results. Large infrastructure projects do not have to degrade nature. A large-area few-decades perspective can produce environmental successes.

The big picture also brings into focus the driving forces or mechanisms of powerful nature, and of powerful humans (Table 3.2). Numerous natural processes are seemingly eternal. Many others seem instantaneous. Very few mainly operate at the human lifetime scale of years to decades. So the natural world without humans is inexorably and powerfully and gradually changing, while also punctuated with major perturbations.

In contrast, the big things we do on land are mainly at the intermediate scale of our vision, years to decades, occasionally centuries. Few natural processes coincide with our timescale activities. Therefore, powerful humans are always fighting (with maintenance and repair budgets) the ubiquitous, inexorable gradual forces at work that slowly return our products to natural conditions. Furthermore, with major repair and replacement budgets, we frequently must deal with nature's big disturbances … often called surprises, even though they are expected.

For infrastructure, road network and rail network systems persist at decades-to-centuries scales, while pipeline, powerline, airport, and dam–reservoir–water systems often function at the shorter time frame of years to decades. Big things have more inertia, and are harder to disrupt, than little things. Pipelines and water supplies are much more subject to disruption than are whole road and rail networks.

LANDSCAPE ECOLOGY TO USE

Since the field of landscape ecology emerged in the mid-1980s, research and the development of principles have accelerated worldwide.[3] In addition, its principles have been incorporated into forestry, landscape architecture, transportation, wildlife management, urban planning, and other fields.

Two areas are especially important in evaluating infrastructure: corridors and networks. Before directly addressing these it is useful to understand natural processes across the landscape, and also the basic spatial patterns produced by nature and by people.[4] Natural processes almost always trace curvy routes and produce curvilinear patterns (Figure 3.2a). The straightest lines on the landscape may be groundwater flows, rapidly moving wind-driven fire in flatland, and geologic faults. Pollinators and wildlife foraging for food move in convoluted routes. Yet some regularity is present since food tends to be patchily distributed, and fine-scale movements within food

patches are characteristic. Eroding small streams tend to be somewhat straight, while meandering rivers have similar-width, smooth-curve convolutions. The landscape pattern (Figure 3.2b) produced by these well-understood natural processes is rich in irregular and fine-textured boundaries, has a wide range of patch shapes and sizes (including large natural patches), and has aggregated, fractal, and other patterns.

Three landscape patterns are mainly molded by humans (Figure 3.2b). The planned, designed, and managed built land is characterized by squares, grids, rectangles, some smooth curves, double lines, and the occasional circle with radiating lines … a simple geometry indeed. Unplanned development, i.e., without an overall plan, results in a mixture of natural and designed patterns, yet many of the natural patterns are degraded by the often inappropriate arrangement of the designed patterns.

An interesting "long-term trial-and-error" pattern exists in some places where over centuries people have lived at moderate or low density consistent with what the land can support (Figure 3.2b). The flat to gently rolling land near San Gimignano, Toscana, Italy is illustrative. Near narrow, curvy roads, residences are separated yet close enough for social interactions. Most residences are surrounded by a domain that provides most of a family's needs for relative local-economy self-sufficiency, and, importantly, the ability to persevere through tough times. Domains tend to have moderately small, compact irregular patches (crops, orchards, woods), plus narrow uninterrupted tree lines and dirt-road corridors linked to the residence. Unfragmented forest is nearby and stream corridors are continuous. The landscape has numerous food-producing species and a diversity of scattered trees and shrubs, both at the scale of the domain and its component parts.

The planned built land pattern (Figure 3.2b), contrasting markedly with that of the natural landscape, is costly to maintain against the eternal natural processes that keep leading toward a natural landscape. Furthermore, this developed land is greatly simplified … much of the natural diversity of pattern has been removed. That means that habitat diversity is low, natural biodiversity reduced, and the diverse natural mechanisms for stability are largely gone.

a. Natural processes across the landscape

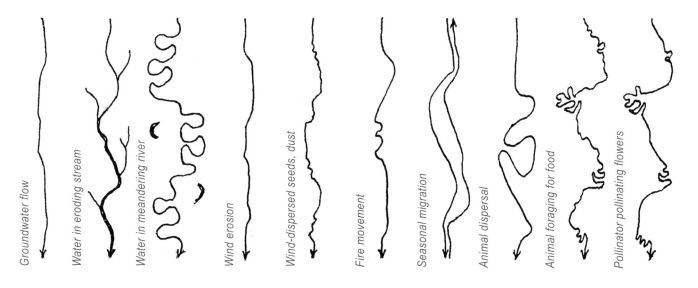

b. Landscape patterns produced by:

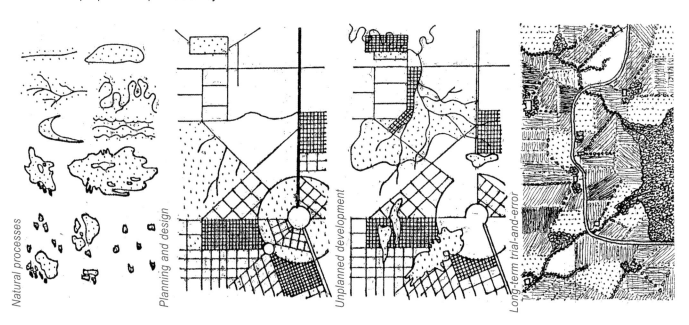

3.2a and b

Natural flows and movements across the land, and four basic types of landscape patterns on the land

Source: adapted from Forman and Hersperger (1997)

Corridors

As simply strips that differ from their surroundings, corridors may be lower (e.g., highway through forest) or higher (raised railway across a grassy plain) than the surroundings.[5] As familiar in landscape ecology, the top-view external corridor form varies in length, curvilinearity, connectivity, width and its variability, environmental gradient or patchiness along its length, sequence of adjacent land types on both sides, distribution of nodes and intersections, distribution of narrows, gap sizes and aggregation, and suitability of land in and around gaps. Each of these has profound effects on corridor function. Also, the internal cross-sectional anatomy of corridors varies in width, height, vertical layering, presence of an interior environment, presence of an internal entity (e.g., stream, road), density, species composition, and height relative to the two adjacent land types. Again the internal structure strongly controls corridor function.

So what are the functions of a corridor, that is, how does it relate to flows and movements? Basically how does it work? Corridors perform five major functions: conduit; barrier or filter; source; sink; and habitat.[6] Edge strips have these same functions, and indeed are a form of corridor.

As a conduit, objects flow or move along a corridor inside or alongside. As a barrier or filter, objects are blocked from crossing a corridor. As a source, objects originate in the corridor and move out into the surroundings. As a sink, it's vice versa. And as a habitat, the corridor is dominated by generalist edge species that survive or thrive close to the two adjoining land types. In short, corridors play especially important roles in the land. Normally corridor width and connectivity are the two most important variables affecting the rates of flows and movements.

Focusing on corridor function, it is useful to differentiate natural corridors (stream corridor, river corridor, woodland corridor, wildlife corridor, animal path) from human corridors [road, railway, powerline (electric transmission), pipeline (oil, gas, electric, water, sewer), dike, canal, hedgerow, windbreak]. Some corridors have elements of both [livestock route, greenway, ride (in European woods), and trail for walking, biking, horseback, ski, snowmobile, motorbike[7]].

Consider five basic corridor types (Figure 3.3). While stream corridors are curvy, railway and pipeline corridors are arrow-straight.

Stream and wildlife corridors are irregular in width and in their boundaries, unlike the other three types. The road corridor has the most distinctive attributes, whereas the railway corridor shares most attributes with other types. Nature is present in skeletal form in the three infrastructure types, yet is especially diverse and functionally active in the stream corridor. Flows and movements along all corridors, as simply strips, are easily disrupted. But only disruptions of the stream and wildlife corridors are serious for nature in the landscape.

Networks

Network theory has developed from many disciplines including geomorphology and railway/road transportation on the ground.[8] Landscape ecology has built on these foundations to understand broad-scale nature. Dendritic networks are illustrated by river systems, from tiny headwater streams to large rivers. Rectilinear networks, in contrast, are produced by people. Structural attributes apply to one or both types, for example: directionality, converging/diverging corridors, curviness, variability in corridor width, number of hierarchical levels, circuitry (loops), mesh size, enclosure size, linkages per node, linkage density, and connectivity.[9] Networks have major conduit, barrier, and habitat functions. Also rectilinear networks change over time, commonly expanding outward, densifying internally, and increasing the number of loops and alternate routes.

Combining large and small nodes with the network of corridors better mimics the real world, both for nature and for infrastructure. Thus for both types, functionally the rate of movement/flow is strongly affected by: location of connected large places (e.g., forest or city), the density of intersections, hierarchies of patch size and of corridor size, and so forth. Three simple node-and-linkage models originating to solve the "traveling salesman's optimal route" problem are useful here.[10] Network connectivity is the degree to which all nodes are connected (gamma index: inverse of the proportion of linkages that must be added to have a completely connected system). Network circuitry is the degree to which circuits or loops are present in the net (alpha index: actual number of loops divided by the maximum possible number of loops). Node linkage indicates

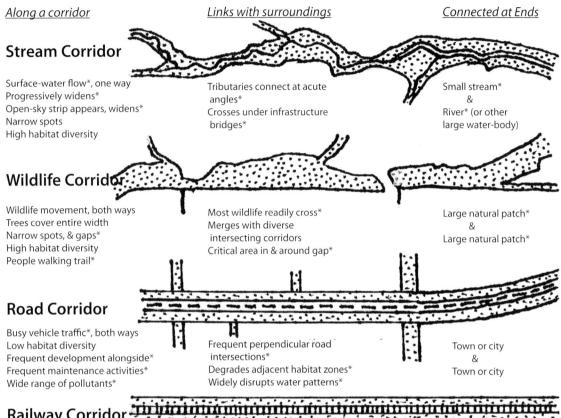

3.3 Five basic corridor types on the land

Notes: stream corridor contains third-order stream with pool-riffle structure, streambanks, heterogeneous floodplain, hillslopes, sometimes strips of adjacent upland. Wildlife corridor = medium width; contains some sensitive interior species. Road corridor contains two-lane paved busy road, slightly raised roadbed, road surface, ditches, open roadside areas. Railway corridor contains two tracks for passing trains, raised sandy railway bed covered with cinders or crushed rock, rails, crossties, opposite facing slopes. Pipeline corridor = buried for oil, gas, water, sewer or electricity; powerline = medium width with high-voltage wires supported by pylon towers. Small-to-medium natural patches and wildlife corridors are commonly attached at intervals to all the representative corridors illustrated here for a moist climate. * = attribute unique to the corridor type considered.

how connected nodes are (beta index: average number of linkages per node). These three simple measures of networks seem usefully applicable to both infrastructure and natural networks.

ROAD ECOLOGY TO USE

Reciprocal effects

Six categories of ways that nature affects infrastructure and infrastructure affects nature are highlighted:[11]

Water and roads/vehicles

Flooding covers roads, destroys bridges and culverts, and blocks traffic. Groundwater saturates roadbeds causing their failure. Freeze–thaw cycles degrade road surfaces. Erosion gullies road shoulders and unpaved roads. Water creates mud that slows or stops vehicles on unpaved roads. Water on road surfaces causes hazardous driving due to hydroplaning and heavy water spray on windshields.

Conversely, roads/vehicles strongly affect nature. Roadbeds blocking subsurface/groundwater flows create or enlarge wetlands. Channelizing streams drains or shrinks wetlands. Rerouting rainwater from road surfaces to roadside drainage ditches then sends large pulses of floodwater to nearby water bodies. Roads alter the shape, size, flows, habitat diversity, and aquatic ecosystems of nearby streams, rivers, lakes, ponds, and vernal pools.

In effect, for water and roads/vehicles, both reciprocal effects are major issues. Nature and infrastructure in this case are strongly in conflict. A high-maintenance, repair, and replacement cost is required to keep the road system, plus the diverse nearby water bodies, both functioning well.

Earth/soil and roads/vehicles

Highway construction involves considerable earth movement creating a raised roadbed, somewhat homogenizing the road right-of-way surface material, cutting upslope banks, and filling downslope.

In this process, erosion of earth/soil material by water or wind is often severe. Later, erosion occurs on the upslope cut-banks and especially on the less-stable unconsolidated fill-slopes. Water and wind erosion also are significant on unpaved roads.

Sediment transport of eroded material affects the functioning of roads and vehicles, including landslides onto road surfaces, fill-slopes that fail, and wind deposits on roads.

Chemicals and roads/vehicles

Roadsalt degrades road surfaces and bridges, and corrodes vehicles. Acid precipitation and periodic chemical spills also cause transportation problems.

But the effects of roads and vehicles on nature are much greater. Chemical pollutants are produced by the road in roadbed and road surface wear, sanding and de-icing agents, plus roadside herbicide, pesticide, and fertilizer use. The structural components of vehicles give off pollutants in engine and parts wear, brake lining wear and tire wear, plus metal plating and rust. Chemicals also emanate from products consumed in driving, including oil, grease, hydraulic fluids, and fuel, as well as from exhaust. So many chemical pollutants … asbestos, cadmium, chloride, copper, phosphorus, PCBs, rubber, zinc, the list goes on. These chemicals then are transported by diverse vectors, producing significant effects especially on nearby soil, plants, animals, surface water bodies, subsurface water, and groundwater.

Aquatic ecosystems and roads/vehicles

Other than hydrology, aquatic ecosystems have little effect on roads/vehicles. In contrast, the transportation effect on the usually sensitive ecosystems of water bodies is extensive. Relocating, straightening, or channelizing streams normally reduces sharply the habitat diversity, including riffle-pool sequences, shaded overhanging banks, sand/gravel spawning beds, shallow backwaters, and deep holes, all of which have major roles in supporting stream biodiversity and fish. Analogous effects occur in other water bodies. Chemicals, from heavy metals, hydrocarbons, toxics, and roadsalt to nitrogen and phosphorus, also widely degrade aquatic ecosystems, truncating

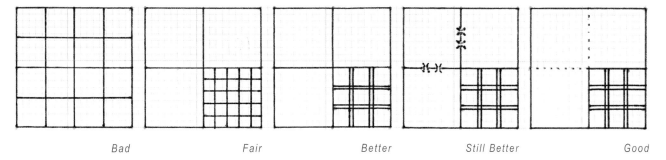

Bad   *Fair*   *Better*   *Still Better*   *Good*

3.4   Options for an ecologically optimum road network form
Notes: the background is entirely natural habitat. All options carry the same total amount of traffic. The first two diagrams have the same total length of small roads, with larger roads included in the other three diagrams. The fourth case has four wildlife underpasses/overpasses, and the last option includes two raised or sunken transport routes (elevated ways, earthways). See text for principles
Source: adapted from Forman (2005)

food webs, blocking light penetration, decreasing oxygen levels, and reducing natural fish populations and movements.

Vegetation and roads/vehicles

While many reciprocal effects occur,[12] overall their importance seems modest. Vegetation controls erosion along roads. Trees and branches occasionally fall on roads. Trees may shade a road surface so ice remains, and may block drivers' vision around curves. China's new expressways often use 2- to 2.5-m-high dense shrub lines in the median, partly to eliminate headlight glare. And roadside management activities typically slow passing traffic.

Roads affect vegetation in diverse ways, such as: homogenized roadside soil reducing plant diversity; management regimes, vehicles, and chemicals favoring generalist edge species; many non-native plants and some rare native species in roadsides; planting distinctive trees, shrubs, and flowers for visual quality; selecting against wetland species by designing to get water quickly away from the roadbed; cutting woody plants in ecological succession to create grassy swaths in roadsides; and dust, roadsalt, and nitrogen that affect vegetation beyond the roadside.

Wildlife and roads/vehicles

Occasionally vehicles collide with large mammals, with bad effects on the animal, vehicle, people, repair cost, medical cost, and insurance cost. Much more often is the pleasure people have in seeing a heron or fox or flying geese or other wildlife *en route*.

Unlike the preceding, major ecological effects of roads and traffic on wildlife are widespread: 1) habitat loss; 2) roadkilled animals; 3) barrier to wildlife movement across the land; 4) decreasing populations in small, fragmented habitats; 5) habitat zone near highways degraded by traffic noise and disturbance; and 6) highly degraded, dangerous roadsides.

In brief, the reciprocal effects in these six categories are strongly tilted toward the negative effects of roads and traffic on nature.

A useful model has emerged that meshes the rigorous design of roadbeds and immediately adjoining space by transportation engineers, with the major patterns and processes of water flows and species movements across the land analyzed by landscape ecologists. This road-effect zone is the zone of influence over which significant road/traffic-caused ecological effects extend.[13] Asymmetric convoluted margins delimit the zone, where material, energy, and species patterns are significantly altered under the influence of wind, water, and behavioral processes. For a 16-mile stretch of highway with about 50 000 vehicles per day west of Boston, the road-effect zone averaged about 300 m width (1000 ft) on each side, and reached >1000 m in spots.

Optimum road network

Instead of focusing on an individual road or road segment, solutions at the road network scale, i.e., in the landscape or region, offer more long-term promise. Measuring road density in the landscape is a first step, but network form is more informative.[14] Although still a research frontier, four principles seem important in determining an ecologically optimum road-network form in a natural landscape (Figure 3.4): 1) concentrate most of the roads in one portion of the landscape; 2) for the same amount of traffic, have fewer and larger roads; 3) insert water and wildlife underpasses/overpasses to partially connect large natural patches; 4) elevate or sink busy transportation routes between large natural areas to eliminate the swath of degraded habitat, and reconnect the large patches into an extensive natural landscape. With these principles, nature should thrive with roads and vehicles.

Railway, powerline, and pipeline corridors

Roads are by far the best-known ecologically of our infrastructure corridors. Railways, powerlines (electric transmission), and pipelines have much in common.[15] All are relatively straight, long, and of constant width. All have regular maintenance effects over their whole width. All are completely connected (no gaps or breaks). All have relatively abrupt boundaries. All are dominated by edge species. All act as filters to wildlife crossing the land. And many are herbicided to control woody plants.

Buried pipelines commonly have much bare surface and erosion, where maintenance activities keep vegetation limited and an earthen service road passes. Powerline corridors with wires supported on tall towers are often largely covered by shrubs, sometimes with small trees, and typically have an earthen service road and some erosion. Various large birds are electrocuted, and many migrating birds are killed by flying into towers. Powerlines and pipelines usually have low habitat diversity and biodiversity at a spot, but, because they cross over heterogeneous land, habitat diversity and biodiversity may be modestly high along the corridor.

Railway corridors usually have rails and crossties on a covering of cinders or crushed rock atop a raised railroad bed of sand and gravel so that water drains away quickly.[16] With rather steep slopes on opposite sides of the elevated bed, habitat diversity at a spot may be modestly high, but is typically low along the monotonous rail corridor. The railway system also usually has a diversity of built objects … brick walls, concrete structures, metal structures, bridges, culverts, stations … where somewhat distinctive lichens, mosses, and other plants grow. Species in a rail corridor, however, must be tolerant of pollution. Moving trains emit loud noises, particulates, gaseous pollutants, hydrocarbons, even sparks that ignite fires. Also trains sometimes hit birds and large mammals.

In essence, landscape ecology has provided much of the conceptual and theoretical foundation for understanding the ecological interactions with corridors and networks. Road ecology has then built upon this and honed in on roads and vehicles in the land, to understand the reciprocal ecological effects of human infrastructure and nature. The final step is to now briefly introduce the ecology of urban regions, where so much of our infrastructure is concentrated.

Urban region ecology to use

Cities worldwide are rapidly spreading outward, devouring their closest and some of their most valuable surrounding resources. Indeed, the city no longer makes compelling sense. It is embedded in an essentially all-built metropolitan area. More to the point, the city intensely interacts with, and is interdependent with, its ring-around-the-city. Flows and movements in both directions are diverse and massive.

Furthermore, proximity is economic value, as well as social and environmental value. Nearby scarce clean water, local food production, and tourism/recreational access pay valuable dividends.

Outward urbanization into a city's urban-region ring seems to be some combination of four spatial processes,[17] represented by growth in: 1) concentric zones; 2) satellite cities; 3) transportation corridors; or 4) dispersed sites. An analysis of 14 natural systems-related variables around 38 cities worldwide found that the first two urbanization patterns are much better, much less degrading, than the latter two. So, either urbanize synchronously around a few satellite cities (slightly the best strategy) or concentrically around the main city, or both. But avoid sprawl, and avoid strip or ribbon development along transportation corridors.

More than half the world's population now lives in urban regions. We have become an urban species, "*Homo sapiens urbanus.*" The urban region is our place. I spend most of my time in the Boston region (Figure 3.5). It has a large distant ecological footprint, yet it also provides a considerable portion of our nourishment … social, cultural and physical. The urban region is our "annual home range." Each year we take different routes through it, so that over years we become familiar with the region, and increasingly appreciate it. In this way we gain a sense of place, a familiarity and an affinity for our place. A sense of place, in turn, leads to caring and stepping forward to make it a better place.

Recently, with frequent explorations of the Barcelona region (Spain) over a 15-month period for a regional ecological planning project, I gained both familiarity and affinity for the region. I had quickly gained a sense of place.

Five major themes were useful in understanding and outlining spatial solutions so that natural systems and their human uses could

3.4 The Boston, USA, urban region
Notes: Atlantic Ocean (right). If the small cities of Manchester (top) and Worcester (left) are included, Boston's urban region is some 100 km (60 mi) in radius, except to the SSW where the large city of Providence (bottom) is generally considered to be a separate urban region
Source: US Government image

flourish long term in that urban region: 1) nature; 2) food (production); 3) water; 4) built systems; and 5) built areas (Table 3.3).[18] Most dimensions of nature and food were relatively straightforward to address using known principles, whereas water was quite difficult due to the extremely wide range of water issues. Only certain components of built systems, relative to natural systems and their uses, were considered at this regional scale. Thus, five locations around satellite cities and one near the main city were pinpointed as especially appropriate for growth. These required developing local transportation systems with public transit, plus a rethinking of the regional transport grids. A new trucking center for redirecting long-distance and local goods to markets seemed valuable. A "green net" of corridors around municipality boundaries was appropriate to help maintain the identity and distinctiveness of municipalities, in an area where all are growing and threatening to coalesce. Nodes of small and medium industry associated with edge parks at the borders of such expanding municipalities provide nearby employment, and in turn minimize commuter traffic on roads. Finally,

Table 3.3 Major themes of an ecological planning project for the Barcelona region

Nature [emerald network]	Food [major production areas]	Water [for nature and us]	Built systems	Built areas
Large natural areas	Large agricultural landscapes	Water supply scarcity, floods	Local transport systems, public transit	Locations for growth, no-growth areas
Diverse corridor connection types	Market-gardening areas on floodplains	Stormwater and sewage combined	Trucking center, commuter rail	Large, medium, small industries
	Agriculture–nature parks	Water quality	Under/overpasses for hikers, local residents	Municipalities, people, nature
	Concentrated greenhouses	Four contrasting river systems	Edge parks, industry nodes, commuters	Floodplain park
		Riparian vegetation, wetlands		

Source: adapted from Forman (2004, 2008)

a dozen key locations were pinpointed for underpasses/overpasses across highways to help reconnect the region for wildlife, hikers, and local residents.

The above-mentioned analysis of 38 urban regions noted different prominent corridor types in three portions of an urban region.[19] For the city and metropolitan area, these were: river corridor with floodplain, highway corridor, railway corridor, and steep slope if present. For the metro-area border and inner urban-region ring, these were: greenbelt (or urban growth boundary), ring of large parks, greenway, and green wedge. For the outer urban-region ring, these were: river corridor, highway corridor (and rectilinear highway network); coastline, pipeline, electric-transmission powerline; and emerald network (large natural patches connected by major water and wildlife corridors). In addition, the small fine-scale corridor types differed in these three concentric portions of an urban region.

Ring highways outside an all-built metro area were more likely around large cities, and more common in Europe than in other geographic areas.[20] The number of multi-lane radial highways also increased with city size. The land surrounding rivers and major streams was mainly agriculture, secondarily built, and few urban regions had more than half of their watercourses protected by vegetation. Reservoirs were the most common water supply for cities, yet half the cities had <40 percent of the water-supply drainage area protected by vegetation.

In cities, infrastructure seems to play an unusual role in supporting biodiversity. Highly designed and maintained familiar places in a city are normally depauperate in species. In contrast, neglected sites, i.e., with little or no design, planning, and maintenance, tend to have the highest biodiversity.[21] Many of these little noticed locations are in less accessible spots near urban railways, highways, canals, and other infrastructure facilities. Urban greenspaces that often include some infrastructure affect the urban heat island. For example, in the summer heat of Berlin, small parks (up to about 30 ha or 100 acres) are approximately 1°C cooler than their surrounding built area, greenspaces of 30–500 ha about 2–4°C cooler, and large greenspaces >500 ha about 5°C cooler.[22] The cooling effect of a large greenspace, such as Berlin's Tiergarten railway nature park area, extends outward several hundred meters, even >1 km.

Finally, in the landscape of an outer urban-region ring in Germany with villages, farming, and forested areas, a new highway catalyzed huge changes.[23] Near the highway, most villages became towns, most towns became small cities, and strip or ribbon development connected some towns and cities. Farmland decreased. And large forests could only remain in a limited area far from the new highway. The new infrastructure thus transformed the land, and undoubtedly created a wide swath of environmental degradation surrounding the highway.

PLANNING AND POLICY

Tomorrow's transportation system

Consider briefly the only two solutions I know for alleviating the mammoth effects of the road system on nature.

Massively mitigate the existing roads-and-vehicles system. Begin with the two major goals of applying road ecology for society: 1) improve the natural environment alongside every road; and 2) integrate roads and traffic with a sustainable emerald network of biodiversity, plus near-natural water patterns, across the landscape. Then let specific mitigations such as the following accumulate. Perforate roads with underpasses/overpasses to re-establish natural wildlife movement patterns. Cut traffic noise effects with quieter road and tire surfaces, along with roadside soil berms. Convert most open roadsides to woody roadsides to increase wildlife habitat and reduce barrier/fragmentation effects (… and always drive at a safe speed consistent with changing conditions along a road). Improve and add numerous culverts to re-establish natural groundwater patterns, stream flows, and fish movements. Remove spur roads and remote roads in every jurisdiction to restore the integrity of large natural areas. Multiplied at the scale of our road system, these and many other mitigations would produce a huge cumulative benefit for nature. Alas, the current rate of implementation is woefully inadequate. Worldwide urbanization, road building, and vehicle use are all vastly outstripping mitigation efforts.

Transform the road system to a netways-and-pods system. Netways are raised ("elevated ways") or at least partially sunken ("earthways") transport routes with electric power embedded in the paved surface to move "pods," essentially lightweight vehicles that can be linked together when desirable and transported with automated control.[24] Netways, only slightly wider than a soccer goal or US football goalposts, facilitate the re-establishment of essentially unimpeded flows/movements of streams, rivers, wildlife, walkers, and vehicles (on local roads) across the landscape. The netway system initially replaces highways with >3000 vehicles per day in remote, rural, and outer-suburban areas, where the most valuable nature thrives and the greatest gain would occur. In addition to the extensive benefits to natural patterns and processes, the system noticeably enhances the safe and efficient transport of people and goods, and additionally provides major energy, water, pollution, food, and recreation benefits that reverberate through society.

The first of these strategies is just entering its rapid-growth phase, and should certainly expand no matter what. The second strategy should promptly launch into its evaluation, planning, and widespread pilot projects phase, in anticipation of a needed upcoming transformation of surface transportation.

Flexibility, stability, adaptability

One of the underlying themes or goals in the Barcelona region ecological planning project[25] was to provide flexibility to get through tough times and adaptability to gradually change over time. Three principles—systems, redundancy, and diversity—helped produce a wide range of results. Systems concepts, including negative feedbacks and hierarchies providing stability, underlay the emerald network, as well as transportation, agricultural, stream/river, and economic systems. Redundancy or multiple similar components provided flexibility, as in the focus on five large agricultural landscapes, ten emeralds for nature, four rivers for clean water, and two valuable floodplain/delta aquifers. Optional routes for flows and movements were also a key. Finally, diversity, as a richness of types providing flexibility and stability, was evident in five types of agricultural landscape, six types of natural emeralds, and five types of satellite cities for growth.

A wide range of principles or guidelines is available to provide flexibility and stability, in addition to adaptability (the capacity to change in response to changing conditions) (Table 3.4). Rarity, redundancy, and diversity highlight the number and types of features. Resistance and resilience are ways to respond to inevitable big changes or potential disruptions. System connectivity and loops (circuitry) highlight connections for flows and movements. And change indicates the human capacity to consciously adjust or alter conditions. Plans and policies that incorporate many of these principles lead to an area's long, robust future.

Table 3.4 Eight strategic planning principles for flexibility, stability, and adaptability, with land-use planning examples listed beneath

Rarity (conserving resource enriches; loss impoverishes)	Redundancy (number of the same type)	Diversity (number of types)	Resistance (small things easily altered; large things more inertia)	Resilience (rapid return after disruption)	Connectivity (connections for flows/ movements among components)	Loops (alternate routes for flows/ movements)	Change (humans adjust/ alter pattern or approach)
Specific strategic resources retained	Two or more nature reserves of each vegetation type	Wide range of resources maintained	Large natural areas and soil protected	Things that have experienced previous disruptions maintained	Transit routes in different directions from a location	Modal choice and alternative routes in transportation	Technology, markets, and products change
Water supply protected		Diversified activities and land uses	Food and fuel storage				

The big picture again

Hand in hand with this approach is the question of making gradual progress piece by piece, or creating big pictures and visions that are only likely to be accomplished at infrequent intervals. Although a combination of the approaches may be operationally desirable, I sense that the commitment to, and socio-economic-political pressures for, the piecemeal approach has truncated our vision. Hardly anyone expects a big-picture plan or policy to appear, or be achieved. A pity, a lost opportunity, and a much more degraded land ahead.

Indeed, many small pieces successfully accomplished only make sense in a narrow spatial context, but are often counterproductive in a broad landscape or regional perspective. American sprawl, many Mediterranean coastal areas, and most spray irrigation in dry areas have mainly resulted from decisions for tiny areas, which in turn have degraded the landscape or region as a whole, as well as the future for both nature and us. Selecting the best among big-picture visions should be a welcome norm. For planners and policymakers, implementing the winners using an adaptive process would be a welcome escape from the endless degradation of our land, and would offer a brighter future.

CONCLUSION

1 Think globally, plan regionally, and then act locally.
2 Dovetail transportation and other infrastructure into nature's prominent patterns and processes of water, wildlife and biodiversity.
3 Mold the land so nature and people both thrive long term.

NOTES

1 R.T.T. Forman, *Land Mosaics: The Ecology of Landscapes and Regions* (New York: Cambridge University Press, 1995). R.T.T. Forman, *Urban Regions: Ecology and Planning beyond the City* (New York: Cambridge University Press, 2008). R.T.T. Forman, Sperling D., Bissonette J.A., *et al.*, *Road Ecology: Science and Solutions* (Washington, DC: Island Press, 2003). A. Farina, *Principles and Methods in Landscape Ecology* (New York: Springer, 2005). J. Davenport, Davenport J.L., eds, *The Ecology of Transportation: Managing Mobility for the Environment* (New York: Springer, 2006).

2 Forman et al., *Road Ecology*.

3 Forman, *Land Mosaics*. Farina, *Principles and Methods in Landscape Ecology*. J. Wu, *Landscape Ecology: Pattern, Process, Scale and Hierarchy* (Beijing: Higher Education Press, 2007).

4 Forman, *Land Mosaics*. R.T.T. Forman, "Coastal Regions: spatial patterns, flows, and a people–nature solution from the lens of landscape ecology." In: *La Costa obliqua: un atlante per la Puglia*, 2010, pp. 249–265. A.F. Bennett, *Linkages in the Landscape: The Role of Corridors and Connectivity in Wildlife Conservation* (Gland, Switzerland, and Cambridge, UK: IUCN—The World Conservation Union, 2003).

5 Forman, *Land Mosaics*. Bennett, *Linkages in the Landscape*. R. Jongman, Pungetti G., eds, *Ecological Networks and Greenways: Concepts, Design, Implementation* (New York: Cambridge University Press, 2004).

6 Forman, *Land Mosaics*.

7 C.A. Flink, Olka K., Searns R.M., *Trails for the Twenty-First Century: Planning, Design, and Management Manual for Multi-Use Trails* (Washington, DC: Island Press, 2001).

8 K.J. Gregory, Walling D.E., *Drainage Basin Form and Process: A Geomorphological Approach* (New York: John Wiley, 1973). P. Haggett, Cliff A.D., Frey A., *Locational Analysis in Human Geography* (New York: Wiley, 1977). J.C. Lowe, Moryadas S., *The Geography of Movement* (Boston: Houghton Mifflin, 1975). E. Pollard, Hooper M.D., Moore N.W., *Hedges* (London: W. Collins, 1974). E.J. Taaffe, Gauthier, H.L., Jr., *Geography of Transportation* (Englewood Cliffs, NJ: Prentice Hall, 1973).

9 Forman, *Land Mosaics*.

10 Forman, *Land Mosaics*. Haggett et al., *Locational Analysis in Human Geography*. Lowe and Moryadas, *The Geography of Movement*. Taaffe and Gauthier, *Geography of Transportation*.

11 Forman et al., *Road Ecology*. H.D. van Bohemen, *Ecological Engineering and Civil Engineering Works: A Practical Set of Engineering Principles for Road Infrastructure and Coastal Management* (Delft, Netherlands: Directorate-General of Public Works and Water Management, 2004). Davenport and Davenport, *The Ecology of Transportation*.

12 P. Aanen, Alberts W., Bekker G.J., *et al.*, *Nature Engineering and Civil Engineering Works* (Wageningen, Netherlands: Pudoc, 1991).

13 Forman, *et al.*, *Road Ecology*. R.T.T Forman, Deblinger R.D., "The ecological road-effect zone of a Massachusetts (USA) suburban highway." *Conservation Biology* (2000): 36–46.

14 Forman et al., *Road Ecology*. R.T.T. Forman, "Good and bad places for roads: effects of varying road and natural pattern on habitat loss, degradation, and fragmentation." *International Conference on Ecology and Transportation 2005 Proceedings* (Raleigh, NC: Center for Transportation and the Environment, North Carolina State University, 2005), pp. 164–174. H. Ellenberg, Muller K., Stottele T., "Strassen-Okologie: Auswirkungen von Autobahnen und Strasse, auf Okosysteme de deutscher Landschaften." *Okologie und Strasse* (1981): 19–122.

15 Forman, *Land Mosaics*. V. Muehlenbach, "Contributions to the syanthropic (adventive) flora of the railroads of St Louis, Missouri, USA." *Annals of the Missouri Botanical Garden* 66 (1979): 1–108. O.L. Gilbert, *The Ecology of Urban Habitats* (London: Chapman & Hall, 1991).

16 Muehlenbach, "Contributions to the syanthropic flora of the railroads of St Louis, Missouri, USA". Gilbert, *The Ecology of Urban Habitats*.

17 Forman, *Urban Regions*.

18 Forman, *Urban Regions*. *Pla territorial metropolita de Barcelona* (Barcelona: Generalitat de Catalunya, 2010). R.T.T. Forman, *Mosaic territorial para la region metropolitana de Barcelona* (Barcelona: Editorial Gustavo Gili, 2004).

19 Forman, *Urban Regions*.

20 Forman, *Urban Regions*.

21 M. Godde, Richarz, N., Walter B., "Habitat conservation and development in the city of Dusseldorf (Germany)." In: H. Sukopp, M. Numata, A. Huber, eds, *Urban Ecology as the Basis of Urban Planning*, (Amsterdam: SPB Academic Publishing, 1995), pp. 163–171.

22 A. Von Stulpnagel, Horbert M., Sukopp H., "The importance of vegetation for the urban climate." In: H. Sukopp, ed., *Urban Ecology*, (The Hague, Netherlands: SPB Academic Publishing, 1990), pp. 175–193.

23 J.A.G. Jaeger, *Landschaftszerschneidung: eine transdisziplinare Studie germas dem Konzept der Umweltgefahrdung* (Stuttgart, Germany: Verlag Eugen Ulmer, 2002).

24 R.T.T. Forman, D. Sperling, "The future of roads: no driving, no emissions, nature reconnected." *Solutions* (2011, in press).

25 Forman, *Mosaic territorial para la region metropolitana de Barcelona*.

4

Quality of Life

ANTHONY KANE

HARVARD UNIVERSITY GRADUATE SCHOOL OF DESIGN

QUALITY OF LIFE, while an intuitive concept, can be difficult to define or measure because its meaning and standards change from country to country, culture to culture, and across disciplines. Within healthcare, quality of life often focuses more specifically on a patient's ability to perform daily activities, whereas studies on the quality of life for cities include broader social and economic issues. In general, quality of life is used to gauge the well-being of individuals, communities, and societies, and it is a key tool in evaluating the third pillar of sustainability; social sustainability. Improving quality of life is the core and fundamental purpose of infrastructure. Infrastructure provides everything from the basic needs of human life to the most extravagant comforts of the modern world. Pipes, mains, and treatment facilities distribute clean water, energy grids light and heat homes, and transportation networks bring food and goods to local markets. Yet the same infrastructure makes possible water parks, indoor skiing in the desert, and first-class leisure travel. How then should quality of life be evaluated in regards to sustainable infrastructure?

In recent decades studies have demonstrated[1] that beyond the ability to provide basic needs greater wealth does not necessarily correlate with greater happiness and that solely economic metrics, such as gross domestic product (GDP) and average income, are not sufficient in evaluating a society's quality of life. This decoupling of over-consumption and happiness makes it possible to achieve environmental, economic, and social sustainability through mutually beneficial solutions. Therefore, preserving the environment does not necessarily come at the cost of the economy or quality of life.

Efforts have been made to measure the subjective aspects of quality of life. In 1972 Bhutan's King coined the phrase "gross domestic happiness" (GNH) in order to explain his goals of achieving a society in harmony with Buddhist spiritual ideals. Since then the Center for Bhutan Studies has pursued research in GNH and in 2008 Bhutan adopted the GNH index, the purpose of which was to "reflect GNH values, set benchmarks, and track policies and performance of the country."[2] The hope was to challenge conventional indicators such as GDP, which are, "heavily biased towards increased production and consumption, regardless of the necessity or desirability of such outputs, at the expense of other more holistic criterion. It is biased against conservation."[3]

In 1996 the Federation of Canadian Municipalities also began developing "a reporting system to monitor quality of life in Canadian communities."[4] The subsequent studies include eight quality-of-life indicators: population resource, community affordability, quality of employment, quality of housing, community stress, health, safety, and participation.

INFRASTRUCTURE CHALLENGES TODAY

Two great challenges face infrastructure development throughout the world today. The first is to provide the basic needs of water, power, food, and waste removal to the hundreds of millions of people in developing countries and in the rapidly growing slums and informal settlements throughout the world. These needs will have to be met with limited resources amidst the challenges of climatic shifts and irregular weather patterns. Studies have warned that shortages in water, energy, and food will increase civil unrest and border disputes throughout many countries, greatly affecting quality of life. In 2007 the organization International Alert published a report identifying 46 countries consisting of a total 3 billion people where climate change could increase the potential of violent conflict.[5] In his Nobel Peace Prize acceptance speech President Barack Obama recognized this threat:

> There is little scientific dispute that if we do nothing, we will face more drought, famine, and mass displacement that will fuel more conflict for decades. For this reason, it is not merely scientists and activists who call for swift and forceful action—it is military leaders in my country and others who understand that our common security hangs in the balance.[6]

The second great challenge of infrastructure is to meet, in a sustainable way, the demands of developed nations accustomed to lives of over-consumption. Adding to this challenge will be the ranks of developing countries like China where increased affluence is driving the massive urbanization of people desiring the luxuries and comforts long enjoyed by the West.

Quality of Life Impacts		Maslow's Hierarchy of Human Need
Information & Education	Becoming	Self-Actualization
Community & Values	Belonging	Esteem
		Love & Belonging
Health & Wellbeing	Being	Safety
		Physiological

4.1   Quality of life impacts and Maslow's "hierarchy of needs"

It is clear that infrastructure's role in providing the basic needs of humanity both safely and securely throughout the world will become increasingly critical to world stability and the maintenance of a high quality of life, for both the developing and developed world. Density and efficiency will be key factors in meeting these challenges. Density has long been recognized as a necessary step in achieving sustainability and preserving the natural world. The adage "not in my back yard" that for years has distributed infrastructure to the periphery, with all the waste and inefficiency it entails, must now be questioned. As world population grows, along with the trend toward greater urbanization, infrastructure will increasingly find itself within the zone of human settlement and its negative impacts on quality of life will need to be mitigated.

EVALUATING INFRASTRUCTURE'S IMPACT ON QUALITY OF LIFE

While the primary purpose of all infrastructure is to provide the service for which it was intended (whether it be clean water, power, safe transport, hygienic removal of waste, etc.) there can be secondary and tertiary impacts on quality of life that should be taken into account. Similar to Maslow's hierarchy of needs these impacts range from basic physiological needs, like personal safety, to more subjective needs, like self-improvement. For the purpose of evaluating sustainable infrastructure this chapter investigates three categories where infrastructure impacts quality of life:

1. Health and well-being
2. Community and values
3. Information and education.

As with Maslow these categories can be grouped as they relate to human needs for being, belonging, and becoming. Health and well-being includes the basic human need of health, safety, and comfort (i.e., "being"). Community and values relates to connecting infrastructure with the culture and identity of a place, and creating a sense of belonging within communities. In this category historic preservation and context-sensitive design are critical. Community and values also encourages a sense of belonging and is necessary for the acceptance of a project into its local community. Concerns in this category include community involvement in decision making, economic benefit for communities through local employment, and good project governance in order to ensure efficient use of resources and minimal disruption to communities. Information and education touch on the higher human needs for self-improvement and becoming the society needed to achieve sustainability. It is clear that technical solutions are not enough to meet demands and that a drastic re-education of societies is necessary. Longstanding biases against locating infrastructure near communities (when appropriate) will need to be challenged as well as promoting efficiency and conservation. As new methods for creating sustainable infrastructure are developed the importance of educating communities on their benefit in order to gain acceptance and support cannot be overemphasized.

HEALTH AND WELL-BEING

As stated previously the primary purpose of infrastructure is to protect human health and well-being by providing clean and safe services whether water, energy, transport, waste removal, or any other form of infrastructure. However, as infrastructure integrates into communities indirect impacts are often overlooked.

Examples can be found in the research conducted by Prof. John Spengler at the Harvard University School of Public Health, which investigates the effects of pollutants on human health. In 2010 Spengler presented at a conference for the Zofnass Program for Infrastructure Sustainability at the Harvard Graduate School of Design on the adverse affects of airport pollutants on neighboring communities.[7] His research also includes the effects of pollutants from fossil fuel burning throughout the USA, from both coal power plants and vehicles. While transportation infrastructure often focuses on the physical safety of networks, such as roads and airports, health risks resulting from air pollutants are not always well understood or taken into consideration. Better understanding of indirect impacts on human health is an important step in improving quality of life.

Human well-being can be a more difficult aspect to quantify than health. As world populations urbanize, infrastructure must do its part to make communities safe and enjoyable places to live. Foremost is the physical safety and security of both occupants and surrounding communities. The United States Environmental Impact Statements (EIS) require assessment of potential accident scenarios and physical safety issues, but these standards can be applied to a far greater range of projects. These assessments should be conducted for both the construction and operation phases of projects and go beyond the internal operations of the project to include surrounding communities. Design features can include natural surveillance and access control, lighting, traffic calming measures, spatial planning for wayfinding, signage, barriers, and many more.[8] For example, streets that give a sense of safety to pedestrians and bicyclists promote sustainable non-vehicular transportation as well as healthy lifestyles. In addition, when infrastructure facilities located within communities are designed to reduce opportunities for crime and promote community activity

and natural surveillance, infrastructure can be seen as a boon to neighborhoods rather than blight. Numerous sustainable rating systems including CASBEE, ASLA Sustainable Sites Initiative, and Estidama Pearl Rating System include credits related to site safety and security.

Also critical in reintegrating infrastructure into urban environments is the adoption of universal design[9] principles, also known as barrier-free designs. The common perception that infrastructure creates urban "dead zones," unoccupied polluted brownfields that promote crime and vandalism, will need to be countered with sustainable and accessible projects. Reducing the restricted space on a site necessary for security and opening space whenever possible to community activity is helpful in gaining acceptance by local communities, educating the public about sustainable infrastructure, reducing crime, and encouraging healthy and vibrant neighborhoods. LEED®, a widely recognized rating system for sustainable design, already promotes universal design principles in its LEED Neighborhood Development rating system.

The prevention of nuisances can also significantly contribute to healthy communities including odor, vibrations, noise, and light pollution. In combination with nuisance prevention efforts should be made to create comfortable outdoor environments providing wind protection, and shade where appropriate. While seemingly trivial these factors can greatly impact quality of life and are already included in numerous of the most widely implemented sustainable development rating systems including ASLA SSI, CASBEE, CEEQUAL, LEED ND, and Pearl. In order to demonstrate the significance of these often overlooked areas Table 4.1 lists credits related to nuisance control and prevention from current major sustainable rating systems and guidelines.

In 2009 San Diego State University published a study from 11 countries showing that city dwellers were 15–50 percent more likely to get moderate to vigorous exercise at least five days a week.[10] In addition, it is clear that dense living will be necessary to reduce consumption of resources and meet sustainability goals. Encouraging urban living by creating healthy, safe, and comfortable communities is critical, and does not solely concern the disciplines of architecture and urban planning. In 2007, according to the New York City Department of City Planning, 7.4 percent of the total

Table **4.1** Nuisance control credits in current rating systems and guidelines

Noise pollution and vibration	Light pollution	Odor pollution	Outdoor thermal comfort
ASLA Sustainable Sites Initiative 2009 Site Design—Human Health & Well-Being Credit 6.7: Provide Views of Vegetation and Quiet Outdoor Spaces for Mental Restoration	ASLA 2009 Site Design—Human Health & Well-Being Credit 6.9: Reduce Light Pollution	CASBEE QUD 1.5.1: Ensuring Good Air Quality, Acoustic and Vibration Environments LRUD 1.3: Prevention of Air Pollution Affecting outside the Designated Area LRUD 1.4.3: Reduction of the Impact of Odor	CASBEE 2007 QUD 1.5.2: Improving the Wind Environment QUD 1.5.3: Securing Sunlight LRUD 1.1: Reduction of Thermal Impact on the Environment outside the Designated Area in Summer LRUD 1.5: Mitigation of Wind Hazard and Sunlight Obstruction Affecting outside the Designated Area
CASBEE Urban Development 2007 LRUD 1.4.1: Reduction of the Impact of Noise LRUD 1.4.2: Reduction of the Impact of Vibration	CASBEE 2007 LRUD 1.6: Mitigation of Light Pollution Affecting outside the Designated Area	CEEQUAL Effects on Neighbors 11.4: Air Pollution, Including Dust and Odors	Estidama Pearl Rating System 2010 Livable Communities LC-R4: Outdoor Thermal Comfort Strategy LC-9: Improved Outdoor Thermal Comfort Resourceful Energy RE-1: Community Strategies for Passive Cooling and RE-2: Urban Heat Reduction
CEEQUAL Effects on Neighbors 1.3: Noise and Vibration	LEED ND 2009 Green Infrastructure and Buildings Credit 17: Light Pollution Reduction		LEED ND 2009 NPD Credit 14: Tree-Lined and Shaded Streets
	CEEQUAL Effects on Neighbors 11.5: Light Pollution		

land area of New York was devoted to transportation and utilities and 25.2 percent devoted to open space.[11] This does not include another 7.3 percent devoted to public facilities and institutions often referred to as "soft infrastructure." Infrastructure cannot be ignored as a significant contributor to the character and quality of life of communities. As urban centers grow, infrastructure will need to increasingly consider issues of health and well-being in communities.

COMMUNITY AND VALUES

This category includes both involving the community in infrastructure development and respecting their local customs and beliefs. The choice of the term "values" attempts to capture in a broad way what might also be considered local culture: both what communities find visually appealing and how they prefer to live their lives. Two important concerns are historic preservation and context-sensitive design. Community involvement provides the mechanisms for learning what a community values as well as gaining their trust and active acceptance of a project. Bringing a community to the table for discussion and then responding to their input benefits the community, the project, and stakeholders. Just as different

4.2 Bicycle parking lot in Amsterdam
Source: AirBete

climates necessitate different approaches to achieving sustainability, different cultures remind us that infrastructure cannot be a "one size fits all" solution.

Whenever possible, historic or cultural assets should be preserved and restored through conservation or adaptive reuse. In the urge to supply communities with the services they require it is important not to strip them of those features that make them unique. As much as green space connects societies to the environment, cultural sites connect them to their shared history and local identity. It is important to remember that the homogenization of communities can breed resentment and the perception that local culture is being dominated or subverted by another has been the source of instability and violent disputes around the world for centuries.

When new projects are developed, context-sensitive guidelines should be developed in collaboration with local planning agencies to address street character, open spaces, building form and character, as well as landmarks and gateways. Just as local climates can provide unique opportunities for creating sustainable designs through efficient use of resources or the harvesting of renewable resources, local cultures can also provide opportunities for both culturally sensitive and sustainable infrastructure. In Amsterdam a longstanding culture

of bicycle use has greatly influenced the transportation infrastructure and city planning. In this case a tipping point has been reached where development caters to bicycles, which in turn increases bicycle use, perpetuating the cycle. For each project it is important to identify cultural tendencies that may influence the frequency or manner in which infrastructure is used in order to take advantage of opportunities to create tipping points, as in Amsterdam, or to ensure infrastructure is utilized efficiently.

In Fuzhou, China, commercial wastewater and sewage was dumped into the city's 80-km network of canals before emptying into the Minjiang River: a not uncommon occurrence in developing world cities. The untreated canal water was a health risk, created unpleasant odors, was visually unappealing, and significantly damaged downstream ecosystems. Rather than pipe the sewage to a remote wastewater treatment facility, in 2002 the city employed John Todd, famous for his work with sustainable wastewater treatment. A living machine, referred to as the Restorer, was created "using 12,000 plants composed of 20 native species. Constructed with a walkway down the center, the Restorer has met water quality goals and created a prized recreation area for the members of the community."[12] The plants, along with koi, bacteria, and an aeration system, treat the water as it flows through the canals. However, along with its treatment goals the project lists improving the aesthetics of the neighborhood as a major achievement. While the city had turned its back on the polluted canals the project was able to re-engage the community with a valuable part of their cultural heritage, improve the quality of the neighborhood, and provide space for healthy leisure activity.

Community involvement is fundamental in gaining acceptance and buy-in for projects. The first step is to establish forums and mechanisms for eliciting community input and feedback. These are important to ensure services are provided when and where necessary. Second, local employment should be encouraged whenever feasible to support local economies and create a sense of ownership and contribution on the part of communities. Third, project governance or management should be conducted to ensure a successful project for all stakeholders.

Efficiency is critical in achieving sustainability and must be informed by community needs, use, and behavioral patterns. Community input and feedback is the best way to determine how to effectively distribute limited resources. While the best of intentions may be at play, infrastructure, such as transportation, that goes unused is not sustainable. Early community involvement can be significant in determining just what type of infrastructure is needed. The solution to a congested roadway is not always to build more roads. Options may include mass transit, high-occupancy vehicle lanes, or even marketing to promote use of existing means of transportation. After all, the most sustainable infrastructure project is the one that does not have to be built. Using community feedback in a critical pre-design phase that explores options can produce low-impact alternatives to conventional infrastructure development.

Whenever feasible local and equal employment should be encouraged during construction, operations, and maintenance to individuals of various skills, backgrounds, and age, including locally owned and operated businesses, and businesses that support youth development, on-the-job training, and green-collar jobs.[13] While not the primary focus of this chapter, it is impossible to entirely disengage economics, and supporting local economies, from supporting vibrant and healthy communities. In addition, engaging local individuals and businesses aids in gaining community support.

Project governance and management should ensure accountability at all levels, effective communication, and timely review and resolution of issues, so as to deliver projects on time, within budget and scope, and up to the intended high quality, performance, and efficiency.[14] While completing a project successfully is naturally the goal of all stakeholders, and perhaps goes without saying, it is important to note that projects striving to meet high standards of sustainability which encounter difficulties often compromise on sustainable features, undermining the initial project goals. Proper management and good communication help ensure the project envisioned is the project delivered, benefiting all stakeholders; especially the community it serves. Often problems can be prevented before they occur and without added cost by taking time before the project begins to establish guidelines. Project managers should clearly identify stakeholders, their roles, and forums for their input. Responsibilities and accountabilities as well as authority to make decisions should be mapped and clear to all parties. In addition, processes for gating and auditing, and authorizing procedures should be established.

Finally, standards for monitoring and assessing the project's progress and compliance with its original goals should be established prior to construction and regularly enforced. These guidelines and plans should be developed early and communicated to all relevant parties in order to minimize conflicts and establish procedures for dealing with conflicts as they arise. If the value of sustainability to the project is communicated early, emphasized throughout project management, and supported by all stakeholders from the project's inception it is more likely to be realized in the end.

INFORMATION AND EDUCATION

While community involvement is important, it should go hand in hand with community education. The wealth of information available today can be overwhelming, making it difficult for the public to have informed opinions. Education efforts should focus on the need for sustainable infrastructure, the need to reduce resource consumption, and informing the public about new and safe infrastructure technology. Information and education can help to mitigate negative impacts and enhance positive impacts on quality of life in the three areas of health and well-being, community and values, and information and education previously identified.

In April 2010 the New York Times published an article on waste incinerators in Denmark that convert trash into heat and electricity. Fitted with filters and scrubbers, these incinerators, such as the one in Hørsholm, are far cleaner than conventional incinerators of only a few years ago. The article sites that more dioxin is released from fireplaces and backyard barbecues than the plants. It also notes that "Denmark now has 29 such plants … and 10 more are planned or under construction. … By contrast no new waste-to-energy plants are being planned or built in the United States."[15] While the merits of these incinerators, relative to other sustainable alternatives, are debatable, they are resisted in the USA largely because of the negative public perception of burning trash. In so far as public opinion on health impacts of infrastructure should be guided by the facts, efforts should be made through information and education to counter unfounded biases.

Likewise, in the area of aesthetics and values, wind turbine construction in the USA is often challenged when communities do not find them visually appealing or complain they ruin scenic views. Here again, other countries like the Netherlands, with centuries' old cultural ties to windmills, are less disturbed aesthetically by wind turbines. While little can be done to alter personal taste, proper information can help communities come to terms with the *actual* aesthetic impact of infrastructure development rather than the *perceived* impact. In addition, educating the public on the benefits of a project to the economy, the environment, and their quality of life can mitigate negative aesthetic opinions.

MOVING FORWARD

Educating communities on the need for sustainable infrastructure is, and will continue to be, a difficult challenge. It will entail a re-evaluation of what a high quality of life truly means. In nutrition it is understood that a high quality of life does not result from eating whatever one desires. Societies have laws because it is understood a high quality of life does not result from doing whatever one likes. Yet in both of these examples the impacts of these actions are felt immediately: poor health, crime, and violence. However, decades of allocating infrastructure to the periphery, of separating communities and the means by which those communities thrive, has disconnected them from the impact of their consumption. Wastewater treatment facilities, landfills, and power plants are all

kept out of sight but their impact on the environment remains. In addition, previously not well understood risks to human health from congestion and airplane exhaust, and other infrastructure that cannot be so easily separated from communities, are coming to the forefront. Fossil fuels and other resources are being consumed at an unsustainable rate to drive the industry providing building materials for infrastructure. The often quoted UN definition of sustainable development as "development that meets the needs of the present without compromising the ability of future generations to meet their own needs" should also be applied to quality of life. Though what qualifies as a high quality of life may differ from country to country, from the developed to the developing world, it is clear that the maintenance of *any* quality of life cannot continue long term unless sustainable. If given the choice between a coal-burning power plant and a wind turbine in their backyard it is not difficult to imagine what most individuals would prefer. However, these are not the choices that most communities currently face. Yet, as populations grow and urbanize, and as billions of people begin demanding their share of world resources, infrastructure will find its way into more and more backyards. The impact of infrastructure on communities, whether through public health or the livability of neighborhoods, will undoubtedly increase. In meeting this challenge, with careful consideration of communities' well-being, their culture, involvement, and by educating them on the need for sustainable infrastructure, a new and better quality of life can be established for both the wealthiest and poorest societies throughout the world and, most importantly, for future generations to come.

NOTES

1 D. Kahneman, Krueger A.B., Schkade D., *et al.*, "Would you be happier if you were richer? A focusing illusion." *Science* 312 (2006): 1908–1910.

2 The Center for Bhutan Studies, *Gross National Happiness*, www.grossnationalhappiness.com.

3 *Gross National Happiness.*

4 Federation of Canadian Municipalities, "The FCM Quality of Life Reporting System: second report quality of life in Canadian communities," March 2001, www.cityindicators.org/ProjectDeliverables.aspx.

5 D. Smith, Vivekananda J., *A Climate of Conflict: The Links between Climate Change, Peace, and War* (Jason Print, 2007).

6 B.H. Obama, "Remarks by the President at the acceptance of the Nobel Peace Prize," Oslo City Hall, Oslo, Norway (December 10, 2009), www.whitehouse.gov.

7 J. Spengler, "Quality of life," Zofnass Program for Sustainable Infrastructure Conference, Harvard University Graduate School of Design, Cambridge, MA, April 22, 2010.

8 A. Georgoulias, Kane A., Mladenova I., *et al.*, "The Zofnass rating system for sustainable infrastructure: analytic credit definitions for environmental sustainability" (report prepared for the Zofnass Program for Sustainable Infrastructure), pp. 117–149.

9 Center for Universal Design, *Guidelines for Use of the Principles of Universal Design*, www.design.ncsu.edu/cud/.

10 J.F. Sallis, Bowles H.R., Bauman A., *et al.*, "Neighborhood environments and physical activity among adults in 11 countries." *American Journal of Preventative Medicine* 36(6) (2009): 484–489.

11 New York City Department of City Planning, "Primary land use tables" (2007), www.nyc.gov/html/dcp/html/landusefacts/landusefactshome.shtml.

12 J. Todd, "Urban municipal canal restorer Fuzhou, China," John Todd Ecological Design, http://toddecological.com/.

13 Georgoulias, "The Zofnass Rating System for Sustainable Infrastructure", pp. 117–149.

14 Georgoulias, "The Zofnass Rating System for Sustainable Infrastructure", pp. 117–149.

15 E. Rosenthal, "Europe finds clean energy in trash, but US lags." *New York Times*, April 12, 2010.

5

Sustainable Wellness: The Convergence of Social and Ecological Well-being

ALEXIOS MONOPOLIS

HARVARD UNIVERSITY

HUMAN BEHAVIOR is at the heart of the global environmental crisis. Therefore, it would seem prudent to incorporate the field of psychology under the umbrella of environmental studies and sustainability science. This will, in turn, enable us to move beyond solely addressing the symptoms of the problem (e.g., global warming, deforestation, or over-fishing) so that we may also begin to tackle the inherently unsustainable nature of human–environmental relations from a fundamental philosophical and behavioral standpoint.

SUSTAINABILITY AND PSYCHOLOGY

The psychological sciences provide a number of tools that environmental policymakers can employ in the creation, promotion, adoption, and maintenance of Ecologically Responsible Behaviors (ERB): any behavioral actions an individual may take that have positive environmental effects. This may include composting, reusing paper and plastic bags (or, preferably, using neither), turning off lights and unplugging electronic devices when not in use, carpooling or riding a bicycle to work, buying second-hand rather than new, farming organically, building green, living simply, etc. ... The ultimate goal of adopting ERBs is to achieve what is referred to as Sustainable Lifestyles (SLs).

SLs are aimed at meeting basic needs, achieving a higher quality of life, minimizing the use of resources, reducing emissions of waste and pollutants, and not jeopardizing the needs of future generations.[1] One way to assess the impact of SL is to perform an ecological footprint analysis aimed at estimating the number of hectares of natural resources that are needed to support an individual's reported level of consumption.[2]

Interestingly, SLs seem to result in not only tangible ecological benefits, but also social and psychological rewards that have not, until recently, been explored in detail. Empirical data collected in a recent study, for example, demonstrates that, on average, Americans who practice one version of SL, known as 'Voluntary Simplicity' (VS), experience approximately 17 percent to 20 percent higher levels of subjective well-being (happiness and life satisfaction) than the average American.[3]

VS is both a lifestyle choice and a cultural movement focused on lightening and unburdening one's life from things and experiences that interfere with a higher quality of life and, instead, concentrating on the things one genuinely needs and cherishes. This is primarily done by deliberately and mindfully reducing one's consumption of goods and services, living with fewer possessions, cultivating non-materialistic sources of satisfaction and meaning, and developing deeper connections with one's social and ecological community. VS is not a lifestyle of deprivation, however, but rather one of sufficiency or enoughness.

The implications of this study and future research examining the correlations between SL and mental health for global ecological sustainability are extensive. The findings may form the basis of a new happiness- or wellness-based frame through which SL can be promoted. This, in turn, will help advance fundamental and socio-ecologically critical shifts in socio-economic attitudes and behaviors. It will also help inform environmental science, management, policy, design, and planning using neglected, albeit vital, tools accessible through the psychological sciences.

THE SCIENCE OF HAPPINESS

The idea of and search for happiness has intrigued philosophers for thousands of years, starting with the Ancient Greeks (e.g., Aristotle's *Nicomachean Ethics*), but it has only been studied and measured in a systematic way within the last few decades.

Aristotle held that all our pursuits as humans were meant to achieve a final, ultimate "good," that of happiness. In 1776, over 2000 years after Aristotle, the *United States Declaration of Independence* argued for "certain inalienable Rights, that among these are Life, Liberty and the Pursuit of Happiness." As such, America was formed on the basis of the search for happiness, and this inalienable right was deemed equal to the rights to life and freedom. In the UK, Jeremy Bentham's utilitarian philosophy helped popularize the idea of happiness. Bentham's "greatest happiness principle" argued that the purpose of politics should be to bring the greatest happiness to the greatest number of people.

Since then, political interest in happiness has persisted within contemporary society. One survey found that 81 percent of the UK population agreed that the government's primary objective should be the creation of happiness, not wealth[4] and David Cameron, Britain's prime minister, solidified the search for happiness on the political agenda by arguing that "It's time we admitted that there's more to life than money, and it's time we focused not just on GDP, but on GWB—general well-being."[5] Furthermore, when college students from different countries were asked to rate the importance of several values on a scale from 1 to 9, happiness came out first with a score of 8.0, slightly above health and love/affection (7.9), but well above wealth (6.8), among others.[6]

Most importantly, happiness is a central criterion of mental health and, thereby, an important factor in achieving a high quality of life. As is discussed in more detail below, happiness is also associated with a wide range of tangible "quality of life" benefits, including enhanced physical health, superior coping skills, better social function, vocational success, and even longer life.[7]

Clearly, for many, happiness is a fundamental object of human existence and the search for happiness continues to be of primary political, social, and individual importance in the world today.

In order to discuss the science of happiness and understand its relationship to "quality of life," it is necessary to first define what is meant by "subjective well-being," the term most commonly used in the sciences to define and conceptualize happiness.

SUBJECTIVE WELL-BEING

Subjective Well-Being (SWB) refers to how people evaluate their lives, positively and negatively, and includes both experienced well-being (momentary affective states and the way individuals feel about experiences in real time) and evaluative well-being (the way individuals remember their experiences after they are over).[8]

SWB is typically measured by asking individuals a single question aimed at eliciting a global evaluation of one's life, such as: "All things considered, how satisfied are you with your life as a whole?" or, "In general, how happy or unhappy do you usually feel? Check the one statement below that best describes your average happiness." Although happiness is in itself intangible, empirical measures of SWB have been shown to have high consistency, reliability, and validity.[9,10] In addition, neuroscientists have been able to assess positive and negative affect using brainwave data. The left prefrontal region in particular is rich in receptors for the neurotransmitter dopamine. Higher concentrations of dopamine, in turn, have been shown independently to be correlated with positive affect.[11] In addition, electrophysiological measures such as electroencephalograms and electromyographic facial recordings also associate with self-reports of SWB.[12]

A positive evaluation of SWB is generally synonymous with happiness, which consists of positive emotions (a state of well-being and contentment) and positive activities (pleasurable or satisfying experience), although happiness itself has a more diverse range of meanings in popular discourse and scholarly literature: "for example, happiness can mean a general positive mood, a global evaluation of life satisfaction, living a good life, or the causes that make people happy, with the interpretation depending on the context."[13]

Happiness itself has two distinct manifestations: *ephemeral* and *authentic* happiness. Ephemeral happiness (or pleasure) refers to brief emotional episodes marked by positive affect, whereas authentic happiness refers to an underlying state of satisfaction with one's life marked by pleasure, engagement, and meaning.[14] Often, what leads to ephemeral happiness at a given moment in time may not be the same as what produces authentic happiness, or long-term positive SWB.

POSITIVE PSYCHOLOGY
AND SUSTAINABLE HAPPINESS

Researchers in the relatively new field of positive psychology have focused on how to promote and increase levels of SWB. Positive psychology can be defined as

the scientific study of the strengths and virtues that enable individuals and communities to thrive. … This field is founded on the belief that people want to lead meaningful and fulfilling lives, to cultivate what is best within themselves, and to enhance their experiences of love, work, and play. Positive Psychology has three central concerns: positive emotions, positive individual traits, and positive institutions. Understanding positive emotions entails the study of contentment with the past, happiness in the present, and hope for the future. Understanding positive individual traits consists of the study of the strengths and virtues, such as the capacity for love and work, courage, compassion, resilience, creativity, curiosity, integrity, self-knowledge, moderation, self-control, and wisdom. Understanding positive institutions entails the study of the strengths that foster better communities, such as justice, responsibility, civility, parenting, nurturance, work ethic, leadership, teamwork, purpose, and tolerance.[15]

All three components are essential to achieving not only high levels of SWB, but also a high quality of life.

Positive psychologists, such as Martin Seligman, have developed a formula for defining happiness that supports the notion that authentic happiness (vs. ephemeral happiness, or pleasure) is a more holistic and valid measure of SWB:

Pleasure + Engagement + Meaning = Authentic Happiness

According to Martin Seligman, there is also a formula for achieving *sustainable* happiness:

$$H = S + C + V$$

In this equation, H is defined as authentic/enduring happiness, S is your set range, C is the circumstances in one's life, and V represents factors under your voluntary behavioral control.

The S variable is, in part, genetically predetermined. Roughly 50 percent of most personality traits can be attributed to genetic inheritance (even though heritability doesn't mean the trait is unchangeable).[16] This "genetic steersman" results in a "happiness thermostat": a fixed and primarily inherited level of happiness (S, the set range) that we eventually revert to despite temporary experiences of SWB beyond or below that level. Similarly, it is often challenging to raise one's level of happiness because of what has been referred to as the "hedonic treadmill": the tendency of humans to rapidly adapt to both positive and negative life experiences (e.g., winning the lottery or becoming paraplegic) and to retain a relatively stable and constant level of happiness regardless of circumstances.

Indeed, there is only a small amount of scientific research focused on if and how SWB can be *increased*, much less *sustained*. Although some of this research has concluded that the pursuit of happiness is all but futile due to our genetic predispositions and the hedonic treadmill, some researchers (including the author of this paper) argue that sustainable increases are indeed possible.

Positive psychologists, for example, maintain that it is possible to make someone happier by as much as 15 percent. In addition, Lyubomirsky believes that an

individual's chronic happiness level is governed by three classes of factors—(1) his or her genetically-determined set point (or set range) for happiness, which is relatively immune to influence, (2) happiness-relevant circumstantial factors (such as location, income, and marital status), which are difficult but not impossible to change, and (3) intentional cognitive, motivational, and behavioral activities that can influence well-being, and are feasible but effortful to deploy.

Lyubomirsky goes on to state that "It is through the intentional activities in the third class that we believe that sustainable increases in well-being are possible."[17]

The fact is that happiness can and *does* improve with time. For example, a 22-year study that followed approximately 2000 healthy veterans found that life satisfaction increased over these men's lives, peaked at age 65, and did not start notably declining until age 75.[18] A positive correlation between age and well-being measures has also been found in a 23-year longitudinal study of four generations of families[19] and in a cross-sectional study of adults aged 17 to 82.[20] Although these data are merely suggestive, they imply the possibility that sustainable changes in well-being may be related to an individual's capacity to resist adaptation.[21]

HAPPINESS AND QUALITY OF LIFE

Perhaps most tellingly, measures of SWB have been closely associated with tangible "quality of life" outcomes and measurements.[22] For example, there is extensive evidence of correlations between SWB and general health.[23] In addition, researchers found that the use of medical services correlated negatively with SWB.[24] This finding was further supported by a critical study demonstrating that SWB was a significant predictor of mental health levels.[25]

SWB is also predictive of a diverse range of behaviors. For example, individuals with high self-reported levels of SWB

are more likely to be rated as happy by friends; more likely to initiate social contacts with friends; more likely to respond to requests for help; less likely to be involved in disputes at work; less likely to die prematurely; less likely to attempt suicide; and less likely to seek psychological counseling.[26]

Furthermore, happy people have stronger social relationships,[27,28,29,30] superior work outcomes,[31,32,33] and more activity, energy, and flow.[34,35,36] They are also less likely to show symptoms of psychopathology[37,38] and more likely to show better coping abilities,[39,40,41,42,43,] to act cooperatively and prosocially,[44,45,46] to have a bolstered immune system,[47,48] and even longer life.[49,50,51]

Clearly, happiness is an important factor in achieving a high quality of life not only in terms of psychological well-being, but also through more tangible outcomes and behaviors.

The inverse correlation is also true. Since SWB is only one of many factors that shape our understanding of "quality of life," it stands to reason that many additional factors representative of a positive quality of life may help promote happiness and life satisfaction.

Numerous happiness studies, for example, point toward social relationships (including a healthy marriage and relationships with friends and family) as the most critical determinant of happiness.[52] Other determinants include job satisfaction and spirituality.[53,54,55,56,57,58]

VALUES AND GOALS

Critical components of SWB are an individual's personal values and goals. These psychological constructs have significant implications for both motivated behavior (e.g., related to sustainability, such as ERB/SL) and personal SWB.[59] One particular framework, highlighting the differences between extrinsic and intrinsic values and goals, is particularly relevant to this paper's discussion on happiness and sustainability.

Individuals who focus on *extrinsic* values and goals are marked by an acceptance and reliance on consumer culture and the organization of one's life to revolve around the pursuit of wealth, the acquisition of possessions, and the attainment of image/status.

Individuals who strive for an *intrinsic* life, however, focus on personal growth, mindfulness, affiliation, autonomy, authenticity, pursuit of fun non-consummatory activities (e.g., hiking, music), family, volunteerism, meaningful work, connection to nature, financial independence, the pursuit of self-knowledge and self-acceptance, environmental and social awareness, intimacy/connection to others, and contribution to the community.

It is important to note, however, that intrinsic and extrinsic values and goals are not synonymous with an inward or outward orientation *per se*. Instead, an intrinsic orientation refers to goals that are generally intrinsically motivated because they satisfy inherent psychological needs associated with a higher quality of life, such as relatedness, autonomy, and competence.[60,61,62,63] As a result, they are inherently satisfying to pursue in and of themselves.[64] Indeed, individuals who reflect a more intrinsic orientation are often fully engaged in outward pursuits, such as community participation and volunteerism, in order to satisfy deeply intrinsic psychological needs such as affiliation and meaning. Extrinsic goals, on the other hand, refer to goals that are focused on rewards, praise, and external attainments.

Of course, most individuals place some level of emphasis on both extrinsic and intrinsic pursuits so the distinction, in practice, is not either/or.

THE MALAISE OF AFFLUENCE

Nevertheless, modern industrial societies place a significant amount of emphasis on extrinsic values and goals. Indeed,

> messages that happiness and well-being come from the attainment of wealth and the purchase and acquisition of goods and services is a pervasive and inescapable fact of modern life. Such messages are intertwined with governmental, educational, media and business institutions, and are infused in our work, home, and leisure time.[65]

In addition, economists, politicians, and many members of society assume that increased wealth leads to increased happiness. If this were true, it would be logical to assume that richer nations are happier than poor ones, that rich people are happier than poor people, and that as individuals increase their wealth, they will also increase their happiness.

In practice, none of these conclusions match reality. Above the $10,000 mark, there is absolutely *no* statistically significant correlation between wealth and happiness, clearly demonstrating that wealth accumulation beyond the degree to which fundamental needs are met does not automatically lead to something "better."[66,67] It is important to note, however, that income obviously matters for individuals living in poverty, not only in terms of happiness but also in terms of quality of life: "There are powerful arguments for more economic growth in countries where a large proportion of the populace lives in poverty. But this should not be construed as an unalloyed endorsement of growth at all costs. The nature of the growth process matters."[68]

Many industrialized nations, including the USA and Japan, whose per capita incomes and GDPs have grown significantly over the last 50 years, have not reported any overall rise in SWB.[69,70] Indeed, in many cases, instead of greater SWB, there have been increases in levels of stress, anxiety, depression, and suicides.[71] Put more dramatically: "despite succeeding in providing much higher incomes for the majority of people [in industrialized countries], those societies are characterized by a pervading and deep-rooted malaise."[72] How is this possible? According to Oropesa: "Malaise is the concomitant of material wealth because people define themselves with what they own instead of what they create."[73]

The unrelenting focus on growth reflects a cultural acceptance of extrinsic values and goals that, in turn, guides individual choices and behaviors, and represents a drive for growth, wealth, materialism, and conspicuous consumption.

Extensive research in the psychological sciences has demonstrated that an extrinsic orientation is associated with less happiness and life satisfaction, fewer experiences of pleasant emotions (and more frequent experiences of unpleasant emotions), physical symptomatology, more drug and alcohol abuse, more narcissism, and more behavior disorders.[74,75,76,77] These phenomena may be a direct result of the inability of an extrinsically oriented lifestyle to fulfill four fundamental psychological needs correlated with a high quality of life. These include security and safety, competence and efficacy, connection to others, and autonomy and authenticity.[78,79,80,81,82,83]

On the other hand, research has also demonstrated that individuals who focus on the pursuit of intrinsic values and goals report greater personal well-being on a host of measures in comparison with those who are extrinsically oriented.[84]

CAN SOCIAL AND ECOLOGICAL WELLNESS BE FOSTERED CONCURRENTLY?

The dominant political discourse by which contemporary industrialized societies are governed supports the notion that there is an inherent tension between the pursuit of human well-being and ecological well-being. Within this context, environmentally responsible behaviors are framed as a self-sacrifice, requiring restraint of our personal desires and, ultimately, our happiness. As long as this framework dominates the discourse, individuals will be faced with tough questions and choices regarding their lifestyles and behaviors because, even though most Americans desire a healthy environment, they also want to be happy.[85]

In practice, however, the apparent trade-off between human and ecological well-being is a false one. Research has already demonstrated the correlation between certain environmental and prosocial behaviors (e.g., frugality and community participation) and increased personal well-being.[86,87] In addition, the most important sources of life satisfaction are non-material in nature. As a result, "the pursuit of happiness does not appear to require consumption-based, environmentally damaging activity."[88] Furthermore, "a set of values oriented more towards intrinsic than extrinsic aims appear to simultaneously benefit both individual and ecological well-being."[89] Indeed, individuals who focus on the pursuit of intrinsic values and goals report greater personal well-being on a host of measures in comparison with those who are extrinsically oriented.[90]

Intrinsically oriented individuals are not only happier but also act in more ecologically responsible ways than do extrinsically oriented individuals.[91,92] As Brown and Kasser point out,[93] higher levels of both SWB and ERB are associated with a more intrinsic, versus extrinsic, orientation. In addition, an intrinsic orientation correlates with greater environmental stewardship in resource dilemma tasks.[94,95]

The inverse has also been demonstrated: in comparison to non-materialistic individuals, those who are materialistic have lower SWB and also engage in fewer environmentally friendly activities.[96] This reinforces the notions that "an intrinsic value orientation may promote both SWB and ERB."[97] Brown and Kasser help explain why an intrinsic goals and values orientation leads to higher degrees of SWB and ERB

> Intrinsic values are, by their very nature, not dependent on material goods for their fulfillment; thus, energy invested in intrinsic pursuits may mean less energy devoted to some of the consumption-based activities reflected in the ecological footprint analysis and certain of the environmentally friendly behaviors assessed here. For example, people holding more intrinsic values are unlikely to be very interested in large "trophy" homes or gas-guzzling vehicles that often reflect ostentatious displays of wealth or image enhancement. Further, the focus on community that is a component of intrinsic value orientation[98] might lead individuals try to decrease the ecological impacts of their behavior so as to benefit future human generations as well as other species.[99]

SUSTAINABLE WELLNESS: UNIFYING THE SOCIAL AND ENVIRONMENTAL DIMENSIONS OF SUSTAINABILITY

Sustainability is defined as the capacity to endure. Sustainable development is further understood as "development that meets the needs of the present without compromising the ability of future generations to meet their own needs."[100] Under conventional models of development, however, "needs" and "quality of life" are measured and defined purely in economic terms: based on access to goods and services.

This formula is both inadequate and dangerous since it promotes unconstrained economic growth at the expense of social, ecological, and individual well-being. The *means* of achieving sustainability are important, but so are the *ends*. Therefore, the relevant metric of sustainability should be "the production of human wellbeing (not necessarily materials goods) per unit extraction from, or imposition upon, nature."[101] Using this metric, the psychological and social sciences, including tools for measuring happiness and assessing overall well-being (psychological, physical, and social), may eventually play an important role in defining and understanding what is meant by "sustainability" instead of relying on narrow, limited, and myopic economic metrics. Social sustainability represents the first part of that equation; a measurement of overall human wellness and environmental sustainability refers to the latter component.

The dominant neo-liberal economic and development paradigm places primary importance on the values of the market (as opposed to those revolving around ecological or social wellness), and ultimately results in an uncompromising emphasis upon economic growth, the conversion of nature to commodity form, the industrialization of all activity, cultural homogenization, commodity and wealth accumulation, and, of course, human alienation and hyper-individualism.

As noted earlier, "more" is no longer synonymous with "better." A number of mental health indicators in many industrialized countries have declined despite GDP growth, and the assumption that wealth and happiness are correlated has been proven false. According to Lance Morrow, "Economic rationales (more = better) that came in with Adam Smith and are now achieving gaudy fruition in globalized hallucinations like the new Shanghai or the Palm Islands of Dubai seem spiritually threadbare—spectacularly pointless. And not only pointless but something worse, stupid."[102] Clearly, we need to take human satisfaction and quality of life, socio-cultural durability/diversity, and environmental health more seriously.

The question therefore is: What does lead to something better—for people and the planet?

This chapter is built on the premise that resources should primarily be used to promote environmental and social sustainability, rather than unconstrained economic growth. Through this process, both environmental quality and quality of life can be increased and sustained. For more information on nations, such as Costa Rica, that have done relatively well in promoting human well-being without significantly and negatively affecting the natural environment, please visit the Happy Planet Index.[103]

RELEVANCE FOR ARCHITECTS, DESIGNERS, AND PLANNERS

Designers, architects, and urban planners often focus their resources on the development of physical structures and landscapes within human communities such as houses, roads, and utilities. A community, however, is not simply a sum total of all its buildings and infrastructure. It is as much a *social* environment as it is a *physical* environment.

Social Sustainability is aimed at enhancing community livability by providing outreach, developing policies, and designing built environments that address both fundamental needs and also the well-being of a community.

At its most fundamental level, Social Sustainability is aimed at developing and maintaining a high quality of life by increasing *social wellness* through the following means:

- providing for basic human needs such as food, shelter, education, and healthcare
- fostering community and promoting social cohesion

- enhancing psychological (and subjective) well-being
- promoting democratic institutions, ensuring transparency, increasing citizen participation/involvement in the political process, and maintaining good governance
- advancing sustainability awareness and engagement programs
- preserving cultural heritage
- revitalizing the local economy
- cultivating education and creativity
- integrating marginalized communities.

Socio-ecological Sustainability is the combination of two sets of goals: those aimed at increasing *social wellness*, as outlined above, and those aimed at increasing *ecological wellness* such as:

- promoting Environmentally Responsible Behaviors (ERBs) and Sustainable Lifestyles (SLs)
- conserving biodiversity and restoring wildlife habitat
- maintaining air and water quality
- reducing consumption and use of resources
- increasing energy efficiency and the reduction of greenhouse gases
- ensuring access to open/natural/wild spaces
- eliminating or reducing sources of pollution
- mitigating the removal of trees and plants, and the introduction of exotic species.

Of course, Socio-ecological Sustainability cannot be created simply through physical design and planning alone, but it can certainly play a far greater role in the design process than it does at present. For example, socially and environmentally sustainable design is not simply about building "green"; it also helps promote ecologically responsible behaviors and environmentally sustainable lifestyles. Similarly, whereas design cannot force the emergence of robust communities, it can, however, help foster social cohesion.

For example, a recent article in the *New York Times* describes a group called La Mesa Verde ("The Green Table"), which visits homes in low-income, predominantly Latino neighborhoods to help residents plant backyard organic gardens and grow their own produce.[104] These gardens, in turn, contribute to economic sustainability by providing inexpensive, readily available food; one participant in La Mesa Verde program described saving $90 a month on grocery bills because of the garden. Furthermore, providing people with the means to accessing inexpensive, healthy foods is important to promoting health equity. An endemic problem in low-income communities of color is lack of access to healthy foods (e.g., fresh produce) and a predominance of cheap, unhealthy foods. This, in turn, exacerbates health inequality.

Participants in the program also describe the social benefits of bringing their families together, of connecting with children and enhancing community connectedness.

Similarly, open space is not just an important tool for conservation; it is also important for human health. In as little as three to five minutes in open space, negative feelings of fear, anger, and sadness are often replaced with feelings of calm and pleasantness.[105]

Trees can even have an impact on crime. By giving people a place to congregate, crime is less likely because witnesses are present. Trees and people-friendly landscaping give residents a chance to get out and enjoy the environment. This puts people outside on the street, watching their neighborhoods, and drives criminals elsewhere.[106]

Additional examples of promising socially and environmentally sustainable and local ventures around the world abound, including a community biosphere reserve in Himalayan India (where locals retain ownership of their land but concurrently develop a conservation program for the area),[107] a world-class public transport system in Brazil that reduced energy use in the city by a quarter,[108] a Guatemalan cooperative that manufactures farm machinery from old bicycles (creating a bicimolino that allows farmers to complete a week's worth of work within a day and a half),[109] and the creation of self-sustaining villages in the Congo, which use local materials and skills to achieve agricultural independence and improve the standard of living for residents.[110]

A WELLNESS FRAME FOR SUSTAINABILITY

Over the last 30 years or so, two main frames/arguments have been used to convince people to lead ecologically sustainable lifestyles. The first is based on *ethics* and essentially argues that humans have no fundamental right to dominate over, transform, and ultimately destroy nature beyond that which is necessary for survival. Logically, it is a sound philosophical argument, but it can only be applied to people who have the capacity (or luxury) for such an ethical framework (a low-income farmer living in Brazil's Amazon rainforest and responsible for the welfare of a large family may not have that luxury).

The second frame is based on *economics*: "buy a hybrid car because it will help the environment—and save you money on gas" or "create a green business so you can be environmentally responsible … and, in the long term, improve your bottom line." This argument also has limited potential for sustained social and behavioral change because it is based on economic principles that can just as easily work against the environment.

As a result, it would clearly be useful to develop a new argument. The long-term aim of this research is to form one based on wellness and, specifically, subjective well-being: in other words, a happiness/wellness frame to promote an intrinsically focused and sustainable lifestyle.

As this chapter has demonstrated: through an intrinsic value and goal orientation, through lifestyles such as Voluntary Simplicity, *one can lead a happier and more sustainable lifestyle beneficial to oneself, society, and the planet.*

In so doing, this chapter creates a pathway for the development of a new happiness/wellness frame through which sustainability and ERB/SL can be effectively communicated to increase the likelihood of a broader paradigm shift from a society of conspicuous consumption to a society of sufficiency and enoughness.

According to Matthew Nisbet,[111] "frames" are "the conceptual term for interpretative storylines that communicate what is at stake in a science-related debate and why the issue matters."[112] At a theoretical and descriptive level, framing research offers a rich explanation for how various actors in society define science-related issues in politically strategic ways … and how diverse publics differentially perceive, understand, and participate in these debates.[113,114,115] For each group, frames help simplify complex issues by lending greater weight to certain consideration and arguments over others.[116]

Within this framing process, the use of values is critical: "scientists and journalists should always emphasize the values-based reasons for a specific policy action."[117] In terms of this essay, the framing of sustainability science and lifestyles will need to employ the framework of intrinsic vs. extrinsic values and goals and, in particular, an emphasis on the value of happiness as a critical component of psychological well-being and quality of life.

Most importantly, frames help create connections: "They suggest a connection between two concepts … such that after exposure to the framed message, audiences accept or are at least aware of the connection. … "[118] Similarly, if a happiness/wellness frame can be further developed to help link the concept of "happiness" with that of "sustainability," environmental scientists, policymakers, and managers may be better equipped to communicate with and persuade a far wider and more diverse audience than the one currently accessible through the ethical and economic frames employed at present.

This chapter represents one small step in that direction.

NOTES

1   O. Mont, "Concept paper for the International Task Force on Sustainable Lifestyles," Third International Expert Meeting on Sustainable Consumption and Production, Stockholm, 2007.

2   M. Wackernagel, Rees W., *Our Ecological Footprint: Reducing Human Impact on the Earth* (Philadelphia, PA: New Society, 1996).

3   A. Monopolis, *Voluntary Simplicity, Authentic Happiness, and Ecological Sustainability: An Empirical Psychological Analysis of Deliberate Reductions in Consumption and the Cultivation of Intrinsic Values on Subjective Well-Being in Addition to a Conceptual Exploration Regarding the Impact of Individual Simplicity and Socio-Economic Localization on Global Ecological Sustainability*, doctoral dissertation, University of California, 2010.

4   M. Easton, "Britain's Happiness in Decline," 2006, www.bbc.co.uk.

5   BBC. "Make people happier says Cameron," 2006, www.bbc.co.uk.

6   E. Diener, Oishi S., "Are Scandinavians happier than Asians? Issues in comparing nations on subjective well-being." *Asian Economic and Political Issues* 10 (2004): 1–25.

7   S. Lyubomirsky, "Sustainable change in long-term positive affect," unpublished NIH Grant Proposal, 2008.

8   D. Kahneman, Riis J., "Living and thinking about it: Two perspectives on life." In: F.A. Huppert, N. Baylis, B. Keverne, eds, *The Science of Well-Being* (Oxford: Oxford University Press, 2005), pp. 285–304.

9   W. Pavot, Diener E., "Review of the Satisfaction With Life Scale." *Psychological Assessment* 5 (1993): 164–172.

10 E. Diener, Lucas R.E., "Personality and subjective well-being." In: D. Kahneman, E. Diener, N. Schwartz, eds, *Well-being: The Foundations of Hedonic Psychology* (New York: Russell Sage, 1999), pp. 213–229.

11 D. Goleman, "Forget money; Nothing can buy happiness, some researchers say." *New York Times*, July 16, 1996, C1, C3.

12 E. Diener, Suh E., Oishi S., "Recent findings on subjective well-being." *Indian Journal of Clinical Psychology* 24 (1997): 25–41.

13 E. Diener, "Guidelines for national indicators of subjective well-being and ill-being." *Journal of Happiness Studies* 7(4) (2006): 397–404.

14 M. Seligman, *Authentic Happiness: Using the New Positive Psychology to Realize Your Potential for Lasting Fulfillment* (New York, Free Press, 2002).

15 The University of Pennsylvania Positive Psychology Center, www.ppc. sas.upenn.edu.

16 Seligman, *Authentic Happiness*.

17 Lyubomirsky, "Sustainable change."

18 D.K. Mroczek, Spiro A., "Change in life satisfaction over 20 years during adulthood: Findings from the VA Normative Aging Study." *Journal of Personality and Social Psychology* 88 (2005): 189–202.

19 S.R. Charles, Reynolds C.A., Gatz M., "Age-related differences and change in positive and negative affect over 23 years." *Journal of Personality and Social Psychology* 80 (2001): 136–51.

20 T. Kasser, Sheldon, K.M., "Of wealth and death: Materialism, mortality salience and consumption behavior." *Psychological Science* 11 (2000): 352–355.

21 Lyubomirsky, "Sustainable change."

22 S. Lyubomirsky, King L.A., Diener E., *Is Happiness a Good Thing? A Theory of the Benefits of Positive Affect* (Department of Psychology, University of California, Riverside, 2003).

23 E. Diener, "Subjective well-being: The science of happiness and a proposal for a National Index." *American Psychologist* 55 (2000): 34–43.

24 W.A. Arrindell, Heesink J., Feij J.A., "The Satisfaction with Life Scale (SWLS): Appraisal with 1700 healthy young adults in the Netherlands." *Personality and Individual Differences* 26(5) (1999): 815–826.

25 M. Eid, Diener E., "Intraindividual variability in affect: Reliability, validity, and personal correlates." *Journal of Personality and Social Psychology* 51 (1999): 1058–1068.

26 R. Frank, "Collective well-being through greater simplicity." In: D. Doherty, A. Etzioni, eds, *Voluntary Simplicity: Responding to Consumer Culture* (Boulder: Rowman & Littlefield, 2003), pp. 83–98, p. 84.

27 D.S. Berry, Hansen J.S., "Positive affect, negative affect, and social interaction." *Journal of Personality and Social Psychology* 71 (1996): 796–809.

28 L. Harker, Keltner D., "Expressions of positive emotions in women's college yearbook pictures and their relationship to personality and life outcomes across adulthood." *Journal of Personality and Social Psychology* 80 (2001): 112–124.

29 G.N. Marks, Fleming N., "Influences and consequences of well-being among Australian young people: 1980–1995." *Social Indicators Research* 46 (1999): 301–323.

30 M.A. Okun, Stock W.A., Haring M.J., *et al.*, "The social activity/subjective well-being relation: A quantitative synthesis." *Research on Aging* 6 (1984): 45–65.

31 C. Estrada, Isen A.M., Young M.J., "Positive affect influences creative problem solving and reported source of practice satisfaction in physicians." *Motivation and Emotion* 18 (1994): 285–299.

32 J.M. George, "Leader positive mood and group performance: The case of customer service." *Journal of Applied Social Psychology* 25 (1995): 778–795.

33 B.M. Staw, Sutton R.I., Pelled L.H., "Employee positive emotion and favorable outcomes at the workplace." *Organization Science* 5 (1995): 51–71.

34 M. Csikszentmihalyi, Wong, M.M., "The situational and personal correlates of happiness: A cross-national comparison." In: F. Strack, M. Argyle, N. Schwarz, eds, *Subjective Well-being: An Interdisciplinary Perspective* (Elmsford, NY: Pergamon Press, 1991), pp. 193–212.

35 S. Mishra, "Leisure activities and life satisfaction in old age: A case study of retired government employees living in urban areas." *Activities, Adaptation and Aging* 16 (1992): 7–26.

36 D. Watson, Clark L.A., McIntyre C.W., *et al.*, "Affect, personality, and social activity." *Journal of Personality and Social Psychology* 63 (1992): 1011–1025.

37 E. Diener, Seligman M.E.P., "Very happy people." *Psychological Science* 13 (2002): 81–84.

38 H. Koivumaa-Honkanen, Honkanen R., Viinamaeki H., *et al.*, "Life satisfaction and suicide: A 20-year follow-up study." *American Journal of Psychiatry* 158 (2001): 433–439.

39 L.G. Aspinwall, "Rethinking the role of positive affect in self-regulation." *Motivation and Emotion* 22 (1998): 1–32.

40 C.S. Carver, Pozo C., Harris S.D., *et al.*, "How coping mediates the effect of optimism on distress: A study of women with early stage breast cancer." *Journal of Personality and Social Psychology* 65 (1993): 375–390.

41 C.C. Chen, David A., Thompson K., *et al.*, "Coping strategies and psychiatric morbidity in women attending breast assessment clinics." *Journal of Psychosomatic Research* 40 (1996): 265–270.

42 B.L. Fredrickson, Joiner T., "Positive emotions trigger upward spirals toward emotional well-being." *Psychological Science* 13 (2002): 172–175.

43 D. Keltner, Bonanno G.A., "A study of laughter and dissociation: The distinct correlates of laughter and smiling during bereavement." *Journal of Personality and Social Psychology* 73 (1997): 687–702.

44 M.R. Cunningham, Shaffer D.R., Barbee A.P., *et al.* "Separate processes in the relation of elation and depression to helping: Social versus personal concerns." *Journal of Experimental Social Psychology* 26 (1990): 13–33.

45 A.M. Isen, "Positive affect." In: T. Dalgleish, M.J. Power, eds, *Handbook of Cognition and Emotion* (Chichester, UK: John Wiley & Sons Ltd, 1999), pp. 521–539.

46 S. Williams, Shiaw W.T., "Mood and organizational citizenship behavior: The effects of positive affect on employee organizational citizenship behavior intentions." *Journal of Psychology* 133 (1999): 656–668.

47 K.M. Dillon, Minchoff B., Baker K.H., "Positive emotional states and enhancement of the immune system." *International Journal of Psychiatry in Medicine* 15 (1985): 13–18.

48 A.A. Stone, Neale J.M., Cox D.S., *et al.*, "Daily events are associated with a secretory immune response to an oral antigen in men." *Health Psychology* 13 (1994): 440–446.

49 D.D. Danner, Snowdon D.A., Friesen W.V., "Positive emotions in early life and longevity: Findings from the nun study." *Journal of Personality and Social Psychology* 80 (2001): 804–813.

50 T. Maruta, Colligan R.C., Malinchoc M., *et al.*, "Optimists vs. pessimists: Survival rate among medical patients over a 30-year period." *Mayo Clinic Proceedings* 75 (2000): 140–143.

51 G.V. Ostir, Markides K.S., Black S.A., *et al.*, "Emotional well-being predicts subsequent functional independence and survival." *Journal of the American Geriatrics Society* 48 (2000): 473–478.

52 C. Hamilton, *Growth Fetish* (London: Pluto Press, 2004).

53 C.D. Ryff, Keyes C.L., "The structure of psychological well-being revisited." *Journal of Personality and Social Psychology* 69 (1995): 719–727.

54 M. Csikszentmihalyi, "If we are so rich, why aren't we happy?" *American Psychologist* 54 (1999): 821–827.

55 Diener, "Subjective well-being."

56 G.D. Myers, "The funds, friends, and faith of happy people." *American Psychologist* 55 (2000): 56–67.

57 R.M. Ryan, Deci, E.L., "Self-determination theory and the facilitation of intrinsic motivation, social development, and well-being." *American Psychologist* 55 (2000): 68–78.

58 Seligman, *Authentic Happiness*.

59 K.W. Brown, Kasser T., "Are psychological and ecological well-being compatible? The role of values, mindfulness, and lifestyle." *Social Indicators Research* 74 (2005): 349–368, p. 350.

60 T. Kasser, Ryan, R.M., "Further examining the American dream: Differential correlates of intrinsic and extrinsic goals." *Personality and Social Psychology Bulletin* 22 (1996): 280–287.

61 E.L. Deci, Ryan R.M., "The 'what' and 'why' of goal pursuits: Human needs and the self-determination of behavior." *Psychological Inquiry* 11 (2000): 227–268.

62 T. Kasser, "Sketches for a self-determination theory of values." In: E.L. Deci, R.M. Ryan, eds, *Handbook of Self-Determination* (Rochester, NY: University of Rochester Press, 2002), pp. 123–140.

63 Ryan and Deci, "Self-determination theory."

64 F.M.E. Grouzet, Kasser T., Ahuvia A., *et al.*, "The structure of goals contents across 15 cultures." *Journal of Personality and Social Psychology* 89(5) (2006): 800–816.

65 T. Kasser, "The good life or the goods life? Positive psychology and personal well-being in the culture of consumption." In: P.A. Linley, S. Joseph, eds, *Positive Psychology in Practice* (Hoboken: Wiley, 2004), pp. 55–67.

66 B. Frey, Stutzer, A., *Happiness and Economics* (Princeton, NJ: Princeton University Press, 2002), Figure 1.4, pp. 74–76.

67 Seligman, *Authentic Happiness*.

68 Hamilton, *Growth Fetish*, p. 27.

69 R. Veenhoven, *Happiness in Nations: Subjective Appreciation of Life in 56 Nations* (Rotterdam: Erasmus University Press, 1993).

70 Myers, "The funds, friends, and faith of happy people."

71 Cross-National Collaborative Group, "The changing rate of major depression." *Journal of the American Medical Association* 268 (1992): 3098–3105.

72 Hamilton, *Growth Fetish*, p. 11.

73 R.S. Oropesa, "Consumer possessions, consumer passions, and subjective well-being." *Sociological Forum* 10(2) (1995): 215–244, p. 216.

74 Kasser and Ryan, "Further examining the American dream."

75 T. Kasser, Ryan R.M., "Be careful what you wish for: Optimal functioning and the relative attainment of intrinsic and extrinsic goals." In: P. Schmuck, K.M. Sheldon, eds, *Life Goals and Well-Being: Toward a Positive Psychology of Human Striving* (Göttingen: Hogrefe & Huber, 2001), pp. 116–131.

76 K.M. Sheldon, Kasser T., "Coherence and congruence: Two aspects of personality integration." *Journal of Personality and Social Psychology* 68 (1995): 531–543.

77 G.C. Williams, Cox E.M., Hedberg V.A., *et al.*, "Extrinsic life goals and health risk behaviors in adolescents." *Journal of Applied Social Psychology* 30 (2000): 1756–1771.

78 A. Bandura, "Self-efficacy: Toward a unifying theory of behavioral change." *Psychological Review* 84 (1977): 191–215.

79 R.F. Baumeister, Leary M.R., "The need to belong: desire for interpersonal attachments as a fundamental human motivation." *Psychological Bulletin* 117 (1995): 497–529.

80 A.H. Maslow, *Motivation and Personality* (New York, Harper & Row, 1954).

81 Ryan and Deci, "Self-determination theory."

82 T. Kasser, *The High Price of Materialism* (Cambridge: MIT Press, 2002).

83 K.M. Sheldon, Elliot A.J., Kim Y., *et al.* "What is satisfying about satisfying events? Testing 10 candidate psychological needs." *Journal of Personality and Social Psychology* 80 (2001): 325–339.

84 Kasser, *The High Price of Materialism*.

85 Brown and Kasser, "Are psychological and ecological well-being compatible?" p. 349.

86 R. DeYoung, "Some psychological aspects of reduced consumption behavior: The role of intrinsic satisfaction and competence motivation." *Environment and Behavior* 28 (1996): 358–409.

87 R. DeYoung, "Expanding and evaluating motives for environmentally responsible behavior." *Journal of Social Issues* 56 (2000): 509–526.

88 Brown and Kasser, "Are psychological and ecological well-being compatible?" p. 350.

89 Brown and Kasser, "Are psychological and ecological well-being compatible?" p. 361.

90 Kasser, *The High Price of Materialism*.

91 M.L. Richins, Dawson S. "A consumer values orientation for materialism and its measurement: Scale development and validation." *Journal of Consumer Research* 19 (1992): 303–316.

92 Brown and Kasser, "Are psychological and ecological well-being compatible?"

93 Brown and Kasser, "Are psychological and ecological well-being compatible?"

94 Kasser and Sheldon, "Of wealth and death."

95 K.M. Sheldon, McGregor H. "Extrinsic value orientation and the 'tragedy of the commons.'" *Journal of Personality* 68 (2000): 383–411.

96 Richins and Dawson, "A consumer values orientation for materialism and its measurement."

97 Brown and Kasser, "Are psychological and ecological well-being compatible?" p. 351.

98 Kasser and Ryan, "Further examining the American dream."

99 Brown and Kasser, "Are psychological and ecological well-being compatible?" p. 361.

100 H. Brundtland, *Our Common Future* (Oxford: Oxford University Press for the World Commission on Environment and Development, 1987), p. 43.

101 R. Paehlke, "Sustainability as a bridging concept." *Conservation Biology* 19 (2005): 36–38.

102 L. Morrow, "Be my neighbor." *New York Times*, April 22, 2007, www.nytimes.com.

103 Happy Planet Index, www.happyplanetindex.org/.

104 P.L. Brown, "In Latino gardens, vegetables, good health and savings flourish." *New York Times*, January 16, 2010.

105 R.S. Ulrich, "Effects of gardens on health outcomes: Theory and research." In: M.C. Cooper, B. Marni, eds, *Healing Gardens. Therapeutic Benefits and Design Recommendations* (New York: John Wiley & Sons, 1999), pp. 27–86.

106 F.E. Kuo, Sullivan W.C., "Environment and crime in the inner city: Does vegetation reduce crime?" *Environment and Behavior* 33(3) (2001): 343–367.

107 B. McKibben, "Reversal of fortune," 2007, www.motherjones.com.

108 J. Rabinovitch, Hoehn J., "A sustainable urban transportation system: The 'surface metro' in Curitiba, Brazil." The Environmental and Natural Resources Policy and Training Project, Michigan State University, 1995.

109 C. Fox, "Pedal power." *Orion*, September–October 2005: 24.

110 A. Petroff, *Localized Economics the Key for Green Development— Report from the Congo*, 2006, www.green-horizon.org/blog/archives/ecology/localized_econo.shtml.

111 M.C. Nisbet, "Framing science: A new paradigm in public engagement." In: L. Kahlor, P. Stout, eds, *Understanding Science: New Agendas in Science Communication* (New York: Taylor & Francis, 2009), pp. 40–67, p. 51.

112 W.A. Gamson, Modigliani A., "Media discourse and public opinion on nuclear power: A constructionist approach." *American Journal of Sociology* 95 (1989): 1–37.

113 Z. Pan, Kosicki G.M., "Framing analysis: An approach to news discourse." *Political Communication* 10 (1993): 55–75.

114 D.A. Scheufele, "Messages and heuristics: How audiences form attitudes about emerging technologies." In: J. Turney, ed., *Engaging Science: Thoughts, Deeds, Analysis and Action* (London: The Wellcome Trust, 2006), pp. 20–25.

115 Nisbet, "Framing science."

116 M. Ferree, Miller F., "Mobilization and meaning: Toward an integration of social psychological and resource perspectives on social movements." *Sociological Inquiry* 55 (1985): 38–61.

117 Nisbet, "Framing science," p. 53.

118 Nisbet, "Framing science," p. 56.

Part 2
Sustainable Practice in Infrastructure Systems

ALL INFRASTRUCTURE is not created equal. For each infrastructure type, there are various projects with numerous components, each with its own impacts on sustainability. One can imagine in water infrastructure the vastly different concerns at play when building a treatment facility versus replacing a principal water supply pipe. In this section, leaders in the field of sustainable infrastructure present their experiences, from water to energy to landscape, explaining the unique opportunities and challenges faced in each infrastructure type. While the previous section outlined the broad scope of sustainability, this section asks the engineers in the field, with their knowledge and experience, the fundamental question: How do we do it?

6

Water Infrastructure and Sustainability

TOM A. PEDERSEN

CDM

INTRODUCTION

Water is our most important natural resource. Civilizations that recognize the centrality of water to life advance; those that lose sight of this precept suffer. Concern over the state of the world's water resources, a topic that had previously been the domain of scientists and engineers, has now entered the public dialog spurred on by the Internet, social media, and the ubiquitous reporting on the state of the environment by the emerging sustainability citizenry.

Signals of an impending water resources and infrastructure crisis have been identified by the United States Agency for International Development (USAID), the United Nations (UN) and others. For example:

USAID reports that urban populations will grow from 3.3 billion in 2008 to about 5 billion in 2030. Most of this growth is expected to take place in under-served city slums and unplanned parts of the world. Recognizing the increasing trend toward urbanization has led USAID to conclude that "rather than planning for urban growth and working to provide land, infrastructure and services for the poor, misguided policies focus on slowing the process of urbanization and unsuccessfully trying to stem the tide of rural to mega city."[1]

According to the UN, water is essential for all socio-economic development and for maintaining healthy ecosystems. As population increases and development calls for increased allocations of groundwater and surface water for the domestic, agriculture and industrial sectors, the pressure on water resources intensifies, leading to tensions, conflicts among users, and excessive pressure on the environment. The increasing stress on freshwater resources brought about by ever-rising demand and profligate use, as well as by growing pollution worldwide, is of serious concern.[2]

In Sick Water? The Central Role of Wastewater Management in Sustainable Development, Corcoran et al. state: global populations are expected to exceed nine billion by 2050. Urban populations may rise nearly twice as fast, projected to nearly double from current 3.4 billion to 6.4 billion by 2050, with numbers of people living in slums rising even faster, from one to 1.4 billion in just a decade. Over a fifth of the global total, 1.6 billion people are expected to live by the coast by 2015. Inadequate infrastructure and management systems for the increasing volume of wastewater that we produce are at the heart of the wastewater crisis.[3]

The United Nations Environment Programme has called for "greener" laws to avert a water crisis and warns that if the international community fails to take action to improve freshwater supplies for drinking, sanitation, and hygiene purposes, as many as 135 million preventable deaths could occur by 2020.[4]

Solomon, in Water: The Epic Struggle for Wealth, Power, and Civilization opines: "Everyone understands that water is essential to life. But many are only just now beginning to grasp how essential it is to everything in life—food, energy, transportation, nature, leisure, identity, culture, social norms, and virtually all the products used on a daily basis. With population growth and economic development driving accelerating demand for everything, the full value of water is becoming increasingly apparent to all. … Every era has been shaped by its response to the great water challenge of its time. And so it is unfolding—on an epic scale—today. An impending global crisis of freshwater scarcity is fast emerging as a defining fulcrum of world politics and human civilization."[5]

The crucial role that cities play in our expanding global economy necessitates the application of improved planning and management for sustainable urban environments. The centrality of water to cities is paramount, and envisioning the water infrastructure for cities of the future requires adoption of new approaches and technologies for the rejuvenation of existing cities as well as for new greenfield eco-city developments.

This chapter addresses the challenges and opportunities to sustainable urban development presented by water and water infrastructure.

WATER RESOURCES

Earth is unique among the planets of our solar system due to the presence of significant quantities of liquid water. Water is required by all but a few living organisms to sustain life and covers 70 percent of the surface of the blue planet.[6] Although less than 1 percent of the earth's water is freshwater available for human use, it amounts to a substantial quantity that is continually replenished by means of the hydrologic cycle driven by solar radiation. This regenerative system results in various forms of precipitation whose distribution is neither uniform spatially nor temporally. For example, 70 percent of California's water supply is derived from the northern part of the state whereas 80 percent of the demand is in the south.[7] Prediction of precipitation frequency and geographic occurrence, important to water resources management, is complicated by a changing climate.

Global water resources, though theoretically adequate to meet all human needs, are of limited availability in certain parts of the world and below that required to sustain life in others. Transporting water from areas of abundance to areas of scarcity is costly and in certain situations poses significant engineering and political challenges. Advances in desalination and regeneration technologies are allowing water to be produced in areas of limited natural supplies; however, energy requirements and production costs pose limitations to widespread adoption of these technologies.

When freshwater supplies are insufficient to meet ecosystem and human demand, water stress or water scarcity results. Water stress is defined by the UN to occur when the water supply drops below 1700 cubic meters per person per year (m³/person/yr); water scarcity occurs when supplies drop below 1000 m³/person/yr.[8] Water scarcity poses its greatest threat to life in arid and semi-arid areas that are prone to climatic extremes like droughts, and brings with it severe environmental degradation, groundwater level depression, and water allocation controversies. The UN estimates that 40 percent of the world will live in water-scarce regions by 2025.

Our planet's ecosystems are adapted to the amount, type, and timing of precipitation received. Exploitation of water resources beyond regenerative capacities leads to disastrous consequences for ecosystems and society. The shrinking of the Aral Sea is perhaps the most widely recognized modern-day example of the unsustainable use of a water resource for the irrigation of cotton.[9] Nearly 70 percent of the earth's freshwater is used for irrigation, 20 percent by industry, and 10 percent for residential use.[10] Human population growth, increasing demand for food, and expanding dependence on irrigated agriculture speaks to the need for more holistic assessments of water resource regenerative capacities, including the consideration on climate change impacts.

Reporting on water use is an important activity for those companies whose stockholders and consumers are holding them accountable for their corporate social responsibility. The World Business Council for Sustainable Development (WBCSD) has stated that "business cannot survive in a society that thirsts" and "business is part of the solution, and its potential is driven by its engagement."[11]

"Water footprinting" is a method-finding application in industry and elsewhere to estimate direct and indirect water consumed and/or polluted per unit of time or product, taking into account freshwater (blue water), evaporated water (green water), and polluted water (gray water). Monitoring water consumption, much like monitoring gasoline or electricity consumption, serves as a driver for conservation for communities, industries, and individuals.

Humans drink about 4 liters/day and another 2000 liters/day of water is used to produce the food each individual consumes on a daily basis.[12] For example, approximately 246 liters of water is required to produce 1 kg of potatoes, and the water embodied in these potatoes is termed "virtual water."[13] The concept that virtual water flows with the product from the point of production to the point of consumption allows for the accounting of the export or import of water from or to a watershed or region. Virtual water amounts to approximately 15,500 liters/kg of beef and 3,900 liters/kg of chicken.[14] The growing recognition that all the earth's natural systems are interdependent and influenced by the activities of civilization is leading to a more complete realization of the importance of better managing all of our natural resources, including water.

WATER MANAGEMENT PARADIGMS

Novotny has defined the following five urban water management paradigms:[15]

1st	Paradigm:	Opportunistic utilization of water where it is found
2nd	Paradigm:	Engineered storage and conveyance
3rd	Paradigm:	Fast conveyance with treatment
4th	Paradigm:	Addressing non-point sources
5th	Paradigm:	Integrated urban water management.

The 1st paradigm is still operable in sub-Sahara Africa and elsewhere in the world where water is scarce or nomadic cultures range. In this paradigm, water infrastructure may be limited to a dug well, and wastewater infrastructure may be a latrine or, more likely, non-existent.

The Roman aqueducts, the most famous water infrastructures of antiquities, represent the 2nd paradigm. In *Water: The Epic Struggle for Wealth, Power, and Civilization* a vivid description of Rome's aqueducts and waterworks is provided along with a discussion on the centrality of these features to the urban development of Rome.[16] Solomon notes that freshwater conveyance in conduits had been in practice hundreds of years before Rome's first aqueduct was built but the "precision, organizational complexity and grand scale" of Rome's set it apart from others that came before. According to Durant,[17] Rome was one of the best managed capitals of its time, despite its corruption, due in part to its water infrastructure that "fed ample water to homes, tenements, palaces, fountains, gardens, parks, and public baths where thousands bathed at once, and that enough water remained to create artificial lakes for naval battles."

The 3rd paradigm represents the systems found in most urbanized areas of the developed world today. The water infrastructure in this paradigm includes storage and conveyance systems as well as treatment plants for drinking water and wastewater. The 3rd paradigm is characterized by systems that move water to consumers from the source or from storage in engineered pipelines. The distance from source to use is typically significant and substantial amounts of energy are needed for water pumping. Wastewater generated in urban centers is quickly conveyed from the point of generation to a wastewater treatment facility prior to discharge of the treated effluent to surface water, ocean, or land, and disposal or reuse of the biosolids generated during treatment. Significant energy input is required for wastewater pumping and treatment processes. Hundreds of thousands of miles of sewer pipe were installed following the end of the Second World War through the 1970s. These aging pipes are in many places reaching the end of their useful life. In fact, the average age of US wastewater pipes is currently 40 years and will be 50 years in 2050 according to USEPA projections.[18]

In communities where wastewater and stormwater sewers are combined, treatment capacity may be exceeded during periods of intense precipitation events, resulting in discharge of inadequately treated wastewaters, referred to as combined sewer overflows (CSO), to rivers and surface water bodies. In the 4th paradigm, engineered solutions, including underground storage caverns, are developed to mitigate the effects of extreme rainfall and runoff, and in combined sewer and separate storm sewer systems. These storage systems are designed to control and equalize flow to allow for required treatment prior to discharge.

Novotny describes the 5th paradigm as integrated urban water management that "adopts a holistic, systems approach to the urban watershed, rather than a functionally discrete focus on individual components (drinking water, sewage, stormwater)."[19]

In theory, an integrated urban water management approach would appear easier to adopt for a greenfield eco-city development as compared to the retrofitting of an existing urbanized area as part of maintenance, renovation, and renewal. In reality, significant challenges exist in both situations as each requires application of new planning and design tools, new water capture, storage, conveyance, treatment and reuse technologies, and advanced stakeholder collaboration methodologies.

6.1   Earth at night, 2001
Source: NASA, http://visibleearth.nasa.gov

WATER INFRASTRUCTURE

Georgoulias and Pollalis define infrastructure as "the set of fundamental physical systems, services and networks that support built environment and protect the natural world and are essential to sustaining a civilized and productive society."[20] Infrastructure includes those works of engineering that we rely on every day such as roads and bridges, as well as engineering wonders such as the Great Wall of China, which is visible from orbiting spacecraft. Viewing earth at night from satellite imagery (Figure 6.1), the effects of infrastructure can be seen in the electric lights of countless villages, towns, and cities, and the transport routes that connect these. Like a neural network through which information flows, the lights on earth map routes, nodes, and centers through which commerce flows. Night lights are particularly concentrated in populated areas, including the eastern seaboard of the USA. These lighted areas depict our energy grid and transportation infrastructure, and serve to outline water bodies, and, by association, water infrastructure routes.

Through the ages, community and city development has centered on sources of water needed for human consumption, crops, and livestock, and support of transportation and commerce. As capabilities and capacities to extract groundwater or convey surface water great distances in engineered systems increased, development spread to areas with less than abundant amounts of naturally occurring surface water resources, including the urban developments in the arid southwest USA (Figure 6.1). The per capita water consumption in arid regions of the USA is significantly higher than that in humid regions of the country, in part because of increased municipal, institutional, and homeowner irrigation of lawns, golf courses, and gardens.

In Figure 6.2 the lights of Europe are concentrated along the seaboards and along major river valleys, and the lights of Egypt provide a stark outline of the Nile River and delta. In the water-scarce Middle East, lights extend from the Mediterranean Sea on the west to the Jordan River Basin in the east. Offshore lights evident in the Arabian Gulf and in the North Sea locate offshore oil drilling operations. What will become clear in future satellite imagery will be the proliferation of "mega cities" defined by the UN as those with populations exceeding 10 million. The number of mega cities in the world increased from two in 1950 to 25 in 2009.

6.2 City lights of Europe
Source: NASA, http://visibleearth.nasa.gov

Satellite imagery provides a high-level view of urbanization and infrastructure sprawl, whereas our daily experiences bring us face to face with readily observable engineered infrastructure in cities around the world. Roadways, subways, railroads, power plants, electric transmission lines and street lights, telecommunication cables and towers, and the ubiquitous cellular telephone antennae are common sights we have become accustomed to seeing as part of the urban landscape. Underground infrastructure on the other hand is for the most part "out of sight—out of mind," except when system failure results in natural gas or steam line explosions, water or sewer main ruptures, stormwater overflow flooding, or wastewater treatment plant odors are detected. Even readily observable water infrastructure systems like water towers, levees, drains, and channels seldom come to mind when operating as designed but make front-page news when ruptured, breached, or overtopped.

Water infrastructure, and the processes that treat our drinking water and wastewater, are among the public services that those in developed nations have come to rely on as a part of everyday life. The systems that treat, distribute, collect, and clean water in the USA are all part of its water infrastructure. Water infrastructure includes those systems and structures that channel, control, capture, convey, treat, distribute, collect, and discharge water. In the USA alone this infrastructure is comprised of 2,400,000 km of pipeline, 16,000 publicly owned municipal wastewater treatment facilities, and 160,000 drinking water treatment plants.[21] Most underground water pipelines in the USA were built nearly a century ago, have a lifespan of 50 to 100 years, and were originally designed for populations half their current size.[22]

Drinking water treatment plant schemes vary depending on the quality of the source water and regulatory regimes but typically include: physical and chemical treatment processes including filtration by sand, diatomaceous earth, and/or membranes for particulate and turbidity control; disinfection by chlorine, ozone, or ultraviolet light for control of bacteria, viruses, and cysts; coagulation, granular activated carbon, and/or nano-filtration for color control; oxidation for taste and color control; air stripping for removal of volatile organic compounds; disinfection by-product control; and conditioning for pH and corrosion control.[23]

Municipal wastewater treatment is provided to about 97 percent of US residents who are served by sewers, the remainder being served by on-site and privately owned wastewater treatment facilities.[24] Municipal wastewater treatment facilities employ a combination of processes such as: physical (screening, mixing, flocculation, sedimentation, flotation, filtration, and gas transfer); chemical (precipitation, adsorption, and disinfection); and biological (aerobic and anaerobic digestion to remove biodegradable organic matter by conversion to gases and for removal of nutrients such as nitrogen and phosphorus into biomass).[25] The biosolids that are collected during the wastewater process are disposed in landfills, or reused in land application for plant fertilizer or soil-conditioning value in liquid, dewatered, composted, or heat-dried pelletized product. Wastewater treatment facilities that use anaerobic, as opposed to aerobic-solids treatment processes, collect methane gas generated through the microbial degradation process for use in process heating or electricity generation. The liquid stream resulting from wastewater treatment is typically discharged to receiving waters, applied to land for groundwater recharge, or for irrigation of crops, golf course turf, or ornamentals.

It has taken many years for the engineering community to raise awareness of the resource value in wastewater treatment biosolids, which until relatively recently had been referred to as sludge. The view of treated effluent as a resource is beginning to make headway even as the "yuck-factor" phrase finds its way into our vernacular in evening television news features and newspaper articles.

Indirect potable reuse is "the planned incorporation of reclaimed water into the raw water supply, such as in potable water storage reservoirs or a groundwater aquifer, resulting in mixing and assimilation, thus providing an environmental buffer."[26] Direct potable reuse is "the introduction of highly treated reclaimed water either directly into the potable water supply distribution system downstream of the water treatment plant, or into the raw water supply immediately upstream of the water treatment plant".[27]

Indirect and direct potable reuse of treated and disinfected effluent will be important to consider during infrastructure planning. Unlike other resources, like aluminum or glass for which society as a whole recognizes and accepts the need to recycle and reuse, water is a resource that once used is considered a waste and referred to as sewage or wastewater regardless of its contaminant load or level of treatment.

INFRASTRUCTURE INVESTMENT NEEDS

In 2002 the United States Environmental Protection Agency (USEPA) reported that a significant funding gap could develop between projected investment and spending needs for drinking water and clean water infrastructure over the period of 2000–2019 if spending and operations practices remained unchanged. The USEPA estimated replacement needs to be $6 billion in 2020 and greater than $10 billion in 2040. The report suggested that the gap would largely disappear if municipalities increase clean water and drinking water spending at a real rate of growth of 3 percent per year over and above the rate of inflation.[28]

The Clean Watersheds Needs Survey 2008 Report to Congress set water quality needs for the nation as of January 1, 2008 at $298.1 billion, representing capital needs for up to a 20-year period for: publicly owned wastewater pipes and treatment facilities; CSO correction; and stormwater management.[29] The cost is distributed among the categories identified in Figure 6.3 and was based on the comprehensive census survey of more than 34,000 wastewater facilities and water quality projects. The need increases from previous estimates are mainly for rehabilitation of aging infrastructure, to meet more stringent water quality standards, and to respond to population growth.

The USEPA reports a 20-year capital improvement need of $334.8 billion for public water system infrastructure needs from January 2007 through December 2026 to continue to provide safe drinking water to the public from the nation's approximately 52,000 community water systems and 21,400 not-for-profit non-community water systems.[30]

In its 2008 testimony to the US House of Representatives Transportation and Infrastructure Committee on "Investing in Infrastructure: The Road to Recovery," the National Association of Clean Water Agencies (NACWA) strongly encouraged Congress to pass an economic stimulus package that included funding for wastewater infrastructure projects to meet the nation's $300–$500 billion funding gap.

President Obama signed the American Recovery and Reinvestment Act of 2009 (ARRA) into law in February 2009, making $275 billion available for federal contracts, grants, and loans. The Recovery Act

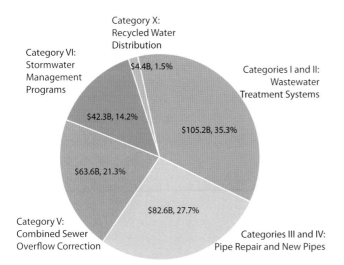

Category X:
Recycled Water
Distribution

$4.4B, 1.5%

Category VI:
Stormwater
Management
Programs

$42.3B, 14.2%

Categories I and II:
Wastewater
Treatment Systems

$105.2B, 35.3%

$63.6B, 21.3%

$82.6B, 27.7%

Category V:
Combined Sewer
Overflow Correction

Categories III and IV:
Pipe Repair and New Pipes

6.3 US water quality capital needs, 2008 through 2030
Source: USEPA, 2008

included significant funding for energy ($70 billion) and transportation ($48 billion) but by comparison only minor funding for drinking water ($2 billion) and clean water ($4 billion) to be managed through State Revolving Funds (SRF).

Local ratepayers fund most wastewater and drinking water treatment needs. Drinking Water State Revolving Fund (DWSRF) and Clean Water State Revolving Fund (CWSRF) monies are designed to supplement, not replace, investment funding by states and localities as well as rate payers. Other funding assistance is available through state-matching funds, bond proceeds, and loan repayments.

In July of 2010 the US House of Representatives passed the "Assistance, Quality, and Affordability Act" (AQUA), which reauthorized the DWSRF program, providing up to $4.8 billion in federal funds over the next three years (HR 5320). AQUA changes to the DWSRF could increase funding to urban water systems for aging infrastructure rehabilitation, replacement, and on-site renewable energy projects The Senate version of the bill (S 1005), which would reauthorize both the drinking water and clean water SRFs, has yet to be passed.

The USEPA's next quadrennial water infrastructure assessment will begin in 2011 to calculate overall needs and allocate federal funds for the DWSRF based on system-specific information on: 1) system inventory and characteristics data including population served, total design capacity, and number of connections; 2) capital improvement projects; and 3) "green" and climate readiness infrastructure projects.[31]

In a 2010 letter to President Obama, Mr Ken Kirk, Executive Director of the NACWA, noted that the nation's water infrastructure needs continue to grow and cited the USEPA-estimated $500 billion gap between current investment and projected needs in water infrastructure through 2020 and the additional need of nearly $300 billion for wastewater and stormwater. The letter refers to studies which show that with every $1 billion invested in water infrastructure, economic ripple effect adds $2.87 to $3.46 billion to the economy as rationale for supporting water infrastructure investments.[32]

The American Water Works Association (AWWA) is promoting the concept of a water infrastructure bank and has stated: "While transportation funding is important, our water systems, although out of sight, cannot be overlooked. These systems are critical for the public health protection, fire protection, economic prosperity and our overall quality of life." In September 2010 President Obama called for the creation of a National Infrastructure Bank to provide increased funding for large-scale road, railway, and aviation infrastructure projects; water infrastructure projects were not included.

In *Infrastructure 2010: Investment Imperative*, the Urban Land Institute and Ernst & Young recommend, among other things, the establishment of a national infrastructure bank, following European models, to promote investment-grade decision making and recruit private capital into infrastructure investments.[33] Establishing a national infrastructure bank could also encourage entry of public private partnerships (PPP) into infrastructure development.

The US General Accounting Office has recently acknowledged that communities will need hundreds of billions of dollars in the coming years to construct and upgrade wastewater infrastructure and a variety of approaches are being explored to finance infrastructure projects, including privately financed public-private partnerships and creation of a national infrastructure bank.[34]

SUSTAINABLE INFRASTRUCTURE

According to the American Society of Civil Engineers "sustainable water resources systems are those designed and managed to fully contribute to the objectives of society, now and in the future, while maintaining their ecological, environmental and hydrologic integrity."[35] The American Water Works Association Sustainability Ad Hoc Committee states that "sustainability means providing an adequate and reliable water supply of desired quality—now and for future generations—in a manner that integrates economic growth, environmental protection and social development."[36]

Sustainable water infrastructure encompasses energy management, climate adaptation, and urban planning. The USEPA sustainable water infrastructure program stresses the need for each utility to improve efficiencies to reduce their overall infrastructure costs, while adopting pricing structures that will produce the revenues to meet their needs.[37] The USEPA's four pillars of sustainable infrastructure are:

1. Better management of water and wastewater utilities
2. Full cost pricing
3. Efficient water use
4. Watershed approaches to protection.

These pillars provide one starting point for development of approaches that will lead to design, construction, and maintenance of more sustainable infrastructure. The Urban Land Institute has identified a number of key points to consider when designing sustainable water infrastructure projects including:[38]

- embrace collaboration among agencies, regions, and communities
- face the reality of added costs to ratepayers
- fix leaks and make necessary upgrades first
- integrate land use into water management
- protect ecosystems
- think comprehensively
- reduce agricultural demand
- moderate household consumption
- encourage conservation and raise rates.

Sustainable water infrastructure can only be realized when conceived, designed, constructed, operated, and maintained within the framework of urban planning. This can only be achieved when the planning and management is conducted in the holistic framework of the urban development, where the built and natural environments are considered concurrently.

WATER-CENTRIC CITIES OF THE FUTURE

Cities require concentration of food, water, energy, and materials that nature cannot provide within a confined area.[39] Water infrastructure, as well as transport and energy, are jointly needed to sustain cities. Our individual views regarding water as a resource are influenced by our local ecosystem setting—proximity to the physical source exploited, and the effort expended, or cost incurred to meet demand. The views of those individuals situated in proximity to large rivers or lakes, or in areas of rainfall abundance, would expectedly differ from those who inhabit desert regions or islands surrounded by oceans. Our views are also shaded by the quality of our water resource, whether it is seen as an agent of health, or a vector of disease.

These divergent views are being brought into focus today more than ever before as society increasingly understands that water must be managed, even locally, as a global resource. As populations grow and the need for food and energy increases, so too does our demand for water. Increasing demand for energy comes with an increase requirement for water at every stage of the value chain: from extraction, to transport, and to generation, whether in hydroelectric, fossil fuel, or nuclear plants, or in the manufacture of the photovoltaic cells or wind turbines that harness renewable energy sources. The "virtual water"—which travels the world from irrigated cotton field, to blue jean manufacturer, to retailer, to consumer, and to recycler—fuels the engine of commerce. Management of the global water resources necessitates an increased appreciation of the embedded water in all the products and services that are crucial to our economies. Moreover, our changing climate necessitates the application of new models and more holistic integrated resource management approaches.

The emergence of the sustainability citizenry, armed with information garnered via the Internet, social media, and soon to be ubiquitous sensors, will exert pressure on politicians, resources planners and managers, and consumers to quickly develop and implement solutions to the water resource challenges.

Bringing these varied perspectives into focus spotlights the need for a more comprehensive and interdependent approach to water management in agriculture, energy, transportation, commerce, recreation, and cities. Implementing an integrated urban water management approach, as envisioned in Novotny's 5th paradigm, will require new technical tools as well as enhanced collaboration of all affected stakeholders. It will require the adoption of new perspectives on every drop of water as it flows through the value chain. It will require that increased permeability be built into new and renovated urban landscapes, and improved flow of information and collaboration between the utilities that manage water. Utilities across the USA, including Charleston Water (South Carolina) and DC Water (formerly the Water and Sanitation Authority of the District of Columbia), realizing the importance of working together are bringing water, wastewater, and stormwater utilities under one umbrella organization. Moving into the future, water and energy utilities partnerships will likely also emerge, especially as the linkage between decentralized energy and water systems becomes more complete.

> According to Brown, "One of the goals of the fifth paradigm is to develop an urban landscape that mimics but not necessarily reproduces the processes and structures present in a predevelopment natural system relying on reduction of imperviousness, increased infiltration, surface storage and use of plants that retain water, interconnected green spaces around urban water resources, and storage-oriented drainage with less reliance on underground conduits and more surface storage, infiltration and flow retardation."[40]

Water is the central organizing element of a healthy and sustainable urban ecosystem. And while we all know that adequate supplies of high-quality water are essential for life itself, we are seeing its importance to the health of the urban environment as a whole—beyond our needs as individuals.

The sustaining life-blood of the urban ecosystem is water. Our emerging understanding regarding the health and sustainability of cities as ecosystems presents significant challenges to our thinking, our expectations, and our roles in the development and protection of the urban environment.[41]

The movement away from large centralized water and wastewater treatment facilities to distributed systems and closed-loop systems will continue to advance, especially as the cost of energy and water treatment and distribution increases and the value of water resources become more evident. Restoring the urban watersheds and water features within cities as part of green infrastructure stormwater systems will point to the importance of ecosystem services to the quality of life. Monetizing the environmental and social benefits of ecosystem services will provide for better decisions to be made regarding urban development and gray and green water infrastructure needs.

"The debate on water policy which has long been dominated by public utilities is now being shaped by progressive private sector companies whose success depends in large part on water availability."[42]

> "One fifth of the world's population, or 1.2 billion people, live in areas of water scarcity, and this is projected to increase to 3 billion by 2025 as water stress and populations increase. There is no option but to consider wastewater as part of the solution. To be successful and sustainable, wastewater management must be an integral part of rural and urban development planning, across all sectors, and where feasible transcending political, administrative and jurisdictional borders. There are few, if any, areas where investments in integrated planning can sustainably provide greater returns across multiple sectors than the development of water infrastructure and the promotion of improved wastewater management."[43]

Sustainable water infrastructure poses complex challenges that require input from experts and stakeholders with diverse perspectives. The Johnson Foundation at Wingspread recently published a call to action that was developed by Freshwater

Summit participants to address the myriad challenges facing the US freshwater resources.[44]

INFRASTRUCTURE SUSTAINABILITY RATING

Measuring the sustainability of a product, service, or project is being considered by a number of organizations. The SustainLane City Rankings provides a relative measure of the sustainability of the 50 most populous US cities based on a rating of the following 16 criteria:[45]

1. City Commuting
2. Metro Transit Ridership
3. Metro Congestion
4. Air Quality
5. *Tap Water Quality*
6. Planning and Land Use
7. City Innovation
8. Energy/Climate Change
9. Knowledge/Communications
10. Local Food/Agriculture
11. Green Building
12. Green Economy
13. Housing Affordability
14. Natural Disaster Risk
15. *Water Supply*
16. Waste Management.

Only two of the criteria deal with water infrastructure related characteristics.

A recent Water Environment Federation (WEF) technical practice update reports that water utility managers are finding that their products and services are being measured increasingly in terms of sustainability, and concludes that "considerable work is needed to help standardize sustainability metrics for the water sector."[46] In another WEF technical practice update (2009) an infrastructure rating methodology is proposed that combines three previously

independent approaches within a watershed for 1) municipal water systems, 2) municipal wastewater systems, and 3) industries. The methodology is as yet untested.[47]

Raucher and Clements evaluated the types of benefits associated with various CSO control strategies by assessing environmental, public health, social, and other benefits to local watersheds and urban-area communities evaluating.[48] Both traditional and green infrastructure approaches to stormwater and CSO management were evaluated to discern which approach would yield the largest net benefit to the community (where net benefits refer to present-value benefits minus present-value costs).

The American Council of Engineering Companies (ACEC), the American Society of Civil Engineers (ASCE) and the American Public Works Association (APWA) have established the Institute for Sustainable Infrastructure to promote sustainability in infrastructure development and redevelopment.

Sustainable infrastructure principles, processes, and programs continue to evolve at a rapid rate to meet the needs of cities and communities, and standardization of approaches will be best achieved through interdisciplinary collaboration.

CASE STUDY—SINGAPORE'S MARINA BARRAGE

Singapore is a 700 square km island-state located at the southern end of the Malay Peninsula. It is a world-renowned shipping port and vibrant city. However, it did not have adequate freshwater resources needed to meet the needs of its growing population. Singapore has treaties in place for importing water from Malaysia, with one set to expire in 2011. Singapore's national water agency, the PUB, in efforts to improve its sustainability and address its water resource needs has established a diversified water supply approach that makes use of four different sources known as the "Four National Taps": 1) water from local catchment areas; 2) imported water; 3) desalinated water; and 4) reclaimed water known as NEWater, a high-grade reclaimed water produced from treated used water that is purified using advanced membrane technologies. This water strategy is aligned with the Singapore

6.4 Singapore's Marina Barrage

Source: PUB, Singapore's national water agency

Urban Renewal Authority's mission to make Singapore a great city to live, work, and play in.[49]

The PUB Marina Barrage project was envisioned more than 20 years ago to address flood control issues, serve as a water supply, and contribute to the lifestyle of the city. Increased catchment area, and subsequently increased water quantity, has resulted from the construction of barrages to separate an estuary from the sea. The estuary area, previously occupied by tidal brackish water, is now being converted to freshwater reservoirs by collecting primarily treated urban runoff.[50] The iconic PUB Marina Barrage shown in Figure 6.4 offers three benefits: water supply, flood control and recreation. It includes the controllable barrage, pumping system, and publicly accessible park, green roof, and educational center powered by solar photovoltaic panels.[51]

CDM served as design engineer and construction manager for the project, which was completed in 2008. The Marina Barrage has created a 100 hectare stable water body in an urban setting. The project was initially designed as a pump station and dam but morphed over the course of planning to a major public facility with multi-agency involvement in the design process. The building was designed to be low profile and iconic to fit in with Urban Redevelopment Authority's long-term goal for this area and to meld into the planned "Gardens by the Bay." Since its official opening on October 31, 2008 through the end of 2009 more than 600,000 people visited the facility.

The success of this project was the result of the strong leadership on the part of the Minister of Environment and Water Resources to carry out this groundbreaking project and the adaptability on the part of PUB engineering staff and their willingness to aggressively tackle the challenges of educating the population on sustainable development.

The Marina Barrage project is an example of how public agencies can adapt their approach to heavy civil engineering projects to provide far wider benefits to the city and population in a "City of the Future" implementation.[52]

NOTES

1   A.M. Garland, Massoumi M., Ruble B.A. *Global Urban Poverty: Setting the Urban Agenda—Comparative Urban Studies Project* (USAID, 2007).

2   UN, "Coping with Water Scarcity: Challenge of the Twenty-first Century World Water Day" (March 22, 2007).

3   E. Corcoran, Nellemann, C., Baker, E., *et al.*, *Sick Water? The Central Role of Wastewater Management in Sustainable Development— A Rapid Response Assessment.* United Nations Environment Programme (UN-HABITAT, GRID-Arendal, 2010).

4   UN. 2010. "Greening Water Law." www.unep.org.

5   S. Solomon, *Water: The Epic Struggle for Wealth, Power, and Civilization* (New York: HarperCollins Publishers, 2010).

6   National Academy of Sciences, "Drinking water: Understanding the science and policy behind a critical resource," 2008, http://water.nationalacademies.org.

7   B. Kingsover, "Freshwater." *National Geographic. A Special Issue. Water—Our Thirsty World* (April 2010): 36–59.

8   UN, "Coping with water scarcity."

9   A. Gore, *Earth in the Balance—Ecology and the Human Spirit* (New York: Houghton Mifflin, 1992).

10 L.R. Brown, *Plan B 3.0—Mobilizing to Save Civilization* (New York: W.W. Norton & Company, Inc., 2008).

11 WBCSD, "Business in the world of water—water scenarios to 2025." Conches-Geneva, Switzerland, 2008, www.wbcsd.org/web/H2Oscenarios.htm.

12 Brown, *Plan B 3.0.*

13 IBM, *Water Global Innovation Outlook Report* (2010).

14 Kingsover, "Freshwater."

15 V. Novotny, "The new paradigm of integrated urban drainage and diffuse pollution abatement." In: *Cities of the Future*, Proceedings of the IWA International Conference on Diffuse Pollution, Belo Horizonte, Brazil, 2007

16 Solomon, *Water.*

17 W. Durant, *The Story of Civilization: Part III—Caesar and Christ. A History of Roman Civilization and of Christianity from their Beginnings to A.D. 325* (New York: Simon & Schuster, 1944).

18 USEPA, "The clean water and drinking water infrastructure gap analysis." US Environmental Protection Agency, Washington, DC (EPA-816-R-02-020, 2002).

19 Novotny, "The new paradigm of integrated urban drainage and diffuse pollution abatement."

20 A. Georgoulias, Pollalis S.N., *Zofnass Program for Infrastructure Sustainability* (Harvard University Graduate School of Design, 2010).

21 GAO, "Wastewater infrastructure financing—stakeholder views on a national infrastructure bank and public–private partnerships." Report to the Ranking Member, Committee on Transportation and Infrastructure, House of Representatives United States Government Accountability Office (GAO, 2010), pp. 10–728.

22 Water Environment Federation, Access Water Knowledge Center, 2010, www.wef.org/AWK/pages_cs.aspx?id=1064.

23 G.P. Fulton, *Water Treatment Plant Design.* American Water Works Association (AWWA) and American Society of Civil Engineers (ASCE) (New York: McGraw-Hill, 2005).

24 GAO, "Wastewater infrastructure financing."

25 Metcalf & Eddy, *Wastewater Engineering—Treatment, Disposal, and Reuse, Third Edition* (New York: McGraw-Hill, 1991).

26 Metcalf & Eddy, *Water Reuse—Issues, Technologies, and Applications* (New York: McGraw-Hill, 2007).

27 Metcalf & Eddy, *Water Reuse.*

28 USEPA, "The clean water and drinking water infrastructure gap analysis."

29 USEPA, "Clean watersheds needs survey 2008 report to Congress" (EPA-832-R-10-002, 2008).

30 USEPA, "Drinking water needs assessment," 2010, http://water.epa.gov/infrastructure/drinkingwater/dwns/index.cfm.

31 USEPA. Federal Register Notice EPA-HQ-OW-2010-0689, September 13, 2010.

32 NACWA. Letter from NACWA Executive Director, Ken Kirk to President Obama, 2010, www.nacwa.org/.

33 J.D. Miller, *Infrastructure 2010—Investment Imperative* (Washington, DC: Urban Land Institute and Ernst & Young, 2010).

34 GAO, "Wastewater infrastructure financing."

35 ASCE, "Sustainable engineering practice—An introduction." *American Society of Civil Engineers (ASCE) Committee on Sustainability* (Reston, VA: ASCE, 2010)

36 AWWA, American Water Works Association Sustainability Ad Hoc Committee. 2009.

37 USEPA, "Sustainable infrastructure website—pillars of sustainable infrastructure," 2010, http://water.epa.gov/infrastructure/sustain/index.cfm; www.epa.gov/water/infrastructure.

38 Miller, *Infrastructure 2010.*

39 Brown, *Plan B 3.0.*

40 P. Brown, "The importance of water infrastructure and the environment in tomorrow's cities." In: V. Novotny, P. Brown, eds, *Cities of the Future: Towards Integrated Sustainable Water and Landscape Management* (London: IWA Publishing UK, 2007).

41 P.R. Brown, "Cities of the future: Improving the machine and tending the garden." Keynote presentation at the Water Environment Federation–International Water Association Cities of the Future 2010 Conference (Cambridge, MA, March 8, 2010).

42 J. Briscoe, "Next generation water policy for business and government." *McKinsey Quarterly* 1 (2010): 66–69.

43 Corcoran, *Sick Water?*

44 Johnson Foundation, "Charting new waters freshwater summit—a call to action to address US freshwater challenges executive summary, report and commitments to action." The Johnson Foundation at Wingspread, 2010.

45 SustainLane. Sustainlane City Sustainability Rankings, 2010, www.sustainlane.com/us-city-rankings/.

46 Water Environment Federation. Access Water Knowledge Center.

47 Water Environment Federation, *Evolving Methodology for Rating Watershed Sustainability in Preparation for Possible Certification— Technical Practice Update.* (Alexandria, VA: Water Environment Federation, 2009).

48 R. Raucher, Clements J. "A triple bottom line assessment of traditional and green infrastructure options for controlling CSO events in Philadelphia's watersheds." In: the 83rd *Water Environment Federation Technical Exposition and Conference Proceedings* (New Orleans, LA, October 2–6, 2010).

49 Urban Redevelopment Authority, *Singapore Storeys—Annual Report.* (Singapore: URA, 2006).

50 Novotny, "The new paradigm of integrated urban drainage and diffuse pollution abatement."

51 B.H. Harley, Kheng Guan Y., "Singapore's Marina Barrage—the community engagement approach as a paradigm for urban solutions in cities of the future." In: *Cities of the Future 2010 Conference Proceedings* (Alexandria, VA: Water Environment Federation, 2010).

52 Harley, "Singapore's Marina Barrage."

7

The Evolution of Urban Water and Energy Infrastructure Systems

JOHN NORTON JR.

MWH

THIS CHAPTER ADDRESSES the evolution and congruence of the urban water and energy infrastructure systems, commonly phrased as the "water–energy nexus." It takes a lot of energy to make water, and it takes a lot of water to make energy, but both resources are under considerable pressures due to a range of significant issues, such as climate and environmental impacts, supply-chain limitations, and socio-economic concerns. Numerous commercial, industrial, and residential developments have been constrained, postponed, or entirely deferred due to water and energy supply limitations, and the rate and relative impact of these concerns is increasing. There have even been concerns of water supply availability in water-rich regions of the world, such as along the Great Lakes, due to the rapid disappearance of the Aral Sea in Central Asia.

This chapter focuses on the technological and social issues driving the evolution of the urban water and energy infrastructure systems, and is separated into five sections, plus a summary and set of references. The first two sections focus on the value of water throughout the water cycle and the evolving energy cost of meeting water system goals from water supply through to wastewater treatment and possible reuse. The third unit describes the congruence of these two issues and describes how local and regional environmental pressures will drive the evolution from the present case. The final two units describe specific implementation scenarios, respectively for capturing the value of water and for integration of non-dispatchable renewable energy.

WATER

Urban water systems represent massive, focused, public investment to withdraw, treat, store, distribute, collect, re-treat, and then discharge water resources. These water systems are almost always centralized, with large standardized treatment facilities that consistently deliver safe, reliable water treatment. Over the years smaller systems have been aggregated into larger systems and the largest treatment facilities often transport treated water or wastewater to and from dozens of communities. For instance, the Metropolitan Water

Reclamation District of Greater Chicago has a system that spans 126 independent cities, including the city of Chicago.

The challenge with these systems is that they provide singular treatment points for the entire water volume, e.g., both the water and wastewater utility treat the entire flow to a single level of treatment, despite the societal demand for a range of water qualities. The latent belief is that water quality is binary, either perfectly clean, or perfectly dirty. With centralized water and wastewater treatment there is no opportunity for capturing the value of water qualities between these two extremes. Society uses, and could benefit from, water treatment and supply at levels between these two extremes. For instance, in water-scarce regions, both grey water harvesting and rainwater harvesting could potentially provide cost-effective augmentation of the water supply to meet non-potable needs. Correspondingly, in water-rich regions, low-impact design (LID) features could draw off stormwater volume to minimize the design capacity and operational costs of large systems sized to treat peak flows. These focused, "sub-scale" treatment systems require a managerial focus more akin to mass production to effectively manage the operations and maintenance of these small systems. The presence of large-scale centralized systems, while cost-effective at meeting their treatment goals due to economies of scale, often dictates a managerial approach at odds with managing multiple quality levels and treatment points distributed throughout an urban system. As a result, most systems are subject to the curse of binary water, the affliction of limited ability or interest to manage water qualities other than those at the fully centralized treatment facilities.

The curse of binary water

The "curse of binary water" implies an inability to consider water qualities other than that within conventional water or wastewater treatment plants. There are two main drivers for this affliction, the existing structure of water utility management, and the economies of scale of both treatment and conveyance operations.

As mentioned above, the presence of large centralized facilities fosters a management structure that is focused on the operations and maintenance of a relatively few large components. This focus emphasizes heavy equipment and training, the near perfect reliability of unit components, and operational reliability over quickness of service. Personnel are often cross-trained to perform multiple maintenance operations since each operation is not performed very frequently, and the maintenance operations themselves can require significant resources and scope of effort.

Economies of scale imply low per-unit treatment cost for larger systems, compared with smaller systems, and there are numerous reasons for this phenomenon. For instance, controls, monitoring equipment, and other devices that must be present are typically the same cost no matter the size of the equipment being controlled, such as payroll software. The cost of centralized collection and distribution facilities are even greater factors in binary water treatment. The cost of conveyance can represent almost 75 percent of the total water system cost and as a result represents a significant expense to be minimized. Conveyance costs are minimized by using single pipe networks for distribution of potable water and collection of wastewater, and thus must use centralized facilities for treatment. In the end, though, the centralized approach also minimizes the capture of the site-specific value of the water qualities generated throughout the collection system.

Water quality is a continuum

The truth is that water quality supply and demand ranges over a continuum. The quality of water demanded ranges from virtually pure water for computer chip manufacturing to fairly contaminated (by organic matter) for agricultural irrigation. We have all washed our hands at a sink that had a sign "not for potable consumption." The water is clean enough for every personal use except for drinking. The water quality of the "poorest" demands range all the way down to high BOD loads used for irrigation or cooling water uses.

Water quality supply also varies, depending on the source, from conventional surface and groundwater to rainwater, grey water, and other recycled water sources. Each of these provides water with distinct chemical, biological, and physical characteristics that must be addressed to meet the needs of the community. Likewise, the water quality demanded by users varies depending on their specific

7.1 Range of water quality generated and demanded
Source: Norton (2008)

needs for chemical and biological purity. An example of some of these contrasting supplies and needs is shown in Figure 7.1.

The value of water

The "value of water" varies based on its suitability for a use and its proximity to a user.[2] The suitability of water to meet a use depends on the quality of its chemical, physical, and biological parameters. There is a range of water quality available and demanded by users throughout the urban water system. A water with fewer contaminants generally can be considered to have higher value than a water with more contaminants, with some variation depending on the type of contaminants (e.g., iron, pathogens).

As a result of the range of water quality that exists, the value of water also ranges over a continuum. Since higher-quality water has higher value than lower-quality water, one can establish a generalized relationship between cost and quality. Figure 7.2 shows this relationship, where the lowest-quality water is generally the water collected at centralized wastewater treatment plants. This water is treated to fairly

Integrated water systems: capture the value of water

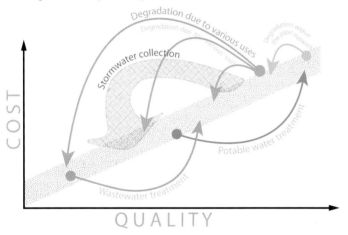

7.2   The generalized value of water throughout the urban system
Source: Norton (2008)[3]

high quality and then discharged to the environment to mix with natural water supplies. This water is better quality than the natural water in the environment due to the US EPA anti-degradation rule. Natural water supplies are then treated by potable water facilities to reach drinking water standards and distributed throughout the urban system to start the cycle once again.

ENERGY

Energy is one of the largest costs of water treatment and is often the largest single operational cost, especially for potable water systems. Sustainable urban water–energy systems are those systems that meet the immediate and long-term needs of consumers within the system and which do so without degrading the system or generating undesirable external impacts. The understanding and implementation of energy management efforts with urban water systems ranges across multiple scales and dimensions. For instance, designing an energy efficient system or implementing renewable

energy generation can require knowledge of everything from water resources to component-level design. While component-level design can, and should, incorporate sustainable design options (such as flexible controls, energy management techniques, and reduction of "imbedded carbon"—the greenhouse gases associated with producing a product), the greatest environmental and energy efficiency will come from system-level analysis that considers all of the relevant environmental costs and benefits. This analysis considers various system designs that incorporate the range of demands and sources, system geometries, contaminant loading, residuals management, and other demands and constraints. It should be specifically noted that while energy consumption is important, the dominating constraint in water system design and operation is meeting water quality goals, specifically permit requirements.

Increasing energy cost of water treatment

Energy costs are expected to increase due to regulatory-driven water quality treatments, increasing pressures to develop marginal sources of water, and degradation of existing water sources. For instance, enhanced disinfection can be achieved by greater chlorination, but at the result of increased formation of disinfection by-products (DBP). Requirements to minimize DBP formation are shifting disinfection methods towards ozonation and UV treatment, followed by chloramination, an effective sequence of processes but one that is also considerably more energy intensive.

Population growth and reduced water supplies have also generated greater pressure to develop marginal sources of water, such as saline water supplies, sea water supplies, and used water sources (water reuse). These water sources are more costly to develop and typically require energy-intensive treatment methods, such as microfiltration, reverse osmosis, and advanced oxidation.

Finally the degradation of existing water supplies will also require increasingly energy-intensive treatment methods. Although the quality of surface water supplies have been increasing for decades, analytical methods have improved to the point where trace amounts of wastewater effluent have been found in almost every water source and thus the apparent quality of the source is degraded. Advanced treatment methods to address these emerging contaminants do exist but—typical to the theme of this chapter—also require greater costs than conventional treatment. The net result of these issues is that the average energy demand per unit of water treated can be expected to increase with time.

Decreasing energy cost of water treatment

In contrast to the increasing cost of water treatment due to increasing treatment requirements is the reduction in treatment cost due to technological innovation. As a result of constant innovation, the typical water treatment unit processes are slowly but constantly improving operational effectiveness. New technologies are resulting in lower energy cost or greater removal efficiency per unit of water volume. For example, reverse osmosis membranes have shown fairly consistent reduction in the energy consumption per unit of water treated. However, not all unit processes have shown such consistent improvement in treatment efficiency. Due to being in a mature stage of product development in recent decades, equipment such as pumps and mixers have shown only minor improvements in process efficiency.

The distribution of innovation-driven efficiency improvements for water treatment processes and components has considerable basis in the product cycle of the technology. Newer treatment technologies and unit processes, although expensive and energy intensive, will also exhibit the greatest efficiency improvements compared with older, more mature product technologies. The implications of this are discussed below.

CONGRUENCE

The water and energy infrastructure systems that undergird our urban communities are a polyglot combination of ancient, old, and new technologies that have evolved into their present form over hundreds of years. The various pipe networks, pump stations, electrical substations, and distribution grids all represent considerable

capital investment and are modified or replaced only through considerable capital investment. Reinvestment is often driven by either increased treatment requirements, or maintenance of existing treatment and conveyance operations. Efficiency and cost savings are often secondary drivers due to the relative permanence of rate structure and customer base, and must therefore present considerable opportunity to overcome institutional inertia and stakeholder resistance. In addition, technological opportunities, such as power demand management, often present latent risks to the operational reliability demanded by the regulators and public, and as such are viewed with suspicion by plant operators.

Contemporary standards and approach

Water and wastewater treatment plant operators are stewards of the public good. Their priorities are treatment standards, organization capability, and human resources. Sustainable design considers the "net environmental benefit" in evaluating, selecting, and implementing treatment systems and options. This benefit is defined as the sum of the positive benefits minus the sum of the negative impacts, and must also be calculated across the entire range of impacted systems. For instance, offsite electrical energy generation results in carbon dioxide and pollutant emission impacts that should be considered in assessing facility design. Various options have various impacts across systems both internal and external to the utility service area. The "best" sustainable design would have the greatest benefits with the least costs across the entire range of impacted systems. One considerable challenge to sustainable design is that specific approaches can have impacts both internal and external to the utility service area, and these impacts vary from design to design. As a result, even when only considering designs that meet relevant regulatory requirements, selected designs might minimize internal impacts but not provide greatest overall benefits due to impacts outside the utility service area.

Most utilities follow the least-cost approach when addressing regulatory requirements. Although utilities are clearly "stewards of the public good," their funding mandates generally preclude funding benefits outside of their service areas. As a result, they are forced to choose service options that might result in greater expenses or operational challenges to other water utilities. For instance, a wastewater utility that discharges just upriver from a potable water utility could meet its discharge permit and yet result in expensive treatment modifications at the potable water utility. An example of this situation is the impact of the Northern Kentucky Sanitation District Number 1 wastewater discharge that is just a few miles upstream of the Cincinnati Water Works intake along the Ohio River. The challenge for these situations is to equitably apportion costs and resources across jurisdictional boundaries, a problem for consensus building using stakeholder workshops.

The future

The future will require agencies to maximize their efficiency based on their local and regional drivers. Just as the criteria defining a sustainable potable water system are unique to a region's geography and climate, the criteria defining a sustainable energy system are unique to a region's geography and climate as well. Water and wastewater utilities face very different water and energy planning scenarios if the resource supply is plentiful or sparse, or if the water quality is excellent or highly degraded. These planning scenarios must reflect the local circumstances of user needs and resource availability. As a result, as wastewater and potable water utilities pursue sustainable processes, they implement distinct goals, evaluation criteria, and trade-off weights in their decision-making approaches. The differences in these approaches, as reflected in the focus and effort of local planning efforts, are due to unique circumstances of geography and climate.[4]

Decision-making factors

System goals

Utilities have very distinct system goals driving their decision-making and planning efforts. A utility pursues goals related to water reuse, water consumption, stormwater management, flood management, stormwater retention, energy use, and other related issues. These goals depend on their specific circumstances and are primarily due to their local geography and climate. For example, regions with significant rainfall focus on stormwater control or urban design features such as green roofs while coastal regions focus on adapting to global warming-induced sea level rise. Undoubtedly utilities have multiple goals and there is significant overlap in goals between utilities of different regions. However, a utility's primary goals are those addressing issues related to their specific geography and climate.

Evaluation criteria

Utilities use evaluation criteria specific to their geography and climate to assess potential alternatives. These evaluation criteria reflect the various functions and capabilities needed by an alternative to meet the system goals. These criteria could be defined as specific attributes or features that meet a required functionality or more broadly such as a quality level or class that could add increasing marginal benefit to an alternative. For example, an evaluation criteria might be relative energy consumption or specific fuel source. Utilities select from among various alternatives based on their assessment of how each alternative performs overall across their entire selection of evaluation criteria.

Trade-off weights

The collective assessment of different evaluation criteria for each alternative is performed using trade-off weights. Trade-offs are necessary with decision-making situations where the alternatives all provide some level of capability across the evaluation criteria and represent the relative weight given one evaluation criteria in terms of another evaluation criteria because of differences in local resources and user demands. For instance, these weights might represent the relative priority given to stormwater treatment versus stormwater prevention. In order to achieve consistency between the various evaluation criteria, trade-off weights are assigned to a specific criteria to represent its relative priority among the entire set of evaluation criteria.

Table 7.1 Characterization of potable water sustainability drivers

		Immediacy of climate change	
		Immediate/near term	Long term
Rough characterization of water resources	Water-rich	Focus: general sustainability issues such as habitat and/or watershed protection, adaptation measures to respond to climate variability/sea level rise	Focus: human health, energy management
			Example region/city: Columbus, OH; Chicago, IL; Midwest
		Example region/city: New York City; Miami, FL; northern coastal cities	
	Water-poor	Focus: non-potable water reuse—quantity and quality issues, local/regional climate modeling	Focus: local/regional climate modeling
			Example region/city: Great Plains (perhaps); financially limited regions or currently uninhabited
		Example region/city: Phoenix; Southern California	

Source: Norton, Ford, and Morris[6]

Regional variation in climate drivers

There are specific differences in policy and implementation between municipal regions based on their potential risk due to climate change.[5] Water-rich regions have a greater emphasis on broader sustainability issues because they have the luxury of a longer time-horizon to modify and optimize their approach based on the failures and successes of the early adapters. Conversely, water-poor regions have immediate concerns with water quality and water quantity issues that drive their policy and planning strategy. Table 7.1 presents a framework contrasting the water management approach for regions of varying water supply and susceptibility to climate change. Note that there are no examples of water-poor regions that do not also have fairly immediate issues with climate change. These cities typically exist on the edge and are extremely vulnerable to even minor fluctuations in water supply due to regional weather variations.

Water abundance versus water scarcity

The availability of regional water supplies drives the planning focus of urban water systems. Almost all water and wastewater utilities have planning issues regarding both stormwater management and developing/maintaining water supply. However, as shown in Figure 7.3, the relative importance of these two issues varies widely depending on the fundamental availability of water: too much or not enough.[7] Areas with excess water invest huge sums to address urban flooding and overflows from combined and/or sanitary sewers. Their water utilities rarely have to address concerns of water volume availability and typically might only need to address water quality issues, for instance if they are supplied from a surface water source. In contrast, water-scarce regions have heavy interest in maintaining and developing water supplies and tend to have fewer significant stormwater management issues. Not all regions are uniformly wet or dry; some areas, regions of Florida for example, have distinct wet and dry seasons and thus have to address both issues.

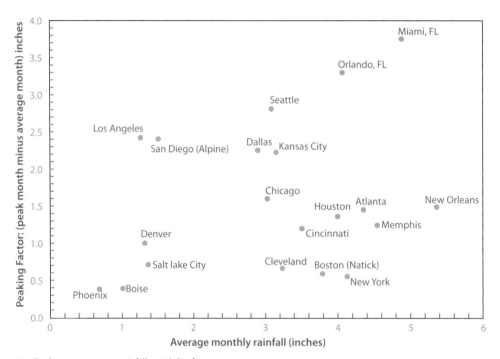

7.3 Peak versus average rainfall variability for various regions
Note: 1971–2000 precipitation averages used
Source: NOAA (2007) (data)

Table 7.2 Characterization of primary urban water focus

		Average rainfall	
		Low	High
Peak rainfall	High	II Capture and store	III Flood control
	Low	I Water reuse	IV Stormwater management

Source: Norton, Ford, and Morris[8]

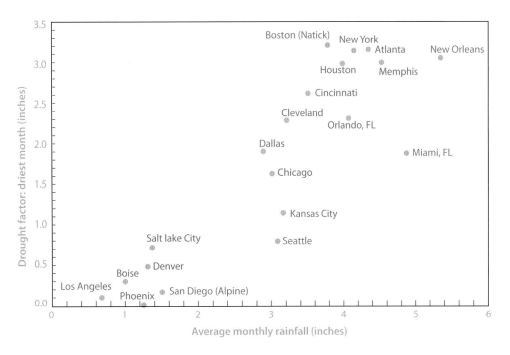

7.4 Variability in rainfall supply: driest month versus average month
Note: 1971–2000 precipitation data used
Source: Norton, Ford, and Morris[10]

The peak and average rainfall data shown in Figure 7.3 can be summarized as a set of four primary focuses for urban water systems. These can be broadly described with unique themes, as described in Table 7.2. For instance, regions in the "Water Reuse" sector have low average rainfall and limited significant rainfall events and thus focus on maximizing their available water via approaches such as water reuse. Sector two "Capture and Store" regions experience low rainfall on average but experience significant rainfall events that can be captured to supplement their available water supply. Sector three "Flood Control" regions experience both high average rainfall and significant peak rain events and are concerned with both stormwater and flood control. Sector four "Stormwater Management" regions have consistently high average rainfall but without the peak rain events typical of the sector three regions

and thus have more focus on general stormwater management. Clearly these regional characterizations ignore important local variations but they do highlight the regional variations that exist as drivers of local efforts.

Regional rainfall variability

Periods of low rainfall typically cause regional water utilities to withdraw greater water volumes than are being recharged. A water utility needs to plan for adequate water supply reserves based on the expected dry periods.[9] There is very good correlation between a region's average monthly rainfall and the rainfall received during its driest month, as shown in Figure 7.4. The driest month typically receives about half the rainfall received during an average month. The data shown have a correlation coefficient of 0.88, but this figure should only be used as an approximation due to the limited population size used in the study.

Coastal versus interior geography

The policy and planning for a sustainable urban water system looks very different for coastal regions compared with interior regions.[11] Coastal cities tend to have much stronger emphasis on climate change and global warming due to the potential impact of sea level rise and increased weather variability on their operations. As a result, they typically have made specific efforts to mitigate their carbon emissions and have taken steps, via policy and planning, to adapt to the most likely climate scenarios. In comparison, inland cities do not have these immediate operational concerns and focus more on broader sustainability issues such as energy-efficient operations and the human health impact of emerging pollutants of concern (EPOCs).

INNOVATION

Advanced treatment systems are more likely to benefit from technological innovation instead of organizational innovation or system restructuring. The reason is that the limitations for successful implementation of advanced treatment systems are primarily based on costs and treatment capabilities, and not changing organizational behaviors or managerial mindsets. By comparison, systems that either capture the value of water or optimize the implementation of renewable energy both require changes in the organizational mindset and conventional thinking. Below are described the implications of both technological innovation and organizational re-thinking in the implementation of these projects.

The rate of technological innovation varies across disciplines due to issues such as physical constraints, economies of scale, relative benefits, and maturity of the discipline. As a result, some

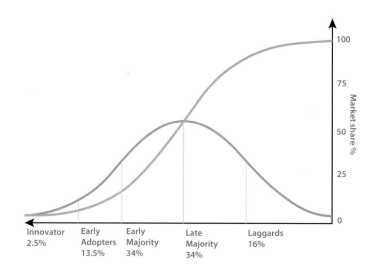

7.5 Graph of technological innovation (s-curve)
Source: adapted from Rogers (1962)[12]

technologies are much more likely to show rapid changes compared to others. The technologies that are most likely to show rapid improvements are those that are relatively new, such as treatment technologies, compared with those that are relatively old, such as pumping or mixing. Figure 7.5 shows the fraction of the applicable population implementing a particular technology. The greatest rate of technological improvement tends to occur during the early majority phase due to the critical mass required for investment in research and development.

INTEGRATION

In contrast to the innovation required for the evolution of treatment systems, the optimal integration of energy generation sources into the water infrastructure will not require technological advances. Instead, integration will require extensive and detailed cross-disciplinary understanding of multiple issues, across multiple domains. This represents a paradigm shift in understanding, in that future planners and designers will be less "subject matter experts" of each relevant domain and more "multiple domain experts" across wide disciplines.

One specific example is the issue of the dispatchability of the energy supply. Non-dispatchable renewable-energy resources are those energy sources that generate energy from external environmental phenomena and not specifically when they are needed. Dispatchable energy resources can be adjusted to meet user demand. Successful integration will require a rethinking and redesign of the water supply and treatment infrastructure based on the most effective use of these energy sources.

Cross-disciplinary planning and design issues

The most significant issue concerning successful integration of variable supply energy sources is the operational flexibility of the underlying system and resultant energy demand. For example, operational flexibility of the water supply system to accommodate variable energy supply could be obtained by a number of methods. One approach could be to have internal storage to accommodate the variations in pump station flow rate due to fluctuations in wind energy generation. This storage could be either point or distributed, e.g., strategically located reservoirs or varying depths of channel flow.

However, this—or any other—design approach will require understanding of multiple issues. For example, variable operations generally result in more frequent maintenance outages for major rehabilitations then required for base-loaded equipment. Some of this is caused by thermal cycling, and some of this is caused by operation under less than ideal conditions with resulting increased fatigue loading.

Case study of planning approach using wind energy

As an example, the domain-specific study components for an application of non-dispatchable energy to power all or part of a municipal water supply system are shown in Table 7.3 overleaf.

These components represent a series of trade-offs between optimized system capacity versus optimized system flexibility. System capacity reflects the size of the pipeline system, the in-system storage volume, and the pump stations. System flexibility addresses the ability of the system to operate with a variable energy supply and the resulting implications on both pump station design and short-term versus long-term water volume transmission and delivery. Optimum system capacity implies the smallest system size that will be able to meet the required average water delivery requirements while optimal system flexibility implies a system with larger components that can compensate for periods of low or no water flow.

Option 1—full grid connection and offset power consumption

In this scenario, the grid connection provides the primary source of power and is sized to meet full electrical demand during periods of quiescent weather conditions. Wind energy is used to offset grid energy demand and the revenue benefit comes from offsetting grid energy purchases. The grid connection will be sized to meet the entire pump station energy demand. The electrical rate could reflect a charge for peak demand that may or may not ever occur, depending on variation in wind energy generation and operation of the pump stations. The pump stations can be operated to optimize water delivery and, since they would be designed to meet constant flow requirements, would have the minimum design capacity. In addition, the required volume of reservoir water storage is minimized.

Option 2—partial grid connection and offset power consumption

In this scenario, the grid connection provides a significant source of power and is sized to meet partial electrical demand during periods of quiescent weather conditions. Wind energy is used to offset grid energy demand and the revenue benefit comes from offsetting grid energy purchases and from both reduced capital connection costs and reduced grid rates due to lowered demand charge. The grid connection will be sized to meet only a portion of the pump

Table 7.3 Overview of power options

Option	Grid (conventional) energy	Connection demand capacity	Pump station capacity	In-system storage	Operational flexibility
Option 1—full grid connection and offset power consumption	WORST—maximum use of grid energy	WORST—maximum peak demand requires largest grid interconnection	BEST—smallest required size to meet flow requirements	BEST—no in-system storage required beyond needed for delivery requirements	BEST—least operational flexibility required, grid energy will be used to "levelize" fluctuations in wind energy
Option 2—partial grid connection and offset power consumption	MODERATE—moderate use of grid energy	MODERATE—moderate peak demand will require moderate grid interconnection	MODERATE—moderately sized pump station to account for periods of low wind energy production	MODERATE—to account for periods of low wind energy production	MODERATE—operational flexibility required to account for variations in wind energy
Option 3—basic grid connection and primary wind power consumption	BEST—minimum use of grid energy	NEAR BEST—minimum grid connection requirement	WORST—largest pump station capacity to accommodate greatest fluctuations in energy supply	WORST—largest in-system storage required to accommodate periods of low wind energy production	WORST—greatest operational flexibility required to accommodate greatest fluctuations in energy supply
Option 4a—primary wind power consumption with emergency on-site power generation	BEST—minimum use of grid energy	BEST—no grid connection requirement	WORST—largest pump station capacity to accommodate greatest fluctuations in energy supply	WORST—largest in-system storage required to accommodate periods of low wind energy production	WORST—greatest operational flexibility required to accommodate greatest fluctuations in energy supply
Option 4b—primary wind power consumption with supplemental on-site power generation	MODERATE—minimum use of grid energy, but potentially substantial use of conventional generator power	BEST—no grid connection requirement	MODERATE—moderately sized pump station to account for periods of low wind energy production	MODERATE—to account for periods of low wind energy production	MODERATE—operational flexibility required to account for variations in wind energy

station energy demand. The electrical rate will reflect a reduced charge for peak demand compared with full grid connection, but will still vary depending on variation in wind energy generation and operation of the pump stations. The pump stations can be operated to meet suboptimal water delivery flow requirements but with the benefit of reduced energy costs. The trade-off is the requirement for more flexible operation, larger minimum design capacity (to cope with flow fluctuations), and potentially the requirement for in-system water storage to account for network slack.

Option 3—basic grid connection and primary wind power consumption

In this scenario, the grid connection provides a base level of power that is sized to meet emergency-system electrical demands such as fire suppression, safety lighting, and similar. Wind energy is used as the primary source of power and the revenue benefit comes from completely offsetting grid energy purchases and from both reduced capital connection costs and reduced grid rates due to lowered demand charge. The grid connection will be sized to meet only the minimum level of pump station functionalities. The electrical rate will reflect a minimal charge for peak demand compared with the other grid connection options, but will still vary depending on applicable grid rate structure. The pump stations would only be operated during periods of wind energy generation and would be oversized, compared with the full or partial grid connection options, in order to provide the same overall flow despite the fluctuations in wind energy generation. The trade-off is the requirement for the most flexible system operation, largest minimum design capacity (to cope with flow fluctuations), and potentially the greatest requirement for in-system water storage to account for network slack.

Option 4a—primary wind power consumption with emergency on-site power generation

In this scenario, there is no grid connection and all supplemental power is provided by on-site emergency generators. The generators can be sized to provide a base level of power that is sized to meet emergency system electrical demands. Wind energy is used as the primary source of power and the revenue benefit comes from completely offsetting grid energy purchases as well as capital connection costs. The pump stations would only be operated during periods of wind energy generation and would be oversized, compared with the full or partial grid connection options, in order to provide the same overall flow despite the fluctuations in wind energy generation. The trade-off is the requirement for the most flexible system operation, largest minimum design capacity (to cope with flow fluctuations), and potentially the greatest requirement for in-system water storage to account for network slack.

Option 4b—primary wind power consumption with supplemental on-site power generation

In this scenario, there is no grid connection and all supplemental power is provided by on-site generators. Depending on system requirements, the generators can be sized to meet partial or even complete pump station energy demands. If desired, the pump stations could be designed without permanent standby generators but with electrical system modifications to allow for easy utilization of portable emergency generators. Wind energy is used as the primary source of power and the revenue benefit comes from completely offsetting grid energy purchases as well as capital connection costs. The pump stations would only be operated during periods of wind energy generation and would be oversized, compared with the full or partial grid connection options, in order to provide the same overall flow despite the fluctuations in wind energy generation. The trade-off is the requirement for the most flexible system operation, largest minimum design capacity (to cope with flow fluctuations), and potentially the greatest requirement for in-system water storage to account for network slack.

SUMMARY

Geographical and situational variability results in considerable inconsistency in the environmental factors and constraints facing large urban systems. For instance, there is considerable variability in water and energy resources across the country. These factors result in very different "best decisions" for different regions of the country. In addition, sustainable planning and decision making concerning large urban systems requires intimate knowledge of numerous cross-disciplinary technologies. As shown in the wind energy example, selection of an optimal solution requires considerable understanding and integration of numerous engineering systems. Standardized sustainability metrics are not likely to either capture these differences or to promote optimal sustainable decision making. Instead, sustainability evaluation methods should require cross-disciplinary efforts to promote understanding across multiple domains.

NOTES

1   J.W. Norton, Jr., "Water, energy, and carbon emissions: Drivers for integrated urban water systems," 2008, World Environmental and Water Resources Congress, May 11–16, Honolulu, Hawaii.

2   J.W. Norton, Jr.,, Weber, W.J., Jr. "Breakeven costs for distributed advanced technology water treatment systems." *Water Research* 40(19) (2006): 3541–3550.

3   J.W. Norton, Jr., "Economic analysis of distributed wastewater treatment units to address emerging contaminants of concern," 2008, Illinois Water Environment Association Annual Conference, March 18–20, Peoria, Illinois.

4   J. Norton, Ford R., and Morris T., "Strategic framework for sustainable urban water system planning considering regional variation in geography and climate," *Proceedings of the 6th IWA Specialty Conference on Wastewater Reclamation & Reuse for Sustainability*, 2007, Antwerp, Belgium: WRRS200, 7, October 9–12.

5   E. Doukakis, "Identifying coastal vulnerability due to climate changes," *Journal of Marine Environmental Engineering* 8(2) (2005): 155–160. K.R. Liso, "Integrated approach to risk management of future climate change impacts," *Building Research and Information* 34(1) (2006): 1–10.

6   Norton, Ford, and Morris, "Strategic framework for sustainable urban water system planning considering regional variation in geography and climate."

7   S. Wolfe, Brooks D., "Water scarcity: An alternative view and its implications for policy and capacity building." *Natural Resources Forum* 27(2) (2003): 99–107.

8   Norton, Ford, and Morris, "Strategic framework for sustainable urban water system planning considering regional variation in geography and climate."

9   M.J. Salinger, "Climate variability and change: Past, present and future—an overview." *Climatic Change* 70(1–2) (2005): 9–29.

10 Norton, Ford, and Morris, "Strategic framework for sustainable urban water system planning considering regional variation in geography and climate."

11 O. Bin, "Real estate market response to coastal flood hazards." *Natural Hazards Review* 7(4) (2006): 137–144. J.S. Yeend, "Coastal natural hazards analysis of risk exposures," *Oceans Conference Record (IEEE)* 1 (1997): 208–212.

12 E. Rogers, *Diffusion of Innovations* (London and New York: Free Press, 1962).

8

Sustainability Aspects of Large-Scale Wind Power Development

GEORGE C. KENDRICK

STANTEC CONSULTING

INTRODUCTION

Renewable energy is often viewed as the ultimate in sustainable development, especially in comparison with the consumption of fossil fuels for power generation, transportation, and heating and cooling. Renewables consist of a broad range of generating technologies, including biomass, geothermal, wind, solar, ocean energy, and hydropower, which collectively now provide about one quarter of total global generating capacity.[1] These energy sources do not consume a finite fuel resource, but tap into sources that are self-renewing or continuous. In fact, with the exception of geothermal, one can argue that all of these renewable energy sources derive ultimately from the sun, for all practical purposes (at least in terms of the duration of the human species) a nearly unlimited energy source.

Despite this seemingly endless fuel supply, measuring the sustainability of large renewable energy projects is a complex undertaking not simply because of the scale of the projects, but also due to the direct and indirect impacts that must be balanced against the benefits of avoiding fossil fuel consumption. For example, the "butterfly effect" from installing a single solar panel becomes more tangible when one considers the repercussions of devoting thousands of acres of land to utility-scale solar photovoltaic collection arrays that modify or eliminate habitats beneath the panels. Offsetting these potential impacts is a complicated mix of potential economic and social benefits.

Wind power, in particular, has moved most dramatically into the worldwide strategic energy mix, driven largely by public policy and economic incentives. Wind energy installations grew at a 27 percent annual rate from 2004 to 2010, making it the fastest-growing renewable energy source in the twenty-first century. From relative obscurity, where wind farms were often seen as a vaguely European curiosity, wind turbines have become a familiar, if not always welcomed, sight in many countries. This global acceleration has placed wind in the forefront of renewable energy development, and has also begun to provide a track record for measuring impacts and sustainability.

This chapter provides a brief overview of the wind power development process, describes the potential impacts from design and implementation choices, and explores sustainability measurements currently available. Although each form of renewable energy has unique characteristics, for the purposes of this discussion we will consider wind power as a surrogate for evaluating sustainability metrics of renewable energy in general.

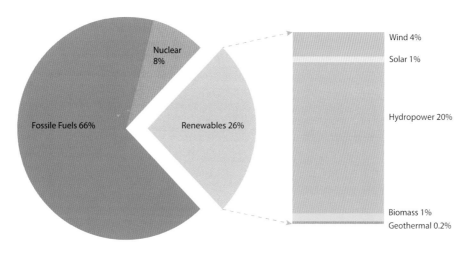

8.1   World electricity-generating capacity by source, 2010

MARKET BACKGROUND

The development of commercial-scale wind farms has rapidly evolved from an exercise limited to portions of Western Europe and driven primarily by government initiatives, to a significant worldwide capital market supported by social initiatives and replete with international developers, major investment banks, and a diverse supply chain of services and products. With growing concerns about global warming and greenhouse gas emissions the carbon-free nature of wind power has attracted significant investment and socio-political support, with worldwide development of wind power increasing ten-fold over the past 10 years.

By the end of 2010, worldwide wind installations totaled 197 GW of generating capacity, with China having 45 GW of installed wind capacity, ahead of the USA (40 GW) and Germany (27 GW).[2] Eleven countries also have offshore wind farms installed or under construction in 2010, totaling 5.5 GW of capacity, led by the UK and Denmark. In Europe, another 16 GW of offshore wind projects have received approval.[3] The National Renewable Energy Lab has identified more than 1000 GW of wind potential off the US Atlantic coast, and more than 900 GW of wind potential off the Pacific Coast, greater than the entire currently installed US electrical capacity in 2009.[4]

Renewable energy standards have emerged in most developed countries, and government programs and subsidies are stimulating continued expansion of wind developments. The European Union (EU) has led the way by establishing a goal of providing 20% of the EU's electricity through renewable energy by 2020.[5] The US Department of Energy (USDOE) evaluated the potential for wind energy to supply 20 percent of the USA's electricity by the year 2030, which would require the installation of 300,000 MW of wind generating capacity. The USDOE report, *20% Wind Energy by 2030*, concluded that such a build-out would result in substantial benefits including reducing carbon emissions, creating jobs, stimulating economic activity particularly in rural areas, and reducing water consumption by the power industry.

From an economic perspective, wind power is a growing force. The renewable energy industry creates thousands of long-term, high-technology careers in wind turbine component manufacturing, construction and installation, maintenance and operations, legal and engineering services, transportation and logistical services, and more. GWEC estimates that about 500,000 people are employed by the wind power industry globally.[6] According to the American Wind Energy Association (AWEA) and USDOE, in 2009 the wind sector invested $17 billion in the US economy and employed 85,000 workers.[7] EWEA, the European equivalent of AWEA, reports similarly dramatic figures.

However, despite the rapid growth, and perhaps as a result of the industry's youth, few quantitative studies of sustainability have been conducted on wind power projects. Creating a sustainability measurement framework requires an understanding of the overall wind project planning and installation process, acknowledgment of stakeholders and their concerns, and an appreciation for the trade-offs associated with wind power development.

THE DEVELOPMENT PROCESS

The development of a wind project is a multi-step process from initial planning, site selection, and permitting, through finance, design, construction, operation, and eventual decommissioning. At multiple points in the planning and design stages, developers and potential investors evaluate project feasibility and risks in terms of economics, environmental impacts, likelihood to receive approvals, and constructability. There are myriad obstacles and potential challenges to wind farms, depending primarily on location, project timing, and, some would argue, luck.

The geographic pattern of wind power expansion has resulted from a variety of factors beyond the wind resource itself. Regional variations in biophysical, political, infrastructural, regulatory, and financial elements have influenced the worldwide distribution of wind projects, and will continue to play a role in the future. In addition, a number of national or regionally focused initiatives reflecting the strategic importance of renewables may shape the future distribution of wind projects even more dramatically. These initiatives include tax incentives, renewable portfolio standards (RPS), and carbon policies.

8.2 Sustainable wind development ideally includes consideration of impacts and benefits at each stage

The successful development of a wind project requires, above all else, wind. Regardless of available investment incentives or tax credits, a commercial wind farm is not economically feasible where the wind resource is unpredictable or below operational thresholds. The technical parameters of individual wind turbine models vary in terms of cut-in speeds and power production curves, but in general developers look for average wind speeds in excess of 6.5 meters per second and capacity factors in the range of 30–35 percent to make a project economically viable.

The windiest spots may not always make the most sense, when balancing engineering costs, local opposition, environmental elements, permit timetables, and getting the power to market. Examples abound where these issues, especially perceived environmental impacts like viewscape degradation, have stymied proposed projects. It is also striking to see similar stakeholder concerns raised by villagers in Turkey, residents in New England, and abutters in Scotland. Siting near densely populated areas may make sense in terms of proximity to market, but local opposition can sink a project through costly appeals, litigation, and delays.

Given these factors, some successful developers have focused on regions where the wind resource may appear less than optimal, yet sites are so unobtrusive and the political climate so favorable that the shortened time-to-construction allows a faster return on investment.

Prospecting for viable sites involves analysis of existing wind data within a region and long-term (usually 12 months or longer) collection of site-specific wind speed data through the installation of temporary meteorological towers with anemometers. Advances in technology have recently increased the use of sound- and laser-based remote sensing systems (i.e., SODAR and LIDAR) capable of evaluating wind speeds up to several hundred meters above ground while avoiding environmental impacts from meteorological tower construction or road building.

Second to wind, grid capacity and transmission have emerged as critical siting factors for most proposed wind farms. Wind resources are not always located near power demand centers, and exploiting these new resources often requires the construction of new long-distance transmission lines. This can result in additional environmental impacts and major socio-economic issues, most notably the potential

The following sections outline typical wind project development steps, each of which provide opportunities for measurable sustainability decisions and analyses.

Planning

In picking a wind power site, selection criteria vary among developers. Obvious siting factors include wind resource, land availability, engineering constructability, environmental issues, permitting requirements, grid capacity, transmission status, turbine availability, and delivery routes. Equally important are regional business elements such as state-renewable energy portfolio goals, power markets, tariff structures, public acceptance, and the local political climate.

requirement for ratepayers in multiple states to share the cost of massive capital investments. For example, in the USA the Midwest Independent Transmission System Operator (MISO; covering fifteen states) recently evaluated a $13 billion project that would add 16,000 MW of wind energy to its system and construct 5000 miles of transmission lines from the Dakotas to New York. Some argue that the enormous potential for offshore wind generation in the Great Lakes and the Atlantic coast precludes the need for such power delivery from the Midwest. In terms of sustainability metrics, the enormous cost of new transmission infrastructure associated with a wind power project must be considered in balance with any avoided costs and fuel savings.

Once a site has been selected, completing appropriate land acquisition becomes the critical task. Developers need to assemble significant land packages to accommodate turbine layouts, access roads, transmission corridors, and operations and maintenance facilities. A developer's appetite (and budget) for lease negotiations and timetables may dictate whether they pursue a project on private or public lands, which also influences the region they select for prospecting.

In many countries, large tracts of public or government-controlled lands are leased for wind project development. The leasing process may involve a non-competitive individual lease application, or a competitive bidding process, particularly for offshore sites. In most leasing situations, a complete environmental impact analysis is required that evaluates environmental and socio-economic impacts, and includes stakeholder consultations.

Private land ownership patterns vary dramatically across the world, ranging from places where individual landowners may own 20,000-acre farms and ranches, to small fragmented holdings in rural areas. In many cases, farmers and ranchers receive lease payments for turbine sites and are able to continue operating their lands for agricultural income. In areas where turbines and access roads are installed along ridges, a ridge owner may benefit financially but abutting landowners might not, unless visual or noise easements are offered in buffer zones. In such areas, the concept of community wind with opportunities for shared ownership is an attractive option for local residents who might otherwise not benefit from a wind project.

The planning stage usually involves an evaluation of environmental issues. Environmental and regulatory constraints differ globally, due to varying population densities, ecosystems and habitats, wildlife species, and degrees of concern about resources. The extent of required environmental studies can influence a developer's choice of regions for their investment.

In developed countries, some environmental issues are directly tied to proximity to populated areas. Noise, visual impact, and shadow flicker are topics of concern unique to certain parts of North America and Western Europe, where electricity consumers live, work, and play within clear sight of wind farms. As a result, projects in these areas may incur additional costs for scientific studies, noise easements, mitigating visual impacts, and legal costs associated with opposition.

Other topics, particularly wildlife issues, are dictated by ecological characteristics and federal or local regulations. In the USA, mortality risk for bat species has emerged as a concern, triggering costly pre- and post-construction scientific studies. In the European Union, similar concerns regarding wildlife impacts exist, and all projects undergo environmental impact assessments (EIAs). Other countries may have a lower degree of scrutiny for projects, where EIAs are typically limited to desktop reviews of available literature and information provided by the developer. Although environmental impacts of offshore projects are only now being evaluated in a rigorous fashion, early indications suggest that the impacts may be minimal on habitats and wildlife, and may be lower than those associated with onshore wind projects.

Permitting is a critical path element, with widely varying requirements for local, county, provincial, and federal permits. Projects near organized communities are often subject to ordinance height restrictions and must seek variances, and if the site is controversial, there is the risk of public-initiated moratoriums or outright bans. Regional, state, or provincial permits are often focused on water quality, wetlands, loss of farmland, impacts to highways, grid integration, and economic benefits. Depending on the regulatory climate, the degree of design and engineering required for permitting varies. In some jurisdictions such as New England, Ohio, and California, where small-scale natural resource impacts are regulated, site layouts and civil engineering often must be completed to 75–80 percent levels at the planning stage to allow an accurate calculation of impact areas. Other locations, especially in developing countries, require less stringent designs for permit review or do not require permits at all. The timing and costs for permitting can determine the likelihood of a project moving forward.

Finance and Renewable Energy Credits

Designing and constructing a commercial-scale wind farm requires significant capital. As a result, financial feasibility is a significant factor controlling the expansion of wind power worldwide. The financial elements of wind development are also inextricably intertwined with government policies concerning renewable energy tax incentives and environmental commodity trading.

Typical costs for building onshore wind farms in developed countries can be in the range of $1.5 million to $2.0 million per MW, which is primarily driven by the cost of turbines, which is in turn heavily influenced by the price of steel and turbine availability. A wind project must also generate enough cash flow during its operating life (typically 20–25 years) to cover the capital costs and provide investors with sufficient return on investment. Most projects negotiate long-term power purchase agreements (PPAs) with utilities or other purchasers at the development stage to ensure a predictable cash flow and provide some level of assurance to investors that the project is feasible.

There are several financing stages for a wind power project, with the highest-risk funds committed at the planning phase when the feasibility and regulatory approvals are uncertain. Funding for this high-risk stage may come from a variety of sources, including internal corporate budgets, venture capital firms, private investors, or government development agencies. For community-scale projects, initial evaluations may be funded through government grant programs, bond issues, contributions from members, or internal cash flow from other operations.

Once a project is deemed viable and has received a permit or license, the investment risk factor is somewhat decreased. Capital requirements increase substantially at this point, however, with typical funding in the range of $150–$200 million for a 100 MW

project. In most cases, a PPA is required before capital financing can be finalized. In 2008–2009 the financial crisis limited access to commercial capital markets for many developers as banks drastically tightened their lending policies for renewable energy projects. To enable more projects to move forward in the face of the tight credit markets, many turbine manufacturers began taking equity positions in high-quality wind farms.

Public sector banks are a significant source of funding for wind projects, and represent a social investment in renewables. For example, the European Investment Bank (EIB) recently committed nearly €300 million ($400 million) toward the financing of the initial phase of the Belwind offshore wind project in Belgium, and nearly doubled its overall renewable energy lending portfolio to €4.2 billion ($5.6 billion). In a similar way, regional development entities such as the World Bank Group, Inter-American Development Bank, Asian Development Bank, Agence Française de Développement (AFD), and the Japan International Development Corporation have committed increased funds for new renewable energy projects in both developing and developed countries.[8]

For community-based wind projects, a variety of creative financing initiatives have emerged, including the issuance of bonds for both municipal projects and non-profit cooperatives. Although typically smaller in scale than major commercial wind projects, these projects may serve as model sustainable projects that provide significant social and economic benefits to a local population. The Vinalhaven Fox Winds project in Maine is an excellent example of a cooperative project that successfully lowered energy costs for local residents, although it also generated opposition from several abutters.

A significant avenue for wind project financing involves tax equity investors who invest in these projects in exchange for federal tax credits. At least 83 countries have some type of tax-related policy to promote renewable power generation. Investment tax credits, reductions in VAT and import duty reductions, and other tax-related incentives provide financial support at the national level, and also at the provincial and state level in Canada, the USA, and Australia. Sustainability metrics should consider economics at both the project and societal scales, and the true cost of any energy option, whether renewable or fossil fuel-based, should include the cost of tax incentives and government support programs.

Production tax credits (PTCs) and feed-in tariffs (FITs) are other methods used by governments to encourage wind development, and are utilized by developers to establish tax equity calculations for financing. PTCs provide incentives for the production of renewable energy in the form of a tax credit based on the amount of electricity generated. FITs go one step further by ensuring access to the grid as well as setting a guaranteed minimum price for sale of renewable power into the grid. PTCs require a project to be in operation before the credits are recognized, although anticipated PTC amounts are critical in determining project profitability and obtaining financing.

The most common incentive policy is the FIT, which has been established in at least 50 countries and 25 states and provinces, and is growing in popularity. FITs are often viewed as the strongest incentive for steady development of renewable energy, but they require strong federal energy policies. Debates surrounding FITs focus on different regional tariffs based on wind resource geography, graduated tariff decreases over time, tariff limitations based on ownership structure, and capacity limits.

Finally, Renewable Energy Certificates (RECs) and related greenhouse gas and Carbon Credit financial vehicles provide additional incentives for developing carbon-neutral renewable energy projects, by allowing a project to monetize environmental benefits. The potential value of these environmental commodities is established for a wind project at the planning stage.

RECs (often called Green Tags or energy credits) represent property rights to the environmental benefits gained from generating electricity from a renewable source, and are sold and traded on specific markets. RECs are traded in both Compliance and Voluntary Markets, with pricing determined by availability and demand.

In Compliance Markets, REC buyers are seeking to meet renewable energy quotas or obligations, which in the USA are driven by Renewable Portfolio Standards (RPS), which have been established in most states. Utilities in those states are required to comply with RPS goals (e.g., 20 percent by 2020) by purchasing RECs from renewable projects, preferably within the state. Compliance Market activity for RECs in the USA is expected to increase exponentially if a national RPS is established.

In Voluntary Markets, REC buyers are typically individuals or companies that simply wish to support renewable energy or offset their carbon footprint on a voluntary basis. In the USA, many such buyers have announced their REC purchases as part of corporate image or branding efforts, and to demonstrate their commitment to sustainability.

Carbon Emission Reduction Credits have also emerged as a growing commodity in world markets as a result of the implementation of the Kyoto Protocol. These credits are sometimes called Carbon Offsets, Carbon Credits, Verified Emission Reductions (VERs), or Certified Emission Reductions (CERs). A central feature of the Kyoto Protocol is the requirement that countries limit or reduce their greenhouse gas emissions. By setting mandatory targets, emission reductions took on economic value and resulted in the establishment of carbon markets. In North America, no national carbon policies are in place, although regional initiatives such as the Northeast's RGGI, and WCI in the West, have fostered fledgling carbon markets. The process of certification and verification for Carbon Credits has been refined under the United Nations Framework Convention on Climate Change (UNFCCC) initiatives, and several review processes are in place worldwide to assist developers in establishing the veracity and market value of their potential VERs and CERs, which are traded in multiple markets.[9,10] As with RECs, Carbon Credits represent a way of monetizing environmental benefits of a wind project, and are also traded on both Voluntary Markets and Compliance Markets. Carbon Credit trading is now a significant market in the EU, and is anticipated to grow in the coming years as other countries, most notably the USA and Canada, eventually consider national carbon initiatives and cap-and-trade policies.

In short, the successful financing of a large-scale wind power project depends on a wide range of factors, and the developer must consider a number of options that may include federal tax incentives, fixed power prices through feed-in tariffs and long-term power purchase agreements, and environmental commodity valuations through the sale of RECs and Carbon Credits.

Design

The design stage for a wind farm involves multiple engineering disciplines and tasks, and achieving a low-impact sustainable design requires an iterative design process that brings together environmental and engineering specialists well versed in green alternatives.

Site conditions dictate the layout and engineering design for a wind farm, which must accommodate wind characteristics, terrain, and land ownership patterns. As with the initial site selection, the wind resource usually is the primary factor in the micrositing of wind turbines, with the aim of optimizing generation capacity. The selection of specific turbine models, tower heights, and blade lengths are also dictated by the wind regime present at the site. Once the optimum turbine layout has been determined, the process of adjusting the layout to avoid and minimize environmental impacts begins.

In places that regulate environmental impacts, field studies are conducted to identify protected natural and cultural resources within proposed disturbance areas. A sustainable design process considers these resources to avoid impacts and demonstrate compliance with permit and license requirements. For projects that seek certification of their Carbon Credits, such avoidance may be a component of the validation process.

For sites located in relatively flat, agricultural terrain, layout offers some flexibility in turbine and road siting, requiring minimal forest clearing or surface disturbance, and thus providing opportunities to minimize soil erosion, sedimentation of streams, water quality degradation, and habitat fragmentation. In steeper terrain, impacts may be greater due to limited turbine placement options. Designing access roads to higher elevations may require significant cut-and-fill, blasting, installing culverts at stream crossings, forest clearing, and stormwater runoff management.

It should be noted that adjusting turbine layouts to avoid specific environmental impacts may result in a decrease in potential power production. For this reason, many developers are reluctant to modify layouts or adjust operational parameters to accommodate environmental concerns unless forced to do so by regulatory requirements, legal challenges, or other opposition. This is particularly true for projects at the margins of profitability. Financial incentives that encourage environmental sustainability may help in this area.

Construction

Once the final engineering design, regulatory permitting, and financing are in place, developers may proceed with construction activities. The construction of a wind farm can take anywhere from 6 to 18 months depending on project scale, weather conditions, and difficulty of access, and is an exercise in complex logistical management, transportation, procurement, staffing, and quality control. The construction of offshore projects, in particular, encounters more complex logistics, hazards, and higher costs. As with any marine project, weather and sea conditions can pose challenges to construction timetables and personnel safety, and require specialized vessels and significant transportation planning and monitoring.

Some major wind developers conduct their own construction management and retain only specialist subcontractors for individual construction steps, while others issue tenders or request for bids to selected construction firms that coordinate entire installations. The selection of a contractor may be based on experience, price, or a best-value approach that incorporates qualifications as well as cost. Other factors that may be considered in bidder selection may include a requirement to exclusively use local subcontractors, such as Ontario's recently-enacted "domestic content" requirement linked to their FIT.

Construction-related jobs can total in the hundreds for a one- to two-year period, with millions of dollars infused into local economies. This information is often provided by developers as part of their stakeholder consultation process and permit applications, to demonstrate the positive aspects of wind power. Private developer First Wind's efforts in this area regarding their Stetson Wind Farm have been particularly visible in the New England region. From a sustainability perspective, such local procurement is a valuable and tangible benefit, as long as local sources can provide appropriate quality and experience.

Protection of environmental resources identified during the planning and design stages may be included in permit requirements, and so many developers of both onshore and offshore projects often must monitor construction activities for compliance. Other construction-related methods of minimizing impacts at onshore sites include re-vegetation with native species, dust control, timing of construction to avoid wildlife breeding and migration periods, and the use of Best Management Practices (BMPs) during construction to reduce erosion and sedimentation. For offshore projects, construction timing may be coordinated to avoid marine mammal migration periods, and monitoring of wildlife activities may be included in compliance activities.

Operations

The operation of a commercial-scale wind farm is usually anticipated to last 20–25 years. Hiring local staff is a goal of most developers as a sign of benefits to the local area, but a significant portion of a terrestrial wind farm's operation is automated and thus typically requires only a small full-time staff, generally fewer than ten employees, to handle both operations and maintenance activities. Offshore projects generally require more staff for maintenance and shore-side support facilities.

The wind industry has recognized a serious shortfall in skilled labor for wind farm operations and maintenance, and regional colleges and universities are logical partners to address that need. Many developers with multiple projects in a region establish partnerships with local educational institutions to help grow training programs and provide scholarships for technicians, engineers, and environmental scientists. Renewable energy programs at institutions such as James Madison University in Virginia, for example, offer courses in wind energy planning and design, along with opportunities for internships and research at local wind farms.

In regions where there is concern about potential wildlife mortality, Curtailment and Adaptive Management strategies are required as part of permit conditions. For example, bird and bat mortality has emerged as a concern in the USA, and most projects are required to conduct post-construction mortality monitoring and modify operations to minimize impacts to wildlife. Adjusting cut-in speeds or shutting down during high-risk periods are potential adaptive management actions. Some developers and turbine manufacturers such as Nordex USA are also developing automated curtailment systems to minimize wildlife risk. As more wind projects are built and monitored in the years ahead, scientists may be able to develop more accurate risk models and help developers meet both operational and environmental goals.

Decommissioning

Decommissioning plans are required as part of many permitting and licensing processes, and bonds are often required from developers to provide financial surety of turbine removal. A complete decommissioning process for an onshore wind project would involve disassembly and transport of turbine components offsite, removal of electrical infrastructure, and restoration of the site including regrading and re-vegetation. As with the construction phase, it is assumed that most wind farms would provide opportunities for local jobs and economic benefits from decommissioning activities.

It is unclear whether full decommissioning would occur at most sites, or whether re-powering of sites with more efficient, or larger, next-generation wind turbines would be more common. Such is the case at the Altamont Pass region of California, where hundreds of small turbines installed in the 1980s and 1990s are gradually being replaced by modern 1.5 MW and larger turbines.

STAKEHOLDERS

There are myriad stakeholders with varying interests in wind farms, including government regulatory agencies, landholders, abutters, conservation organizations, taxpayers, and investors. The most successful developers identify and engage stakeholders early in the planning stages, whether required or not, to help secure support for a project, identify concerns, and develop solutions.

In most developed countries, the responsibility for regulating energy projects rests with federal agencies. The developer who can avoid environmental impacts may not need to consult with these agencies, but may run the risk of third-party lawsuits concerning potential violations of federal laws, especially in the area of federally protected wildlife.

If a wind project is proposed for federal lands in the USA and a wind lease is desired, the stakeholder list may grow to include not simply the stewardship agency (such as the Bureau of Land Management), but also entities who have interest in the land's severable estate resources. In the western USA, federal lands generally have separate surface rights, water rights, mineral rights, oil and gas rights, geothermal rights, and timber rights, any of which could be leased to a third party prior to or after a wind farm is developed. Thus, a proposed wind farm may encounter stakeholders such as forest products firms, oil and gas companies, geothermal developers, transmission entities, highway departments, and groups concerned about recreational trails, wilderness areas, and wildlife conservation areas, all of whom will want assurance that their resources are minimally impacted or appropriately compensated.

State, provincial, or regional agencies may also become involved in project reviews at the planning and permitting stages. Many of these entities are concerned with natural and cultural resource protection, noise, water quality, erosion and sedimentation, visual impacts, effects on recreation and tourism, tax revenues, infrastructure upgrade costs, and job creation.

In North America and Europe, electrical grid integration for a wind farm requires review and approval from the regional grid operator and the appropriate state public utility commissions (PUCs). These stakeholders are concerned with the project's ability to deliver reliable power to the grid and the system's ability to accommodate that power, as well as the cost structure of power purchase agreements (PPAs) that may affect ratepayers in the region. The latter is a key factor in sustainability measurement.

Non-governmental organizations (NGOs), including conservation groups and wind power advocacy organizations, are emerging as important stakeholders in wind power development. Environmental and scientific non-profits such as Audubon, Union of Concerned Scientists, and World Wide Fund for Nature (WWF) support wind power in appropriate locations, while balancing the need to conserve and protect natural resources. For example, the WWF was instrumental in supporting the design of sustainability review processes, including the Gold Standard, for Carbon Credit certifications. Local chapters of conservation organizations occasionally face internal policy dilemmas when a proposed wind farm that would help reduce global carbon emissions may also negatively impact an endangered wildlife species. Partnering with such NGO stakeholders early in a project is emerging as an important strategy to identify concerns and develop potential solutions, such as purchasing conservation lands, which can allow projects to move forward.

Perhaps the most important stakeholders in terms of sustainability are local residents and abutters, who are primarily focused on how the project will directly affect their lives and livelihoods. In the era preceding regulatory controls, sustainable goals, and public advocacy, local residents were often the last to be consulted about an energy project. However, local stakeholders are now usually involved in consultation early in the planning stages for a wind farm. Local stakeholders are most often concerned about lease payments, noise easements, visual impacts, health effects, property values, recreational access, continued current use (e.g., grazing or farming), and economic benefits versus costs. Addressing local concerns is a measurable element under several Carbon Credit review processes such as the Gold Standard CER and VER processes, where documentation of local stakeholder consultation is a requirement for certification.[11]

It is instructive to recognize that there is a significant gap between the public's embrace of renewable energy as a concept, and their acceptance of a nearby wind farm as a reality. This gap may be responsible for delays in wind power expansion in many regions. As Wolsink (2007) has noted, public opinions throughout Europe show significant support for renewable energy and wind power, yet the planning and installation of individual wind farms is fraught with opposition.[12] Focusing on the public's apparent positive attitude toward wind energy, developers and regulators often cite either a failure in communication or a selfish "Not In My Back Yard" (NIMBY) reaction from local residents as the root of local opposition. While there may be some who oppose wind farms for personal reasons, Wolsink suggests that the visual impact of wind project on landscape values, as well as emotional concerns about fairness and equity, may be the driving forces behind local opposition, as opposed to selfishness. Again, outreach and consultation are the keys to identifying and mitigating concerns early in the planning process.

SUSTAINABILITY METRICS

Evaluating the sustainability of wind power, or any other energy development, requires an examination of the environmental, economic, and social aspects of not just the development itself and the fuel that runs the generator, but also the project's supply chain characteristics, fabrication and construction-related impacts, project operations, and the potential indirect and cumulative impacts of a full industry build-out. A variety of methods exist for evaluating portions of energy project sustainability goals and achievement, but no single method is widely used for wind-specific comprehensive sustainability metrics.

Several third-party verification processes are available for calculating and certifying greenhouse gas emissions and Carbon Credits for renewable energy projects, such as the Green-e Climate Protocol for Renewable Energy,[13] and the Clean Development Mechanism Gold Standard.[14] Most processes do not incorporate quantitative ecological resource valuations into the assessment process.

The Global Reporting Initiative, or GRI, is another standardized, albeit producer-validated, approach to reporting sustainability factors including environmental, economic, social, governance, and human rights. The overall GRI approach is applicable to any industry, and GRI provides sector-based Indicator Protocols (IPs) to measure sustainability in specific markets. For example, GRI's environmental IPs for utilities include evaluations of materials, water, biodiversity, emissions, waste, and transportation.[15] However, the GRI method is voluntary and self-reporting, not subject to third-party verification, and thus may not allow accurate comparisons between projects, companies, regions, or markets.

Perhaps the most applicable sustainability review process for renewable energy in place today is the Gold Standard, which focuses on the United Nations Framework Convention on Climate Change (UNFCCC) Clean Development Mechanism (CDM) that forms the basis for worldwide carbon emission credits and associated trading markets. Since its inception in 2006, the CDM has registered more than 1000 projects and is anticipated to produce CERs amounting to more than 2.7 billion tons of CO_2 equivalent in the first commitment period of the Kyoto Protocol, 2008–2012.[16]

The Gold Standard is currently the only independent standard designed to ensure that Carbon Credits are verifiable and projects make measurable contributions to sustainable development worldwide. Similar to the Forest Stewardship Council's approach toward Forest Certification labeling,[17] the Gold Standard's objective is to add branding and a label to existing and new Carbon Credits, which can then be bought and traded by countries that have made a binding commitment to the Kyoto Protocol.

In addition to meeting specific criteria regarding a project's renewable characteristics, timing, and economic reliance on Carbon Credits ("additionality"), a project must also "make a net-positive contribution to the economic, environmental, and social welfare of the local population that hosts it" to be eligible for Gold Standard Certification.[18] This emphasis on the contribution to sustainable development differentiates the Gold Standard from other greenhouse gas reduction review standards. Gold Standard project developers are also required to engage stakeholders in consultation meetings and respond to local concerns. Only projects with an overall positive impact on the environment, social networks, and local economy can be certified under Gold Standard criteria.

As renewable energy continues to penetrate global markets, and as more countries such as the USA embrace mandatory carbon emission controls, comprehensive measures of sustainability for large-scale wind energy projects will need to be further refined and standardized.

The following section provides a sampling of some issues and concerns that face developers and stakeholders in assessing sustainability metrics for wind farms, organized into the three primary categories of sustainability; environmental, economic, and social welfare.

ENVIRONMENTAL BENEFITS ANALYSIS

Most renewable energy technologies are so new that there is not enough information to predict impacts. For example, hydropower has long been viewed as a renewable source of energy, yet identifying and measuring the sustainability aspects of hydropower has only recently (within the past two decades) begun through more rigorous environmental impact assessments and stakeholder involvement at the planning stages, and through efforts such as the Low Impact Hydro certification process. We now know that damming free-flowing river systems may result in impacts such as inundating historic or archaeological features, blocking fish passage and reducing spawning habitats, or changing water flows and affecting the recreational use of downstream reaches. Sustainability evaluations must consider these kinds of impacts.

For wind projects, potential environmental impacts include habitat loss, wildlife mortality, wetland and stream degradation, soil erosion, stream degradation, and impacts to cultural resources. At each stage of wind development, however, there are opportunities to evaluate, avoid, or mitigate these impacts.

Pre-construction environmental surveys that focus on wildlife and habitats are an important aspect of sustainable development for wind farms. By identifying potential risks to wildlife at the pre-construction stage, resource agencies can analyze possible resultant large-scale (i.e., population-level) impacts on species, and a developer can design appropriate curtailment measures to minimize those impacts. Conservation and mitigation measures for wildlife impacts may include acquisition of conservation lands, habitat restoration or creation, preservation of critical roost or breeding areas within a project boundary, or developer contributions to conservation organizations. The costs for each of these measures can be determined and factored into economic models.

Some developers, such as Iberdrola Renewables, have developed formal Avian and Bat Protection Plans (ABPPs) that establish corporate guidelines for the design and operation of their wind farms to minimize risk to bird and bat species. ABPP guidelines may address turbine siting, road widths, habitat conservation, forest clearing, pre- and post-construction monitoring, tower lighting, transmission line design, and options for curtailment. Most ABPPs are developed in consultation with government resource agencies and stakeholders like conservation NGOs.

At the planning and design stage, site layouts can be designed to minimize soil disturbance, avoid wetlands and protected habitats, reduce cut-and-fill and associated blasting of ridgetops, and minimize stormwater runoff and erosion. Sustainable practices in design may include minimizing turbine blade laydown/assembly areas, using narrow crawler-mounted cranes to minimize road widths, co-locating operation and maintenance (O&M) buildings near substation clearings where possible, and installing collector systems along or under access roads rather than across undisturbed areas.

It should be noted that adjusting turbine layouts to avoid environmental impacts can result in a potential reduction in power-generating capacity. Thus, in the absence of a rigorous environmental review or permitting process, developers who are focused solely on economic return rather than a holistic sustainability evaluation may choose to ignore environmental issues and proceed with their project as originally designed regardless of negative impacts. Although several Carbon Credit CER and VER review protocols consider environmental impacts as part of the certification process, in many cases only cursory EIAs are performed in keeping with the host country's regulatory environment, which can result in an inconsistent impact analysis on a worldwide basis.

At the construction stage a variety of opportunities exists to enhance environmental sustainability. Since the fabrication of wind turbine components generally does not use recycled materials, the life cycle aspects of turbines involve mining of iron ore, coal, steel mill operation, petroleum for composite blade manufacture, copper for collector systems, transmission lines, substations, etc. To offset these non-sustainable aspects, construction procurement managers can focus on green options for a variety of other purchases including recycled materials, FSC-certified forest products for buildings, and native species for re-vegetation. The construction manager can also use intelligent transportation planning to reduce fuel consumption, re-flag wetlands and educate subcontractors to avoid impacts, and time the construction work to avoid migratory or breeding periods. It may not be feasible to use recycled steel for turbine components, but reviewing the sustainable track records of major component suppliers and using that information in supplier selection may also be worth considering.

During the operation phase of a wind project, adaptive management and curtailment are the dominant environmental measures, although green procurement of supplies, and intelligent transportation and low-impact maintenance activities can be utilized by operators where possible. As previously mentioned, elimination of turbines from a design, or curtailment of operation during wildlife migration periods can reduce project revenues. Best practices in this area are still emerging, but include methods of identifying the times of year and physical characteristics of high-risk collision periods, and scaling back operations only when those factors are present. Such actions by developers should be considered an important sustainability measure.

ECONOMIC BENEFITS ANALYSIS

From an economic sustainability perspective, one needs to consider the potential values (in both avoided-cost dollars and carbon footprint reduction) related to displacement of conventional energy sources and how those values may improve the sustainability metrics for wind. For example, a wind farm typically provides intermittent electricity that can replace generation from a thermal plant, thus displacing fuel costs and reducing carbon emissions. The avoided costs of fuel, in particular, are an important aspect of evaluating long-term wind economics.[19]

However, a wind farm usually cannot fully replace the need for the thermal plant's existence as a baseload generator available on calm days. Wind power generation in many regions also tends to peak at night and drop off during higher peak demand periods in daytime. In evaluating avoided cost elements of wind power, more specifically the savings related to avoiding fuel consumption, avoided costs would be realized primarily during off-peak hours, and baseload from conventional fuel facilities would still be required.[20] Thus, an individual wind farm investment may not fully replace a conventional power station, but a geographically diverse portfolio of wind projects, which provides more continuous power delivery, might.

Van Kooten and Timilsina[21] outline a "levelized cost approach" to evaluating wind power economics. Initial capital costs for wind development may exceed those of conventional fuel plants on a per-MW basis, particularly if one includes costs for land acquisition or extending transmission and grid connections to remote windy regions. However, a levelized cost includes not just investment

and capital costs, but also O&M costs and, most importantly, fuel costs. Whereas capital and fixed O&M costs are proportional to the capacity of a generation facility, variable O&M and fuel costs are functions of electricity output. Under a levelized cost analysis, wind power can be competitive with conventional power generation due to 1) decreasing capital costs of developing wind projects, 2) potentially higher fossil fuel prices over the long term, and 3) a global move toward accounting for the environmental costs and benefits of power generation through greenhouse gas limits and carbon trading.

In a similar way, a Life Cycle Assessment (LCA) approach provides a rational framework for evaluating sustainability on a quantitative basis. Keoleian and Spitzley[22] have outlined a quantitative method for tracking resource consumption and the costs of environmental impacts at all stages in a project's life cycle, from initial planning and procurement through construction, operation, and decommissioning. Existing Carbon Credit certification and audit processes capture some of these accounting metrics in verifying a wind farm's output and equivalent carbon savings, but most wind developers do not have the project management frameworks in place to track full life cycle costs and benefits, particularly when it comes to environmental impact valuations.

The ancillary social costs of regional transmission infrastructure development must also be considered in renewable energy economic analyses. As mentioned above, the US transmission infrastructure is currently inadequate to support a full expansion of wind, solar, hydroelectric, and geothermal energy, primarily because those resources are generally located at significant distances from power demand centers. The construction of large-capacity transmission lines will require enormous capital investment, and will incur significant allocated costs to taxpayers and ratepayers throughout the country.

A host of interrelated tax incentive and tariff policies provide support for renewable energy development, but these also have a social cost that should be considered under an overall sustainability evaluation. Of course, similar incentives and favorable tax policies have been in place for decades worldwide for a wide range of industries and infrastructure, such as transportation and oil and gas. In addition, governments routinely provide a range of services and actions (such as weather forecasting, development of the interstate highway system, marine research, etc.) that benefit specific industries without an imputed cost. Allocating appropriate costs to wind power that reflect the taxpayer's share of incentives may help ensure fairness in comparisons.

As an example, Stantec recently developed a sustainable energy framework for a foreign government that evaluated current and potential future mixes of conventional and renewable energy options as well as conservation measures, incentives, and tariff policies. The overarching goal was to reduce the country's dependence on fossil fuels, and thus reduce energy costs, improve energy security, and enhance sustainability. As part of the study, Stantec reviewed feed-in tariffs (FITs) and metering rules for utilities purchasing renewable power from small distributed generation units. "Net metering," which is in place throughout the world including the USA, is essentially equivalent to setting a FIT at the retail rate. The result of net metering, however, is that the utility pays considerably more than avoided cost for power, and so the total cost of the electricity supply goes up, and those customers who do not have distributed generation end up subsidizing those who do. From a sustainability perspective, this might not be a positive benefit. As an alternative, Stantec recommended that the price the utility was required to pay should be no more than its avoided cost (which is generally the avoided fuel cost), and to implement that policy it would be necessary to meter separately the power that the customer buys from the utility, and the power the utility buys from the customer, since they are charged at different prices. The result would be encouragement of renewable development, and a fair and equitable sharing of the costs and benefits across the population.

SOCIAL WELFARE BENEFITS ANALYSIS

Perhaps the most challenging aspects of sustainability lie in addressing the myriad concerns of host communities and quantifying social benefits. As described above, positive public perception of renewable energy does not always translate into warm embraces for a local wind farm. Sustainability metrics must consider stakeholder involvement and investment in a project, and evaluate the degree to which local concerns are addressed and social benefits are realized.

Abutters and local residents most often express concerns about loss of property values due to visual degradation of the landscape, loss of land use for agriculture or recreation, possible health impacts from noise and low-frequency vibration, impacts on local roads and other infrastructure, and destruction of habitats and wildlife mortality. They also may raise issues of fairness concerning the export of power to distant locations and consumers, who benefit from the renewable power, while local residents bear the brunt of negative impacts. Some of these points are valid or at least debatable, while others can be addressed through low-impact design or education.

The trade-offs of renewable energy are similar to any infrastructure development, and providing stakeholders with avenues for discussion and understanding of potential compromises is a critical step in sustainability. For example, wind projects usually enable local property owners to maintain the current use of their land, such as farming or timber harvesting, while creating a new source of clean energy that provides additional income through new jobs. Developers also often seek to hire local residents during the construction and operation phases, providing positive social benefits to the community and employment opportunities.

Utility-scale wind farms modify the landscape, however, and the acceptance of their visual character varies. In Europe, windmills have been part of the social landscape for hundreds of years, and are widely accepted. Some people see wind turbines as graceful symbols of energy independence, while others detest them as signs of industrialization in previously undeveloped or pristine landscapes. Because of the non-quantitative nature of visual impact assessment, it remains a thorny subjective issue for wind projects.

The postulated decline in property values near wind farms has not been substantiated in the USA to date and a handful of studies have sought to disprove the concept, yet it remains a concern of abutters, particularly those who do not host a wind turbine on their property and thus do not receive a lease payment. To mitigate concerns of abutters, some developers establish noise and buffer zones extending up to one kilometer from a turbine string, and secure noise easements or visual easements from landowners within the buffer in exchange for an easement payment. Other mitigation measures for visual impacts can include shifting turbines lower on a ridge to reduce their visibility, eliminating turbines in visually offensive locations, designing roads to minimize their visibility, and preserving or replanting vegetation. Again, shifting or eliminating turbines may result in a negative economic impact due to decreased power production.

Wind farms typically pay substantial property taxes, which can provide the host community with sizeable funds to improve roads, fire departments, schools, libraries, health centers, water systems, and other beneficial social infrastructure. Energy facility values typically depreciate over time, however, resulting in steadily declining tax revenues over the 25-year lifespan of a wind project. Thus, local communities may wish to consider wind farm tax revenues as windfalls to be invested in infrastructure or in rainy-day funds, rather than relied upon as baseline operating funds.

Finally, the opportunity to educate and employ future generations is an important social sustainability factor. Students at local universities and technical schools benefit from training programs, job shadowing, internships, and co-op education–work programs focusing on wind technologies. Many wind developers are working with local educational institutions to establish such programs, providing both financial support and technical advice to educators in these areas, and contributing funds for student scholarships. The dollar value of such measures is easily determined. Other opportunities also exist for educating our very youngest citizens. Wind projects provide visible, tangible, and understandable examples of how our society can address future energy needs in a sustainable way. By providing financial support and outreach to local schools, offering field trips to wind farms, establishing education centers at wind facilities, or installing interpretive signage along roadways that pass beneath wind projects, developers can contribute to the education of the next generation of energy users who need to learn everything they can about the opportunities, choices, and ramifications of society's energy decisions.

CONCLUSION

Wind energy projects offer the promise of low-impact, sustainable electricity generation, but the successful development of these projects hinges on myriad economic, environmental, and social factors. Developers must consider wind resources, grid capacity, environmental impacts, stakeholder concerns, and availability of capital when planning a new project, and the availability of tax incentives and viable carbon markets play key roles as well.

From an economic perspective, the levelized cost of electricity for large-scale wind power now compares favorably with conventional fossil fuel power generation, primarily due to wind power's avoided costs of fuel. The recent worldwide recession temporarily deflated oil and natural gas fuel prices, but few energy prognosticators believe that fossil fuel prices will remain at depressed levels for the next 25 years. The rapid rise of fuel prices in 2010 reflecting the nascent economic recovery suggests that the days of affordable oil and gas are numbered. As capital markets rebound, investments in wind power should remain strong if returns on investment look favorable. Tax incentives and subsidies for wind power are also expected to continue in the near future, reflecting society's commitment to move toward a more sustainable energy future.

The potential environmental impacts of wind power are a growing concern in certain regions, especially with regard to wildlife impacts, but scientific knowledge and appropriate mitigation measures are steadily emerging as the industry matures. Stakeholder consultations and proper siting remain critical elements in the planning process, and will grow in importance as the geographic density of wind projects increases. All energy development results in some level of impact, of course, but the challenge for environmental analysis lies in weighing the relative impacts and sustainability metrics between renewable sources like wind power versus alternatives like coal mining, shale gas extraction, or offshore oil drilling.

The social benefits and impacts of wind developments can be challenging to measure, but they are key components of a sustainability analysis. Some of the perceived negative social impacts of wind are qualitative, such as the potential visual impacts of turbines on a landscape, while others can be quantified, like increased noise levels at the homes of nearby residents. Community benefits, in contrast, are often tangible and readily measured in terms of reduced electricity costs, tax revenues, jobs gained, and improvements to local roads. Yet projects that are community based may also need to wrestle with issues of fairness and compensation for abutter impacts. As with environmental impacts, the knowledge gained from wind development over the past decade can help provide a framework for understanding potential local costs and benefits.

Perhaps the most revealing sustainability measure for wind power will require a long-term and larger-scale analysis of global wind development. Society tends to focus on obvious, short-term phenomena, but the worldwide benefits of renewable energy may take decades to evaluate, especially in the context of reduced carbon emissions, improved air quality, restoration of habitats, and improved living conditions and opportunities for residents in development areas. If we are serious about leaving a sustainable world for our children and grandchildren, however, we must continue to pursue the path of sensible renewable energy, while balancing the costs and benefits of our energy choices.

CASE STUDY 1
THINK LOCALLY, ACT GLOBALLY:
STETSON WIND FARM, MAINE

The 50 MW Stetson onshore wind project was developed in a rural location in the northern New England region, on private lands managed for timber harvesting. The region faces significant economic challenges, relying heavily on a resource-extraction based economy, and has one of the highest unemployment rates in the state of Maine. The project's developer, First Wind, espouses an environmental ethic of low-impact design and community outreach as part of its mission, and development of the Stetson project followed this approach. The site's low-elevation ridge provided acceptable wind resources, a large intact private landholding, and low visibility from surrounding roads and communities. The engineering and environmental teams produced multiple site layouts designed to avoid and minimize impacts to natural resources, consulted with agencies and stakeholders, and the developer reached out to the

local towns and committed to hiring local firms for the project. Of approximately $65 million spent for construction, engineering, and development services, about $50 million was spent within the state of Maine, providing a significant economic boost to the region during the design and construction phases. In addition, the firm has hired local residents for the operations team, contributes significant tax revenues to the host communities, established relationships with educational institutions, and has funded scholarships for technical training programs in the state. The project's RECs have been purchased by a number of commercial and non-profit entities in the region. Although the project is not eligible for CDM-based Carbon Credits due to the US non-participation in Kyoto Protocols, it would probably receive Gold Standard certification based on the environmental, economic, and social welfare benefits provided.

Source: www.firstwind.com/html_templates/map.html

CASE STUDY 2
POWER TO THE PEOPLE:
FOX ISLANDS WIND, VINALHAVEN, MAINE

The island community of Vinalhaven, located 15 miles off the coast of Maine, has a year-round population of about 1500 residents and is home to the largest lobstering fleet in Maine. Built on a long history of fishing and a bygone era of granite quarrying, Vinalhaven today relies on the lobster industry and tourism for its economic well-being. High fuel and electricity costs on the isolated island posed challenges to the community's economic and social sustainability, however, since lobstering consumes expensive diesel fuel that must be delivered by ferry, and electricity is provided by undersea cables at triple the rates found on the mainland. To foster energy independence and lower the cost of energy, a community wind project was undertaken by the local Fox Islands Electric Cooperative. With technical support from the state, NGOs, and local residents, the co-op investigated wind resources, secured land, obtained financing through government incentives and the issuance of bonds, and developed plans through an extensive community stakeholder process. Support for the project was nearly universal throughout the community, but some controversy has emerged regarding noise impacts to abutters and their concerns about decreased property values, health effects, and landscape changes. Installation and operation of the wind farm has resulted in a successful 30 percent reduction in electric bills for most residents, but concerns remain about the sustainability aspects of a project that some have characterized as a "social experiment" that has fragmented personal relationships in the tight-knit island community. The project is emerging as a potential model for community wind development in the region, particularly for similar island communities, but has also raised questions about stakeholder rights, due process, and the moral implications of impacting individuals for the greater good.

Sources: www.foxislandswind.com; www.fiwn.org

CASE STUDY 3
CARBON CERTIFICATION AND STAKEHOLDER CONSULTATION IN TURKEY: SOMA WIND PROJECT, TURKEY

The 90 MW Soma Wind project under construction in the Aegean region of western Turkey consists of 36 turbines over a project area of 150 hectares, with turbines located in two rural communities. Developed by Bilgin Energy Power Generation Inc., the project initially received a grant from the US Trade and Development Agency (USTDA) supporting a feasibility study and environmental/social development impact assessment, and subsequently has been validated under the CDM as a Gold Standard VER project. Turkey is encouraging the development of sustainable renewable energy through a Renewable Energy Law that established a feed-in tariff, ensured grid access, and relaxed restrictions on foreign investment of renewables in the Turkish power sector. The project has met additionality criteria by requiring Carbon Credits as part of its economic feasibility, and will assist Turkey in moving toward its stated renewable energy target of 20 percent by 2023 with significant annual Carbon Credits verified for the project's operation. As part of the Gold Standard review process, the developer conducted an environmental impact analysis, and conducted stakeholder consultations in local villages where information on the environmental and social aspects of the project was presented. The local stakeholders raised questions and concerns common to other global regions, including damage to local roads, electromagnetic effects, noise impacts on livestock, continued use of the land for grazing, local job opportunities, construction effects such as dust and contaminants, and impacts to wildlife. In addressing these concerns, the developer provided educational information and also agreed to a number of measures and best practices to mitigate impacts. These measures included rehabilitation of local roads, fencing turbine enclosures and allowing continued grazing and agricultural use, building small reservoirs for livestock use, watering roads to reduce dust, using non-carcinogenic lubricants and recycling waste, and giving priority to local firms and residents for both construction work (60 jobs) and operations (15 positions). In addition, the developer proposed to monitor possible impacts to migratory birds by engaging one villager for each part of the project to conduct mortality searches during migration seasons. The Soma project is currently included in carbon investment portfolios by a number of third-party entities such as the Sustainable Travel Network, a non-profit organization that provides carbon offsets to travelers by purchasing Carbon Credits from CDM certified projects throughout the world.

Sources: www.bilgin.com.tr/eng; https://gs1.apx.com/mymodule/ProjectDoc/EditProjectDoc.asp?id1=655; www.sustainabletravelinternational.org/documents/projects_turkey.html.

NOTES

1 REN21, *Renewables 2010 Global Status Report* (Paris: REN21 Secretariat, 2010).

2 GWEC, *Global Wind 2010 Report* (Brussels: GWEC, 2011).

3 GWEC, *Global Wind 2010 Report.*

4 USDOE, *20% Wind Energy by 2030: Increasing Wind Energy's Contribution to US Electricity Supply*, Washington, DC: DOE/GO-102008-2578, 2008.

5 Center for Resource Solutions, "Green-e® climate protocol for renewable energy," www.green-e.org/docs/climate/Green-e_Climate_Protocol_for_RE.pdf, July 28, 2010.

6 GWEC, *Global Wind 2010 Report.*

7 USDOE, *20% Wind Energy by 2030.* American Wind Energy Association, *Green Power Superhighways: Building a Path to America's Clean Energy Future*, joint publication of the American Wind Energy Association and the Solar Energy Industries Association (Denver: AWEA, 2009).

8 REN21, *Renewables 2010 Global Status Report.*

9 CDM, "Clean Development Mechanism approved baseline and monitoring methodologies," United Nations Framework Convention on Climate Change, http://cdm.unfccc.int/methodologies/PAmethodologies/index.html, December 29, 2010.

10 Center for Resource Solutions, "Green-e® climate protocol for renewable energy."

11 CDM, "Clean Development Mechanism."

12 M. Wolsink, "Wind power implementation: The nature of public attitudes." *Renewable and Sustainable Energy Reviews* 11(6) (2007): 1188–1207.

13 Center for Resource Solutions. "Green-e® climate protocol for renewable energy."

14 CDM, "Clean Development Mechanism."

15 GRI. "Global Reporting Initiative reporting framework," www.globalreporting.org/ReportingFramework, July 30, 2010.

16 CDM, "Clean Development Mechanism."

17 Forest Stewardship Council, "FSC principles and criteria for forest stewardship," www.fsc.org/fsc/how_fsc_works/policy_standards/princ_criteria, July 28, 2010.

18 CDM, "Clean Development Mechanism."

19 T. Bodell, "Why we can't avoid avoided costs," PennWell Electric Light and Power, www.elp.co.m/index/display/article-display/9555126175/articles/electric-light-power/volume-88/issue-2/columns/why-we_can_t_avoid.html, 2010.

20 M. Milligan, Kirby, B., *Calculating Wind Integration Costs: Separating Wind Energy Value from Integration Cost Impacts.* National Renewable Energy Lab Technical Report NREL/TP-550-46275, July 2009.

21 G.C. Van Kooten, Timilsina G.R., "Wind power development: Economics and Policies," *Policy Research Working Paper Series 4868* (Washington, DC: World Bank, 2009).

22 G.A. Keoleian, Spitzley D.V., "Life cycle based sustainability metrics." In: M.A. Abraham, ed., *Sustainability Science and Engineering: Volume 1, Defining Principles* (Amsterdam: Elsevier, 2006), pp. 127–159.

9

Sustainable Solid Waste Infrastructure

MICHAEL W. MCLAUGHLIN AND LISA K. MCDANIEL

SCS ENGINEERS

WHEN THINGS ARE DISCARDED, they enter the solid waste infrastructure. In some communities, the solid waste management system consists of a means of collection, a means of disposal, and little else. Other communities supplement the basic solid waste infrastructure by including intermediate measures to remove valuable components of the waste stream, or to convert portions of the waste stream to other forms such as compost or energy. Which forms of solid waste infrastructure are the most sustainable? Is a municipal solid waste (MSW) landfill more or less sustainable than a waste-to-energy (WTE) plant? Is either of these more or less sustainable than a compost facility?

Experienced solid waste professionals would object to the questions raised above. They would correctly note that alternatives such as material reuse and waste minimization—not making solid waste in the first place—would be preferred to the alternatives listed above. They would observe that only a portion of MSW can

be composted, or that any solid waste management approach will have residuals that will require management in a landfill. And what about recycling, such as selling components of MSW to be used as feedstock for manufacturing instead of using virgin materials? How does that concept fit into the solid waste infrastructure?

These are not simple questions to answer. In fact, it seems these questions turn into arguments as often as not. But perhaps there are some general truths to be gleaned from the reams of data assembled by the experts.

SOLID WASTE GENERATION

On a per-capita basis, the USA generates more MSW than other developed nations. The US Environmental Protection Agency (USEPA) estimates that each US resident produces 4.3 pounds of MSW each day. By comparison, the average MSW generation for 17 other developed countries is about 3.5 pounds per person per day.[1]

The components of MSW in a given community will differ from national statistics, and may vary over time as the population demographics change. In addition, MSW varies with the season (e.g., relatively little yard trimming waste is generated in the winter in much of the USA). That said, many MSW planners use national annual MSW characteristics as a starting point in the planning process. Figure 9.1 shows the breakdown of MSW components "as generated" in the United States in 2008, as estimated by USEPA.

According to USEPA, the USA discards about 54 percent of the MSW it generates, recycles 34 percent, and burns the rest. These are national numbers, and any given jurisdiction likely has a different mix. With respect to recycling in particular, different commodities are recycled at different rates in different parts of the country. Collectively, according to USEPA, the USA recycles almost all of the automobile batteries it uses, and about 74 percent of the office paper, 60 percent of the yard trimmings, 66 percent of the steel cans, and 51 percent of the aluminum cans generated.[2]

At the other end of the spectrum are commodities such as food waste (2.5 percent recycled), plastics (7.1 percent), and wood (14

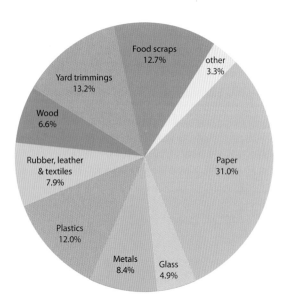

9.1 Total MSW "as generated" (before recycling) in the USA

Source: *Municipal Solid Waste Generation, Recycling, and Disposal in the United States: Facts and Figures for 2009* (EPA-530-F-010-012, December 2010)

percent). There are challenges to recycling these materials in an environmentally responsible manner, as discussed below.

THE SOLID WASTE HIERARCHY

Figure 9.2 shows the classic and widely accepted hierarchy of preferred approaches to MSW management. Reduced to its essence, the hierarchy is based upon resource allocation considerations. Under this approach things should be produced sparingly or not at all. Once produced, things should be used until they are no longer suitable for their given purpose, whereupon they should be handed down to someone else to use some more. At the end of their useful life, things should be recycled into other useful goods. That which cannot be recovered and recycled should be burned for its energy value, some of the residuals beneficially used for other purposes, and the leftovers should be placed in a properly designed landfill.

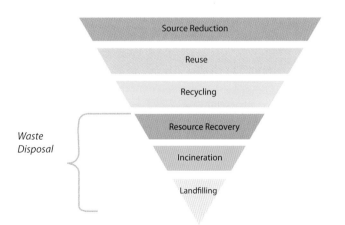

9.2 Solid waste management hierarchy
Source: *Fairfax County Solid Waste Management Plan 2004–2024*, Figure 3-1

The most important consideration in designing an MSW infrastructure is public health and safety. Modern life would not be possible without safe, reliable, and sanitary systems for collection, processing, and disposal of MSW. Economic considerations also are important, but protection of public health and safety is paramount.

Source reduction and reuse

Normally, those responsible for MSW management in a community do not have the option to manage only a select portion of the MSW. They must provide a safe and reliable system that accounts for everything that people put in the trash. For example, policymakers can forbid residents from putting nickel-cadmium batteries into the MSW stream, but as a practical matter it is not possible to sort through tons of collected trash to see if any nickel-cadmium batteries are present despite the law forbidding such disposal.

On the other hand, it is possible (at some cost) to educate the public about materials that should be segregated from the trash and to provide a convenient means of separate collection. The easier it is for people to comply with requirements to keep certain materials out of the solid waste stream the more likely they will comply. But, at the end of the day, the MSW management professional has to manage the MSW stream "as generated."

As mentioned earlier, the average US resident produces a little less than a pound of excess MSW each day, as compared with waste generation rates in other developed countries. A pound of waste not generated is a pound of waste that does not have to be managed by the MSW infrastructure.

One opportunity for source reduction would be to use less packaging, because most packaging ends up in the trash. There are tradeoffs, of course, since less packaging might result in more damage or spoilage of goods in transit (and thus more waste).

Some communities encourage citizens to come to a central facility and take discarded items left by others that they can use. Some regard this practice as a version of the old-fashioned "Commons," where citizens can gather and socialize on Saturday morning while doing something good for the environment by collecting discarded materials for reuse. Such areas can include covered areas to protect items like used furniture from the elements. Many charity groups operate collection centers where used goods can be taken for distribution to the less fortunate or sold to raise funds for the charity. Extending the useful life of goods in this manner reduces the amount of waste to be managed.

Recycling and composting

Another consideration regarding reducing packaging is the effect fewer materials will have on recyclables. For example, some jurisdictions have noted that, despite their best efforts to collect aluminum cans or plastic beverage containers, the percentages recycled on a weight basis are declining or staying the same. As it turns out, the difference often is the average weight of the aluminum can, which has been declining in recent years. It now takes many more cans to achieve the same weight of recycled aluminum than in the past. This phenomenon is called "light weighting," and sophisticated MSW managers have begun to factor it into their recycling reports to the public.

Recycling paper, aluminum, and other commodities reduces the need to consume energy and virgin materials to produce these commodities, with a dramatic reduction in greenhouse gas (GHG) emissions as a result. USEPA has published a simple tool called the Waste Reduction Model (WARM) to assist MSW planning professionals in estimating GHG emission reductions associated with recycling different materials. WARM calculates GHG emissions for baseline and alternative waste management practices, including source reduction, recycling, combustion, composting, and landfilling.[3]

Diverting yard waste (and food waste) to compost also can result in GHG reductions because carbon dioxide produced during composting is considered biogenic or natural (not anthropogenic or man-made), and carbon stored in compost remains sequestered in soils for at least some period of time. However, some have noted that compost facilities can generate anthropogenic methane and nitrous oxide (potent GHGs), thus offsetting some (perhaps 20 percent) of the GHG and other emission reductions that would otherwise be expected.[4]

Each time a truck burning diesel fuel comes by a home or apartment building to pick up trash or yard waste or recyclable materials, there are GHG and diesel exhaust emissions (not to mention economic costs) associated with the collection event. If the collected materials are transported to an interim facility, such as a transfer station or a material recovery facility (MRF) where recyclables are separated, there are also economic costs and GHG emissions associated with that step.

Recycling and compost programs have limits, of course. If a community produces 50,000 tons of MSW annually, and the MSW stream contains only 1.5 percent aluminum (the national average), it would be impossible to recycle more than 750 tons of aluminum. The community would be better than the national average if it recycled 200 tons of aluminum each year (the national average for aluminum would be 20 percent, or 150 tons per year[5]). Similar constraints apply to other commodities—one cannot recycle more than one generates, and it is only possible to recycle a fraction of that because it is impossible to segregate all of a particular material from an MSW stream.

A common tool for serious MSW planners to estimate the limits of a recycling program is a waste characterization study, or "waste sort." Often conducted over several seasons, a waste sort collects statistically based samples of wastes to determine the characteristics of the MSW stream in a community at a particular point in time. Normally a waste sort is based on dividing the MSW stream samples into component categories of interest and weighing each resulting portion. In some cases, additional information is collected (e.g., physical or chemical characteristics, numbers of beverage containers for a light weighting study, etc.).

Both recycling and composting require facilities to process collected materials. Common complaints of neighbors of such facilities include the associated truck traffic, both bringing material to the facility and removing commodities or products after processing, odors, disease vectors, and noise. Proper facility siting (e.g., with access to major roads, centrally located to minimize transportation routes to and from the facility) can ameliorate somewhat the concerns over truck traffic. Proper facility design and operation can mitigate the potential for odors, disease vectors, and noise.

Some materials require more processing than others and more stringent controls for processing in an environmentally responsible manner. One example is food waste, which is currently recycled at a rate of 2.5 percent. Large-scale food waste compost facilities require careful design and operation to avoid creating health hazards (e.g., disease vectors such as rats), odors, and significant emissions of volatile organic compounds that contribute to air quality issues. There are not many such facilities in the USA and regulations governing proper design and operation of food waste compost facilities are not as well developed as for other kinds of solid waste facilities (e.g., landfills, MSW combustors, or yard waste compost facilities).

Waste to energy

Modern WTE facilities incorporate state-of-the-art air pollution control technologies with high-temperature incineration, metals recovery, and ash management to reduce MSW mass by about 90 percent. Two basic approaches are used to burn MSW as fuel. One removes unsuitable materials and metals from the MSW and shreds and processes the remainder into pellets of refuse-derived fuels (RDF) that are fed into boilers where they are burned. The other approach uses shovels to load MSW without significant processing into large hoppers that in turn are fed into large boiler chambers (mass burn). Facilities using this approach recover metals after the MSW is burned.

Several public and private entities are experimenting with technologies that promise to convert MSW into synthetic gas (useable as an energy source) and inert materials (useable as aggregate), but large-scale demonstrations of these technologies on heterogeneous (not source-separated) MSW have yet to be successful.

As with recycling and composting facilities, the common complaints expressed by WTE facility neighbors have to do with truck traffic (both bringing MSW to the facility and carrying ash and recovered metals from the facility), noise, and odors. In addition, neighbors typically are concerned about air emissions from the facility and the resulting health effects for their families.

Landfills

Eventually, some portion of the trash generated must be taken to a landfill for final disposal. A WTE facility reduces the weight of the trash by 90 percent, but the residual materials must be managed somewhere (along with any air pollution control residuals that the facility generates).

Modern landfills include liners to minimize leakage into the environment. They include measures to cover wastes at the end of each work day to reduce the potential for litter and disease vectors. They collect and manage liquids that drain from wastes (leachate). Organic materials that are buried in a landfill will decompose over time under anaerobic conditions and produce gas containing carbon dioxide and methane. While the carbon dioxide portion is considered natural or biogenic, the methane portion of decomposition gas from landfills is considered a potent[6] anthropogenic or man-made GHG. Many landfills collect and burn most of the methane they generate, but some landfills do not have landfill gas collection and control systems. Some landfills burn gas in flares, and other landfills utilize landfill gas to generate electricity (e.g., in engines or turbines) or thermal energy (e.g., in boilers).

Where landfill gas is burned as a fuel (offsetting fossil fuels), the GHG emissions associated with the landfill can be negative—the landfill is doing more good than harm in terms of GHG emissions. In addition, a significant amount of the carbon disposed in a landfill is sequestered indefinitely, thus keeping carbon out of the atmosphere.

QUALITY OF LIFE

With respect to MSW management, most would say that their quality of life would be optimized with an "out of sight, out of mind" approach. No one wants to manage or collect garbage at their home any more than is absolutely necessary, and no one wants the garbage of others managed where they can see or smell it.

One response is that a modern approach to MSW management will minimize garbage odors altogether. Indeed, most modern MSW management facilities are designed and operated without significant odor complaints once the MSW enters the facility. In part this is because facility designs should incorporate sufficient land buffers to separate the facility from neighbors. Facility designs also often incorporate negative air pressures to assure that odors do not leave the building (in the case of transfer stations, mass burn facilities, RDFs, and MRFs) before they are removed by treatment.

Modern landfills often include gas collection and treatment because these can help reduce or eliminate odors from decomposing MSW. When a landfill stops receiving MSW, it must be closed, maintained, and monitored for some period of time (the "post-closure period") in accordance with MSW regulations.

During the post-closure period, some landfills can be used as open space for other purposes (e.g., golf courses, parks), and sometimes such post-closure uses are built into formal landfill plans as a way of offsetting the impact an operating landfill might have had on its neighbors. In other words, in exchange for living near a landfill for ten or fifteen years, the community will have the use of the resulting open space indefinitely following closure.

Some might complain that MSW facilities are unattractive, but they need not be eyesores. In fact, some are quite the opposite. An MSW facility with abundant landscaping, or incorporating ecosystems into the facility (e.g., constructed wetlands for stormwater or even leachate treatment), can preserve view sheds and enhance habitat. For example, Byxbee Park in Palo Alto, California, is a former landfill that consists of recreational trails and public art. Some say that the park offers spectacular views of San Francisco Bay.

Closed landfills can also provide topographic relief in flat areas. Mount Trashmore in Virginia Beach, Virginia, is an example of a public park that some regard as an enhancement over the flat coastal plain provided by nature. Certainly steps can be taken to augment habitat and otherwise enhance the quality of life for members of the community.

RESOURCE ALLOCATION

Resource allocation in the context of MSW management has to do with resource conservation. The Figure 9.2 hierarchy lists MSW management alternatives in order of preference. The best MSW management alternative in terms of resource allocation is to avoid creating MSW through source reduction, followed by reuse and recycling. Next come WTE facilities (mass burn or RDF). Incineration without energy recovery and landfills are at the bottom of the scale in terms of resource allocation.

PRESERVATION AND ENHANCEMENT OF NATURAL WORLD

Proper management of MSW reduces degradation of the natural world by humans. For much of recorded history waste was discarded into waterways and open sewers, or allowed to pile up and burn in the form of an open dump on the edge of a settlement. By contrast, modern sanitation, including safe and effective MSW management systems, reduces the potential for litter and trash to affect the natural world.

In the hierarchy of MSW alternatives all but landfills are normally considered temporary uses of land. Transfer stations, MRFs, compost facilities, mass burn facilities, and RDF plants all can be closed and the land reused for other purposes without elaborate measures. However, landfills are considered long-term uses that will affect the land long after closure. Construction atop a closed landfill has been performed successfully at scores of landfills, but it requires special precautions for foundation settlement and landfill gas migration control for decades following closure.

Table 9.1 Solid waste management unit costs

Element	Unit costs		
	Unit	Cost ($)	CO_2e emissions (lbs)
Collection[1]	Per pickup	2	1.0
Transfer station[2]	Per ton	15	10.0
Recycling (MRF)[3]	Per ton	100	-7000.0
Compost[4]	Per ton	40	-500.0
WTE facility[5]	Per ton	60	-300.0
Landfill w/LFGE[6]	Per ton	25	-700.0
Landfill w/flaring[7]	Per ton	26	-300.0
Landfill w/o GCCS[8]	Per ton	25	3000.0

Notes:

1 Collection assumes pickup at single family homes and transport to facility, e.g., 500 homes would cost $1000 to collect and truck would emit 500 lbs CO_2e (equivalent to about 25 gallons of motor fuel consumed) per collection day.

2 Transfer station assumes operation of facility to consolidate collected waste into transfer trailers and transport to facility 50 miles distant, with empty trailer on return. If truck conveys 40 tons of MSW per load and emits about 400 lbs CO_2e per round trip (equivalent to about 20 gallons of fuel per round trip), then transportation emissions would be about 400/40 or 10 pounds per ton of MSW handled. Ignore building energy load and associated emissions.

3 Assume materials diverted for recycling are proportionate to MSW fractions generated and include aluminum, steel, glass, plastic, mixed paper, and carpet. Dollar cost based on experience over long term (commodity sales prices can fluctuate widely with resulting impact on net cost). CO_2e cost is based on blend of materials and EPA September 2006 Exhibit 3-8, with transportation emissions subtracted.

4 Compostable materials include food waste and yard waste (collectively about 25 percent of typical MSW composition). CO_2e cost based on EPA September 2006 Exhibit 4-6 with transportation emissions subtracted. This GHG emission factor ignores any methane or nitrous oxide emissions from composting (which may mean GHG savings are overstated by about 100 lbs CO_2e/ton).

5 WTE assumes mass burn facility. CO_2e cost based on EPA September 2006 Exhibit 5-6 for mixed MSW with transportation emission subtracted.

6 Landfill w/LFGE assumes landfill gas collection system and collected gas is used to produce electricity. CO_2e cost is based on EPA September 2006 Exhibit 6-8 for mixed MSW with transportation emissions subtracted.

7 Landfill w/flaring assumes landfill gas collection system and collected gas is simply flared. CO_2e cost is based on EPA September 2006 Exhibit 6-8 for mixed MSW with transportation emissions subtracted.

8 Landfill w/o GCCS assumes no landfill gas collection system. CO_2e cost is based on EPA September 2006 Exhibit 6-8 for mixed MSW with transportation emissions subtracted.

CLIMATE CHANGE

The GHG implications of different MSW management alternatives include both direct GHG emissions (e.g., fossil fuel used in collection trucks) and indirect GHG effects (e.g., avoided GHG emissions by using recycled instead of virgin feedstocks). Table 9.1 provides some simplistic unit costs and GHG emission factors to help illustrate the differences.

Consider an example community of 60,000 residents with 15,000 households that takes all 50,000 tons of trash it generates each year to a nearby landfill that does not collect landfill gas. The town collects trash once each week from each household. As shown in Table 9.2, the annual cost of the current system is about $2.8 million per year, with GHG emissions of about 68,500 metric tons of carbon dioxide equivalent (MT CO_2e) per year.

Table 9.2   Solid waste management planning annual baseline

Element	Portion of waste handled	Unit costs			Extended costs	
		Unit	Cost ($)	CO_2e emissions (lbs)	Cost (K$)	MT CO_2e
Collection		Per pickup	2	1	1560	355
Transfer Station		Per ton	15	10	0	0
Recycling (MRF)		Per ton	100	-7000	0	0
Compost		Per ton	40	-500	0	0
WTE Facility		Per ton	60	-300	0	0
Landfill w/ LFGE		Per ton	25	-700	0	0
Landfill w/ Flaring		Per ton	26	-300	0	0
Landfill w/o GCCS	100%	Per ton	25	3000	1250	68,182
Totals	100%				2810	68,537

Note: Population 60,000; calculated generation rate 4.6 lbs/person/day; 50,000 tons/year waste generated; 15,000 households; 1 weekly pickup/household

Table 9.3   Solid waste management planning transfer station and landfill with gas utilization alternative

Element	Portion of waste handled	Unit costs			Extended costs	
		Unit	Cost ($)	CO_2e emissions (lbs)	Cost (K$)	MT CO_2e
Collection	100%	Per pickup	2	1	1560	355
Transfer station	100%	Per ton	15	10	750	227
Recycling (MRF)		Per ton	100	-7000	0	0
Compost		Per ton	40	-500	0	0
WTE facility		Per ton	60	-300	0	0
Landfill w/LFGE	100%	Per ton	25	-700	1250	-15,909
Landfill w/flaring		Per ton	26	-300	0	0
Landfill w/o GCCS		Per ton	25	3000	0	0
Totals	100%				3560	-15,327

Note: population 60,000; calculated generation rate 4.6 lbs/person/day; 50,000 tons/year waste generated; 15,000 households; 1 weekly pickup/household

Table 9.4 Solid waste management planning recycling, composting, transfer station, and landfill with gas utilization alternative

Element	Portion of waste handled	Unit costs			Extended costs	
		Unit	Cost ($)	CO_2e emissions (lbs)	Cost (K$)	MT CO_2e
Collection	100%	Per pickup	2	1	4680	1064
Transfer Station	60%	Per ton	15	10	450	136
Recycling (MRF)	25%	Per ton	100	-7000	1250	-39,773
Compost	15%	Per ton	40	-500	300	-1705
WTE Facility		Per ton	60	-300	0	0
Landfill w/ LFGE	60%	Per ton	25	-700	750	-9545
Landfill w/ Flaring		Per ton	26	-300	0	0
Landfill w/o GCCS		Per ton	25	3000	0	0
Totals	100%				7430	-49,823

Note: population 60,000; calculated generation rate 4.6 lbs/person/day; 50,000 tons/year waste generated; 15,000 households; 3 weekly pickups/household

Table 9.5 Solid waste management planning mass burn WTE alternative

Element	Portion of waste handled	Unit costs			Extended costs	
		Unit	Cost ($)	CO_2e emissions (lbs)	Cost (K$)	MT CO_2e
Collection	100%	Per pickup	2	1	1560	355
Transfer Station		Per ton	15	10	0	0
Recycling (MRF)		Per ton	100	-7000	0	0
Compost		Per ton	40	-500	0	0
WTE Facility	100%	Per ton	60	-300	3000	-6818
Landfill w/ LFGE		Per ton	25	-700	0	0
Landfill w/ Flaring		Per ton	26	-300	0	0
Landfill w/o GCCS		Per ton	25	3000	0	0
Totals	100%				4560	-6463

Note: population 60,000; calculated generation rate 4.6 lbs/person/day; 50,000 tons/year waste generated; 15,000 households; 1 weekly pickup/household

Now, consider the effect of using a transfer station to consolidate MSW for transport to a regional landfill some distance away that has a landfill gas collection and control system using landfill gas to make electricity. As shown in Table 9.3, the total costs and emissions would be $3.6 million ($800K more) and minus 15,000 MT CO_2e per year (a reduction of 83,500 MT CO_2e per year over the current system). On a per MT CO_2e basis, the added cost of this alternative is about $10/MT.

What about recycling? Could the GHG emissions of the MSW management system be reduced even more by instituting separate collections for recyclables and yard wastes (a total of three collections per week from each household)? For purposes of this analysis, assume that 25 percent of the trash collected could be diverted for recycling and 15 percent diverted for composting (a total diversion rate of 40 percent), and that the rest of the trash goes to the transfer station and regional landfill considered in the previous example. Table 9.4 shows the MSW system with these assumptions.

Primarily due to the extra collections, annual costs for this alternative increase to about $7.4 million, with annual emissions of about minus 50,000 MT CO_2e. This alternative reduces GHG emissions by about 35,000 MT CO_2e per year over the previous example, but at an added annual cost of about $3.8 million. On a per MT CO_2e basis, the added cost of this alternative is about $110/MT.

We should also compare the recycling and compost option with the current system. The recycling and compost option would cost about $4.6 million more than the current system, but would reduce annual GHG emissions by 103,500 MT CO_2e. This works out to a unit cost of about $44 per MT CO_2e.

How would WTE (mass burn) compare? Table 9.5 assumes that the town implements once per week collection and takes its trash to a local WTE plant. The cost of this alternative is about $4.6 million ($1.8 million more than the baseline current system), and GHG emissions are about minus 6500 MT CO_2e (75,000 MT CO_2e less than the current system). On a per MT CO_2e basis, the added cost of this alternative is about $24/MT when compared with the current system.

Several markets exist where GHG "credits" can be purchased from those who invested in voluntary GHG reduction projects. At the moment, the market for GHG credits in the USA is far below either $44 or $110 per MT CO_2e, and few experts think it will reach those levels any time soon. The $24 per MT CO_2e cost of the WTE option is also far above the current market for GHG emission reduction credits in the USA, but it is in the range of where some experts believe the market may move in the years ahead (i.e., using the European Union credit trading experience as a benchmark).

The best choice in terms of cost-effective reductions in GHG emissions might be to invest in a landfill gas collection and flaring system for the existing local landfill. The small additional cost for gas control (on the order of $100,000 per year) would result in reducing GHG emissions by about 75,000 MT CO_2e each year. Assuming that the gas collection and control system is not otherwise required by regulations or business as usual, the emission reductions that cost about $1 per MT CO_2e to create could likely be sold for several times that amount on the open market.[7]

CONCLUSION

Measures of sustainability—Quality of Life, Resource Allocation, Preservation and Enhancement of the Natural World, and Climate Change—offer the MSW planner useful tools when evaluating MSW management options. Traditional thinking—emphasizing (for example) resource allocation—might drive decisions toward use of preferred options such as recycling and composting.

However, it is more complicated to select a sustainable solid waste infrastructure than traditional thinking might suggest. Recycling and composting can account for only a portion of the MSW waste stream. Emerging technologies offer promise for converting solid wastes into useable materials with no residuals requiring landfilling, but these new technologies have not been proven on the scale that would be required for most communities. If residuals must be managed in a landfill in any case, a sustainable approach to solid waste management must include landfilling for at least a portion of the waste stream.[8, 9]

NOTES

1 US Environmental Protection Agency, *Municipal Solid Waste Generation, Recycling, and Disposal in the United States: Facts and Figures for 2009* (EPA-530-F-010-012, December 2010).

2 US Environmental Protection Agency, *Municipal Solid Waste Generation.*

3 WARM is available for download or use on USEPA's website (http://epa.gov/climatechange/wycd/waste/calculators/Warm_home.html).

4 I. Miller, Angiel, J., "Municipal yard trimmings composting benefit cost analysis," *BioCycle* (July 2009).

5 To reconcile these numbers with the earlier statement that the USA recycles 51 percent of aluminum beverage containers, note that beverage containers account for only 54 percent of the aluminum found in MSW. The other 46 percent of aluminum in MSW is recovered in negligible amounts.

6 Methane is considered 21 to 25 times more potent than carbon dioxide as a GHG.

7 P. Sullivan, *The Importance of Landfill Gas Capture and Utilization in the US*, Council for Sustainable Use of Resources, Earth Engineering Center, Columbia University (April 2010).

8 Fairfax County (Virginia) Department of Public Works and Environmental Services, *Solid Waste Management Plan 2004–2024* (June 2004).

9 US Environmental Protection Agency, *Solid Waste Management and Greenhouse Gases: A Life-Cycle Assessment of Emissions and Sinks, Third Edition* (September 2006).

Sustainable Transportation Infrastructure

SUSANNAH KERR ADLER, MEG CEDEROTH, KATHERINE HENDERSON, AND SCOTT SNELLING

PARSONS BRINCKERHOFF

INTRODUCTION: DEFINING SUSTAINABLE TRANSPORTATION

This chapter focuses on the practical application of sustainability goals and principles in three areas of transportation infrastructure: 1) roads and highways; 2) inter-city passenger and freight rail systems (railroads); and 3) intra-city transit systems, including rail and bus (transit).[1] While each of these transportation modes has its own specific definitions and practices around sustainability, some goals are common. These goals, outlined in Table 10.1, provide important clarification for this industry beyond the general definitions of sustainability.

When considering how to address the sustainability of transportation infrastructure, two big-picture assumptions must first be addressed: 1) that roads and highways are inherently unsustainable, such that nothing can be done to improve them; and 2) that railroads and transit are inherently sustainable, such that nothing is left to be done. While each of these assumptions has some foundation, neither should be used to justify "business as usual."

Table 10.1 Sustainable transportation infrastructure—goals

For users:	Choice and affordable options Access for all
For the environment:	Efficient use of resources Habitat conservation/protection
For communities:	Environmental justice Context-sensitive design Community engagement/focus
For businesses:	Short- and long-term success of local businesses Short- and long-term success of transportation agencies

CHALLENGES AND OPPORTUNITIES

There are some general sustainability challenges that apply to all transportation infrastructure projects. For example, these projects require an extended planning and design process. By construction time, the original design standards will be outdated, and the built project will not reflect the "cutting edge" of sustainable design. An additional challenge relates to construction activities: railroad and transit represent some of the most energy-intensive construction activities.

To help combat these challenges, transportation organizations must first engage in collaborative planning efforts at the local level to increase emphasis on land use and transit-oriented development. When designing new roads, rail lines, and public transit systems, a collaborative stakeholder process should be used to ensure that a transportation facility fits its setting. Further, all transportation systems, facilities, and vehicles should be designed for flexibility, including system expansion, increased user demand, and alternative uses of supporting facilities. Wherever possible, transportation organizations should encourage non-single-occupant-motor-vehicle transportation, incorporating connections to pedestrian and cycling networks, rail, buses, transit, and airports, and promoting the use of high-occupancy vehicles and low-emission vehicles.

When designing transportation infrastructure, teams should apply all relevant sustainable site design principles, with particular emphasis on minimizing the need for cut-and-fill, selecting highly efficient equipment, and carefully planning for waste segregation and erosion and sedimentation control during construction. Materials used in transportation infrastructure should be easy to maintain, environmentally friendly, and economical, with long service lives. Design teams should give particular attention to the life cycle costs of transportation projects. By accounting for the operation, maintenance, and decommissioning phases of infrastructure, life cycle cost analysis facilitates long-term efficient solutions, versus those based solely on lowest initial cost.

Once infrastructure is in service, new modeling techniques should be applied to optimize operations. Over time, transportation organizations should continuously measure and reduce energy consumption and greenhouse gas emissions from all facilities/vehicles. Even small changes during the operations and maintenance phase can have a major impact over the long life of infrastructure systems.

Mode-specific considerations

Much discussion has focused on our country's detrimental reliance on the automobile, and the fossil fuel use and sprawling network of highways and roads supporting this reliance. It seems to be a practical reality that road networks will continue to grow for as long as societies grow, and will exist in some form for as long as societies exists. Therein lies an opportunity: to improve the performance of these long-lasting systems, which will continue to have impacts far into the future.

A particular area of opportunity for sustainable design of roads and highways is stormwater control systems. Design teams should incorporate systems that absorb and filter stormwater within the road or highway right-of-way. Technologies that can accomplish this include impervious pavement, infiltration trenches, retention ponds, constructed wetlands, and vegetated swales. This is preferable to the conventional method of allowing stormwater to wash pollutants from pervious pavements and quickly return, untreated, via storm sewers to streams, rivers, and lakes.

When compared with roads, transit systems and railroads, both passenger and freight, begin with an advantage. This advantage stems, in part, from fuel source and system efficiency. Some parts of the rail network are electrified, and some transit systems run on electricity. In areas where the energy profile includes a high percentage of renewable energy, hydro, or nuclear power, this results in low operational emissions of greenhouse gases. In terms of transit and fuel choice, many agencies have begun to "green" their fleet by purchasing hybrid and biofuel-adapted vehicles. In addition, for commercial reasons, transit and rail systems are seeking increasing efficiency. Finally, whether diesel or electric, rail and transit systems have significantly more vehicle capacity, and therefore can efficiently carry more passengers (or freight) per gallon of fuel compared with other modes.

These advantages notwithstanding, there are meaningful improvements that the railroad and transit industries should incorporate to dramatically improve the long-term viability of their facilities and organizations. Railroads can diminish operational greenhouse gases by electrifying their system, contracting for 100 percent electric power, switching over from diesel, and using their right-of-way to generate renewable energy. When optimized, only walking beats railroad in terms of greenhouse gases emitted per passenger mile.

Railroads can also consider implementing "infrastructure condominiums," in which the right-of-way and distribution network is shared and optimized across freight, high-speed, and commuter passenger rail. This strategy reduces redundancy in transmission infrastructure. In addition, rail agencies can implement high-speed rail to transfer passengers from short-haul air to rail, thereby decreasing air travel and road congestion. Other opportunities to improve the sustainability of railroads include the use of "smart grids" to optimize traction power, and recycling and/or refurbishing vehicles to minimize resource use and waste.

Similarly, transit agencies have numerous opportunities to improve the sustainability of their infrastructure.[2] In general, they should provide a safe, attractive, easy-to-navigate rider environment to attract and maintain ridership. In all operations, transit systems should conserve energy through innovative, more efficient, lighter-weight vehicles and component design, and minimize transmission losses throughout. Further, transit organizations can "right-size" parking by sharing with residential and commercial developments, and providing preferential parking for shared car services, carpools, vanpools, etc. They can implement new technologies, such as regenerative braking systems that capture energy from braking vehicles and feed it back into the power distribution system. Other creative opportunities are available; for example, a transit agency could partner with a local power utility (perhaps via a pilot project) to micro-generate and transmit electricity for transit system use.

MAKING IT HAPPEN: MARKET DRIVERS

Moving toward more sustainable transportation infrastructure does not happen by accident, and generally requires several different external factors ("market drivers") applying pressure in concert. At present, a variety of policy, financial, and social market drivers are pushing change in the transportation infrastructure industry.

Policy

Political and regulatory pressures on the transportation industry as a whole begin at the White House, and are influencing all governmental agencies to an increasing degree. The Obama–Biden administration has emphasized the principles of livability, energy efficiency and independence, and "green transportation" in White House statements and key legislation such as the American Recovery and Reinvestment Act (ARRA). These priorities have spurred other legislation and Executive Orders such as the American Clean Energy and Security Act and Executive Order (E.O.) 13514, *Federal Leadership in Environmental, Energy, and Economic Performance*, which requires all federal agencies to implement a Strategic Sustainability Plan for their organization.

Congress has worked on several bills that would regulate carbon emissions through a cap-and-trade scenario, reflecting the growing interest from its constituents in utilizing financial markets to value environmental goods. Additionally, new federal interagency partnerships are emerging to tackle sustainability issues, such as the Interagency Partnership for Sustainable Communities. Through this agreement, the US Environmental Protection Agency (EPA), the US Department of Transportation (DOT), and the Department of Housing and Urban Development (HUD) are coordinating federal housing, transportation, and other infrastructure investments to apply a set of six "livability principles" (see Table 10.2).

At the level of individual federal agencies, the EPA is pushing sustainability through regulation and its ongoing greenhouse gas reporting program (40 CFR 98), which applies to all transportation sectors. DOT is applying the livability principles listed above via programs tailored to its highway, transit, and rail divisions. The

Federal Highway Administration (FHWA) is defining and promoting sustainable highway practices through two key programs: the Sustainable Highways Criteria and Tools program, which will define and promote a set of highway-specific sustainability practices, and the Safe Routes to School program, which funds projects to address safety concerns associated with walking and biking to school. The Federal Rail Administration (FRA) is primarily focused on improving the fuel efficiency of its systems. For its part, the Federal Transit Administration (FTA) published a Transit Green Building Plan and collaborated with the American Public Transportation Association to implement a consistent methodology for transit agencies to account for greenhouse gas emissions.

The DOT is backing its sustainability agenda with targeted funding programs, most notably the TIGER (Transportation Investment Generating Economic Recovery) Discretionary Grant Program. In February 2010, the DOT awarded on a competitive basis $1.5 billion of grants for surface transportation capital investment. The selection criteria included sustainability, livability, and innovation. Due to the success of this innovative program, funds have been

Table 10.2 EPA–DOT–HUD Interagency Partnership: six principles of livability

---

Provide more transportation choices to decrease household transportation costs, reduce dependence on oil, improve air quality and promote public health

Expand location- and energy-efficient housing choices for people of all ages, incomes, races, and ethnicities to increase mobility and lower the combined cost of housing and transportation

Improve economic competitiveness of neighborhoods by giving people reliable access to employment centers, educational opportunities, services, and other basic needs

Target federal funding toward existing communities—through transit-oriented and land recycling—to revitalize communities, reduce public works costs, and safeguard rural landscapes

Align federal policies and funding to remove barriers to collaboration, leverage funding, and increase the effectiveness of programs to plan for future growth

Enhance the unique characteristics of all communities by investing in healthy, safe, and walkable neighborhoods, whether rural, urban, or suburban

---

allocated for a second round of grants, dubbed TIGER II. A related transit-specific program is called TIGGER: Transit Investments for Greenhouse Gas & Energy Reduction. This program provides $100 million in discretionary grants to transit agencies for capital projects that reduce the agency's energy consumption and/or greenhouse gas emissions.

Political shifts toward sustainability are appearing at the local level as well, supported by corresponding regulations. For example, many jurisdictions are updating their building codes to require "green" design, often according to the US Green Building Council's Leadership in Energy and Environmental Design (LEED) criteria. These building code changes mandate that new facilities, including transportation-related buildings, are designed and built to meet specific environmental performance standards. Other state/local policy changes that affect the transportation industry include California codes that define land use in relation to environmental and energy impacts (e.g., SB 375), and state-wide energy efficiency targets (as in New York). State and local DOTs and Metropolitan Planning Organizations (MPOs) have also demonstrated their commitment to sustainability by building hundreds of LEED-certified green buildings, ranging from office headquarters (California), highway rest areas (Virginia), and maintenance buildings (New York City). DOTs, such as Washington State DOT, are now looking for ways to apply the lessons of third-party "green" certification programs to their road and highway projects. Authorities, such as the Port Authority of New York and New Jersey, have also implemented sustainability initiatives, including developing sustainable design guidelines for the range of their infrastructure projects.

Financial

Next are financial realities, which are perhaps the most critical motivator for changing behavior, especially in difficult economic times. On a macro-economic scale, emerging markets for renewable energy and Carbon Credits, plus the push to tie financial instruments to environmental protection, have the potential to radically shift business behavior over time. Federal transportation subsidies with environmental performance requirements, such as those described

above, are a temporary but powerful way to develop the industry's best practices and implementation experience.

Perhaps the most important financial shift, however, is happening at the level of individual transportation organizations and infrastructure projects. The improving return on investment associated with sustainable transportation projects is allowing transportation organizations, individuals, and businesses of all sizes to consider innovative materials, building methods, fuels, and other solutions previously deemed cost prohibitive. The changing math is due to factors including: long-term savings on operations/maintenance; reduced permitting time/cost when regulations are proactively met and communities are proactively engaged; and savings achieved by design/build programs. Mounting success stories within the industry, such as the case studies below, will continue to push it toward more sustainable practices in the future.

The International Association of Public Transportation (UITP) provides a useful definition in this context: "Sustainable development is how you plan for the future while still operating in the now." The use of the term "operations" here helps underscore the everyday, functional aspects of sustainability—and the idea that lofty ideals cannot be pursued in a vacuum without explicit incorporation of business objectives. For transit, there are several aspects to the "bottom line": ridership, cash flow, operations, and safety. These priorities are tied to the goals of social justice, economic viability, and environmental protection. All are integral to ensuring the long-term viability of the industry.

Social

Finally, there are widespread and growing social pressures for all businesses to operate more overtly with the future in mind. This is especially true in the infrastructure industry, which operates so visibly in the public realm. Stakeholders are increasingly demanding environmental and community sensitivity, and will hold up permitting processes where this is deemed lacking. Transportation-related agencies and consultancies are also experiencing pressure from within—progressive thinking from staff expecting their workplace to exemplify their personal values. Attracting and retaining the best talent will increasingly require all organizations to be proactive and accountable to sustainability goals, both within their internal operations and in their external projects.

No one of these market factors alone is enough to shift behavior and produce more sustainable transportation systems. In fact, even with all of them taken together, we are only beginning to see the types of behavior changes and infrastructure outcomes that are needed. But the market has changed enough to encourage some "front runners," several of which are detailed in case study form below.

MAKING IT HAPPEN: ORGANIZATIONAL CHANGE

The market drivers described above are putting pressure on transportation organizations to change their priorities. But sustainable project outcomes will only happen when these organizations make lasting change to the way they do business. In order to achieve the required culture shifts sustainability must be integrated into every facet of an organization. Some important steps in this process include:

- make the business case based on return on investment and integrate sustainability as a part of the organization's strategic objectives
- identify a sustainability champion within the organization coupled with the proper human and/or financial resources and mandates
- establish an outreach program (awareness raising and education) on sustainability for all staff
- undertake a sustainability inventory of your organization to identify current resources and achievements
- set a baseline year, and goals for continual improvement
- formulate mode-specific certification programs and solicit commitments from partner organizations (e.g., APTA Sustainability Commitment)
- establish a protocol for implementation during construction
- advertise the message to system users and the general public.

CONCLUSION

Ultimately, sustainability must be tailored to each industry, transportation mode, and infrastructure project. This represents a process, not a specific product. The transportation infrastructure industry is showing signs of progress toward sustainability, driven by political, regulatory, financial, and legacy pressures. The industry is making rapid technical advances and—just as importantly—is learning how to support and sustain this progress with organizational changes and behavior shifts. Achieving a smarter transportation system requires the engagement and commitment of many stakeholders and a substantial culture shift for both transportation users and providers.

PROJECT CASE STUDIES
Cooper River (Arthur Ravenel Jr.) Bridge, Charleston, South Carolina

As the lead designer for the Cooper River (Arthur Ravenel Jr.) Bridge in Charleston, South Carolina, PB applied several environmental best practices. This award-winning bridge has the longest cable-stayed span in North America of 1546 feet (471 meters) and has a 100-year design life. Public involvement and stakeholder engagement was accomplished with a Context-Sensitive Solutions (CSS) process. Accordingly, bicycle and pedestrian facilities were included due to the grassroots support revealed by CSS. The concrete mix used for this structure has high percentages (up to 43 percent) of industrial by-product cements, which include fly-ash, silica fume, and steel blast-furnace slag. The lighting for this signature bridge was designed to minimize disruption to turtle nesting and bird migration patterns. Over 80 percent of the replaced bridge material was reused to produce an artificial ocean reef to provide habitat and stimulate diving. The Design–Build project delivery method encouraged innovation and efficiency through competition. Other best practices included: wetland restoration, biodegradable oil in the construction equipment, noise minimization, erosion control, tree relocation, and repurposing brownfields for new parks.

Doyle Drive Environmental and Design Study

PB served as the lead consultant on the Doyle Drive Environmental and Design Study, performing preliminary engineering and environmental documentation for the replacement of 1.5 mile Doyle Drive (US 101) located in the Presidio of San Francisco, California. As part of the Environmental Impact Statement/Report, PB suggested proactive strategies for Doyle Drive that would anticipate California legislation and regulatory guidance on climate change. Additionally, PB and other joint-venture staff developed a sustainability program for the project, including greenhouse gas emission reduction strategies, material selection evaluations, construction waste management targets, a sustainability performance and goals-tracking mechanism, and exploration of potential certification schemes and award programs.

California High Speed Rail

As part of its role as program manager for the California High Speed Rail project, PB assessed air quality, including greenhouse gases, for the planned 800-mile-long high-speed train system that will connect San Diego, Los Angeles, Sacramento, and San Francisco. The air quality analysis included a detailed regional emission study that considered both the increased power demands needed to operate the system and associated shifts in plane and roadway traffic.

Corona Maintenance Shop and Car Washer, Queens, New York

PB was the designer of record that achieved LEED certification for the Corona Maintenance Shop and Car Washer in Queens, New York. Specific resource-saving strategies in PB's design included a photovoltaic system that meets 5 percent of the building's electricity needs, a fuel cell that can operate independently of the local utility's grid, natural lighting and ventilation, rainwater capture and reuse of gray water on site for the car wash. The facility is among the first rail maintenance shops in the USA to achieve LEED certification.

Rosa Parks Transit Center, Detroit, Michigan

PB was responsible for conceptual and final design of the celebrated Rosa Parks Transit Center in Detroit, Michigan. PB also performed construction-phase services on behalf of the Detroit Department of Transportation (DDOT). The facility honors Rosa Parks, an activist widely credited with beginning the civil rights movement in the USA and a resident of Detroit for more than 40 years. The transit center provides convenient connections among 21 city bus routes, taxis, and other regional bus systems. Funnel-shaped translucent canopies offer protection from the weather, maximize natural light and a feeling of openness, and channel rainwater to landscaped areas.

NOTES

1 In this chapter "rail" or "railroad" refers to heavy-rail commuter and freight systems that are inter-city/long-haul. "Transit" refers to intra-city systems such as light- and heavy-rail, streetcar/tram, bus, and/or paratransit.
2 T. Feng, ed., "Transit sustainability guidelines," Transit Sustainability Working Group, http://134.67.99.207/region9/greenbuilding/pdfs/TransitSustainabilityGuidelines.pdf.

Transportation: Aviation/Airports

JAMES S. GRANT ET AL.[1]

HNTB CORPORATION

AIRPORT INFRASTRUCTURE PRESENTS OPPORTUNITIES TO SOAR WITH SUSTAINABILITY

Aviation advancements and airport development are critical for people's ability to travel quickly, easily, and affordably. The efficient transport of cargo is similarly important to the world's economic viability. If aviation is to remain the preferred long-distance transportation choice—and we expect it will for the next several decades, based on current demographic trends and consumer behavior—then improvements in aircraft fuel economy, emissions, flight times, and the overall passenger experience are key.

In addition, the growth of air traffic will necessitate massive infrastructure projects over the next several decades. Business-as-usual projections for carbon dioxide (CO_2) emissions from global aviation are estimated to increase at 3.1 percent per year over the next 40 years, resulting in a 300 percent increase by 2050.[2] The industry consensus expects aviation—defined by revenue passenger miles—to double from 2009 volumes by 2030 to 2032.[3] Airport development will be a matter of great competitive significance, and it must be linked to a broader transport strategy that includes rail, road, and shipping systems.

In this section, we'll first provide a foundational understanding of basic airport infrastructure systems and then describe guidelines for considering sustainability in related planning, design, and construction projects. The desired economic and social outcomes will vary for each project and location, so it's difficult to cite a specific target metric. Among the factors used to measure the economic and social impact are payroll generation, specific job categories, revenue sources, and the volume of passengers, aircraft, and cargo.

TRANSPORTATION ACCOUNTS FOR A THIRD OF CLIMATE-CHANGING EMISSIONS

Because of its near-total dependence on petroleum fuels, the US transportation sector is responsible for about a third of America's climate-changing emissions.[4] Globally, about 13 percent of manmade CO_2 comes from cars, trucks, airplanes, ships, and other vehicles.[5] Global aviation accounts for 3 percent to 5 percent of total world greenhouse gases (GHGs), based predominantly on fuel burned in aircraft engines.[6]

As we examine airport infrastructure sustainability options, it may be helpful to understand the different ways airport infrastructure can be considered—by type of infrastructure, by stakeholder, and by project category.

Airport infrastructure is grouped into airside, civil-landside, and building categories. Civil-landside includes roads, bridges, parking structures, parking lots, signage, landscaping, fencing, and utilities. Airport infrastructure often is integrated with light rail, cargo, trucking, and marine transportation systems.

Projects also are divided by stakeholder responsibility. For example, airports can be run by cities, counties, states, aviation authorities, and port authorities. Within these organizations are departments of aviation, airport tenants, and federal agencies, such as the Transportation Security Administration (TSA) and Federal Aviation Administration (FAA), which often execute airport design and construction projects. Major airport growth and rehabilitation projects offer excellent opportunities to improve the overall infrastructure sustainability performance.

Airport projects typically break down into specific categories. The first is buildings—both occupied and non-occupied—and those used for fuel storage and dispensing. The next category is civil features, which includes "landside" features such as roads and fencing and "airside" features such as runways, aprons, and airport utilities. In addition, projects are divided by those sponsored by tenants, such as airlines and concessions, and those sponsored by government agencies, such as the FAA (runway status lights projects, for example) and TSA (security screening programs). Finally, many airport projects involve construction and maintenance, such as landscaping, airfield cleaning, and waste management.

EVERY PROJECT PHASE
CAN INCORPORATE SUSTAINABILITY

Funding and financing must be sustainable, too

The essence of airports' financial sustainability is the ability of the airport operator to provide the facilities and operational services required to meet the long-term air service demands of its community while protecting the long-term financial viability of the organization. Any environmental sustainability plans must fit into the funding and ongoing financing of airport projects.

Key in the definition of the financial parameters is an understanding of the operating revenues and capital funding sources available to the airport and the potential threats and disturbances to revenue sources. The long-term financial viability of airports is achieved through building diversified sources of revenue and stable sources of capital funding.

To further promote financial sustainability, capital-funding plans should attempt to capture the broad range of funding options that are available. Airport funding typically comes from four revenue sources:

1. Airport improvement program grant appropriations from the FAA, which represent a national redistribution of ticket and fuel taxes, collected from the aviation passengers and aircraft users to airports.
2. State and local grants, primarily from state-imposed fuel taxes.
3. Passenger facility charges, which are user fees imposed on passengers by airports and collected by airlines through the total airfare on a ticket.
4. Operating revenues, such as rents and fees paid by the airlines using the facilities and commercial operators at the airports, retail and food concessionaires, rental car companies, and ground transportation operators.

Given the magnitude of most airport capital programs, the construction of individual projects is frequently financed through general airport revenue bonds, which are supported by pledges to repay bondholders through airport operating revenues or passenger facility charges.

Looking forward, airports are likely to find an ever-increasing requirement for maintaining and rehabilitating aged facilities. Effective facilities maintenance and selective enhancements such as systems retrofitting to reduce energy use or boost capacity can significantly reduce operating costs and thereby support both the long-term financial viability and sustainability of the facilities.

Airports are generally governed by elected or appointed officials who serve on their boards as commissioners or directors. They are responsible for general oversight, policy formation, and approval of the annual airport budget. The board of commissioners has the ultimate authority over airport funds and is, therefore, an important constituency for any efforts to improve the sustainability of airport infrastructure. Some airports also have a separate airport advisory committee, which is made up of representatives appointed by elected officials from communities surrounding the airport. It may advise the board on matters of public concern and help formulate and recommend priorities for the capital improvement and expansion of the airport.

Global economy relies on air travel; planning is critical

Air travel is essential to the global economy, and airport planning, therefore, is critical. In a December 2009 *Airport Business* article, Tonci Peovic, CEO of Zagreb Airport, said, "For the sake of a sustainable airport network in Europe, don't forget that one mile of road takes us nowhere, but that one mile of runway takes us everywhere."[7]

Airport planning encompasses the strategic, business, financial, facilities, environmental, community, and social aspects of providing a fully functional airport system to meet the current and future needs of the local economy that it serves. Planning for future aviation infrastructure begins with a clear understanding of a region's existing and future air travel needs and translating that into specific facility (runways, terminals, etc.) requirements. But these facility needs also must be balanced with financial, social, and environmental considerations. While airport infrastructure provides a vital function for the regional economy, facility development and utilization can have negative impacts on the local environment and communities. It is the role of the airport planning to work with the airport sponsor and all key stakeholders to understand and work through the various issues.

While most airport facility planning efforts over the past 40 years have focused on new airport facility development, such as new runways and terminals, today's airport planning issues are more focused on renovation and redevelopment. In fact, many airports are faced with the decision to rebuild or renovate an existing terminal versus building an entirely new building.

A key part of the planning process is the inclusion of the airport stakeholder. Airport stakeholders play a critical role in the planning, approval, and funding of the airport's capital development program. Consequently, their involvement in the planning process is critical to the overall success of the program. The key stakeholders listed here are among the typical participants in the planning process. Their involvement and the timing of their involvement vary by project and location.

Managing multiple stakeholders can be challenging

- The airport planning team will lead the effort, anticipate and plan for future land use, and maximize site flexibility. Planners are responsible for articulating the tradeoffs between the various alternatives and assisting the airport sponsor through the decision process with input from the stakeholders. With a properly structured planning process, sustainability is an integral part of the effort.
- The role of the environmental advisory team is to provide input on federal, state, county, and local laws governing the protection of the environment. This includes Environmental Protection Agency (EPA) laws such as the Clean Air and Water acts.
- Maintenance and operation teams provide input on the life cycle aspects of the concepts.
- Airport tenants and users provide input on program requirements and lessons learnt related to facility operations.
- Members of other projects that may be affected often provide their input, as well. For example, when a sustainability project

such as an HVAC replacement is going on, planners would be wise to consider how it might integrate with lighting replacement or asbestos remediation projects that need to happen during similar timeframes.

- Local officials have a responsibility to ensure the orderly development of the airports within their jurisdiction and to advise on impacts to the community.
- Community participants are often brought in to voice comments on the plan.
- Regulatory agencies, including the FAA, TSA, and EPA, provide input on planning studies. The FAA approves the activity forecast, airport layout plan, airport noise studies, leads the federal environmental processes, and provides input on air traffic management procedures and related facility needs. The TSA is responsible for security in all modes of transportation and provides input on related facility development elements.

The planning stage also is the time to assess existing conditions, set sustainability goals, and plan studies to ensure an outcome that properly addresses sustainability. A sustainability checklist is one way to help planners identify and record sustainability goals and selected technical strategies for each project. Checklists summarize the required performance standards, the optional performance standards, and comparative criteria for the evaluation of alternative concepts. For examples of sustainability checklists, review the Los Angeles World Airports (LAWA) guide, "LAWA's Sustainable Airport Guidelines," at www.cscos.com/pdf/other/LAWA_Sustainable_Airport_Guidelines.pdf. (Boxes 11.1 and 11.2)

Project design/delivery

In the USA, 95 to 99 percent of airport design projects involve additions or rehabilitations. China, which is building up to 10 new airports a year, has a far greater potential for significantly affecting sustainability in airport design.

Regardless of what design method is selected (design–bid–build, design–build or construction management at risk), the consultant must meet a standard of performance. The standard of performance

BOX 11.1
Case study
LAX makes sustainability part of its business strategy

California—always an innovator—leads the way in making sustainability every bit as important to its airport plans as financial success, customer satisfaction, safety, and economic leadership. As the "international gateway" in southern California, the Los Angeles International Airport is determined to build its international and domestic business by expanding Tom Bradley International Terminal and respective airside areas to attract the new, larger A380 aircraft from Asia and Australia.

The LAX master plan balances the public's call for no expansion and fewer impacts into their neighborhoods with the airport's need to modernize and improve related ground access, safety, and security. Completion of improvements in the current plan will allow LAX to accommodate up to 78.9 million annual passengers, 3.1 million annual tons of cargo, and 2300 daily operations by 2015. Under the Enhanced Safety and Security Alternative, LAX will contribute $64 billion annually to the regional economy by 2015, $32 million more than the economic output generated without the master plan.

Among the airport's plans are design alternatives that mitigate many environmental concerns involving energy and water consumption and air emissions. Planners are considering self-generation systems that produce power and thermal energy, reduction in potable water through increased use of reclaimed water, thermal energy storage, use of alternative fuels (electricity and biofuels), 34,5kV utility power distribution and peak demand reduction schemes. Retro-commissioning of aging building systems has been identified as a key strategy to lower energy costs and achieve rapid payback periods, as well.

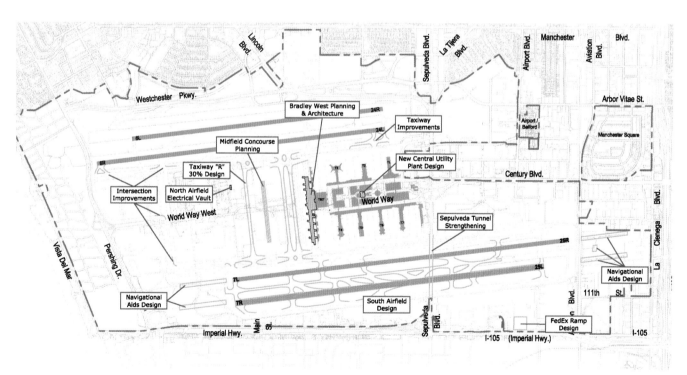

11.1 Bradley West
Note: Los Angeles International Airport has applied sustainability guidelines to several recent projects, including LEED® Silver Certification for the TBIT renovation, safety upgrades on the airfield, and energy improvements in the new central utility plant

includes regulatory requirements by federal, state, or local agencies and engineering and architecture codes and standards. It also may include sustainability measures.

Projects are ready for design once they:

- align with the airport's strategic plan
- meet the life cycle cost requirements
- include a reasonable scope, schedule, and budget definition
- have been vetted by the department of aviation planning group and key stakeholders.

The Chicago and Los Angeles international airports have developed their own sustainable airport planning, design, and construction guidelines for implementation on all airport projects. In addition, both airports have established their own rating systems. Designs need to reference the requirements of the sustainability guidelines and integrate them into the plans and specifications. Airport planners also may want to consider linking vendor payment to achievement of sustainability goals for air quality, energy or water conservation.

Land use is a critical issue in designing new airports and additions. While minimizing the size of the built environment and maximizing green space seems an obvious goal for sustainability, the positive tradeoff isn't so direct. For example, new air traffic management technology may reduce land use by allowing for runways to be closer together, while safely maintaining independent operations. More efficient takeoffs and landings also mean a potential increase in ground congestion, however, and the solution to that issue is more taxiways and aprons.

It's important to consider the distinct roles of each design stakeholder. The airport project manager will lead the design team. Airport representatives for each engineering discipline will participate

11.2 Manual covers
Note: The Chicago and Los Angeles international airports have developed their own sustainable airport planning, design, and construction guidelines for implementation on all airport projects

Terminal 5 at Heathrow International Airport is the largest single construction project in Europe. Its planners incorporated several sustainability practices into the construction process:

- more than 300,000 metric tons of aggregate was processed and recycled on site from demolition materials and waste concrete
- crushed green glass from domestic household recycling banks was used as a base for the terminal's site roads
- about 6.5 million cubic meters of earth were moved during the project. This earth has been used to backfill excavations and to landscape the terminal
- waste materials were segregated on site, and 85 percent of the waste from the project has been recycled.

Source: "Case study 12: A large building with a small footprint on the environment," Airports Council International, July 2007, www.aci.aero.

McCarran International Airport considered a demand-side system to manage its electrical costs. Recent electric tariffs had increased summer "on-peak" demand charges. A demand-side management system may reduce costs by limiting airport demand during high peak time periods. Alternatives include producing power on site, shifting demand to cheaper time periods through thermal energy storage systems, and simply cutting back non-essential loads such as lighting or escalators.

in design meetings, submittal reviews, sustainability assessments, utility capacity checks, other project coordination and schedule, budget, and quality checks. Key stakeholders from operations and maintenance, flight line, airlines, concessions, tenants, rental cars, and others also will participate in team meetings as needed. Finally, the engineer of record will take the construction documents through the plans examiner's office to complete permit review. This effort is typically done at 90 percent level design. Final construction documents are submitted for bid and advertisement.

Even construction phase gets in on the game

Final construction documents are used during the construction process to communicate the work to the contractor, clarify contractor requests for information, review contractor equipment submittals, and prepare the record set of the actual installation. They also will include any sustainability guidelines. Sustainable construction guidelines may include specifications for everything from training and inspections to sustainability standards for traffic management, dust reduction, noise minimization, and endangered-species protection.

During the design phase, the stakeholders list narrows to include the airport construction manager, the contractor, and airport representatives, who provide services to support the contractor. (Box 11.3)

Operational efficiencies affect longevity

Efficient management and monitoring of airport infrastructure is the key to minimizing disruptions to operations and maintaining the longevity of the facilities and equipment. LAWA, for example, adopted a facilities asset enterprise management system. It calls for inventorying LAX assets, performing a condition assessment on the assets and establishing a strong preventive maintenance program. Its goal is to reduce emergency repair costs. (Boxes 11.4 and 11.5)

BOX 11.5
Case study
Hamburg Terminal 1 design innovates to save energy, water

Hamburg is Germany's fourth largest airport, with nearly 12 million passengers a year. When it designed its new Terminal 1 building in 2005, it included a number of energy-saving features.

- It uses a water-based cooling system that is about 15 percent more efficient than an air-based system. Using water to cool the space is more efficient than cooling incoming and re-circulating air. In winter, warm water circulates through the same system to ensure comfortable year-round temperatures.
- It has a "thermo-labyrinth" system to pre-heat outside air in winter and pre-cool summer outside air. By transferring heat from incoming summer air to the cooler ground, the thermo-labyrinth reduces the annual energy needs of Terminal 1 by 1450 megawatt hours.
- All water needs in the toilets and washroom facilities are met by an energy-saving rainwater utilization system.

Source: "Case study 7: Energy saving technology in new terminal," Airports Council International, April 2007, www.aci.aero.

CLEAR METRICS INCREASE ODDS OF HITTING SUSTAINABILITY GOALS

Airport sustainability goals vary depending on size, geography, and strategic role. Most airports, however, would be interested in implementing innovative and cost-effective environmental solutions, improving their overall operational sustainability, increasing their business value through improved sustainable performance, incorporating sustainable design and construction practices in their projects, and monitoring and measuring their sustainable progress. One way to increase the odds of achieving sustainability goals is to develop a set of comprehensive performance standards applicable to the needs of the airport. These standards will help integrate sustainable practices into the airport culture.

In developing a set of sustainable performance standards, it is prudent to focus on the desired outcomes. A sustainable airport is one that:

- reduces waste
- reduces greenhouse gases
- reduces energy consumption
- reduces water consumption
- conserves natural resources
- prevents pollution
- uses resources efficiently
- creates public benefits
- generates community outreach programs
- strengthens the local economy
- measures and monitors sustainability performance
- strives for continuous improvement.

Set concrete targets for airside planning and design

Here are some examples of the airside sustainability goals that airport stakeholders might consider setting.

- Reduce the distance traveled by aircraft and decrease taxi times to and from runways and terminals to reduce GHG and other hazardous emissions.
- Eliminate choke points in the airfield system that cause delays. Provide alternative taxiway options to provide flexibility in getting the correct aircraft to the runway end (moving it ahead of other aircraft) for departure when the airspace slot is available for that aircraft.
- Provide terminal gate infrastructure to provide aircraft power and conditioned air. Aircraft parked at the gate require 400 Hz power to operate onboard systems. Depending on the climate, aircraft also require pre-conditioned air or heat (Alaska). If these systems are not available, the aircraft will run its auxiliary power unit and burn aviation jet fuel at the gate, which contributes to GHG.
- Provide infrastructure for alternative-fueled ground support equipment (GSE). This includes baggage trailer tractors, aircraft tugs, baggage loaders, and various support equipment. GSE commonly operates on diesel, gas, or propane fossil fuels. The airport and airlines may enter into a memo of understanding where the airport agrees to install electric quick-charging stations and the airlines agree to replace their fleet with new electric battery-operated equipment, which will reduce GHG.
- Install underground hydrant fueling systems to supply aviation jet fuel from the fuel farm to the aircraft. Hydrant fueling systems reduce the number of tanker truck trips on airport grounds. Portable fuel hydrant trailers can be parked at each gate to replace the fossil-fueled hydrant trucks. This option reduces truck emissions, GHG and airport congestion.

Airlines, too, must participate

Airlines also can take specific infrastructure-related steps to dramatically affect sustainability.

They can consider replacing less efficient aircraft, for example. Airbus produces a long-range aircraft (A380), which carries more passengers per mile than any other commercial aircraft, resulting in a drop in per-passenger operating costs of 15 to 20 percent per Airbus. The A380 single-class passenger capacity is up to 840, and the three-class configuration carries 555. Boeing produces the B747-8, which carries 415 passengers. It's made with carbon-reinforced fiber and is estimated to be up to 20 percent more fuel efficient than its aluminum counterpart. Boeing also makes a B787 from carbon-reinforced fiber, making it up to 20 percent more fuel efficient than similar aluminum models.

In addition, airlines can reduce or replace fossil fuels in their existing ground service equipment, which commonly use diesel fuel. Biodiesel blends of B10 (10 percent biodiesel and 90 percent diesel) and B20 can be used safely in this equipment. B100 also may be used, but additives are recommended for freeze protection, power boost, and reduction of the mono-nitrogen oxides NO and NO_2 (also called NOx). Interestingly, the California Air Resource Board does not recognize any GHG reduction with the use of current biofuels, even though the EPA credits biofuels with a 57 percent reduction over fossil fuels.

Reducing the amount of Jet A they use also can have a significant impact. Aircraft are by far the largest GHG contributor associated with airports (85 to 90 percent). Blending Jet A with sustainable biofuels for use in aircraft can significantly reduce GHG. Bio-derived synthetic paraffinic kerosene (bio-SPK) performs as well as or better than typical petroleum-based Jet A. Tests in several commercial airplane engine types using blends of up to 50 percent petroleum-based Jet A/Jet A-1 fuel and 50 percent sustainable biofuels were successful, as well. The American Society of Testing and Materials has certified a blend of 50 percent bio-SPK with Jet A.

Finally, airlines can implement strategies to reduce flight distances with customized airspace arrival and departure routes using advanced navigation technologies (NextGen). While this is beneficial from a cost and GHG perspective for the airlines, it is often at issue with established aviation noise patterns around airports, which can make this a difficult task to accomplish. While aircraft are getting quieter, more precise routes still increase the consistency and repetition of flights over specific locations, which can create challenges for the local community.

Locating alternative fuel suppliers onsite can reduce carbon footprint

Airport managers would be wise to consider opportunities to attract sustainable alternative-fuels suppliers and users at their airport grounds. This would give airports a readily available supply of alternative fuels to reduce their carbon footprints. In addition, they could generate new business revenue as they become concentrated demand centers for alternative fuels.

Consider, for example, the high level of fuel consumption at airports. Aircraft consumption of Jet A is the single largest contributor to GHGs at airports. Large hub airports, such as Chicago O'Hare, Hartsfield–Jackson Atlanta, and Los Angeles (LAX), consume more than 4 million gallons of Jet A per day on average. In addition, airports have many other fossil fuel ground transportation modes that produce GHGs, including ground service equipment, airport fleet maintenance vehicles, rental cars, shuttle buses, taxis, limousines, and passenger vehicles. The combination of these multi-modal transport users makes airports attractive "concentration demand centers" for alternative fuels.

The largest operating renewable fuels production facility in the USA is Imperium Renewables, with a nameplate capacity of 100 million gallons per year.[8] Renewable-fuels suppliers depend on large production capacities and equivalent markets to achieve economic success. This capacity is well within a major airport's multi-modal transport user demand, not to mention the cost savings attributed to fuel deliveries.

Federal law also supports this idea. Under the Energy Independence and Security Act (EISA) of 2007, the Renewable Fuel Standard (RFS) program increased the volume of renewable

---

BOX 11.6
Case study
bio-SPK performs as well as Jet A

Boeing and a team from across the aviation industry released a study in 2009 citing the superiority of bio-derived SPK.

- Bio-SPK fuel blends used in the test flight program met or exceeded all technical parameters for commercial jet aviation fuel. Those standards include freezing point, flash point, fuel density, and viscosity, among others.
- Bio-SPK fuel blends had no adverse effects on the engines or their components.
- Bio-SPK blends have greater energy content by mass than typical petroleum-derived jet fuel—which potentially could lower fuel consumption per mile.

The conversion formulas for Jet A[10] demonstrate the potential GHG savings:

- 1095 lbs CO_2 per gallon of Jet A
- 18,355 lbs CO_2 per gallon aviation gas
- total lbs of CO_2 × 0.0004536 metric tons/lbs = metric tons CO_2.

Source: "Boeing and industry study shows biofuels perform effectively as jet fuel," Boeing Media Room, http://boeing.mediaroom.com/index.php?s=43&item=714.

---

fuel required to be blended into transportation fuel from 9 billion gallons in 2008 to 36 billion gallons in 2022.[9] It is a matter of time before alternative fuels become commercially available and economically scalable for use in aircraft. (Box 11.6)

Airports can't forget ground transportation dependencies (airport stakeholder perspective)

- Minimize roadway congestion to reduce vehicle emissions and respective GHG.
- Design roads for increased life cycle to reduce auto accidents due to damaged roads, decrease maintenance costs, and minimize the airport carbon footprint.
- Provide public transportation access to reduce GHG from private vehicles and land development impacts from automobile use, minimize traffic congestion, reduce air and water pollution, and reduce parking space requirements.
- Reduce parking capacity by decreasing private vehicle usage, GHG, and consumption of natural resources.
- Support fuel-efficient vehicles and consider using biofuels or electric vehicles to reduce GHG and consumption of natural resources.
- Plan future land use in the event of an airport closure or sale. Evaluate potential future uses for the land, structure, and building components to increase the land value potential.

From landscaping to social responsibility, sustainable possibilities are endless

These additional topics may also be considered:

- managing stormwater
- making landscaping changes to reduce water requirements, add native vegetation, etc.
- reducing heat islands by replacing dark materials with light-reflecting materials
- increasing water efficiency and conservation
- improving energy efficiency and conservation through mechanical systems
- inventorying emissions and developing mitigation strategies
- improving social responsibility factors such as job creation, public health, community engagement, education, etc. (Box 11.7)

> **BOX 11.7**
> **Case study**
> **Paris Airport taps geothermal power**
>
> The Paris Orly Airport, located above the Dogger aquifer that contains warm groundwater, was planning, in 2010, to tap into its natural supply for heated water in its terminal buildings. It's expected to save about 40 gigawatt hours of gas and avoid up to 9000 metric tons of CO_2 emissions annually.
>
> Source: "Aéroports de Paris taps into geothermal power," *Green Flight Times* 1 (January–May 2010): 3.

Environmental metrics traditionally based on FAA concerns

Commercial service airport environmental metrics are based traditionally on compliance with the FAA's prevalent environmental concerns, which include:

- 1990 Clean Air Act Amendments 42 USC 7401–7671 for both mobile and stationary sources
- National Environmental Policy Act
- National Pollutant Discharge Elimination System Permit
- hazardous substances and air pollutants, including the 1990 Oil Pollution Act and Clean Water Act, along with others
- underground and aboveground storage tanks, including the Resource Conservation and Recovery Act and 40 CFR for Underground Storage Tanks
- wetlands, including the Clean Water Act.

New legislation by Congress is expected to drive many additional environmental metrics. They are likely to include mandated GHG inventory and reporting. As a result, GHG reduction planning will be critical to airport planning strategy.

In addition, airports need to be aware of their current and forecasted carbon footprints, compared with a base year. In the state of California, the base year is 1990 in support of the Kyoto Protocol on Global Warming. The much-debated US Climate Bill, which included 2005 as the base year, did not reach the President's desk. It passed the US House but failed to pass the US Senate. The US Supreme Court ruled carbon dioxide as a pollutant to be regulated by the EPA on April 2, 2007. Using a quantitative approach to understanding where each airport stands with respect to its current, future, and baseline CO_2 levels will only strengthen each airport's business strategy going forward.

Some of the key environmental performance indicators for airports are:

- total CO_2 output per passenger for the construction (including supply chain)
- total energy consumption during construction (including supply chain)
- total water consumption during construction
- total CO_2 output per passenger (including the energy mix for all electrical consumption)
- consumption of electrical energy per passenger
- water consumption per passenger
- consumption of heat or air condition energy per passenger (in context with outside temperatures)
- tons of de-icing agents per passenger (in context with aircraft size and outside temperatures)
- percentage of recycling of de-icing agents
- kg of un-recycled waste per passenger
- percentage of renewable energy
- percentage of green roofs where possible
- percentage of passengers and employees using public transportation.

As a general rule, the boundaries of a GHG emissions inventory define the sources, their operational characteristics, and ultimately the outcome of the assessment. There has been little precedence for establishing this parameter for airport-related studies. Figure 11.3 shows three boundaries of the GHG emissions inventory:

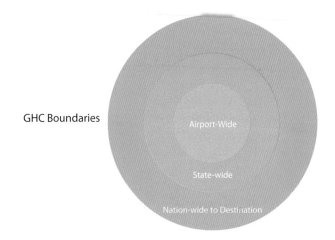

GHC Boundaries

11.3 Boundaries of SBA GHG emissions inventory
Note: Santa Barbara Municipal Airport planners considered the operation's GHG emissions from the local, state, and national perspectives

- Airport-wide—this category includes operations and facilities that are associated with airport-owned or leased property and comprise emissions attributable to aircraft, GSE, and on-site motor vehicles. For aircraft, this encompasses the entire landing and takeoff cycle (i.e., up to an altitude of 3000 feet or three to five miles from the runway ends), even though some of these emissions occur outside the airport boundaries. Also included in this category are emissions associated with electrical use by the airport and its tenants.
- State-wide—this includes the category of "airport-wide" emissions, and for aircraft it also includes cruise emissions within the state regarding the USA. For off-site, airport-related motor vehicle trips, this also includes those out to a distance of eight miles from the airport (or a round-trip distance of 16 miles).
- Nationwide—this includes the categories of airport- and state-wide emissions and also includes aircraft cruise emissions to the destination airports that are located outside the state's border.

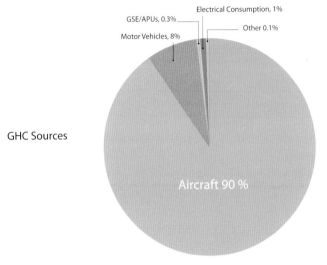

GHC Sources

Aircraft 90 %

GSE/APUs, 0.3%

Electrical Consumption, 1%

Other 0.1%

Motor Vehicles, 8%

11.4 SBA GHG emissions inventory by source category (as CO_2e)
Note: SBA nationwide inventories show the majority of GHG
emissions are from aircraft, followed by motor vehicles in a distant
second place

11.5 DIA solar PV array
Note: DIA leased property to a third party to install solar PV as a
hedge against increasing electric rates. The array also is a highly
visible sign of the airport's effort to "go green"

Figure 11.4 shows the percentage of GHG emissions at Santa Barbara Airport (SBA) by source category. Aircraft represent 90 percent of the overall total, followed by motor vehicles at 8 percent, electrical consumption at 1 percent, GSE/auxiliary power unit at less than 1 percent, and other miscellaneous sources at less than 1 percent.

Another new standard is the state Renewables Portfolio Standard (RPS). This regulation requires the increased production of energy from renewable energy sources, such as wind, solar, biomass, and geothermal. States differ in the percentage of renewable energy required in a given year. Some states do not yet have an RPS. The US House Climate Bill includes a national RPS equal to 15 percent minimum. Airports can partner with utility companies to help meet the RPS requirement in their state by contracting with private parties to finance, install, operate, and maintain renewable energy generation systems on airport property.

Utility bills are often one of the highest operating costs for an airport, after labor and vendor contracts. Energy conservation, self-generation, and renewable energy alternatives can help reduce

these costs. And, airports can lower their capital investment in new utility projects through federal grants, utility rebates, incentive programs, and private-party renewable energy projects.

Denver International Airport (DIA) has installed two solar photovoltaic (PV) arrays. The first, shown in Figure 11.5, is a 2-megawatt (MW) ground-constructed system on 7.5 acres. The second system is a $7 million, 1.6-MW solar PV array that is expected to provide 100 percent of the electricity needed by the airport's fuel farm (a "net-zero" system). Both projects were financed and installed by a third party that will maintain them for 20 years. DIA benefits by reducing current energy costs, getting a "hedge" on rising electric rates, and increasing investment income. Xcel Energy benefits by purchasing the renewable energy credits and moving closer to Colorado's renewable portfolio standard requirement. (The Colorado State Senate has passed H.B.1001, increasing the state's RPS to 30 percent by 2020.) The third party profits on the deal by obtaining a 30 percent federal grant, depreciating the asset and selling the renewable energy credits to Xcel Energy.

BOX 11.8
Key sustainability practices for energy

1. Mandate aggressive end-use efficiency: improve efficiency of energy services to reduce energy demand. Smart meters and utility rate schedules give consumers price choices regarding their use of energy.
2. Diversify domestically: shift to domestic energy resources. Use renewable and conventional carbon-free supplies. Standardize and certify sustainable products.
3. Modernize energy networks: modernize distribution systems. Install high-voltage grids that supply remote solar and wind power to cities. Encourage smart, local micro-grids with demand-side management control and locally distributed generation and electrical storage. Focus on installing power production systems at the demand sites.

Source: Stephen Connors, "Energy transitions and transformations," *MIT Faculty Newsletter* 21(5) (summer 2009).

Airports can benefit from sustainable-energy practices. For example, many airports charge tenants on a square-footage basis. As soon as utility meters are installed on a tenant's leased space, the tenant will begin to conserve energy and reduce its bills. Smart meters, combined with utility rate structures, will only enhance energy savings. Consider self-generation systems to produce power on site and consume the power at the airport to reduce the carbon footprint and possibly save on electricity costs. (Box 11.8)

PRACTICAL BARRIERS TO TECHNOLOGY AND ECONOMIC POTENTIAL PERSIST

Our ability to make some of the suggested sustainability improvements to airport infrastructure and operations overall is limited by the economic and practical issues presented by many of the renewable energy sources and public policies currently in play. While we are making improvements every day, some of these issues won't be solved until we learn how to bring certain technologies to scale or we put taxation systems in place to force improvements that would not otherwise be economically viable.

One example is the sustainability of biofuel. Biofuels are made from first-generation feedstocks, which are food based. As the demand for biofuels increases, the price of some food products such as corn and soybeans rises, in turn raising prices for consumers. In addition, sustainable biofuels are hard to certify, and few standards exist. The Roundtable on Sustainable Palm Oil is one standard, but many other crops used in making biofuels have no sustainable guidelines. Some of the cheapest feedstocks come from Malaysia, where indigenous tribes were forced off their land and rainforests were destroyed to plant palm trees. The USA formerly offered a Federal Blenders Credit equal to $1 per gallon of biodiesel to encourage US consumption. US refiners sold their biofuel to Europe, however, where they could get a better price than in the USA, even though the incentive was coming from US taxpayers.

Another issue under hot debate is some countries' lack of restrictions on the number of aircraft accommodated at each airport. In the USA, for example, laws require public facilities to be equally available to everyone. This results in most US airports being required to accept all requested landings—scheduled or not—which can lead to landing delays and increased emissions. In the European Union, conversely, airlines bid for limited airport slots, which results in a more orderly flow of traffic and fewer landing delays. To be successful in achieving sustainability goals worldwide, we will need full global participation and consensus on the targets, approach, and validation of reducing GHGs. (Box 11.9)

Our ability to create and maintain affordable, sustainable alternative energy and water systems overall is a challenge, as well. Along with this challenge come the associated increasing

BOX 11.9
Case study
Hawaii sets goal to meet 70 percent of energy demand at home

Hawaii's governor signed a Memorandum of Understanding with the US Department of Energy (DOE) in 2008 for the Hawaii–DOE Clean Energy Initiative. The goal is to decrease energy demand and accelerate use of renewable, indigenous energy resources in Hawaii for residential, building, industrial, utility, and transportation end-use sectors, so that efficiency and renewable energy resources will be sufficient to meet 70 percent of Hawaii's energy demand by 2030.

The DOE defines biofuels as a renewable energy source. The Hawaiian Clean Energy Initiative RPS states that no more than 30 percent of the Hawaiian electric utilities' total RPS may come from imported biofuels consumed in utility-owned units. This worthy goal was meant to encourage local jobs in farming biofuel crops and refining biofuel feedstocks on the islands. Growing first-generation biofuel crops is cost prohibitive in Hawaii, however, just as sugar cane was. Other countries, such as Brazil, can grow the crops much cheaper. In addition, to make an economical biofuel refining facility in Hawaii, sales must reach 100 million gallons per year. Imperium Renewables built such a plant in Grays Harbor, Washington, and the plant continues to operate today through one of America's worst economic downturns.

Source: "Hawaii and DOE sign agreement to promote Hawaiian clean energy," EERE Network News, January 28, 2008, http://apps1.eere.energy.gov/news/news_detail.cfm/news_id=11547.

BOX 11.10
Case study
UK airport installs willow farm

The East Midlands Airport in the UK has launched a willow farm to produce fuel for a biomass boiler. It's expected to produce about 280 metric tons of wood fuel annually, saving 350 metric tons of CO_2. The airport also has committed to making its ground operations carbon neutral by 2012. In addition, it has received permission to plan four on-site wind turbines.

Source: "UK's first airport willow farm," *Green Flight Times Edition* 1 (January–May 2010): 3.

NASCENT LEGISLATIVE, TECHNICAL DEVELOPMENTS TO CATALYZE EFFORT

Several nascent legislative and technical developments will catalyze the airport sustainability effort.

Legislative

- The 2007 Energy Independence and Security Act calls for an increase in the use of biofuels from 11 billion gallons per year to 36 billion gallons by 2022. Biofuels can be blended with or replace diesel fuels in airport GSE, service vehicles, shuttle buses, and rental-car fleet vehicles. In addition, biofuel blends with jet fuel in aircraft are proven to work well.
- The proposed Boxer–Kerry Energy/Climate Bill caps GHG emissions below 2005 levels by 3 percent in 2012, 17 percent in 2020, and 80 percent by 2050. The bill sets new energy efficiency standards for buildings to reduce energy by 50 percent

need for jobs creation in the USA and Europe, and increasing global energy demands, not to mention the regulatory changes required to implement new energy and air transportation technologies. (Box 11.10) by 2016. This bill will make renewable energy projects more attractive to install on airport property.

- State and city clean-energy initiatives and utility incentive programs are proliferating for both economic and sustainability reasons.

Technical

The next generation of air traffic management technology has the potential to dramatically affect the efficiency of modern air travel.

"NextGen," as it's called by US industry insiders, essentially moves air traffic management from the land to the skies. Instead of relying on ground-based radar and audio broadcasting systems, the new technology uses satellite-based global positioning, data networking, and digital communications. It has the potential to affect several environmental factors. More efficient flight paths mean planes will be in the air for shorter periods, reducing fuel use, emissions, and noise. More efficient communication will provide for advance planning and decision making, which will lead to more efficient use of airspace and reduced delays. NextGen also has great promise for increasing airport capacity and decreasing land use. For example, existing regulations require a 4300-foot parallel separation between runways for independent bad-weather operations. With global positioning and digital communications providing more precise airplane location data, the requirement could be as little as 2000 feet.

Finally, NextGen technology can potentially make ground delay programs (GDPs) more efficient. Ground delays can reduce GHG emissions by grounding aircraft rather than having them hold in the air when weather conditions or other factors indicate the flight will not be able to land at its destination. Ground delays can significantly affect overall air traffic, however, delaying the primary flight and adding to ground congestion and affecting flight arrivals and departures in the originating location. In addition, the current air traffic management technology is not able to respond quickly to weather changes, so delays often go on much longer than necessary. NextGen technology includes "System-wide Integration Management" (SWIM) that will provide better real-time data sharing

among aircraft, airports, and air traffic controllers, which should make GDPs more efficient. The FAA has identified SWIM as an area of emphasis for implementation by 2018.

These advancements in airplane, airport, and air traffic systems will significantly reduce the environmental impact of airports, improve safety, and make air travel more convenient for everyone. Some airlines, flight-based businesses, and airports are implementing selective portions of the technology already. Full phase-one US implementation of the core set of avionics necessary to support these operational capabilities is scheduled for 2020.

CONCLUSION:
AIRPORT INFRASTRUCTURE CAN CONTRIBUTE TO PRESERVATION, CLOSED-LOOP CYCLE OF THE NATURAL WORLD

Ultimately, with airport infrastructure and all built environments, we must seek to preserve the natural world through use of materials that can be "up cycled" versus recycled—to retain their high quality in a closed-loop industrial cycle versus downgrading them into a mixture of materials.

We believe that airports can become sustainable—economically, socially, and environmentally. To make sustainability a priority for decision makers, we must treat sustainability as a competitive advantage and driver for innovation.

Each perceived barrier to sustainability has an incentive counterpart. For example, economic barriers can be overcome through federal grants, third-party financing, and utility rebates. Regulatory barriers can be countered with renewable energy opportunities and an improved understanding of the airport's carbon footprint. Educational and organizational barriers need to be addressed with training and mindset changes.

The most sustainable choice is not always intuitive and can shift with evolving technology or new information. Maintaining sustainable practices will require strong leadership, cultural change, and training. But the payoff—preservation of the natural world—will well be worth the effort.

NOTES

1   Additional contributors to this chapter: Gregory H. Albjerg, PE, Susan
    Warner-Dooley, AAE, IAP, Michael D. Feldman, CM (AAAE), Ronald C.
    Siecke, PE, Paul A. Yarossi, PE, Brian R. Cox, and Julie Bartels Smith.
2   D. McCollum, Gould G., and Greene D., "GHG emissions from aviation
    and marine transportation: mitigation potential and policies," Pew
    Center on Global Climate Change, www.pewclimate.org/technology/
    report/aviation-and-marine.
3   Federal Aviation Administration, "FAA aerospace forecast fiscal
    years 2010–030," www.faa.gov/data_research/aviation/aerospace_
    forecasts/2010-2030/media/2010%20Forecast%20Doc.pdf.
4   US Environmental Protection Agency, "2010 US greenhouse
    gas inventory report," http://epa.gov/climatechange/emissions/
    usinventoryreport.html.
5   International Transport Forum, "Greenhouse gas reduction strategies
    in the transport sector," www.internationaltransportforum.org/Pub/
    pdf/08GHG.pdf.
6   McCollum, Gould, and Greene, "GHG emissions from aviation and
    marine transportation."
7   T. Peovic, "Europe's airports key engines to restore economic growth,"
    Airport Business, December 2009.
8   Marketwire, "Imperium Renewables resumes production of biodiesel,"
    www.marketwire.com/press-release/Imperium-Renewables-Resumes-
    Production-of-Biodiesel-1129521.htm.
9   US Environmental Protection Agency, "Renewable fuel standard,"
    www.epa.gov/otaq/fuels/renewablefuels/.
10 "Guidebook on preparing airport greenhouse gas emissions
    inventories," Airport Cooperative Research Program, Report 11,
    Transportation Resource Board, 2009.

Sustainability in Ports, Freight, and Logistics

ERIN HYLAND AND JOE BRYAN

HALCROW

PORTS AND LOGISTICS

Ports and logistics centers are nodes within the global supply chain. Overall, this network is a complex web balancing consumer supply and demand. The entire network is built from decisions made and influenced by a variety of actors, both local and international. These decisions influence the structural and physical form as well as the operations, including routing and mode choice. The sustainability of the supply chain as a whole, and the nodes individually, reflect the various choices made throughout the life cycle of infrastructure development. As with any project or system in which multiple actors have inputs, the definition and extent of sustainable choices is contingent upon tradeoffs and stakeholder perspectives.

Port authorities, shipping companies, terminal operators, railway operators, haulers, and transport agencies have had growing interest in increasing sustainability throughout their supply chains. Many are implementing sustainable or "green" strategies. This is in response to cost-control efforts and to increased customer demand for sustainability, as well as to regulations and citizens interested in limiting adverse environmental impacts.

Sustainability in ports and logistics requires consideration of climate change, both mitigation (carbon reduction strategies) and adaptation (resiliency and risk management), resource and energy efficiency, and impacts or benefits to the environment and community. Comprehensive strategies in turn necessitate analysis and integration of supply chain networks, transportation systems (air, rail, highway, port), land use and development policies, and operations and procurement choices. Complex tradeoffs and operating decisions influence the supply chain network. What follows is an overview of basic infrastructure components, the types of decision makers and choices being made, and the way in which these components are interrelated and may influence the sustainability of the node and the network.

12.1 Container terminal—stacked yard, cranes along berth
Source: Halcrow

DEFINING PORTS AND LOGISTICS FACILITY INFRASTRUCTURE ASSETS

A maritime port is a terminal node within the supply chain network, where goods move into or out of one land-based network in order to move to another. By definition, a port is the intersection of a number of systems. Most commonly a maritime port refers to a seaport engaged in foreign and domestic trade. However, the term also includes facilities along rivers, canals, and lakes. Ports may specialize in certain types of cargo, such as containers, petroleum, bulk, and breakbulk products, or automobiles, and they may also be military facilities. Because waterborne vessels normally carry much larger quantities of goods than freight vehicles moving on land, ports also perform a cargo consolidation and deconsolidation function.

The physical infrastructure at a port can be classified as "on-dock" or "off-dock," which describes the relationship to the waterfront. Depending upon the cargo handled and the specific operation, there will be differences in equipment type and other structures, for example pipeline connections and storage tanks would be specific to a liquid fuel terminal. On-dock generally refers to the boundaries within a terminal gate, and off-dock refers to the port facilities outside of the terminal gate. The pieces work in concert to move imported goods from an ocean-going vessel, through a terminal, and onto the land-based transportation network via rail or truck in order to reach a final consumer. For export goods, the process is reversed.

The on-dock components of a terminal include physical structures as well as cargo-handling equipment.

- *Docks and wharfs*—a bulkhead and retaining wall creates a hard edge along which ships dock at berths. Cranes operate along the wharf to move goods to and from the ships. Most cranes are electric, and powered by the grid. Docked ships run auxiliary engines to power their operations while in-port. This results in berthing, or hoteling, emissions.
- *Yard*—a paved storage area where cargo is stored either before being loaded onto a ship or before being picked up and sent inland. Various types of cargo handling equipment operate within the yard. For container terminals, the general classification is between wheeled or grounded. Some facilities operate a combination of the two. In wheeled operations, yard tractors move containers, which are stored on chassis, parked side-by-side for retrieval by drivers. In terms of density, or containers per acre, wheeled operations are less efficient. In a grounded operation, containers are stacked in the yard. Stacking height and yard density are dictated by operating type. A grounded operation might use straddle carriers, Rail Mounted Gantry (RMG), or a Rubber-Tired Gantry system. The operating equipment is typically diesel powered, but can be electric.
- *Gate*—a processing center through which all goods are tracked when arriving at, or departing from, a terminal. Trucks stop to have the cargo they are carrying logged and tracked. Depending upon the volume of containers and the efficiency of the gate to process the trucks, queues may form with, in worst cases, trucks idling for hours.
- *On-dock rail*—some terminals have rail lines within the gate where goods are loaded directly onto intermodal rail connections and moved inland.
- *Buildings*—there is often a variety of physical structures on-dock. These may be management buildings, customs buildings, or warehouse structures within a terminal.

The off-dock components of a terminal are located outside the gate, and often include ancillary activities associated with goods movement. These may be located in close proximity to the terminal, but many of these facilities are also sited inland as core parts of the larger logistics network. Such off-dock or logistics facilities may include:

- *Distribution center (DC)*—a large, specialized facility where goods are held and assembled into deliveries to retailers, wholesalers, or directly to consumers. DCs perform staging, consolidation, and unitizing functions, can be involved in final-stage manufacturing (such as packaging and labeling of goods), and may double as an operating terminal for an associated truck fleet.
- *Warehouse*—a structure that stores goods or merchandise. Some warehouses have multiple users, some of whom may

carry out more processing activities, but, typically, warehouses are inventory holding points.

- *Cross-dock*—a staging facility where inbound items are not received into stock, but are prepared for shipment to another location or for retail stores. Cross-docking facilities are used to reconfigure and consolidate goods for further distribution.
- *Drop yard*—a site used by carriers for equipment storage and load staging, but with no transfer of goods. A drop yard can be as simple as a fenced parking lot with perhaps an office trailer, and are often handoff points between local and intercity drivers.
- *Rail and highway*—additional infrastructure within the logistics network includes intermodal yards, rail lines, and roadways, over which goods are moved.

PORT AND LOGISTIC OWNERS, AND BOUNDARIES OF INFLUENCE

There is a variety of stakeholders and decision makers involved with port and logistic facility development and operations. The myriad of potential owners adds to the complexity and challenge of pursuing green strategies at a facility, and reinforces the need for collaboration. A summary of the boundaries of influence typical to stakeholders within a port is outlined below.

- *Port authority*—there are two primary port models, especially in the USA. In some cases, the port authority owns the land and also manages and operates the terminal facility. In such cases, the port authority has control over the development of the facility from the design phase through to operations. The port authority can choose equipment types and set hours of operation, subject to labor agreements. The other operating model is the landlord port. The port authority owns the land, but the facility is developed and operated under a long-term agreement with an independent terminal operator. Operators may have specific operating requirements in the lease terms. The port authority may look for opportunities to work with its tenants on developing common projects of interest. Port authorities often have regulatory or policy-making influence, and commonly are arms of government. They are often working to balance competing objectives, including sustainability, regional economic development, and financial returns.
- *Leased terminal operators*—in landlord ports, these operators control terminal development and operations subject to the terms of their agreement. The terminal operators negotiate with shipping lines for cargo contracts, and plan and operate the facilities.
- *Private terminal operator*—there are some port facilities that are entirely privately held. Private terminal operators have the same responsibilities as do leased terminal operators, but are not subject to lease terms and agreements with the port authority. Petroleum facilities are a prominent example of this type.
- *Shipping/cruise lines*—operate the vessels carrying cargo between ports. Shipping lines determine vessel routing, in terms of the ports at which to call, as well as the types of vessels to operate. This includes fuel type, sailing speed, and all matters of travel. In non-bulk and breakbulk services, shipping lines also own or control the marine container that bears the cargo, and sometimes the truck chassis that carries the container to and from port. The size and type of containers, and the rules and charges that lines set for use of their equipment, have a substantial influence on land miles traveled to, from, and around the port, and on real estate required for equipment storage.
- *Labor unions*—dockworkers, or longshoremen, in North America are unionized. The labor unions negotiate terms that affect gang size, technology deployment, hours of operations, and other aspects of terminal operations. As a result, for a terminal operator or port authority to pursue changes in operations, including where improved sustainability is sought, labor unions will typically need to participate in discussions.
- *Truckers/carriers*—the drivers bringing and retrieving cargo may be individual owner-operated entities, or employees of a larger carrier company. The trucker or carrier makes vehicle decisions such as fleet replacement, fuel choice, and other technology enhancements that may make the vehicle more fuel efficient. They also design operating routes and service patterns that affect the way the vehicle uses fuel, and the miles it travels in the accomplishment of work.

- *Warehouse and distribution centers or other tenants*—the owners or operators of facilities may be involved in the development of the buildings, the siting choice, and ultimately long-term operations that affect energy and water consumption.
- *Rail operators*—rail operators decide which ports to serve, and invest in infrastructure,[1] locomotives, and rolling stock. This includes fleet decisions, such as the incorporation of cleaner engines.
- *Transportation agencies*—units of government that typically lead investment in the roadway network connecting to port and logistics facilities. They may influence congestion through management programs, or infrastructure expansion. Transportation agencies may designate truck routes in or around communities.
- *Environmental agencies*—oversee permitting and regulatory compliance in the design and development stages of a project, and may be involved with monitoring during the operations stages.
- *Municipal planning/economic development*—local agencies may regulate or limit land use in certain areas, or provide economic incentives for activities that generate jobs and regional growth, including port expansion.
- *Military*—national military services may own and operate a port (and in this sense function as a form of port authority). In the USA, the engineering corps of the army also is charged with the maintenance of coastal and inland waterways. The depth maintained in waterways influences the size and type of vessel that can serve a port, and the act of dredging to preserve or increase depth presents environmental risks and disposal requirements.

Addressing severe congestion at a port facility is an example of a challenge that might require collaboration between multiple stakeholders in order to enact a policy change. As a result of port congestion, long truck queues form at the port's gate while trucks await processing. Emissions from idling add to air pollution and the noise and traffic decreases quality of life for the surrounding community. The local highway network is already congested, and the port's growing cargo volume is worsening traffic as a result of increased truck trips, especially during rush hour. A landlord port authority is considering options to alleviate the problem, and would like the terminals to extend gate hours and operate on weekends when there is less commuter traffic. Such a plan would avoid otherwise necessary construction of an additional lane and exit ramp on the nearby highway, but there would be other costs.

In order to advance this plan, the port authority needs to engage with the terminal operator and the labor unions. Were gate hours extended, there might be additional costs, as labor contracts have clear overtime shifts. Increased labor costs could reduce an operator's profitability, or they might be passed onto the shippers through increased cargo handling fees. An increase in shipper fees might negatively affect the volume of cargo coming to the port if shippers determined an alternative route was more cost-effective. A decrease in volume could adversely impact job levels if too great. In addition, the port authority would consult warehouse and distribution center operators. Changes to port facility operating hours would likely be more effective if the warehouse and distribution centers adjusted their hours to correspond. Truck drivers need a place to take and secure shipping containers if they pick them up from the port during off-peak hours, as they do not want to hold the cargo for additional periods of time. As a result, the port authority's attempts at alleviating congestion are more likely to be successful through partnership and cooperation from the other actors.

WHAT IS SUSTAINABILITY IN PORTS AND LOGISTICS?

At a broad level, the way a port or logistics facility is developed or operates has both social and environmental impacts, as well as cost or financial considerations. Port and logistic centers are drivers of regional economic growth and employment, and many decisions come down to tradeoffs between labor, energy, and financial resources. Ports themselves are a complex of specific, interconnected facilities on designated land, and both the land and facilities may be added to, redeployed, or subtracted over the course of time. A facility's efficiency can be measured and impacted by the construction approach, materials used, and technology options employed throughout project development and operations. The types of impacts, and mitigating solutions, vary over the course of the asset life cycle, but there are numerous factors that may be considered and approaches employed.

During the *design phase*, land use tradeoffs may be considered for siting the facility. Brownfield sites may be redeveloped, or locations with access to rail and multi-modal transportation networks may be selected to facilitate more efficient inland goods distribution. Other factors considered and mitigated or minimized in designing sustainable solutions are stormwater management, impacts to the marine environment and native species, vulnerability to flooding and sea level rise, and emissions from vessels, cargo handling, and distribution. Designs try to use recycled content where possible, to use more durable materials, and to minimize the adverse impacts of dredging or fill around wetlands. On-site power generation may be incorporated.

During *construction*, efforts may be made to reduce energy consumption of construction equipment or to reduce emissions, noise, and congestion by delivering materials by water. Dredging impacts may be mitigated through use of technology to lessen turbidity and adverse water quality impacts, or through reuse as fill, where possible, to lessen handling and disposal requirements. Worker safety is an important consideration throughout all project phases.

At the *operations* stage, there are numerous factors that can be measured and sustainable strategies that may be employed. Many of the sustainable solutions for freight systems fall into four categories: technology-based solutions including alternative fuels and newer vehicles and equipment, infrastructure-based solutions which focus on improvements to physical networks and efficiency, flow-based solutions such as traffic management and improvements to the efficiency of operating networks, and demand-based solutions such as pricing incentives and modal substitution.[2] Ports are employing combinations of these solutions to improve their sustainability.

An operational port's land use efficiency can be measured in terms of cargo throughout per acre. Yard densification can be increased through adoption of higher-stacking equipment. In some cases, an existing facility may be re-developed to increase capacity within the existing footprint, thereby avoiding additional construction and resource consumption.

A variety of strategies may be adopted to reduce operating emissions. Newer crane technology is increasingly efficient. These cranes are completely electric, and, in the most advanced ports, load containers directly onto electric trolleys where they are moved to the yard and into the stacks, and ultimately to trucks or rail. Where all of the handling equipment is electric, the on-dock emissions can approach zero. A tradeoff, however, may be in jobs, as an automated facility requires fewer longshoremen to operate.

Other facilities have employed equipment running on alternative fuels. The Ports of Long Beach and Los Angeles demonstrated the first application of LNG cargo-handling equipment, which decreased criteria air pollutants. Another technology implemented was a flywheel energy storage system on yard handling equipment, which decreased emissions and had significant fuel savings.[3]

Incentivizing shipping lines to slow steam into port, thereby lessening fuel consumption, is another strategy employed by ports. The Port of Long Beach instituted a Green Flag Vessel Speed Reduction Incentive Program that required vessels to abide by a 12-knot speed limit within 20 miles of the facility. Participating lines received discounted dockage rates, and, by 2006, the port reported 90 percent compliance.[4]

An operating terminal may also pursue strategies to lessen vehicle idling and the associated air quality impacts. Ships need to run power while being worked by cranes, and truck drivers may need to wait to pick up or deliver their cargo. A number of ports, especially on the US West Coast, have introduced alternative maritime power (AMP) or cold ironing. Electricity is supplied from shore to run lights, heating, air conditioning, and hot water requirements for the vessel, and the diesel engines can be shut off. The shipping lines incur costs to retrofit a vessel to be connected to shore power. At the same time, cold ironing increases demand on the local grid. As a result, terminal operators need to consider the costs associated with installing sufficient electrical capacity and shoreside connections to accommodate vessels. The origination of power supply is another factor in thinking holistically about a facility's sustainability and overall environmental footprint. While cold ironing may reduce emissions in the immediate vicinity, in some cases it may move the impact upstream to a power plant.

12.2 RTG stacks
Source: Halcrow

Similar efforts are being employed to decrease truck idling emissions as well. Electric plug-in pedestals or emissions capture systems offer truck drivers a cost-effective alternative to power their vehicles. Technology systems, such as IdleAire and Shorepower, two examples of external power systems, increasingly are being installed at truck stops and distribution centers throughout the USA. Ports including Los Angeles, Long Beach, Seattle, Tacoma, Oakland, and New York and New Jersey have adopted Clean Trucks programs aimed at replacing the older, and most polluting, portion of the truck fleets serving their facilities.[5]

At the *decommissioning* stage, ports may be redeveloped. Given their industrial history, many facilities have toxic materials or contamination that require proper disposal. Other materials may be recycled. Existing structures may be adaptively reused for light industrial or other activities.

DRIVERS FOR SUSTAINABILITY

There are a number of drivers underlying efforts to incorporate sustainability into port and logistics facilities. For many ports, sustainability initiatives form part of a response to challenges to growth and constrained capacity. With limited land available for development and limited capital to invest, operators are choosing strategies that increase efficiency while lowering operating costs. In addition, efforts to mitigate pollution, congestion, and other adverse environmental impacts help to lessen community opposition to port development.

There are stringent regulatory requirements for waterfront development that guide much of the design phase. More recently, there have been regulatory requirements addressing carbon emissions. California's landmark Energy Act AB 32, passed in 2006, features a roadmap for meeting a target of reducing emissions to 1990 levels by 2020. In 2010, the Environmental Protection Agency announced new rules for heavy vehicle fuel efficiency that would require a 20 percent reduction in carbon dioxide emissions by 2018 for over-the-road tractor-trailers.[6]

Stakeholder perception and brand also encourages sustainable practices. An increasing number of companies are issuing corporate social responsibility or sustainability reports, and are monitoring their overall impacts. Many large-scale shippers and manufacturers are influencing behavior throughout the supply chain, by requiring their carriers and vendors to adopt and demonstrate sustainable practices. These practices, especially focused on fuel usage in the operational stage, generate cost reductions and efficiency improvements that are often the primary motivators for adoption. Densification of cargo and off-peak operations are further examples of sustainability initiatives attractive to ports and industry, the former because it allows more product to be delivered by the same volume of carriage, the latter because it allows freight vehicles to run in uncongested conditions. Both breed productivity gains in transport and energy use. For-profit companies need a business case to drive their sustainability programs, yet that case can be made from the advances in asset utilization, cost, and brand position that efforts like these can yield.

Finally, public and private interest coincides around the point of fuel and carbon efficiency. The freight industry has always cared about its fuel efficiency because it is a primary and growing component of cost, but that has meant little to the residents of neighborhoods and the passengers on roads who would rather send freight out of its way so as to not mingle with it. However, residents increasingly take a different view of greenhouse gas emissions, and could wish to see freight miles reduced in order to bring emissions down. As industry begins to translate fuel utilization into carbon efficiency, it becomes able to make common cause with the citizenry.

CONCLUSION

Ports are complex nodes in the transportation network. They are comprised of multiple pieces under the jurisdiction of many parties. There are any number of strategies that may be employed to increase the sustainability of a port throughout all stages of project development. These include reusing or delivering material in less impactful ways, minimizing their physical footprints, decreasing overall energy consumption and resulting emissions, and ensuring resiliency in the face of climate change and sea level rise. However, the complex infrastructure network and the number of parties involved requires collaboration and partnership for successful implementation.

NOTES

1   Rail companies control both operations and physical network in much of the world, but in "open access" environments such as Europe the two functions are performed by different entities.
2   T.R. Leinbach, Capineri C., "The global economy and freight transport flows." In: T.R. Leinbach, Cristina Capineri, eds, *Globalized Freight Transport: Intermodality, E-commerce, Logistics, and Sustainability* (Cheltenham, UK: Edward Elgar Publishing Ltd, 2007).
3   H. Tomley, Maggay K., "Green initiatives in port operations" presentation to AAPA 2009 Safety Ops IT Seminar, http://aapa.files.cms-plus.com/SeminarPresentations/2009Seminars/09OpsSafetyIT/Maggay_Tomley.pdf.
4   D. Sereno, "Sustainability and environmental stewardship" presentation to AAPA Port Sustainability Task Force, January 10, 2007, http://aapa.files.cms-plus.com/PDFs/Sereno_Sustainability.pdf.
5   A. Chiarello, Tracy D., "Improving air quality for communities" presentation at 2010 Harbors Navigation and Environment Seminar/GreenPort Americas, http://aapa.files.cms-plus.com/SeminarPresentations/2010Seminars/10HNEGreenports/Chiarello_Tracy.pdf.
6   J.M. Broder, "New US standards take aim at truck emissions and fuel economy," *New York Times*, October 26, 2010.

Ecological Infrastructure

CHRISTOPHER BENOSKY AND SHAUN O'ROURKE
AECOM

ECOLOGICAL INFRASTRUCTURE

Infrastructure allows water, power, food, and transportation to be available to society. We have become accustomed to these services and traditionally view these technical, built systems as our true infrastructure. This traditional 'gray' infrastructure of power lines, roads, sewers, levees, and ports provide essential services yet they are often planned and designed in opposition to, or in isolation from, existing natural systems.

Each type of infrastructure has a distinct series of boundaries that need to be drawn to understand its influence on society and the environment. It's how these boundaries are drawn on the landscape that has the greatest effect on the overall measurement of infrastructure performance.

The landscape is uniquely positioned to act as the mitigating force in defining the performance of traditional infrastructural systems. It is not only the landscape functioning as a plane that all technical and built systems sit on, in, or suspend over but also a volume that has tremendous influence. The landscape and natural systems have the ability to enhance the performance of traditional infrastructure if they are harnessed and integrated with foresight and purpose.

Society has become accustomed to, and proud of, the ability to alter landscapes to allow precise measurement and overall control. This is at direct odds to the charge provided to designers who are encouraged to screen or hide infrastructure in favor of an untouched "natural" landscape.

NEW PARADIGM

According to the US Census Bureau (2008), the global population exceeded 6 billion in 2000, and is expected to reach 9 billion by 2050. Increased population places greater pressure on available land and often results in a conversion of undisturbed lands into uses that are purely anthropogenic. Although there is great pressure, an alternative to this conversion of important ecosystems is needed.[1] New constraints and drivers for design and planning such as population rise and the potential effects of climate change are altering traditional patterns and approaches. Complex models and processes for helping to understand the potential effect of these challenges continue to be developed, yet the solutions need to be simple and immediate.

This is a watershed moment where we have the ability to model and understand the effects of our design decisions on terrestrial habitats, air and water quality, and socio-economic conditions. The effectiveness of these models is only as great as the design and planning outcome that manifest and evolve at the site. A true paradigm shift in looking to natural systems as the driver for infrastructure development is a significant social hurdle, yet necessary in the application of a holistic approach to infrastructure. Just as landscapes are continually evolving in response to environmental conditions, infrastructure systems need to be resilient and adaptive as well. A focus on a multifunctional, high performance landscape could be a driver for offering specific design guidelines based on the goal of achieving ecological, cultural, and production functions within a given space.[2]

Natural systems have been providing infrastructure for our planet well before we became reliant on the heavily engineered systems of today. From the dawn of time, the earth has drawn and utilized energy from the sun, natural processes have absorbed and cleansed stormwater, wind and river systems have provided transportation corridors, and now it is time that we as designers and planners distil and refine these processes to their essence and work with nature to harness the great potential of these natural systems within the landscape and develop a true "green" infrastructure.

CHALLENGES

There is a historic perception of heroism in the building of structures that can keep natural forces at bay. This notion has permeated throughout modern time and it was particularly evident through the 1930s and 1940s when bridge and dam building were the focus of the Works Progress Administration. Solely focusing on the insertion of engineered built structures has taken our perspective away from looking at the landscape as a whole. This is ever present in current construction practices and patterns of super-highways, dams, and transmission line corridors today. These highly visible projects are often at the forefront of media and political attention but it is the lost spaces or horizontal "voids" within constructed landscapes where the greatest opportunities lie. Landscapes have the potential to aid in the creation of ever-productive, high-performing, and functional infrastructure systems. Attention needs to be turned to these lost landscapes.

A 2006 national report on brownfields redevelopment titled *Recycling America's Land*[3] reported that there were more than 400,000 sites with real or perceived environmental hazards dotting the American landscape. These lands are often associated with infrastructure or industry that is developed to provide critical societal services such as waste treatment or energy production. This legacy is estimated to be worth more than $2 trillion in devalued property. This is particularly true in the New York City area where there has been a tremendous focus placed on reinventing these "voids" and creating productive urban landscapes. A dominant driver for this movement is the renewed attention turned to environmental health and well-being within our urban environments.

PERFORMANCE

The confluence of systems and forces is where overall performance can be optimized. We need to define a new perspective and measure of success when designing and building infrastructure systems. Instead of relying on hard engineered solutions with large ecological footprints to meet easily defined and measurable outcomes we should be integrating natural systems into these solutions to mitigate the scale of infrastructure. The integration of ecology into large-scale infrastructure is not always simple and often it is difficult to measure success. Success and performance of ecological infrastructure is not static; this type of infrastructure must be able to evolve and adapt to changing conditions. Environmental fluctuations can have a negative effect on ecological infrastructure; however, the potential for increasing performance in the infrastructure over time due to maturity and resiliency in the newly created ecosystem is also great, if designed and constructed appropriately. Metrics and key performance indicators developed in traditional language and scale are currently being developed for green infrastructure to allow for comparison and optimization.

We are living in an increasingly complex world where we need to be nimble, quick, and responsive to ever-changing economic, environmental, climatic, and social conditions. How we design and plan our cities of the future and the architecture of their infrastructure has great impact at all scales, from the lot, to the city, to the region, and even globally. As mentioned earlier, where we draw our boundaries of impact is critical to measuring the overall performance or, even more critically, the overall success of infrastructure projects. Our ability to view complexity as opportunity will ultimately be our legacy. The ability of species, populations, and communities to respond to changing conditions is largely moderated by the spatial configuration of habitats within the larger landscape, and by the scale at which individual organisms perceive the landscape.[4] We need to be smarter and think not only of singular infrastructure types such as roads and telecommunications but also of a complex web of networks, corridors, and nodes that can accommodate multiple uses and be designed to create resiliency in the landscape.

These networks create a mosaic of spaces that if not viewed through the lens of optimization are lost to the support systems that accompany large-scale infrastructure. These support systems are often of the same scale as the constructed infrastructure itself. Conduit networks, maintenance facilities, and right of ways are necessary components of infrastructure performance, yet they are inserted within the landscape without investigating the potential for crossing the boundaries of disciplines.

The design and planning profession has the responsibility to raise awareness of this need and to demonstrate ideas that will spur the concerted response that is necessary. Integrating public access and recreation into these lands that are set aside for a singular infrastructure presents a new amenity. The rethinking of conventional drainage systems can provide space for networks of open space shared by people and working biological systems at little increased cost.[5] By bringing conventional drainage systems to the surface, daylighting streams and rivers, we can create natural systems that cleanse the water as it flows through the landscape, and in the process create opportunities for riverfront parks and recreation areas where people can live, work, and play

PRODUCTIVE URBAN LANDSCAPES

According to the United Nations Population Fund, more than half the global population is now living in cities. The world is urbanizing at a rate never before seen. Cities around the globe are increasingly consuming the planet's freshwater, land, and other natural resources, while serving as leading contributors of greenhouse gas emissions. Sprinkled within cities is a patchwork of underutilized or vacant spaces that range from small to large, and are ripe for remediation, restoration, and reuse. It is critical to look at these spaces not as independent and insignificant parcels or corridors but as a collection or mosaic of productive lands that cumulatively can have a great benefit when viewed holistically at the city, regional, and global scale. There is an ever-present need for creating productive urban realm landscapes, such as streetscapes, parks, rain gardens, and urban farms—elements that provide significant levels of ecosystem services and socio-economic benefits.

The planning and design of high-performing, productive landscapes can directly improve the livability of cities by promoting recreation opportunities, providing locally available fresh foods and clean air and water, while contributing to overall social and economic vitality. This has been evident in cities like New York through the creation of PlaNYC 2030, announced in December 2006. This comprehensive, aggressive, and forward-thinking plan has announced critical initiatives addressing key land, water, transportation, energy, air, and climate change issues within the city.

One example of a landscape-based approach to sustainability and environmental health is increasing the overall tree canopy coverage within our cities. This is a critical, tangible, and achievable way to mitigate many of the negative environmental impacts of the built environment. By improving our urban forest, we can improve air quality through the interception of particulate matter and the reduction of VOCs, sequester carbon from source polluters, decrease stormwater runoff volumes, and reduce the urban heat island effect.

The critical issues when developing landscape strategies within our cities are identifying available land, procuring the appropriate plant material for implementation, planting strategies and techniques, and maintenance practices. Many cities are now looking to initiate programs to increase tree canopy coverage, urban farming, and wildlife habitat, but goals need to be set that are obtainable and environmentally and economically sustainable. Without addressing these critical issues, green infrastructure from the start will fail or greatly underperform at the expense of the taxpayers, city, or other funding source. Lessons learnt from programs across the USA, including PlaNYC, need to be documented within an adaptive management framework. A tremendous amount of planning and analysis work on the anticipated benefits of green infrastructure exists. This data is valuable in determining the potential return, yet the benefits calculated are not site based or relevant to maintenance practices. Best-management practices for implementation are critically needed to ensure that projects are viable, self-sufficient, and sustainable.

REPRESENTATIVE PROJECTS—DIVERSE ENVIRONMENTS FROM DISTINCT GEOGRAPHIES[6]

Three representative AECOM projects have been chosen to highlight the integration of natural processes into the design and construction of landscapes around the world. The three projects represent three distinct project types from diverse geographies.

Lower Lea Valley regeneration; 2012 Olympic and Paralympic Games Master Plan and Legacy Master Plan Framework

Threaded with canals, roads and rails links, water pipes, sewers and electricity pylons, the Lower Lea Valley has long been the service entrance for London. At the start of the new century it was a run-down and melancholic place, but with the growth of the capital shifting eastwards it provided the opportunity for one of Europe's largest regeneration projects, a home for the new 2012 Olympic Park and a new park for London.

The vision on how to effect positive, long-lasting, and sustainable change was rooted in the landscape's history and the area's most prominent and potent feature—its water. The goal was to revitalize this neglected area by creating 35,000 new homes and as many as 50,000 jobs along with schools, healthcare facilities, community centers, and sporting amenities. Expected to take a generation to complete, the sustainable scheme will also include improved public transport and transport infrastructure, and better connection to the rest of the capital. The vision's seven themes included Water City celebrating the area's rivers and canals and completing the missing link connecting the Lea Valley Regional Park with the Thames as a continuous green corridor. The second theme in the vision was the identification of Thriving Centers, including Stratford and Canning Town, where new development could be concentrated. The third was Neighborhoods and Communities where mixed-use schemes would ensure an improved quality of life for all. Other themes focused on creating active and dense areas of industry and employment opportunities, improved communications, and social, economic, and environmental sustainability. The final theme was the

2012 Olympic and Paralympic Games. The regeneration strategy was well underway before the Games were a consideration, but they were incorporated in the vision as an important catalyst for regeneration of the wider area.

The opportunities document provided clarification on the social, economic, and regeneration challenges and the scale of effort that would be required to effect significant, lasting, and positive change.

The land designated for the Olympic Park (more than 230 hectares) occupies around one fifth of the whole Lower Lea Valley regeneration zone and flanks a 2-km stretch of the River Lea. In addition to having the river at its heart, the site incorporated a network of canals and a tangle of infrastructure including pylons, roads, sewers, and rail. It was disfigured by run-down buildings and dereliction, and was surrounded by poor and badly served communities. Local neighborhoods were identified as some of the poorest, youngest, and most ethnically diverse in the entire city. They suffered from lack of jobs, a lack of amenities, and limited public transport connections with other local areas and the rest of London. Significant parts of the land were contaminated with pollutants from decades of low-value industry and landfill, including thousands of tons of rubble dumped here following the widespread destruction caused by the German Blitz in the 1940s during the Second World War.

Ideas evolved to create a new park around the upgraded river and networks of canals. Work on the public realm would be accompanied by improving local transport infrastructure to link the district with the center of London and neighboring communities. With the 2012 Olympic and Paralympic Games as a catalyst for regeneration and a profound and lasting change, investment would be accompanied by the creation of a distinctive and positive image for the area.

The creation of the park involved a complex sequence of compulsory purchase orders to acquire the site, followed by a systematic clearing and remediation of the land. This included excavating, treating, and clearing around 1.5 million cubic meters of soil, eradicating an infestation of Japanese knotweed and other invasive species, reusing around 90 percent of the site, removing more than 50 pylons and placing electricity cabling in two underground tunnels more than 6 km in length, and cleaning up more than 8 km

13.1 Shape of things to come
Note: the legacy of staging the 2012 Olympic and Paralympic Games in London will include a beautiful new park in the east of the capital. While some of the main sporting venues, such as the Olympic Stadium, will be reduced in size and retained, the site of temporary venues will become areas for development

13.2 Biodiversity
Note: habitat protection enhancement and creation have been carefully considered throughout the design process, which included a biodiversity action plan. Occasional tree and shrub planting provide structural diversity and cover, benefiting species such as birds. Flower-rich grassland is an important aspect of the site's existing ecology. A high herbaceous component provides greater diversity of nectar, seed, and food plants

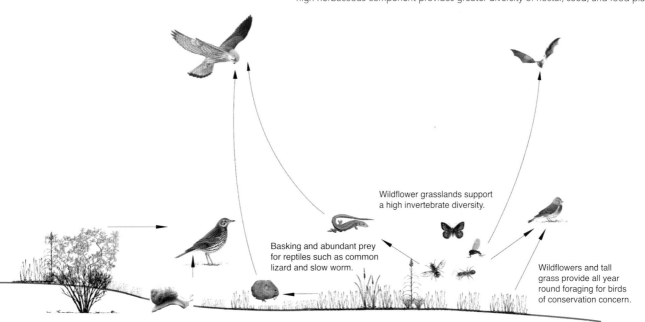

Wildflower grasslands support a high invertebrate diversity.

Basking and abundant prey for reptiles such as common lizard and slow worm.

Wildflowers and tall grass provide all year round foraging for birds of conservation concern.

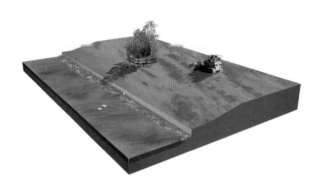

13.3 Wetland landscape

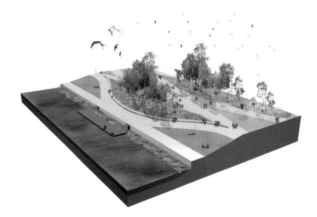

13.4 Landscape transformation
Note: images show the progression of works on a riverbank section of
the site where areas of natural habitat are preserved and enhanced,
and where the brownfield land is made ready for the Games. Figure
13.4b shows the land in the Games mode with the broad concourse
at the upper level and walkways closest to the water. After the Games
the site is transformed into the legacy state where temporary parts of
the concourse are removed and trees and plants gain stature as the
park matures

of waterways. In addition, work was carried out to improve wildlife
habitat and biodiversity with extensive planting of native species
including oak and ash, willow, birch, hazel, holly, blackthorn, and
hawthorn. It was ensured that construction work followed established
sustainability principles using recycled materials and that 50 percent
of materials by weight were transported by sustainable means,
including by waterways and rail.

The creation of the park is underpinned by environmental,
economic, and social sustainability with the goal of minimizing
any adverse impacts during the design and construction of the
park, its venues, infrastructure, and surrounding housing to leave
a lasting, high-quality place incorporating the principles of Green
Infrastructure throughout its overall fabric.

In terms of environmental sustainability, key gains include
transformation of the near-derelict site and bringing the land into
public use by creating significant new green space in East London.
All construction has been carried out to maximize the careful

use of resources such as using recycled material and optimizing opportunities for the efficient use of water. In addition the new utilities infrastructure was designed to meet the long-term needs of this part of the Lower Lea Valley, ensuring that 20 percent of the total energy demand from the permanent Games facilities will be met by new on-site renewable energy sources. At the heart of the park's infrastructure is the Energy Centre with a biomass boiler and a combined cooling, heating, and power plant for the Aquatics Centre and 2012 Olympic Stadium. Other aspects of the environmental sustainability included a network of cycle ways and footpaths, and a range of improvements to the public transport system including the high-speed Javelin train's 7-minute journey to Central London, an extension to the Docklands Light Railway, increased capacity on the Jubilee Line, and the upgraded Stratford International Station. All these improvements were planned and designed to work with the landscape and improve the overall ecological health of the region, taking advantage of the landscape infrastructure to tie the necessary engineered and built, hard systems with the newly created and restored natural systems.

PlaNYC Reforestation Initiative, New York City

On Earth Day 2007, New York's Mayor Bloomberg released PlaNYC 2030, a holistic set of 127 initiatives that addressed six key areas of sustainability for the city: land, air, water, energy, transportation, and climate change. One of these initiatives, the PlaNYC Reforestation Initiative, has the long-term aim of foresting more than 800 hectares of public land across the five boroughs by 2017. This initiative is one of the three components of the Million Trees NYC project, which aims to increase New York City's canopy coverage from 24 percent to 30 percent by planting trees on streets, on privately owned land, and on public land. The production on this project has been remarkable both for its breadth and its depth. The first step was the production of GIS maps, site rankings, and databases to serve the client in locating and selecting appropriate sites for meeting the 1500 acre mandate.

Next, a team was sent out to collect key data about all considered sites to provide a preliminary assessment of ground conditions, focusing on existing soil and existing invasive plants. This data was mapped in GIS and meticulously catalogued in a database. In conjunction with site selection and assessment, three diverse pilot sites were selected for fast-track implementation—the Hutchinson River Parkway, Kissena Corridor Park, and Willow Lake in Flushing, Queens. These pilot sites have not only served as a test for the effectiveness of species selection, spacing, and invasive control measures, but also for imbedding research plots. The New York City Parks Department Natural Resources Group recognized the opportunity that this project had to serve as a living experiment for monitoring the effectiveness and success of the implementation of urban reforestation design decisions. Within each of the pilot sites research plots have been imbedded at a variety of scales to allow for ongoing data collection. This application will allow for critical data to be collected about growth and mortality rates, invasive species, and the effectiveness of site preparation techniques. The data collected start to bridge the gap that currently exists between analysis and best-management practices for implementing large-scale urban planting programs.

The outcome of this phase of the plan is a book with the working title of *New York City Forest Restoration Guidelines.* The book will

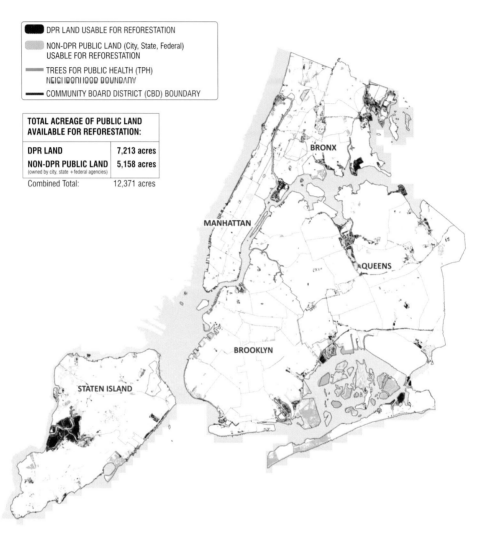

DPR LAND USABLE FOR REFORESTATION

NON-DPR PUBLIC LAND (City, State, Federal) USABLE FOR REFORESTATION

TREES FOR PUBLIC HEALTH (TPH) NEIGHBORHOOD BOUNDARY

COMMUNITY BOARD DISTRICT (CBD) BOUNDARY

TOTAL ACREAGE OF PUBLIC LAND AVAILABLE FOR REFORESTATION:	
DPR LAND	7,213 acres
NON-DPR PUBLIC LAND (owned by city, state + federal agencies)	5,158 acres
Combined Total:	12,371 acres

BRONX

MANHATTAN

QUEENS

BROOKLYN

STATEN ISLAND

13.5 Greening the city
Note: bringing nature into the city, the PlaNYC Reforestation Initiative is to encourage tree planting throughout the New York area. Work has been completed to assess ground conditions, identify suitable sites, and publish a comprehensive guide on implementing the planting

be a comprehensive how-to manual, addressing a broad range of topics from urban forest typologies and invasive plant control techniques, to the nuances of designing parks as forest. The book will serve practitioners and policymakers as the project evolves over the coming decade, and will help dictate how urban reforestation and landscape infrastructure will be incorporated into the densely built environment of New York City's five boroughs.

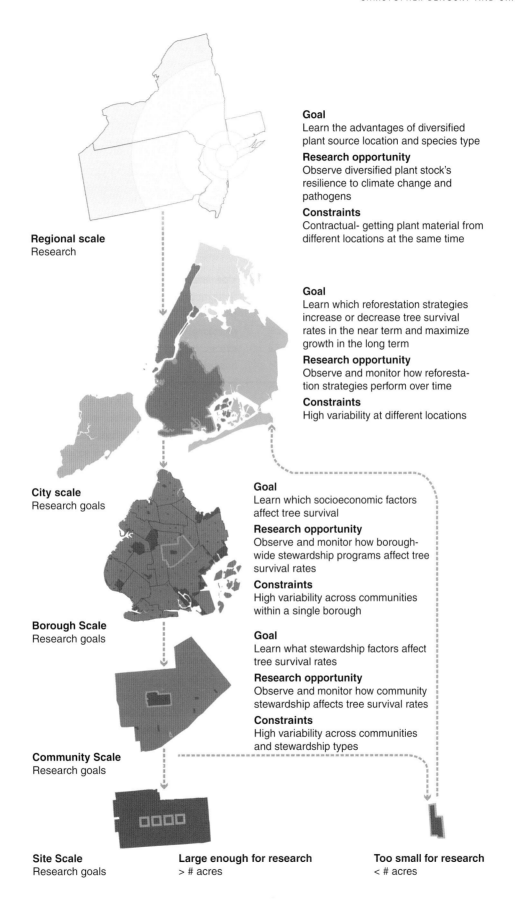

Regional scale
Research

Goal
Learn the advantages of diversified plant source location and species type

Research opportunity
Observe diversified plant stock's resilience to climate change and pathogens

Constraints
Contractual- getting plant material from different locations at the same time

City scale
Research goals

Goal
Learn which reforestation strategies increase or decrease tree survival rates in the near term and maximize growth in the long term

Research opportunity
Observe and monitor how reforestation strategies perform over time

Constraints
High variability at different locations

Borough Scale
Research goals

Goal
Learn which socioeconomic factors affect tree survival

Research opportunity
Observe and monitor how borough-wide stewardship programs affect tree survival rates

Constraints
High variability across communities within a single borough

Community Scale
Research goals

Goal
Learn what stewardship factors affect tree survival rates

Research opportunity
Observe and monitor how community stewardship affects tree survival rates

Constraints
High variability across communities and stewardship types

Site Scale
Research goals

Large enough for research
> # acres

Too small for research
< # acres

13.6 Function and beauty
Note: the water treatment system is designed to be highly functional and beautiful. It creates a buffer zone around the huge industrial facility. Boardwalks make it possible to gain access deep within the site to enjoy the water and a variety of wetland plants and wildlife, particularly the wildfowl attracted to the site

Shanghai Chemical Industrial Park Natural Wastewater Treatment System, Shanghai, China

In a fusion project uniting landscape design, environmental expertise, water engineering, and academic knowledge, a natural wetland treatment system has been created to improve industrial wastewater, the first system of its kind in China. This highly functional installation also provides the ecological, landscape, and recreational benefits of a beautiful wetland park.

With its lush reedbeds and extensive sequence of lakes, ponds, and weirs, along with boardwalks and a new visitor center, this wetland park is located within one of Shanghai's largest petrochemical industrial complexes, providing a welcome green oasis for staff and the local community. In addition to providing an attractive recreational space and wildlife habitat, this wetland also works hard as a natural wastewater treatment system for the industrial park. This facility is home to more than 40 petrochemical and pharmaceutical production plants run by international blue-chip companies including global giants Bayer and BP.

Combining the skills of landscape architects, engineers, ecologists, and academics, the natural treatment system creates a model for the polishing and recycling of treated industrial wastewater at a rate of more than 22,000 cubic meters per day. Innovative design components include shallow-water oxidizing ponds for biochemical oxygen demand (BOD), and nitrate and heavy metal removal. The system design evolved in response to growing environmental awareness in China, public concerns about issues of health and safety and water quality, and the willingness of forward-thinking industries to adopt a responsible attitude toward the impact of a booming economy on the environment.

Located southeast of Shanghai along the north coast of Hangzhou Bay, the Shanghai Chemical Industrial Plant (SCIP) has been established as one of the country's first industrial zones specializing in the development of petrochemical and fine-chemical businesses. The owners and managers of the gigantic 3000 hectare complex generated a brief for a water treatment system that would purify industrial wastewater effluent to a level suitable for recycling within the industrial park, thereby reducing the overall

13.7 Wetlands system
This working landscape is an attractive and enjoyable place for the industrial plant's employees. As it flows from the industrial facilities through the system, wasted water is channeled through a primary treatment plant before it enters the natural wetlands system. This initial cleaning process ensures that effluent is of a consistent quality before it enters the wetlands, with many key pollutants removed from the water

water demand, or for discharge into the ecologically sensitive Hangzhou Bay. Achieving these goals would improve effluent to the Level IV National Standard for Surface Water Quality (NSSWQ). Any proposed treatment system must also ensure compliance with groundwater and soil standards.

During work on the treatment system design, it became clear there was an opportunity to broaden the scope of the project beyond its purely functional infrastructure requirements. Using the latest ideas in ecological engineering, it was possible to take the innovative step of combining the new wastewater facility with the provision of natural wetlands as wildlife habitat and a recreational space for the park's employees and visitors, and also to benefit local communities living adjacent to the park. The treatment system is also of interest to the scientific community, and a research center has been established as part of the wetland area.

The design of the 30 hectare wetland system follows a long, linear, L-shaped route along the park's boundary, providing a green buffer for neighboring residential areas. Wastewater from the industrial park has already undergone the first phase of cleaning before it reaches the wetlands. While this treatment removes much of the ammonia, BOD, and total phosphorous (TP) from the effluent, wastewater entering the wetland treatment system is still highly saline, and contains significant concentrations of chemical oxygen demand (COD) and nitrates. The treatment system provides wastewater "polishing" to remove these remaining pollutants. The wetlands are also designed with a degree of treatment flexibility, as effluent water quality and volume is likely to change as new industrial facilities come on-stream. Therefore, the system can accommodate these variations, maintaining discharge standards with minimal operational changes.

On entering the wetlands, wastewater passes through a research area, before flowing slowly through two large, shallow ponds where pollutants are oxidized, and then flowing through a long sequence of wetland cells. Here, different planting blocks that include bulrushes, reeds, and wetland grasses act as natural filters. These plant species were selected for their saline tolerance and also their filtering function, with different species able to remove different pollutants from the water. In the final phases of the system, water enters a network of open ponds and broader swathes of flowering wetland vegetation. This botanical wetland can be explored by boardwalks and bridges that are connected to the wetland visitor center with its conference, meeting, and education rooms. Viewing platforms within the center, and also on the central island of the botanical wetland, enable visitors to observe the abundant and diverse wildlife attracted to the wetlands. By the end of the process, most of the water is returned to the industrial park for reuse, with any excess being released into Hangzhou Bay.

A rigorous operation and monitoring program is in place that offers a quick response to water quality changes. Researchers assess the effluent from each industrial facility before it enters the natural treatment system. The chemical, physical, and biological condition of the wetlands is also checked to avoid the buildup of pollutants in the water or soil. Continuous research is conducted to track removal rates of specific water effluent constituents such as heavy metals and organics, and to refine the system to target specific pollutants. Finally, water quality is closely monitored at points throughout the wetland system to minimize the risk of accidental pollution discharge.

This landmark project took advantage of the landscape surrounding the chemical facilities and turned it into a productive part of the facilities infrastructure, reducing the demand on hard, engineered structures and using natural systems to integrate the landscape within the infrastructure. Even in the early stages following construction, this innovative natural treatment system has attracted considerable interest from other industries in China, and has set a new benchmark in the country for ecological engineering, water treatment, and the development of "green" infrastructure.

SUMMARY

The traditional "gray" infrastructure of power lines, roads, sewers, levees, and ports that provides essential services is often planned and designed in opposition to, or in isolation from, existing natural systems. As greater funding becomes available to repair and replace the aging traditional infrastructure, a great potential and opportunity exists for incorporating the natural systems within the landscapes that surround these projects. The creation of multifunctional, high performance landscapes that not only place emphasis on the efficiency of built infrastructure, but also on the use of natural systems to increase ecological function is critical to our future.

As available land becomes scarce and increasingly more complex due to environmental, economic, and social constraints, infrastructure projects need to be designed and delivered in tandem with the landscape and the natural processes within them. Natural processes should not be viewed as a constraint to hard, engineered solutions, but as opportunities to harness the energy and sustainable natural processes that have been at work on our planet since its creation.

The overall success of large-scale infrastructure projects needs to be measured by the overall productivity of the site, the region, and the globe as a whole. It is no longer acceptable to look at a site's performance individually. While individual elements can be designed to increase productivity or ecological performance, systemic productivity and performance can only occur and be evaluated at the landscape scale. It is at this scale that built structures and ecology are able to interact and function to create a true ecological infrastructure.

NOTES

1   S.T. Lovell, Johnston D.M., "Designing landscapes for performance based on emerging principles in landscape ecology." *Ecology and Society* 14(1) (2009): 44.
2   Ibid.
3   The United States Conference of Mayors. *Recycling America's Land: A National Report on Brownfields Redevelopment.* Vol. VI (Washington, DC, 2006).
4   E. Kiviat, MacDonald K., "Biodiversity patterns and conservation in the Hackensack Meadowlands, New Jersey." *Urban Habitats* 2(1) (2004): 28–61.
5   G.L. Strang, "Infrastructure as landscape." *Places* 10(3) (1996): 8–15.
6   Adapted from AECOM's "The Bigger Picture." F. Sweet, *The Bigger Picture: Designing Better Places.* AECOM Design and Planning (Formerly EDAW) (London: Black Dog Publishing, 2009).

Part 3
Assessing Urban Infrastructures

AS THE TERM "sustainability" catches on and claims of sustainability become widespread, the need for a means of assessing infrastructure sustainability has become pressing. Given the heterogeneous nature of infrastructure projects, determining an appropriate method for assessment has serious challenges. This section presents these challenges as well as current environmental evaluation methods that can offer insight and act as guides. Environmental impact cannot be entirely divorced from monetary concerns and a pairing with economic assessment presents the opportunity to assess the value of sustainable infrastructure. The Zofnass Rating System for Sustainable Infrastructure is described here as an example for future infrastructure assessment; it represents a bold step towards advancing the cause of sustainable infrastructure.

14

Issues in Assessing Urban Infrastructures

THE ZOFNASS PROGRAM TEAM[1]

HARVARD UNIVERSITY

INTRODUCTION

This chapter discusses some of the issues that must be considered in developing a system for assessing and rating the relative sustainability of infrastructure projects with respect to environmental, economic, and social considerations.

WHAT IS SUSTAINABLE INFRASTRUCTURE?

What is meant by sustainable infrastructure? This question actually has two important parts. One is what is meant by "sustainable" and the other is what is "infrastructure." In the past, the term infrastructure generally meant publicly funded physical works that were shared by the residents of a city or town, such as roads, bridges, water supply, wastewater, electrical and telephone service, street lighting, and so on. These projects were almost always funded by tax dollars and designed and constructed by public agencies. Not usually included in this earlier definition were other community facilities, such as hospitals or schools. Today, definitions of infrastructure have been expanded to include all things needed for a society to function, including both the traditional or "hard" infrastructure elements—roads, bridges, utilities—but also the less tangible "soft" infrastructure elements—the systems and facilities for education, healthcare, transportation, and even financial systems—upon which a fully functioning society depends.

As for the definition of "sustainable," help comes from the United Nations (UN), which defines sustainable development as "development that meets the needs of the present without compromising the ability of future generations to meet their own needs."[2] This simple concept of using what is needed to sustain today's society without taking future generations' ability to sustain themselves is often used to describe sustainability in general. But how does this concept apply to sustainable infrastructure projects in practice? One organization is attempting to answer this question.

The Practice, Education and Research for Sustainable Infrastructure (PERSI) organization is an alliance of professional and standards organizations that was formed for the purpose of promoting sustainability in infrastructure. Operated by the American Society of Civil Engineers, PERSI defines infrastructure as "constructed facilities and natural features that shelter and support most human activities: buildings of all types, communications, energy generation and distribution, green spaces, transportation of all modes, water resources, and waste treatment and management." PERSI also defines sustainability of infrastructure projects as "the challenge of meeting human needs for natural resources, industrial products, energy, food, transportation, shelter, and waste management while conserving and protecting external and internal environmental quality and the natural, economic and social resources essential for future human need."[3]

PERSI's definition of infrastructure and its comprehensive description of sustainability seem to provide guidance for framing the issues that should be addressed in the development of a system to assess, rate, and reward the relative sustainability of infrastructure projects.

ASSESSMENT PERSPECTIVE

What are primary assessment perspectives with respect to project planning, design, construction, and use stages? It is obvious that high levels of sustainability cannot be accomplished after a project has been designed. Decisions made in the early phases of a project's inception and planning can have great impact on its eventual sustainability. Therefore, whenever possible, sustainability should be an integral part of the planning, design, documentation, and construction phases of an infrastructure project. Assessments could be performed in each phase of a project's life cycle such as:

- planning and conceptualization
- design and documentation
- construction
- operation and maintenance.

SCOPE OF ASSESSMENT

What should be the scope of a sustainable infrastructure assessment and rating? Should it be local, regional, or even global? On the one hand, sustainability principles encourage the application of the broadest possible perspective in assessing an infrastructure project because everything that is built in some way affects the environment, although often this is not obvious at the time. Decisions about which materials to use in a project can have large implications up the supply chain. This is particularly important when considering the sustainability of large-scale projects, such as highways, which consume enormous quantities of materials based on a single specification. On the other hand, from a practical standpoint, it seems logical that not every infrastructure project can be assessed and rated in the broadest terms of sustainability. For example, should all of the "soft" elements of infrastructure—such as the educational system—be considered when assessing the degree of sustainability of, say, a new bridge project? What of a bridge project that also includes a stretch of new highway leading to it? Or further, what if the infrastructure project includes a bridge, highway, plus the utilities, such as water, wastewater, electrical, and telephone service, to serve a new housing development? Should the presence or absence of soft infrastructure elements be part of assessing and rating the sustainability of such a project? An infrastructure sustainability assessment and rating system will have to address these questions if it is to be widely accepted and implemented.

STAKEHOLDERS

The sustainability of an infrastructure projects has many stakeholders. In addition to the public and society in general, they include sponsors, owners, developers, customers, partners, suppliers, communities, users, investors, the environment, and future generations. Stakeholders include those who pay for the project through taxation or investment, those who will use and benefit from the project, and those who are indirectly affected by its construction and operation. Each of these groups is affected in some way because of the effect that any infrastructure project has on the climate and use of resources. Stakeholder interests should be considered when developing a system for assessing and rating the sustainability of an infrastructure project, but how best to accomplish that may be a challenge.

ASSESSORS

Who should make assessments of an infrastructure's sustainability? There are several options. One option would be a voluntary self-assessment by the sponsor or developer of the project. This would compare the sustainability of the project against a recognized, uniform set of guidelines or checklists. This is similar to the "ENERGY STAR"[4] voluntary labeling program sponsored by the US Environmental Protection Agency (EPA) and the US Department of Energy (DOE), which was originally designed to promote energy-efficient products but has been expanded to include new homes and commercial and industrial buildings. Compliance and certification rely on the integrity of the self-assessing applicant. Another option would be self-assessment by a trained and licensed member of the sponsor or developer team but with independent validation by a trained third-party assessor. This is similar to the methodology required by the Civil Engineering Environmental Quality and Assessment (CEEQUAL) rating system developed in the UK.[5] This approach provides the public and industry with greater confidence that a project has achieved a stated level of sustainable performance because a disinterested evaluator has verified the assessment. Yet another option would be a fully independent third-party assessment performed by a trained and/or licensed assessor without any influence or assessment by the sponsor or developer. This option offers the greatest assurance of any sustainability rating and award, but would likely prove cumbersome because the assessor would have to become knowledgeable about the project without benefit of the insider's view.

The second option seems more applicable to the assessment of infrastructure sustainability because it would involve validation by a trained third-party assessor with no vested interest in the outcome, and a trained inside assessor who knows the details of the project. This approach will ensure conformance with the sustainability standards, lend credibility within the industry, and provide the public with greater confidence that the sustainability rating and any subsequent award or certificate are based on merit.

REWARDS, AWARDS, AND PENALTIES

Awards and certificates of achievement provide sponsors and developers of infrastructure projects with incentives to seek higher levels of environmental sustainability. Just as LEED® certification or ENERGY STAR rating of a new building enhances its public image and garners industry respect, an infrastructure project will likewise benefit from such recognition. It can enhance a project's image, assist in its funding, and help gain public support. A project that is subject to regulatory approval may be more likely to be accepted if it is recognized to be highly sustainable by a credible authority.

Awards and certificates can also serve as models for other infrastructure projects. The knowledge that a project's sustainability might be compared with other projects can spur a developer to emulate the achievement. Competition in this sense would have a positive impact on the environment. Awarding exceptional sustainable performance, processes, or approaches can result in the development of industry standards of achievement and best practices. Financial incentives, such as tax credits and abatements, can provide additional motivation to the infrastructure developer.

There are a number of reasons why a sponsor or developer of an infrastructure project will want to pursue an award for improved sustainability of an infrastructure project, such as:

- recognition that project sponsors respect the environment and society's interests
- demonstration that a project's sustainability compares favorably with or exceeds other infrastructure projects
- improvement of public image by communicating the achievement of high scores on a recognized sustainability standard

- communication to industry and public that construction of the project attempts to mitigate its environmental impact
- encouragement for other infrastructure project sponsors to seek greater sustainability.

The issue of whether to penalize infrastructure projects for failing to achieve certain levels of sustainability is problematical. First, what agency would assess the penalty? Would it be the municipal, state, or federal government? Second, how would infrastructure sponsors be assured the system is and remains fair? Third, would the agency use police power to enforce compliance with subjective sustainability standards? At the federal level the EPA and the DOE have power to enforce in certain areas, and some states and municipalities have enacted statutory requirements for certain elements of sustainability. However, how might one devise a system that fairly and equitably rewards or punishes an infrastructure project that addresses the vagaries of all aspects of sustainability, such as needs of society, the use of resources today to the detriment of future generations, and who decides what standard to use? Would the police power of the state be used to pursue criminal justice for failure to comply with those sustainability standards? What if an offense is discovered years after a project is complete? Further, most infrastructure projects involve not-for-profit, tax-exempt, public agencies, which complicates the enforcement and penalty discussion. It is easy to imagine a litigious nightmare of suits and countersuits. It seems far better to use a voluntary approach like those used by most building assessment and rating systems today that motivate sustainable behavior through incentives, awards, recognition, and peer pressure by celebrating success rather than punishing failure.

DIMENSIONS OF ASSESSMENT

The dimensions for assessment can be complex. Infrastructure projects can be large scale and require years to complete. Such projects can require the use of substantial resources and can have large impacts on the environment. In the broadest sense, sustainability might be assessed in terms of resource allocation, climate effect, impact on the natural world, and effect on the quality of human life, today and in the future. The metrics of infrastructure sustainability might be assessed and rated along a number of dimensions, such as:

- Energy
- Land Use
- Materials
- Landscape
- Cultural Heritage and Archeology
- Transportation
- Water and Waste
- Community and Neighborhood
- Ecology and Biodiversity
- Project Administration and Management.

There are several methods that can be used to assess and rate the sustainability of an infrastructure project. A simple list of desired environmental and sustainable actions applicable to any project might be used. This could be a set of principles against which a project is evaluated by counting the number of principles the project incorporates. The more principles incorporated, the greater the sustainability of the project. This approach gives equal importance to each action. Another method would be the use of a more detailed list of sustainable actions that are weighted in terms of importance. This is similar to the LEED approach.[6] Certain actions are awarded more points than others. This approach requires the rating authority to assign weights or points to each action. These weights might be determined by a consensus of experts. Possibly the most interesting approach would be a science-based methodology that benchmarks a project over its useful life, measuring the new project against an ideal using data from actual projects. This life cycle approach would require greater cost and analytical rigor but could yield a more scientifically satisfying result. Japan's Sustainable Building Consortium CASBEE system employs such an approach.[7] Whatever approach is used, it should be based on sound and proven sustainability principles that can be applied with fairness and equity across all projects.

SUMMARY

This chapter highlights some of the issues that should be considered in the development of a sustainability assessment and rating system for infrastructure projects. In the broadest sense, infrastructure projects have many stakeholders and should be assessed in terms of environmental, economic, and social sustainability. An important early step in the process will be the development of a clear definition of what constitutes sustainable infrastructure for the purposes of assessment. Not only must that definition describe the "hard" infrastructure components, but it must also contain descriptions of the "soft" infrastructure elements that will be assessed. This latter definition may prove to be the most difficult. Assessments should be continuous throughout an infrastructure project's life cycle, beginning at the earliest conceptualization phase. The assessment system should rate the one-time sustainable actions and decisions, and the ongoing operating effects of those decisions. Ideally, an infrastructure sustainability assessment system will be based on science, and benchmark proposed projects against actual performance data. Finally, the assessment system that uses incentives and rewards for achieving greater sustainable performance is preferable to legal enforcement and punishment of non-performance. Given the right combination of reward and recognition, a sustainable assessment and rating system could inspire infrastructure project sponsors and developers to achieve greater sustainability to the benefit of all members of society.

NOTES

1   Richard Jennings wrote this chapter as a part of his work in the Zofnass
    Program for Infrastructure Sustainability at the Harvard University
    Graduate School of Design.
2   United Nations General Assembly, "Towards sustainable development."
    *Report of the World Commission on Environment and Development:
    Our Common Future*, www.un-documents.net/ocf-02.htm.
3   Practice, Education and Research for Sustainable Infrastructure (PERSI),
    "PERSI memorandum of understanding," www.persi.us.
4   US Environmental Protection Agency, "Designing commercial buildings
    to achieve Energy Star," www.energystar.gov.
5   The Civil Engineering Environmental Quality and Assessment Scheme
    (CEEQUAL), "The CEEQUAL assessment," www.ceequal.com.
6   US Green Building Council, "LEED rating system," www.usgbc.org.
7   Comprehensive Assessment System for Building Environmental
    Efficiency, "CASBEE rating system," www.ibec.or.jp/CASBEE.

15

Current Environmental Evaluation Approaches

THE ZOFNASS PROGRAM TEAM[1]

HARVARD UNIVERSITY

INTRODUCTION

There are a surprisingly large number of sustainability rating systems in use today. Most of these rating systems are designed to assess the sustainability of new buildings. Some also address neighborhood or urban development. Only a few address the sustainability of infrastructure projects.

The most familiar rating system in the USA is LEED®, which stands for Leadership in Energy and Environmental Design. Developed in 1993 and administered by the US Green Building Council (USGBC), LEED has been widely promoted and adopted. It has become the "gold standard" of sustainability in America. LEED Silver, Gold, and Platinum building certifications are coveted indicators of a building's environmental "friendliness." Most people in the design and construction industry are familiar with this rating system. In other parts of the world, however, different rating systems are considered the standard. In fact, there are more than one hundred sustainability rating systems in existence worldwide, with new ones under development.

Virtually all sustainability rating systems have been developed by independent organizations or separate government bodies established to design, administer, and promote the use of the particular approach. Most rating systems rely on a quantitative scoring technique to assess the relative sustainability of a project. However, sustainability rating systems vary considerably in the level of detail and sophistication. Some rating systems, such as LEED, use a checklist to assess a building's relative sustainability, without regard to a project's operational life cycle or detailed analysis of future operations. The more points accumulated, the higher the sustainability rating. Other rating systems require deeper analyses and employ different assessment approaches, using such techniques as life cycle costing, whole-building design, and other approaches that attempt to provide greater insight into a project's sustainability over its useful life. Each rating system has advocates and critics, largely depending on how well the system has been promoted and adopted in a geographic region. Regardless of the approach or techniques employed, most of the rating systems attempt to provide a basis for comparing and rewarding the relative sustainability of a project in order to encourage the development of more environmentally friendly projects.

Few of the rating systems in existence today address the sustainability of infrastructure projects for a number of reasons. New buildings are more easily analyzed yet consume substantial resources in their construction and operation. Buildings also have more defined and compact physical boundaries. By contrast, infrastructure projects vary greatly in type, size, and scope, are difficult to assess, and the definition of what constitutes an infrastructure project has been fluid in recent decades. Further, new building projects were plentiful and more visible when environmental assessment and rating systems were developed. However, as infrastructure projects have become more numerous, and the dimensions of their potential environmental impact more understood, the need for a standard infrastructure sustainability rating system is growing. A number of the building rating system sponsors have added rating systems to assess the sustainability of larger-scale multiple building projects, neighborhoods, and communities.

THE RATING SYSTEMS

This chapter provides an overview of the major sustainability rating systems in use today, the relative merits of each, and whether they relate to infrastructure projects. In addition, a list of all known rating systems is provided. Approximately 120 rating systems were found to be either in use or under development at this writing. Most of these rating systems are subject to continuous revision and refinement to reflect the changing needs of users and the goals of the sponsoring agencies.

Despite the large number of sustainability rating systems identified, only a few have been widely adopted. Below, the more familiar rating systems are reviewed, and, when available, the rating system that specifically addresses infrastructure projects or urban and neighborhood development is described. For example, LEED for Neighborhood Development is described in lieu of the LEED for New Development. Seven rating systems were selected for review:

- CASBEE for Urban Development
- LEED for Neighborhood Development

- Cascadia: the Living Building Challenge
- Green Globes™
- BREEAM
- CEEQUAL
- AGIC Infrastructure Sustainability Assessment.

The chapter ends with a list of the rating systems identified. However, because of the evolving nature of sustainability and environmental concerns, this list will likely be out of date soon after publication.

CASBEE FOR URBAN DEVELOPMENT

Description

CASBEE is the acronym for Japan's Comprehensive Assessment System for Building Environmental Efficiency. Conceived in 2001 by the Institute for Building Environment and Energy Conservation with support from the Japan Ministry of Land, Infrastructure, Transport, and Tourism (MLIT), CASBEE is sponsored by the Japan GreenBuild Council (JaGBC)/Japan Sustainable Building Consortium (JSBC), and is administered by Japan's Institute for Building Environment and Energy Conservation (IBEC).

The CASBEE system was designed to achieve four primary objectives:[2]

1. Award high assessments to superior buildings to provide incentives to designers and others
2. Be as simple as possible
3. Be applicable to buildings in a wide range of applications
4. Consider issues and problems peculiar to Japan and Asia.

CASBEE is unique because in addition to providing assessment tools to encourage reducing the environmental impact of new building projects, it provides assessment tools for more subjective elements such as interior comfort and scenery.

The CASBEE assessment tools themselves were developed using the premise that assessment can continue throughout the life cycle of a building and should consider both the environmental quality of the building itself as well as the environmental impact of the building on its surrounding environment.

The "CASBEE Family" is the name for the collection of assessment tools, including CASBEE for Pre-design, CASBEE for New Construction, CASBEE for Existing Building, and CASBEE for Renovation, among others. Each tool is designed for a separate purpose and target user, and is intended to accommodate a wide range of uses (offices, schools, apartments, etc.) in the evaluated buildings.

CASBEE recognizes two "spaces" for assessment purposes. The "internal", or private property space, is defined as the building and its site. This space is termed the environmental quality of the building and its immediate site. The "external" or public space is the area outside the site that can be negatively impacted by the building project, such as adjacent buildings or public space. This space is deemed the environmental load of the building. For assessment purposes CASBEE defines the internal space as "Q—Building Environmental Quality and Performance" and the external space as "L—Building Environmental Loadings." CASBEE assesses a project based on: 1) energy efficiency; 2) resource efficiency; 3) local environment; and 4) indoor environment. These categories are further divided into six subcategories for the building and the space outside the project boundary. Scores are based on criteria for each assessment item. A five-level scoring system is used. A score of 3 indicates average. The assessment score of each item is weighted and takes into account "the level of technical and social standards at the time of assessment."[3] CASBEE defines the sustainability of a building project as the "Building Environmental Efficiency" (BEE), which is determined by the ratio of the Q-scores over the L-scores.

Based on the BEE score, CASBEE assigns a letter grade to signify the relative environmental efficiency or sustainability of a building using the following scale: Excellent (S), Very Good (A), Good (B+), Fairly Poor (B-) and Poor (C).

The CASBEE assessment tools are designed to be used at various phases of a project's development. An assessment is performed at the "Pre-design" phase and takes into account the business, cultural, social, and natural environment before the building is designed. A further assessment is performed during the "Design" phase, and, finally, an assessment is performed during a "Post-design" phase to evaluate and verify the actual sustainability of a project.

The CASBEE Family

The "CASBEE Family" refers to a set of CASBEE environmental assessment tools. Each tool is designed for a specific application and intended to accommodate a wide variety of project types. The CASBEE rating tools available today are:

- CASBEE for New Construction
- CASBEE for Existing Building
- CASBEE for Renovation
- CASBEE for Heat Island
- CASBEE for Urban Development
- CASBEE for an Urban Area + Buildings
- CASBEE for Home (Detached House)
- CASBEE Property Appraisal.

CASBEE for Urban Development

CASBEE for Urban Development is a relatively new tool for assessing the environmental impact or sustainability of groups of buildings. This tool is intended for use on multiple buildings and large-scale developments to encourage improvement of environmental performance on an urban scale. It has a number of applications: an environmental assessment tool for area development projects; an environmental labeling tool; a planning and assessment tool for energy-saving urban-scale remodeling plans; and a tool to support city planning to encourage sustainable urban development. It can also be used to guide improvement of environmental performance of urban redevelopment projects, special urban renewal zones, and comprehensive design of merged sites. In the future, CASBEE for Urban Development projects may serve as examples to guide the improved sustainability of entire cities.[4]

CASBEE organization

The CASBEE organization is composed of government and academic participants who serve in various capacities. Its assessment tools undergo continuous review and refinement through its committees.

Reference documents

The CASBEE reference documents and analysis tools are available for download from the CASBEE website: www.ibec.or.jp/CASBEE/english/method2E.htm.

Summary

CASBEE is used primarily in Japan. It is intended to be adopted by local and regional authorities, much like a model building code, and modified to reflect local conditions. Unlike some other sustainable assessment systems, CASBEE does not yet have a certified assessor program.

CASBEE is unique in that it takes into account more subjective environmental elements, such as interior comfort and scenery. It is also gives consideration to the environmental impact of new projects on their surrounding buildings and public spaces. Finally, it is a life cycle assessment system that can be used throughout a project's life cycle.

LEED FOR NEIGHBORHOOD DEVELOPMENT

Description

LEED is a widely recognized USA-based series of rating and certification systems used for the independent verification that new buildings, renovation projects, interior spaces, and new neighborhood developments achieve certain levels of sustainability. LEED is a registered trademark of the USGBC. The mission of LEED is articulated at the USGBC website as "To transform the way buildings and communities are designed, built and operated, enabling an environmentally and socially responsible, healthy, and prosperous environment that improves the quality of life."[5] A consensus-based rating system, LEED addresses five areas of sustainability: sustainable site development, water savings, energy efficiency, materials and resources selection, and indoor environmental quality.

With 78 regional chapters in the USA, the USGBC asserts that LEED is "the preeminent program for rating the design, construction and operation of green buildings." According to the USGBC, some 35,000 projects totaling 4.5 million square feet worldwide participate in the LEED system.[6]

Using independent third-party "Accredited Professionals," LEED rewards projects with certifications that serve as indicators of the relative sustainability of a project in terms of "energy savings, water efficiency, CO_2 emissions reduction, improved indoor environmental quality, and stewardship of resources and sensitivity to their impacts." There are more than 100,000 LEED Accredited Professionals worldwide.[7]

Although first designed to encourage greater sustainability of new buildings, the relatively new LEED for Neighborhood Development (LEED-ND) is a separate rating system that USGBC developed to encourage and assess the sustainability of new neighborhood and community developments. It incorporates the principles of smart growth, urbanism, and green building. According to the USGBC, LEED for Neighborhood Development "extends the benefits of LEED beyond the building footprint into the neighborhood it serves."[8]

Developed in a collaborative endeavor by the USGBC, Congress for the New Urbanism (CNU), and Natural Resources Defense Council (NRDC), LEED-ND goes beyond individual building projects and

Table 15.1 LEED-ND certification levels

Points	Certification level
40–49 points	LEED-ND Certified
50–59 points	LEED-ND Silver
60–79 points	LEED-ND Gold
80–106 points	LEED-ND Platinum

Source: USGBC website, www.usgbc.org

encourages improved sustainability of neighborhood developments. After commencing a pilot program in 2007 with approximately 240 participating projects, the LEED for Neighborhood Development rating system was officially placed in service on April 29, 2009. Like the other LEED rating systems and tools, LEED-ND uses a point-based approach to determine the relative sustainability of a new community or neighborhood development.

Like the other LEED rating systems, points are awarded for incorporating certain elements and strategies in a project. LEED-ND awards points in the following categories: Smart Location and Linkage; Neighborhood Pattern and Design; Green Construction and Technology; and Innovation and Design Process. A total of 106 possible points can be earned, which can result in one of the certification levels shown on Table 15.1.

These levels of certification are the same as the certification levels for new buildings and renovation projects. However, unlike the other LEED rating systems, the LEED for Neighborhood Development rating system requires that projects seeking certification advance through a progression of phases to achieve certification. At the end of the first phase, Stage 1, a neighborhood development can receive a conditional approval of a LEED for Neighborhood Development plan. At the end of Stage 2, a project can be pre-certified as a LEED for Neighborhood Development plan. Finally, at the end of Stage 3, the project can become a LEED-certified project. This three-step process is unique among the set of LEED assessment tools.

The LEED-ND rating system focuses on the larger perspective of urban and neighborhood development. It attempts to reduce urban sprawl, limit vehicle miles traveled, and, unlike other LEED rating systems, includes a major focus on social justice issues. Smart growth and new urbanism principles run through the rating system. LEED-ND encourages the design of compact yet attractive communities, mixed land uses, walkable neighborhoods, housing for various income levels, alternative transportation, development of existing communities, and more open spaces, among other progressive urban planning initiatives.[9]

LEED-ND rating system principles

- Revitalize existing neighborhoods.
- Reduce land consumption.
- Reduce automobile dependence.
- Promote pedestrian activity.
- Improve air quality.
- Decrease polluted stormwater runoff.
- Build more livable, sustainable communities for people of all income levels.

LEED for Neighborhood Development rating categories

"Smart Location and Linkage" has 30 possible points:

- Prereq 1:   Smart Location (required)
- Prereq 2:   Proximity to Water and Wastewater Infrastructure (required)
- Prereq 3:   Imperiled Species and Ecological Communities (required)
- Prereq 4:   Wetland and Water Body Conservation (required)
- Prereq 5:   Agricultural Land Conservation (required)
- Prereq 6:   Floodplain Avoidance (required)
- Credit 1:   Brownfield Redevelopment (2 possible points)
- Credit 2:   High-Priority Brownfield Redevelopment (1 possible point)

- Credit 3:   Preferred Locations (2–10 possible points)
- Credit 4:   Reduced Automobile Dependence (1–8 possible points)
- Credit 5:   Bicycle Network (1 possible point)
- Credit 6:   Housing and Jobs Proximity (3 possible points)
- Credit 7:   School Proximity (1 possible point)
- Credit 8:   Steep-Slope Protection (1 possible point)
- Credit 9:   Site Design for Habitat or Wetlands Conservation (1 possible point)
- Credit 10: Restoration of Habitat or Wetlands (1 possible point)
- Credit 11: Conservation Management of Habitat or Wetlands (1 possible point).

"Neighborhood Pattern and Design" has 39 possible points:

- Prereq 1:   Open Community (required)
- Prereq 2:   Compact Development (required)
- Credit 1:   Compact Development (1–7 possible points)
- Credit 2:   Diversity of Uses (1–4 possible points)
- Credit 3:   Diversity of Housing Types (1–3 possible points)
- Credit 4:   Affordable Rental Housing (1–2 possible points)
- Credit 5:   Affordable For-Sale Housing (1–2 possible points)
- Credit 6:   Reduced Parking Footprint (2 possible points)
- Credit 7:   Walkable Streets (4–8 possible points)
- Credit 8:   Street Network (1–2 possible points)
- Credit 9:   Transit Facilities (1 possible point)
- Credit 10: Transportation Demand Management (2 possible points)
- Credit 11: Access to Surrounding Vicinity (1 possible point)
- Credit 12: Access to Public Spaces (1 possible point)
- Credit 13: Access to Active Public Spaces (1 possible point)
- Credit 14: Universal Accessibility (1 possible point)
- Credit 15: Community Outreach and Involvement (1 possible point)
- Credit 16: Local Food Production (1 possible point).

"Green Construction and Technology" has 31 possible points:

- Prereq 1: Construction Activity Pollution Prevention *(required)*
- Credit 1: Certified Green Buildings *(1–3 possible points)*
- Credit 2: Energy Efficiency in Buildings *(1–3 possible points)*
- Credit 3: Reduced Water Use *(1–3 possible points)*
- Credit 4: Building Reuse and Adaptive Reuse *(1–2 possible points)*
- Credit 5: Reuse of Historic Buildings *(1 possible point)*
- Credit 6: Minimize Site Disturbance through Site Design *(1 possible point)*
- Credit 7: Minimize Site Disturbance during Construction *(1 possible point)*
- Credit 8: Contaminant Reduction in Brownfield Remediation *(1 possible point)*
- Credit 9: Stormwater Management *(1–5 possible points)*
- Credit 10: Heat Island Reduction *(1 possible point)*
- Credit 11: Solar Orientation *(1 possible point)*
- Credit 12: On-Site Energy Generation *(1 possible point)*
- Credit 13: On-Site Renewable Energy Sources *(1 possible point)*
- Credit 14: District Heating and Cooling *(1 possible point)*
- Credit 15: Infrastructure Energy Efficiency *(1 possible point)*
- Credit 16: Wastewater Management *(1 possible point)*
- Credit 17: Recycled Content in Infrastructure *(1 possible point)*
- Credit 18: Construction Waste Management *(1 possible point)*
- Credit 19: Comprehensive Waste Management *(1 possible point)*
- Credit 20: Light Pollution Reduction *(1 possible point)*.

"Innovation and Design Process" has 6 possible points:

- Credit 1: Innovation in Design *(1–5 possible points)*
- Credit 2: LEED Accredited Professional *(1 possible point)*.

The project totals have 106 possible points.

Reference documents

The LEED-ND rating system is described in *LEED for Neighborhood Development Rating System. Pilot Version* (US Green Building Council, Congress for the New Urbanism, National Resource Defense Council, 2007). This document is available for download at the LEED website: www.usgbc.org.

Summary

LEED as a name and trademark has been well-promoted. As a result it has become widely accepted as the gold standard of sustainable building. Many design professionals have become LEED Accredited Professionals and integrated the LEED principles into their designs. Owners and developers frequently seek LEED certification of their new buildings, not only to demonstrate their sensitivity to sustainability issues but also as marketing and promotional tools to attract lenders and tenants. With the publication of the LEED-ND system, elements of infrastructure sustainability are beginning to be addressed by LEED.

The point values of the various LEED categories of sustainability are sometimes questioned because they can appear somewhat arbitrary. LEED does not provide insight into the reasoning behind the relative values that are assigned to the achievement of one sustainable element over another. For example, in the LEED-ND rating system, only 1 point can be earned for the reuse of historic buildings, or taking into consideration solar orientation, or ensuring infrastructure energy efficiency in a new development. However, 8 points can be earned for providing walkable streets in a neighborhood. Certain projects might make more use of the credit related to the reuse of historic buildings, or construct highly energy efficient infrastructures. Either action, although having a positive effect on the total environmental impact of the project, under LEED-ND would earn just one point toward their certification.

CASCADIA: THE LIVING BUILDING CHALLENGE 2.0

Description

The Cascadia Living Building Challenge 2.0 is a green building standard that covers a wide range of projects from small remodeling projects to entire neighborhoods, and leads to a green building certification. Conceived and authored by Jason F. McLennan prior to joining Cascadia, the Living Building Challenge is today administered by the Cascadia Green Building Council and its recently founded International Living Building Institute (ILBI). Cascadia maintains that the Living Building Challenge 2.0, which is intended to go beyond LEED certification, is the first green building certification program to include "urban agriculture, social justice and universal access issues as mandatory requirements." A recently added section to the Living Building Challenge 2.0 incorporates Universal Design principles and attempts to help "end economic segregation of public and semi-public places."

Cascadia promotes the design, construction, and operation of buildings that are environmentally responsible, profitable, and healthy places to live, work, and learn throughout Alaska, British Columbia, Washington, and Oregon.

The Cascadia Green Building Council, named for the Cascadia bioregion in the Pacific Northwest region of North America, was founded in 1999 as one of three original chapters of the USGBC. Cascadia primarily serves Alaska, British Columbia, Washington, and Oregon, and maintains branches in 14 cities in the Pacific Northwest. It is also a chapter of the Canada Green Building Council.

The Living Building Challenge 2.0 rating system

The Living Building Challenge 2.0 rating system is founded upon a simple question with large implications: "What if every single act of design and construction made the world a better place?"[10] Toward this end, a set of performance criteria is defined for certification of a project. Seven performance elements, or "petals," make up the Living Building Challenge 2.0 standard:

1. Site
2. Water
3. Energy
4. Health
5. Materials
6. Equity
7. Beauty.

The flower petals analogy is used to illustrate the challenge to owners, architects, design professionals, engineers, and contractors to design and construct new projects that are as efficient and elegant as a flower. The seven flower petals are subdivided into a total of twenty "Imperatives," each addressing a specific environmental topic that must be accomplished for certification.

The Living Building Challenge 2.0 imperatives can be applied to all building and project types—renovations, existing building, new construction, infrastructure projects, parks, or landscape and community development projects. However, for assessment purposes, one of four project typologies must be chosen:

1. *Renovation*—projects that do not involve the complete building, such as residential kitchen remodeling, single-floor tenant build-out, or historic renovations.
2. *Landscape or Infrastructure*—projects that are "non-conditioned," such as open-air parks, amphitheaters, roads, and bridges.
3. *Buildings*—new or existing building construction projects.
4. *Neighborhood*—projects that contain multiple buildings on a contiguous site or in a neighborhood, such as college or university campuses, corporate office parks, and business and industrial districts, or even villages or towns.

Unlike LEED, the Living Building Challenge does not rely on credits or a scalar point scoring approach but instead challenges the project to achieve a set of prerequisites for certification. Also, unlike LEED, the Living Building Challenge offers only one level of certification. The Living Building Challenge certification program is not considered an alternative to other rating systems but is rather a challenge for achieving additional levels of sustainability through concerted effort. LEED certification is considered only a first step.

The Living Building Challenge is a top-down approach that seeks to define an ideal state of sustainability. The conditions for certification are both implicit and explicit. For instance, the prerequisite of Net Zero Energy is an explicit requirement of the Living Building Challenge, but implicit in that requirement are many strategies that should be pursued to make the building as energy efficient as possible.

It is important to note that the Living Building Challenge certification is based on actual building performance, not theoretical projections or calculations. Projects seeking a Living Building certificate must be in operation for at least one year prior to the assessment and demonstrate compliance through actual operating results.

The Living Building Challenge 2.0 petals and imperatives

Site
- Limits to Growth.
- Urban Agriculture.
- Habitat Exchange.
- Car-Free Living.

Water
- Net Zero Water.
- Ecological Water Flow.

Energy
- Net Zero Energy.

Health
- Civilized Environment.
- Healthy Air.
- Biophilia.

Materials
- Red List.
- Embodied Carbon Footprint.
- Responsible Industry.

- Appropriate Sourcing.
- Conservation + Reuse.

Equity
- Human Scale + Humane Places.
- Democracy + Social Justice.
- Rights to Nature.

Beauty
- Beauty + Spirit.
- Inspiration + Education.

Reference documents

The Living Building Challenge 2.0 guide is available for download from the International Living Building Institute website: www.ilbi.org/the-standard/LBC2-0.pdf.

Summary

The Living Building Challenge 2.0 is a guide to sustainable design and building that encompasses a wide range of projects, from small additions to whole neighborhoods, and which can lead to a Living Building certification. Unlike LEED, Living Building Challenge 2.0 offers only one level of certification and it challenges the design and construction industry to seek a higher level of sustainability through compliance with a series of prerequisites or imperatives.

Cascadia is seeking to expand its influence to national and international levels. The Cascadia organization has many connections and affiliations. The Cascadia Green Building Council, the Living Building Challenge 2.0, the International Living Building Institute, the Canada Green Building Council, the USGBC and the LEED rating systems are all part of or affiliated with Cascadia.

Like other sustainable rating systems, the Living Building Challenge is constantly under review and subject to revisions as the state of sustainability and technology changes. Like its name, the Living Building Challenge itself is a living document.

GREEN GLOBES

Description

Green Globes is an interactive online assessment and rating system for buildings that is used in the USA and Canada. It claims to be a revolutionary system to guide the design and operation and management of green buildings. It originated with the Building Research Establishment Environmental Assessment Method (BREEAM) Canada for Existing Buildings, developed by the Canadian Standards Association (CSA) in 1996. In 2000, Green Globes for Existing Buildings was introduced as an online assessment tool. In that same year, the Canadian Department of National Defense and Public Works and Government Services began developing Green Globes for use in the design of new buildings. In 2002 a team that included Arizona State University, the Athena Institute, BOMA (Building Owners and Managers Association), and several Canadian federal departments including Public Works and Governments Services and Natural Resources Canada further revised and refined Green Globes into the rating and assessment tool that is in use today.[11]

In the USA, Green Globes is administered by the Green Building Initiative (GBI), which has the rights to develop and distribute it throughout the USA. In Canada, the Green Globes system for existing buildings is operated under the name BOMA BESt and is administered by BOMA Canada. Other Green Globe products in Canada are administered by ECD Jones Lang LaSalle.

Because Green Globes is a rating and assessment tool for buildings, it is used mostly by real estate developers and property managers. BOMA BESt for existing buildings has been adopted by the Canadian federal government for all of its buildings.

The Green Globes rating system

The Green Globes rating system is an internet-based interactive assessment and rating process that uses an online questionnaire exclusively to collect information and generate reports. Questionnaires are completed by the user and then reviewed and validated by trained third-party assessors. The certification process includes

Table 15.2 Green Globes scale

Percentage of points	Number of Green Globes
35 to 54%	One Green Globe
55 to 69%	Two Green Globes
70 to 84%	Three Green Globes
85 to 100%	Four Green Globes

Source: Green Globes website, www.greenglobes.com

validating the information submitted in the questionnaire, review of the project's drawings and specifications, energy modeling, and a tour of the building. Existing buildings can commence the validation and certification process immediately. New buildings can commence the process at the end of the construction document phase with final certification at the end of construction.

Green Globes uses a point system to award a building one to four "green globes." The number of globes awarded is based on the percentage of a maximum of 1000 points that are achieved according to the scale shown on Table 15.2.

The majority of points that are available toward Green Globes certification are related to energy use. The Green Globes system benchmarks projects against the EPA Target Finder database, which contains operational data from existing higher-performing buildings. Green Globes asserts that this is a truer measure of a building's performance over using the ASHRAE 90.1 hypothetical standard. In addition to assessing the energy performance of a building, Green Globes also assesses the application of efficient-energy technologies, the building's space efficiency, and microclimate design.

Green Globes offers five categories of assessment tools:

- *Design of New Buildings or Significant Renovation*—assessment tool for new buildings or extensive remodeling of existing buildings
- *Building Emergency Management Assessment (BEMA)*—assessment tool for rating building emergency management systems

- *Management and Operation Existing Buildings (including BOMA BESt)*—assessment tools for existing buildings
- *Building Intelligence (BIQ™)*—assessment tool for building automation and intelligence. Produces the Building Intelligence Quotient (BiQ)
- *Green Globes Fit-up*—assessment tool for new construction or the remodeling of commercial interiors.

Reference documents

The various Green Globes assessment and rating tools are available for a fee from the organization's website: www.greenglobes.com.

Summary

Green Globes is primarily a commercial and institutional green building assessment and rating system used in Canada and the USA. It is unique in that it is exclusively an online interactive rating system. It began as an assessment tool for existing buildings. Today, it is used on large and small commercial and institutional building projects such as offices, schools, universities, libraries, and multifamily buildings. Unlike other rating systems, Green Globes processes existing building management and operations as well as new construction. Green Globes uses a unique interactive online questionnaire approach, and provides third-party verification and certification of the building data that is entered in the online questionnaire. It employs a point system to award one to four green globes as a measure of relative building sustainability. It is also used by owners and building managers to compare the relative sustainability of multiple buildings in a portfolio.

BREEAM

Description

BREEAM, which is the acronym for "BRE Environmental Assessment Method," is a UK-based sustainability rating and certification system for buildings and communities. BREEAM claims to be the most widely used environmental rating and certification system for buildings in the world, with some 110,000 BREEAM-certified buildings existing today. This compares with 35,000 LEED participating green building projects.[12]

Established in 1990 by the BRE (Building Research Establishment) in the UK, BREEAM began as a rating system for buildings but has since introduced rating systems for multiple buildings and entire communities.

Various versions of BREEAM are tailored for different regions of the world including the UK, Europe, and "the Gulf." BREEAM notes, however, that its assessment systems can be adapted to any country. BREEAM is used for mostly non-residential buildings but it offers residential assessment tools. BREEAM uses evidence-based research as the basis for its rating systems unlike the consensus-based approach used by LEED.

The BREEAM rating system

BREEAM uses a five-level scoring system in all of its assessment schemes to award a number of "stars" for certification. Project assessments are graded on the scale shown on Table 15.3.[13]

BREEAM requires that its certification assessments be performed by "Licensed" or "Qualified BREEAM Assessors," or by those who are qualified under its relatively new assessor category called a BREEAM Accredited Professional, or BREEAM AP.

BREEAM publishes technical manuals to guide certification of a wide range of project and building types, called "schemes," including:

- Communities
- Courts

Table 15.3 BREEAM Scoring

Score	Grade	Stars
<25	Unclassified	None
25–40	Pass	One star
40–55	Good	Two stars
55–70	Very good	Three stars
70–85	Excellent	Four stars
75	Outstanding	Five stars

Source: BREEAM Communities Scheme Document, www.breeam.org

- Education
- Healthcare
- Industrial
- Office
- Prisons
- Refurbishment
- Residential
- Retail
- Other Buildings.

BREEAM Communities assessment system

Recognizing the growing importance of the broader scope of sustainable communities and infrastructure, BREEAM recently introduced a separate assessment protocol for communities, neighborhoods, and residential, non-residential, and mixed-use developments. BREEAM Communities is intended to assist planning authorities ensure that new large-scale, multiple building developments meet sustainability goals established by the planning authority and includes assessment of environmental, social, and economic sustainability in the following categories:[14]

- *Climate and Energy (built-form mitigation and adaptation)*
  - Flood Risk Issues
  - Passive Design Principles
  - Water Consumption Management
  - Energy Consumption Management
  - Infrastructure
- *Community (consultation processes and local community involvement)*
  - Inclusive Communities
  - Community Consultation
  - Information/Ownership
- *Place Shaping (local area design and layout)*
  - Land Use
  - Form of Development
  - Open Space
  - Inclusive Design
  - Mix of Use
- *Transport (sustainable transport options)*
  - Public Transport
  - Cycling Requirements
  - General Policy
  - Car Parking
  - Traffic Management
- *Ecology (protection of the ecological value of the site)*
  - Ecological Survey
  - Biodiversity Action Plan
  - Native Flora
  - Wildlife Corridor
- *Resources (sustainable use of resources)*
  - Impact of Materials
  - Waste Management (Operation and Construction)
  - Water Resources Management
  - Pollution Issues
  - Land Remediation
- *Business (local and regional economic issues)*
  - Business Investment
  - Employment
  - Business Facilities
  - Connectivity

- *Buildings (overall sustainability performance of buildings)*
  - Residential Buildings (CSH or EcoHomes)
  - Non-Domestic Buildings (BREEAM).

The BREEAM Communities assessment and certification is a two-phase process. The first phase is an "Interim Certificate" phase, which is encouraged but optional, and is the certification of the project at the early preliminary planning stage. This is intended to preliminarily assess the sustainability of the project against the stated goals of the planning authority, thus providing an early indicator of the key issues that will need to be addressed for final certification. The "Final Certificate" phase is a detailed planning assessment and certification state that is mandatory in order for the project to receive a BREEAM Certificate. It is not required that projects obtain an Interim Certificate before seeking a Final Certificate but BREEAM encourages the two-step process.

Reference documents

BREEAM publishes technical manuals and assessment guides that are available for download from its website: www.breeam.org.

Summary

The BRE Environmental Assessment Method or BREEAM is a widely used environmental assessment and certification system that is applicable to a variety of building and project types, called schemes, including new communities and multi-building developments. Although widely used in the UK it is applicable to any country. In fact, BREEAM claims to be the most widely used assessment system for buildings in the world. BREEAM Certification requires assessment by qualified third-party assessors that are licensed by BREEAM. BREEAM offers different schemes tailored to different project types. Like LEED for Neighborhood Development, BREEAM Communities has been created to address elements of infrastructure sustainability. However, like all other environmental rating and assessment systems, the various BREEAM schemes are under

constant review and revision reflecting advances in technology and sustainability.

CEEQUAL

Description

The Civil Engineering Environmental QUALity Assessment and Award Scheme, or CEEQUAL, is a UK-based environmental assessment and awards program for improving environmental performance in civil engineering and public projects. Developed in 2003 by the Institution of Civil Engineers (ICE) with the support of the UK Government, CEEQUAL seeks to encourage the delivery of greater sustainability in project scoping, design, and construction. CEEQUAL is used in the UK and the Republic of Ireland.

The CEEQUAL system rewards civil engineering and public project clients, designers, and constructors when they exceed the minimum legal and environmental requirements and achieve distinctive environmental and social standards. To date 61 awards have been bestowed on completed projects. Another 22 interim project awards have been granted and 180 assessments are underway.[15]

CEEQUAL cites four main benefits that result from using its assessment and awards program, including:

1. Enhanced reputation and public image through communication of a company's environmental, sustainability, and socially responsible goals and policies.
2. Improvements to projects and best practices through the use of life cycle costing, reduction of waste, improved resource efficiency, and reduced environmental complaints.
3. Demonstration of a commitment to the environment by clients, the project team, the companies involved, and the industry.
4. Enhanced team spirit resulting from working toward a common goal of "we must score well here" and the rewarding of project teams that go "the extra mile."

CEEQUAL assesses environmental and sustainability elements such as land use, ecology, use of water, energy and carbon, waste reduction and management, landscape, noise and dust, cultural heritage, and social issues including neighborhood impact and community relations. CEEQUAL can be used to assess roads and railways, water supply and wastewater treatment, airports, power stations, coastal and river projects, retail and business parks, and is applicable to projects of any scope or scale. For example, the CEEQUAL system is being used to assess the infrastructure for the London 2012 Olympic Park project.

The CEEQUAL rating system

The CEEQUAL assessment and rating system relies on the research and experience of BREEAM. Unlike BREEAM and other rating systems, however, CEEQUAL offers only one rating scheme rather than different schemes for different project types.

CEEQUAL is a self-assessment system. It requires the involvement of a trained CEEQUAL Assessor, most often a member of the project team, and a separate CEEQUAL-appointed Verifier who validates the assessment. Qualification as a trained CEEQUAL Assessor requires completion of a 2-day CEEQUAL Assessor training course and passing an examination at the end of the course.

Originally a spreadsheet-based system, beginning in late 2010 all CEEQUAL assessments will be performed using a new online assessment tool using the CEEQUAL Manual, which is available for download.

The CEEQUAL system rates performance of environmental, sustainability, and societal elements in 12 main categories, which are weighted for scoring purposes (see Table 15.4).

Five types of CEEQUAL awards are available:

- *Whole Project Award*—applied for by client, designer, and principal contractor
- *Design Award*—applied for by the lead designer
- *Construction Award*—intended to be sought by the main contractor
- *Design and Build Award*—for integrated contracts

Table 15.4   CEEQUAL category weights

Category	Weight
Project Management	10.9%
Land Use	7.9%
Landscape	7.4%
Ecology and Biodiversity	8.8%
The Historic Environment	6.7%
Water Resources and the Water Environment	8.5%
Energy and Carbon	9.5%
Material Use	9.4%
Waste Management	8.4%
Transport	8.1%
Effects on Neighbours	7.1%
Relations with the Local Community and other Stakeholders	7.4%

Source: CEEQUAL website, www.ceequal.com

- *Client and Design Award*—also available as an Interim Award.

CEEQUAL assesses the margin by which a team or project exceeds minimum legal or prescribed requirements. Achieving the minimum level of sustainability will result in a low score. Likewise, because of the realities of environmental issues, a perfect score is also not possible. The CEEQUAL Award is based on the percentage of the maximum score possible for a project as agreed by the Assessor and Verifier as shown on Table 15.5.

For an Excellent Award, the actual percentage score achieved by the project is printed on the award certificate as a further incentive for project teams to seek greater sustainability of their projects. Upon granting an award, CEEQUAL hosts public award certificate

Table 15.5 CEEQUAL Award percentage margin

Percentage margin	Rating
Exceed by 25%	Pass
Exceed by 40%	Good
Exceed by 60%	Very Good
Exceed by 75%	Excellent

Source: CEEQUAL website, www.ceequal.com

presentations, often in tandem with another professional or public event.

Reference documents

The CEEQUAL Manual and other information is available from the CEEQUAL website at www.ceequal.com.

Summary

The CEEQUAL assessment and rating system is one of the few rating systems that most specifically addresses infrastructure projects. Although used in the UK and the Republic of Ireland, it offers valuable principles and guidelines to assess the sustainability of infrastructure projects in other countries.

AGIC INFRASTRUCTURE SUSTAINABILITY ASSESSMENT

Description

The AGIC Rating Scheme is an Australian-based infrastructure assessment and rating system currently under development by the Australian Green Infrastructure Council (AGIC). Once operational it will provide a methodology for independently validating and rewarding improved sustainability of infrastructure projects. This rating system is included here because it is one of the few environmental assessment and rating systems that specifically addresses infrastructure projects and as such can inform the development of other sustainable infrastructure rating systems for use in other countries.

The AGIC Rating Scheme assesses the environmental consequences and sustainability of a broad range of infrastructure project types, such as:

- roads, rail, bridges, and tunnels
- ports and wharves
- airports
- distribution grids
- water infrastructure and resource management
- waterway management.

The AGIC rating system

The AGIC Rating Tool is a points-based rating system that will be part of the AGIC Rating Scheme. AGIC intends to publish a technical manual and scoring spreadsheet that will describe eligibility criteria, rating points, and the process for validating a project. The AGIC recently announced that government funding has been received for further development of the Rating Scheme. AGIC also announced that it plans to release an automated checklist called the "Quick Guide," which covers 136 considerations of the seven AGIC Rating Scheme categories and is intended to guide users in the adoption of sustainable features into projects. AGIC also plans to publish case studies to serve as exemplars.[16]

Like other rating systems, the AGIC Rating Scheme will be a self-assessment system. The scoring spreadsheet and application for award will be initially completed by an "accredited AGIC Assessor." The assessment and application will be reviewed and validated by an "accredited AGIC Verifier." To become an accredited AGIC assessor, a candidate must complete a one-day AGIC assessor course, which includes training in use of the AGIC Rating Tool. Upon successful completion of the process, the AGIC will award a certificate as an indication of a project's sustainability achievements.

The AGIC Rating Tool assesses a project's sustainability across seven main categories. At the time when this chapter was written the seven main categories had 27 subcategories:[17]

1. *Project Management and Governance*
1.1 Purchase and Procurement
1.2 Reporting and Responsibilities
1.3 Making Decisions
1.4 Climate Change Adaptation
1.5 Knowledge Sharing and Capacity Building
2. *Economic Performance*
2.1 Value for Money
2.2 Due Diligence
2.3 Economic Life
3. *Using Resources*
3.1 Energy Use
3.2 Water
3.3 Material Selection and Use
4. *Emissions, Pollution, and Waste*
4.1 Greenhouse Gas Management
4.2 Discharges to Air, Water, and Land
4.3 Land Management
4.4 Waste Management
5. *Biodiversity*
5.1 Functioning Ecosystems
5.2 Enhanced Biodiversity
6. *People and Place*
6.1 Health, Well-being, Safety
6.2 Natural and Cultural Heritage Values
6.3 Participatory Processes
6.4 Positive Legacy
6.5 Urban and Landscape Design
6.6 Knowledge Sharing
7. *Workforce*
7.1 Safety, Health, and Well-being of Workforce
7.2 Capacity Building
7.3 Increased Knowledge of Applied Sustainability
7.4 Equity

Resources

Further information on the AGIC Rating Scheme and the AGIC Tool can be found at the AGIC website: www.agic.net.au.

Summary

Although the AGIC Rating Scheme for infrastructure projects is not yet operational, with recent government funding approval it appears the rating system will be published. The AGIC system, along with CEEQUAL, is among the few environmental and sustainability assessment and rating systems specifically designed for infrastructure projects.

CONCLUSION

There is a plethora of organizations promoting green building and a large number of sustainable assessment, rating, and certification systems in existence today. More are being developed. Many of these organizations and systems are regional in nature but others are expanding beyond geographic borders. Few of these groups and systems have concentrated on sustainable infrastructure. However, this is changing. There is growing interest in developing environmental assessment, rating, and certification systems to encourage and reward improved infrastructure sustainability. Right now only a few rating systems specifically address sustainable

Table 15.6 Sustainability rating system types

Category	
Sponsorship	Public body Private enterprise
Application	Single system for all project types Multiple systems for different project types
Methodology	Self-assessment Third-party validation required
Assessor	No license or accreditation required Licensed or accredited assessor required
Recognition	No awards or certificates Awards or certificates of achievement

infrastructure, such as CEEQUAL and the under-development AGIC. Further, a number of rating systems that were initially developed for individual building assessment are being expanded to include larger-scale projects such as multiple building developments, neighborhoods, and even entire communities and at least part of their infrastructures. Recently the American Public Works Authority (APWA) announced a green scorecard manual for public works projects. Collaborating with organizations such as the American Association of Civil Engineers, the CEEQUAL Assessment and Award Scheme, the International Federation of Consulting Engineers (FDIC), the US Federal Highway Administration, and the US Army Corps of Engineers among others, this green scorecard will be a rating tool for sustainable infrastructure that is applicable to a broad range of public projects.[18]

Sustainability rating systems can be classified in terms of type of sponsorship, rating system applicability, methodology, qualification of assessors, and whether or not an award or certificate is granted for achieving certain levels of sustainability (see Table 15.6).

It is clear that there is great interest in environmental and

sustainable assessment and rating systems for buildings. Owners, designers, and builders all seek recognition for their sustainable achievements. With growing awareness of the environmental impact of infrastructure developments, public bodies, developers, designers, and builders of these types of projects increasingly seek recognition for their sustainability efforts.

PARTIAL LIST OF SUSTAINABLE RATING SYSTEMS AND PRINCIPLES

The following is a partial list of sustainable assessment systems, guidelines, and environmental principles currently available. Although not exhaustive, this list includes frequently encountered sustainability assessment and rating tools as well as those under development.[19]

- AGBR (Australia Greenhouse Building Rating).
- AGIC Rating Scheme (Australian Green Infrastructure Council).
- BCA Green Mark (Singapore).
- BREEAM (Building Research Establishment Environmental Assessment Method).
- BREEAM Canada.
- BREEAM Green Leaf.
- Calabasas LEED.
- CASBEE (Comprehensive Assessment System for Building Environmental Efficiency, Japan).
- Cascadia: the Living Building Challenge.
- CEEQUAL (Civil Engineering Environmental Quality and Assessment).
- CEPAS (Comprehensive Environmental Performance Assessment Scheme).
- Earth Advantage Commercial Buildings (Oregon).
- EEWH (Ecology, Energy Saving, Waste Reduction and Health, Taiwan).
- EkoProfile (Norway).
- Energy Star (US Environmental Protection Agency).

- ESCALE.
- European Committee for Standardization.
- GBTool.
- GEM (Global Environmental Method).
- German Energy Savings Standards.
- GOBAS (Green Olympic Building Assessment System).
- Green Building Rating System (Korea).
- Green Globes.
- Green Globes Canada.
- Green Globes US.
- Green Leaf Eco-Rating Program.
- Green Star Australia.
- Harvard Green Campus Initiative.
- HK Beam (Hong Kong Building Environmental Assessment Method).
- IGBC (India Green Building Council).
- International Organization for Standardization.
- Labs21.
- LEED (Leadership in Energy and Environmental Design).
- LEED Canada.
- LEED India.
- LEED Mexico.
- Model Green Home Building Guidelines (National Association of Home Builders).
- MSGB (the State of Minnesota Sustainable Building Guidelines).
- NABERS (National Australian Built Environmental Rating System).
- Pearl Rating System.
- PGBC (Philippine Green Building Council).
- Practice, Education and Research for Sustainable Infrastructure (PERSI).
- PromisE.
- Protocol ITACA.
- RMI (Rocky Mountain Institute).
- Rocky Mountain Institute Guidelines.
- SBAT (Sustainable Buildings Assessment Tool).
- Scottsdale Green Building Program.
- SPEAR.
- SPiRiT (Sustainable Project Rating Tool).
- TERI Green Rating for Integrated Habitat Assessment.
- TQ Building Assessment System (Total Building Assessment System).
- UNEP SBCI.

US Government initiatives and guidelines

- California Integrated Waste Management Board Green Building Program.
- Collaborative for High Performance Schools (CHPS).
- Database of State Incentives for Renewables and Efficiency.
- Federal Energy Management Program—Greening Initiatives/ Tools.
- Federal Greening Toolkit.
- Field Guide to Sustainable Construction.
- Green Buildings BC.
- Greening Federal Facilities.
- Maryland Environmental Design Program.
- Minnesota Sustainable Design Guide.
- National Renewable Energy Laboratory.
- New Jersey Clean Energy Program.
- New York State Energy Research and Development Authority (NYSERDA).
- New York State Green Building Tax Incentive Initiative.
- OECD Project on Sustainable Buildings.
- Oregon Department of Energy.
- Pennsylvania Buildings—Governor's Green Government Council.
- Performance Contracting Legislation by State.
- US Air Force Environmentally Responsible Facilities Guide.
- US DOE and US EPA—Energy Star program.
- US DOE Building Technologies Program.
- US DOE Energy Efficiency and Renewable Energy (EERE).
- US DOE High-Performance Commercial Buildings: A Technology Roadmap.
- US EPA's Environmentally Preferable Purchasing (EPP).
- US GSA—Great Lakes Region—Build Green.

- US GSA Sustainable Design and LEED.
- US National Park Service—Guiding Principles of Sustainable Design.
- US Naval Facilities Engineering Command—design policy.
- Whole Building Design Guide.

Life cycle analysis and costing products

- ATHENA Sustainable Materials Institute.
- BEES (Building for Environmental and Economic Sustainability) [NIST].
- BuildingGreen.com—Life Cycle Assessment.
- California Life Cycle Cost Assessment Model.
- Cradle to Cradle.
- ENVEST (Environmental Impact Estimating Design Software) [UK BRE].
- GREENGUARD Environmental Institute.
- LCA Center.
- Life Cycle Analysis of Wood Products.
- LISA (LCA in Sustainable Architecture).
- MBDC.
- UNEP SBCI (Sustainable Buildings and Construction Initiative).

Sustainability principles

- Biomimicry Principles.
- The CERES Principles.
- Charter of Rights and Responsibilities for the Environment.
- Deep Ecology Principles.
- The Earth Charter.
- The Five Principles of Ecological Design.
- The Hannover Principles.
- The Houston Principles.
- ICC Charter and ISO 14000.
- International Council of Local Environmental Initiatives.
- The Natural Step.

- The Netherlands National Environmental Policy Plan (NEPP).
- Ontario Round Table on Environment and Ecology (ORTEE).
- Permaculture Principles.
- The Precautionary Principle.
- The Sanborn Principles.
- The Todd Principles of Ecological Design.

NOTES

1   Richard Jennings, Holly Wasilowski, Shelby Doyle, Mary Gourlay, Ann Shi, and Leeta Mohanty wrote this chapter as a part of their work in the Zofnass Program for Infrastructure Sustainability at the Harvard University Graduate School of Design.
2   Excerpted from the CASBEE website. www.ibec.or.jp/CASBEE/english/overviewE.htm/.
3   CASBEE website.
4   CASBEE website.
5   USGBC website: www.usgbc.org.
6   According to the USGBC website: www.usgbc.org/DisplayPage.aspx?CMSPageID=124.
7   USGBC website: www.usgbc.org.
8   USGBC website: www.usgbc.org.
9   See *Principles of Smart Growth* at www.smartgrowth.org; *The Principles of New Urbanism* at the Congress for the New Urbanism at www.cnu.org; and the Natural Resources Defense Council at www.nrdc.org.
10 International Living Building Institute website: www.ilbi.org.
11 Green Globes website. www.greenglobes.com.
12 From the USGBC website: www.usgbc.org/DisplayPage.aspx?CMSPageID=124.
13 BREEAM Communities Scheme Document at www.breeam.org.
14 See the Certification Scheme for BREEAM Communities www.breeam.org.
15 CEEQUAL website: www.ceequal.com.
16 AGIC. *e-Newsletter*. June 2010. www.agic.net.au/agic_newsletter_june_2010.pdf.
17 www.agic.net.au/Tool.htm, accessed June 29, 2011.
18 FIDIC News. "Sustainability infrastructure rating system to be developed." March 3, 2010. www1.fidic.org/news/content.asp?ArticleCode=083Pr&Rubrique=Practice&Date=03/03/10&lang=en.
19 This list was compiled by graduate students Shelby Doyle, Mary Gourlay, Ann Shi, Leeta Mohanty, and Holly Wasilowski as a part of the Zofnass Program for Infrastructure Sustainability at the Harvard University Graduate School of Design.

16

The Zofnass Rating System for Infrastructure Sustainability and Decision Making

ANDREAS GEORGOULIAS AND JILL ALLEN

HARVARD UNIVERSITY GRADUATE SCHOOL OF DESIGN

INTRODUCTION AND OVERVIEW

In recent years, "sustainability" has become a widely used term, and environmental design has become more prevalent and broadly implemented. This trend has been accompanied by a shift in design at the building scale. Environmental design and sustainable buildings have become commonplace, and some cities require new construction to surpass a specified sustainability baseline. Sustainability rating systems such as LEED® have played a significant role in this process, educating citizens, providing a means to quantify sustainability at the building scale, and facilitating the adoption of sustainable design.

Largely missing from these developments, however, has been infrastructure, the base network for cities and buildings. Infrastructure directly and indirectly impacts many aspects of sustainability, and achieving a sustainable future must include developing alternative and renewable options for energy production, reducing consumption of our limited water resources, and finding ways to reduce our dependence on private transport. The need for a closer look at the environmental consequences of infrastructure coincides with a crisis in infrastructure in the USA. American infrastructure is showing signs of aging and is in dire need of modernization, as indicated by the cumulative "D" rating given to the country's infrastructure by the American Society of Civil Engineers during 2009.[1]

The need for modernization is crucial because, without immediate attention, social and economic growth within the States will be constricted. The private sector appears to be positioned to invest in such growth but faces a lack of political and other guidance. A sustainability rating system could help fill this gap, but because of fundamental differences between infrastructure and individual buildings (network characteristics, difficulty of boundary definition, greater resource consumption for construction and operations, longer life cycles, larger scales), existing building rating systems are not applicable to infrastructure projects. An infrastructure-specific sustainability rating system is needed to provide a means to quantify sustainability for infrastructure projects and facilitate the adoption of sustainable practices and technologies.

This chapter focuses on the development of the Zofnass Rating System for Sustainable Infrastructure. The chapter begins with a brief history of the Zofnass Program and description of its research method. This is followed by a summary of the early academic literature that focused on infrastructure sustainability frameworks. Next, the overall Zofnass Rating System framework is described, followed by a snapshot of the rating system today. This section describes the framework's four system categories—Resource Allocation, Natural World, Climate Change, and Quality of Life—in more detail and gives preliminary lists of the credits for each category. After that, existing economic and environmental assessment tools are surveyed for their potential to be incorporated within the Zofnass Rating System framework. The chapter concludes by explaining the next steps and ongoing challenges facing the Zofnass Rating System for Sustainable Infrastructure.

ZOFNASS PROGRAM HISTORY AND RESEARCH METHOD

With a great awareness of the need for research on sustainable infrastructure, Paul and Joan Zofnass made a generous donation to Harvard University's Graduate School of Design. The Zofnass Program for Sustainable Infrastructure was founded in 2008 as a result of their gift. The Program extends its activities to several other schools of Harvard, including Public Health, Government, Business, and the Center for the Environment. The Zofnass Program follows an applied-research approach and conducts research through a combination of quantitative and qualitative methods. Instead of conducting basic research, the Zofnass Program follows an applied, hybrid approach that better reflects the complexity and interconnectedness of the variety of systems under study, providing original contributions on theory and practice of sustainability at the city and infrastructure levels. Through field research, the Zofnass Program collects and analyzes data about system performance, technology application, user behavior, and costing and operations. Research findings are presented through case studies, reports, and comparative analyses, and knowledge produced is disseminated through conferences, publications, graduate-level courses, and workshops. Although the Zofnass Program has produced several reports, papers, and case studies, the core outcome of the Program is the Zofnass Rating System for Sustainable Infrastructure.

LITERATURE REVIEW:
SUSTAINABILITY AND INFRASTRUCTURE

The research process of the Zofnass Rating System began with a literature review. The goals of this early research were to develop an understanding of the relationship between sustainability and infrastructure, and more importantly to begin to think about how to structure a rating system for sustainable infrastructure. Topics researched included: general models of sustainability, sustainability definitions, infrastructure sustainability, and climate change and infrastructure.

Several papers address general models or frameworks for defining sustainability. Vanegas[2] finds that sustainability is comprised of five interrelated subsectors: people, industrial base, resource base, natural environment, and built environment. These elements are part of a larger system that includes spatial scale, temporal scale, economic and financial systems, environmental systems, and ecological systems. The BEQUEST (Building Environmental Quality Evaluation for Sustainability through Time) system finds four underlying sustainable development principles: minimal damage to the environment, equity among the stakeholders, participation of as much of the society as possible, and a concern for future generations (both human and natural).[3] Similarly, the Bossel report discusses the many dimensions of sustainability: environmental, material, ecological, social, economic, legal, cultural, political, and psychological.[4] All these papers share similar ideas with the generally accepted breakdown of sustainability into three categories: economic, social, and environmental. Their definition of sustainable development also expresses the interconnected nature of these three areas; to them a sustainable idea leads to an "economically feasible, socially viable, and environmentally responsible project outcome."

The relationship between sustainability and infrastructure is clarified by Vanegas, who says ideas about sustainability must

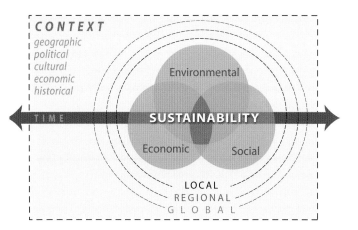

16.1 The three dimensions of sustainability through context and time

be examined in regard to three aspects of infrastructure: what it does (products, goods, and services), how it does it (operations, procedures, and practices), and with what (natural resources required). These general models are useful for two main reasons. Ugwu refers to the potential of models to promote alternates to conventional practices (which tend to encourage unsustainable means) by providing a method to translate sustainable objectives into action.[5] On the other hand, Dasgupta and Tam[6] find that a model can present a hierarchical system, which can offer a useful means of deciding among alternatives. In their method, mandatory screening indicators (regulatory and project specific) and judgment indicators (environmental and technical) are used in succession to decide between alternatives.

Models also allow the development of key performance indicators. These indicators are crucial to translating sustainability concepts into concrete objectives at the project scale. Ugwu and Haupt[7] find that a large gap currently exists between theory and practice, and posit that this gap exists because of stakeholders' education (not focused on sustainability concepts), a short-term focus rather than long-term focus when making decisions, and a lack of flexible, user-friendly tools to facilitate quantitative analysis and decision making. Subsequently, Ugwu and Haupt present a method for translating categories of sustainability into a weighted system of indicators. After dividing sustainability into six main categories and approximately thirty subcategories, they mailed this list to different groups (including architects, engineers, "the public") and asked respondents to rank the importance of each item to "sustainability" on a scale of 1 to 5. Ugwu and Haupt found that nearly all of the items were significant aspects of sustainability, as each regularly scored greater than a 4 on their scale. Societal aspects of sustainability, however, tended to receive slightly lower rankings by all groups (with the exception of "public sector" respondents).

The results of the survey provided a means of assigning a weight to each indicator, where higher weights reflected greater perceived importance to a sustainable outcome. It has to be added that the survey approach gains support from stakeholders for the system, since it is based on their thinking, but that it potentially suffers from a lack of a scientific basis, especially if survey respondents are not well educated about sustainability. This suggests a tradeoff between consensus and science, similar to what rating systems in the USA, such as LEED, might suffer from. A second method for creating indicators is described by Sahely et al., who use a quantitative time series approach. In this process, indicators are chosen and satisfactory ranges for each item are defined. Next, data is collected for each indicator over time and expressed as a time series, which is analyzed using statistical measures. The model then allows users to calculate the relative sustainability of a system using weighted criteria.[8]

Another group of papers deals with the issue of infrastructure provision, mainly focusing on developing countries. Panayotou[9] believes that the private sector is an important provider of infrastructure in developing countries. He points out inherent structural differences between buildings and infrastructure, and finds that these differences tend to create problems. These problems are exacerbated when infrastructure is provided by the public sector, because it tends to be inefficient and costly. Vives[10] picks up on this same idea and argues for private provision of infrastructure. His paper examines specifically the recent surge of private provision of infrastructure in developing countries, investigating whether this increase signals a fundamental shift in the way infrastructure is provided or is simply a passing fad. These issues and concepts will become very important when

considering the user groups of an infrastructure sustainability rating system and who the primary decision maker in applying such an assessment tool would be.

Finally, the "social" aspect is very important in defining sustainability. The "Report of the World Summit" in 2002 resulted from an international conference organized by the United Nations in Johannesburg and provided insight about political interpretations of sustainability.[11] In this report, sustainability is described in broad terms and focuses on non-contentious issues in order to gain international support. The report focuses on three basic goals (each with measurable, more detailed subgoals): eradicate poverty (improve human health), change unsustainable patterns of consumption and production, and protect and manage the natural resource base of economic and social development.

TOWARDS THE ZOFNASS FRAMEWORK FOR INFRASTRUCTURE SUSTAINABILITY ASSESSMENT

Having studied the existing literature, the Zofnass Program research team followed two paths in seeking to delineate a framework for assessing sustainability. First, we followed a "grounded research" approach, developing a preliminary sustainability assessment framework through research, meetings, and focus group workshops with expert faculty from Harvard and with select firms from the engineering industry. We identified four main categories to encompass sustainability: Resource Allocation, Climate Change, Natural World, and Quality of Life. We then identified principal issues or topics for consideration within each category; we debated their applicability to infrastructure through several focus groups with academic and industry participants over several months. We concluded by proposing a set of credits that would cover the most crucial issues for environmental sustainability as it applies to infrastructure projects.

In parallel, we studied existing sustainability rating systems for building projects. It should be noted at this point that our research was not able to identify any rating system specifically for infrastructure projects. After the identification of more than 100 existing rating systems and methods for building projects, we decided to study six in detail: BREEAM, CASBEE, Cascadia, CEEQUAL, Green Globes™, and LEED (in alphabetic order). Through detailed analysis of credit definition and scope, measurement methods employed, and issues covered or left out, we learned a great deal about how our metrics should be positioned. We noticed that each rating system did not have an entirely unique set of credits; although no two systems were identical, some credits appeared in similar forms in multiple systems.

The major choice facing the team at this point was whether to create a different rating system for each type of infrastructure or to design an overarching framework of categories that could be used to rank the sustainability of all types of infrastructure. We chose the latter approach after discussions with engineers and faculty. The overall framework approach would provide a common basis for comparing sustainability across infrastructure types and would recognize the synergies that exist between various types. Integrated infrastructures (for example landfill gas to energy, or transportation combined with stormwater management) often create opportunities for sustainable behavior, and the second approach would provide a more holistic measurement of a project's sustainability than if each infrastructure type was assessed independently.

Infrastructure systems

As the Zofnass Rating System focuses on infrastructure projects, we aimed to create a rating system that would address their specific characteristics. We started by drafting our own definition of infrastructure. Infrastructure is a broadly and sometimes loosely defined term, and we wanted a working definition to help us create a rating system that would be inherently different from building rating systems. Definitions from major organizations and institutions provided a starting point.

The US Environmental Protection Agency (EPA) definition falls more on the technical and project side. According to the EPA,[12]

> The term infrastructure refers to the substructure or underlying foundation or network used for providing goods and services;

especially the basic installations and facilities on which the continuance and growth of a community or state depends. Examples include roads, water systems, communications facilities, sewers, sidewalks, cable, wiring, schools, power plants, and transportation and communication systems.

On the other hand, the World Bank definition is closer to a systems and outcome approach. The World Bank[13] calls infrastructure the "sectors including energy, information and communications; mining, transportation, urban development, and water supply and sanitation, but education, health, and other social services, as well as finance, public administration, and law, are treated separately."

As part of our research approach, we asked faculty and industry representatives which of these definitions is closer to their understanding of infrastructure and which definition could help us achieve our mission. The feedback we received was divided amongst the two, so we had to pick a middle ground. Our working definition of infrastructure is *the set of fundamental physical systems, services, and networks that support the built environment and protect the natural world and are essential to sustaining a civilized and productive society.*

Within that definition, we had to identify the principal infrastructure categories or types that we would focus our rating system on. We started with a typical civil engineering classification, looking at energy, water, waste, transportation, landscape, and information infrastructures. Within each type we listed the various systems and technologies that exist. Figure 16.2 illustrates the concept.

A key component of our analysis immediately emerged. Through our workshops it became apparent that synergies and overlays of infrastructure systems had a significant potential contribution to sustainability. It was not enough to study and optimize a given infrastructure within its typological confines; the analysis had to expand in a multi-layered approach in which infrastructure systems would be grouped based on their synergistic potentials. As such, we started by separating energy systems in power generation and distribution. Then we combined energy, water, and waste due to their similar storage and distribution needs, as well as their input–output relationships (waste-to-energy, hydropower, wastewater treatment facilities, etc.). In a similar fashion, *landscape and transportation*

ENERGY	WATER	WASTE	TRANSPOR-TATION	LANDSCAPE	INFORMATION
geothermal	potable water distribution	solid waste	airport	public realm	telecommunications
hydroelectric	capture and storage	recycling	roads/highways	parks	internet /phone
nuclear	water reuse	hazardous waste	bike/pedestrian	ecosystem services	satellites
coal	stormwater management	collection and transfer	railways	other	data centers
natural gas	flood control	other	public transit		sensors
oil/refinery	other		ports		other
wind			waterways		
solar			other		
biomass					
other					

16.2 Infrastructure categories

| ENERGY | WATER | WASTE | TRANSPORTATION | LANDSCAPE | INFORMATION |

Integrate water and waste into energy due to their interconnected nature and their transmission and storage needs. Consider landscape and transportation as interrelated due to their land use planning needs

16.3 Synergies between infrastructure systems

were grouped together due to their significant requirements for land. Figure 16.3 depicts an initial grouping of infrastructure types. Of course this is not the only way to classify infrastructure types, and future developments in technology will most certainly suggest novel and more efficient groupings.

Our last infrastructure type, information, was viewed as the system that overlays on all other types. Our view was, and still is, that information is the new utility and that its collection, distribution, and management will enable more sustainable features, elements, and operations within all other infrastructure types.

Through our workshops, a recurring discussion topic was the very nature of infrastructure as a network. Several participants agreed

that this is one of the primary differentiators between infrastructure and building projects. A building project can be easily defined by its walls and site boundaries. For infrastructure such limits are very difficult to identify. The network nature of infrastructure creates an inherent boundary definition problem. Where does it start and where does it end? What are the project boundaries? The issue gets more complicated when assessing the impacts of an infrastructure project. Different characteristics, attributes, and outcomes of an infrastructure project will have a different zone of influence on the environment.

To face this challenge, we classified infrastructure projects by their spatial and geometric characteristics. We identified infrastructure

Geometry	Diagram	Example
Point		independent facility
Line		single road
Network		road network
Point + Network		power plant and distribution grid
Polygon		airport

16.4 Defining the boundary of infrastructure projects

16.5 Boundary of infrastructure effects

systems that are indeed networks. A street grid, a water distribution system, and a power transmission grid are good examples. However, other infrastructure systems are spatially confined in a site and their boundary is much clearer: an airport, a seaport, and a power generation facility are good examples in this category. And some infrastructure types may come very close to a point on a map, such as the antennas of telecommunication infrastructure. Of course, several systems are a combination of these classification types, containing a network with points and nodes. Figure 16.4 illustrates the concept.

The impact of infrastructure systems on the environment becomes easier to assess by utilizing this spatial/geometric classification.

Zones of influence for each infrastructure element are derived from their spatial type (network, area, or point) and the relationship between the elements of each infrastructure type. Then the characteristics of the environment, such as sensitivity to stimuli, degree of bio-connectivity, etc., define zones of influence in another way. An overlay of the two generates the final boundary for each infrastructure type, as shown in Figure 16.5.

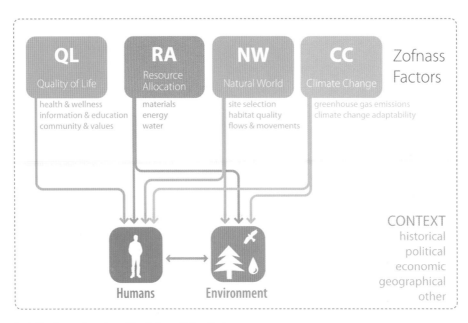

16.6 The four categories of the Zofnass Rating System

Zofnass Rating System framework overview

The Zofnass Rating System is organized around a series of distinct *categories*. The four Zofnass categories—Resource Allocation, Natural World, Climate Change, and Quality of Life—reflect the specific impacts of infrastructure on the environment and the local community.

Within these categories, separate credits are listed. *Credits* include items such as "reducing carbon emissions" and "using recyclable materials." *Points* are then awarded based on project design and performance for each credit. *Certification* is awarded based on the total number of points earned.

The Zofnass Rating System strives to provide an overarching framework to quantify sustainability for all infrastructure types, from power plants and transmission lines to landfills and sidewalks. Specific credit items and point allocation will vary, however, depending on the infrastructure type. Because of the inherent differences between the diverse categories of infrastructure, the Zofnass Rating System will ultimately be tailored specifically to each individual infrastructure type.

Sustainability issues emerge at many points during the life cycle of infrastructure, and the Zofnass Program addresses the factor of *time* within the rating system framework. This is important because infrastructure projects take longer to plan, design, and construct than individual buildings, because of their longer life cycles and

larger areas. Infrastructure is also built to last longer and cover an ever-expanding set of human needs. Existing building-level rating systems tend to focus on design decisions and calculations, but every phase of an infrastructure project has crucial impacts on sustainability. Including time within the Zofnass Rating System is crucial to ensure that all impacts are measured. To take time into account, the Zofnass Rating System divides credits into relevant phases. A separate assessment stage is provided for the four major phases of a project: planning/design, construction, operations, and decommissioning.

One credit may apply in different ways during different phases. For instance, carbon emissions during the design phase from consultant travel can differ a lot in scale and impact from emissions during the construction phase from bulldozers and trucks, or from emissions during operations from day-to-day processes. Including time within the system is crucial to capture each of these impacts over the entire life cycle of an infrastructure project.

Because of the varying duration of each phase, the Zofnass Rating System will certify each phase separately. This method is preferable for two main reasons. First, speed of assessment and time to get a certification is important: a project's operation phase may be crucial to sustainability, but waiting to issue certification until a project is complete and operating undermines some of the motivation behind the certification process. Similarly, waiting until a project is decommissioned to award certification would take

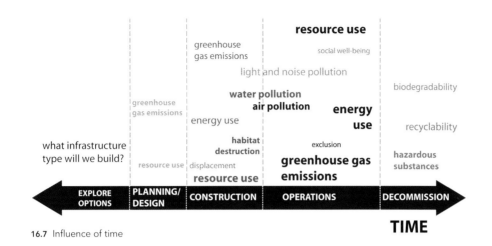

16.7 Influence of time

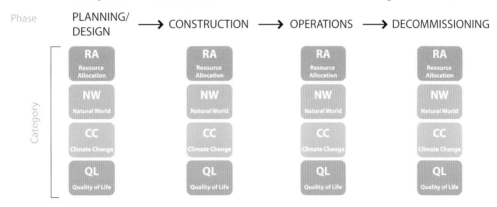

16.8 The Zofnass Rating System through the different project delivery stages of infrastructure

much, much longer. Owners may wish to achieve a high rating to demonstrate a sustainable vision to financiers, so a rating could be needed before construction starts. A rating system that stops when construction ends, however, would not fully capture the impact of a project on the environment. Certifying each phase separately resolves these issues. Second, assessing operations independently allows for existing infrastructure facilities and networks to be eligible for certification. This expands our system to include both new and existing infrastructure.

Certifying phases separately also allows for *different user groups* to become involved with the system. During design and planning,

the engineering firm will be primarily responsible for undertaking certification, and this accountability will shift to the contractor and operator in later phases. These groups will report infrastructure design decisions and performance measurements, which will then be verified and evaluated by an independent, third-party rating system assessor. The concept is illustrated in Figure 16.9.

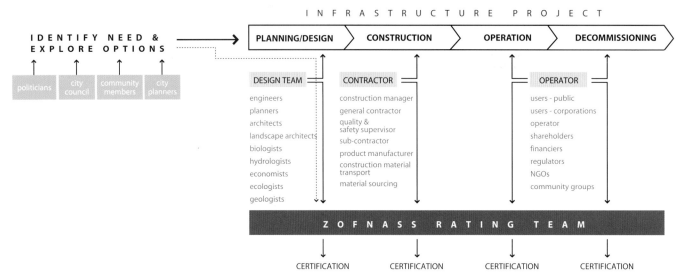

16.9 Stakeholders of the assessment process

How the Zofnass System works

Credits and points

Each credit is worth a set number of points that varies depending on the importance or impact of what the credit assesses, and also on the type of assessment: qualitative, quantitative, or yes/no. Points are awarded based on sustainable performance or prescriptive intent, and more points equate to a more sustainable outcome. For quantitative credits (such as reduction of carbon emissions or energy use), relative performance of similar infrastructure projects provides a method of assigning points. Specifically, projects are awarded points on a scale of 1 to 5. One point would be offered for meeting a baseline value, relative to comparable infrastructure projects. If the project met or exceeded the top quartile of all similar infrastructure projects, additional points would be awarded. Performing better than all other comparable projects would receive additional points, but even attaining commonly held "ideal goals" (carbon neutral, net zero waste, etc.) would not be sufficient to attain maximum points. The highest points would be reserved for projects that did more than simply have "no" effect on their surroundings. To receive 5 points on a given

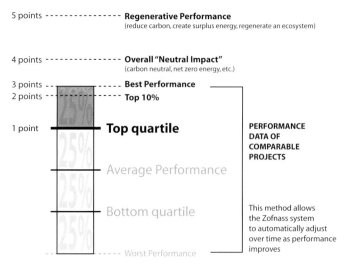

16.10 Credit allocation

credit, a project would actually need to enhance its environment (by absorbing excess atmospheric carbon, for example). This system would additionally have the advantage of automatically adapting over time as industry performance improves; being in the top quartile of projects would require increasingly better performance.

This method of assigning points is limited in two ways. First, the long life cycle of many infrastructure projects complicates the assessment process. At what moment should a project be compared to a baseline defined by comparable projects? Would the comparison be prescriptive, and based upon projected performance during the design phase, or would it require demonstrated performance after construction? Adapting over time is a desirable quality, but if benchmark standards were continually changing, it would be difficult for project teams to know what goals to set (particularly if the team aimed for a given number during the design process but comparison did not happen until the operation phase, when performance could be verified). Second, this type of relative performance system is best suited for quantifiable metrics with a given value range. Credits that are qualitative or binary (yes/no) would be difficult to address in the same way.

Weights

After points are awarded, they are adjusted based on a given set of weights. Figure 16.11 illustrates the concept. Local/regional context is the first driver of weights. Differences between locations and regions result in different sustainability impacts, so it is important for the Zofnass System to be adaptable. For instance, minimizing potable water consumption is important for all areas of the US but could be critical for Western states. Any credit relating to water use will be given increased weight in these dry areas.

Objective standards are a second driver of weights where scientifically feasible. This method would be most relevant to pollutant-related credits and could take into account commonly accepted thresholds for human or wildlife harm, or chemical potency. For example, greenhouse gas emission describes the relative impacts of a gas relative to carbon dioxide on climate change: carbon

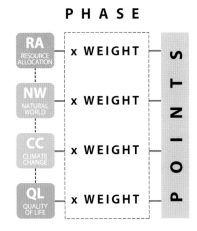

PHASE

16.11 Applying weights to the four Zofnass categories

dioxide has a global warming potential of 1, whereas methane has a global warming potential of 23.[14] This measurement means that if equal amounts of carbon dioxide and methane are released into the atmosphere, the methane will contribute 23 times more to global warming than will the carbon dioxide.

Other possible weighting mechanisms include stakeholder input to allow a local community to define what is important to them, and infrastructure types and scales, where certain credits would be more important to a given infrastructure type, or above a given project size. In all of these cases, allowing for local adaptability and customization comes at the expense of global comparability and standardization.

Explore options

As the Zofnass System expanded to include all phases of an infrastructure project, we realized that some of the very earliest decisions about a project can be crucial to sustainability. Infrastructure projects arise out of a perceived need, but what if this need could be addressed more effectively, efficiently, or sustainably in a different way? We named this phase *"explore options"* to recognize that a given need may be matched by many different solutions. Explore options precedes planning/design in the Zofnass framework. Instead

203

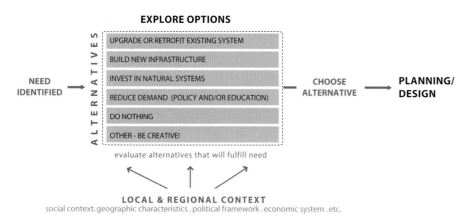

EXPLORE OPTIONS

ALTERNATIVES

- UPGRADE OR RETROFIT EXISTING SYSTEM
- BUILD NEW INFRASTRUCTURE
- INVEST IN NATURAL SYSTEMS
- REDUCE DEMAND (POLICY AND/OR EDUCATION)
- DO NOTHING
- OTHER - BE CREATIVE!

NEED IDENTIFIED →

CHOOSE ALTERNATIVE →

PLANNING/ DESIGN

evaluate alternatives that will fulfill need

LOCAL & REGIONAL CONTEXT
social context. geographic characteristics . political framework . economic system . etc.

16.12 The explore options phase

of a new infrastructure project, alternatives could include upgrading an existing system or solutions that don't involve construction, such as policy changes or public education. Examining and evaluating different alternatives is crucial to ensure that the most sustainable option is selected. For example, the "greenest" new power plant is not sustainable if it is not necessary. Figure 16.12 depicts the explore options assessment phase.

To illustrate the concept, let's take the hypothetical example of unacceptable congestion levels on a local highway. What can be done to alleviate the congestion? And how would the explore options phase help the community make a decision? First, available options should be identified. In this case, there are several alternatives, some involving significant construction and others employing non-structural solutions. Lanes could be added to the existing road, or a completely new road could be built. Perhaps charging a toll could help alleviate congestion. If the road has a wide median, a rapid-transit bus system could be constructed in it. On the other hand, a public education campaign could encourage community members to bike and walk more. Or congestion may be reduced in the future by more careful land use planning. With many options to choose from, the question becomes: which one of these alternatives is the most sustainable for this particular community?

To answer this question, the community should evaluate each option in terms of how effectively it will address the given need and what the impacts would be, both negative and positive. Perhaps, after weighing all their options, the community might decide that adding a rapid-transit bus system in the median will reduce congestion, as well as greenhouse gas emissions, by removing vehicles from the road.

Although explore options has potentially the greatest impact on overall project sustainability, its assessment has proven contentious because of the varied stakeholder groups who are influential during its

duration. Specifically, the influence of politics and political motivation has caused concern. For these reasons, explore options will provide a recommended procedural framework, which will include guidelines for performing the analysis of the phase and a set of alternatives that should be considered. These alternatives will include (but will not be limited to): upgrade/retrofit existing system, build new infrastructure, invest in natural systems, reduce demand (utilizing policy and/or education measures), and do nothing. Users will be encouraged to explore other options as well. Specifying broad categories of alternatives ensures that a range of options is considered and helps to educate users, owners, politicians, and communities about cutting-edge technologies and ecological solutions.

Explore options will be a prerequisite for planning/design certification only. Credit for completing it will be awarded as long as the procedures laid out by the Zofnass Program are followed, and it will not evaluate whether the "best" decision was made. This process will be very similar to the environmental impact statement which is already required for federal or federally funded projects, and is also a procedural rather than substantive requirement.

A SNAPSHOT OF THE ZOFNASS SYSTEM TODAY

The Zofnass Rating System for Sustainable Infrastructure has undergone several revisions since the program started in 2008. Figure 16.13 illustrates the rating system as it now stands (February 2011). Additional revisions are likely as work on the system is ongoing.

Infrastructure impacts the local environment and community in multiple ways. The Zofnass Rating System classifies these impacts into four major categories. *Resource Allocation* deals with the materials and resources consumed by the infrastructure (during construction

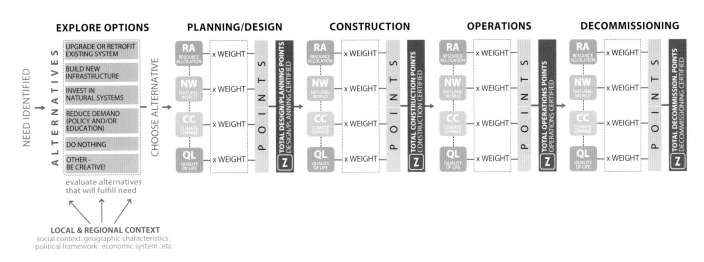

16.13 The Zofnass Rating System

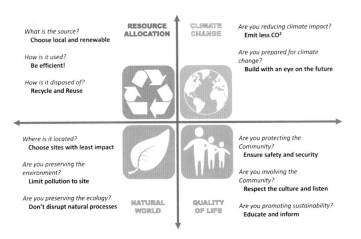

16.14 The four main categories of the Zofnass Rating System and the principal questions they answer to

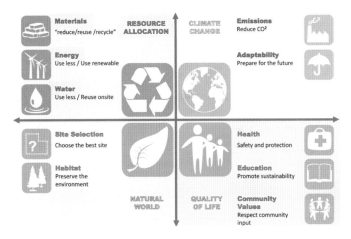

16.15 The four main categories and subcategories of the Zofnass Rating System

and operations). *Climate Change* focuses on mitigating climate change by reducing greenhouse gas emissions and adapting to climate change. *Natural World* addresses the impacts an infrastructure project has on its site and nearby areas (due to site selection, construction practices, or operational processes). *Quality of Life* looks at how the infrastructure project interacts with the local community. Resource Allocation, Climate Change, and Natural World deal with environmental sustainability; credits within Quality of Life address aspects of social and economic sustainability. Figures 16.14 and 16.15 show the four main categories of the Zofnass Rating System, the key questions that they cover, and their respective subcategories.

Resource Allocation

Resource Allocation is the first category of the Zofnass Rating System. The general objective of this category is the optimal allocation of resources, the one that has the least impact on the current environment and maximizes the potential of future generations to have access to the resources they will need. Resource Allocation deals with the use of materials, water, and energy from infrastructure projects. This category encourages the efficient use of materials, water, and energy that are obtained from renewable resources, contribute to a long-lasting and durable operation, and are non-toxic to people and the environment.

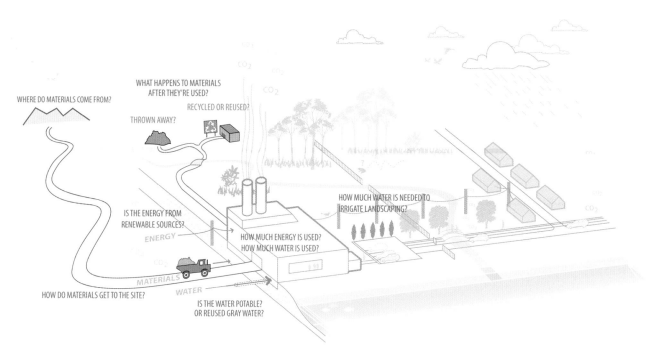

WHERE DO MATERIALS COME FROM?

WHAT HAPPENS TO MATERIALS
AFTER THEY'RE USED?

RECYCLED OR REUSED?

THROWN AWAY?

IS THE ENERGY FROM
RENEWABLE SOURCES?

ENERGY

HOW MUCH WATER IS NEEDED TO
IRRIGATE LANDSCAPING?

HOW MUCH ENERGY IS USED?
HOW MUCH WATER IS USED?

MATERIALS

WATER

HOW DO MATERIALS GET TO THE SITE?

IS THE WATER POTABLE?
OR REUSED GRAY WATER?

16.16 Schematic representation of the issues addressed by the Resource Allocation category

The Resource Allocation category deals with several issues. Figure 16.16 illustrates the concept. Minimizing the total amount of material used should be a prime consideration for infrastructure projects. Reducing the total size of a facility will decrease the total amount of resources needed to construct the project. Reducing material use must be balanced with safety, stability, and durability. Reducing overall energy and water use is similarly crucial. However, while reducing total consumption is vital, it is also imperative to consider the source of all materials, energy, and water. Materials obtained from far away should not be used if the same type and quality of material are available locally. Using power from non-fossil fuel sources is favored, and reducing potable water use is important as well. Two projects that both require 1 MW of electricity to operate are not equal if one project obtains its electricity from hydropower and another from a coal power plant.

Regardless of the amount of material used and its source, some materials are simply worse for humans and the environment than others. This fact is also important for the Resource Allocation category. The most toxic and polluting materials are prohibited by the Zofnass System, and other materials that have a negative impact on the environment over their life cycle are discouraged. Overall environmental impact includes effects from extraction, manufacturing, use, disposal, and other phases of a material's life cycle. Life Cycle Assessment (LCA) provides a useful framework

for analyzing the cumulative impact of a product/material on the environment, but its use is limited currently by a lack of available data. When more data is available and the evaluation process is more standardized, this tool will provide a streamlined method for comparing the environmental impact of different materials/products. Other characteristics of materials that make them more favorable for use include having a higher percentage of recycled or reused content, the ability to be recycled/reused at end of life cycle, durability, and adaptability.

Continuing to maintain, repair, and upgrade infrastructure over time is important to ensure efficiency and optimal performance. Monitoring performance and making adjustments when needed helps minimize material, energy, and water use over the life cycle of the infrastructure project.

The Resource Allocation category is divided into three subcategories: Materials, Energy, and Water. Each of the subcategories includes a set of quantifiable metrics. Table 16.1 lists the credits of the Resource Allocation category.

During the industry peer review process, concerns have been raised about the potential overlaps between this section and Climate Change, especially with regard to measurement of carbon emissions. Energy use is examined in both Resource Allocation and Climate Change categories, but Resource Allocation focuses on the quantity of energy and its source, whereas Climate Change measures the

Table 16.1 The Resource Allocation category credits

Credit name	Intent	Metric
R1: Materials		
R1.1: Reuse materials	Reuse materials and products in order to reduce material extraction and waste	Percentage of reused content by weight or volume
R1.2: Use less materials	Reduce overall material consumption of project	Percentage of reduction over business as usual case
R1.3: Use durable materials	Develop and implement a comprehensive long-term strategy and plan of action for material maintenance and durability	Plan (yes/no). Scale ranking thoroughness and rigor of the plan
R1.4: Use recycled materials	Use recycled materials and products in order to reduce material extraction and waste	Percentage of recycled content by weight or volume
R1.5: Use regional materials	Utilize materials that are extracted, manufactured, or grown within a specific distance from the project	Percentage of material by volume/weight, coming from a specific distance
R1.6: Use sustainably certified materials	Utilize materials from a certified source and purchase from a supplier utilizing sustainable practices	Percentage of material by weight or volume from accepted certified sources
R1.7: Manage construction waste	Implement best-management practices to sort waste and divert from landfills	Percentage of construction waste diverted from landfills
R1.8: Innovate or exceed credit requirements	Implement innovative sustainable practices on the allocation of material resources in project	Achieves exemplary performance or employs innovative solutions
R2: Energy		
R2.1: Reduce energy use	Reduce overall energy consumption of project	Percentage of reduction over a business as usual case
R2.2: Use renewable energy	Meet energy needs through renewable energy sources on site	Percentage of total energy use from renewable sources
R2.3: Commission electrical/mechanical systems	Commission energy systems to ensure efficient functioning and extend their useful life	Third-party commissioning (yes/no)
R2.4: Monitor energy performance	Implement means to monitor energy performance during operations	Documentation of system in the design and validated after construction
R2.5: Innovate or exceed credit requirements	Implement innovative sustainable practices on the allocation of energy resources in project	Achieves exemplary performance or employs innovative solutions
R3: Water		
R3.1: Reduce water use	Reduce overall water consumption, particularly potable water consumption	Percentage of reduction over a business as usual case
R3.2: Reuse water on-site	Reuse graywater on-site or treat wastewater on-site for reuse	Percentage of water use from graywater
R3.3: Utilize water-efficient landscaping	Provide water-efficient landscape design through plant selection, irrigation technologies, management, and the use of recycled water	Percentage of reduction from a midsummer baseline case
R3.4: Commission water systems	Commission water systems to ensure efficient functioning and extend their useful life	Third-party commissioning (yes/no)
R3.5: Monitor water system performance	Implement means to monitor water performance during operations	Documentation of system in the design and validated after construction
R3.6: Innovate or exceed credit requirements	Implement innovative sustainable practices on the allocation of water resources in project	Achieves exemplary performance or employs innovative solutions

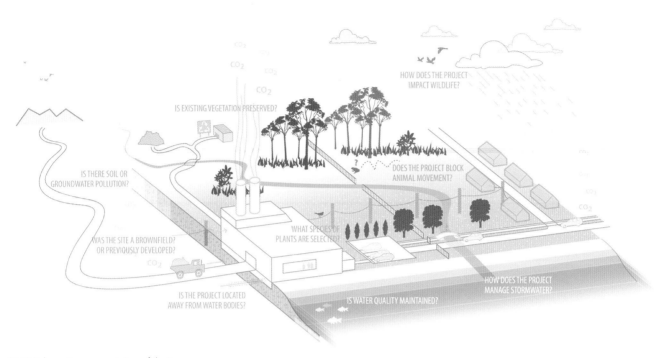

16.17 Schematic representation of the issues
addressed by the Natural World category

emissions generated by its use. Another ongoing question is whether other factors should be considered "resources" and, therefore, part of the Resource Allocation category. Labor and technology were initially included in this category but were later omitted due to difficulties in quantifying their impacts on sustainability (which is a more sustainable approach: using more technology or using more people?). One industry member felt "financial resources" belonged in this category, but we have decided to have "cost" as a parallel assessment to the four categories of the Zofnass System framework, as it will be described later on.

Natural World

Natural World is the second category of the Zofnass Rating System. The general scope of this category is to preserve and enhance the ecological systems that sustain life. The Natural World category focuses on the impact of infrastructure projects on local/regional ecosystems and plant/animal life. Infrastructure should promote the rejuvenation of degraded ecosystems, minimize fragmentation and disruptions to ecosystems that provide habitat and support biodiversity, and employ strategies of conservation that engage hazard avoidance and mitigation. Landscape ecology can provide a valuable framework for analyzing the spatial impacts of an infrastructure

project on the environment in this category. Infrastructure affects the natural world due to its site selection, operating processes, and impact on its surroundings (for example, roads may catalyze future suburbanization along them).

Site selection is crucial for infrastructure projects, which may impact vast geographic areas. Figure 16.17 illustrates the concept. Infrastructure projects should avoid disturbing wetlands or temporary waters (vernal pools, etc.) because these sensitive areas perform important ecosystem services and provide critical habitat for many plant and animal species. Parks, national forests, and other protected areas should be avoided as well. Other local areas or features may play important functions in local ecosystems but may not necessarily be protected by laws or regulations. Infrastructure project teams should work with a local biologist or ecologist to identify areas that are of ecological significance. For example, a section of old-growth forest with a unique combination of plant species may provide significant habitat for wildlife, and infrastructure site selection should avoid this area. The remediation of brownfield sites, sites previously contaminated by industrial or commercial uses, helps the local environment and as such is encouraged by the Zofnass Rating System.

The impacts of infrastructure may extend beyond its physical boundaries, and site selection should take this into account. Even if a project does not physically touch an area, care should be taken

Table 16.2   The Natural World category credits

Credit name	Intent	Metric
NW1: Site selection		
NW1.1: Prepare site assessment	Conduct a comprehensive site assessment of the project site	Thoroughness and rigor of assessment in all relevant categories
NW1.2: Mitigate site impact	Develop and implement a comprehensive site impact mitigation plan	Subjective evaluation of extent to which impacts have been mitigated
NW1.3: Protect wetlands and water bodies	Prevent or mitigate the effects of development in or around wetlands and water bodies	Location of site on or within standards for proximity to wetlands (yes/no)
NW1.4: Conserve prime habitat	Minimize impacts to parks, national forests, and other protected areas outside of site	Percentage of site deemed prime habitat
NW1.5: Maximize use of developed sites	Encourage density and protect habitat by selecting previously developed sites	Percentage of site previously developed
NW1.6: Maximize use of contaminated sites	Select and remediate a site that has been environmentally contaminated or designated as a brownfield	Percentage of site designated as brownfield
NW1.7: Innovate or exceed credit requirements	Implement innovative sustainable practices on site selection of project	Achieves exemplary performance or employs innovative solutions
NW2: Habitat		
NW2.1: Assess regional habitats and watersheds	Implement a comprehensive regional assessment to determine impacts beyond the site boundaries including animal movements and watershed quality	Conduct study with a qualified environmental professional (yes/no)
NW2.2: Preserve/protect habitat connectivity	Mitigate the impact of habitat encroachment by providing means for local fauna to access pre-development habitat and prevent the subdivision of natural habitats and promote habitat preservation and consolidation	Percentage of site retained as contiguous habitat and meeting standards set for animal access points
NW2.3: Prevent soil contamination	Prevent the introduction of contaminants into the ground soil	Implement best practices to prevent soil contamination
NW2.4: Use appropriate vegetation	Limit the introduction of non-native and invasive species, minimize artificial landscapes, and encourage the restoration of natural habitats	Documentation of appropriate vegetation (yes/no)
NW2.5: Preserve natural waterways	Preserve the natural flow of hydrologic systems	Project does not in any way impact local water flows
NW2.6: Protect water quality	Minimize damage to, and contamination of, water sources and aquatic ecosystems	Percentage of effluent reduction over a business as usual case
NW2.7: Utilize stormwater best practices	Develop and implement a stormwater management plan that addresses peak and average rainfall on site	Do not exceed current stormwater velocity or contaminant levels
NW2.8: Maximize pervious surfaces	Reduce the use of surface covering materials, including paving, of low permeability and the total amount of impervious surfaces on site	Percentage of site that is pervious including green roofs
NW2.9: Balance earthwork	Reduce pollution and site disruption caused by transporting soil off-site	Percentage of disturbed soil retained on-site
NW2.10: Minimize site damage	Develop and implement a comprehensive Construction Management Plan to minimize environmental impacts during construction	Thoroughness and rigor of construction impact plan and documentation of site ecology
NW2.11: Innovate or exceed credit requirements	Implement innovative sustainable practices on habitat quality affected by project	Achieves exemplary performance or employs innovative solutions

to ensure that the infrastructure will not harm the feature or area in other ways. For example, grading necessary to construct a road could alter water flows and disrupt the hydrology of water bodies. Similarly, a power plant near a state park could negatively impact the air quality within the park. Infrastructure should be sited to avoid direct and indirect impacts on important ecological areas. If avoiding sensitive areas is not possible, mitigation measures should be taken. The sites selected for mitigation or the new features created should be of comparable quality to those that were impacted by the infrastructure. The location and quality of mitigation areas is critical, and infrastructure teams should work with local biologists, ecologists, and planners to determine the best location for new conservation land.

Habitat quality includes the quality of air, soil, groundwater, surface water, and vegetation. Infrastructure projects should eliminate or minimize pollutants and emissions that degrade these elements. Noise, light, and air pollution can adversely impact wildlife and should be minimized or eliminated. Infrastructure projects should not increase local temperatures or alter local microclimates (e.g., they should avoid the heat island effect). Soil and groundwater should be protected from contamination, and hazardous waste should not be buried. Minimizing soil compaction during construction is important as well. Infrastructure should not adversely impact surface water quality with pollutants and sediments, with regard to its turbidity, temperature, quantity, or nutrient levels (especially phosphorous and nitrogen). Water withdrawals from surface or groundwater sources should not decrease water levels significantly. Existing vegetation should be preserved, and impervious surface cover should be minimized to the extent possible. New vegetation should be carefully selected and appropriate for the location. Care should be taken to avoid introducing invasive species or inadvertently facilitating their spread. Invasive species, such as zebra mussels in the Midwest, kudzu in the South, and phragmites in the Northeast, can have detrimental impacts on habitat quality by choking out native species and disrupting ecosystem function.

Additional issues of importance include habitat connectivity, stormwater management, and watershed impacts. Infrastructure projects should minimize habitat fragmentation and promote habitat connectivity. Projects, particularly transportation infrastructure and other network types, should consider animal movements. Roads, for instance, should include underpasses or overpasses to allow for safe wildlife crossings. These crossings should be situated to correspond to likely animal movement routes and sized appropriately for expected animal users. Stormwater flow is another consideration for infrastructure projects. Infrastructure should reduce stormwater runoff through on-site strategies. Projects should mitigate the impacts of stormwater runoff on local water bodies and prevent adverse effects on water quality throughout their watershed.

The Natural World category is divided into two subcategories: Site Selection and Habitat. Each of the subcategories includes a set of quantifiable metrics. Table 16.2 illustrates the credits of the Natural World category.

Uncertainties within the Natural World category include the omission of environmental health and the problem of boundary definition. Including humans within Natural World has been a matter of ongoing debate. Human health and well-being seem to fit neatly within Quality of Life, but there is great potential for overlap with the Natural World category. Air and water pollutants harm animals and people alike. A key argument for keeping people and wildlife in separate categories is that different thresholds are considered harmful for each. In any case, care must be taken not to double-count items. Defining the boundary of infrastructure projects is a difficult topic with important ramifications for the Natural World category. Clearly, infrastructure projects' effects extend beyond property lines, but where should the line be drawn? Impact area and boundary definition will vary according to infrastructure type, if for example it has the network characteristics of a road grid or the nodal significance of an airport. Additionally, the relevant boundary may differ for different chemicals, compounds, or substances. For instance, air pollution may travel for many miles depending on prevalent wind patterns, but noise pollution will tend to be confined to the immediate project surroundings. Determining the appropriate scale of examination is likewise critical. A regional or local scale is more appropriate for the Natural World category, whereas global impacts will likely fall within the Climate Change category.

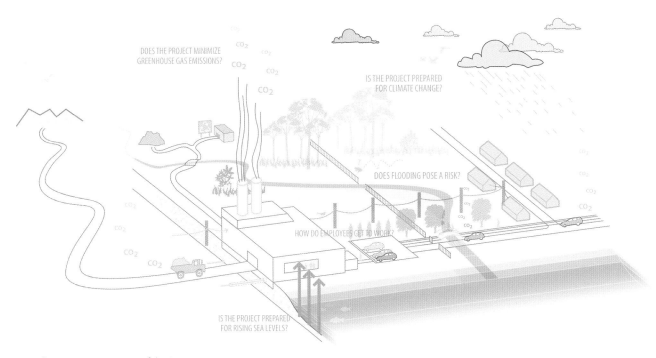

16.18 Schematic representation of the issues
addressed by the Climate Change category

Climate Change

Climate Change is the third category of the Zofnass Rating System. The general scope of this category is to minimize long-term climate change caused by human activities and infrastructure, and to promote infrastructure projects that are adaptable and resilient to future conditions that may result from climate change. Figure 16.18 illustrates the concept.

Climate Change focuses on two major topics: reducing greenhouse gas emissions and promoting climate change adaptability. The 2007 report released by the Intergovernmental Panel on Climate Change (IPCC) states simply and emphatically: "Human-induced warming of the climate system is widespread."[15] The major cause of climate change is "very likely" the increase in greenhouse gases in the atmosphere and "very unlikely" to be the result of natural forces alone. Greenhouse gases, including carbon dioxide (CO_2), water vapor, methane (CH_4), nitrous oxide (N_2O), and ozone (O_3), alter the atmospheric composition and prevent radiation from the earth from escaping into the atmosphere. The significant and rapid increase of greenhouse gases after the industrial revolution is attributable to human activities (IPCC FAQ 2007). Infrastructure contributes to a significant portion of greenhouse gas emissions— either directly by producing energy through combustion or indirectly

by providing a transportation network that encourages the use of automobiles. Reducing total emissions is critical to minimizing climate change.

The Zofnass Rating System documents infrastructure greenhouse gas emissions from multiple sources: energy consumption, transportation, and waste products. Emissions will be measured in carbon dioxide equivalent values (CO_2e) to simplify comparisons. Focus is on reducing emissions during all stages of a project's life cycle, including design, construction, operations, and decommissioning. Other means of reducing emissions will be considered, including carbon sequestration and carbon offsets.

Climate change is expected to impact global climate in three key ways: changes in long-term average annual conditions (mean temperature or annual precipitation), increases in climate variability (fluctuations in precipitation), and increases in more extreme weather events. Infrastructure adaptability refers to its ability to withstand these changes and remain functional. In analyzing adaptability, Smit *et al.*[16] state that there are three important questions to ask: 1) Adapt to what? What are the consequences of climate change that will necessitate adaptive strategies? 2) Who or what adapts? What is the system that is being adapted? And 3) How does adaptation occur? What is the process of adaptation? What are the decision-making parameters? Credits dealing with adaptability will include

Table 16.3 The Climate Change category credits

Credit name	Intent	Metric
CC1: Emissions		
CC1.1: Reduce greenhouse gas emissions	Develop and implement a comprehensive long-term strategy and plan of action for reducing total greenhouse gas emissions	Percentage of overall CO_2 reduction achieved by strategies
CC1.2: Improve transportation efficiency	Develop and implement a comprehensive transportation demand management plan (TDM) and promote transportation efficiency	Plan outlining strategies and/or measures for reducing VMT, congestion/parking, and promoting reduced-emissions vehicles
CC1.3: Use fuel-efficient vehicles	Utilize reduced emissions and/or high fuel-efficiency vehicles for project-related transportation	Percentage of reduced emmissions vehicles used. Follow Low Carbon Fuel Standards or equivalent if applicable
CC1.4: Enhance public transport	Provide safe, secure, convenient, and efficient public transit lanes, facilities, and waiting areas	Percentage increase in projected public transit use over comparable project type
CC1.5: Enhance pedestrian/bicycle routes	Provide safe, secure, convenient, and efficient biking and walking areas, paths, and promenades	Subjective ranking of walkability and bike lane improvements
CC1.6: Capture carbon	Implement Carbon Capture and Storage (CCS) and Carbon Sequestration technologies	Percentage of carbon emissions captured
CC1.7: Utilize carbon offsets	Purchase carbon offset credits from qualified sources	Percentage of carbon offset credits used
CC1.8: Reduce construction-related transportation	Implement strategies to reduce transit during construction	Percentage of transportation (distance and tonnage) reduced over a business as usual case
CC1.9: Innovate or exceed credit requirements	Implement innovative sustainable practices on the reduction of greenhouse gas emissions in project	Achieves exemplary performance or employs innovative solutions
CC2: Climate adaptability		
CC2.1: Assess climate change threat	Develop and implement a comprehensive Climate Impact Assessment and Climate Adaptation Plan	Plan (yes/no). Scale ranking thoroughness and rigor of the plan
CC2.2: Design for long-term climate change	Design infrastructure systems to be resilient to gradual climate change and perform adequately under altered climate conditions	Plan (yes/no). Scale ranking thoroughness and rigour of the plan
CC2.3: Prepare for extreme weather events	Implement self-reliance strategies in anticipation of extreme weather conditions and natural disasters related to climate change	Can project survive for designated time period in a " failure/disaster scenario"? (yes/no)
CC2.4: Mitigate heat island effect	Minimize surfaces with SRIs under set limit to reduce localized heat accumulation	Percentage of surfaces that meet SRI criteria
CC2.5: Innovate or exceed credit requirements	Implement innovative sustainable practices on the adaptability of the project to long-term climate change	Achieves exemplary performance or employs innovative solutions

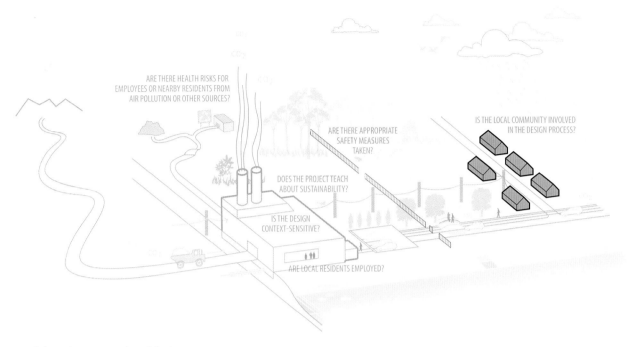

ARE THERE HEALTH RISKS FOR
EMPLOYEES OR NEARBY RESIDENTS FROM
AIR POLLUTION OR OTHER SOURCES?

IS THE LOCAL COMMUNITY INVOLVED
IN THE DESIGN PROCESS?

ARE THERE APPROPRIATE
SAFETY MEASURES
TAKEN?

DOES THE PROJECT TEACH
ABOUT SUSTAINABILITY?

IS THE DESIGN
CONTEXT-SENSITIVE?

ARE LOCAL RESIDENTS EMPLOYED?

16.19 Schematic representation of the issues
addressed by the Quality of Life category

conducting a climate change impacts assessment plan and increasing self-reliance. The impacts assessment plan will include testing for extreme scenarios and developing backup plans for failure. The focus of this category is essentially on a macro scale; for this reason, durable and adaptable material implementation will fall within the Resource Allocation category.

The Climate Change category is divided into two subcategories: Emissions and Climate Adaptability. Each of the two subcategories includes a set of quantifiable metrics. Table 16.3 lists the credits of the Climate Change category.

Uncertainties within the Climate Change category result from the inherent uncertainty of the degree and impacts of climate change. The science behind climate change is still developing, and likely scenarios are still under investigation. No one knows for certain how much or how quickly the climate will change or what the impacts of these changes will be. The Zofnass Program will use the best available information to guide its credits dealing with climate change.

Quality of Life

Quality of Life is the fourth category of the Zofnass Rating System. The general scope of this category is to maximize the quality of life of those who use or are affected by infrastructure projects, both now and in the future. Within this framework the Zofnass Program views infrastructure as having a dual function: first to cover a given need, and second to provide this service at an acceptable quality level.

The Quality of Life category recognizes the impacts infrastructure projects may have on local residents, employees, and user groups. Figure 16.19 illustrates the concept. These impacts may be physical, economic, or social. Emissions and other pollutants from infrastructure may have adverse impacts on community health, especially for nearby residents. Air pollution and water pollution may lead to asthma, cancer, bronchitis, and other health problems. Infrastructure's effects are not only negative, however. Positive results from infrastructure projects can include community education, community outreach, knowledge creation, and worker training. Displaying the environmental performance of an infrastructure project may also help facilitate positive changes in user behavior.

Community involvement should be sought by infrastructure owners. Community members (both users and non-users) should be considered important stakeholders in the decision-making process

Table 16.4 The Quality of Life category credits

Credit name	Intent	Metric
QL1: Health		
QL1.1: Protect air quality	Prevent the introduction of contaminants into the air near communities	Evaluation of type of air pollutant, its effects, and proximity to humans
QL1.2: Enhance site/neighborhood safety	Ensure safety and security on site and its direct vicinity	Plan (yes/no). Scale ranking thoroughness and rigor of the plan
QL1.3: Enhance public space quality	Provide for outdoor climate comfort by minimizing excessive or inadequate exposure to sun and wind	Evaluation of comfort improvements
QL1.4: Enhance public space accessibility	Encourage use of, and ensure universal and barrier-free access to, public space	Evaluation of site's accessibility
QL1.5: Minimize noise and vibrations	Prevent excessive noise and vibration	Percentage of noise and vibration reduction over "no action" scenario
QL1.6: Minimize light pollution	Prevent excessive light and glare	Lighting meets minimum standards for safety but does not extend beyond site boundaries
QL1.7: Minimize odors	Prevent unpleasant odors that can arise from specific industrial and natural processes	Evaluation of odor prevention plan. Scale ranking thoroughness and rigor of plan
QL1.8: Innovate or exceed credit requirements	Implement innovative sustainable practices on health and wellness	Achieves exemplary performance or employs innovative solutions
QL2: Education		
QL2.1: Implement community outreach	Promote the understanding of the project's specific sustainable features and processes, and of broader sustainability impacts	Establishment of local partnerships for effective communication with community (yes/no)
QL2.2: Implement sustainable practices training	Train construction workers and project employees on appropriate sustainable practices	Evaluation of training level provided
QL2.3: Display sustainability performance	Educate the public about sustainability indicators and facilitate behavioral change	Provide publicly accessible and comprehensible information about sustainability performance of project
QL2.4: Innovate or exceed credit requirements	Implement innovative sustainable practices on informational and educational capacity of project	Achieves exemplary performance or employs innovative solutions
QL3: Community values		
QL3.1: Preserve cultural sites	Preserve and/or restore significant historical and cultural assets	Conduct a survey of cultural and historical assets, and preserve or restore all historical and cultural assets of note (yes/no)
QL3.2: Plan for growth impacts	Assess potential future development the project may encourage and its impact on regional environment and communities	Narrative demonstrating and understanding the awareness of growth impacts (yes/no)
QL3.3: Implement context-sensitive design	Design project to visually complement and/or enhance its surroundings while minimizing negative impacts on scenery	Establish and implement guidelines for context-sensitive design (yes/no)
QL3.4: Implement integrated-project approach	Ensure an effective, transparent, and accountable project management structure incorporating feedback from important project team members early in design	Follow industry best-practice guidelines for integrated project approach (yes/no)
QL3.5: Solicit community feedback	Engage community stakeholders in meaningful participation during all the project stages	Evidence community feedback was incorporated or considered (yes/no)
QL3.6: Encourage local employment	Ensure equal opportunities for employment to the local community	Percentage of employment provided by local workers
QL3.7: Innovate or exceed credit requirements	Implement innovative sustainable practices on community and values considerations of project	Achieves exemplary performance or employs innovative solutions

(during design as well as during operation). Infrastructure owners should work to ensure equal access (availability and quality) to all; exclusionary practices should be avoided.

Context-sensitive design is important to infrastructure design. Infrastructure is driven primarily by engineering parameters, but its visual and functional impact on immediate surroundings should be considered during the design process. Local context and community feedback should contribute to design decisions. A positive example of community-influenced infrastructure design is the Puente Hills Landfill in Los Angeles, California. The largest operating landfill in the country, Puente Hills has worked closely with the two neighboring communities to minimize the visual impact of the landfill. The result is a unique vegetation strategy, with the two sides of the landfill receiving dramatically different treatment in accordance with the desires of the respective communities. The first community desired a densely vegetated edge, so one side of the landfill features rapidly growing, extremely dense tree, vine, and underbrush species. From the first neighborhood's vantage point the landfill resembles a forested hill. The opposite side of the landfill, however, is planted entirely with native vegetation as requested by the second neighborhood.

The Quality of Life category is divided into three subcategories: Health, Education, and Community Values. Each of the subcategories includes a set of quantifiable metrics. Table 16.4 illustrates the structure of the Quality of Life category.

The difficulties posed in the Quality of Life category, as reiterated by industry feedback, arise chiefly from their qualitative character. Choosing metrics and defining point values is challenging. Other issues with Quality of Life include the aforementioned difficulty of separating human, animal, and plant health. The apparent overlap between the Quality of Life and Natural World categories may prove confusing to users of the Zofnass Rating System. Finally, boundary definition within Quality of Life is problematic for the same reasons as mentioned previously at the Natural World category. Infrastructure has impacts beyond property lines, and choosing the boundary for investigation is challenging.

The Zofnass Rating System credit list

Using the Zofnass System requires three basic steps.

First, consider each credit and determine points earned. Teams begin by considering each credit and determining whether or not the project meets it (the methods of evaluating credit attainment are clearly outlined in the Rating System). When a project satisfies a credit, it earns the points associated with that credit.

Second, calculate the project's score by dividing the earned points by the total points. After looking at all the possible credits, the team adds up the total number of points they earned and divides by the total number of points available. This calculation tells what percentage of points the team earned. The percentage of points earned is the project's "score."

Third, interpret the results. The Zofnass Program will provide guidance about how to interpret these scores (i.e., to determine whether a score is exemplary or mediocre). If the team is unsatisfied with the result, they may choose to go back and alter their design to earn additional points.

RESOURCES   19 Credits

promotes the use of resources which:
* *minimizes impacts on the current environment, and*
* *does not compromise the ability of future generations to have access to the resources they will need.*

1 MATERIALS
- ☐ R1.1   Reuse Materials
- ☐ R1.2   Use Less Materials
- ☐ R1.3   Use Durable Materials and Systems
- ☐ R1.4   Use Recycled Materials
- ☐ R1.5   Use Regional Materials
- ☐ R1.6   Use Sustainably Certified Materials
- ☐ R1.7   Manage Construction Waste
- ☐ R1.8   Innovate or Exceed Credit Requirements

2 ENERGY
- ☐ R2.1   Reduce Energy Use
- ☐ R2.2   Use Renewable Energy
- ☐ R2.3   Commission Electrical / Mechanical Systems
- ☐ R2.4   Monitor Energy Performance
- ☐ R2.5   Innovate or Exceed Credit Requirements

3 WATER
- ☐ R3.1   Reduce Water Use
- ☐ R3.2   Reuse Water On-Site
- ☐ R3.3   Utilize Water-Efficient Landscaping
- ☐ R3.4   Commission Water Systems
- ☐ R3.5   Monitor Water System Performance
- ☐ R3.6   Innovate or Exceed Credit Requirements

CLIMATE CHANGE   14 Credits

* *reduce greenhouse gas emissions*
* *promote climate change adaptability*

1 EMISSIONS
- ☐ CC1.1   Reduce Greenhouse Gas Emissions
- ☐ CC1.2   Improve Transportation Efficiency
- ☐ CC1.3   Use Fuel-Efficient Vehicles
- ☐ CC1.4   Enhance Public Transport
- ☐ CC1.5   Enhance Pedestrian/Bicycle Routes
- ☐ CC1.6   Capture Carbon
- ☐ CC1.7   Utilize Carbon Offsets
- ☐ CC1.8   Reduce Construction-Related Transportation
- ☐ CC1.9   Innovate or Exceed Credit Requirements

2 CLIMATE ADAPTABILITY
- ☐ CC2.1   Assess Climate Change Threat
- ☐ CC2.2   Design for Long-Term Climate Change
- ☐ CC2.3   Prepare for Extreme Weather Events
- ☐ CC2.4   Mitigate Heat Island Effect
- ☐ CC2.5   Innovate or Exceed Credit Requirements

☐/19   **TOTAL RESOURCES**   +

☐/14   **TOTAL CLIMATE CHANGE**   +

16.20 The Zofnass Rating System credit checklist

NATURAL WORLD 18 Credits

minimize the negative impacts of infrastructure on local and regional ecosystems by:
- *promoting the rejuvenation of degraded ecosystems,*
- *minimizing fragmentation and disruptions to ecosystems, and*
- *mitigating problems causes by its construction or operations.*

1 SITE SELECTION
- ☐ NW1.1 Prepare Site Assessment
- ☐ NW1.2 Mitigate Site Impact
- ☐ NW1.3 Protect Wetlands and Water Bodies
- ☐ NW1.4 Conserve Prime Habitat
- ☐ NW1.5 Maximize Use of Developed Sites
- ☐ NW1.6 Maximize Use of Contaminated Sites
- ☐ NW1.7 Innovate or Exceed Credit Requirements

2 HABITAT
- ☐ NW2.1 Assess Regional Habitats and Watersheds
- ☐ NW2.2 Preserve/Protect Habitat Connectivity
- ☐ NW2.3 Prevent Soil Contamination
- ☐ NW2.4 Use Appropriate Vegetation
- ☐ NW2.5 Preserve Natural Waterways
- ☐ NW2.6 Protect Water Quality
- ☐ NW2.7 Utilize Stormwater Best Practices
- ☐ NW2.8 Maximize Pervious Surfaces
- ☐ NW2.9 Balance Earthwork
- ☐ NW2.10 Minimize Site Damage During Construction
- ☐ NW2.11 Innovate or Exceed Credit Requirements

 QUALITY OF LIFE 19 Credits

maximize the quality of life of those who use, or are affected by infrastructure projects by:
- *minimizing environmental health impacts and promoting safety and security,*
- *engaging the local community in decision-making, and*
- *employing and training local workers*

1 HEALTH
- ☐ Co1.1 Protect Air Quality
- ☐ Co1.2 Enhance Site/Neighborhood Safety
- ☐ Co1.3 Enhance Public Space Quality
- ☐ Co1.4 Enhance Public Space Accessibility
- ☐ Co1.5 Minimize Noise and Vibrations
- ☐ Co1.6 Minimize Light Pollution
- ☐ Co1.7 Minimize Odors
- ☐ Co1.8 Innovate or Exceed Credit Requirements

2 EDUCATION
- ☐ Co2.1 Implement Community Outreach
- ☐ Co2.2 Implement Sustainable-Practices Training
- ☐ Co2.3 Display Sustainability Performance
- ☐ Co2.4 Innovate or Exceed Credit Requirements

3 COMMUNITY VALUES
- ☐ Co3.1 Preserve Cultural Sites
- ☐ Co3.2 Plan for Growth Impacts
- ☐ Co3.3 Implement Context-Sensitive Design Strategies
- ☐ Co3.4 Implement an Integrated-Project Approach
- ☐ Co3.5 Solicit Community Feedback
- ☐ Co3.6 Encourage Local Employment
- ☐ Co3.7 Innovate or Exceed Credit Requirements

☐ /18 **TOTAL NATURAL WORLD** + ☐ /19 **TOTAL QUALITY OF LIFE**

TOTAL CREDITS EARNED:

$$\frac{\boxed{}}{70} = \boxed{\%}$$

TOTAL POSSIBLE CREDITS:

ZOFNASS SCORE

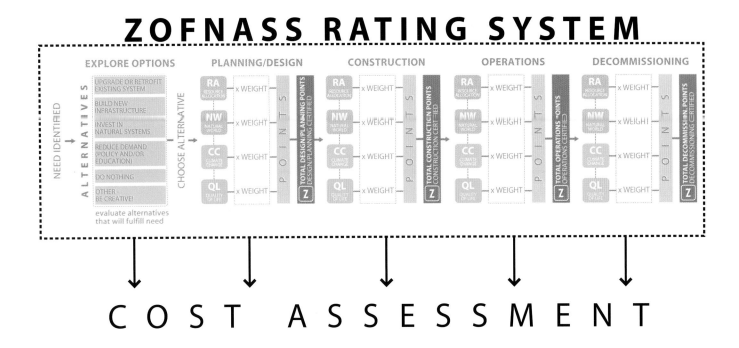

16.21 Parallel cost assessment

Economics and cost

Throughout the development of our rating system, industry collaborators stressed the need to include "economics" in the Zofnass Rating System. Eventually we realized that, while cost is an important consideration, it does not need to fall directly within the Zofnass System. Instead, a parallel economic framework can provide a means of assessing costs. Life cycle costs and cost–benefit analysis provide useful assessment tools for sustainability cost assessment. With a parallel system, sustainability information and economic data together provide well-rounded information to guide decision making. Cost accounting will be a completely separate system, and cost information will remain confidential and will not influence Zofnass project certification in any way.

POTENTIAL TO INCORPORATE EXISTING ASSESSMENT TOOLS

Many techniques to quantify and assess economic costs and environmental impacts have already been developed. The Zofnass Rating System could benefit by incorporating some of the existing tools into its framework where an existing tool fulfills a goal of the system. Incorporating existing tools rather than developing new techniques is preferable for several reasons. Existing tools have been in use for many years and provide established, standardized assessment methods. Industry professionals are, in most cases, already familiar with the techniques. In some cases, users will already be using the techniques with infrastructure projects. Zofnass could include these tools without adding any extra burden on the user. The existing tools with the greatest relevance to the Zofnass System are environmental impact assessment (EIA), life cycle assessment, and life cycle costing. This section will describe these three techniques, their applications, their advantages and limitations, and potential relevance to the Zofnass System.

EIA/EIS | Environmental Impact Assessment / Environmental Impact Statement

	Alternative A	Alternative B	Alternative C
describe environmental impacts	• environmental impact 1 • environmental impact 2 • environmental impact 3 • environmental impact 4 • environmental impact 5	• environmental impact 1 • environmental impact 2 • environmental impact 3	• environmental impact 1 • environmental impact 2 • environmental impact 3 • environmental impact 4
may include social(quality of life)/ economic impacts	• social impact 1 • social impact 2	• social impact 1 • economic impact 2 • economic impact 3	• economic impact 1 • economic impact 2
describe mitigation measures	• mitigation measures	• mitigation measures	• mitigation measures

<< **compare alternatives** >>

+

any additional factors can also be considered …

DECISION

16.22 The Environmental Impact Assessment process

Environmental Impact Assessment

EIA is a change-oriented, procedural tool used to evaluate alternatives. An environmental impact statement (EIS) reports the results of an EIA. These tools have been in use since the 1970s and offer a way to evaluate potential environmental impacts of actions. Environmental impact statements were a component of the National Environmental Protection Act (NEPA) passed by Congress on January 1, 1970. NEPA is a cross-cutting, action-forcing statute requiring federal agencies to take a "hard look" at the environmental impacts of their decisions. Conducting an EIS is a purely procedural, rather than substantive, requirement; agencies must adequately outline the environmental impacts of their decisions, but NEPA does not mandate any particular decision be made.

As described in NEPA, an environmental impact statement is a mandatory step in the USA for "major federal actions with significant impact on the environment." The key points of this requirement are that it applies only to federal actions that are considered "major" with an expected "significant impact" on the environment. Federal actions can include the adoption of policies, the adoption of formal plans, the adoption of programs, or the approval of specific projects.

Projects receiving federal funds, such as some road improvement projects, often also require an impact statement.

Environmental impact statements assess specific projects and allow an organization to understand alternatives. These statements are open ended and require a detailed description of expected environmental impacts. Impact statements should also contain descriptions of possible mitigation measures for a project's expected impacts, but agencies have no legal responsibility to undertake these measures. The requirement to conduct an EIS is a purely procedural obligation; an agency can, after conducting an EIS, decide that an alternative with the worst environmental impact is still preferable. Typically, an EIA focuses solely on environmental impacts, but it could possibly also include economic and social impacts.

Opinions about the effectiveness of NEPA and its requirement of impact statements are mixed. Supporters say NEPA has brought about modest but important changes to agency decision making. To its critics, however, impact statements tend to be self-serving and do nothing to affect the decisions of agencies. Another concern about impact statements is their impact on project delivery. Adding another step to the process inevitably delays projects. Finally, impact statements are designed to consider issues project by project, and some argue that this approach may miss the big picture. Incremental impacts alone may not significantly impact the environment, but the cumulative effects of many small actions have the potential to affect the environment.

EIA provides an ideal framework for our "Evaluate Need" step that precedes the go/no go decision. This well-established technique provides a procedural framework to evaluate the environmental impacts of alternative projects. Furthermore, because many infrastructure projects receive federal funds, some projects may already be legally required to conduct an EIA. This step could be a procedural requirement like the existing EIA, or we could require that decision makers choose the alternative they believe will have the least impact. Perhaps some economic consideration should be included at this step if it is to be more than procedural.

Life cycle assessment

Life cycle assessment (LCA) is an analytical tool used to assess the environmental impacts and resources used throughout a product's life from raw-material acquisition through production, use, and disposal. LCA is a fairly standardized procedure. ASTM's *Standard Guide for Environmental Life Cycle Assessment (LCA) of Building Materials/Products* (ASTM E1991-05) and ISO's *Principles and Framework* (ISO/DIS 14040) and *Requirements and Guidelines* (ISO/DIS 14044) outline standard practices for conducting LCAs. Both public and private entities use LCAs. Public organizations use LCAs to support development of environmental legislation and regulation, to provide consumer information, or to develop criteria for environmental taxes, standards, or eco-labeling programs. Private companies tend to use LCAs to help with product development and marketing.

This technique consists of three major steps: goal and scoping definition, inventory analysis, and impact assessment.[17] Goal and scoping definition includes defining boundaries (subjective) and determining the functional unit (the unit of interest, for example the packaging required to hold 100 ml of a soft drink). Second, during inventory analysis, researchers make a model of the product's life cycle showing all the environmental inflows and outflows. This stage is objective in nature and aims to quantify inputs and outputs that cross system boundaries.[18]

The third step, impact assessment, requires impact data that is based on scientific research. This stage aims to objectively quantify the relative environmental impacts of different substances. Most methods for accomplishing this are based on calculating a weighted sum of the inventory results. Weight can be based on relative harmfulness, maximum allowable concentration, mitigation costs, or target levels of different substances. The method with the widest acceptance for this stage is impact categories and equivalency factors. For this, every item in the life cycle model is first classified in an impact category. Potential environmental impacts fall into the general categories of resource depletion, human health impacts, and ecological impacts.[19] After classification, the effect of each item in the inventory on each impact category is quantified, typically with the use of equivalency factors. These factors are based on scientific research, not subjective weights. Finally, the different impact categories are weighted subjectively so they can be compared. Representing the relative importance of the categories to the group performing the analysis, these weights reflect social values and preferences.

Following the impact assessment, the improvement assessment step includes a systematic evaluation of the needs and opportunities to reduce the negative environmental impacts that occur during the product's life cycle. Some research points to the need for preference data during this step, so that decision makers can make decisions that reflect society's values and preferences. This analysis may include quantitative and qualitative measures of improvement, such as changes in product design, raw material use, industrial processing, consumer use, and waste management.

Obtaining accurate and reliable data and information can be difficult, and presents a substantial barrier to undertaking an LCA. Data collection and validation typically accounts for about three-fourths of the total cost of a study. Fortunately, data can be shared once it is collected, and collaboration between firms has the potential to significantly reduce data costs. However, firms must

LCA | Life Cycle Assessment

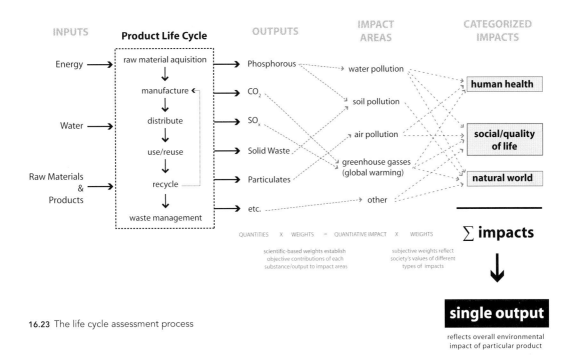

16.23 The life cycle assessment process

have an incentive to work together, and this may be less likely to happen in highly competitive industries. LCAs cost significant time and money, and companies must believe they will realize some tangible benefits from the results before investing in a study. LCA promises to be less costly over time as data is accumulated and made available for future studies.

Although they have been used for several decades, LCAs are still criticized for their underlying characteristics and focus. The LCA by definition considers only environmental issues, but other issues (especially economic) must be considered when making decisions. Some believe LCA's lack of economic considerations limits its relevancy as a decision-making tool. As Gregory Norris explains, "Even if we only care about environmental performance, we must consider the variable economics of alternatives, in order to identify the decisions through which our limited resources can achieve the best environmental performance."[20] Another criticism of LCA is its ability merely to expose tradeoffs rather than point to better solutions. For example, disposable diapers create more solid waste in landfills, but cloth diapers lead to greater overall water use and groundwater pollution (with detergents). LCA is still limited in its ability to recommend either type of diapers. This

shortcoming emerges in part because LCA is intended to be used as an analytical and accounting tool, not a decision-making framework. Finally, data deficiencies today limit the ability of companies to conduct LCAs. Often, companies are forced to rely on confidential, unpublished data, but doing so limits the ability to verify their results (this is particularly problematic if the intended use of the LCA is marketing).

LCA's ability to evaluate the environmental impacts of a product would fit neatly within the Zofnass System's resource allocation category. With this tool, the environmental impacts of each of the project's materials can be quantified to a single number. These numbers could then be combined with the total quantity of each material, and the resulting outcomes could be summed across materials. These calculations would lead to a single output that would represent the total environmental impact of the materials within the project. Social/quality of life impacts would possibly need to be added to the existing LCA framework so that the output would reflect all values that the Zofnass Program deems important.

LCA ideally would be undertaken by each product's manufacturer and then incorporated into Zofnass calculations. Obtaining data

LCCA | Life Cycle Cost (LCC) Analysis

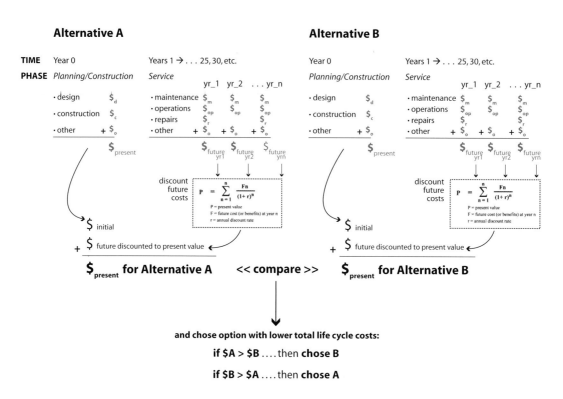

16.24 The Life Cycle Costing Process

from manufacturers rather than asking project engineers/contractors to conduct LCAs would be desirable for three reasons. First, data supplied by manufacturers would only need to be obtained once, so project decision makers would not need to spend significant time and money duplicating the LCA process. Second, relying on a single set of data would increase reliability and eliminate the possible discrepancies that might occur between different engineering firms each conducting their own LCAs on identical products. Third, manufacturers are presumably more capable and knowledgeable about conducting LCAs, so results would be more consistent and reliable.

Life Cycle Cost Analysis

Throughout our meetings with industry, the importance of incorporating economic considerations into our model has been stressed. The most appropriate existing assessment technique to

address these concerns is Life Cycle Cost Analysis (LCCA).

LCCA is an analytical technique typically used to decide between alternatives by comparing the total discounted economic costs of each alternative over its life cycle (design, construction, operation, and disposal). Accordingly, key variables include: costs (initial and future), time (planning/construction and service), and the discount rate (the rate of interest reflecting the investor's time value of money). A suggested means to obtain an appropriate discount rate is to use the US Department of Energy's real discount rate, published annually in the *Energy Prices Indices and Discount Factors for Life-Cycle Cost Analysis*. The life cycle cost technique first emerged in the 1960s and is still in wide use today.

The procedure for conducting a LCCA is relatively straightforward:

1. Define the scope of the problem/project.
2. Define the requirements of the cost model.
3. Collect the required data.

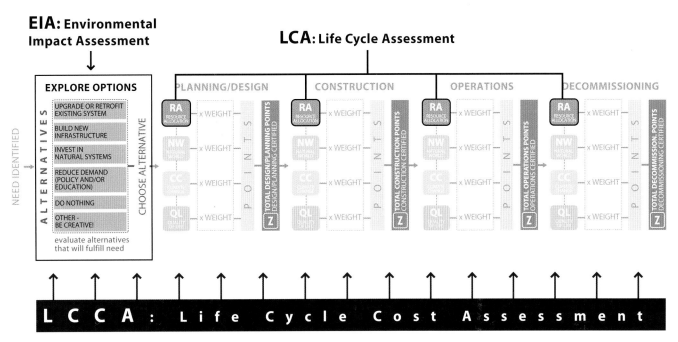

16.25 Potential to integrate tools into the Zofnass Rating System

4. Develop estimated costs for each year.
5. Discount future costs to present value.
6. Sum the present values of all future costs.
7. Evaluate results and make a decision.

Using this technique, future expenditures for several alternatives can be easily compared. Using similar cost categories and life cycle lengths for different alternatives is important so the costs of the alternatives can be compared accurately. Cost categories include:[21]

• acquisition costs—research and development costs, non-recurring investment costs, recurring investment costs
• sustaining costs—scheduled and unscheduled maintenance costs, facility usage costs, and disposal costs.

ASTM's *Standard Practice for Measuring Life-Cycle Costs of Buildings and Building Systems* (ASTM E917-05e1) provides technical standards for conducting LCCAs. Two important aspects of this technique are that, in its conventional use, it does not include benefits (only costs) and it only considers economic costs (that accrue *directly* to the user). Potentially it could be expanded to include social, environmental, and external costs as well.

LCCA could be used at key decision points throughout the process to weigh the economic costs of alternatives. In this way, economics could be incorporated into the decision-making process. LCCA would be compatible with the life cycle-oriented environmental assessment techniques within the Zofnass Rating System. Cost analysis would function as a separate but parallel system to the rating system, as shown in Figure 16.21. In this manner, Zofnass could remain relevant yet avoid addressing economics directly within its rating system framework.

Figure 16.25 illustrates the potential to incorporate these three techniques (E/A, LCA, LCC) into the Zofnass framework.

NEXT STEPS OF
THE ZOFNASS SYSTEM DEVELOPMENT

Critical feedback from faculty and industry participants through the peer review process has been invaluable in bringing the rating system to its current state. However, the development of the Zofnass Rating System is ongoing, and several challenges still exist. From the beginning, we have tried to balance model complexity with usability. The Zofnass Rating System must be rigorous enough to accurately portray sustainability concepts, relationships, and even feedback loops. The system's thoroughness and complexity, however, must not be a barrier to use. Usability is the key to the ultimate adoption of a rating system.

A similar challenge is how editable, transparent, and/or invisible the assessment calculations should be. Making calculations visible would increase apparent complexity, but hiding them could provoke criticism and hinder educational opportunities. A step beyond making calculations visible could be to make them editable to certain parties. In this way, local governments could customize the Zofnass Rating System to suit local conditions, concerns, and priorities. However, if the Zofnass Rating System were to be customizable, oversight would be needed to maintain a comparable level of stringency across regions. Making certification too easy in some locations would dilute the value of the Zofnass Rating System as a whole. A related challenge is the tension between adaptability and standardization. How much should local context influence outcomes? Is it important to be able to compare infrastructure projects across regions? These are questions we must answer as we move forward.

Existing rating systems currently function as checklists in which credits are attained after decisions have already been made. Creating a rating system that functions as a decision-making tool, however, could have dramatic consequences on behavior and choices. The idea of a rating system as a decision-making tool is a significant change, and some industry participants have questioned whether it is possible or even desirable. "A rating system inherently means being blind to process and only looking at final results," one industry representative told us. "A decision-making tool, on the other hand, is inherently about process. You cannot have both."

Challenges in creating a decision-making tool include: the need for continual, real-time feedback; the probable need for a more complex model to provide this feedback; and the need to include additional factors (possibly even cost) within the model to allow for holistic decision making. The result would be a rating system that functions more as a program than a checklist.

Until now, we have focused on creating an overarching framework for all infrastructure types. Taking into account the differences between infrastructure types is important as we move forward. Each infrastructure category has distinct issues relating to sustainability, and the rating system will need to be tailored specifically for each type. Maintaining a balance between an overall framework and specificity will be an ongoing challenge. The prevalence of coupled infrastructure projects will also need to be taken into account. Landfills today may also generate power or include recycling facilities. Wastewater treatment facilities may also act as a water source, providing recycled water for non-potable uses such as irrigation, industrial processes, and decorative fountains.

As the Zofnass Rating System is adapted to each infrastructure type, existing project performance databases will be needed to determine baseline levels of certification. If our credits focus on rewarding performance levels in the top quartile of comparable infrastructure projects, knowing where that line sits is crucial. Gathering sufficient data to establish minimum, maximum, and average values of performance is necessary. Additionally, if regional context is entered as a factor into the rating system, databases must be sortable by region. Each geographic unit must contain a sufficient number of similar projects to allow calculation of performance thresholds.

Perhaps the most critical challenge is to identify the underlying motivation of future users of the Zofnass Rating System. Is attaining a sustainability certification a financial incentive for municipal bond ratings, asset value, or marketability? Would a company with a certified power plant be able to charge a premium for "green" energy? Or is certification simply seen as "the right thing to do"? Understanding incentives is crucial for ensuring the widespread adoption of the Zofnass Rating System.

CONCLUSION

This chapter presented the Zofnass Rating System for Sustainable Infrastructure, developed at the Harvard Graduate School of Design after the generous donation of Paul and Joan Zofnass in 2008. The Zofnass Rating System aims to impact the infrastructure and built environment industries at a time critical for our civilization and environment. As the world's resources are diminishing and countries experience massive demographic challenges, infrastructure will be a key determinant of the viability and sustainability of our cities and nations. Whether the need is for refurbishment and upgrade of systems, built decades ago, or to build new infrastructure to sustain newly constructed cities, the core function and value of infrastructure can never be distant from a sustainability mandate.

In our efforts to develop the Zofnass Rating System we strived to maintain a global approach and generate a framework that can address the world's challenges. We also aimed to create a system that is sensitive to local context and current needs. Our work has not been easy, nor is it complete. The Zofnass Rating System, at the moment of writing, is being tested in several case studies of real projects in the USA, Europe, the Middle East, and Central Asia. We expect certain details, metrics, and measurement techniques to change. However, we are also confident that the overall framework we have developed is robust and flexible enough to incorporate future changes. Our vision was always projective, looking at alternative scenarios of how our futures will be. This is still the energy that moves us forward.

NOTES

1   American Society of Civil Engineers, "2009 report card for America's infrastructure," www.asce.org/reportcard.

2   J. Vanegas, "Road map and principles for built environmental sustainability." *Environment, Science, and Technology* 37 (2003): 5363–5372.

3   V. Bentivegna, Curwell S., Deakin M., *et al.*, "A vision and methodology for integrated sustainable urban development: BEQUEST." *Building Research and Information* 30(2) (2002): 83–94.

4   H. Bossel, *Indicators of Sustainable Development: Theory, Methods, and Applications.* (Winnipeg: International Institute for Sustainable Development, 1999.)

5   O. Ugwu, Kumaraswamy M., Wong A., *et al.*, "Sustainability appraisal in infrastructure projects: Development of indicators and computational methods." *Automation in Construction* 15 (2006): 239–251.

6   S. Dasgupta, Tam E., "Indicators and frameworks for assessing sustainable infrastructure." *Canadian Journal of Civil Engineering* 32 (2005): 30–44.

7   O. Ugwu, Haupt T., "KPIs and assessment methods for infrastructure sustainability." *Building and Environment* 42 (2007): 665–680.

8   H. Sahely, Kennedy C., Adams B., "Developing sustainability criteria for urban infrastructure systems." *Canadian Journal of Civil Engineering* 32 (2005): 72–85.

9   T. Panayotou, "Role of the private sector in sustainable Infrastructure development." United Nations Development Program Environment Discussion Paper No. 39 (1998).

10 A. Vives, "Private infrastructure: Ten commandments for sustainability." *Infrastructure* 1(3) (1996).

11 United Nations, "Report of the World Summit on Sustainable Development. Johannesburg, South Africa, 2002," United Nations publication sales No. E.03.II.A.1, New York, 2002, http://daccess-ods.un.org/access.nsf/Get?Open&DS=A/CONF.199/20&Lang=E.

12 US EPA, "Definition of 'infrastructure' for purposes of the American Recovery and Reinvestment Act of 2009," www.epa.gov/ogd/forms/Definition_of_Infrastructure_for_ARRA.pdf.

13 World Bank, "What is infrastructure?" www.worldbank.org/html/prddr/trans/janfebmar03/box1pg3.htm.

14 IPCC, "Climate change 2001: Synthesis report. A contribution of Working Groups I, II, and III to the Third Assessment Report of the Integovernmental Panel on Climate Change" [R.T. Watson and the Core Writing Team (eds)] (Cambridge: Cambridge University Press, 2001).

15 G.C. Hegerl, Zwiers F.W., Braconnot P., *et al.*, "Understanding and attributing climate change." In: S. Solomon, D. Qin, M. Manning, *et al.*, eds, *Climate Change: The Physical Science Basis. Contribution of Working Group I to the Fourth Assessment Report of the Intergovernmental Panel on Climate Change* (Cambridge: Cambridge University Press, 2007).

16 B. Smit, Burton I., Klein R., *et al.*, "An anatomy of adaptation to climate change and variability." *Climatic Change* 45 (2000): 223–251.

17 G. Rebitzer, Ekvallb T., Frischknechtc R., *et al.*, "Life cycle assessment part 1: Framework, goal and scope definition, inventory analysis, and applications." *Environment International* 30 (2004): 701–720.

18 J.J. Lee, O'Callaghan P., Allen D., "Critical review life cycle analysis and assessment techniques and their application to commercial activities." *Resources, Conservation and Recycling* 13(1) (1995): 37–56.

19 P. Miettinen, Hamalainen, R.P., "How to benefit from decision analysis in environmental life cycle assessment (LCA)." *European Journal of Operational Research* 102 (1997): 279–294.

20 G.A. Norris, "Integrating economic analysis into LCA." *Environmental Quality Management* 10 (2001): 59–64.

21 P. Barringer, "A life cycle cost summary." International Conference of Maintenance Societies 2003, www.barringer1.com/pdf/LifeCycleCostSummary.pdf.

17

Economic Assessments of the Value of Sustainability

JOHN WILLIAMS,*† STEPHANE LAROCQUE† AND LIDIA BERGER†

*COLUMBIA UNIVERSITY SCHOOL OF INTERNATIONAL AND PUBLIC AFFAIRS; †HDR

INTRODUCTION TO ENVIRONMENTAL ACCOUNTING

In June 1995, the United States Environmental Protection Agency (EPA) released a document entitled, "An introduction to environmental accounting [EA] as a business management tool: Key concepts and terms" (EPA 742-R-95-001). Produced as part of EPA's Environmental Accounting Project, the document's intent was to serve as a "primer" on the environmental accounting activities at several companies in North America. The document was designed to aid stakeholders in at least two ways: "(1) to orient readers to key concepts often referred to as environmental accounting, and (2) to explain how the terms that refer to environmental accounting are currently being used, so that confusion about the terms does not impede progress in understanding and applying core concepts."[1] The EPA makes the point that "the term environmental accounting has many meanings and uses"[2] and goes on to discuss national income accounting and EA as a means of informing internal business decisions.

The report suggests that "environmental costs are one of the many different types of cost businesses incur as they provide goods and services to their customers. Environmental performance is one of the many important measures of business success."[3] While this emphasis on business is to be applauded, decisions made while developing or retrofitting infrastructure that supports economic activity, as well as environmental remediation and restoration, climate adaptation, and mitigation, are sorely lacking in ability to measure, monetize, and articulate full sustainable costs and benefits (across the triple bottom line of environment, community, and economy) associated with a given action.

The EPA is correct in its assumption that, "Many environmental costs can be significantly reduced or eliminated as a result of business decisions, ranging from operational and housekeeping changes, to investment in "greener" process technology, to redesign of processes/products. … Environmental costs may be obscured in overhead accounts or otherwise overlooked."[4] The EPA cites a number of other reasons that include benefits to human health, design of more preferable processes and services, competitive advantage, and better overall environmental management, which are just as relevant and possibly impactful in infrastructure development. Given that the work cited dates back more than 15 years, only marginal progress has been made in bringing EA to the forefront of decision making regardless of sectors. This lack of progress can be attributed at least partially to shifts in economic conditions, public policy, stakeholder priorities, and overall lack of standardization in terms, tools, and transparent processes.

The remainder of this chapter will focus on the need for a common understanding and approach to assessing sustainable benefits of infrastructure-related decisions. It will begin with an overview of current terminology followed by a review of prevailing practices (cost–benefit analysis and Life Cycle Cost Analysis), examples of methodologies and common denominators (ORC, True Impact, Sigma, AICE's Total), and an introduction to HDR's Sustainable Return On Investment framework (evolution, steps, inputs and outputs, applied examples). There is also a section on steps to standardization and on tradeoffs in choosing environmental accounting approaches.

KEY DEFINITIONS

There are gaps between work already done by the federal government and private sector, and the emerging sustainable infrastructure industry that are rooted in basic terminology and process. EA is in essence an "umbrella" term that reflects at least five contexts that are redefined below.

National Income Accounting (NIA)—a macro-economic measure focused on goods and services as an indicator of societal well-being. Gross Domestic Product (GDP) is an example. The GDP is a measure of how goods and services flow through an economy (without fully accounting for the non-cash and externalities associated with economic activity). More specifically in this context, National Income Accounting would make use of physical or monetary units to refer to the consumption of the nation's natural resources, both renewable and non-renewable or, "natural resources accounting."[5]

Financial Accounting (FA)—enables companies to prepare financial reports for use by investors, lenders, and others. Private and publicly held companies report information on their financial condition through documents governed by the US Securities and

Exchange Commission, with input from the industry's self-regulatory body, and the Financial Accounting Standards Board. Generally Accepted Accounting Standards are the basis for this reporting. Environmental accounting in this context refers to the estimation and public reporting of environmental liabilities and financially material environmental costs.[6]

Managerial or Management Accounting (MMA)—the process of identifying, collecting, and analyzing information, primarily for internal purposes.[7] Management Accounting can involve data on costs, production levels, inventory and backlog, and other vital aspects of a business needed to plan, evaluate, and control in a range of ways including directing management decisions, and controlling and motivating behavior to improve business results.[8]

Environmental Management Accounting (EMA)—the identification, collection, analysis, and use of two types of information for internal decision making: physical information on use, flows and destinies of energy, water, and materials including wastes; and monetary information on environment-related costs, earnings, and savings.[9] According to Burritt, "organizations generally use EMA (or a variant) with a common purpose in mind—to improve information that supports management of their environmental performance so as to improve environmental impacts, reduce costs, and enhance profits as well as organizational reputation."

Sustainability Accounting (SA)—the generation, analysis, and use of monetized environmental, social, and economic performance.[10] Sustainability Accounting and EMA can be used separately or together depending on the decision makers' needs. Further, growing pressure to reveal potential environmental risks/liability associated with publicly traded companies and entities seeking certain types of insurance coverage are likely to place additional emphasis on sustainability in FA and MMA. Specifically regarding sustainable infrastructure decisions, the micro-economic nature of these programs requires a look that shifts emphasis away from NIA to the direct cash, non-cash, and externalities associated with local/infrastructure-based alternatives analysis. As a result, some combination of all of these practices is required to provide the decision support needed to create sustainable infrastructure. That final combination must transparently and objectively address costs and benefits, probabilities of outcomes, and risk associated with direct, non-direct, and "hidden"

or external outcomes to the greatest extent possible in monetary terms, to enable productive comparisons. A hybrid definition and related methodology addressing all of these requisites/attributes has yet to be solidified or standardized.

SUSTAINABILITY BUILDING BLOCKS

Evidence exists that the hybrid definition/methodology referred to above is emerging (see examples described in this chapter) and will likely be built on applications of two commonly accepted analytical practices: business case analysis and Life Cycle Cost Analysis (LCCA).

Traditional models such as business case analysis and LCCA fall short in justifying sustainable decisions because they consider only cash impacts, lack transparency, and do not account for uncertainty. Business case analysis is designed to calculate return on investment from direct cash costs and benefits, and does not account for less tangible items or benefits that are "hidden" from traditional cash flow. LCCA incorporates changes to direct cash flows over a project's entire life cycle. These include initial capital expenditures and replacement capital, changes to annual operations, and maintenance expenses such as utility bills and decommissioning costs. These impacts are then adjusted for the time-value of money to measure financial return on investment (FROI).[11]

Calculating the value of sustainability in infrastructure projects take these measures into account but several other elements must be added to reveal the full value or Sustainable Return on Investment (SROI). Measuring sustainability in a way that is helpful to decision makers involves adding the monetized value of non-cash benefits such as changes in greenhouse gas and air contaminant emissions, health and safety effects, water saved, and worker productivity. The following metrics are valuable outputs calculated for direct-cash, non-cash, and external costs and benefits of a given initiative or project:[12]

- net present value (NPV)—the net present value of an investment, calculated as benefits less costs, with both expressed in present-value monetary terms

- Return on Investment (ROI)—the ratio of the net value of an investment relative to the cost of the investment
- discounted payback period (DPP)—the period of time required for the discounted return on an investment to recover the sum of the original investment
- internal rate of return (IRR)—the discount rate at which the net present value of a project would be zero
- benefit to cost ratio (BCR)—the overall "value of money" of a project, expressed as a ratio of the benefits of a project relative to its costs, with both expressed in present-value monetary terms.

These metrics can help to inform the creation of "green" business cases that public officials can use to articulate the value of FROI as well as SROI attributes in light of other funding priorities and stakeholder interests. Further, they will help in revealing the value associated with specific applications for competitive grant programs. In addition to the metrics described above, the "green" business case could also include: the net costs and benefits of the proposal; the probability that outcomes will be achieved; impacts on jobs (traditional/"grey" and green jobs); the likelihood that sustainable benefits would be realized without new investment (additionality); potential of the proposal to produce energy production/distribution or consumption savings or lead to the development of renewable energy alternatives; contributions to other sustainable costs or benefits (water, waste, high-performance buildings, land use, vehicle miles traveled).

Projects with features that could increase the resiliency of critical services (i.e., mass transit, power, water treatment and distribution) during extreme events should be clearly identified. Green business cases that stress these contributions to the health and security of a host community should be recognized for significant added value that can be stated in monetary terms.

Further, while job creation is generally considered to be a positive attribute, in traditional cost–benefit analysis, as well as SROI, they are viewed as a "cost" of the proposed action since the resources required to fund those jobs must be drawn from some other priority. Regardless, policy and infrastructure decision makers would be wise to include detailed analysis (conducted separately from the sustainability calculations) in the green business case, as funding agencies view green jobs as a major plus.

IDENTIFYING, MEASURING, AND MONETIZING ENVIRONMENTAL COSTS AND BENEFITS

P.J. Simmons and M.R. Rangaswami, in their publication "Show me the money,"[13] have collected examples of ways in which decision makers are seeking to justify investments in green initiatives. Their report includes a series of tools aimed at revealing the business value of specific investments. It describes the shortcomings of traditional analysis, the need to outline the logic and assumptions behind each case, steps to measuring and monetizing key metrics, and ways to address non-financial costs and benefits. Success stories include experience from the FUJITSU Green Cost Index; ORC Worldwide's Return on Health, Safety and Environmental Investments Model; True Impact Web-based ROI Calculator and other software tools; Bob Willard *Sustainability Advantage* Worksheets; SIGMA Sustainability and Environmental Accounting Guides; American Institute of Chemical Engineers' Total Cost Assessment Methodology; BP and Jan Bebbington's Sustainability Assessment Model ; Mark J. Epstein's *Making Sustainability Work* Method for Risk measurement and Valuation; and HDR, Inc.'s Sustainable Return on Investment framework (see details and case examples in sections below).

These examples and more reveal a number of common elements that offer a strong hint to the direction of emerging practices:

- identification of project goals
- definition of scope and boundaries of analysis
- identification of alternatives under consideration
- establishment of steps in the assessment process
- collection of financial and non-financial inputs
- assessment of related risks
- building consensus
- obtaining feedback from key stakeholders.

Each approach uses its own combination of elements. All face a similar challenge in that standardization will be hampered by the need to customize the approach to fit specific markets and geographies. The balance of this chapter will focus on a specific framework that has been applied widely in the sustainable infrastructure sector.

INTRODUCING HDR'S SUSTAINABLE RETURN ON INVESTMENT FRAMEWORK—A MEANS OF ASSIGNING MONETARY VALUE TO THE TRIPLE BOTTOM LINE

In 2007, the morning after a local election, HDR, Inc.[14] representatives met with the economic development director for a large town on New York's Long Island. When asked about the newly re-elected town supervisor's goals for his new term, the director quickly said, "We will be a green community where you will want to live, work and raise your family." When asked for details on what would constitute a "green" community, the director had a difficult time explaining the strategies that would be deployed. It became apparent that articulating a green community vision was difficult without the ability to explain specifically and in monetary terms what the tangible benefits would be. This Long Island town was not the only example to be found of public officials with big "green" plans but lacking the ability to answer the question "What is in it for us?" in a way that stakeholders could understand and support.

This need is shared by the leaders of thousands of communities, utilities, authorities, state and federal agencies, NGOs, and the private sector: how to measure green or establish a monetized value of sustainability. Research revealed the EA work mentioned earlier, but little evidence existed of a framework that would work well for sustainable infrastructure development. This framework needed to address direct-cash, non-cash, and external costs and benefits associated with a given project or program. It had to be informed by detailed knowledge associated with work in the built/infrastructure environment, as well as work in environmental restoration, adaptation, and mitigation, it needed to provide a means for addressing the more difficult to estimate "hidden" benefits, and it needed to provide a means for building credibility and confidence associated with projected outcomes. Most importantly, it had to be transparent and simple enough for most decision makers to use, yet flexible enough to accommodate the variation in data input required to reflect local conditions and priorities.

HDR's Decision Economics practice group (a large team of economists specializing in the development of cost–benefit and business case analysis decision support tools) was challenged with creating what is now referred to as the Sustainable Return on Investment framework or SROI (not to be confused with Social Return on Investment, which has gained some popularity in academic circles) and with applying it, first, on a test basis and then on live projects at a variety of scales.

By summer 2008 HDR made significant progress and reached out to the Clinton Global Initiative (CGI) to make a Commitment to Action to bring the SROI framework to live projects and to release its intellectual property rights into the public domain.[15] HDR also enlisted participation from Columbia University and Mayor Thomas Menino from the City of Boston as partners in a process of testing and evaluating the framework. In September 2009, at the CGI Annual meeting, HDR launched SROI. Since 2010 HDR has worked with CGI, Columbia University, and Harvard's Graduate School of Design to accelerate diffusion of the framework through educational, network, and database initiatives. Elements of the framework have been applied to projects of many sizes and types with an aggregate value of more than $6 billion. A detailed description of the framework is provided below. The HDR SROI process involves four distinct steps.

1. Development of the structure and logic of costs and benefits over the project life cycle. This involves determining the costs and benefits that result from the proposed investment and creating a graphical depiction to quantify these values.
2. Quantification of input assumptions and assignment of risk/uncertainty. This step involves building the preliminary outline of the SROI model, populating the model with initial data assumptions, and performing initial calculations for identified costs and benefits (financial, social, and environmental).
3. Facilitation of a Risk Analysis Process (RAP) session. This is a meeting, similar to a one-day charrette, which brings together key stakeholders to reach consensus on input data values and calculations to be used in the model.
4. Simulation of outcomes and probabilistic analysis. The final step in the process is the generation of SROI metrics, including Net Present Value, Discounted Payback Period, Benefit–Cost Ratio, and the Internal Rate of Return, in addition to the traditional financial metrics. Financial metrics are included as a point of comparison and to transparently and comprehensively illustrate the relative merits of all potential investments being analyzed.

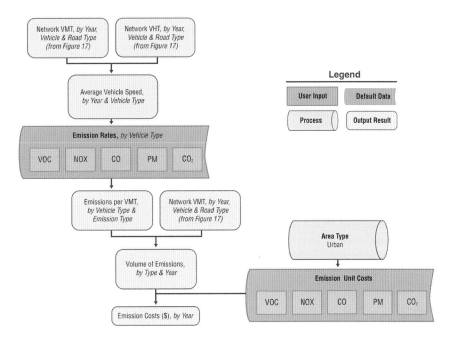

17.1 Example of a structure and logic diagram

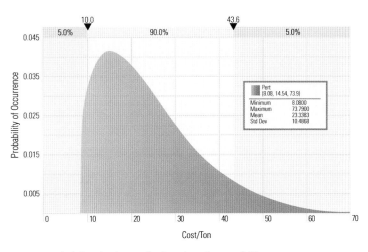

17.2 Probability distribution for the value of a ton of CO_2

Step 1: structure and logic of the cost and benefits

A "structure and logic model" depicts the variables and cause and effect relationships that underpin the forecasting problem at-hand (see Figures 17.1 and 17.2). The structure and logic model is written mathematically to facilitate analysis and also depicted diagrammatically to permit stakeholder scrutiny and modification during Step 3.

Step 2: central estimates and probability analysis

Risk analysis and Monte Carlo simulation techniques can be used to account for uncertainty in both the input values and model parameters. All projections and input values (quantities and pricing) are expressed as probability distributions (a range of possible outcomes and the probability of each outcome), with a wider range of values provided for inputs exhibiting a greater degree of uncertainty. Of note, each element is converted into monetary values to estimate overall impacts in comparable financial terms and discounted to translate all values into present-value terms.

Table 17.1 Example of data input sheet

Quantify input data assumptions

Quantify input data distributions	Data sources	Over 8000 architects, engineers, scientists, and economists Meta-analysis of third-party research and data Financial and insurance markets Contingent valuation, i.e., willingness to pay surveys Bayesian analysis/expert opinion

Colorado electric power generation (2005)—total (all plants)

Category	Metrics	Median	Comment
Plant annual net generation	MWh	49,632,186	EPA: eGRID2007 Version 1.0 Plant File (2005 data)
Plant annual total non-renewable net generation	MWh	47,528,394	EPA: eGRID2007 Version 1.0 Plant File (2005 data)
Plant annual total renewable net generation	MWh	2,103,792	EPA: eGRID2007 Version 1.0 Plant File (2005 data)
Plant annual hydro net generation	MWh	1,293,231	EPA: eGRID2007 Version 1.0 Plant File (2005 data)
Plant annual biomass net generation	MWh	34,327	EPA: eGRID2007 Version 1.0 Plant File (2005 data)
Plant annual wind net generation	MWh	776,234	EPA: eGRID2007 Version 1.0 Plant File (2005 data)
Plant annual solar net generation	MWh	0	EPA: eGRID2007 Version 1.0 Plant File (2005 data)
Plant annual geothermal net generation	MWh	0	EPA: eGRID2007 Version 1.0 Plant File (2005 data)
Total retail sales	MWh	48,353,236	EPA: eGRID2007 Version 1.0 Plant File (2005 data)
Exported	MWh	1,198,342	Implied
Direct use	MWh	80,608	Direct use is commercial or industrial use of electricity
Plant annual net generation less direct use	MWh	49,551,578	Implied

Colorado electric power generation—GHG and CAC—total (all plants) (2005)

Category	Metrics	Median	Comment
Plant annual NO_x emissions	Tons	72,523	EPA: eGRID2007 Version 1.0 Plant File (2005 data)
Plant annual SO_2 emissions	Tons	62.898	EPA: eGRID2007 Version 1.0 Plant File (2005 data)
Plant annual CO_2 emissions	Tons	46,988,461	EPA: eGRID2007 Version 1.0 Plant File (2005 data)
Plant annual CH_4 emissions	Tons	583	EPA: eGRID2007 Version 1.0 Plant File (2005 data)
Plant annual N_2O	Tons	726	EPA: eGRID2007 Version 1.0 Plant File (2005 data)
Plant annual PM 2.5 emissions	Tons	5441	EPA 2005 National Emissions Inventory. Tier Summaries
Plant annual PM 10 emissions	Tons	7391	EPA 2005 National Emissions Inventory. Tier Summaries
Plant annual VOC emissions	Tons	887	EPA 2005 National Emissions Inventory. Tier Summaries

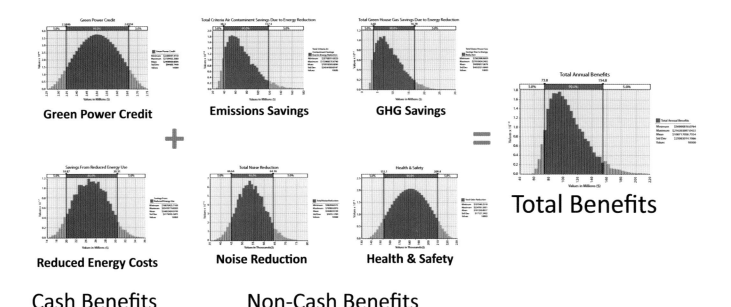

Green Power Credit   **Emissions Savings**   **GHG Savings**

Reduced Energy Costs   **Noise Reduction**   **Health & Safety**

Cash Benefits   Non-Cash Benefits   Total Benefits

17.3 Combining probability distributions

Specifying uncertainty ranges for key parameters entering the decision calculus allows the SROI framework to evaluate the full array of social costs and benefits of a project while illustrating the range of possible outcomes to fully inform decision makers.

Each variable is assigned a central estimate and a range to represent the degree of uncertainty. Estimates are recorded on Excel-based data sheets (see Table 17.1). The first column gives an initial median. Likely high and low values are also determined to define an uncertainty range representing a 90 percent confidence interval—the range within which there exists a 90 percent probability of finding the actual outcome. The greater the uncertainty associated with a forecast variable the wider the range.

Probability ranges are established using both statistical analysis and subjective probability. Probability ranges do not have to be normal or symmetrical. In other words, there is no need to assume a bell-shaped normal probability curve. The bell curve assumes an equal likelihood of being too low and too high in forecasting a particular value. For example, if projected unit construction costs deviate from expectations, it is more likely that the costs will be higher than the median expected outcome than lower.

The Excel-based risk analysis add-on tool @Risk transforms the ranges depicted in Figure 17.3 into formal probability distributions (or "probability density functions"), helping stakeholders understand and participate in the process even without formal training in statistical analysis.

The central estimates and probability ranges for each assumption in the forecasting structure and logic framework come from three sources, as described below.

- The best available peer-reviewed third-party information from a variety of sources, including the Environmental Protection Agency, the Department of Energy, the Federal Highway Administration, the Bureau of Labor Statistics, financial markets, universities, think tanks, etc.
- Historical analysis of statistical uncertainty in all variables and an error analysis of forecasting "coefficients," which are numbers that represent the measured impact of one variable (say, fuel prices) on another (such as the price of steel). While these coefficients can only be known with uncertainty, statistical methods help uncover the level of uncertainty (using diagnostic statistics such as standard deviation, confidence intervals, and so on). This is also referred to as "frequentist" probability.

- Subjective probability (also called "Bayesian" statistics, for the mathematician who developed it) in which a frequentist probability represents the measured frequency with which different outcomes occur (i.e., the number of heads and tails after thousands of tosses). The Bayesian probability of an event occurring is the degree of belief held by an informed person or group that it will occur. Obtaining subjective probabilities is the subject of Step 3.

To explain the HDR process to monetize the value of non-cash benefits, an example of how the dollar value of a ton of CO_2 was monetized in a recent project follows.

The probability distribution for CO_2 was modeled using a PERT distribution that required three key data points: an expected median or 50th percentile value; a low value representing the 5th percentile; and a high value representing the 95th percentile. A meta-analysis of more than 200 recent scientific estimates of the social cost of CO_2 helped in the determination of the most appropriate data points.

The upper and lower bounds used two well-established yet extreme views of the theoretical impact of an incremental ton of CO_2 on the planet, based on two respected sources:

- lower: $8.08/ton in 2008 USD (source: William D. Nordhaus, *A Question of Balance: Weighing the Options on Global Warming Policies*, 2008, Table 5-4)
- upper: $73.79/ton in 2008 USD (source: Nicholas Stern, *The Economics of Climate Change: The Stern Review*, 2006).

Both values are based on calculation of expected damage from climate change. The most comprehensive damage studies include such factors as the greater intensity of hurricanes, impacts of changes in temperature and precipitation on food production, recreation and amenities, and the increased burdens of disease. Estimates include adjustments for the risk of low-probability, high-consequence events such as abrupt climate change. The primary difference between the estimates is in the discount rate used to value future impacts.

For the median price, the current market price as quoted on the European Climate Exchange (ECX) based on the cap and trade system

in place in Europe was used. This is based on a judgment that it is only a matter of time until a cap and trade system is implemented in the USA, making this the best proxy for the eventual impact on US firms. In this case, the median price used was $14.54 USD/ton (ECX price for a ton of CO_2 as of January 21, 2009, was €11.22 adjusted by the Federal Reserve exchange rate of 1$US=€1.2963). It should be noted that both the CO_2 market price and the exchange rate fluctuate greatly, resulting in regular adjustments to the median price used by HDR. Using these three values with a PERT distribution results in a mean price of just over $23 USD/ton.

Step 3: expert evaluation: the RAP© session

The third step in the SROI process involves the formation of an expert panel to hold a charrette-like one- or two-day meeting that HDR calls the Risk Analysis Process (RAP) session. We use proprietary facilitation techniques to elicit risk and probability beliefs from participants about:

1. The structure of the forecasting framework
2. Uncertainty attached to each input variable and forecasting coefficient in the framework.

In 1), experts are invited to add variables and hypothesized causal relationships that may be material, yet missing from the model. In 2), panelists discuss a protocol where initial central estimates and ranges that were provided to panelists prior to the session are modified based on subjective expert beliefs.

Examples of typical RAP session participants include the project team, technical specialists, financial experts, technical specialists, economists, outside experts, public agencies and officials, business groups, and project skeptics.

Step 4: simulation of outcomes and probabilistic analysis

Traditional financial analysis takes the form of a single "expected outcome" supplemented with alternative scenarios. The limitation of a

SROI adds to traditional financial anaylsis the monetized value of non-cash benefits and externalities

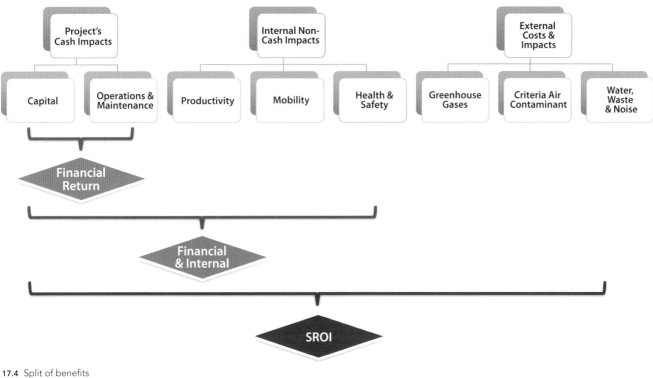

17.4 Split of benefits

forecast with a single expected outcome is clear—while it may provide the single best statistical estimate, it offers no information about the range of other possible outcomes and their associated probabilities. The problem becomes acute when uncertainties surrounding the underlying assumptions of a forecast are material.

Another common approach to provide added perspective on reality is "sensitivity analysis." Key forecast assumptions are varied one at a time, in order, to assess their relative impact on the expected outcome. A concern with this approach is that assumptions are often varied by arbitrary amounts. A more serious concern with this approach is that, in the real world, assumptions do not veer from actual outcomes one at a time, but rather the impact of simultaneous differences between assumptions and actual outcomes is needed to provide a realistic perspective on the riskiness of a forecast.

Risk analysis provides a way around the problems outlined above. It helps avoid the lack of perspective in "high" and "low" cases by measuring the probability or "odds" that an outcome will actually materialize. A risk-based approach allows all inputs

to be varied simultaneously within their distributions, avoiding the problems inherent in conventional sensitivity analysis. Risk analysis also recognizes interrelationships between variables and their associated probability distributions.

In Step 4, final probability distributions are formulated by the risk analyst (Economist) and represent a combination of probability information drawn from Steps 2 and 3. These are combined using simulation techniques (called Monte Carlo analysis) that allow each variable and forecasting coefficient to vary simultaneously according to its associated probability distribution (Figure 17.4). The result is a forecast that includes estimates of the probability of achieving alternative outcomes given the uncertainty in underlying variables and coefficients.

Table 17.2a   Example of a summary of SROI financial and economic outputs

SROI	Current design	Alternative	Notes
Annual value of benefits	$1,284,097	$1,388,514	The total value of the benefits in one year
Energy reductions	$474,470	$516,241	Cash benefit
Water reduction	$80,039	$80,039	Cash benefit
Greenhouse gas savings	$163,461	$177,654	Non-cash benefit
Air pollutants savings	$558,039	$606,492	Non-cash benefit
Savings from reduced water use	$8088	$8088	Non-cash benefit
Net present value	$15,773,620	$13,798,340	PV benefits/PV all costs
Return on investment	39.3%	18.0%	Average rate of return on capital investment
Discounted payback period	4.6	7.7	Time in years + discounted cash flow
Internal rate of return (%)	31.0%	18.1%	Discount rate marking NPV = 0
Benefit to cost ratio	4.7	2.8	PV benefits/PV costs

FROI	Current design	Alternative	Notes
Annual value of benefits	$554,870	$596,193	The total value of the benefits in first year
Net present value	$4,353,935	$1,391,047	PV benefits/PV all costs
Return on investment	15.9%	5.5%	Average rate of return on capital investment
Discounted payback period	12.9	25.0	Time in years to positive discounted cash flow
Internal rate of return (%)	14.2%	6.8%	Discount rate marking NPV = 0
Benefit to cost ratio	2.0	1.2	PV benefits/PV costs

SROI OUTPUTS FOR THE CLIENT

The SROI analysis produces results that address both financial and sustainable criteria using many popular financial/economic metrics described earlier in the chapter. They include Net Present Value, Return on Investment, Discounted Payback Period, Internal Rate of Return, and Benefit/Cost Ratio.

Table 17.2a and 17.2b show key risk-adjusted outputs for a client from an SROI study. The first group provides the mean expected SROI results, i.e., those that correspond to the "triple bottom line." Benefits are included in calculating these metrics, including real cash benefits, non-cash benefits, and externalities. The second group provides the mean expected FROI results, which account for traditional cash benefits, equivalent to a traditional LCCA.

Table 17.3 shows various non-financial metrics that can be provided, such as annual amount of greenhouse gases and pollutants expected to be avoided or the number of jobs and/or "green" jobs expected to be created.

Using the SROI process allows decision makers the ability to prioritize worthy—but competing—projects for funding based on the maximum financial and societal returns. In the following example, a project's outcome metrics are synthesized into an intuitive risk analysis model based on return on investment. Figure 17.5 illustrates the total possible values for the project.

1. Compare the FROI and SROI. In this example, the mean sustainable return on investment is more than double the traditional return on investment.
2. Evaluate non-cash benefits, such as improvements in employee health and productivity, and the benefits to the larger community.
3. Assess the statistical likelihood that return will fall within an 80 percent confidence interval. In this example, sustainable return on investment ranges from 15 percent to 34 percent.

Table 17.2b Example of a summary of SROI financial and economic outputs

Item	Sustainable technology/design element	Impact	Net present value (8.8% nominal discount rate)		Net present value (4.8% nominal discount rate)	
			SROI	FROI	SROI	FROI
1	Thermal storage	Load shifting to reduce electricity cost. It saves water consumption	($2,277,950)	($2,768,156)	($1,423,265)	($2,446,650)
2	Co-generation option #1 (full load)	Load shifting of the full electricity load from the electric utility to natural gas (full load)	($7,519,001)	($29,128,501)	$11,115,030	($34,064,372)
3	Co-generation option #2 (peak shaving)	Load shifting of the peak electricity load from the electric utility to natural gas (peak shaving)	($9,960,971)	($14,754,989)	($11,599,363)	($21,409,068)
4	Heat recovery chiller	Produces electricity and reduces natural gas and water consumption	$9,451,008	$5,373,148	$20,496,349	$11,402,984
5	Energy recovery ventilator	Reduces electrical and natural gas consumption	$758,508	($492,549)	$2,627,693	($66,722)
6	Ground source heat pump	Reduces electrical and natural gas consumption	$2,531,891	$532,460	$7,480,615	$3,314,412
7	Solar hot water	Reduces electrical consumption. However, increases water consumption	($130,196)	($297,640)	$158,474	($215,818)
8	Solar photovoltaics	Produces electricity. However, increases water consumption	($2,658,852)	($3,240,496)	($2,531,472)	($3,776,996)
9	Geothermal direct heating	Reduces natural gas consumption. However, increases electrical consumption	($1,375,199)	($1,936,041)	($228,491)	($1,512,578)
10	HVAC exhaust energy recovery wind turbines	Produces electricity	($1,015,939)	($1,573,125)	($658,058)	($1,857,096)
11	On-site graywater and wastewater reclamation, treatment, and re-use	Reduces water consumption. However, increases electrical consumption	($768,573)	($3,116,302)	$1,323,187	($3,554,027)
12	Dishwasher water recovery and re-use	Reduces water consumption. However, increases electrical consumption	($59,432)	($82,115)	($94,223)	($141,415)
13	Recycling station on site	Diverts waste from landfill. However, increases electrical consumption	$1,199,726	$929,241	$2,916,764	$2,354,488
14	HEPA filtration at all air handling units in patient-care areas	Reduces hospital-acquired infections. However, increases electrical consumption	$38,151,331	$73,577	$79,618,918	$276,584
15	Hydrogen peroxide vapour cleaning	Reduces hospital-acquired infections. However, increases electrical consumption	$121,065,684	$1,966,018	$253,166,523	$4,999,118

Table 17.3 Example of a summary of SROI non-financial outputs

Environmental	Annually	Notes
Tons of CO_2 emissions avoided	3943.6	Number of tons of carbon dioxide avoided based on the energy savings
Tons of CH_4 emissions avoided	0.1	Number of tons of methane avoided based on the energy savings
Tons of N_2O emissions avoided	0.1	Number of tons of nitrous oxide avoided based on the energy savings
Tons of SO_2 emissions avoided	14.3	Number of tons of sulphur dioxide avoided based on the energy savings
Tons of NO_x emissions avoided	4.4	Number of tons of nitrogen dioxide avoided based on the energy savings
Tons of PM 2.5 emissions avoided	1.0	Number of tons of particulate matter avoided based on the energy savings
Tons of VOC emissions avoided	0.1	Number of tons of volatile organic compounds avoided based on the energy savings
Gallons of freshwater saved	1,640,602	Number of gallons of freshwater saved
Tons of waste avoided	23	Number of tons of waste avoided

Social	Annually	Notes
Number of injuries avoided	1	Number of potential injuries avoided due to the project
Hours of productivity saved	16,783	Number of productive hours saved due to the project

Economic	Annually	Notes
Jobs created	2781	Number of incremental new jobs created (FTEs)
Green jobs created	33	Number of incremental new "green" jobs created (FTEs)
Equivalent barrels of oil saved	11,436	Equivalent number of barrels of oil saved based on the energy savings

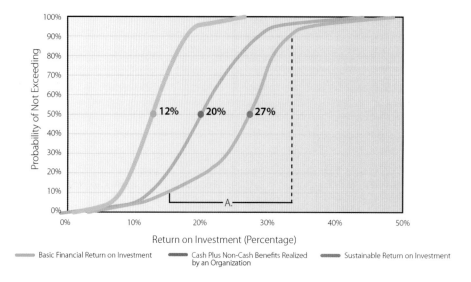

17.5 The sustainability "S" curve

SROI FRAMEWORK CASE STUDIES

City of Boston/Boston Redevelopment Authority[16]

The City of Boston received American Recovery and Reinvestment Act (ARRA) funding across multiple departments and functions, so the Boston Redevelopment Authority Research Division and HDR Decision Economics conducted an SROI analysis to estimate near-term economic impacts and longer-term sustainability benefits of these investments. While the redevelopment authority has used the Regional Economic Model to gauge economic impact of the City's various investments since 1999, it did not have a modeling framework for broader environmental and social benefits. SROI provided this framework. Sustainability benefits were measured for four city departments totaling $87.6 million in ARRA funding, with a total leveraged investment of $162.9 million:

The Energy and Environmental Department
SROI was measured for most of this department's $6.2 million in ARRA funding, including a residential energy retrofit program, a small-business energy program, LED street lights, and installing solar energy infrastructure. Direct benefits primarily include reduced kilowatt-hours and related emissions reductions.

The Boston Transportation Department
SROI was estimated for the Dorchester Avenue project, which reduces traffic delays at intersections and related emissions. Other direct benefits include energy savings from LED lights and reduced accidents.

The Department of Neighborhood Development
This department uses ARRA funding primarily as a gap-financing mechanism to facilitate and accelerate mixed-use development projects. Primary focus was on developing a LEED®-standard energy efficient building that will accelerate development of a vacant parcel in Jamaica Plain.

The Boston Housing Authority
This department's portfolio includes modernizing multi-family residential buildings and new construction of energy-efficient residential properties. Sustainability benefits were measured in terms of reduced kWh, therms of gas and fresh water used in low-flow toilets.

The direct sustainability benefits were estimated to be substantial over time, with annual benefits in 2015 of:

- 34.4 million fewer kWh of electricity consumed
- 277,000 fewer therms of gas used
- 23,750 hundreds of cubic feet of water preserved
- 25,120 fewer tons of greenhouse gas emissions.

By far the largest benefits category is a direct energy bill cost savings of more than $5.7 million a year. Reduced air pollutants save nearly $3 million a year, reduced water and sewer bill costs are more than $2.4 million per year combined, and reduced greenhouse gas emissions $0.9 million per year.

Aggregate net present value is more than $208 million, more than $111 million for the Dorchester Avenue project alone, with a 4.5 discounted payback period of approximately five years. The internal rate of return is estimated at 38 percent across the four departments, with even stronger returns for the Transportation Department, Housing Authority, and Energy and Environmental Department.

Fort Belvoir Community Hospital, Fort Belvoir, Virginia[17]

The Norfolk District of the US Army Corps of Engineers and HDR-Newberry Joint Venture charged with designing the Fort Belvoir Community Hospital, the Walter Reed Hospital replacement, asked HDR Decision Economics to provide an SROI analysis of energy and water conservation measures for the new hospital. The study was conducted jointly with a Life Cycle Cost Analysis (LCCA) as required by the Federal Energy Management Program.

In this study, the energy model called "Performance Rating Method model" or baseline was compared with the following two energy model alternatives:

- an "as designed" model of the building with updates
- a model called "Current Design 30%," reflecting the "Current Design with Updates" energy measures and an additional energy measure—in this case a solar photovoltaic system—needed to meet the 30 percent energy use reduction required by the Energy Policy Act 2005.

The joint LCCA and SROI analyses found that the combined energy conservation methods in both energy models were justified from the economic and societal standpoints.

The LCCA found that the savings-to-investment ratio is greater than 1, the adjusted internal rate of return is higher than the real discount rate (3 percent), and both the simple payback and discounted payback were reached during the study period (two years of construction and 25 years of service). The LCCA results were confirmed by the FROI analysis contained within the SROI analysis.

The SROI analysis showed that after accounting for externalities, conservation measures would have less impact on human health and the environment than a typical building complying with minimum ASHRAE requirements. The study also evaluated the proposed solar photovoltaic system as a stand-alone energy conservation method using LCCA, and found it would not be economically justified if it was the exclusive energy conservation measure.

Metropolitan Transportation Authority, State of New York[18]

The Metropolitan Transportation Authority (MTA) serves New York City, the Hudson Valley, Long Island and southern Connecticut. As part of its report, *Greening Mass Transit and Metro Regions*, conducted in partnership with the Blue Ribbon Commission on Sustainability, the MTA recommended developing an SROI model that can be used to select green initiatives in a manner compatible with the MTA's standard accounting practices.

One hypothetical example used by HDR Decision Economics was a simple one—swapping out 1700 light bulbs at Grand Central Station for energy-efficient compact fluorescent light bulbs (CFLs). Seven hundred bulbs would be switched from 60 W to 15W CFLs, and 1000 would be switched from 100 W to 20 W CFLs. In addition, the new light bulbs would require annual replacement instead of monthly replacement. The impacts were evaluated over a ten-year timeframe. These impacts included the annual expense of purchasing light bulbs, annual electricity cost, and reduced environmental emissions, including carbon, nitrogen oxide, sulfur dioxide, volatile organic compounds, and particulate matter.

The SROI analysis found that this initiative would reduce annual electricity consumption by nearly 980,000 kWh each year, equivalent to 294 tons of carbon emissions. Over the ten-year timeframe, this is equivalent to nearly 3000 tons of carbon. The social benefit was measured at $8500 in the first year and increased to $11,000 per year by the tenth year. Over the ten-year period, the value of the other reduced emissions is an additional $15,000.

Total cost savings incurred by switching to CFL light bulbs was estimated at $1.46 million. Total social value of reduced emissions was estimated at an additional $115,000 over this period, $100,000 of which is attributable to carbon. The cost of the CFL light bulbs is recovered immediately, and the social return is substantial.

Johns Hopkins[19]

The Johns Hopkins University SROI study grew out of the university's campus-wide Sustainability Initiative. As part of the initiative, the School of Medicine saw value in the US Green Building Council's LEED program and sought LEED certification for several of its facilities. When the university engaged HDR Architecture to develop LEED applications for four laboratory buildings, university and HDR team members realized the value of quantifying the relationship between better environmental fit and lower operational costs, and engaged the HDR Decision Economics group to calculate the project's SROI.

Using a 20-year economic simulation model, the project team identified all of the costs and benefits associated with sustainable initiatives at the four buildings. These included efficient lighting, variable air volume systems, heat recovery wheels, a recycling program, grey water system, and low-flow fixtures. Research determined the proper values of each input and how to quantify and incorporate them into the model. Inputs were also developed for increased productivity made possible by reduced sick days.

The SROI analysis discovered that 57 percent of the sustainable benefits would accrue to reduced energy use. Improved health and increased productivity accounted for 41 percent of the benefits, and water efficiency and waste reduction accounted for 1 percent each.

The analysis also determined a mean or average value of $3.6 million of benefits per year. Using the S curve to determine all possible outcomes showed that the median/50th percentile result was also $3.6 million, with an 80 percent confidence interval ranging between $3.1 million and $4.1 million. This means that there is an 80 percent chance the actual benefits will fall within that range.

The Net Present Value calculation, derived by discounting the project's cash flow over a 20-year period, showed a mean expected SROI value of $37.8 million, meaning that society will be the equivalent of $37.8 million better off (in today's dollars) over the course of the next 20 years as a result of these initiatives.

STEPS TO STANDARDIZATION

The issue of the lack of widespread standardization of sustainability measurement was raised at the beginning of this chapter. This is a primary challenge for the entire infrastructure industry, which must be addressed in order to expand and sustain momentum toward more responsible development that responds to societal needs today without jeopardizing the interests of future generations. While there have been moves in both the public and private sectors to quantify triple bottom line impacts, much of the work to date is focused on macro-level economics and the evaluation of national level policies (e.g., the Clean Air Act) rather than at the micro-economic project level.[20] Often, these analyses are conducted *ex post* to assess the external benefits of programs, rather than *ex ante* to inform decision making.[21] Although this methodology

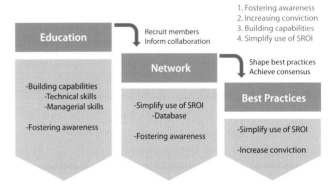

Broad Adoption of Sustainability Measurement and Communication

17.6 Strategies to achieve the diffusion of the SROI framework

works in theory, it could be more standardized and needs to be adopted on a broader scale.[22]

Private sector companies are using a growing number of established frameworks to report specific environmental impacts, carbon emissions, and social impacts including factory health and safety conditions. The public sector and infrastructure decision makers are struggling to measure and articulate the benefits that support their plans. In both sectors a large proportion of spending decisions remain based on a FROI, not on external benefits.[23] In order to achieve a higher level of acceptance into routine practice, sustainability measurement must gain broad acceptance by decision makers. The objectives of such outreach programs should include:

- fostering awareness
- increasing conviction
- building capabilities
- simplifying the use of frameworks.

Three practical strategies will achieve these objectives (Figure 17.6).[24] Work is currently underway with a group of organizations aimed at developing the education, network, and best-practices database on a significant scale. In years to come those efforts will lead to broad adaptation and self-perpetuation beginning with the educational element followed by network collaboration and the growth of a database.

SUMMARY

Accounting for environmental costs and benefits has been a priority since the early 1990s. As awareness of the importance of sustainability has emerged, there has been an associated desire to measure "green" or the value of investments in the triple bottom line. While different cost–benefit and life cycle-based frameworks and methodologies have been developed, a specific approach to measuring sustainability associated with infrastructure development has yet to be standardized. Economists at HDR, Inc. have developed and applied the Sustainable Return on Investment or SROI framework on a variety of scales for infrastructure and building projects. They have collaborated with the Clinton Global Initiative, City of Boston, Columbia and Harvard Universities to disseminate the framework into the public domain. They are also working with academic institutions and social entrepreneurs to create education, network, and database development opportunities that accelerate progress toward standardization of the methodology. As more and more infrastructure decision makers apply the methodology, their stakeholders will become accustomed to programs that are prioritized and selected on a basis of the total value of the social, environmental, and economic implications or return to user communities

NOTES

1   United States Environmental Protection Agency, office of Pollution Prevention and Toxics, *MC 7409* (Washington, DC: 20460 EPA 742-R-95-001, June 1995), p. viii.
2   Ibid., p. 1.
3   Ibid., p. 1.
4   Ibid., pp. 1 and 2.
5   Ibid., p. 4.
6   Ibid., p. 4.
7   Institute of Management Accountants Statement on Management Accounting, No. 1A
8   United States Environmental Protection Agency, *MC 7409*, p. 5.
9   S. Schaltegger, Burritt R., "Caption 20: corporate sustainability accounting, a catchphrase for compliant corporations or a business decision support for sustainability leaders?" In: *The 2005 IFAC Guidelines on Environmental Management Accounting, Improving Decision Flows to Support Decisions* (United Nations Expert Working Group on EMA, 2005), p. 2.
10 Ibid., p. 2, and *The Forum for the Future.*
11 J. Williams, Larocque S., "Calculating a sustainable return on investment." *Journal of Public Works and Infrastructure* 2(2) (2009): 98.
12 Ibid., page 99.
13 "Show me the money: demonstrating green business value to skeptics," Corporate ECOFORUM Research Series, November 2009.
14 HDR, Inc. is an international architecture, engineering, and consulting firm.
15 CGI is a not-for-profit, non-partisan organization founded by former President Clinton to bring leaders including heads of state, philanthropists, corporations, and NGOs together to collaborate to solve many of the world's problems as related to health, education, poverty, energy, and the environment. Members of CGI are required to make Commitments to Action to undertake initiatives that are new, significant, measurable, and aligned with CGI priorities.

16 Boston Redevelopment Authority, *Economic and Sustainability Benefits of Boston's ARRA Investments* (Boston: BRA, 2010).

17 HDR Decision Economics, *Sustainable Return on Investment and Life-Cycle Cost Analysis of: The Energy and Water Conservation Measures for the Proposed Fort Belvoir Community Hospital* (Ottawa, Canada: US Army Corps of Engineers—Norfolk District, 2010).

18 Metropolitan Transportation Authority, *Greening Mass Transit and Metro Regions: The Final Report of the Blue Ribbon Commission on Sustainability and the MTA* (New York: MTA, 2009).

19 HDR Decision Economics, *Evaluation of Johns Hopkins University Campus Sustainability Investments* (Ottawa, Canada, November 11, 2008).

20 C. Kolstad, *Environmental Economics* (Oxford: Oxford University Press, 2000).

21 A. Boardman, Greenburg D., Vining A., *et al.*, *Cost–Benefit Analysis Concepts and Practice* (Upper Saddle River: Pearson Education, Inc., 2006).

22 A.M. Cofield, Ellison H., Jansen F., *et al.*, "Sustainable return on investment: A pathway towards widespread sustainability measurement and communication" (Columbia University Capstone Workshop, spring 2010), p. 4.

23 Ibid., p. 4.

24 Ibid., p. 8.

Part 4
Design and Planning for Infrastructure Sustainability

AS IS ALWAYS THE CASE, one must toil in the now while keeping an eye on the future. The means and methods for creating sustainable infrastructure and for developing an assessment tool exist today but require implementation. Nevertheless, new challenges and opportunities await us. Individual sustainable infrastructure projects will need to become integrated into entire sustainable cities. Existing cities will need to be retrofitted to become ecological centers. The very goals and values associated with the current culture of consumption must be checked and re-evaluated. This section presents some of the new and fascinating challenges, both practical and theoretical, that await us. As our understanding of these new challenges increases so does our hope for better solutions and the future of sustainable infrastructure.

18

Sustainable Cities:
Oxymoron or the Shape of the Future?

ANNISSA ALUSI, ROBERT G. ECCLES, AMY C. EDMONDSON, AND TIONA ZUZUL[1]

HARVARD BUSINESS SCHOOL

ABSTRACT

Two trends are likely to define the twenty-first century: threats to the sustainability of the natural environment and dramatic increases in urbanization. This paper reviews the goals, business models, and partnerships involved in eight early "eco-city" projects to begin identifying success factors in this emerging industry. Eco-cities, for the most part, are viewed as a means of mitigating threats to the natural environment while creating urban living capacity by combining low carbon and resource-efficient development with the use of information and communication technologies (ICT) to better manage complex urban systems.

INTRODUCTION

Urbanization presents one of the most pressing and complex challenges of the twenty-first century. How cities are designed, managed, and used is likely to shift substantially based on demands created by two powerful trends. One trend involves a growing awareness of a threat to the sustainability of the Earth's natural environment; the second is the rapid rise in the number of people moving into and living in cities. Combined, these trends call for massive development of new buildings and infrastructure, along with new social and cultural institutions, to accommodate vast numbers of city dwellers without irreparably harming the natural environment.

In particular, rapid population and economic growth in the developing world pose profound implications for the future of human society. About 90 percent of urban growth worldwide occurs in developing countries, which are projected to triple their existing base of urban areas between 2000 and 2030.[2] It is estimated that, by 2025, China alone will add 350 million people to its urban population—more than the population of the entire USA today.[3]

The pathway taken by urban development over the next few decades will play a crucial role in the trajectory of worldwide greenhouse gas emissions and natural resource depletion. Cities consume 60 percent to 80 percent of the world's energy production,

and with the urban population of the developing world projected to reach more than 5 billion people by 2050, ideas about how to combine urbanization and sustainability are of critical and immediate importance.[4]

In response, around the world a few companies and government bodies have begun to explore the creation of "ecocities"—a term that overlaps and is sometimes used interchangeably with "smart cities" or "sustainable cities." According to the declaration of the World Ecocity Summit 2008 in San Francisco, an eco-city:

> is an ecologically healthy city. Into the deep future, the cities in which we live must enable people to thrive in harmony with nature and achieve sustainable development. People oriented, ecocity development requires the comprehensive understanding of complex interactions between environmental, economic, political and socio-cultural factors based on ecological principles. Cities, towns and villages should be designed to enhance the health and quality of life of their inhabitants and maintain the ecosystems on which they depend.[5]

As this encompassing description implies, the term eco-city remains loosely defined.[6] A second, similar definition comes from the World Bank "Eco[2] Cities" report: "Ecological cities enhance the well-being of citizens and society through integrated urban planning and management that fully harnesses the benefit of ecological systems, and protects and nurtures these assets for future generations."[7] Both definitions include environmental and social components, and emphasize the importance of urban planning and management.[8]

Some observers have suggested that threats to the environment can be mitigated by eco-cities, which might provide "needed structural change for transition into a post-carbon economy."[9] To consider this possibility, we examined eight eco-city projects currently under development. We reviewed both what these early efforts have in common and how they differ, as a first step in identifying factors that may affect the success of future eco-cities. As elaborated below, eco-city projects typically include carbon emissions reduction and resource efficiency targets, economic development goals, and unique city designs to promote healthy, socially sustainable communities, as well as to gain recognition for sustainability. Whether or not these targets can be reached remains an open question. Is the juxtaposition of sustainability and urbanization an oxymoron, or the shape of things to come? The projects described below present evidence that a substantial number of thoughtful, deeply expert individuals and experienced organizations are betting on the latter.

DRIVERS AND COMPONENTS OF ECO-CITY INITIATIVES

The World Bank launched the Eco^2 Cities Program to "provide practical and scalable, analytical and operational support for cities in developing countries to achieve ecological and economic sustainability"[10] based on four key principles: 1) a city-based approach; 2) an expanded platform for collaborative design and decision making; 3) a one-system approach; and 4) an investment framework that values sustainability and resiliency. The program's goals include assessing the economic viability of eco-cities to explore the possibility that eco-cities might attract global businesses and allow lower costs relative to traditional cities, while withstanding resource, climate, and economic shocks. The World Bank plans to partner with governments, NGOs, and private sector organizations to help pilot Eco^2 Cities develop.

Attempts to define the attributes of eco-cities include a joint initiative between the Clinton Climate Initiative and the US Green Building Council that suggested the following:

100 percent carbon-neutral energy production; an interconnected transport system and land-use pattern that shifts people from cars to walking, cycling and public transport; a zero-waste management system; resource conservation, including maximizing water and energy efficiency and preserving open land, wildlife and plant habitats; and using environmentally sound building materials, preferably locally sourced.[11]

Although these compelling attributes are not yet widely endorsed, there are two dominant themes associated with most eco-city projects: the use of green buildings to reduce greenhouse gas emissions, and the use of ICT to better manage and operate the cities.

Green building has been the focus of much government attention over the past few years. In May 2010, the European Union (EU) announced a mandate for "nearly zero-energy buildings," which will apply to all new public buildings in the EU after 2018 and to all new homes and offices in 2020.[12] The European Commission, the executive branch of the EU, is responsible for designing specific regulations for "minimum energy" buildings. In the USA, the General Services Administration, responsible for the federal government's buildings and real estate, embraced sustainable-design principles by mandating that all new construction and major renovations be compliant with LEED® Gold standards.[13] While the EU is a step ahead of the USA in its requirements, governments in both regions are likely to continue to exert a major influence on the type of design and urban development that eco-cities seek to achieve.

China's Ministry of Construction established the China Green Building Council in 2008, to establish a LEED-like rating system as a step toward pursuing stricter environmental standards for construction and promoting clean-tech development.[14] The government's goal is "to cut energy use of buildings by 65 percent by 2020, using the average energy efficiency of Chinese buildings in 1980 as the base point."[15] The four largest cities in China—Beijing, Shanghai, Tianjin, and Chongqing—will work to cut building energy use by 65 percent before the end of 2010. As the World Bank estimates that 50 percent of new building construction globally will occur in China by 2015, this is a massive undertaking and could open up numerous "eco-friendly" development opportunities in China in the coming years.

Smart infrastructure, or the use of ICT to better manage complex systems ranging from traffic patterns to the electric grid, is a related field that plays a central role in eco-city development. A key component is the integration of wireless sensors, which can collect and transmit information from almost any object, including utility lines, water pipes, roads, and buildings. Using sensors, advanced computer software interprets raw data to "monitor and optimize" these kinds of complex systems. In this way, computers will "become intelligent instruments of control, [linked] to data-generating sensors throughout the planet's infrastructure,"[16] resulting in enormous reductions in greenhouse gas emissions and wasted natural resources.

The Climate Group's SMART 2020 plan identified ICT within cities as a resource that could cut global emissions by 15 percent by 2020, and the research firm IDC estimates that the smart infrastructure field will amount to $122 billion over the next two years.[17] For example, IBM has been a leader in the digital infrastructure field and many of its advances apply to city-related technologies. IBM has undertaken projects across the globe under the umbrella of its "Smarter Planet" initiative, including smart grid software, working with cities on water management systems, and implementing "smart" traffic systems in major cities.[18]

Another example is technology giant Cisco's interest in the eco-city realm. Executive Vice President, Cisco Services, and Chief Globalization Officer, and head of Cisco's "Smart+Connected Communities" initiative Wim Elfrink estimated that "at least $500 billion will be earmarked for instant cities over the next decade, with $10 billion to $15 billion allotted for network plumbing alone." CEO John Chambers predicted that the smart-grid market itself "may be bigger than the whole Internet."[19] More broadly, Cisco sees its entire Smart+Connected Communities initiative as a potential $30 billion opportunity, including revenues from installation of infrastructure—notably highways, bridges, railroads, airports, utilities, and dams—and "selling the consumer-facing hardware as well as the services layered on top of that hardware."[20]

ECO-CITY DEVELOPMENTS

The development of eight eco-city initiatives provides early experiments from which we can learn. This section thus reviews Dongtan, Tianjin Eco-City, Nanjing, and Meixi Lake District in China; Masdar City in Abu Dhabi; New Songdo City in South Korea; Sitra Low2No in Finland; and PlanIT Valley in Portugal. While not exhaustive, the list presents a reasonable sample of early eco-city projects. Our aim is to assess these geographically diverse initiatives, beginning with the earliest ones, and to examine their

aims, business models, and partnerships, so as to identify factors associated with the development of successful eco-cities.

New Songdo City

Background and goals

Plans for New Songdo City, located on a man-made island about 40 miles from Seoul, South Korea, began in 2000. The 1500-acre city's anticipated population is 430,000 by 2014, and its overall development goal is "Compact, Smart, and Green." Plans are to emit only one-third the greenhouse gases of a similar size city, with plans for green homes and commercial buildings developed by GE Korea. The city lies within the Incheon Free Economic Zone to attract businesses and foreign investment, and aims to "position South Korea as the commercial epicenter of Northeast Asia."[21]

Governance and financing

In 2001, the City of Incheon gave development rights to a 70/30 partnership between developer Gale International and construction manager POSCO E&C, a Korean steelmaker.[22] The project has an estimated cost of $35 billion and in 2006 Morgan Stanley became the first financial institution to make a direct cash investment, totaling $350 million.[23] At that time, $1.5 billion in construction had already been financed through a syndicated loan extended by a group of 26 financial institutions.

Partnership network

Kohn Pederson Fox was selected as the master architect for the New Songdo International Business District, but several architects, including KlingStubbins, HOK New York, and Dong-II Architects, took charge of individual projects in the city.[24] Arup, an engineering and design consultancy with expertise in sustainability, was engaged to support engineering and design work on the downtown area of the city. Cisco emerged as the major technology player in the city, with plans to develop a "Cisco Global Center for Intelligent Urbanization" in New Songdo. Cisco plans to completely digitize the city by covering

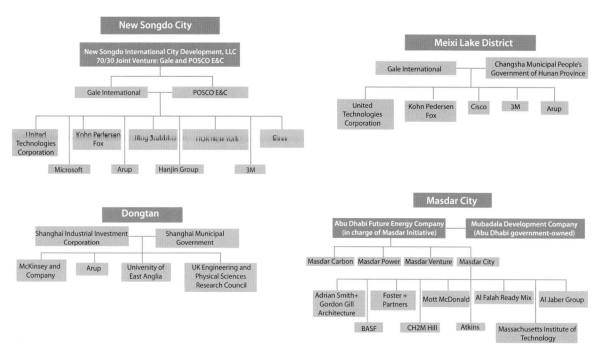

18.1 Key statistics

it in sensors so that it "runs on information"—meaning that Cisco's "control room" would act as the "brain" of the city.[25] New Songdo would be a key part of Cisco's Smart+Connected Communities initiative—including revenue from installing infrastructure and also selling consumer hardware and services.

New Songdo City features the Songdo International Business District (IBD), organized through a Memorandum of Understanding (MOU) between Gale International, United Technologies Corporation (UTC), and Hanjin Group.[26] The IBD was launched in August 2009 and is intended to fill the need for an international business hub in Northeast Asia due to the massive business growth in nearby cities such as Beijing, Shanghai, and Tokyo. Songdo IBD aims to attract multinational corporations by providing hotels, schools, technology infrastructure, and convention centers of the highest caliber, and by employing leading urban planning and sustainable design firms to create an "unparalleled quality of life."[27] Two other major technology companies, Microsoft and 3M, have agreed to partner to create a world-class health facility, Songdo International City Hospital, within the city. (See Figure 18.1 for a diagram of partnership networks for each city.)

Status

As of 2009, 60,000 residents and 418 companies and research centers either had relocated to New Songdo or announced plans

to do so, and by 2014 the second phase of development was targeted for completion.[28] The city plans to include 10 foreign universities, eight Korean universities, four international schools, and 17 theaters, at some point in the future.

Dongtan

Background and goals

Dongtan City, China, presents one of the earliest and most widely publicized sustainable urbanization projects. In 2005, the Shanghai Municipal government gave a tract of land on Chongming Island to the Shanghai Industrial Investment Company (SIIC), China's state-run investment arm. Chongming Island is situated about nine miles from Shanghai's financial district and covers nearly 33 square miles—an area about three-quarters the size of Manhattan.[29] The government instructed SIIC to develop a plan for the land, thus beginning the project of Dongtan City.

The city's original stated goal was to be a "renewably powered, car-free, water-recycling" city that could serve as a sustainable city model for the world, housing 25,000 residents by the 2010 Shanghai World Expo and 500,000 by 2050.[30] According to SIIC, the broader idea was "to skip traditional industrialization in favor of ecological modernism."[31]

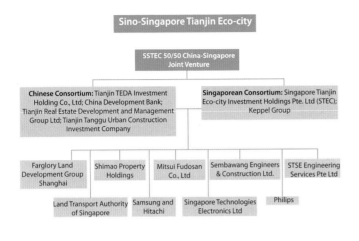

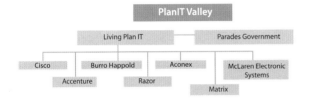

Governance and financing

In 2010, SIIC was the second largest real estate holder in China and, as the developer of the Dongtan City project, was solely responsible for appointing companies to the project. SIIC first hired consulting firm McKinsey & Company to be involved in its process of considering different design and engineering firms to take on the project. Eventually, with the recommendation of McKinsey, SIIC offered the lead design role to Arup. Finally, SIIC and Arup signed partnership agreements with HSBC and UK investment bank Sustainable Development Capital LLP for financing.

Partnership network

Arup oversaw the key design and sustainability aspects of the Dongtan project: "urban design, planning, sustainable energy management, waste management, renewable energy process implementation, economic and business planning, sustainable building design, architecture, infrastructure and even the planning of communities and social structures."[32] The intended collaboration between SIIC and Arup received significant political support and publicity. On November 9, 2005, in a ceremony in London at Number 10 Downing Street in the presence of Prime Minister Tony Blair and visiting Chinese President Hu Jintao, the two companies signed a contractual agreement to develop the world's first "eco-city" and also collaborate on sustainable development projects in the future.

Over time, SIIC spent over $1 billion building a bridge and tunnel connection between Chongming Island and Shanghai, connecting the site to one of the most rapidly growing mega cities on the planet. The partners grappled with complex issues, including who would live in Dongtan, what sort of jobs would be created, how to make the city commercially viable, and how to make it replicable.[33]

The project planned to focus on education, including building a Dongtan Institute for Sustainability. Dongtan's educational initiatives received support and assistance from the Engineering and Physical Sciences Research Council (EPSRC), the primary UK funding body for engineering and physical sciences. The EPSRC, Arup, and SIIC agreed to form research networks to study the process of developing a sustainable city and collaborate to address the associated challenges.[34] Arup and SIIC also signed an MOU with the University of East Anglia carbon reduction team in the UK to collaborate on the Dongtan Sustainable Technologies and Renewables (STAR) Project, which would include a renewable energy station in the city.[35]

Status

Despite the partnerships and planning, delays pushed the construction start date back from 2006 to 2009. As of 2010, implementation of Arup's master plan seemed stalled. Peter Head, a key project leader from Arup, said in an interview that to his knowledge the plans were indefinitely on hold and that SIIC had not informed Arup of the reasons for this. Chen Lianglu, a Communist Party leader in Shanghai, who played a large role in procuring the Chongming Island land for development by SIIC, was arrested for fraud in 2006, perhaps creating political tension that helped derail the project timeline. There has also been speculation about funding and environmental challenges. Chongming Island is home to important wetlands, making development less environmentally friendly than developers would have liked.[36]

Masdar City

Background and goals

The government of Abu Dhabi began one of the most famous—and most widely criticized—eco-city projects to date. The 2.7 square mile Masdar City, located in a desert 10.5 miles from downtown Abu Dhabi, was designed to house 40,000 residents, along with hundreds of businesses and a research university, and to serve as a clean-tech city cluster. Masdar City officials stated that the city's goal "is to serve as a model for other sustainable urban development, assist the wider Abu Dhabi in lowering its eco footprint, contribute to Abu Dhabi's economic diversification and establish the emirate as a global hub for renewable energy and clean technology."[37] Initially, Masdar City had a $22 billion price tag and a projected completion date of 2016.

The government originally announced that the city would aim to be zero-carbon, powered entirely by renewable energy, car-free, and produce net-zero waste. Plans for the city were later revised to achieve more modest, if still ambitious, sustainability performance indicators. These include reducing overall energy demand by 50 percent, embodied carbon (emissions caused by building materials and products) by 30 percent, and operational carbon (emissions caused by the city's day-to-day operations) by 50 percent, compared with what Masdar City officials describe as "business as usual" in Abu Dhabi.[38] Aside from energy, Masdar City's planners hope to reduce water and landfill waste by 30 percent and 50 percent respectively. Also, Abu Dhabi won the right to host the headquarters of the International Renewable Energy Agency (IRENA), an organization with a mandate to "promote the widespread and increased adoption and sustainable use of all forms or renewable energy," within Masdar City.[39]

Governance and financing

The plan for Masdar City was conceived by the government of Abu Dhabi and administered by Masdar, a wholly-owned subsidiary of the Mubadala Development Company, a government-owned investment vehicle that manages a multi-billion dollar portfolio of projects to support the growth and economic diversification of Abu Dhabi. Masdar is comprised of five integrated units, including Masdar City, Masdar Carbon, Masdar Capital, Masdar Power, and Masdar Institute of Science and Technology. Masdar describes itself as "a commercially driven enterprise that operates to reach the broad boundaries of the renewable energy and sustainable technologies industry" and "seeks to become a leader in making renewable energy a real, viable business and Abu Dhabi a global centre of excellence in the renewable energy and clean technology category."[40]

The Abu Dhabi government set aside $15 billion for Masdar, about $4 billion of which was allocated to Masdar City. Other forms of financing will presumably provide the remainder of approximately $19 to $20 billion anticipated total price tag.[41] The city is designated as a special economic zone that allows 100 percent foreign ownership and zero taxes in an effort to encourage economic investment and to attract international companies.[42]

Partnership network

In 2006, Masdar selected London-based Foster + Partners to design the city, help set sustainability standards, and design the Masdar Institute campus. Design of the Masdar Headquarters building was awarded to Adrian Smith + Gordon Gill Architecture; Atkins took on the infrastructure design concept, while Mott McDonald handled infrastructure consulting. CH2M Hill was selected as the program managers, with the Al Jaber Group managing infrastructure construction.[43]

Several technology companies are participating in the city's development, particularly on demand-side energy solutions. Masdar City and Siemens signed a strategic partnership agreement to work on an innovative power grid and advanced building technologies development project for the first phase of Masdar City. Siemens also plans to locate its Middle East headquarters in the city. General Electric (GE) works with Masdar's shareholder, Mubadala, across a range of fields. GE and Masdar City are investigating ways to reduce peak power demand through the use of GE smart home appliances; GE stated it has "developed a line of 'smart' appliances that automatically react to pricing signals from the utility and delay or reduce wattage of high-consumption tasks until lower-cost, off-peak periods."[44] GE plans to build its first Ecomagination Center, which "will develop innovative technologies and services to help ensure the sustainability of our planet" in Masdar City.[45] Masdar City also partnered with Al Falah Ready Mix, which is manufacturing low-carbon concrete required for the City's first phase. Finally, BASF, an international chemicals and materials company, was named Masdar City's "preferred supplier" of construction materials and system solutions, and also plans to open an office in Masdar City.[46]

Masdar developed the Masdar Institute (MI), the Middle East's first graduate research institution dedicated to renewable energy and environmental technologies, in partnership with the Massachusetts Institute of Technology (MIT). Located in Masdar City, the MI is supported by MIT's Technology and Development Program. A second class of graduate students, for whom tuition is free, entered the MI in the fall of 2010.

Status

The city's original timeline included six development phases, beginning with the development of the MI, the Masdar Headquarters, and the initial residential, office, and community infrastructure in the first phase. The first buildings of the MI were set to open in 2009, with full build-out expected by 2016.

Masdar project leaders scaled back some ambitions and adjusted their original timelines, facing financial challenges in 2010.[47] They pushed the construction finish date back from 2016 to 2021–2025. The *New York Times* reported that Masdar was reconsidering its plan to generate all power on-site, and that computer-driven "personal transit pods" intended to connect the entire city might be rolled out at a more limited scope.[48] Several directors of various aspects

of Masdar left the organization.[49] In July 2010, Masdar's CEO Dr. Sultan Ahmed Al Jaber announced that, although delivery dates and some of the city's sustainability performance benchmarks would not be achieved immediately, the vision of Masdar City remained the same. Masdar officials attributed these changes to the global economic crisis and a weakened Middle East property market,[50] coupled with lessons learned in building the first phase of the Masdar Institute Campus, noting that the crisis suggested "it made no sense, either commercially or from an eco-sustainability perspective, to insist on the original zero-carbon, zero-waste goals in the short term, when current technology would make achieving such targets enormously expensive and thus largely irrelevant to any other sustainable urban development project."[51]

Masdar City officials have stated that Phase 1 of the city should be completed in stages through 2015.[52] This should include doubling the size of the MI's current campus, and constructing the Masdar Headquarters building (which will house IRENA), an office building, and several residential and commercial buildings. Masdar expects that Phase I will accommodate 7000 residents and 15,000 commuters; at full build-out in 2021–2025, they expect around 40,000 residents and 50,000 commuters.[53]

Sino-Singapore Tianjin Eco-City

Background and goals

In 2007, only a few years after announcing the Dongtan project, the Chinese government made plans for another eco-city, Sino-Singapore Tianjin Eco-City, on a site about 25 miles from the Tianjin city center, 95 miles southeast from Beijing, and less than a ten-minute drive to the Tianjin Economic-Technological Development Area (TEDA). The city's mission revolves around "Three Abilities" (practicability, scalability, and replicability) and "Three Harmonies" (harmony with economic development, harmony with the environment, and harmony with society). The city's plans for sustainable development include six dimensions: intelligent city, clean water, ecology, clean environment, clean energy, and green building.

Governance and financing

The structure of Tianjin Eco-City differs from Dongtan—hinting that the Chinese government learned from its first highly publicized and unsuccessful eco-city experience. Tianjin Eco-City is a joint collaboration between the Chinese and Singaporean governments, agreed to by Singapore Prime Minister Lee Hsien Loong and Chinese Premier Wen Jiabao in November 2007. The groundbreaking ceremony occurred just ten months later. The project is structured as a 50/50 joint venture between a Chinese consortium and a Singaporean consortium, called Sino-Singapore Tianjin Eco-City (SSTEC).

The Chinese are led by the state-run Tianjin TEDA Investment Holding Co., Ltd (Tianjin TEDA), and other partners include China Development Bank, Tianjin Real Estate Development and Management Group Ltd, Tianjin Tanggu Urban Construction Investment Company, Tianjin Hanbin Investment Co. Ltd, and Tsinlien Group (Tianjin) Assets Management Co., Ltd. The Singaporean consortium is led by an entity called the Singapore Tianjin Eco-City Investment Holdings Pte. Ltd, in turn led by its majority stakeholder, the Keppel Group. The Keppel Group is a Singaporean company involved in property, infrastructure, and investments, and is partially owned by state investor Temasek.

While Tianjin TEDA originally owned the land, the SSTEC joint venture is the official master developer for the eco-city. The progress of Tianjin Eco-City indicates that developers are managing the project by land parcels, which are controlled by different private developers—and it seems that SSTEC is trying to involve many major corporations. Financing is being handled primarily by the China Development Bank, and by May 2010 the project had about $1.5 billion of registered capital.[54] SSTEC plans to develop several economic incentives to attract residents and companies to the city, including tax incentives, housing rebates, R&D funding, and subsidies for businesses.

Partnership network

In 2009, several real estate-focused companies formed partnerships with SSTEC through an MOU (Memorandum of Understanding). One of these was Ascendas, Singapore's primary business space solutions provider, with plans to develop and market an Eco-Business Park in the city. The park plans provide space and resources for the offices or headquarters of world-class companies, particularly those focused on energy and other environmental issues. Other partners include Shimao Property Holdings, China's leading foreign-funded property developer, Mitsui Fudosan Co., Ltd, Japan's largest real-estate developer, and Shanghai Broadway Packaging and Insulation Material Co., Ltd, which plans to develop a green technology center. Additionally, Taiwan's largest property developer, Farglory Land Development Group Shanghai, proposed to create a "live, work and play" center, intended as the city's primary space for leisure activities.

Additionally, SSTEC formed partnerships to study and work on reducing the city's energy usage with energy and technology companies, including PV World (a Singapore-based manufacturer of wafer-based photovoltaic solar modules), First DCS Pte. Ltd. (a Singaporean company that plans to develop heating and cooling systems for the Eco-Business Park), Sembawang Engineers and Constructors Pte Ltd (to study feasibility of a planned billion-dollar solar polysilicon production plant), and Envision (a Chinese company working on energy-efficient glazing systems). Other technology companies involved through "strategic partnerships" and/or MOUs are Philips (test-bedding and application of energy-efficient lighting and consumer lifestyle solutions for sustainability), Hitachi (eco-solutions for homes, electric vehicle charging, building energy management, smart grid, and water), Samsung C&T Corporation (developing an eco-residential project), Singapore Technologies Electronics Limited (intelligent building/transport systems), and STSE Engineering Services Pte. Ltd (overseeing pneumatic waste collection systems). The Land Transport Authority of Singapore plans to advise on transportation for the eco-city, including a public transport system and hybrid/electric vehicles for both public and private usage. A primary focus of the eco-city is on education, with plans for a new university that will offer doctoral and master's degree programs in sustainable design.

Status

The Tianjin Eco-City project is continuing to sign tenants and expects its first wave of residents in 2011. Completion of the initial phase of the project, about three square miles, is expected within the next three to five years, and the entire 11.5 square miles is planned for completion within 10 to 15 years. According to Wang Bao, a Chinese environmental activist, the Tianjin eco-city has realistic design schemes and expectations, making it China's most promising eco-city project to date. Furthermore, Bao believes that the project developers "have scientific methods of ensuring that the development is in line with their green targets—and the Singapore leaders frequently come to check the progress."[55]

Sino-Singapore Nanjing Eco High-Tech Island

Background and goals

Nanjing Eco High-Tech Island (Nanjing Ecocity) is another Chinese eco-city being developed by a joint partnership with Singapore. It is about two square miles in size and four miles from Nanjing, the capital of southern Jiangsu province. This eco-city's goal is "to establish a platform for the sustainable development of high-tech, smart industries under an ecologically conscious environment."

Governance and financing

In November 2007, a bilateral platform—the Singapore–Jiangsu Cooperation Council—was launched to promote collaboration between Singapore and Jiangsu on the project. International Enterprise (IE) Singapore signed an MOU with the Nanjing Municipal People's Government agreeing to jointly undertake a feasibility study of the Eco High-Tech Island. The final agreement was formed in 2009, and the city is slated for completion in three phases by 2020. Three Chinese banks—Bank of China, Industrial and Commercial Bank of China, and Bank of Shanghai—extended an RMB 7.2 billion credit line to the Singapore–Nanjing Eco High-Tech Island Joint-Venture Company.

Partnership network

The Nanjing municipal government procured the land, and the real-estate developers are Singapore Intelligent Eco Island Development and Nanjing Jiangdao Investment & Development Company.[56] Singapore Intelligent Eco Island Development is a private joint-venture company formed by Yanlord Land Group (real-estate developer), Sembcorp Industrial Parks (industrial development and engineering), and Surbana Land (design/architecture of the city). Other companies involved include G-Energy Global, ST Engineering, Etonhouse International, AVI Tech Electronics, and Ivy Group (a Hong Kong-based firm that plans to develop educational systems for the city).[57]

Status

In October 2010, the Singapore–Jiangsu Cooperation Council was renewed for three years, to promote further "economic collaboration in urban planning and development, environmental services, logistics, commercial tourism/hospitality projects."[58] The council also announced in October 2010 that the official launch of housing construction for Nanjing Eco High-Tech Island had recently taken place.

PlanIT Valley

Background and goals

PlanIT Valley is a prototype smart city being planned for a site in the municipality of Paredes, about ten miles from the center of Porto, Portugal, by a start-up high-technology company called Living PlanIT. In 2008, the company acquired the right to purchase 4200 acres from the municipal government of Paredes as the site for PlanIT Valley. The anticipated completion date is 2015, by which time the city plans to accommodate around 150,000 residents.[59]

PlanIT Valley was designed as a research-focused city in which Living PlanIT and its partner companies would base research and development operations to test new technologies and services for sustainable urban development. According to Living PlanIT, the city was designed to be the world's first "living laboratory of sustainability."[60] Company founders Steve Lewis and Malcolm Hutchinson are former software executives who bring a technology perspective to the business of developing cities, and are focusing on the development of what they call an "Urban Operating System" (UOS). The UOS is intended to function as the city's central "brain" by collecting information from all urban systems, storing it in the UOS data center, and efficiently managing the systems through a software platform.

Governance and financing

Living PlanIT is running the project, which received special investment status from the Portuguese government as a "Project of National Interest," with strong support from all levels of the Portuguese government including the Municipality of Paredes and various national agencies in Lisbon.[61] The city aims to be green and has extensive plans for alternative energy usage and water/energy efficiency, as well as a goal of diverting 80 percent of trash to energy production or recycling (in comparison to the current average of 5 percent per city).[62] Living PlanIT plans to build pre-made smart infrastructure technology and sensors into all the city's facets—from concrete foundations blocks to the energy supply to transportation systems.[63] The total expected cost of this venture is $8 billion to $10 billion.

Living PlanIT and its partner ecosystem plan to develop several revenue streams to fund the Valley. Living PlanIT estimates the revenue produced from real-estate leases in PlanIT Valley will represent less than 5 percent of total revenues.[64] Revenue streams, such as partner fees, participation fees, and equity sharing, are planned to be supplemented with small amounts of debt capital from banks. The conversion of $8 million worth of salaries to employees to equity means that venture capital funding has not been needed to date.

Partnership network

PlanIT Valley's business model depends on "creating an ecosystem of large and small company partners that will focus on creating products and services for sustainable urbanization."[65] It has already established partnerships with companies including Cisco, Accenture, UK engineering firm Buro Happold, and McLaren Electronic Systems, which manufactures sensors. The goal is for these companies to work together in PlanIT Valley to develop city-solution technologies and the UOS platform, and to tackle similar city-building projects elsewhere.

As Lewis said, "You create a platform, you license it to partners, they augment it, they drive it, and we pick up a royalty … we provide a software model to the entire industry."[66] He aims to sign 14,000 partners eventually, to participate in the company's plan to "code cities like software—in which buildings, sensors, and traffic applications alike are connected through the cloud."

Status

PlanIT Valley received the Project of National Interest designation in September 2009, an asset valued at 8 million on the company's balance sheet.[67] Land acquisition and zoning for the commencement of construction were underway in 2010. PlanIT Valley has been divided into 25 "Waves," with the first Wave involving the purchase of 90 acres of land and the building of R&D centers, schools, and retail, residential, and entertainment facilities, expected to be completed by the first quarter of 2012. The project's target goal was to have the majority of PlanIT Valley completed by the end of 2015.

Meixi Lake District

Background and goals

In February 2009, Changsha Municipal People's Government of Hunan Province and real-estate developer Gale International signed an agreement to develop an eco-city called Meixi Lake District in Changsha, the capital of Hunan province in south-central China. Meixi Lake District expects to eventually house 180,000 residents in 1675 acres.

According to Kohn Pedersen Fox, the city's designer, Meixi Lake proposes to offer "a new model for the future of the Chinese city."[68] It plans to focus on combining the features of a metropolis and a natural setting, and plans to feature innovative transport networks, a smart grid, urban agriculture, and waste energy recovery.[69] Furthermore, Changsha is a booming city of over 65 million residents, so the project planners see major opportunities for the economic development of the Meixi Lake District.

Governance and financing

Gale International signed an agreement with Changsha Municipal People's Government of Hunan Province to "plan, develop and operate" Meixi Lake, which Gale called "an ecological city."[70] China Merchants Bank (CMB) promised to extend RMB 10 billion in new credit to key projects and enterprises in Meixi Lake over the next five years.[71]

Partnership network

Kohn Pedersen Fox and engineering firm Arup plan to work together on the city's design. Cisco envisages extending its New Songdo City partnership with Gale into the Meixi Lake project. Here, Cisco plans to "deploy video networking technology and energy management software tools city-wide and meld municipal systems, such as education, health care, transportation and hospitality into a common network."[72] Wim Elfrink of Cisco's Smart+Connected Communities initiative reported that Cisco plans to begin by focusing on six to seven of the 20 services the company believes can be linked. United Technologies Corporation plans to provide energy-saving elevators and water-cooled air conditioning, which can reportedly cut energy use by 20 percent; 3M is developing digital signs and "stick-on film" for use in both Meixi Lake and New Songdo City.

Status

The project, in early planning stages, is expected to be completed in 2020.

Sitra Low2No

Background and goals

Low2No plans to be a mixed-use eco-development in Helsinki, Finland, about the size of a large city block. In 2006, a master plan for the redevelopment of Jätkäsaari, an industrial port area, was approved, and the Low2No site lies within this region. Low2No's goal is to create a successful prototype of a low- to no-carbon district. The project intends to "spur innovation in the field of energy efficiency and sustainable development."[73] The project does not expect to make a profit; its primary goal is to catalyze sustainable development in Finland by learning from the project and enacting new financial policies to make low-carbon ventures economically viable. The development's leaders hope this will encourage other developers to tackle similar projects in the future.

Governance and financing

Unique because of its innovative financing model and partnerships, Low2No was initiated by Sitra, Finland's government-run venture capital fund and investment firm. Sitra is supervised by the Finnish Parliament, and its projects are funded by endowment capital and returns from capital investments. Sitra's tasks are to promote the welfare of Finnish society through stable and balanced development in the growth of the country's economy. Sitra has identified energy and low-carbon development as a major area of interest. A team led by Arup won a competition in 2009 to design the Low2No carbon-neutral district.

Partnership network

Other members of the winning team included international sustainable finance consultancy Galley Eco Capital, architecture firm Sauerbruch Hutton, and design consultancy Experientia. Sitra partnered with SRV, one of the biggest real-estate developers in Finland, and VVO, Finland's largest provider of rental buildings, to develop the project. SRV and VVO are traditional companies focused on the bottom line of building sellable developments while Sitra is focused on transforming Finnish industry and spurring clean-tech and economic development.[74] SRV and VVO do, however, aim to become leaders in sustainable construction and residential development. Executive Director of Sitra's Energy Program, Jukka Noponen, stated, "With this project Sitra encourages cities and the real estate and building industry to tackle these ambitious goals in their projects."[75]

The creation of new financial policies to support green development is a crucial desired outcome of the project, and Galley Eco Capital started this process by developing "ways to create a reliable pipeline of green mortgage, environmental, energy and carbon finance capital for Jätkäsaari."[76] All decisions for Low2No have input from multiple project partners and are made through a five-frame "lens," which includes Inspired Design, Social Innovation, Environmental Responsibility, Economic Viability, and Replicability/ Diffusion.

Status

After the design competition, Sitra moved on to planning and scoping phases focused on the project proposal and general project guidelines, such as sustainability frameworks and carbon protocols. The government hopes to see the completion of ten successful low- or zero-carbon developments similar to Low2No in the five years after Low2No is completed. Sitra plans to use the number of these developments as one metric of the project's success.[77]

DISCUSSION

The government agencies, developers, urban planners, designers, builders, technologists, and financiers involved in the projects discussed above have launched urban development efforts that are unprecedented in kind, if not in scale. Although the deliberate creation of cities from scratch has notable precedents in the form of new towns, company towns, capital cities, and other planned communities, the idea of building full-scale "smart" and "sustainable" cities is still new and the viability of such efforts remains unproven. If projects such as those reviewed here and summarized in Table 18.1 prove successful, they may give rise to a new industry of eco-city development, the success of which will surely depend upon novel, complex collaborations between public and private sector organizations. Integrating knowledge in fields as disparate as computing, sensor technology, architecture, engineering, real-estate development, materials, energy, finance, and management, such collaborations will require innovative business models to design, develop, and manage cities that are economically, socially, and environmentally sustainable. Many challenges related to governance and civic engagement will have to be addressed.

The emergent industry created by "sustainable urbanization" activities is likely to function more like a natural ecosystem than a traditional marketplace.[78] This has implications for how companies and other organizations succeed over the long term. Yet, today, companies and other entities working to create this new industry must operate without the kind of knowledge players in established industries take for granted, such as accepted best practices and recognized performance standards.[79] As a result, the entities responsible for the development of each project have made notably different choices about the ways to define, organize, deliver, finance, and administer their initiatives.

Variations across the eight eco-city projects suggest both opportunities and challenges in such initiatives. We identified differences in financing, in extent of public–private sector collaboration, in relative emphases on technology versus real estate development, and in replicability. The projects also have interesting features in common: most notably, all are located close to major urban centers. Yet, their differences may be more informative in our

Table 18.1 Key statistics

Eco-city (start date)	Nearest major city (distance)	Land size	Project leader	Estimated cost	Anticipated residents	Premise	Completion date and status
New Songdo City (2001)	Seoul (40 miles)	1500 acres	Gale International	$35 billion	430,000	International business district	2014; under construction
Dongtan (2005)	Shanghai (16 miles)	21,250 acres	Shanghai Industrial Investment Corporation	NA	25,000 by 2010, 500,000 by 2050	Model sustainable city	Stalled
Masdar (2007)	Abu Dhabi (10.5 miles)	1730 acres	Masdar	$19 billion	40,000	Clean-tech cluster in model sustainable city	2025; six buildings operational, with residents
Tianjin Eco-City (2007)	Tianjin (25 miles)	7360 acres	SSTEC	NA	350,000	Education	2018–2023; continuing
Nanjing Eco-City (2008)	Nanjing (4 miles)	1280 acres	Singapore–Jiangsu Cooperation Council	NA	NA	High-tech, smart industries in an ecologically aware environment	2020
PlanIT Valley (2008)	Porto (20 miles)	1670 acres	Living PlanIT	$10 billion	150,000	Research	2015; planning
Meixi Lake District (2009)	Changsha (within city limits)	4200 acres	Gale International	NA	180,000	Model future Chinese city	2020; early planning
Low2No (2009)	Helsinki (within city limits)	5.4 acres	Sitra	TBD as part of design process	60% of space designated residential	Low or no carbon district	2012; in design

search for the key factors that will explain success. With these early reflections, our aim is to provide a foundation for future research to evaluate eco-city success.

Financing

Financing remains one of the greatest challenges facing eco-city initiatives. Although benefits of eco-city developments may be realized over the long term, the staggering capital requirements of such projects—estimated between $10 billion for PlanIT Valley and $35 billion for New Songdo City—typically require both public and private sector involvement. The projects we reviewed have approached this challenge in different ways. In some models—notably Masdar City,

Nanjing, Meixi Lake, and Tianjin Eco-City—governments provided a significant portion of the funding through state-owned banks or direct public sector financing. Although Masdar City is currently funded by the government, those involved anticipate private developers and third parties will provide most development capital after the completion of Phase I, when Masdar City will revert to the role of master developer responsible for infrastructure and other city-wide services.[80] New Songdo and PlanIT Valley, on the other hand, rely upon investments and capital from international companies, although the South Korean and Portuguese governments have provided incentives through various forms of indirect support and tax relief. Low2No also has support from its own state-based venture capital fund. All eight initiatives anticipate some revenues from real-estate sales, long-term leases, and office rentals, while some include technology-based royalties to offset the capital requirements. Whether these projects will secure financing in an appropriate time-frame remains uncertain; moreover, the optimal capital structure cannot be determined from these data.

Partnerships: integrating public and private sectors

The complexity and scale of an eco-city initiative necessitate cooperation among multiple entities, including companies of varying types, sizes, and nationalities, and government entities at the city, regional, and national levels. In most of the eco-city projects we studied, public–private partnerships (PPPs) were initiated by governments working with companies ranging from real-estate developers, architects, technology experts, financial institutions, and other service providers. The balance between the private and public sectors varies across projects. Dongtan, Masdar City, and Low2No are primarily government initiatives. Besides providing much or all of the financing, governmental entities are responsible for administering the project and selecting the other parties. Nanjing and Tianjin are led by joint ventures between consortia in China and Singapore. Although these consortia include private sector corporations, each is led and managed by a state-owned company. Finally, New Songdo and PlanIT Valley are supported by the Korean and Portuguese governments, respectively, but spearheaded by private companies driving financing and development, and working to recruit other partners.

Each of these three models—projects led by a single government, dual-government joint ventures, and private sector companies—present distinct challenges. According to Asanga Gunawansa of the National University of Singapore, the standard PPP models common in traditional infrastructure projects, where the government recruits private companies that contribute to project development, may not work well for eco-cities.[81] Gunawansa offered reasons, including: eco-city projects require a unique type of public acceptance to entice residents and businesses in the long term; a completed city will require high levels of maintenance; and it is difficult to bind developers and end-users to the desired regulations for sustainability features and standards. Government-led projects may be ill-equipped to face these challenges. Such initiatives are also threatened by mismatched expectations, poor communication, and misunderstandings between the private and public entities. Peter Head, an Arup director, reflected on his experience working with the Chinese government in Dongtan: "China does everything by the rules handed down from the top. There is a rule for everything. The width of roads, everything. … We wanted to change the rules in Dongtan, to do everything different. But when it comes to it, China cannot deliver that."[82]

Initiatives developed through joint ventures between governments face similar issues. Coordination between private and public entities from two different countries can result in a lack of coordination and cooperation. While the innovative partnership structure behind Tianjin Eco-city, for example, appears to be working relatively well, there have been reports of "disharmony" between the Singaporean and Chinese consortia, possibly caused by friction from different work cultures and differing opinions on how fast the project should develop.[83]

Finally, initiatives led by the private sector face a separate set of challenges. Coordinating a network of private companies without the institutional authority of a governmental entity at the center, and garnering sufficient financial support without the backing of a government-owned bank, might prove challenging. Partnership models where value is delivered through a network of collaborating companies are rare in any industry, and, to succeed, eco-city initiatives spearheaded by private companies will have to develop new governance structures and frameworks for coordination.

Real-estate development emphasis

Most of the eco-city projects discussed here are based on a real-estate development model. Although many promise social and economic benefits to separate them from pure property development projects—including Masdar City's focus on becoming a global clean-tech cluster and New Songdo's free economic zone—six of the eight projects (Dongtan, Tianjin, Nanjing, Masdar City, New Songdo, and Meixi Lake) rely on real-estate sales and rentals as the means for eventually repaying banks and other capital providers. Several initiatives, including Masdar City, New Songdo, and PlanIT Valley, also intend to offer government-based economic and tax incentives to encourage corporations to locate offices there, driving demand for both office space and residential real estate.

Two projects do not rely on real estate as the primary driver. The Low2No project instead develops an economically viable low-carbon model, albeit with a real-estate component. Sitra partnered with SRV to deliver a well-designed and professionally developed project, and to encourage other developers to follow a sustainability-oriented approach. However, the Low2No development does not expect profit on real-estate sales. Real estate is envisioned as a means to foster Sitra's end of testing methods of sustainable development for others' learning.

Similarly, while Living PlanIT intends to work with developers to lease and sell real estate in PlanIT Valley, property development is not the major driver of its business model. Living PlanIT's leaders believe PlanIT Valley will become economically self-sustaining through a business model based largely on the software industry, comprised of revenue-sharing arrangements, royalties for the use of intellectual property (IP) developed by Living PlanIT and its partners, annual partner fees, and PlanIT Valley participation fees. Living PlanIT's model for PlanIT Valley is an interesting alternative for eco-city development.

Technology emphasis

A study by Booz & Company and the World Wildlife Foundation found that an up-front investment of $22 trillion dollars in green urban transportation and residential technology would save $55 trillion in future infrastructure spending.[84] Most eco-city projects aim to realize these kinds of savings through the development of city-based technologies. However, the level of emphasis on technology R&D, in particular on the application of new "clean" and "green" technologies, varies across these eight projects. Dongtan is at one end of the technology spectrum. Despite expressed dedication to R&D programs and technology initiatives, the initiative has not yet recruited technology companies, involving only real-estate developers, designers, and engineers.

The Masdar City, Nanjing, Tianjin Eco-City, New Songdo, and Meixi Lake projects, in contrast, engaged technology companies early to develop innovative technological solutions and R&D centers. Although technological solutions, from smart buildings to renewable power plants, are planned features of the completed cities, these are not intended to be a primary driver of Nanjing's and Tianjin Eco-City's business models. There is greater emphasis on technology in New Songdo and Meixi Lake, which tout the application and development of connected urban technologies as central to their visions. New Songdo and Meixi Lake are key players in Cisco's Smart+Connected Communities initiative, designed to be part of Cisco's common infrastructure in order to allow for the coordination, control, and optimization of a wide range of urban services. Masdar City officials stated that "Masdar City specifically seeks to be a test-bed for new technologies," including the use and application of smart sensors and city-wide power and utility management systems.[85]

Finally, technology is the very foundation of Living PlanIT's business model and thus at the core of the PlanIT Valley project. While New Songdo and Meixi Lake will make extensive use of new technologies, PlanIT Valley is a research city that will showcase existing new and to-be-developed technologies of Living PlanIT and its partners, including Cisco's networking technologies, McLaren Electronics' sensor technologies, and Living PlanIT's UOS, intended to optimize resource allocation within the city. IP licensing fees and revenue-sharing arrangements from the application of these technologies are intended to form the foundation of the company's revenues.

While the success of these models and technology initiatives remains uncertain, observers have noted that interconnected systems raise serious security issues.[86] The integration of sensors into all aspects of a city—everything from traffic signals to windows to vehicles to people—raises concerns about privacy, government surveillance, and disastrous security breaches.[87] Even Sam Palmisano, CEO of IBM, acknowledged, "Some citizens have expressed discomfort at living in not a safer society but a 'surveillance society.'"[88] While companies such as IBM and Cisco hope to resolve these issues, how citizens will react to living and working in entirely connected communities remains unknown.

Replicability

These initiatives differ greatly with regard to replicability. Certain projects are intended to create a unique eco-city. Masdar City officials hope the city will provide a "model for sustainable urban development regionally and globally," and that its business model and technology will demonstrate the commercial viability of eco-cities.[89] Although they are offering consulting services to developers, they lack plans to pursue similar projects elsewhere. On the other hand, the Chinese government's involvement in over a third of the initiatives reviewed here reflects industry estimates that China needs to build 500 new cities over the next several decades—100 with populations over one million.[90] Although each Chinese eco-city is conceived as a one-off, the Chinese government appears to be learning from each venture—moving, for example, to a collaborative model with Singapore perhaps as a result of the problems it experienced in Dongtan. Although each Chinese eco-city may not be replicated exactly, the government's experience with them might lead to a greater understanding of the appropriate strategies for sustainable urbanization.

The governments and businesses involved in Low2No, New Songdo, and PlanIT Valley, on the other hand, are less interested in building a single eco-city than in developing strategies and business models for building new eco-cities and making existing cities more sustainable. The projects vary in the extent to which their keystone partners—Sitra, Gale International, Cisco, and Living PlanIT—intend to be involved in these future ventures. Sitra does not intend to build any urban developments other than Low2No. It has been clear, however, about its hopes that Low2No can serve as an economic model or a showcase for future initiatives spearheaded by independent developers. One of Sitra's stated goals is to encourage similar initiatives; indeed, the project's founders explain that they will measure its success partially on whether its model of sustainable development spreads to other developers and other countries.[91] Gale International and Cisco, the primary drivers behind New Songdo, are explicit about their intent to develop similar eco-cities in the future: "We're trying to replicate cities," Elfrink at Cisco stated.[92] Indeed, Meixi Lake is seen as the first of many anticipated New Songdo-like cities. Living PlanIT also hopes PlanIT Valley can serve as a "showcase" for sustainable urbanization, and that its business model and technologies will be replicated around the world. While Living PlanIT hopes to be involved in some of these ventures, it also hopes its partners will eventually build cities on their own—utilizing (and paying for) the IP developed through PlanIT Valley.

There are many challenges to developing replicable business models for sustainable urbanization. We identify four that are particularly important. One is getting access to enough land in the right location at the right price—a necessary but not sufficient condition. A second is the great variation in how development occurs under different political systems. Lessons learned in Portugal will not translate directly to China, for example. Third, lessons from new eco-cities will need to be adjusted for projects done in existing cities or the urban retrofit market. Each setting provides its own opportunities and constraints. Fourth, and in our view the biggest challenge of all, is establishing a new economic model for eco-cities. Every new city needs an economic foundation based on jobs. Not every new eco-city can be a research city whose purpose is the development of new technologies for building other eco-cities. To thrive, a city requires a range of jobs, spanning multiple sectors, such as technology, financial services, retail, entertainment, education, and healthcare. And every eco-city similarly needs a clear economic model, as well as features that attract both businesses and residents. Sectors likely to play crucial roles in new eco-cities include healthcare (and related industries like biotechnology and pharmaceuticals), light or heavy manufacturing, natural resources, and tourism. Yet, too many eco-city projects are implicitly or explicitly based on a real-estate development model—a kind of "if we build it they will come" approach that often lacks serious consideration of who will come and why.

Limitations and future research

This chapter reviewed the goals, business models, and partnerships involved in eight eco-city projects to identify common features of initiatives in this emerging industry. In brief, these projects were conceived as a means of creating urban living capacity while mitigating threats to the natural environment—by combining principles of low-carbon and resource-efficient development with the use of information and communication technologies to better manage complex urban systems.

The tentative nature of the ideas we have put forward reflects the embryonic state of the eco-city industry.[93] We lack crucial knowledge about these initiatives. How will they be governed? How will residents' security be protected? Will they achieve their goals of economic, social and environmental sustainability? How will residents respond to living in heavily planned communities? What governance structures and financing schemes will lead to success? What business models are most replicable? We hope that scholars will pursue these important questions as eco-cities continue to develop and take shape.

We believe that eco-cities provide fertile territory for future collaborative research by urban planners, designers, engineers, public policy experts, sociologists, and management researchers. Through our review of eight early and still unfolding projects, we have sought to identify factors that characterize and differentiate eco-cities as a small contribution to understanding the challenges and opportunities of sustainable urbanization.

We gratefully acknowledge useful comments from Harley Blettner, Jock Herron, Steve Lewis, Jan Jungclaus, Warren Karlenzing, Sara Al Khalufi, Jean Rogers, and Marco Steinberg. All errors remain our own.

NOTES

1 Authorship is alphabetical.
2 World Bank, "Eco^2 cities," http://web.worldbank.org/WBSITE/ EXTERNAL/TOPICS/EXTURBANDEVELOPMENT/0,,contentMDK:22643 153~pagePK:148956~piPK:216618~theSitePK:337178,00.html.
3 McKinsey Global Institute, *Preparing for China's Urban Billion*, March 2009.
4 Carbon Disclosure Project and Accenture, *The Case for City Disclosure*, November 2010, via www.greenbiz.com/business/ research/report/2010/11/01/carbon-disclosure-project-case-city-disclosure#ixzz156q0mBRe.
5 "San Francisco ecocity declaration," *Ecocity Media* (blog), May 15, 2008 (9:13 p.m.), http://ecocity.wordpress.com/2008/05/15/san-francisco-ecocity-declaration.
6 R. Register, *Ecocity Berkeley: Building Cities for a Healthy Future* (Berkeley: North Atlantic Books, 1987).
7 H. Suzuki, Dastur A., Moffatt S., *et al.*, *Ecological Cities as Economic Cities*. Eco^2 Cities, conference edition, 2009.
8 "San Francisco ecocity declaration."
9 2020 Climate Leadership Campaign, "International EcoCities," http://2020climatecampaign.org/content/international-ecocities.
10 World Bank, "Eco^2 cities."
11 F. Harvey, "Green vision: The search for the ideal eco-city," *Financial Times*, London, September 7, 2010, www.ft.com/cms/s/0/c13677ce-b062-11df-8c04-00144feabdc0.html.
12 P. Harrison, "EU agrees mandate for 'nearly zero energy' homes," Reuters, Brussels, May 19, 2010, www.reuters.com/article/ idUSTRE64I6LO20100519.
13 The US Green Building Council developed Leadership in Energy and Environmental Design (LEED®) as a green building certification system. Buildings are rated Platinum, Gold, Silver, or Certified based on the number of points achieved.
14 "Eaton's Asia HQ achieves new green building standard in China," *GreenerBuildings*, August 11, 2010, www.greenbiz.com/ news/2010/08/11/eatons-asia-hq-achieves-new-green-building-standard-china.
15 R. Chalons-Browne, "China takes world lead in clean energy as others fear to finance," *Asian Power*, July 12, 2010, http://asian-power.com/ environment/commentary/china-takes-world-lead-in-clean-energy-others-fear-finance.

16 S. Lohr, "Bringing efficiency to infrastructure," *New York Times*, April 29, 2010, www.nytimes.com/2009/04/30/business/energy-environment/30smart.html.

17 The Climate Group, *SMART 2020*, 2008. SMART 2020 launched a framework "for developing ICT solutions. Through standards, monitoring and accounting (SMA) tools and rethinking (R) and optimizing how we live and work, ICT could be one crucial piece of the overall transformation (T) to a low carbon economy."

18 Lohr, "Bringing efficiency to infrastructure."

19 G. Lindsay, "The new urbanism: New Songdo and creating cities from scratch," *Fast Company* (February 2010): 88–95.

20 Ibid.

21 Songdo IBD, "A global business hub," www.songdo.com/songdo-international-business-district/why-songdo/global-business-hub.aspx.

22 J. Han, "Songdo's tallest building project in jeopardy," *Korea Times*, July 24, 2009, www.koreatimes.co.kr/www/news/biz/2010/04/123_49049.html.

23 A. Perotta, "Morgan Stanley invests $350M in multibillion dollar South Korea project," *All Business*, September 12, 2006, www.allbusiness.com/operations/facilities-commercial-real-estate/4418763-1.html.

24 Green by Design, "HOK New York designs first commercial building in Korea aiming to achieve LEED Platinum criteria," http://greenbydesign.com/2007/12/18/hok-new-york-designs-first-commercial-building-in-korea-aiming-to-achieve-leed-platinum-criteria/.

25 Lindsay, "The new urbanism," p. 90.

26 C. Go-eun, "Sustainability effort in Songdo international business district," *Korea IT Times*, October 19, 2007, www.koreaittimes.com/story/3475/sustainability-effort-songdo-international-business-district.

27 Songdo IBD, "A global business hub."

28 K. Mee-yoo, "Incheon to be NE Asia hub," *Korea Times*, February 26, 2010, www.koreatimes.co.kr/www/news/nation/2010/06/281_61524.html.

29 S. Hart, "Zero-carbon cities," *Architectural Record*, March 2007, http://archrecord.construction.com/tech/techFeatures/0703feature-1.asp.

30 F. Pearce, "Greenwash: The dream of the first eco-city was built on fiction," *Guardian*, April 23, 2009, www.guardian.co.uk/environment/2009/apr/23/greenwash-dongtan-ecocity.

31 Ibid.

32 Green Progress, "Arup and SIIC sign accord to develop further sustainable cities in China," November 9, 2005, www.greenprogress.com/green_building_article.php?id=579.

33 C. Wright, "Dongtan: China firms up eco-city proposal," *Euromoney*, March 4, 2008, www.euromoney.com/Article/1886972/Dongtan-China-firms-up-eco-city-proposal.html.

34 EPSRC Dongtan Sustainable City Networks: Coordination framework, EPSRC grant reference EP/F01936X/1, http://gow.epsrc.ac.uk/ViewGrant.aspx?GrantRef=EP/F01936X/1.

35 "Arup and SIIC engage British consultants to provide renewable energy supply for the world's first sustainable city in China," *Mondaq Business Briefing*, March 3, 2006, www.highbeam.com/doc/1G1-143081521.html.

36 P. French, "China's eco-towns: Green communities—to go eco, think small," *Climate Change Corp*, February 3, 2009, www.climatechangecorp.com/content.asp?ContentID=5942.

37 Masdar's Marketing and Communications team, personal correspondence with the authors, February, 2011.

38 Ibid.

39 IRENA. www.irena.org/Menu/index.aspx?PriMenuID=13&mnu=Pri.

40 Masdar. "Background," www.masdar.ae/en/Menu/index.aspx?MenuID=42&CatID=12&mnu=Cat.

41 Masdar's Marketing and Communications team, personal correspondence with authors.

42 Ibid.

43 Environmental News Service, "Bush previews Abu Dhabi's planned carbon neutral, car free city," January 14, 2008, www.ens-newswire.com/ens/jan2008/2008-01-14-01.asp.

44 GE News Center, "Smart appliances help consumer get smart about energy costs," May 26, 2010, www.genewscenter.com/content/Detail.aspx?ReleaseID=10394&NewsAreaID=2.

45 Ibid.

45 General Electric. 2011. www.ge.com/innovation/masdar/index.html.

46 Masdar's Marketing and Communications team, personal correspondence with authors.

47 J. Mandel, "Financial woes crimp celebrated Middle East 'green city,'" *New York Times*, March 17, 2010, www.nytimes.com/gwire/2010/03/17/17greenwire-financial-woes-crimp-celebrated-middle-east-gr-91007.html.

48 Ibid.

49 B. Prior, "Masdar update: the green city in the Middle East struggles with dust and departures," *Greentechsolar*, July 26, 2010, www.greentechmedia.com/articles/read/masdar-update.

50 K. Stacey, "Masdar: 'No silver bullet' for problems facing cleantech city," *Financial Times*, October 27, 2010, http://blogs.ft.com/energy-source/2010/10/27/masdar-no-silver-bullet-for-problems-facing-cleantech-city/.

51 Masdar's Marketing and Communications team, personal correspondence with authors.

52 Ibid.

53 Ibid.

54 H. Garcia, "China–Singapore eco-city bags new international funding support," *EcoSeed*, July 23, 2010, www.ecoseed.org/en/living-green-article-list/article/6-living-green/7654-china-singapore-eco-city-bags-new-international-funding-support.

55 G. Ng, "Greenwashed? Are China's eco-cities really green?" *Straits Times*, August 14, 2010.

56 V. Wee, "Singapore group inks Nanjing eco-island pact," *Business Times* via *Times Business Directory of Singapore*, May 26, 2009, www.timesbusinessdirectory.com/Singlenews.aspx?DirID=86&rec_code=388976.

57 GovMonitor, "Singapore and China step up collaboration in

environmental services sector," November 25, 2009, www.thegovmonitor.com/world_news/asia/singapore-and-china-step-up-collaboration-in-environmental-services-sector-16636.html.

58 GovMonitor, "Singapore boosts collaboration with Jiangsu, China," October 24, 2010, www.thegovmonitor.com/world_news/asia/singapore-boosts-collaboration-with-jiangsu-china-41201.html.

59 G. Lindsay, "A city in the cloud: Living PlanIT redefines cities as software," Fast Company, August 20, 2010, www.fastcompany.com/1684055/a-city-in-the-cloud-living-planit-redefines-cities-as-software.

60 Living PlanIT, "PlanIT Valley: Next generation intelligent city," http://living-planit.com/planitvalley.htm.

61 Ibid.

62 H. Knight, "The city with a brain," New Scientist, October 9, 2010.

63 "Living on a platform," The Economist, November 4, 2010, www.economist.com/node/17388308?story_id=17388308.

64 Harley Blettner, interview with Robert Eccles, February 2011.

65 R. Eccles, Edmondson A., "A bold new model for sustainable cities," Harvard Business Review HBS Faculty blog, July 22, 2010 (9:40 a.m.), http://blogs.hbr.org/hbsfaculty/2010/07/a-bold-new-model-for-sustainable-cities.html.

66 Lindsay, "A city in the cloud."

67 Blettner interview with Eccles.

68 Kohn Pedersen Fox, "Meixi Lake master plan," www.kpf.com/project.asp?T=8&ID=135.

69 McGraw Hill Construction, "Innovation 2010 big and super green: From buildings to cityscapes," http://construction.com/events/innovation2010/speakers.asp.

70 Gale International, "Meixi Lake district," http://gale.mydelphic.com/home/projects/meixi-lake-district.aspx.

71 Hunan Government, "China Merchants Bank awards a 3 billion credit line to help build Meixi Lake area," press release, February 23, 2009, www.enghunan.gov.cn/wwwHome/200902/t20090223_152717.htm.

72 E. Woyke, "Very smart cities," Forbes, September 3, 2009, www.forbes.com/2009/09/03/korea-gale-meixi-technology-21-century-cities-09-songdo.html.

73 Low2No, A Sustainable Development Design Competition, www.low2no.org/competition/downloads/Low2No_overview.pdf.

74 Jean Rogers, interview with Tiona Zuzul and Amy Edmondson, January 28, 2011.

75 Sitra, "€60m low carbon building project in Helsinki," press release, April 6, 2010, www.cisionwire.com/sitra/60m-low-carbon-building-project-in-helsinki.

76 Galley Eco Capital, "Galley Eco Capital helps Helsinki to reduce carbon emissions," September 2, 2009, www.galleyecocapital.com/2009/09/galley-eco-capital-helps-helsinki-to-reduce-carbon-emissions.

77 Jean Rogers, interview with Annissa Alusi, August 2010.

78 M. Iansiti, Levien R., The Keystone Advantage (Boston: Harvard Business School Press, 2004).

79 T. Zuzul, Edmondson A., "Strategy as innovation: Emergent goals formation in a nascent industry" (Harvard Business School Working Paper, 2011).

80 Al Khalufi, personal correspondence with authors.

81 A. Gunawansa, "Contractual and policy challenges to developing ecocities," Sustainable Development 18(2) (2010).

82 Pearce, "Greenwash."

83 SSTEC, "No discord, no concord between Singapore and Chinese teams," January 20, 2010, www.tianjineco-city.com/en/news_center/sstec_coverage/958.aspx.

84 N. Pennell, Ahmed S., Henningsson S., "Reinventing the city to combat climate change," Strategy+Business, autumn 2010, www.strategy-business.com/article/10303?pg=all.

85 Al Khalufi, personal correspondence with authors.

86 T. Yigitcanlar, Han J.H., "Managing ubiquitous eco cities: Telecommunication infrastructure networks, technology convergence and intelligent urban management systems" (unpublished, 2009).

87 "Horror worlds," The Economist, November 4, 2010, www.economist.com/node/17388328.

88 Ibid.

89 Masdar's Marketing and Communications team, personal correspondence with authors.

90 Lindsay, "A city in the cloud."

91 Marco Steinberg, interview with Tiona Zuzul, February 7, 2011.

92 Ibid.

93 Zuzul and Edmondson, "Strategy as innovation."

19

Intelligent Infrastructures

DIMITRIS PAPANIKOLAOU[1]

MIT

IT HAS BEEN a common misbelief that intelligence and coordinated behavior is the result of a single mind's activity. In his seminal work *The Society of Mind* Marvin Minsky described a new model to explain intelligence consisting of a distributed social network of connected agents, the behavior of whom is driven by their personal goals, beliefs, and constraints as a response to external stimuli. Minsky argued that intelligence is thus not a single-mind phenomenon, but instead the product of properly wired collective behavior. Today, current research on distributed sensor networks uses market mechanisms and basic micro-economic behavior as the means to create emergent patterns of collective intelligence for managing resource allocation among the sensor nodes. How can these ideas be used to create smarter urban environments?

SMART CITIES

As William Mitchell points out, *Smart Cities* are intelligent networked urban environments that can be more responsive to the needs of their inhabitants by providing customized services on demand, making thus a more sustainable use of their resources.[2] They can do that by collecting and analyzing data from human behavior patterns through dense neural networks of sensors and microcontrollers, evaluating the data based on some higher-level goals, and providing the output back to the users to affect their behavior, closing thus a big control feedback loop. For example, smart power grids can sense consumption patterns from smart meters, correlate them with current production patterns to forecast the system tendency, and dynamically modify electricity tariffs between buyers and sellers for valley filling and peak shaving. Likewise, networks of smart domestic appliances can monitor consumption and production patterns, and determine the best time for time-elastic operation such as defrosting, washing, etc. Or, smart vehicle sharing systems can estimate fleet distribution asymmetry and incentivize users accordingly to rebalance the fleet.

Controlled behavior through feedback is not a new idea; Norbert Wiener formalized it in *Cybernetics*. For example, when you touch with your finger a hot surface your sensor cells will react, sending pain signals to your brain cells, which will evaluate their magnitude, and send back accordingly orders to your hand's muscle actuator cells to react. Nowhere in this feedback loop exists one single cell yet all cells collaborate to create what seems to be from outside a cognitive behavior. What is new though here is the idea that this cognitive behavior can be collaboratively achieved by distributed urban infrastructure systems to create responsive environments that behave as single organisms. But if this is the case, then where does coordinated behavior come from and how can it be achieved? Most of the required technology is here; it is time now to think how to put the pieces together to make them work.

Three areas of current research shape the emerging field of smart environments: first, *ad hoc* distributed networks of sensors, microcontrollers, and actuators that can sense, compute, control, and communicate; second, human–computer interaction interfaces that allow end-users to actively engage in these networks through portable or embedded smart devices, formulating thus human–machine ecosystems; third, mechanism design and computational economics for creating policies to coordinate goal-seeking collective behavior and understanding stability of these ecosystems. In this chapter we present the concept of collective intelligence in urban infrastructures and discuss some of their key theoretical principles, technologies, and questions.

URBAN INFRASTRUCTURES

Urban infrastructure networks are the nerves and veins of cities that carry information and vital resources to and from their functional units to work. As Mitchell points out, cities once consisted of mere organs, skeleton and skin in which inflow of resources and outflow of waste took place through man and animal muscle power. In the industrial era cities developed extensive mechanized supply systems of hydraulic pumps, fuel-burning motors, and power grids to provide energy and resources and remove waste, which were manually monitored and controlled. Today, in the digital age cities are developing electronic nervous systems that digitally monitor and control the organs and supply systems.[3] The next step is to develop the collaborative patterns of intelligence that will allow them to coordinate sophisticated behavior.

Urban infrastructure networks consist of *transmission* links and *storage* nodes that reallocate scarce resources or commodities between nodes to provide service to the beneficiaries of the nodes. Transportation networks reallocate vehicles from origins to destinations to provide users with mobility; hydraulic networks pump in fresh water from ponds to households while pumping out wastewater from households to processing plants to vitalize inhabitants; electrical grids transport energy from power plants to households to provide users with power to work; data cables send information bits to and from computer registries and logic gates to allow end-users to communicate. Transmission through links is actuated by motors, pumps, or electric power sources, while storage in nodes is held by parking spaces, reservoirs, batteries, or computer memory registries.

LEVEL OF SERVICE AND CAPACITY LIMITATIONS

Citizens don't need infrastructures; instead they want the services infrastructures provide when they need them. Since demand patterns are often unpredictable, and different citizens need certain services at different times and locations, the efficiency of the infrastructure system in delivering the service relies on its ability to rapidly adapt to those spatiotemporally changing patterns. However, due to limits in the capacity of both transmission and storage technologies there will always be trade-offs as demand grows; an increase in demand for a service would lead to decreasing marginal gains from that service to people as infrastructure limitations kick in. For example, limits in transmission bandwidth bring congestion trade-offs: more cars in the streets will transport more commuters but throughput speed decreases as streets get more congested.

Similarly, limits in storage capacity bring overflow trade-offs: since land is scarce, the average parking space per user diminishes as more users buy vehicles, taking up vital public urban space. In fact, urban economists know well that there is no such thing as sufficient capacity for an infrastructure system: the larger it gets, the more its demand grows such that a new saturation level occurs, inhibiting its further growth. For example, constructing wider streets increases urban development, attracting even more vehicles until a new traffic congestion level comes that eventually restrains further development. Therefore, creating self-sufficient systems is not always about endlessly increasing their infrastructure capacity, but often about inventing new organizational policies for cleverly regulating the goals and desires of their users.

CONTROL AND POLICY

Since service must always flow from some parties to others, it turns out that performance is not only a technical issue but also a political and strategic design one. Adoption of most urban infrastructures is always a trade-off between the costs of private ownership and the inefficiencies of public services. For example, on one hand the high cost of private vehicle ownership compared with their low utilization rates, and the increasing parking requirements compared with the decreasing available urban land, make private automobiles an unsustainable solution for the future of dense urban environments. In the USA the average household has nearly two vehicles, which spend around 90 percent of their time parked while they require three to five times their footprint in urban land to be able to travel from an origin to a destination.[4] On the other hand, public service networks compromise everybody to receive the service at the same time as decided by a single authority. For example, in public transit others decide for you when, where, with whom, and how you will move; schedules are inflexible, and service coverage is often driven by political motivations rather than social needs. As a consequence, many areas become privileged while other areas remain underserved. In addition, the true social costs of public transportation, hidden in complex taxation, are often much higher than their seemingly low-priced fares.

THE PRESENT

So far, most urban infrastructural systems have been hierarchical, highly regulated, and topologically centralized: a single power plant powers tens of thousands of households; a public transport carrier controls hundreds of transit lines to mobilize a city. Control arbitration is difficult, and bottlenecks, when they occur, can have catastrophic chain reaction consequences. In August 1996 a minor failure in a single power transmission line in Oregon caused, through a domino effect, a massive failure in the entire West Coast from Canada to New Mexico, interrupting service to 7.5 million people.[5] Moreover, since energy production can not just stop when you turn off your switch, and since energy storage technology is still expensive, a central power plant must constantly overproduce electric power to avoid the economic consequences of undersupply, wasting inconceivable amounts of (often) non-renewable energy. Furthermore, users are passive recipients of service deprived from any sort of control and often unaware of their own consumption patterns. The first (and current) generation of power grids does not allow bidirectional data communication; there is no way that one edge may monitor the demand or supply of the other in real time. They are not responsive nor can they sense or compute. Like a broken telephone game, information from one edge to the other will be both outdated and inaccurate due to the system's inherent latency and lack of technological tools for advanced controlling. Moreover, arbitration complexity in centralized systems also increases disproportionally as the system grows: a single telephone service provider will rewire phone calls from each individual caller to receiver, but as the number of users increases, rewiring complexity will escalate exponentially.

THE FUTURE

However, today a new generation of intelligent urban infrastructure systems is emerging that will be able to predict bottlenecks, overflows, or shortages caused by unbalanced demand patterns using sensors, and control accordingly user behavior through sophisticated incentive policies and ubiquitous communication platforms. These sustainable infrastructures will primarily consist of distributed *ad hoc* sensor networks coupled with decentralized production, consumption, and storage abilities that will exhibit self-optimizing behavior with minimum central intervention. As an example, domestically owned renewable power generators and rechargeable high-density batteries, equipped with smart sensor meters, can turn each connected household into a potential energy producer or storage provider that can competitively sell, buy, store, or consume energy resources on demand. Thus, the end-user turns from a passive service receiver to an active stakeholder, the decisions and actions of whom may affect the performance and efficiency of the overall system's ecology. The question however is how can these individual stakeholders be informed about what is collectively optimal given the absence of a central authority? Two fundamental principles can create a sustainable, cooperative, infrastructure ecosystem: *sharing* and *incentivizing*.

Sharing

Sharing, or *fractional ownership*, is a method for sharing the cost, while increasing utilization of a large resource allocation system when the aggregate demand for resources is greater than the system's supply capacity. Sharing empowers the end-user to freely decide when, where, or how to reallocate, produce, or consume a resource within an infrastructure system. Typically, a sharing system involves a policy that allows fractional ownership rights over the allocated resources and a network of depositories where shareholders can deposit or withdraw these resources. Banking systems with bank accounts, freight rental service networks with their trucks, and airports with their luggage carts, are only a few of the many current examples. Recently, sharing has entered public transit systems as a complementary way to provide customized personal mobility with the form of one-way bike-sharing programs, while one-way car sharing is now starting. One-way vehicle sharing systems utilize a decentralized network of parking stations and a fleet of shared vehicles. Users can pick up a vehicle from any station and drop it off at any other station (one-way trips).

Despite their great convenience sharing systems have drawbacks too. Lack of cooperation and individual selfish behavior are not able to sustain welfare in sharing systems. For example, in vehicle sharing since departures and arrivals vary randomly in stations, eventually vehicles are all ending at the stations with no demand.[6] This inventory imbalance not only decreases throughput, but it also increases trip time as drivers search for parking spaces. To maintain the level of service a vehicle-sharing system needs to constantly feed origin points with vehicles while draining destination points from occupied parking spaces. While it is possible to centrally monitor bikes and periodically redistribute them with trucks, this is clearly not a viable solution for larger vehicles such as cars. Not only is it operationally complex, but also it is expensive: either the fleet needs to be too large or the redistributions need to be too frequent. In addition, continuous redistributions keep vehicles away from the system, reducing further service capacity. As a consequence, many vehicle-sharing systems end up wasting more resources sustaining their performance than the value of the service they provide.

Incentivizing

If users in a sharing system had a common way to evaluate the impact of their actions in the performance of the system, then decision making would be straightforward, individual actions would not worsen collective output, and cooperation would emerge. Incentive-based strategies such as dynamic pricing have been successfully employed in decentralized resource allocation networks with limited capacity as a means to create feedback mechanisms to regulate demand patterns: congestion pricing zones, smart grids of renewable energy resources, eBay-style online auctions, and carbon trading programs, are just a few of the many successful examples.

To calculate pay-offs, information from both the users' actions and the nodes' condition must be known. This can be done at the individual level if nodes in the network can talk to each other. Distributed networks of smart domestic appliances equipped with sensors and cheap microcontrollers can easily perform basic computation and propagate information through gossip algorithms,[7] creating ubiquitous inhabitable environments of distributed computation, a concept otherwise known as the *internet of things*.[8] Duncan Watts showed that designing such scalable *small-world* networks where any pair of nodes can be linked through a path of maximum six steps is easy.[9] For example, networks of parking stations may calculate parking prices by observing inflow and outflow of vehicles, average it with their neighbors, and communicate this information back to the users through handheld devices.[10] Information thus brings a powerful tool for decentralized control.

Calculating pay-offs using sophisticated smart infrastructure would have trivial value if this information could not be perceived effectively by the end-users to affect their decisions. Creating ubiquitous communication platforms of portable mobile devices using intuitive user interfaces is the key component for closing the feedback loop in intelligent distributed infrastructure systems.

In what follows we will see how these two principles can be applied by discussing *Mobility on Demand (MoD)*, a research direction for intelligent shared urban transportation systems that the Smart Cities group of the MIT Media Laboratory has been developing since 2003.

MOBILITY ON DEMAND: INTEGRATING URBAN INFRASTRUCTURE NETWORKS

MoD is an integrated proposal for the future transportation scheme of dense urban environments that consists of a decentralized network of rapid charging stations, a shared fleet of lightweight rechargeable electric vehicles, and an intelligent fleet management system.[11] MoD allows users to conveniently pick up a vehicle from any origin station and drop it off at any other destination station. Each station in MoD is equipped with an Uninterruptible Power Supply (UPS), a high-capacity battery that can slowly charge with energy from the urban electrical grid during off-peak hours and rapidly charge vehicles during daytime parking. Vehicles thus can rapidly pull energy from a charging station, transport it in their batteries, and push it back to another charging station in less than 15 minutes. Each vehicle's battery can store up to 10 KWh, enough energy to power a household for one entire day, offering thus not only a tremendous energy storage buffer for smart power grids of renewable energy resources but also an emergency energy reallocation system (Vehicle to Grid technology). Therefore, MoD consists of three synergetic urban infrastructure networks: a one-way vehicle-sharing system, the smart power grid of the charging stations, and the energy transportation network of the vehicles' batteries (Figure 19.1).

To address fleet and energy distribution asymmetries MoD uses price incentives to motivate users to drive vehicles to the stations that most need them, while discouraging them to drive vehicles to stations that do not need them, and an intuitive graphical user interface to effectively communicate location-based price information. Similarly to a market economy, prices adjust to parking needs. Each station locally computes a pick-up and a drop-off price based on its inventory change rate, its available energy resources, and the price competition with its neighbor stations; these two components are then added to the standard trip fare as a negative or positive percentile discount. Therefore, some trips can be more expensive while other trips may even pay back money to the users (Figures 19.2 and 19.3). There are no trucks, nor employees involved in the fleet redistribution. MoD is essentially a self-organizing system operated by its users for its users.

19.1 Mobility on Demand

MoD's prices are discounts off the trip fare, not fixed prices; thus, they have the same behavioral impact on trip decision making independently from the trip's length. Users can access online price information at the stations, on their handheld mobile devices, or at desktop computers with internet access. Users can either prepay during pick-up (thus locking the price) if they know their destination station in advance, or they can pay during drop-off, allowing the price landscape to change during trip time. MoD thus does not force users to use it; it does not aim to replace existing transportation options. Instead it aims to offer more options to users, creating a market competition environment among transportation options. Users that consider a trip to be expensive may simply opt out, choosing to perform the trip using another option (e.g., walking, taxi, public transit, or private automobile).

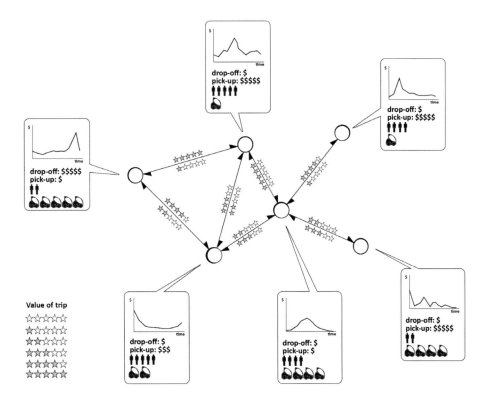

19.2 The market economy of trips

Source: William Lark, Jr. and Michael Lin, MIT Media Lab, Smart Cities

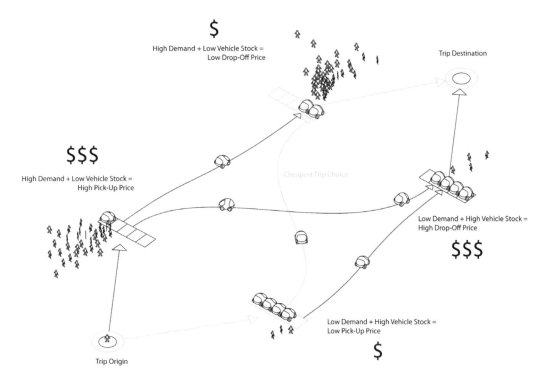

19.3 User case

LANDSCAPES OF PAY-OFFS: VISUALIZING INFORMATION

Understanding the pay-off landscape is necessary for users of MoD to bring it into a sustainable equilibrium. Smart Cities has been developing PriceScape, an intuitive web-based Graphical User Interface that uses dynamic heat-map and contour display for communicating location-based price information to users. Isometric price curves or color zones describe areas with the same parking discount rates. Like the analogy of navigating through a price landscape, climbing from valleys to hills is expensive, while descending from hills to valleys is rewarding. Traveling between locations of the same level is neutral (Figure 19.4). Users can scroll in time to see the dynamic trend of it. PriceScape is not a recommender, nor an expert system; it does not suggest to users what to do; however, it helps them to perceive their pay-offs to assist their decision-making process.

MOD ECONOMICS

How would users make decisions given this pricing context? Each urban trip is inevitably a combination of at least two options (one of which is always walking) and users will select that combination which minimizes total trip costs. As an example, consider a user traveling with a MoD system from an origin O to a final destination D (Figures 19.5 and 19.6). The user will select an in-between drop-off station Q if and only if the total time-adjusted trip cost from the origin to the drop-off station with MoD (including the parking discount) plus the time-adjusted trip cost from the drop-off station to the final destination with the substitute (e.g., bus, taxi, walking, etc.), are in sum less or equal than the original time-adjusted cost that the user would pay to travel from the origin to the final destination with MoD (Figure 19.5). Since users evaluate time differently based on their level of income, each user would select a unique drop-off station for a given price condition.

19.4 User interface in vehicle and portable devices

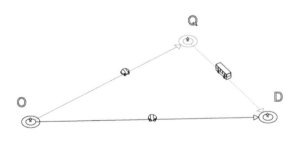

19.5 The decision-making process

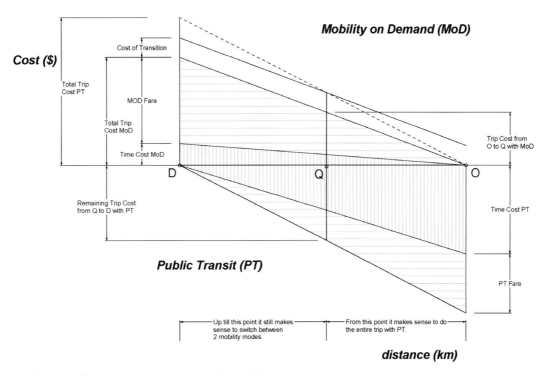

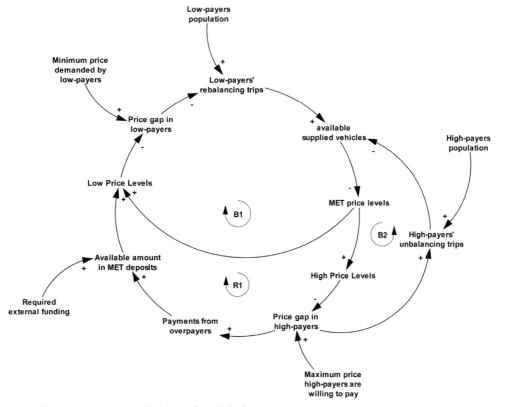

19.6 Market equilibrium between two transportation models

19.7 Causal-loop diagram explaining behavior of a vehicle-sharing system

MoD, as other intelligent infrastructure systems, is in fact a form of a *strategy game*. Decisions of individual price-taking users change the price landscape affecting decision making of other users. Contemporary urban economic theory[12] suggests that users with sufficient information would make decisions that minimize their time-adjusted costs, eventually bringing the system into an *equilibrium* state where no further action can be taken to increase their pay-offs. In that ideal state, the excess of money from the overpaying users plus any additional external funding should match exactly the reward demanded from the underpaying users. Moreover, the overall throughput performance of the system will depend on their price sensitivity; the higher the demand elasticity, the better the performance will be.

Income distribution greatly affects equilibrium in MoD. While the high-level prices for the high-payers are determined directly by the stations, the low-level prices that are offered to the low-payers are determined by the stations and the available pool of funds in the MoD deposits. These funds increase by the high-payers and decrease by the low-payers. This simply means that MoD cannot pay back endlessly to low-payers; it can only pay back money to the extent that this money exists in the system deposits, financed by the high-payers. To solve this issue either the system might need to be larger, or an additional external source of funding may be required. This can be provided either by increasing the standard MoD fare, or by utilizing external funding sources such as advertising etc. Figure 19.7 shows a causal-loop diagram that graphically explains this important concept. Polarity of arrows indicates how the effect is related to the cause. Loops can be either self-reinforcing (R) or self-balancing (B). B1 and B2 balancing loops determine the equilibrium between low-payers and high-payers. However, R1 reinforcing loop may drain available funds, reducing rewards offered to low-payers, which would reduce their willingness to rebalance vehicles dragging down the system into a lower-performance equilibrium state.

DISCUSSION:
WHERE DOES INTELLIGENCE COME FROM?

Intelligence is typically associated with the ability of a system to adapt to the changing conditions of its environment. As our societies become more complex, it is becoming increasingly evident that urban infrastructures capable of foreseeing their goals, understanding their needs, and reflecting back to their users with incentives for motivating their actions will be essential in creating sustainable and responsive environments to human needs. Intelligent infrastructures are in essence networked, distributed resource allocation markets consisting of two parties: those who control the stocks at the nodes, and those who control the flows at the links. It is the mutual interaction of those two parties guided by their personal goals, beliefs, and constraints that eventually determines the system's intelligence and the level of its sustainability.

But what is sustainability? For sure, it is not just about being green, or simply reducing CO_2 emissions. Sustainable infrastructures are infrastructures able to sustain themselves; those whose aggregate generated value can outweigh their aggregate operational, societal, and environmental costs. If this is the case, then the issues that we should start reasoning about in the future should focus on understanding the circumstances under which such systems can indeed become sustainable, as well as understanding what types of social equity they may bring.

NOTES

1   The author wishes to acknowledge Professor William J. Mitchell, Kent
    Larson, and the Smart Cities group for all the help and guidance on this
    work. Figure 19.2 credits: William Lark, Jr. and Michael Lin, MIT Media
    Lab, Smart Cities. All other figures are courtesy of the author.

2   W.J. Mitchell, *City of Bits: Space, Place, and the Infobahn* (Cambridge:
    MIT Press, 1996).

3   W.J. Mitchell, Casalegno F., *Connected Sustainable Cities* (Cambridge:
    MIT Mobile Experience Lab Publishing, 2008).

4   US Department of Transportation, *National Household Travel Survey:
    Summary of Travel Trends* (2001), pp. 11–15.

5   D.J. Watts, *Six Degrees: The Science of Connected Age* (New York:
    W.W. Norton & Company, 2004).

6   A. Kaltenbrunner, Meza R., Grivolla J., *et al.*, "Bicycle cycles and
    mobility patterns—Exploring and characterizing data from a community
    bicycle program," 2008, http://arxiv.org/abs/0810.4187.

7   P. Levis, Culler D., Patel N., *et al.*, "Trickle: A self-regulating algorithm
    for code propagation and maintenance in wireless sensor networks."
    In: *Proceedings of the 1st USENIX/ACM Symposium on Networked
    Systems Design and Implementation* (NSDI, 2004).

8   N. Gershenfeld, *When Things Start to Think* (New York: Henry Holt &
    Company, 1999).

9   Watts, *Six Degrees.*

10 D. Papanikolaou, *Mobility on Demand: Sustainable, Self-Optimizing,
    Vehicle Sharing Systems.* Poster presented at 2nd International
    Sustainability Conference (MIT, 2010).

11 W.J. Mitchell, *Mobility on Demand: Future of Transportation in Cities*
    (Cambridge: MIT Media Laboratory, 2008).

12 D. DiPasquale, Wheaton W.C., *Urban Economics and Real Estate
    Markets* (Upper Saddle River, NJ: Prentice Hall, 1995).

20

Landscape Infrastructure: Urbanism Beyond Engineering

PIERRE BÉLANGER

HARVARD UNIVERSITY GRADUATE SCHOOL OF DESIGN

INCREASINGLY, ecology is coming into focus as a strategy and system in the design of urban infrastructures and performance of urban economies.[1] This contemporary change is largely attributable to the massive transition from industrialization to urbanization worldwide in the past century made visible by three cumulative shifts: the rise of environmental concerns since the 1970s, the crisis of public works planning in the 1980s, and the erosion of post-war engineered structures from the 1990s onwards, whose legacy total more than 2.2 trillion dollars in urgently needed reinvestment.[2,3] Contributing to the rising agency of the field of landscape, this transition is further amplified by the effects of population pressures such as regional dispersal, transnational migration, geopolitical borders, and capital flows, as well as from environmental pressures such as carbon consumption, atmospheric emissions, chemical effluents, groundwater depletion, floods, droughts, sea level rise, soaring energy costs, and rising food prices. Although tremendous attention has been given to the magnitude of these challenges, the scale and frequency of infrastructural disasters and technological accidents continues to rise at an alarming rate. The upward sloping timeline of events in the past three decades is the most blatant indicator: sudden power outages in the Northeast, rolling blackouts in the Southwest, bridge collapses in the Midwest, as well as oil spills, hurricanes, and levee breaks along the Gulf Coast.[4]

These growing incidences are exacerbated by outmoded patterns of land development upheld by the spread of standardized, end-of-pipe engineering, Euclidean land use zoning, and uncoordinated, reactionary planning. The industrial structure of cities today—vertical, centralized, and inflexible—further explains the unchecked and unseen dependence on centralized systems of water abstraction, waste landfilling, oil import, food processing, soil depletion, and uniform transportation at the expense of pre-urban, pre-industrial endowments of biophysical resources.[5]

Consequently, we have recently begun to better understand how Fordist modes of production and Taylorist principles of efficiency have oversimplified the ecology of urban economies and underplayed the social role of urban infrastructures, by way of marginalizing and suppressing the living, biophysical systems. At the center of this ecological divide are the historic practices of engineering and planning that operated well into the twentieth century, under the tenets of efficiency and control through centralization. Often considered in isolation, the disparate and disastrous events that mark the end of the twentieth century index the inherent effects of ecological complexity of urbanization associated with contemporary technologies, biophysical systems, climate change, regulatory frameworks, public works management, and population dynamics. Yet, despite infrastructural overload and chronic underfunding, demand for mass housing, mass mobility and mass communications persists.[6] Ironically, the horizontal spread of low-rise urban populations continues.

Stemming from the overexertion of civil engineering[7] and inertia of urban planning[8] vis-à-vis the pace of urban change,[9] and coupled with the exhaustion of the environmental lobby,[10] there is an urgent need for the rethinking of current models of city building towards contemporary patterns of spatial distribution that meet new and existing demands with current resources. Putting into question the conventional capacities of any single discipline to address the magnitude of urban challenges and ecological complexities today, this chapter proposes the compound, collaborative formulation of landscape infrastructure as a contemporary field of practice that addresses the flows of urban economies and dynamics of global ecologies. To accomplish this objective, this chapter first outlines prevailing paradigms in the scientific disciplines of engineering and planning, and how they conditioned cities as a socio-technological problem through measures of control and efficiency. A brief survey of shifts that occurred during the proto-urbanization of North America in the twentieth century are brought forth to redefine the conventional notion of urban infrastructure and expand it as a landscape of systems, services, scales, resources, flows, processes, and dynamics, which support and cultivate urban economies. In light of the massive infrastructural transformation occurring worldwide, the chapter concludes with a series of strategies and projections that reclaim the landscape of urban infrastructure along with pragmatic and immediate advantages for contemporary practice.[11]

20.1 Urban Hazards: the devastating effects of Hurricane Ike on the shoreline of the Gulf Coast
in 2008 near Houston-Galveston, Texas, the third costliest storm event in the history of the US
Source: ©2008 NOAA

20.2 Horizontal Urbanization: view of the expanding urban region of the Greater Toronto Area (GTA) showing the logistics zone of the
Pearson International Airport lining Highway 401, with fog rising from the forest ravines of the Etobicoke-Mimico Creek watershed
Photo: ©2007 Pierre Bélanger

MEASURES AND METRICS

Infrastructure has grown in complexity *vis-à-vis* the current urbanization of the world. It is both a response to, and generator of, horizontal forms of development, in part due to the transnational distribution of technologies and techniques of urban engineering. Although it is often relegated to mere background or unseen substructure of urban development, infrastructure is the interface by which we interact with the biological and technological world. However banal they are, taps, pipes, wires, sewers, sidewalks, curbs, roads, verges, ditches, sidewalks, medians, spans, pylons, highways, landings, landfills, tunnels, power plants, treatment plants, airports, are the technological spaces—the hardware—that compose the urban world. Simultaneously, urban infrastructure is both site and system. It is designed, constructed, and continuously reconstructed. While we may argue on how it actually works, or sometimes how it works even too well, its influence has exerted itself most often to the point of invisibility, often obscuring the connection with the software of social environments and biophysical resources. Rarely do we actually see the entire watershed that supplies the water that we drink or bathe in; nor do we see the subsurface soils that we walk on that underlie roads or regions; nor do we see the power of a coal mine from a power plant that generates the electricity when we turn the lights on.

Central to the reconsideration of urban infrastructure are the historic roles that civil engineering and urban planning have played as the most prominent city building professions of the nineteenth and twentieth centuries. As twin disciplines, they have both exercised tremendous influence in the shape of cities and urban regions during the past two centuries.[12] To begin, a summary of baseline principles of urban planning and civil engineering is instructive:

1. Standardization—the singularity of infrastructure as a linear and closed system, designed exclusively on efficiency and economy. The normalization of dynamic systems and externalization of other dynamics or wastes and organic systems are effectively reduced to use-value functions, utility efficiencies, or mechanical operations.[13] Standards are therefore developed for purposes of maintenance and self-preservation as opposed to management and modernization.

2. Mono-functionality—the singularity of land uses leads to economic, ecological, and sometimes social segregation. Dynamic systems become parceled and closed off, externalizing the larger set of biophysical and socio-economic services that intrinsically depend upon their interconnectivity to function. Excessive regulation of land use has further stifled economic development and, despite its original intention, contributed to patterns of low-density urban development.[14]

3. Permanence—as well as they seem to work and as solid as they may appear, standardized infrastructures and mono-functional land uses are inflexible to change, demonstrating a considerable level of fragility towards unexpected hazards, accidents, and disasters. Through the illusion of safety and certainty created by specialization and standardization, centralized infrastructures and dense aggregations—such as the reliance on one specific type of energy source or water distribution system for example—often expose larger concentrations of urban population to greater risk.[15]

Notwithstanding the scale of their influence, civil engineering and urban planning have respectively formed the functional architecture and regulatory framework that underlie the legislative governance and physical construction of cities today. Yet, over time, the implementation of legal controls and standards of efficiency has gradually contributed to the rigid, inflexible, and detached nature of cities from greater landscape ecologies and regional climates. As Gene Moriarty discusses in *The Engineering Project*, "the modern engineering enterprise is primarily a colonizing project," both self-aggrandizing and totalizing.[16]

From engineering to design

Through the hegemony of efficiency and scientific positivism,[17] civil engineering has become central to the design of urban environments as the premier design service discipline.[18] How it attained this unwavering status is remarkable, given how very little attention the profession or its parent associations have given to social conditions, political ideologies, or theoretical discourses. Its relative absence of manifestos alone is both surprising and suspect. Compared with other fields of design such as architecture and urban design or the social sciences and regional planning that are arguably over-theorized,[19] civil engineering has made leaps and bounds by literally operating without theory. In the absence of critical discourse,[20] quantitative logic and numerical precision have become the foundations for achieving accuracy, efficiency, and safety. Since the cost–benefits of civil engineering services represent less than 1 percent of the life cycle cost of a project, it is rather difficult to contest the economic value of these services where they are viewed as an investment.[21] However central this logic may be, its foundation also relies on the isolation of variables and the exclusion of less quantifiable and more complex information through reductionism and externalization of dynamic forces.

Post-Taylorism

The decontextualization of urban infrastructure is important and critical to recognize as an overlooked side effect of engineering techniques, and, to a certain extent, planning policies. Underlying this condition are linear notions of utility and efficiency stemming from technological determinism and technocratic control. Hierarchical methods of management and vertically oriented administration, borne from the industrial era of Taylorist principles, were premised on the improvement of production through rationality, numerical logic, and standardization of the production process and work flows. Central to industrial economies were notions of planning, predictability, centralization, and control; principles that influenced the development of factories, production processes, and even military strategies, during the rise of mechanization, automation, and Fordist methods of mass production at the turn of the twentieth century. While scientific, centralized approaches to management and manufacturing resulted in a series of short-term and direct economic gains, in the long term it excluded other environmental processes that pre-dated and pre-conditioned industrial economies: the pre-industrial ecology of resources, the immediate impacts of

large infrastructural networks, culture of labor organizations, social innovations, post-production wastes, regional de-industrialization, and international outsourcing.

This practice has more recently been challenged with the disastrous effects of maintenance deferrals, deregulatory frameworks, and growing risks made visible by bridge collapses, or major chemical spills. Recent events such as the sudden collapse of I35W Bridge in 2007 on the Mississippi River or the fly ash slurry spill in 2008 at the Kingston Coal Plant have demonstrated the limits of engineered controls, and the shortcomings of rational efficiency. Its over-exertion has now made apparent the impermanence and limited lifespan of infrastructure.

In response to these externalities, a post-Taylorist discourse has emerged in the past decades both as a critique of the tenets of efficiency and control, as well as catalyst for decentralized ecological strategies that move beyond engineering and planning. In an attempt to bridge the gap between economy and ecology, the potential for more networked patterns of spatial distribution and more decentralized methods of decision making is radically changing the landscape of urban economies and production. There are more diverse and more flexible modes of production, higher-quality services, featuring just-in-time production, business process re-engineering, call centers, simultaneous engineering and asynchronous teamwork, across different networks.[22,23]

Infrastructural apartheid

Further to the re-reading of urban infrastructure and professional disciplines, common assumptions about sustainability need to be challenged. Crystallized by publications such as the Club of Rome's *Limits to Growth* (1972) or Paul Ehrlich's *The Population Bomb* (1968), principles of city building such as density and compactness,[24] growth and permanence,[25] stability and security,[26] have been so far unchecked and should be rethought. Often carrying moralistic or ideological overtones, these notions are questionable in terms of their value as governing principles in design. At their core, these principles are rooted in traditions of military engineering and wartime planning.[27] For example, it is crucial to understand that the discipline of civil

20.3 Infrastructural Squatting: a 5-kilometre long, extra-legal settlement along the public right-of-way of Quezon City's
Republic Avenue, within metropolitan Manila in the Philippines, where road development was formerly planned
Source: ©2011 DigitalGlobe

engineering emerged from the glut of military engineers from West Point during a prolonged period of peace at the end of the nineteenth century.[28] In traditions of military engineering, defense imperatives led to the delineation of biophysical environments along clear divisions between dry and wet land, or high and low ground. Traditions in water management, topographic earthworks, centralized fortifications, and flood control are some of the most important contributions that French military engineering has passed down to techniques of civil engineering, underpinning the work of the US Army Corps of Engineers.[29] Although engineering practices may command a sense of military-like authority, the unwavering adherence to quantitative calculation and hierarchical control has its limitations. It overlooks the social and ecological dimensions that often lie outside the bounds, edges, scopes, and peripheries of its facilities. For all of its accuracy and precision, civil engineering is actually handicapped by an exclusive reliance on efficiency at the expense of other, equally important social, spatial, ecological factors. The natural smoothness and seamlessness of Western infrastructure—whether the expansion of a highway or the diversion of a river—question the neutrality of civil engineering. In several parts of the world, infrastructures ranging from roads and bridges to airports and power plants have been often implemented and strategically located to serve a small, powerful elite at the expense of a larger, often poorer majority.[30] Effects of the All-American Canal along the US–Mexico border, Highway 443 in Palestine, or Republic Avenue slums in Manila are samples of the physical divides created by urban infrastructures. Their unintended consequences have resulted in forms of spatial apartheid, social marginalization, and in some cases, civil strife.

SHIFTS AND PROCESSES

The historic lack of engagement of infrastructure as a territory of design stems from its dystopic and banal nature. Traditionally, urban design has concentrated on the design of streets, blocks, and buildings as the locust of urban development while overlooking the potential of infrastructure as great enabler, the glue of urbanization.[31]

Decentralization

In the past century, increasing demands for urban services of transportation and mobility have originated from the expansion of cities on their periphery, where more than 60 percent of the European and more than 80 percent of the American population live today.[32] Ever since the exhaustion of the City Beautiful Movement at the end of the nineteenth-century Industrial Revolution,[33] the population explosion that soon followed—the urban bomb—radically transformed the making of cities. Planning in America emerged from an infrastructural boom during a period when cities like Chicago, Los Angeles, Boston, and New York were doubling and tripling in population.[34] Gangs were rampant, motorization was just on the horizon, but, more importantly, the dramatic rise in urban populations during the 1920s marked a turning point. For the first time in America's history, US demographers recorded the official transition from rural to industrial to urban economies in less than a century.[35] More than 50 percent of its population lived in urban areas. Notwithstanding crime and congestion, the multiple, concurrent demands for drinking water, waste management, energy generation, food distribution, and transportation corridors placed significant pressures upon the services of growing, congested cities. Control of these conditions seemed imperative, leading to the separation of urban services into distinct, more manageable categories, divisible through the inception of public works departments.

Upward-sloping and double-digit growth from famine-era migration[36] necessarily resulted in planning policies and zoning regulations premised on the control, containment, and constraint of urban growth. Height restrictions, density limits, and land use compatibilities were naturally formalized as part of the specialization of a professional planning discipline. Steeped in a core–periphery understanding of cities, urban planning drew from its inheritance of Old World principles of centralized city development, as well as the legacy of prisons and hospitals (the earliest forms of public planning through architecture) as models of socio-spatial control.[37] Master planning would consequently be predisposed as a social science.

Usurping the goals of the American Civic Association and the grandeur of the City Beautiful Movement, the new planning institution saw the substitution of ground-level development with hierarchical control. It capitalized on the separation of government powers that form the backbone of the US Constitution, to place authority in the hands of city governments. Although local governments were the largest stakeholders and beneficiaries of master planning, their objectives were soon subverted. The compound effect of squalid inner-city conditions, individual mobility, cheap low-rise housing, and de-industrialization fueled processes of outbound horizontal growth of urban populations along transportation corridors and new lines of access. This sprawl leaped over so-called growth boundaries, flowing beyond city limits, and threatening the imposed political boundaries that no longer contained horizontal urbanization. Seen as uncontrollable, growth became the new urban problem.[38] The incapacities and inflexibilities of master planning were further demonstrated by the contradictory rise of population checks, excess condemnation, and police power.

Unplanning: zoning, after Euclid

In the urban decentralization of cities, the task of planning relied on the neat separation of services with individual land use classifications. Faith in scientific planning and administrative control led to the establishment of basic single-use categories according to Euclidean planning principles: residential, commercial, and industrial. Cities took on new dimensions, raising more questions about the use of master plans as instruments of control and management reliant on use-values at the precise moment when, as John Kenneth Galbraith captured in *The New Industrial State* (1967), "capital [and power] became more important than land."[39] Dependent on jurisprudence, the planning discipline has irreversibly become entrenched in legislation, land use economics, and social sciences.[40] Consequently, geography and ecology were divorced from the basis of planning for the future altogether.[41] With rising preservation interests and constant indictments of suburban land development, this divide is growing wider. Planning methods have more recently failed to gain traction vis-à-vis the speed of urban expansion, housing, and infrastructural developments or the environmental pressures taking place.

From this divide, between the large-scale jurisprudence of planning and the smaller-scale technocratization of engineering, is a vacuum of unaddressed urban challenges. From groundwater abstraction in the Midwest States to river pollution of the Rio Grande to sewage flows in the Great Lakes, these demonstrate the regional pressures from urbanization beyond the ever-present divide of political jurisdictions, public works departments, and property boundaries.[42] Twentieth-century planning has been, for the most part, relegated to a generation of lawyers and economists reliant on an overarching legal or economic world view. Not unlike engineers, planners too have failed to see the greater synergies made possible by a more ecological, more integrative lens that couples and synthesizes different spatial, biophysical conditions with social and economic concerns.

From plans to processes

As a landscape, the fragmented, diffuse, and often transboundary pattern of urbanization has further demonstrated the weakness of nation states in facing massive urban change, as well as the fading power of the post-war welfare state to exercise influence or direct patterns of urban growth. Gradually, from the fading of federal power, the boundaries between public jurisdictions and private forces of development are dissolving when dealing with large-scale infrastructural projects. Physical boundaries of territories are often limited by state jurisdictions or federal agencies whose boundaries were established by wars or conflicts more than a century ago. Historically, resources such as rivers, coastlines, and water bodies served as military or geopolitical boundaries, or were marginalized as backwaters. This political preconditioning explains

why water courses and water bodies have historically been reduced to singular functions of sewage or navigation, contributing to the relative invisibility of biophysical resources, habitats, and ecotopes: systems that depend on systemic interconnectivity. As a result of these exclusions, biophysical systems are partitioned and parceled into defined areas, often categorized or restricted to bounded sites of conservation or recreation. The static boundaries of political jurisdictions now stand in sharp contrast to the fluid, dynamic patterns of urban growth whereby the flows of water, waste, energy, and food transcend geopolitical borders.

From sub-urbanization to super-urbanization

In parallel with the loosening of engineering's grip on the complexity of urban conditions, the planning of cities is now falling short due to an outgrowth of regulatory boundaries, an inflexibility to adapt to rapid change, and an incapacity to maintain existing infrastructures. Most pronounced in "older" economies of the New World and "newer" economies of the Developing World, the inertia of the planning profession is putting into question the regulatory regimes of cities, as the rise of ecological intelligence and systems thinking make connections across the economic and legislative borders.[43] What has been overlooked in the discourse on decentralization and urban dispersal, one that has been skewed by blanket dismissals of sprawl, is the general advantage afforded by the regionalization of urban conditions. In support of urban agglomerations earlier last century, regional urbanist Howard W. Odum documented the characterization of overlapping ecological, economic, or social regions "as a technique of decentralization and redistribution of population, industry, wealth, capital, culture, and of bigness, complexity, and technology."[44]

Often poorly understood, the global phenomenon of decentralization and the "flattening of the density gradient" stems from the leveling of socio-economic structures in the twentieth century. It is a process occurring across "a more dispersed landscape [that] has afforded many people greater levels of mobility, privacy, choice."[45] The increase in individual purchasing power thanks to consumer credit and the birth of instant communication made

20.4 Dezoning: demolition of GM's Fisher automotive body plant in Euclid, Ohio to make way for new expanding
institutional campuses and business parks in the suburbs of Cleveland in the vicinity of Lake Erie
Photo: ©2008 Pierre Bélanger

possible by network technology systems[46] have thus contributed to a horizontal pattern of urbanization that functions largely as an alternative to the "densely settled cities that were the norm at the end of the nineteenth century."[47]

From this larger lens, the process of urbanization is best understood as a transition from former industrial economies of supply towards urban economies of demand that has occurred in the past century. From this shift, we can propose that the current rise of urban economies is a reaction to the Fordist modes of production and Taylorist modes of management that have dominated the past century. As a natural response to these models of control and containment, the decentralization of cities and the expansion of urban economies at the regional scale provide major benefits, where super-urbanization opens new territories for occupation, renewal, and redistribution.

From control to contingency

The rethinking of efficiency, the basis of engineering, and of control, the historic focus of planning, is yielding more strategic and more contingent formats of design.[48] Legal and regulatory frameworks are being counterbalanced by pressing concerns about the carbon footprint of cities and the limited lifespan of infrastructure. The view of cities as closed systems, composed of a few controllable variables, is succumbing to a growing body of knowledge and expertise on dynamic, distributed, ecological systems.

With the inability of planning to counteract or control the spread of urban form and capital through growth or shrinkage at the onset of the twenty-first century,[49] it is clear that planning tasks will merge with the more influential parent discipline of landscape architecture, further augmented by softer forms of civil engineering. From this position, zoning as well as dezoning may take on unprecedented roles in the design of regions—either coastal, continental or oceanic—at super-urban scales. They will transition from being tools of prevention to instruments of projection through forces that may eventually yield a richer, more productive set of ecologies.

FIELDS AND FLOWS

As a result of the diversification of urban economies and decentralization of their service infrastructure, we have been witnessing in the past three decades the decoupling of centralized planning from state authorities. Naturally, we are also witnessing the waning of national identities associated with great public works, such as the highway systems and other great engineering feats,[50] followed by the decoupling of infrastructure as an exclusive domain of practice of civil engineers. From this flattening of urban administration and engineered hierarchy, a set of new regionalized identities are emerging that privilege diversity and differentiation, most evident in a more visible landscape of resources, cultures, territories, and innovations.[51]

In order to initiate a more ecologically responsive, socially expedient, culturally relevant, and fiscally effective reorganization of urban lands, how then can we rebundle and redesign essential urban services—from water resources and waste cycling, energy generation and food cultivation, mass mobility and network communications—as living landscapes that span the divide between economy and ecology facing contemporary cities?

Regionalization

From this re-questioning and re-reading of the dominant principles of the past two centuries, and the disciplinary cleavage created by the complexity of current urban conditions, rises the field of landscape, a multi-disciplinary and cross-scalar horizon where forces converge: the ecological with the economic, the social with the political, the organic with the technological. Here, the horizontal nature of the field of landscape avoids disciplinary cul-de-sacs, rendering irrelevant the historic oppositions between concepts such as city and country, rural and urban, natural and human, modern and historic.

By employing a wider view, we can expose how the landscape of urbanism lies beyond the grey matter of cities, operating dynamically across several overlapping regions. This vantage opens a wider and deeper view of urban economies and urban footprints. Resource flows

20.5 Farms, Factories, Workshops: the pattern of subsistence farms in the contemporary logistics and manufacturing hub of Zhengzhou, China, where over 30 percent of land within existing ring roads is designated for agricultural use by food security policy
Source: ©2011 GeoEye

from across watersheds, energy demands, and food provision from continental sources index the greater extents of urbanization.

When viewed over time, this super-urban vantage sheds light on the interconnections of infrastructure, spatially and temporally. Largely perceived as smooth, seamless, and permanent, infrastructure networks are, in fact, extremely fragile and short lived. Spatial conventions that are borne from the techno-bureaucratic factions of public works departments (waste, water, energy, food, and transport agencies) and inherited from classical, Old World notions of civil engineering, or from the socio-political mechanisms of legislative

zoning and master planning inherited from military ideologies and wartime strategies, are deliberately put into question.

So far, in the discourse of urban reform, considerable attention has been given to the hard systems of urban support such as roads, sewers, and bridges, evident in national investment policies[52] and private investment in waste treatment and water delivery systems. A parallel discourse has emerged in design, planning, and engineering on the value of softer, leaner infrastructures premised on ecology as the catalyst of infrastructural reform and the driver of urban morphology.[53]

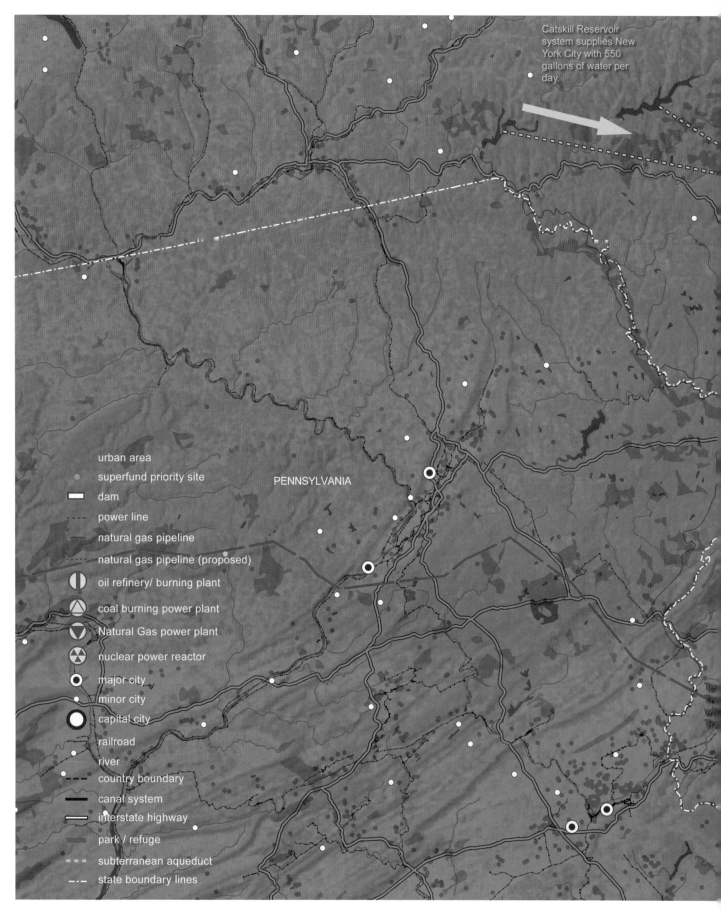

Catskill Reservoir system supplies New York City with 550 gallons of water per day.

PENNSYLVANIA

urban area
• superfund priority site
▬ dam
---- power line
—— natural gas pipeline
······ natural gas pipeline (proposed)
◑ oil refinery/ burning plant
◭ coal burning power plant
▽ Natural Gas power plant
◈ nuclear power reactor
◎ major city
• minor city
◎ capital city
railroad
river
---- country boundary
—— canal system
══ interstate highway
park / refuge
▪▪▪ subterranean aqueduct
–·– state boundary lines

20.6 Urban Footprints: the networks of energy, waste, water, food and mobility that service the New York–New Jersey region
Diagram courtesy of Jonathan Scelsa, 2011

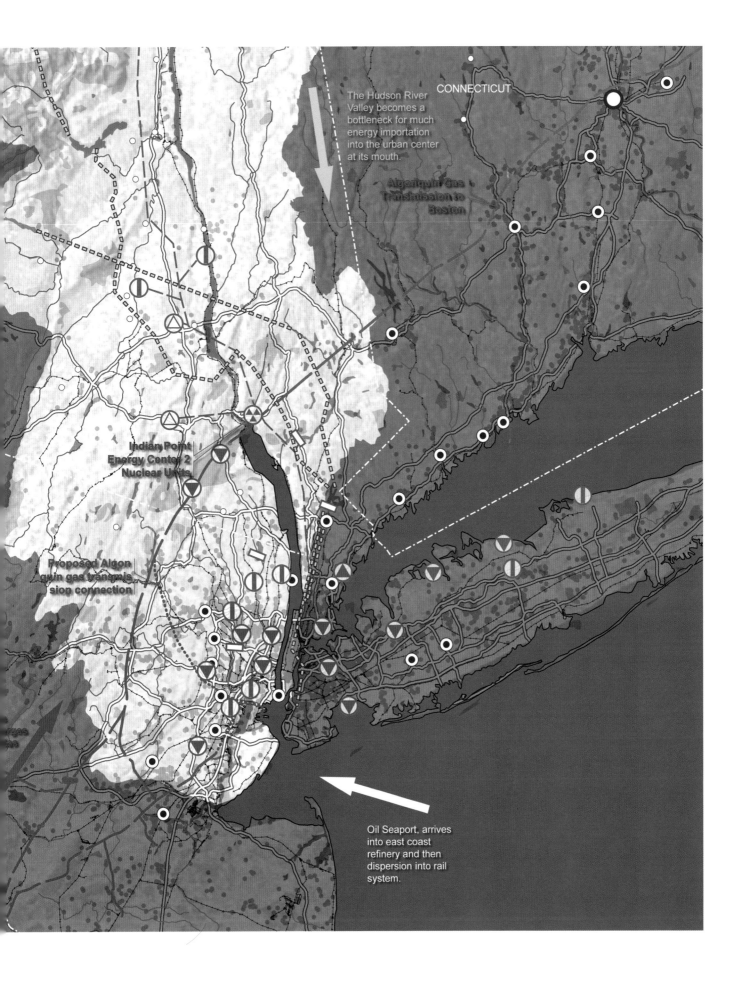

CONNECTICUT

The Hudson River Valley becomes a bottleneck for much energy importation into the urban center at its mouth.

Algonquin Gas Transmission to Boston

Indian Point Energy Center 2 Nuclear Units

Proposed Algonquin gas transmission connection

Oil Seaport, arrives into east coast refinery and then dispersion into rail system.

20.7 Ecological Zoning: Aerial view of Donau-Auen wetlands bordering the Danube, a riparian system that protects Wien's City Centre, the Vienna International Airport, and the Schwechat vineyards from the perennial risk of 1 to 7-metre flood levels
Image: ©2011 DigitalGlobe, ©2011 GeoEye

In the wake of ongoing restructuring of city centers toward more decentralized and dispersed spatial patterns, cultural thinker and theorist Sanford Kwinter projects:

that infrastructural demands are not only becoming exponentially more importunate today but that these infrastructural demands are breeding and mutating in kind and not only in degree. We have no choice today but to deal with the new "soft" infrastructures: of knowledge infrastructure, program infrastructure, cultural infrastructure, virtual infrastructure. The demand for design and de-design—in our over-engineered, over-mediated world is both enormous and pervasive, yet the majority of architects still respond to it with the medieval language of the stoic, autonomous building. Today's design world is stratified, with an emerging class structure, its associated embedded conflicts, and an emerging new proletariat increasingly separated from the principle means of production.[54]

Risk and complexity

Often operating on extraordinary scales, and precipitated by the onslaught of global urbanization, the basic attributes of urban infrastructure and large-scale public works (roads, canal, bridges, dams for example) conjure a sense of plain and simple awe.[55] By

20.8 Farmland and Power: the first commercial scale public utility wind field in Michigan built by
John Deere Renewables on land leased from cooperative sugar beet farmers near Bad Axe

Source: Don Coles, Great Lakes Aerial Photography, 2008

virtue of its bigness alone, as urbanist Rem Koolhaas observes, infrastructure "instigates a regime of complexity" that mobilizes the full intelligence of design, less dependent on "meticulous definition, the imposition of limits, but about expanding notions, denying boundaries."[56] Pragmatically, the field of landscape—both cross-collaborative and trans-scalar—provides the instrumental equipment to best handle the complexity precipitated by contemporary urbanization.

In the high-risk technological landscape of the twenty-first century, however, it is ironically the unassuming attribute of dumbness—the relative ease of understanding and interpreting a strategy—that serves as design's greatest asset in its *accouplement* with infrastructure.[57] If civil engineering has worked in the past, it has achieved its status

by simplicity and straightforwardness. In the current reallocation of public sector work to the private sector market and more collaborative forms of project delivery, the advantage that infrastructure affords, both as a construction and as a concept, is that it further transcends the conventional boundaries associated with public works and private properties by referring to underlying conditions and challenges that are specific and common to both.

This is the greatest service that infrastructure promises as an emergent design territory. Yet, in order to do so, design must be more opportunistic in its borrowings from predominant disciplines, and leverage disciplinary knowledge outside the formal limits of its own capacities while engaging more synergistic collaborations.[58] Identified over a decade ago by Gray L. Strang in a special edition of *Places Magazine*, the advantage of appropriating infrastructure as landscape is heightened since:

> the amount of funding for renovating public infrastructure is likely to far exceed the amount that will be available for buildings, parks and open space. Large budgets can be used to produce urban design that simultaneously solve utilitarian problems, and help repair cities and regional landscapes at a scale not dreamed of since the days of the great dams.[59]

Circular economies and resource flows

Underlying this latent potential is the horizontal nature of landscape both as scale and system. The synthetic capacities of landscape conflate both infrastructure and ecological process, enabling the reclamation of formerly abandoned sites with the intensification of new ones. As a scale, the field moves from the bio-molecular to the global geographic, by way of urban, ecological regions. It operates across the disciplines of engineering at the smallest level to policy planning at the highest level. As a system,[60] the scale of landscape is operationalized through ecological intelligence. In contrast to closed, industrial systems of production from economies of mass production, it is as an open system of exogenous and endogenous flows. Like an operation system, its software and hardware come in the form of points, patches, or planes of interventions or as networks and zones of influence, sometimes fluid or fragmented, gradual or temporal. Surfaces of intervention are often unconstrained; climate works as a conditioner rather than a constraint. At its extreme, the field of landscape can potentially be subversive, where aesthetics are embedded through patterns and processes of latent biodynamics. Through connections, expansions, contractions, and projections, urban conditions become synonymous with constructed ecologies. Wastes and excesses, the surpluses of urbanization, become absorbed into a re-circulating economy of secondary and tertiary materials, through downcycling and upcycling.

PROJECTIONS AND PROTOECOLOGIES

From this horizon, we can begin to see how the processes of urban agglomeration and decentralization work as strategies of distribution and dispersal in response to the legacy of Old World models of urban centrality that failed to adapt to the rising demands of contemporary population pressures, modes of production, communication networks, and biophysical systems. The vertical growth that characterized much of the nineteenth and twentieth centuries is being eroded by the horizontal nature of income and population distribution across larger areas, and the inefficiencies and inequalities often associated with compact, exclusive, or unaffordable city centers. Here, the processes of decentralization—whether by strategies of distribution or dispersal[61]—provide capabilities and opportunities to open a new territory where patterns and processes drive new morphologies in the future.[62]

Landscape as infrastructure

Emerging from these ecological imperatives and economic exigencies, the project of landscape infrastructure proposes an expanded operating system for contemporary cities where the full complexity of biodynamic processes and resources are visualized and deployed across the full footprint of urbanism and the life cycles of infrastructure. As a theoretical evolution of the reformist discipline of landscape architecture at the beginning of the twentieth century, landscape infrastructure engages the full capacity of post-Euclidean planning and global contextualism of capital flow while exploiting the techno-spatial capacity of twenty-first-century civil engineering in order to deploy ecology as the agent of urban renewal and expansion. Departing from conventional bureaucratic and centralized forms of civic administration, this contemporary formulation foreshadows a more flexible, cooperative, and process-driven agency for the design disciplines with a co-commitment to the metrics of design, research, and implementation. From this position, design strategies can be launched between two extremes: short, immediate interventions that are graduated and sequenced over long periods of time with large, durable geopolitical and ecological effects. Design—including the research that precedes it—becomes strategic, capable of integrating multiple scales of intervention at once.

Still relatively nascent, the field of landscape supports a multitude of possibilities and protocols of engagement with this project. Despite the death-of-distance thesis foreshadowed in the late 1990s by globalization and communication networks,[63] the landscape of geography, ecology, and urbanism figures more prominently today than ever before. Professionally and culturally, the recognition of landscape's directive capabilities in contemporary design culture is growing, especially with the rapidly growing understanding of ecological complexity worldwide.[64] When considered outside the confines of disciplinary professionalization, a wider, more open-ended and diversified understanding of the field will liberate it from its past dependencies and borrowings on the architecture and urban planning disciplines as surrogates for its own history and evolution. If we consider infrastructure as a constructed landscape of channels, pipes, grids, and networks that extend across vast territories and that precondition urban life, then we can borrow from several disciplines—urban geography, civil engineering, public administration, botany, horticulture—and combine that knowledge with biophysical resources to form the essential services of urban regions and construct new histories and new lineages. In this way, landscape becomes a beta-structure of processes, an instrumental pattern that shapes the urban world in which we live while enabling us to perceive it differently.

Indexing ecology

Rendering visible the living systems that underlie urban economies is a critical practice. As a projective method, representation through the mapping of complex levels of information is instrumental to the design of infrastructure and ecology. Whether by diagrams or maps, composite imaging provides an important alternative to the conventional orthographic methods of visualization inherited from engineers and architects. Those methods were intended exclusively as construction documents—blueprints that privileged drawings as contracts for the production of legal information

through representation. Conversely, a recent body of work has begun to rethink the historic or exclusive role of the drawing as contractual document to consider drawings of disclosure and public communication.[65] In the public works realm, the visual communication of strategies, and the research that supports it, has become, in and of itself, an essential design practice.

The visibility of flows, processes, and systems underlies much of the work to be done, especially when displaying vast movements of information and people or managing huge volumes of natural resources that are often operating in remote or underground environments or at scales too large for the naked eye.

New, multimedia modes of representation are seeking to redefine the conventions of design historically rooted in technical drafting or pictorial imaging. Architectural historian and theorist Kenneth Frampton reveals the purpose of this expanded representational role:

> At broad scales, the creative use of landscape representation to project alternative futures for urban form, infrastructure investment, ecological restoration and environmental management can be a powerful counter to the technocratic dominance of other forms of knowledge. The understanding of the particularity and distinction of local and regional landscapes can provide a point of resistance to the homogenizing effects of globalization.[66]

For example, the rise of master planning during the era of the City Beautiful Movement led to the domination of single, orthographic points of view that often excluded context and time. Constrained by a limited repertoire of design instruments (streets, blocks, and buildings) these historically imposed limits on design overlooked powerful ecological flows and geographic patterns operating at large scales that cut across property boundaries. In contrast to the specificity of planometric forms of representation, the section provides a much more flexible means of communication, prototyping change across a large scale. The section, with all of its attendant variations (cutaways, developed, expanded, and longitudinal), acts as a graphic interface between the surface and subsurface. It simultaneously reveals the invisibility of what is below ground or underwater, and translates what is downstream and what is upstream.

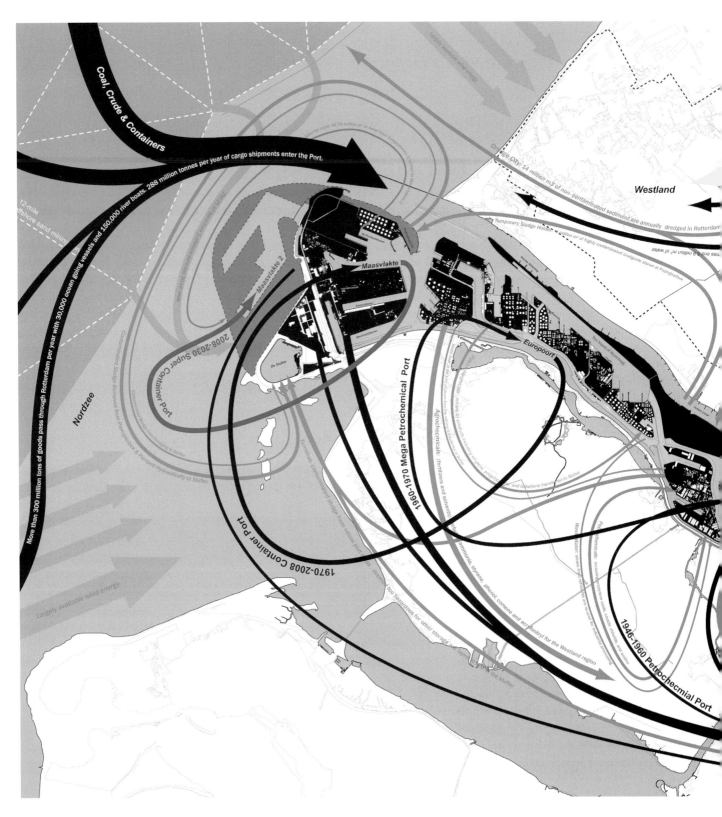

20.9 Flows, Reflows and Backflows: the aggregated landscape of waste cycling, material movements, and resource exchanges developed during the past five centuries of growth throughout the Port of Rotterdam

Source: ©2010 OPSYS

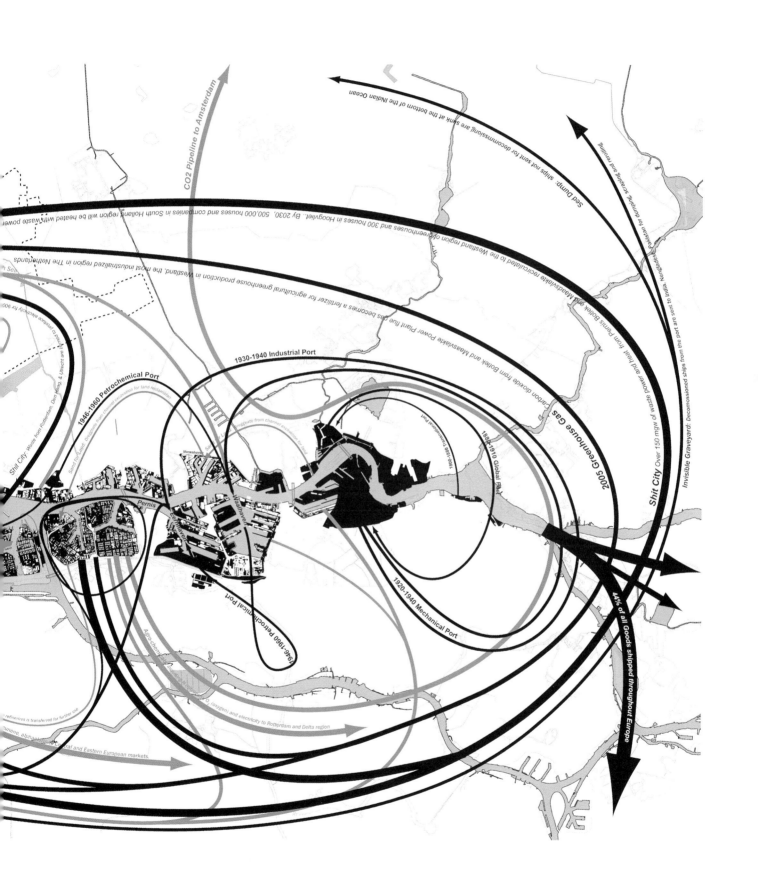

CO2 Pipeline to Amsterdam

Sea Dump: ships not sent for decommissioning are sunk at the bottom of the Indian Ocean

By 2030, 500,000 houses and companies in South Holland region will be heated with waste power

500,000 houses and 300 houses in Hoogvliet. By 2030, 500,000 houses and companies in South Holland region will be heated with waste power

the Westland region of greenhouses and Maasvlakte recirculated to the Westland region in The Netherlands

in Westland, the most industrialized region in The Netherlands

flue gas becomes a fertilizer for agricultural greenhouse production in Westland, the most industrialized region in The Netherlands

Carbon dioxide from Botlek and Maasvlakte Power Plant flue gas becomes a fertilizer for agricultural greenhouse production

Carbon dioxide from Botlek and Maasvlakte Power Plant flue heat from Pernis Botlek and Maasvlakte

to produce electricity for 900

1930-1940 Industrial Port

1946-1960 Petrochemical Port

Sand for land. Dredging from channel excavation for land reclamation

Sand for land. Dredging from channel excavation for land reclamation

2005 Greenhouse Gas

Shit City: Waste from Rotterdam, Den Haag, & Utrecht are

Shit City Over 150 mgw of waste power

Invisible Graveyard: Decomissioned ships from the port are sent to India. Neshbadb, Pakistan, for dumping or scrapping and building

Pernis

Waalhaven

Merwehaven

1880-1890 Transnational Port

1880-1910 Global Port

1946-1980 Petrochemical Port

1920-1940 Mechanical Port

Agro-chemical

O (oxygen) and electricity to Rotterdam and Delta region

refineries is transferred for further use

nunne, alphen

tral and Eastern European markets.

44% of all Goods shipped throughout Europe

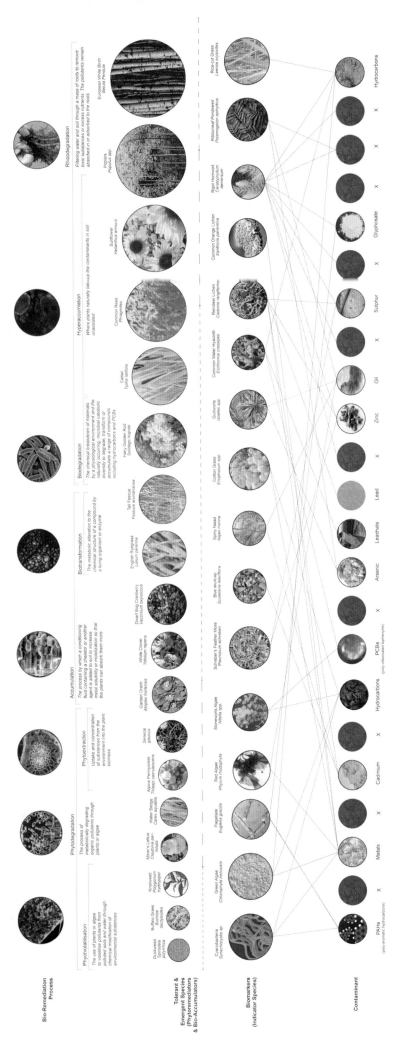

20.10 Bioindication: relational diagram of contaminant-sensitive plant species as vegetal indices of bioavailability and hyperaccumulation

Source: ©2010 OPSYS

For these reasons, sectional strategies have become the privileged interface between the complexity of the subsurface below (soils, foundations, wires, conduits, tunnels, pipelines) and the banality of the surface above (curbs, edges, surfaces, manholes, posts, grates, markings). Small and often minuscule changes of surface profiles in cross-section can have pronounced effects across vast distances when seen from above, or experienced from the ground.

Dynamic conditions that were most often characterized as constraints are now being projected as major opportunities, especially when laid out across time. Therefore, it is not surprising that hybrid formats of representation—from sectional profiles to oblique aerial views to cutaway sections—have liberated the field from the stronghold of orthographic drawings and engage the design of relationships, associations, and synergies across a multitude of sites. Foreshadowed by James Corner, mapping itself takes on a double agency as process and projection:

> Mappings have agency because of the double-sided characteristic of all maps. First, their surfaces are directly analogous to actual ground conditions; as horizontal planes, they record the surface of the earth as direct impressions. … By contrast, the other side of this analogous characteristic is the inevitable abstractness of maps, the result of selection, omission, isolation, distance and codification.[67]

Through visualization and intervention, contemporary practice will rely on both the design and designation of new territories. The collaborative and interdisciplinary process of mapping becomes the program of the project, making it relatively fast and easy to think big. Modes of representation—such as design scenarios, section profiles, and construction sequences—which enable a level of precise approximation and strategic generalization, can exploit situations of uncertainty and indeterminacy, collaboration and leadership. Time becomes, in and of itself, a medium, and time zones instrumental to the orchestration of large-scale effects through simple interventions. Operating on prolonged time scales, the vegetal dimension of design—encompassing the horticultural, the botanical, the silvicultural, the fluvial, the agronomic—can then be integrated as organic infrastructure at scales that were previously overlooked and undervalued.

20.11 Dual Infrastructure: cross-sectional strategy showing the dualization of land uses proposed
for the intensification of industrial landscapes throughout the network of portlands in Rotterdam

Source: ©2010 OPSYS

20.12 Time-scale: visual timeline of milestones in world energy during the past five hundred years as a result of technological innovation, world politics, energy resource substitution and decentralized power sources

Source: ©2010 OPSYS

2020

2030

of Predictions
f Pentagon report,
how that by 2035,
il reserves will be
followed by natu-
ound 2050.

Oil Titans
Six countries Saudi Arabia,
Iran, Kuwait, the UAE, Iraq
and Russia control 40% of
total world oil production.

Polarities
Energy consumption gr
by almost 60 perc
almost 2 b
basi

Water Wars

goodbye nuclear
hello hydrogen

5385 km/l

biofuel bonanz

gas from grass

wind rush

propulsion

fusion

LE GROS EOLIEN
NON MERCI

BELUGA PROJECTS

Telefonica

1960
the Organization of Petroleum Export-
ing Countries (OPEC) is established by
Iraq, Iran, Saudi Arabia, Kuwait and
Venezuela.
1964 LNG
First international trade of liquefied
natural gas begins.

1969 Solar Furnace
Using an array of plane mirrors, rays of
sunlight are captured and focused to
an area the size of a cooking pot with
temperatures reaching up to 3,000
degrees Celsius.

1971 DOE
US President Jimmy Carter creates the
Department of Energy.
1974 Energy as National Security
Nixon calls for a second Manhattan
Project to lead the US to energy self-
sufficiency by 1980.

1977 Strategic Reserves
US begins to maintain an emergency
petroleum supply following the 1973
Oil embargo.
1980 Eight-Year War
Saddam Hussein's Army attacks Iran
over long standing rivalries.

1982 Law of the Sea
United Nations' Convention
overturns the 'freedom of the
seas' and defines rights and
responsibilities of nations towards the world oceans.

1989 Spill
The Exxon Valdez oil tanker hits a reef
off the Alaskan coast, spilling 10 million gallons of crude oil in Prince William Sound, costing over $6.5 billion
in cleanup costs and damages.

1991 Farming Air
Vindeby, the world's first offshore wind
farm, is built in Denmark.
1994 EEZ
International Law of the Sea establishes
200-mile zone as standard Exclusive Economic Zone for all countries.

2002 The China Factor
A new industrial superpower emerges as a co
petitor for control over global oil reserves.
2005 Hydrogen Miles
On June 26, PAC-Car II sets a new world rec
in fuel-economy with 5385 km/l consuming
of hydrogen at an average speed of 30km/l

alization
I Highway Act mandates
n of a 43,000-km Inter-
nse Highway System en-
e entire United States

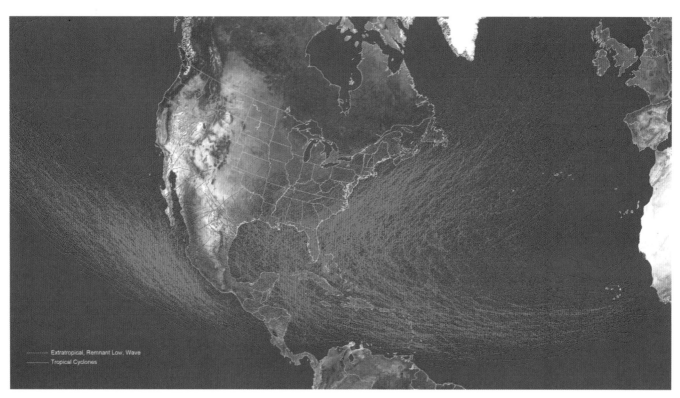

20.13 Hurricane Alley: historic paths of major storm events since 1851 forming across the Atlantic Ocean,
a climatic pattern responsible for an average of 13 hurricanes each year (including Katrina, Ike, and Andrew)
Source: ©2008 NOAA

Infrastructural ecologies: fluid, biotic, contingent

Once the sole purview of the profession of civil engineering, infrastructure—the management of water, waste, food, transport, and energy—is taking on extreme relevance for the design practices in the context of the changing, decentralizing structures of urban-regional economies. Food production and energy networks can no longer be engineered without considering the cascade of waste streams and the cycling of raw material inputs. Industries, landfills, land farms, and logistics areas can no longer be designed without their wastesheds. Highway networks, sewage systems, and subdivisions can no longer be planned without their watersheds. Simply put, urban regions cannot shrink or expand without employing the geographies and climates of continental landscapes that eventually shape them.

Designation of territories, zones of intervention, and modes of organization become soft design processes that eventually lead to the formation of new spatial morphologies and performative ecologies.

Over time, we can engage infrastructure as a landscape with strategic interventions that span extremely short and immediate intervals, sliding across different scales. At the exact moment construction ends, when blueprints are implemented, the penultimate objective of design management can begin. More often than not, design should be under-detailed leaving raw, open, and often incomplete the assembly for unknown site circumstances and social change, where the beauty of the project lies in its banality and openness to change. As a medium, time becomes a dimension of design management and superintendence that is slow but enduring.

Design becomes telescopic, sliding across different scales, systems, and strategies that are no longer defined by professional or political boundaries but rather by trans-disciplinary, trans-boundary collaborations. In contraposition to the hard, fixed infrastructures, this interpretation provides the room for the design of softer, looser ecological systems, with a concentration on the effects at macro- and micro-levels. Borne from performance and productivity, newly recognizable morphologies and topologies of the infrastructural landscape—*meshes, webs, nodes, conduits, gardens, and fields*—

are most often hybrids of invariable types molded by additional processes of flow, trade, exchange, conveyance, mobility, and communications. Through this lens, we can begin opening a territory of new scales, systems, and synergies, upstream or downstream across the gradient of urban economies.

Invoking the unfinished project of landscape[68] as a geospatial and geobotanical practice with the softer, more fluid field of ecological systems pioneered by Sauer, Odum, and Bailey,[69] the *double entendre* of the landscape infrastructure project maintains an operative, polyfunctional objective dedicated to urban expansion and contraction through land use synergies and biophysical dynamics. Sponsoring transboundary crossover, this nascent field implies a dual identity for single-use infrastructure along corridors of movement, where a synthesis of ecology preconditions the detail of implementation, where long-term resource management is as important as the short-term mobilization of capital, and where the commonwealth of public systems presides over the uncoordinated guise of self-interests, requiring the sustained engagement from public and private motives. Transcending jurisdictional boundaries, the integrative and horizontal enterprise of landscape infrastructure enlists geographic zoning, boundary realignments, strategic design, subsurface programming, sectional thickening, and ecological engineering as some of the most influential mechanisms in the structural transformation of urban regions to effect change on the large-scale operational and logistical aspects of urbanization. Staging uncertainty and harnessing contingency become the new urban imperatives, through the design of resilient and flexible edges, margins, and peripheries.

From this position, this augmented capability explains the establishment of a more precise approach to the field of complex data without sacrificing the generalized levels of interpretation and reuse of the work. It further enforces a level of general approximation that defies the current convention of basing precise measures on undefined information, or the "institutionalized black boxing of models."[70] In the most extreme circumstances, the field of landscape demonstrates its agility as *le plan libre par excellence*.[71]

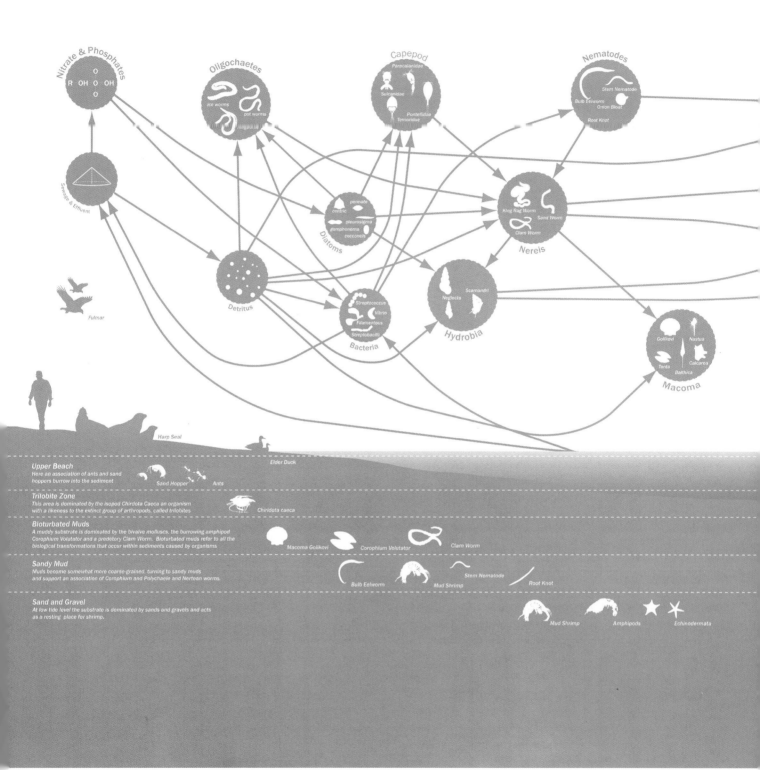

20.14 Food Web: diagram of shoreline gradients, land use relationships, biodiversities and feeding patterns of aquatic species in estuaries, at the base of marine ecosystems

Source: ©2010 OPSYS

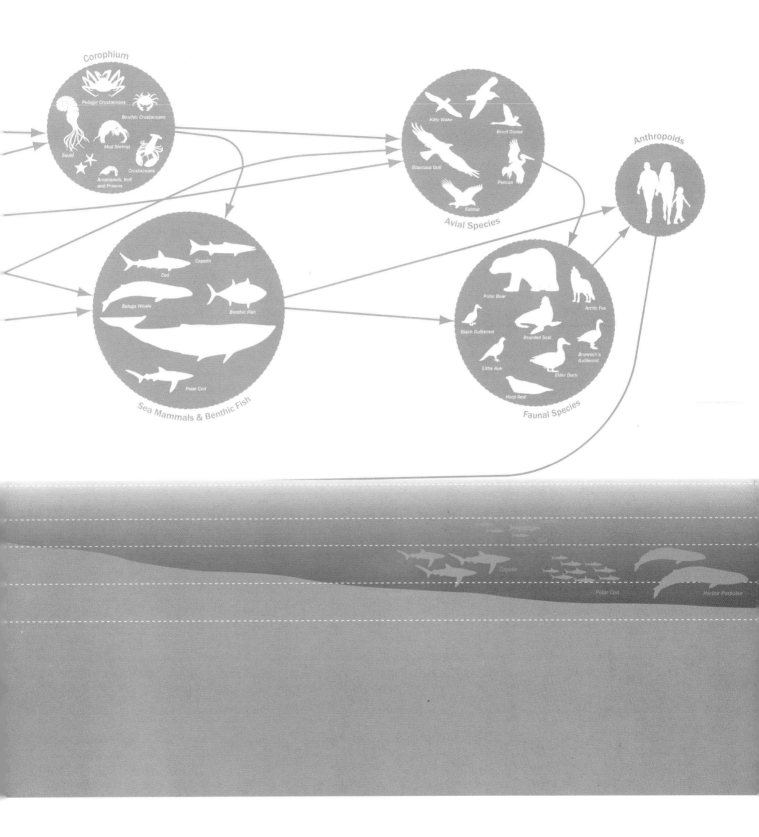

20.15 Intelligent Flooding: upswelling of the Danube River along the edges of the Donau-Insel, a flood
protection island that deflects and distributes high water away from the historic centre of Vienna and
transportation crossings, towards the National Parklands downriver
Photo courtesy of Wolfgang H. Wögerer, Wien, 2009

Post-carbon public works

Embodied by projects such as the Works Progress Administration
(WPA) and other programs of FDR's New Deal—a historic period
that defined US history through its infrastructural undertakings—
the era of national public works is over. The great public works
that have defined the identity of America, or any great nation,
are crumbling. Perpetuated by the discipline of civil engineering,
national infrastructure projects are unrealistic, fading away in the
background of increasing ecological complexity. The perceived
promise of security and stability of centralized infrastructure, and

its affiliation to notions of permanence and vertical growth, no
longer provide the foundation for the more horizontal, distributed
urban economies.[72]

The construction of urban ecologies and reclamation of biophysical
processes provides much greater flexibility and adaptive potential.
In the wake of this loosening grip of engineering and the weaker
position of planning, the estimated $5.5 trillion project of urban
renewal in North America, which will see the reconstruction of
more than 200 billion square feet of space, as well as the defense
of more than 2.5 billion people living within coastal zones, presents
an unprecedented opportunity.

20.16 Post-Fordist Infrastructure: aerial view of linear greenways and flood management zones of the Buffalo Bayou system, underlying the I-45 highway interchange in Houston, Texas, a project spearheaded by a public-private partnership of civic, environmental, governmental, and business representatives
Image: ©2011 United States Geological Survey

If we are to mold the future, beyond a few exceptional precedents, this project will involve the merger of the landscape of living systems and the territory of urban infrastructure, as interface to the contemporary conditions.

By design, the project of landscape infrastructure will be contingent on several processes and practices across an expanded "plane of services and performances":[73]

1. Flexibilities: the division between land use classifications (residential, commercial, industrial) and characteristics (wet/dry, high/low) will have to make way for overlaps, interconnections, and exchanges. Flexible, more porous formats of construction, design, and maintenance that privilege ecological systems will enable tidal fluctuation, moisture variations, climactic regimes, biodiversity and social functions to flourish and grow.

2. Synergies: the dismantling and decoupling of bureaucratic land use controls and the decentralization of engineered infrastructure must make way for straightforward and practical reclamation of biophysical processes and reintegration of ecological flows. To generate multi-functionality and inter-operability, design scenarios will have to combine hardware and software to expand the effects, spin-offs and offsets of strategies. Moving beyond carbon

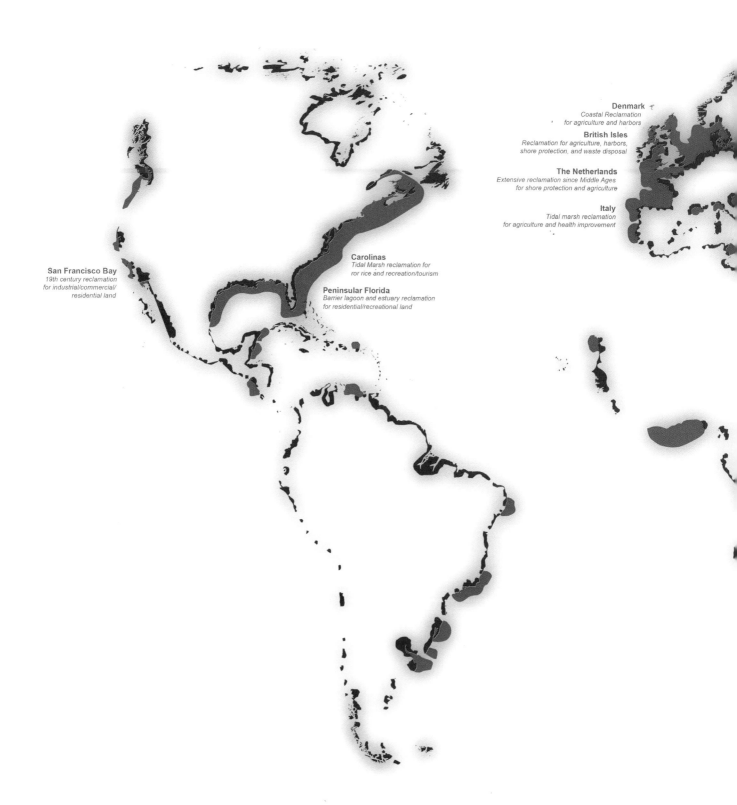

Denmark
*Coastal Reclamation
for agriculture and harbors*

British Isles
*Reclamation for agriculture, harbors,
shore protection, and waste disposal*

The Netherlands
*Extensive reclamation since Middle Ages
for shore protection and agriculture*

Italy
*Tidal marsh reclamation
for agriculture and health improvement*

Carolinas
*Tidal Marsh reclamation for
ror rice and recreation/tourism*

San Francisco Bay
*19th century reclamation
for industrial/commercial/
residential land*

Peninsular Florida
*Barrier lagoon and estuary reclamation
for residential/recreational land*

20.17 Risk Landscape: coastal regions of the world showing current hypoxic zones (grey) and areas of potential
sea level rise or storm surge (red), where more than 60% of the world's population will be living by 2030
according to the United Nations

Source: OPSYS, with data from NOAA, NASA, UNDP

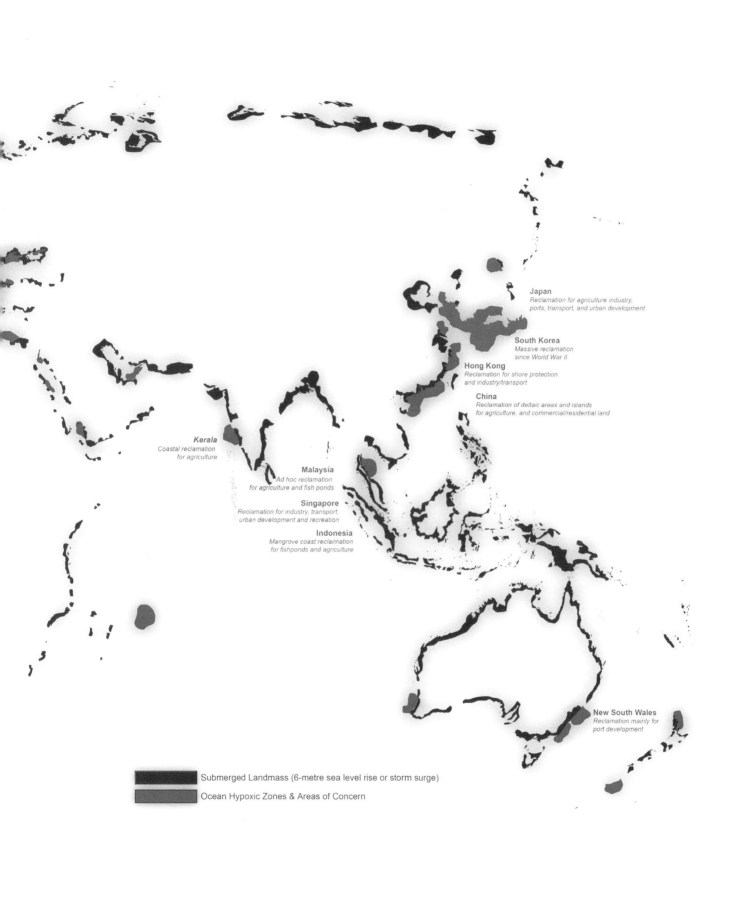

Japan
Reclamation for agriculture industry,
ports, transport, and urban development

South Korea
Massive reclamation
since World War II

Hong Kong
Reclamation for shore protection
and industry/transport

China
Reclamation of deltaic areas and islands
for agriculture, and commercial/residential land

Kerala
Coastal reclamation
for agriculture

Malaysia
Ad hoc reclamation
for agriculture and fish ponds

Singapore
Reclamation for industry, transport,
urban development and recreation

Indonesia
Mangrove coast reclamation
for fishponds and agriculture

New South Wales
Reclamation mainly for
port development

Submerged Landmass (6-metre sea level rise or storm surge)

Ocean Hypoxic Zones & Areas of Concern

20.18 Post-Carbon Resource Park: view of the Svartsengi Geothermal Power Station in southwestern
Iceland where geothermal effluents are re-circulated through a public health spa and wastewater
lagoon, rich in blue-green algae, mineral salts, and fine silica muds
Source: ©2009 Stephen Bunch

dependence, we can begin to see buildings become batteries, highways as rolling warehouses, landfills as goldmines, suburbs as stormwater sponges, forests as carbon sinks, city coastlines as estuarine aprons. Requiring suppleness, infrastructural ecologies must employ existing capabilities and existing resources to be easily implementable and replicable.[74]

3. Cross-collaborations: while no single discipline or designer can lay claim to the design of infrastructure in the future, its complexity alone generates the potential for interdisciplinary partnerships and cultural cross-fertilization. Synergistic reasoning, strategic design, and integrated social agency will loosen boundaries

between public and private jurisdictions and open new possibilities for strategic project partnerships. Focusing on the synthesis of ecology, engineering, and economy, complex responsibilities are spread out and risks shared across a more lateral network of professional liabilities.

4. Speeds and scales: the exchange of resources, materials, and information will drive the modification and reprogramming of urban surfaces to accommodate greater auto-mobility and auto-diversity as a result of increasing modes of mobility by way of the separation of different speeds of movements. Surface differentiation, markings, and codifications at one end, and

infrastructure of mobility at the other, will radically transform the built environment in the future.[75] Communication networks and polycentric nodes of knowledge are generating live–work patterns that, in contrast to the centralized 9-to-5 industrial model, are increasingly distributed and dispersed.

5. Distribution and disaggregation: urban densities will persistently decline and regions spread wider as long as incomes increase and transportation remains relatively inexpensive.[76] The slackening of political and regulatory controls will help shape urban expansion, decongestion, fragmentation, or diffusion. Through ecological engineering, those processes enable the formation of more hybridized morphologies and new financial mechanisms that join owners, users, stakeholders, and regulators, over time.

6. Regionalization: the dismantling of historical divide between city center and periphery, or the differentiation of cities from other cities, in order to engage the different footprints of urbanism and life cycles of infrastructure, to acknowledge the impermanence and flexibilities of growth, as well as continental forces, beyond the grey zones of cities on road maps. When factoring resource regions and biodynamic flows, infrastructural networks and social innovations, the restructured understanding of economic forms ultimately relies on the reclamation of capital flow as an intrinsically ecological strategy.[77] The visibility of resource urbanism will bring closer the sources of resource extraction with end uses and spaces of consumption.

Ecologies of scale

In spite of the adolescence of the city building disciplines, the Athenian Oath that has been restraining urban designers for the past 2000 years can finally loosen its grip and make room for new instruments and methods for intervening at geospatial scales, beyond the city and into contemporary urban territories. The linear, fixed, and closed mechanisms of the industrial economy are quickly fading in the background of more flexible, circular, and networked systems of urban economies. Releasing the pristine ideals of the city from the crutches of security, permanence, or density opens a horizon of new social equities and regional synergies—a whole range

of projects beyond that of a few exceptional precedents. Moving beyond conservation or preservation, the ecological imperative instigates the design of relationships, where associations and synergies become infrastructural. Softer, more fluid forms of urban configurations generate open, flexible infrastructures where risk becomes an opportunity, and morphology is based on contingency and indeterminacy of climate fluctuations.

Signaling a critical tipping point, the re-examination of historical practices reveals that the landscape of biological processes and natural resources that are integral to larger, regional systems cannot, and should not, be segregated from the discourse or the design of urban infrastructure. To learn how to slide across scales, across disciplines, or across jurisdictions, the metrics, processes, and protoecologies presented here offer preliminary examples of how designers can operate across the greatest and fullest extent of design over time: from the largest scales of geography and regions to the engineering and genetics of the smallest size. Through the redesign of infrastructure, our work in the future lies in the re-coupling, re-configuration, and re-calibration of these processes. Urgent and pressing, the project of the ecological restructuring of these systems—where transportation departments collaborate with conservation agencies, or where port authorities partner with fisheries organizations, or where power corporations work with waste recycling organizations—is a necessary corollary to the next generation of post-Fordist, post-Taylorist infrastructures.

We can posit a more fluid understanding of urbanization formed by new forces and flows such as capital and mobility, speed and communications, power and production, toxicity and ecology, contamination and cultivation, energetics and synergies, war and wealth, societies and networks that can be considered the main drivers and denominators in the design and construction of contemporary urban ecologies operating across different scales, magnitudes, and borders, with regional, continental, and global capabilities.

In the wake of the over-planning, over-regulation and over-engineering of the past century, it is clear that the strategic engagement of the landscape of living systems as urban infrastructure is already moving ahead by governments and engineering consultancies worldwide, and being adopted by professional design offices and academic researchers. Either in slums, suburbs, or skyscrapers,

20.19 Estuarine Urbanism: the oyster cultivation region of Marennes-Oléron, located off the eastern coast of the Atlantic, in between the estuaries of La Charente and La Seudre River, whose yield accounts for almost 45% of the entire French oyster industry
Data source: ©2011 GeoEye, ©2011 IGN-France, ©2011 TeleAtlas

paradigms are changing: dispersal substitutes density, pace instead of space, sequence over speed, design instead of technology, concurrency over control, culture instead of growth. In short, ecology is urbanism's best insurance policy; landscape is infrastructure's most flexible strategy. For if we don't pay attention to the effects of global change and engage urban networks as constructed ecologies, it is not "we" who will design the future flows of urbanization, but rather "they" who will be designing us.

NOTES

1   In "The renewal of landscape" (1931), urban theorist and critic Lewis Mumford recognized early on the foundation role of landscape in the shape of urban economies: "Now there are three main ways of modifying and humanizing the visible landscape. One of them is by agriculture and horticulture; it involves the orderly arrangement of the ploughed field, and the wood lot, the meadow and the pasture, the road and the enclosure. When these functions are undertaken consciously and intelligently, as they were by the country gentlemen of England in the eighteenth century, for example, they lead to landscape design. The second method is by city development and architecture; and the third is by works of engineering—bridges, viaducts, canals,

highroads, docks, harbors, dams. These three modes intermingle, and it is impossible to neglect one without spoiling the effect of others. What is a beautiful city with bad drains, or a fine concrete highway in a barren landscape?" See Lewis Mumford, *The Brown Decades: A Study of the Arts of America, 1865–1895* (New York, NY: Dover Publications, 1931), pp. 60–61. More recently, the inter-related writings on landscape, infrastructure, and ecology by Alan Berger, James Corner, Richard Forman, Chris Reed, Nina-Marie Lister, Eduardo Rico, Kelly Shannon, and Charles Waldheim have provided important contributions to this *fin de siècle* discourse.

2   For more information on this crisis, see *America in Ruins: The Decaying Infrastructure* (Durham: Duke Press Paperbacks, 1983) by Pat Choate and Susan Walter, and *Report Card for America's Infrastructure* (2009) by the American Society of Civil Engineers, www.infrastructurereportcard.org.

3   The capital stock of public US infrastructure is currently between 30 to 40 trillion dollars, an average of 100,000 USD per capita. See James Heintz, Robert Pollin, and Heidi Garrett-Peltier, "How infrastructure investments support the US economy: employment, productivity and growth" (Amherst, MA: Political Economy Research Institute, 2009).

4   On the role of failure and disaster in engineering, see Henry Petroski, *To Engineer is Human: The Role of Failure in Successful Design* (New York, NY: Vintage Books, 1992).

5   For a longer discussion, see David Harvey, "Flexible accumulation through urbanization, reflections on post-modernism in the American city" in *Post-Fordism: A Reader* edited by Ash Amin (Cambridge, MA: Blackwell, 1994), pp. 361–386.

6   According to the Organisation for Economic Co-operation and Development (OECD), US infrastructure ranks 23rd in the world. See Fareed Zakaria, "Are America's best days behind us?" *Time* (March 3, 2011): 28.

7   Looking beyond the current paradoxical condition of twentieth-century engineering, it is clear that "there is no 'end of engineering' in the sense that it is disappearing. If anything, engineering-like activities are expanding. What is disappearing is engineering as a coherent and independent profession that is defined by well-understood relationships with industrial and other social organizations, with the material world, and with guiding principles such as functionality. … Engineering emerged in a world in which its mission was the control of non-human nature and in which that mission was defined by strong institutional authorities. Now it exists in a hybrid world in which there is no longer a clear boundary between autonomous, non-human nature and human generated processes." See Rosalind Williams, *Retooling: A Historian Confronts Technological Change* (Cambridge, MA: MIT Press, 2003), p. 31.

8   The re-reading of engineering has naturally followed a concurrent course in the profession of urban planning. This contemporary view is captured by Charles Siegel in his discussion of the legacy of over-planning of the American landscape in *Unplanning: Livable Cities and Political Choices* (Berkeley, CA: Preservation Institute, 2010).

9   In his Norton Lectures (1938–39), Swiss-trained architectural historian and Harvard Professor Sigfried Giedion observed the proximity of civil engineering to the practice of urban planning dating back to the nineteenth century when "construction was ahead of architecture in expressing, often unconsciously, the true constituent forces of the period. The engineer has often been nearer to future developments than the town planner, who has too frequently been concerned exclusively with the reorganization of the body of the city itself." See *Space, Time, and Architecture: The Growth of a New Tradition* (Cambridge, MA: Harvard University Press, 1941), p. 823.

10 Maurie J. Cohen argues that the American environmental lobby, as a loosely associated group of small organizations, failed to gain any significant traction in its causes due to an overwhelming reliance on adversity and resistance to urban development. See "Ecological modernization and its discontents: The American environmental movement's resistance to an innovation-driven future" in *Futures* 38 (2006): 528–547.

11 Gary L. Strang, "Infrastructure as landscape," *Places* Vol. 10, No. 3 (summer 1996): 15.

12 In *Space, Time, Architecture* (Cambridge, MA: Harvard University Press, 1941), Giedion recognized the significance of this turning point more than a half century ago: "the world has now become aware of the impasse to which we have been led through an emphasis on purely rational thought. We have become conscious of the limits of logic and rationality. We again realize that the principles of form are based on more profound and significant elements than rigid logic. … What we have to do in the realm of architecture is to find a method of linking rationality with the organic in such a way that the organic becomes dominant and rationality is reduced to a menial position" (pp. 872–873).

13 For example, more than 30 percent of freshwater is lost in piping systems through conveyance.

14 Wayne Bachis, "Enabling urban sprawl: Revisiting the Supreme Court's seminal zoning decision Euclid v. Ambler in the 21st century," *Virginia Journal of Social Policy and the Law* Vol. 17, No. 3 (spring 2010): 373–403.

15 The 2003 blackout in the Northeast demonstrated that most major cities only carry a two- to three-day supply of perishable food. See New York City Emergency Response Task Force, "Enhancing New York City's emergency preparedness: A report to Mayor Michael R. Bloomberg" (October 2003), www.nyc.gov/html/om/pdf/em_task_force_final_10_28_03.pdf.

16 For more on the colonization effect of the engineering project as a form of "hypermodernism," see Gene Moriarty's chapter, *The Engineering Project: Its Nature, Ethics, and Promise* (University Park, PA: Pennsylvania State Press, 2008), p. 85.

17 Positivism entails a scientific belief based on rational logic and verifiable evidence, and it is closely affiliated with linear forms of Taylorist management and Fordist production. In *Beyond Engineering: How Society Shapes Technology* (New York: Oxford University Press, 1997), Robert Pool describes the limits of positivistic views inherent to

twentieth-century engineering by explaining how "non technical factors have come to exert an influence that is unprecedented in the history of technology … the past century has seen a dramatic change in Western society, with a resulting in people's attitudes towards technology. As countries have become more prosperous and more secure, their citizens have become less concerned with increasing their material well-being and more considered about such aesthetic considerations as maintaining a clean environment. … The result is that the public now exerts a much greater influence on the development of technologies—particularly those seen as risky or otherwise undesirable—than was true one hundred, or even fifty, years ago" (p. 7).

18 Designers must acknowledge the hierarchy associated with the design of urban systems, where the numbers alone provide an indication of the food chain of the disciplines and the prominence of civil engineering. For example, according to their respective associations, professional membership in 2010 included 26,700 landscape architects, 38,400 urban and regional planners, 141,000 architects, 551,000 construction managers, and 971,000 engineers (combining civil, mechanical, industrial, electrical, environmental). See the Bureau of Labor Statistics, *Occupational Outlook Handbook, 2010–11 Edition*, www.bls.gov/oco/.

19 For example, consider one of the earliest texts in the social sciences by Louis Wirth, "Urbanism as a Way of Life" in *The American Journal of Sociology*, Vol. 44, No. 1 (July 1938): 1–24.

20 The traditional reliance on landmarks and annual reviews of large public works projects as the unifying discourse of the civil engineering discipline has more recently been put into question. In *Civil Engineering Practice in the 21st Century: Knowledge and Skills in Design and Management* (Reston, VA: ASCE Press, 2001), Neil S. Grigg *et al.* provide an important direction in disciplinary discourse as they rethink the role of civil engineering in society.

21 Neil S. Grigg, *et al.*, p. 103.

22 Jean-Louis Paucelle, "From Taylorism to post-Taylorism: Simultaneously pursuing several management objectives," *Journal of Organizational Change Management* Vol. 13, No.5 (2000): 452–467.

23 The turn of the century rise of the design laboratory, a midway point between the factory and the studio, promises considerable potential in the formation of flexible project teams dedicated to specific spatial and ecological challenges. See Peter Galison and Caroline A. Jones, "Factory, laboratory, studio: Dispersing sites of production," in *The Architecture of Science* (Cambridge: MIT Press, 1999): 497–540.

24 For a comprehensive critique of the notions of density and compactness in contemporary urban design, see Rafi Segal, "Urbanism without density" in *Architectural Design AD* Vol. 78, No. 1 (January –February 2008): 6-11. Segal provides a thorough discussion of the counterproductive distinction between the urban and the non-urban, which is thoroughly assessed in favor of degrees, distributions, and gradients of urbanization.

25 For a comprehensive rethinking of growth as an economic driver of urbanization and the notion of stability, see Andrea Branzi's "Weak and diffuse modernity: The world of projects at the beginning of the 21st Century" (Milan: Skira, 2006) and Charles Waldheim's "Weak Work: Andrea Branzi's 'weak metropolis' and the projective potential of an 'ecological urbanism,'" edited by Mohsen Mostafavi with Gareth Doherty (Cambridge, MA: Harvard GSD/Lars Müller, 2010), pp. 114–121.

26 See "Dimensions in global urban expansion," in Shlomo Angel with Jason Parent, Daniel L. Civco, and Alejandro M. Blei, *The Persistent Decline in Urban Densities: Global and Historical Evidence of 'Sprawl'* (Cambridge, MA: Lincoln Institute of Land Policy, 2011).

27 A brief but concise account of engineering's early influence in North America and European antecedents can be found in John Stilgoe's *Common Landscape of America, 1580 to 1845* (New Haven, CT: Yale University Press, 1982): pp. 121–128.

28 See Todd Shallat, "The West Point connection," in *Structures in the Stream: Water Science, and the Rise of the US Army Corps of Engineers* (Austin, TX: University of Texas, 1994): pp. 79–116.

29 We may also attribute the overexertion of civil engineering techniques to concurrent innovations in steel and concrete construction after the Industrial Revolution, evolving rapidly from traditional practices of earthworks and topographic engineering.

30 For an in-depth critique of the so-called seamlessness of infrastructure, see Paul Edwards, "Infrastructure and modernity: Force, time and social organization in the history of sociotechnical systems," in *Modernity and Technology*, edited by Thomas J. Misa, Philip Brey, and Andrew Feenberg (Cambridge, MA: MIT Press, 2003), pp. 185–226.

31 See Stan Allen, "Infrastructural urbanism," in *Points + Lines: Diagrams for the City* (New York, NY: Princeton Architectural Press, 1999), pp. 46–89.

32 See Joel Kotkin, "Urban legends: Why suburbs, not dense cities, are the future," *Foreign Policy* (September/October 2010).

33 The events at the First Planning Conference in 1909, with the ensuing conflicts between social reformer Benjamin Clarke Marsh and Frederick Law Olmsted, Jr., provide an important understanding of the waning of architecture's influence and the rise of planning at the beginning of the twentieth century. See Stuart Meck and Rebecca C. Retzlaff, "A familiar ring: A retrospective on the First National Conference on City Planning (1909)," *Planning and Environmental Law* Vol. 61, No. 4 (April 2009): 3–10.

34 See Raymond Mohl's *The Rise of Urban America* (Lanham, MD: Rowman & Littlefield, 2006).

35 "Urban population now exceeds rural, more than 51 per cent live in cities and towns, the Census Announces," *New York Times*, January 14, 1921.

36 Between 1880 and 1890, almost 40 percent of the townships in the USA saw a decrease in rural population as a result of urban migration. The National Census revealed that, in 1920, half of the country's

population lived in cities and suburbs instead of rural areas. See Margo J. Anderson, *The American Census: A Social History* (New Haven, CT: Yale University Press, 1990) and Ken Ringle, "Unearthing America's urban roots; Archive releases pivotal 1920 census," *Washington Post* (March 3, 1992).

37 See Norman Johnston, *Forms of Constraint: A History of Prison Architecture* (Champaign-Urbana, IL: University of Illinois Press, 2000) and Jeremy Bentham's classic "Panopticon" (1787 Letters) in *The Panopticon Writings*, edited by Miran Bozovic (London: Verso, 1995), pp. 29–95.

38 Throughout his career, the renowned urban planner C.A. Doxiadis capitalized on the perpetuation of urbanism as a global problem. See "The universal urban crisis" in his study on Detroit and the Great Lakes Megalopolis, *Emergence and Growth of an Urban Region*, Vol.3: *A Concept for Future Development* (Detroit, MI: Detroit Edison Co., 1970), pp. 3–8.

39 John Kenneth Galbraith, *The New Industrial State* (New York: Houghton Mifflin Company, 1967), p. 388.

40 Richard T. LeGates describes well the scientific origins of city planning in *Early Urban Planning, Volume 9* (London, UK: Thoemmes Press, 1935).

41 The profession of urban planning divorced itself from the foundations of geography by retreating into the social sciences. Except for Canada, the mid-twentieth century also saw the closure of geography departments altogether across North America. The most pronounced example of this was at Harvard University where the geography department closed in the 1940s with the attendant rise of urban and regional planning departments, including those at MIT, University of North Carolina, Michigan State University, and University of Washington. See Jill Pearlman, *Inventing American Modernism: Joseph Hudnut, Walter Gropius, and the Bauhaus Legacy at Harvard* (Charlottesville, VA: University of Virginia Press, 2007).

42 Urbanism in North America is often recounted through the discipline of urban planning, which stems from the social sciences or through the discipline of urban design, rooted in architecture. In the context of North America, both of these mainstream lineages overlook the important influence that wartime planning and military engineering have had on the shape of the North American urban landscape, at the height of the USA's imperial growth and economic supremacy.

43 The growth and presence of large regulatory agencies such as the US Environmental Protection Agency and US Army Corps of Engineers are representative examples.

44 Howard W. Odum and Harry Estill Moore, "The rise and incidence of American regionalism," in *American Regionalism: A Cultural-Historical Approach to National Integration* (New York: Henry Holt & Company, 1938), p. 5.

45 In *Sprawl: A Compact History* (Chicago, IL: University of Chicago Press, 2006), Robert Bruegmann discusses at great length the inevitability of sprawl and how efforts to thwart it may be doomed.

46 See Thomas L. Friedman, *The World Is Flat: A Brief History of the Twenty-First Century* (New York: Farrar, Straus & Giroux, 2005).

47 Bruegmann, p. 220.

48 In his essay "Irony and contradiction in an age of precision," James Corner discusses the advantages and drawbacks of metrics in design, especially when flexibility and risk are involved, in *Taking Measure across the American Landscape* (New Haven, CT: Yale University Press, 1996), pp. 25–37. See also Robert Pool's discussion on control and collaboration in *Beyond Engineering: How Society Shapes Technology* (New York: Oxford, 1997), pp. 215–248.

49 Charles Siegel discusses this observation in "The failures of planning" and "The failure of growth" in his *Unplanning: Livable Cities and Political Choices* (Berkeley, CA: Preservation Institute, 2010).

50 See Todd Shallat, "Prologue: A nation builder," in *Structures in the Stream: Water, Science, and the Rise of the US Army Corps of Engineers* (Austin, TX: University of Texas, 1994), pp. 1–9.

51 This phenomenon is manifest in the rise of the Sun Belt, the Broiler Belt, Washington's Internet Alley, the Great Lakes Region, the California Delta as well as the rise of regional cultural publications such as *Garden & Gun*, *Space Coast*, or *Highway Star*.

52 The economic stimulus plan under the American Recovery and Reinvestment Act by the Obama Administration is comparable to the National Industry Recovery Act of 1933 conceived under Roosevelt after the Great Depression and the Dust Bowl Decade. See "The New New Deal" issue of *Time Magazine* Vol. 172, No. 21 (November 24, 2008).

53 The search for formal, spatial orders in design mainly stems from a lopsided understanding of modernization as a utopic state rather than as an ongoing process of transformation that incorporates non-formal logics, most often associated with a more operative view of ecology, with softer morphologies such as flow patterns, organizations, and synergies.

54 Sanford Kwinter, *Far from Equilibrium: Essays on Technology and Design Culture* (Barcelona, Spain: Actar), p. 39.

55 Rem Koolhaas, "Bigness or the problem of large," in *S,M,L,XL* (New York, NY: Monacelli Press, 1995), p. 498.

56 Rem Koolhaas, "Whatever happened to urbanism?" in *S,M,L,XL* (New York, NY: Monacelli Press, 1995), p. 969.

57 Key to this understanding is the difference between engineering and design. On one hand, engineering is premised on the notion of "closed systems," whereby all the scientific aspects that can be controlled are enlisted as part of the scope of work and where all the other variables are externalized. On the other hand, design is a form of synthesis that often revels in complexity when dealing with diffuse, indeterminate, fluctuating processes or dynamics, most often found in biophysical processes, social networks, or urban conditions.

58 The separation of surface and structure is synonymous with the separation of civil engineering from urban design (analogous to the rupture between the exterior and the interior in current architecture). Alternatively, design can disclose and reveal subsurface conditions,

namely through networks of access, vegetal systems, and degrees of permeability. Whereby land uses have formerly been laid out in plan, we can begin to design geographic territories in section across vast scales, where minute changes in profile can have significant effect over long distances.

59 Strang, "Infrastructure as landscape," p. 15.

60 Identified early on in the work of systems ecologist, Howard T. Odum. See "Energy, ecology, economics," *Ambio* Vol. 2, No. 6 (1973): 220–227.

61 In "The pattern of the metropolis" (1961), Kevin Lynch proposes that "the pattern of urban development critically affects a surprising number of problems, by reason of the spacing of buildings, the location of activities, the disposition of the lines of circulation. Some of these problems might be eliminated if only we would begin to coordinate metropolitan development so as to balance services and growth, prevent premature abandonment or inefficient use, and see that decisions do not negate one another. In such cases, the form of the urban area, whether concentrated or dispersed, becomes of relatively minor importance." See Kevin Lynch, "The pattern of the metropolis," in *Daedalus* Vol. 90, No. 1, The Future Metropolis (winter, 1961): 79–98.

62 Overemphasis on vertical form and growth through density obscured the importance of civil engineering in the construction of large-scale projects, especially during the megastructures movement of the 1960s. In *Megastructure: Urban Futures of the Recent Past* (New York, Thames & Hudson, 1976), Reyner Banham recounts: "The architectural concept of the megastructure, popular several years ago, was roughly that of a skeletal framework comprising the essential functions of the building, into which are inserted the individual, more or less temporary, installations. The advantages of the megastructure are that the individual is provided with necessary facilities and also a greater freedom of choice." Additionally, exactly ten years earlier, notable landscape geographer and theorist J.B. Jackson proposed landscape as megastructure: "The megastructure is *prior* to the individual installation and presumably, more lasting. Few of us realize that there is another kind of megastructure in terms of the whole environment; one of the oldest creations of man. This megastructure consisting of the environment organized by man can be called the public landscape. A more correct term would be the political landscape, but since we associate that word not within citizenship as we should, but with politicians and politics, the term public is more effective." See John Brinkerhoff, "The public landscape (1966)," in *Landscapes: Selected Writings* by J.B. Jackson edited by Ervin H. Zube (Amherst: The University of Massachusetts Press, 1970), p. 153.

63 Frances Cairncross, *The Death of Distance: How the Communications Revolution Will Change Our Lives* (Boston, MA: Harvard Business School Press, 1997).

64 In the past decade, Landscape Architecture departments have experienced double-digit growth rates and are enjoying considerable demand on their faculties as they incorporate and integrate urban development within ready-made, ecologically based curricula. As a result of this reorientation, the traditional, inflexible disciplines of urban design and planning are becoming more isolated and their influence is waning.

65 See James Corner, "The agency of mapping: Speculation, critique and intervention," in *Mappings* edited by Denis Cosgrove (London, UK: Reaktion Books, 1999), pp. 231–252.

66 Kenneth Frampton, "Towards a critical regionalism: Six points for an architecture of resistance," in *The Anti-Aesthetic. Essays on Postmodern Culture* edited by Hal Foster (Port Townsend, WA: Bay Press, 1983).

67 Corner, Ibid., pp. 214–215.

68 The project of landscape infrastructure is seen here as the natural and new convergence of landscape architecture, ecological planning and civil engineering.

69 For a collective account of their contributions, see Jeff Dozier and William Marsh, *Landscape: An Introduction to Physical Geography* (Reading, MA: Addison-Wesley Publishing, 1981), Carl Ortwin Sauer, *Agricultural Origins and Dispersals*, Bowman Memorial Lectures Vol. 2, Ser. 2. (New York, NY: The American Geographical Society, 1952), Liberty Hyde Bailey, *The Horticulturist's Rule-Book; A Compendium of Useful Information for Fruit Growers, Truck Gardeners, Florists, and Others* (Norwood, MA: Norwood Press, 1895).

70 Mary P. Anderson, "Groundwater modelling: The emperor has no clothes," *Ground Water* Vol. 21, No. 6 (November 1983): 669.

71 Borrowing from two historic strategies, this formulation conflates the notion of "*le plan libre*" expressed by Le Corbusier in his "Cinq points de l'Architecture moderne" in *Vers Une Architecture* (1923) where he discusses the freedom gained on the ground plane through the use of concrete construction and load-bearing walls. Second, it borrows from the free-soil movement of the mid-nineteenth century that emerged from Jeffersonian agrarian ideals that equate land and freedom through free speech, free society, and the equal division of land.

72 For example, the original efficiency that was once relied upon the use of fertilizers in the production of large, monocultural crops is now contested. The organic urbanism of Havana, or *organopónicos*, is one of its best examples. As the former communist colony in the Antilles, the island of Cuba developed a unique decentralized strategy for the cultivation of food in the absence of imported petro-chemical fertilizers and machinery necessary for intensive agriculture. Since the late 1980s, with the collapse of the Soviet bloc and a punitive US trade embargo, Cuba has undergone a major structural reorganization of its agriculture and food production system, which has privileged the resurgence of small urban and regional farms along with a series of agrarian formats across a range of scales. See Hugh Warwick, "Cuba's organic revolution," *The Ecologist* Vol. 29, No. 8 (December 1999).

73 Andrea Branzi, "The hybrid metropolis," in *Learning from Milan: Design and the Second Modernity* (Cambridge, MA: MIT Press, 1988), p. 24.

74 Drawing from the example of the Great Lakes Region in the USA and Canada, the emergence of bio-industries, waste economies, and urban

ecologies will be dominant drivers of economic growth and urban structure in the future of shrinking cities and decentralizing urban regions. See Pierre Bélanger, "Regionalisation," *JOLA—The Journal of Landscape Architecture* (fall 2010): 6–23.

75 Marcel Smets and Kelly Shannon, *The Landscape of Contemporary Infrastructure* (Rotterdam, Netherlands: NAI Publishers, 2010).

76 Shlomo Angel with Jason Parent, Daniel L. Civco, and Alejandro M. Blei, *The Persistent Decline in Urban Densities: Global and Historical Evidence of "Sprawl"* (Cambridge, MA: Lincoln Institute of Land Policy, 2010).

77 In *Ecology and the Accumulation of Capital: A Brief Environmental History of Neoliberalism* (prepared for the workshop, "Food, Energy, Environment: Crisis of the Modern World-System," Fernand Braudel Center, Binghamton University, 9–10 October), Jason W. Moore explains this conceptualization much further in his critique of the historically flawed differentiation between environmentalism and industrial society by bluntly stating a new way of thinking whereby "capitalism is an ecological regime" (p. 4). For Moore, capitalist development is best understood when seen as complementary to a specific mode of environmental transformation where there is a generative relation between accumulation and transformation.

315

Shaping the Built Environment and Infrastructure to Improve our Quality of Life

BILL VALENTINE[1]

HOK

THE WORLD NEEDS our help. It's time for planners and architects to focus our skills on improving people's lives.

Quality of life has three main components: social, sustainable, and affordable. When we reach a balance among these three elements that make up the triple bottom line, we can achieve a rich quality of life. Planners, architects, and engineers can enhance all three aspects of people's lives through careful design of the built environment and its supporting infrastructure. This is something we desperately need to do.

Let's use the USA as an example. This country has tremendous natural resources, scenic views, a terrific variety of climates—it's a fantastic geographic location on earth. The problem is that its people are ruining it. As 4 percent of the world's population, the USA consumes up to 25 percent of its resources. It consumes these resources 20 percent faster than our earth can support renewal.

Somewhere along the way, people got the misguided notion that the only way to have a good life is to consume. People of even modest incomes can buy everything they ever dreamed of in megastores. They crave more "stuff" and will do anything to get it. So people buy more, work more, and sink further into debt. In the USA, consumer entitlement is close to being a national religion. Ironically, all the world's major religions contain moral teachings against over-consumption.

The conspicuous consumption in the USA has serious environmental, financial, political, and health implications. Statistics show Americans die earlier and spend more time disabled compared with other developed countries. According to the *CIA's World Factbook*, the life expectancy of Americans is 78.24 years, ranking 49th of 224 countries. Compounding the damage is that our behavior is emulated by countries all over the world.

MOST ARCHITECTS ARE COMPLICIT

Unfortunately, most large architectural practices are not helping our culture. In fact, many are making it worse. We've created a country full of McMansions inhabited by people who believe happiness comes from a luxury SUV sitting in a four-car garage

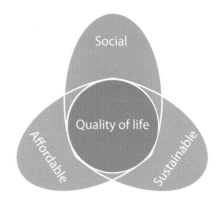

21.1 The three main components of quality of life

that has more square footage than the average American home from the 1950s.

Some architects believe that bigger is better. So they build massive, curvy buildings with expansive atriums that compromise our sense of scale and place. Enormity has developed an unfortunate but real cachet.

The Getty Center in Los Angeles is an attractive building and Richard Meier, the architect, is very talented. This giant new $1 billion marble and glass museum complex, which was built on a greenfield site, is certified as a LEED® (Leadership in Energy and Environmental Design) Silver project. Yet the Getty Center uses a huge amount of resources in a place where beleaguered elementary school teachers don't have the resources they need to teach their students. We have our priorities wrong.

In 2007 there was a design competition for the $1 billion-plus Transbay Terminal transit center and skyscraper project in downtown San Francisco. The three finalists were Richard Rogers, SOM, and Cesar Pelli, the eventual winner. Each firm designed attractive high-rises. However, I believe that none of them asked the right question related to sustainability and quality of life: "Is building a high tower in San Francisco the right thing to do? Is taller really better?"

When my architect friends visit San Francisco, they often ask about the great buildings they should see. To me it's a short list: simple but magnificent structures like the San Francisco City Hall and the Ferry Building. San Francisco is one of the world's best cities because of the wonderful neighborhoods, not the individual structures. Instead of taking over, the buildings in San Francisco fit into their environments.

It's certainly important to plan for density and wise land use. But only a small percentage of San Francisco's buildings are high-rises. The real city is low, with most buildings less than 40 feet tall. Yet it is dense enough to create vibrant neighborhoods and provide housing near public transit, employers, retail, and other amenities.

HOK actually developed the master plan for that Transbay Terminal project. As architects, we are nearly all complicit. By creating expensive buildings that scream, "Look at me!" we are encouraging people to consume more. To quote Walt Kelly's famous Pogo cartoon character, "We have met the enemy and he is us."

OPPORTUNITIES IN THE CRISIS

In these difficult economic times, environmental issues are leapfrogging to the forefront. There is a renewed need to be frugal and to use less steel, concrete, and other materials. The priorities of the economy and ecology are finally coming together.

Our government leaders are instituting more environmentally friendly policies. Large corporations like Walmart are thinking about the environment and throwing their weight behind powerful sustainability initiatives. The mainstream media is covering sustainability. We need to use this interest as a lever for making sustainability even more important in our culture.

Until the Second World War, our "waste not, want not" culture used resources intelligently and efficiently. Today, necessity is creating an environment in which we must re-embrace that philosophy. This is a time when meaningful change can happen.

Designers know better than anybody that limits inspire creativity. I believe we can help trigger significant improvements to our quality of life and help resolve this crisis by enthusiastically promoting "less" in the buildings and infrastructure we design.

BUILDING LESS

The idea of curbing our consumption does not mean we have to live dull, gray existences in ominous buildings that resemble post-Stalin Moscow housing blocks.

Designers know that the simplest ideas can be humanistic, attractive, and, most importantly, helpful. This requires achieving clarity in design, flexibility over time, and reduced reliance on building systems. In my mind, less is the elegance of simple, clear solutions that also happen to be smaller.

I urge designers to have the courage to challenge clients' program assumptions and ask the questions, "Do you really need to build this? Maybe there's another way to accommodate your needs? Or maybe the solution doesn't have to be so grandiose? We can build it smaller than you think or, better yet, we can recycle an old building."

Developing smaller buildings without all the unnecessary "statement" space is the first step toward conserving land and materials. Do hospitals need lofty atriums? Do airports need gigantic ticketing halls? Do corporate office facilities need to be monuments? Only what is truly needed should be built. If we are going to build something new, we should design it to be durable and long lasting, and use affordable local materials.

This philosophy would seemingly conflict with the need to earn as much fee as possible in order to function as a profitable design firm. But it is our obligation and, ultimately, I believe this will be good business. Designers are in the business of providing thought leadership. If we can demonstrate to a client that they don't need to build a new facility, we might take a short-term business hit. But in the long term, these clients will think of us as thought leaders and come back to us when they really do need the building. When that time comes, it will be our responsibility to show them ways to do it more efficiently while spending less. Let's deliver smaller, smarter, more inexpensive buildings that still satisfy all their program needs.

The current economic climate has created an environment in which clients cannot afford to build what they need, let alone throw money at an architect's whims. Budget consciousness can drive this idea of using less.

The idea of designing less is *the* essential concept of green design. It resonates with the goals of sustainability and LEED requirements by using less land, square footage, materials, energy, and water.

Designers should not look down on real people. Let's look up to them by creating buildings that they enjoy and are comfortable with, that fit into their neighborhoods and inspire their communities. Let's design for the greater good.

This doesn't mean stripping away the elements that make our buildings beautiful. But we can design structures in simpler, more thoughtful ways that work with, instead of against, nature, which never wastes. Janine Benyus, a principal and co-founder of the Biomimicry Guild, makes a point that in nature nothing is wasted. Every single thing—whether it's a ray of light, the dropping of a worm, a decaying leaf or a root—is useful. If we think about creating spaces that are useful in our culture as opposed to wasteful, we'll devise solutions that are completely different.

SCALING DOWN OUR INFRASTRUCTURE

At some point in the not-too-distant future, we will need to curb fossil fuel consumption. Can we power our current infrastructure with renewable energy instead of coal and without continuing to deplete our natural resources? I don't think so. We will have to use less while supporting a fast-growing world population.

Our country's infrastructure is largely designed to support the suburban, automobile-focused lifestyle, which consumes vast amounts of energy. In his book *Deep Economy*, Bill McKibben writes that we need to establish new, more localized economies that are good for people and the environment. We need to "get local" before our fossil fuel-based infrastructure implodes. With federal and state budget deficits swelling and the government having trouble maintaining the already deteriorating US infrastructure, this implosion may already be underway.

Designers will need to help fix suburbia, encourage infill, and create more human-scaled cities and towns that use less land, materials, and roads. Rather than repairing and expanding highways, we should infill the suburbs and invest in rail and other mass-transit systems.

A current global trend is the building of compact new towns focused on sustainability. The infrastructure becomes critical, with ideas about generating energy through solar, wind, and other systems: recycling, stormwater management, and waste reduction becoming as important as creating walkable, higher-density neighborhoods.

CATALYZING A CULTURAL SHIFT

Architects are already designing more energy-efficient, environmentally responsible buildings. Now we need to help scale back our infrastructure by designing buildings at scales and densities that bring together people and inspire them to live new, more local lifestyles. Scaling down our lifestyles and buying local is healthier and more economically sound—a win-win solution for everybody.

Though we can't legislate "less" in our culture, we're at a tipping point. To paraphrase Winston Churchill, we're at the end of the beginning.

The idea that architects can change culture and society through design is not new; neither is minimalism. But this is a rare time in modern history when these ideas and the "power of less" message could actually take hold in the building industry. I want designers to use our creativity and influence to catalyze a move toward less with our clients that, when our citizens see the benefits of designing this way, spreads across society and penetrates into people's hearts and minds. If we can make a difference in curbing consumption and trigger a cultural shift toward simplicity, our success could send ripples across the world.

NOTE

1   A 49-year veteran of HOK, Bill Valentine serves as a passionate advocate for sustainability while leading the design of several projects each year.

22

Why Ecological Urbanism? Why Now?

MOHSEN MOSTAFAVI

HARVARD UNIVERSITY GRADUATE SCHOOL OF DESIGN

PREAMBLE

The world's population continues to grow, resulting in a steady migration from rural to urban areas. Increased numbers of people and cities go hand in hand with a greater exploitation of the world's limited resources. Every year, more cities are feeling the devastating impacts of this situation. What are we to do? What means do we have as designers to address this challenging reality?

For decades now, reminders have come from many sources about the difficulties that face us and our environment. The Brundtland Report of 1987, scientific studies on the impact of global warming, and former US Vice President Al Gore's passionate pleas have all made their mark. But a growing concern for the environment is matched by a great deal of skepticism and resistance. The USA has not only failed to ratify the Kyoto Protocol, but it is also, along

with Canada and many of the Gulf States, among the largest per capita users of energy resources. The failure of the Copenhagen Summit to produce a legally binding agreement further confirms the scale of the challenges that lie ahead. The concept of "one planet living" can only be a distant dream—and not just for the worst offenders, but for everyone else as well.

Architects have been aware of the issues for some time, of course, but the proportion of those committed to sustainable and ecological practices has remained small. And, until recently, much of the work produced as sustainable architecture has been of poor quality. Early examples were focused mainly around the capacities of simple technologies to produce energy and recycle waste. Sustainable architecture, itself rudimentary, often also meant an alternative lifestyle of renunciation, stripped of much pleasure. This has changed, and is changing still. Sustainable-design practices

22.1 Syncrude Oil Sands Mining Operations
Source: David Dodge, The Pembina Institute

319

are entering the mainstream of the profession. In the USA, LEED® certification—the national standard for the evaluation of sustainable buildings—is being more widely applied. But there remains the problem that the moral imperative of sustainability and, by implication, of sustainable design, tends to supplant disciplinary contribution. Thus sustainable design is not always seen as representing design excellence or design innovation. This situation will continue to provoke skepticism and cause tension between those who promote disciplinary knowledge and those who push for sustainability, unless we are able to develop novel ways of design thinking that can contribute to both domains.

The second issue concerns scale. Much of the work undertaken by sustainable architects has been relatively limited in scope. LEED certification, for example, deals primarily with the architectural object, and not with the larger infrastructure of the territory of our cities and towns. Because the challenges of rapid urbanization and limited global resources have become much more pressing, there is a need to find alternative design approaches that will enable us to consider the large scale differently than we have done in the past. The urban, as the site of complex relations (economic, political, social, and cultural), requires an equally complex range of perspectives and responses that can address both current conditions and future possibilities. The aim of this book is to provide that framework—a framework that through the conjoining of ecology and urbanism can provide the knowledge, methods, and clues of what the urban can be in the years to come.

ECOLOGICAL URBANISM

Is that not an oxymoron in the same way that a hybrid SUV is an oxymoron? How can the city, with all its mechanisms of consumption—its devouring of energy, its insatiable demand for food—ever be ecological? In one sense the "project of urbanism," if we can call it such, runs counter to that of ecology, with its emphasis on the interrelationship of organisms and the environment—an emphasis that invariably excludes human intervention. And yet it is relatively easy to imagine a city that is more careful in its use of

resources than is currently the norm, more energy efficient in its daily operations—like a hybrid car. But is that enough? Is it enough for architects, landscape architects, and urbanists to simply conceive of the future of their various disciplines in terms of engineering and constructing a more energy-efficient environment? As important as the question of energy is today, the emphasis on quantity—on energy reduction—obscures its relationship with the qualitative value of things.

In other words, we need to view the fragility of the planet and its resources as an opportunity for speculative design innovations rather than as a form of technical legitimation for promoting conventional solutions. By extension, the problems confronting our cities and regions would then become opportunities to define a new approach. Imagining an urbanism that is other than the status quo requires a new sensibility—one that has the capacity to incorporate and accommodate the inherent conflictual conditions between ecology and urbanism. This is the territory of ecological urbanism.

THREE NARRATIVES

There is ample evidence all around us of the scope of the challenge we face. A while ago, a single issue of the *Guardian* newspaper in the UK by chance carried three articles that addressed fundamental questions of sustainability.[1] Such stories are now typical of what one reads on a daily basis and constitute the norm rather than an exception.

The first, by Canadian political journalist Naomi Klein, explored the connections between the invasion of Iraq and the oil boom in Alberta. "For four years now, Alberta and Iraq have been connected to each other through a kind of invisible see-saw," says Klein. "As Baghdad burns, destabilizing the entire region and sending oil prices soaring, Calgary booms." Klein's article gives a glimpse of a large territory being laid to waste in the search for oil. Alberta has "vast deposits of bitumen—black, tarlike goo that is mixed up with sand, clay, water and oil … approximately 2.5 trillion barrels of the stuff, the largest hydrocarbon deposits in the world." The processes involved in turning these tar sands into crude are both complex and costly. One method involves open-cast mining. For this, great forests have to be leveled and the topsoil removed before huge, specially designed machines dig out the bitumen and place it in the world's largest two-story dump trucks. The tar is then chemically diluted and spun around until the oil rises to the top. The waste products, the tailings, are dumped in ponds that according to Klein are larger than the region's natural lakes. A second method involves the drilling of large pipes that push steam deep underground to melt the tar before a second pipe transfers it through various stages of refining. Both of these processes are much more expensive than conventional oil drilling; they also produce three to four times the amount of greenhouse gases. Despite this, they became financially viable after the invasion of Iraq, and resulted in Canada overtaking Saudi Arabia as the leading supplier of oil to the USA. The "success" of this enterprise has led the Pembina Institute, a non-profit think tank that advances sustainable energy solutions, to warn of the threat to an area of boreal forest as large as the state of Florida. More recently the Institute, together with Ecojustice, has presented evidence documenting the damaging effects of oil-sands development on Alberta's freshwater resources. The extent of this environmental devastation, encompassing land, air, and water—all in aid of relatively cheap oil for the consumer and hefty profits for the oil companies—is a vivid reminder of the urgent need for future conurbations to discover and design alternative and efficient ways of using energy resources.

The second story involved the construction of a high-rise residence in Mumbai for one of India's richest tycoons, Mukesh Ambani, chairman of the country's largest private-sector company, the Reliance Group. The building, called Antilla after a mythical island, is equivalent in height to a 60-story tower block. Besides providing accommodation for Ambani, his mother, his wife, three children, and 600 full-time staff, it comes with its own helipad, health club, and six floors of parking. The family's proposed move from its current residence, a mere 14 stories high, has been given additional impetus by the rapid growth of the Indian economy and the simmering rivalry between Mukesh Ambani and his brother. According to Praful Bidwai, a local newspaper columnist quoted in the article, "there is growing anger about such absurd spending," as the divide between rich and poor is becoming obscene. Even

the name of this "house" suggests the idea of separation and the desire for autonomy from the rest of Mumbai. But is there such a thing as our "individual share" of the resources that our cities have to offer? What are the guidelines for evaluating the impact of a building on the city, not just in terms of its aesthetic appearance but also in relation to its ethical performance?

The third story was about the making of a film, Grow Your Own, which chronicles the progress of a group of traumatized asylum seekers as they work their inner-city allotment gardens in Liverpool. The film was inspired by the research of a psychotherapist, Margrit Ruegg, who runs a refugee support center. Her experience had shown the therapeutic as well as the physical benefits of gardening. "Many [refugees] had left such places as Somalia, Angola and the Balkans in horrific circumstances," says Carl Hunter, one of the producers of the film. "War had robbed them of their homes, their families and, in many cases, their identities. Margrit's experience was that, in the confinement of a room with a desk and a chair, the refugees clammed up. But once she'd had the idea of giving them each a little plot of land, they were able, over time, to open up to her." The story of these allotments is not simply limited to the lives of the refugees but is in turn entangled with the local community—with the tensions and conflicts between people of diverse cultural and ethnic backgrounds. In tending to their vegetables on the plots, alongside their neighbors, the participants are able, in a modest and unsentimental way, to construct a collaborative and productive ground for communication and integration.

These three stories are all facets of the multiple realities that our individual and group actions shape in the context of the contemporary urban domain. Taken together, they illuminate Gregory Bateson's argument that, in contradistinction to the Darwinian theory of natural selection, "the unit of survival is organism plus the environment."[2] A broader articulation of Bateson's ideas can be found in Félix Guattari's The Three Ecologies, a profound yet concise manifestation of a relational and holistic approach to our understanding of ecological issues. Guattari's ethico-political concept of "ecosophy" is developed in the form of three ecological "registers" (environment, social relations, and human subjectivity). Like Bateson, Guattari places emphasis on the role that humans play in relation to ecological practices. And, according to him, the appropriate

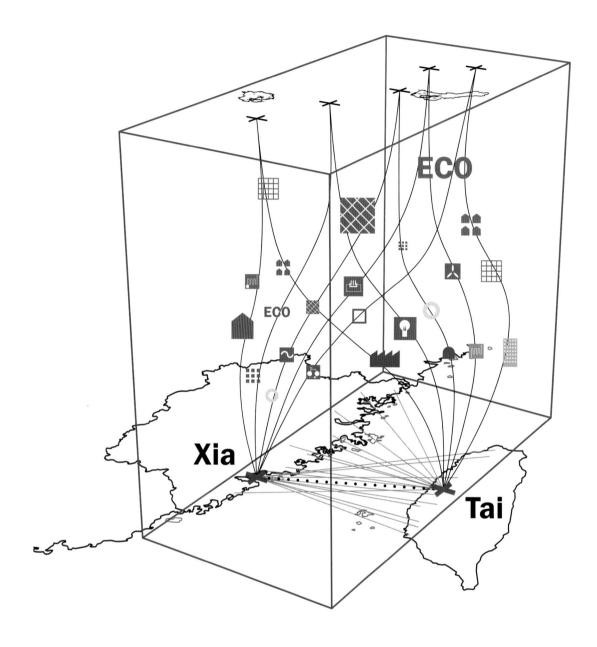

22.2 The Taiwan Strait Climate Change Incubator
Note: the TSCCI maps a complex web of economic, cultural, and
ecological connections across the Taiwan Strait and exploits these
ecologies in developing sustainable prototypes at the urban scale
Source: Raoul Bunschoten/Chora architecture and urbanism

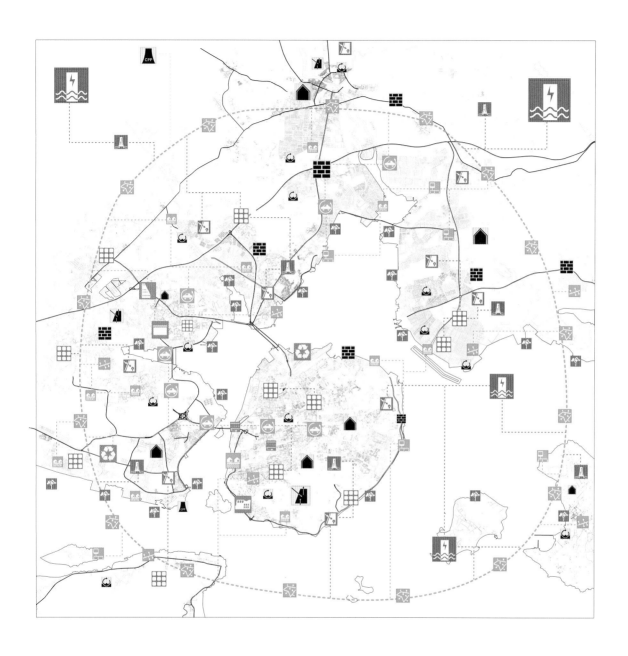

22.3 Xiamen City Energy Master Plan
Note: a series of urban prototypes are financed using the Clean
Development Mechanism, a policy under the Kyoto Protocol that
allows industrialized countries to gain emission-reduction credits for
engaging developing countries with sustainability
Source: Raoul Bunschoten/Chora architecture and urbanism

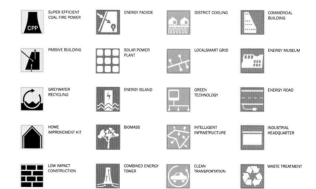

response to the ecological crisis can only be achieved on a global scale, "provided that it brings about an authentic political, social and cultural revolution, reshaping the objectives of the production of both material and immaterial assets." [3]

One of the most important aspects of Guattari's argument concerns the interrelations between individual responsibilities and group actions. An emphasis on the role of the "ecosophic problematic," as a way to shape human existence within new historical contexts, leads to a proposed reformulation of the "subject." In place of the Cartesian subject, whose being is solely defined by its thinking, Guattari has "components of subjectification" who engage with real "territories of existence," that is, with the everyday domains of their lives and actions. These alternative processes of subjectification are not rooted in science but instead embrace a new "ethico-aesthetic" paradigm as their primary source of inspiration.

Guattari's position, developed at the end of the 1980s, is as much a criticism of a depoliticized structuralism/postmodernism that "has accustomed us to a vision of the world drained of the significance of human intervention" as it is an ethical and aesthetic project that promotes the "reshaping of the objectives of the production of both material and immaterial assets." Such a radical approach, if applied to the urban domain, would result in a form of ecological design practice that does not simply take account of the fragility of the ecosystem and the limits on resources but considers such conditions the essential basis for a new form of creative imagining.

Extending Guattari's suggestion that the "ecosophic problematic" has the capacity to define a new form of human existence, we might consider the impact of the ecological paradigm not only on ourselves and our social actions in relation to the environment, but also on the very methods of thinking that we apply to the development of the disciplines that provide the frameworks for shaping those environments. Every discipline has the responsibility to constantly create its own conditions of progress—its own instabilities—and today it is valuable to recognize that we have a unique opportunity to reconsider the core of the disciplines that help us think about the phenomenon of the urban: urban planning and design.

The prevailing conventions of design practice have demonstrated a limited capacity both to respond to the scale of the ecological crisis and to adapt their established ways of thinking. In this context, ecological urbanism can be seen as a means of providing a set of sensibilities and practices that can help enhance our approaches to urban development. This is not to imply that ecological urbanism is a totally new and singular mode of design practice. Rather, it utilizes a multiplicity of old and new methods, tools, and techniques in a cross-disciplinary and collaborative approach toward urbanism developed through the lens of ecology. These practices must address the retrofitting of existing urban conditions as well as our plans for the cities of the future.

In recognizing the productive values of the relationships between reality and this project, the methods of ecological urbanism include the feedback reciprocities that Henri Lefebvre described as "transduction." [4] Take the case of the Promenade Plantée in Paris, the precursor of the High Line in New York City, where a disused railway line, part of which is on top of a viaduct, has been transformed—reused—as an urban park that traverses a variety of conditions and prospects. Given the undulating topography of the city, the promenade affords an ever-changing sectional relationship to its surroundings. As a result, the park produces a different experience of the city compared, for example, with that of a Parisian boulevard. This is achieved through the discovery and construction of stark juxtapositions and contrasts that include the experience of the city from different horizon lines.

This type of urban recycling of the remnants of the industrial city benefits from the unexpected and given context of the site that needs to be remade, a context far from a *tabula rasa*. In these examples, the site acts as a mnemonic device for the making of the new. The result is a type of relational approach between the terrain, the built, and the viewer's participatory experiences. Other examples of this type of development include the Downsview competition in Toronto, and the Forum area of the North East Coastal Park project in Barcelona, designed by Ábalos and Herreros, which combines infrastructure and public space by juxtaposing a municipal waste management complex with a new waterfront beach on the site of an artificial landfill.

A reference point for many such contemporary projects is the unbuilt competition entry for the Parc de la Villette by OMA. The architects claim that their 1982 proposal was not for a definitive

22.4 The Promenade Plantée in Paris
  Note: a disused railway line has been reused as an urban park
  (images taken before and after)
  Source: Atelier Parisien d'Urbanisme (Apur)

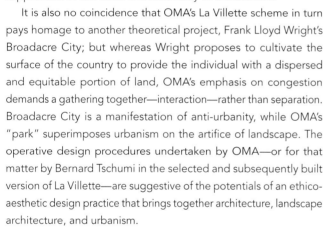

park but for a "method" that combined "programmatic instability with architectural specificity,"[5] a condition that would eventually generate a park. In essence, the design involved the conceptual and metaphorical turning on its side of the section of Manhattan's high-rise Athletic Club, with its variegated program spread horizontally rather than vertically. This process also included a rethinking of the relationship between architecture and landscape, through a suppression of the three-dimensionality of architecture.[6]

It is also no coincidence that OMA's La Villette scheme in turn pays homage to another theoretical project, Frank Lloyd Wright's Broadacre City; but whereas Wright proposes to cultivate the surface of the country to provide the individual with a dispersed and equitable portion of land, OMA's emphasis on congestion demands a gathering together—interaction—rather than separation. Broadacre City is a manifestation of anti-urbanity, while OMA's "park" superimposes urbanism on the artifice of landscape. The operative design procedures undertaken by OMA—or for that matter by Bernard Tschumi in the selected and subsequently built version of La Villette—are suggestive of the potentials of an ethico-aesthetic design practice that brings together architecture, landscape architecture, and urbanism.

Despite these examples, one could argue that the traditional divisions between architecture, landscape architecture, planning, and urban design are still necessary for the formation and accumulation of specific disciplinary knowledge. But each individual discipline is of limited value in responding to the range and diversity of contemporary urban issues. The pitfalls of acting in isolation become especially evident in the extreme conditions of the most densely populated conurbations around the globe, where it is much harder to identify disciplinary boundaries. While a collaborative mode of working among various areas of design expertise is mandatory in thinking about the contemporary and future city, the transdisciplinary approach of ecological urbanism gives designers a potentially more fertile means of addressing the challenges facing the urban environment.

Yet another key characteristic of ecological urbanism is its recognition of the scale and scope of the impact of ecology, which extends beyond the urban territory. The city, for all its importance, can no longer be thought of only as a physical artifact; instead,

22.5 Andrea Branzi's *Pineta di Architettura*—discontinuous architecture,
without perimeter and without function
Source: Andrea Branzi

we must be aware of the dynamic relationships, both visible and invisible, that exist among the various domains of a larger terrain of urban as well as rural ecologies. Distinctions between rural and urban contingencies can lead to uncertainties and contradictions—calling for unconventional solutions. This regional, holistic approach, with its consequent national and global considerations, demonstrates the multi-scalar quality of ecological urbanism. Much of the knowledge necessary for this mode of design practice can be gained from disciplines such as environmental planning and landscape ecology, with an emphasis on biodiversity. But this must be supplemented with advances from a host of other fields, from economics to history, from public health to cultural studies and (despite Guattari's warnings)

the sciences. The insights found at the interface of these disciplines will ultimately provide the most synthetic and valuable material for alternative multi-scalar design strategies.

The visionary Italian architect and urbanist Andrea Branzi has for many years espoused the advantages of a different approach toward the city—one that is not reliant on a compositional or typological approach. Rather, for Branzi it is the fluidity of the city, its capacity to be diffuse and enzymatic in character, that merits acknowledgment. In a series of projects that deliberately blur the boundaries between the disciplines (and are as much indebted to art practice as they are to agriculture and network culture), Branzi has proposed an adaptive urbanism based on their symbiotic relationship. A key feature of this type of urbanism—like the agricultural territory—is its capacity to be reversible, evolving, and provisory. These qualities are necessary in response to the changing needs of a society in a state of constant reorganization. In particular, the open areas that are no longer in use in many cities, such as New Orleans, could become productive domains where residences, workplaces, and spaces of leisure could be intertwined. Branzi's curating of the urban territory is in some sense a form of art practice, where the parallelism with agriculture is presented in a highly conscious manner that is fully aware of its aesthetic and visual qualities. It is a form of nature that resists naturalism and uses its references to the agricultural territory in an operative and temporal way.

More specifically, the blurring of boundaries—real and virtual, as well as urban and rural—implies a greater connection and complementarity between the various parts of a given territory. Conceptually akin to acupuncture, the interventions in and transformations of an area often have a significant impact beyond perceived physical limits. Thinking simultaneously at small and large scales calls for an awareness that is currently unimaginable in many existing patterns of legal, political, and economic activity. One of the major challenges of ecological urbanism is therefore to define the conditions of governance under which it could operate that would result in a more cohesive regional planning model.

The network of relations among multiple localities at different scales provides a window onto the ways in which we could reconsider the implications of developments such as sprawl. According to a recent study, "New York City has 47,500 vacant land parcels totaling more than 17,000 acres, New York City faces an acute housing shortage, and the fastest growing part of the New York area is in the Pocono Mountains of north-eastern Pennsylvania. There, far from the city core, forests are being cleared for big box stores, high-speed roadways, and low-density subdivisions for long-distance commuters."[7] What is the impact of this form of automobile-based living on the health of the community? One effect can be seen in the alarming rate of increase in the proportion of Americans who are overweight, from 24 percent in 1960, to 47 percent in 1980, to no less than 63 percent today. Surely the problem of obesity is fueled by the ongoing development of residential communities with so much emphasis on the automobile and so little encouragement of walking. Other factors include the general lack of investment in public transport in the USA compared with most European countries, where urban and regional infrastructures are seen as necessary provisions for the citizens.

These figures show the importance of density as a determining criterion of ecological urbanism. The importance of long-range planning, together with the potential benefits as well as challenges of denser, more compact cities, necessitates a much closer collaboration between the public and private sectors. Although an increasing number of private development companies, for ethical as well as financial reasons, are now espousing the values of sustainability, their concerns are often focused on the technical performance of individual buildings rather than on the larger territory. The articulation of long-range public policies defined by an ethico-aesthetic principle—on topics such as density, use, infrastructure, and biodiversity—will therefore require a greater imaginative involvement than has been the norm in the past.

Because the public sector deals with the operations and maintenance of existing cities, it bears primary responsibility for considering alternative ways of addressing these issues. Many progressive cities already have active sustainability policies and procedures for the greening of the urban environment. But most of these plans are largely pragmatic, with a focus on energy reduction or the addition of green spaces. The question is: Could such efforts be transformed by the approach of ecological urbanism? Couldn't the everyday elements, needs, and functions of the city be creatively imagined in new and unconventional ways that are not simply subjugated to the imperatives of the ecological?

British architectural historian and critic Reyner Banham, for example, argued that the form of a city matters little as long as it works. This for him was especially the case with Los Angeles, which he believed broke all the rules. Banham wrote and spoke brilliantly about the city, with the enthusiasm of a serious tourist. His *Los Angeles: The Architecture of Four Ecologies* discovers the logic and the spectacle of this horizontally expanding metropolis.[8] It is hard to imagine many other examples of urban sprawl today that match the sense of impermanence, mobility, and fantasy that LA presented in the late 1960s and early 1970s (and to some degree today). But Banham's contextualization of the evolution of Los

Angeles is itself a call for our openness to unexpected models of urban development—ones that are opportunistic in their modes of practice and use of available resources.

During the sixteenth century, the city of Rome had an ambitious plan linking the private initiative of watering the extensive gardens of the wealthy with the provision of external wall fountains for the mass of the people: water was both a necessity and a source of pleasure—as exemplified in later manifestations such as the fountains at San Carlo alle Quattro Fontane or in Piazza Navona. This is of course still the case today, but we have become more disconnected from the pleasures of water in our cities, oblivious to either its sources or its distribution. And this invisibility, this stealth quality, applies to most other resources and services as well. One can point to some contemporary parallels with the Roman example, such as the formation of pocket parks in the city of New York, or a range of major waterfront developments such as those in Baltimore, San Francisco, Monaco, Dubai, Singapore, and Sydney, but on the whole we underutilize the unexpected opportunities afforded by ecological practices as well as the location, functions, and daily operations of maintaining our cities. Our approach to the city has become more anesthetized, lacking the sense of wonder and achievement that characterized many urban projects in the past. We still cling to the inheritance of an Enlightenment philosophy that, for example, regarded cemeteries in the midst of the city as unhealthy and unhygienic, something to be banished to the outskirts at the first possible opportunity.

Given the limitations of space, perhaps it is not unreasonable that we do the same today, not just with the bodies of the dead but also with the waste of our own consumption. Who really has a sense of the mountains of garbage that are produced by most cities (unless you happen to have been in Naples during one of the frequent strikes by city workers): out of sight, out of mind. If we don't see the garbage of our culture, both literally and metaphorically, then we are not confronting the reality of what that garbage actually says about us. One can only imagine that in New York City, with its enormous appetite for fast food and takeout, the relation between consumption and waste would produce some frightening statistics. But this interrelation can also be seen as an ethico-aesthetic, cultural, and environmental project, an opportunity based on viewing the garbage as a measure of who we are, rather than as yet another difficulty, a hindrance to be overcome technically. We must find new ways not only of dealing with the problems of waste management and recycling but also of addressing garbage more forensically, for traces, clues of what we are doing to ourselves. What kind of foods are we consuming, for example, and in what manner?

We have already witnessed an increasing interest in new ways of producing food closer to and within cities. The global transportation and distribution of food is being supplemented by more local growers, whose farmers' markets create temporal events in many cities. But in some places, such as Havana, urban allotments and other forms of productive urban landscapes are being cultivated in a more large-scale and commercial manner than ever before. These developments provide the possibility of designing such terrains as the continuation of the urban territory—in part, as new forms of public space. Detroit, an example of a shrinking city, has been the site of various experiments in urban farming on the ever-expanding terrain between the remnants of its residential fabric. One can also imagine that a city like New Orleans, devastated by Hurricane Katrina and with little likelihood of major reconstruction any time soon, is ripe for such a project—for an urbanism that can address the vast areas of sparsely populated territory with productive and other forms of biologically diverse urban landscapes just as effectively as it can those areas still populated by a resilient community. These spaces also carry a potential for social interaction and healing that is presumably not dissimilar to the example of the allotment gardens in Liverpool.

Yet much more common than decreases in the urban population are examples of sharp rises, particularly in Asian cities, in line with the tripling of the world's population during the last century alone. The rate of population growth in many cities is so dramatic that conventional methods of planning are unable to respond to their rapid rates of transformation. The challenge of ecological urbanism is to find ways of effectively responding to these conditions. While in some instances, such as the *favelas* of Rio de Janeiro or the markets of Lagos, these cities can construct their own informal productive logics, they can nevertheless benefit from large-scale strategies that not only take account of the ecological impact of rapid urbanization but also provide the necessary resources and restorative actions for the well-being and recreation of the citizens.[9] These strategies have a long tradition, dating back to the early part of the last century and the work of Patrick Geddes, who argued for an ecological approach toward the planning of large cities. Similarly, ecological urbanism has the potential to respond to and transform other criteria that affect and shape cities, such as geography, orientation, weather, pollution, sound, and smell.

Just as geographical orientation often determines the prosperity of cities, so it can, together with other factors, produce a large degree of variability in the definition of ecological or urban practices. For example, in the case of African cities, according to AbdouMaliq Simone:

> while it is clear that the pursuit of structured plans, development agendas, and rational decision-making require economic supports and political will often lacking in impoverished societies, the apparent provisionality of African urban life also masks the degree to which residents capitalize on some of the most elemental facets of "cityness" itself ... whereas planning discourses center largely on defining, consolidating, and articulating a given position in relation to others, the urban game for many Africans is to become nodes of gravity that draw attention not by standing still and defending niches, but by an ability to "show up," make oneself present, no matter the circumstances, in a kind of social promiscuity.[10]

The "informality" of many African cities points to the importance and value of participatory and activist planning by citizens. This type of bottom-up, "extraterritorial" urbanism, developed outside conventional legal and regulatory frameworks, often produces novel and ingenious solutions to urban life. It invariably also produces major problems, such as poor standards of health and hygiene. Can we not incorporate the lessons learnt from the informal and provisional character of these cities into our future plans? Ecological urbanism must provide the necessary and emancipatory infrastructures for an alternative form of urbanism, one that brings together the benefits of both bottom-up and top-down approaches to urban planning.

22.6 Vegetable market, Lagos; new state infrastructure, Ordos, Inner Mongolia
Source: Charlie Koolhaas

What is a standard norm or value in parts of Africa may be unacceptable or uncommon elsewhere. The traditions, for example, of the growth of Islamic cities did not result in a singular and identifiable pattern of urban development. Rather, they were highly dependent on variable local contingencies such as climate and materials. The pitfalls of nostalgia notwithstanding, the uneven development of much of the Gulf region today, with its of conditions and circumstances connected to urban development in various parts of the world.

Gregory Bateson, writing some 40 years ago, spoke of both the need for flexibility and the difficulties in achieving it. [11] For Bateson, maintaining flexibility—of ideas, systems, and actions—was like being a tightrope-walker: to remain on the wire, you have to continually shift from one condition of instability to another, adjusting certain variables along the way (in the case of the tightrope-walker, the position of the arms and the rate of movement). But the skill of the acrobat also grows through practice and repetition—what Bateson calls the "economy of flexibility." This describes a set of practices that have survived through repeated use and come to mind spontaneously, without much introspection. And it is the dynamic interrelationship between flexibility and formed habits—habits that must be open to their own conditions of instability and change—that produces the ecology of ideas as an evolutionary process. The production of these ecologies and of ecological urbanism depends on both certain traditions of practical knowledge and the flexibility to respond to a host of networked physical and non-physical variables.

Some designers have already shown how this might work in practice. French architect Jean Renaudie, for example, developed an architecture of social housing in the 1960s and 1970s that, instead of the typical, anonymous high-rise block, was based on a dense, organic arrangement of building clusters. These buildings both in the south of Paris as well as the south of France present a radical, visionary departure from the modernist idea of "existence minimum," which over time had become debased and pedantic. Renaudie designed his buildings according to a complex geometric pattern that placed as much emphasis on the outdoor areas—the terraces and gardens between the apartments—as it did on the apartments themselves. At first, such novel care and attention to the design of low-income housing was criticized by potential inhabitants, who argued that Renaudie's design was not in keeping with the ethos of the working class. Today, of course, the buildings represent a desirable community of mixed-income residences. The buildings themselves are also one of the best examples of the use of nature in a high-rise context. Their organizational structure demonstrates the benefits of the flexibility and diversity of relations between the inside and the outside as well as their inseparability from politics.

22.7 Centre Jeanne Hachette, Ivry-sur-Seine, Paris. Jean Renaudie, c. 1975
Source: Gabriele Basilico

fetishism of the object, compares unfavorably to the principles and sensibilities of earlier traditions. The need for differentiation demands that ecological urbanism not take the form of fixed rules but promote a series of flexible principles that can be adapted to the circumstances and conditions of a particular location. Instead of the wholehearted use of an imposed, imported form of planning, non-Western nations would benefit from a more careful re-examination of the conditions, rites, and progressive social relations that are more or less specific, but not limited to their region. Today we face a situation where there is an erasure of differentiation and a surprising degree of apparent sameness

More recently, French President Nicolas Sarkozy announced a plan for the creation of a new sustainable Greater Paris, a domain that according to Sarkozy does not belong to a single party or group, but to everyone. Despite the political subtexts of his intentions, the idea of Paris as an environmentally sensitive and integrated economic region that can merge the city with its blighted suburbs and beyond is one of the most ambitious urban planning projects of recent years. To explore this agenda, a number of architects, landscape architects, and urbanists were asked to consider Paris as the sustainable city for the post-Kyoto era. Regardless of their individual merits, the projects presented by these teams, which were exhibited at l'Institut français d'architecture, provide concrete examples of what could be done. The early emphasis on projects rather than policies is a recognition of the value of projective possibilities for the physical development of the region. This type of speculative design is a necessary precondition for making radical policies that are embedded in imaginative and anticipatory forms of spatial practice.

A key feature of the overall plan is its focus on the pragmatic necessities and liberating potentials of mobility and infrastructure by proposing the creation of a 90-mile (145-kilometer) automated rail system that would circle Paris, connecting its business centers and suburbs as well as providing additional links to the heart of the city. Given the context of the riots in 2005, creating better connections between the suburbs and the city will be a step toward greater social mobility. It is in part the lack of connectivity of social housing slums that renders them as isolated "camps" whose inhabitants are "imprisoned" within a larger territory. Whether this project will be able to survive its economic and political realities (who will finance it? who will rule the new metropolis?) has yet to be seen.

The ethico-aesthetic dimension of ecological urbanism—defined through the registers of mental, social, and environmental ecology—is directly concerned with the articulation of the interface, the liminal space, between the urban and the political. Unlike some other forms of revitalization, such as the City Beautiful Movement in the past or New Urbanism today, this approach does not rely on the image, nor on social homogeneity and nostalgia, as its primary sources of inspiration, but rather recognizes the importance of the urban as the necessary site of conflictual relations. Political

22.8 Olafur Eliasson, the New York City Waterfalls (Brooklyn Piers), 2008
Source: Olafur Eliasson, the New York City Waterfalls (Brooklyn Piers), 2008, commissioned by Public Art Fund, © Olafur Eliasson, 2008. Photo: © Bernstein Associates, Photographers, courtesy of Public Art Fund

philosopher Chantal Mouffe makes a valuable distinction between "the political" and "politics." She says that by "the political, I refer to the dimension of antagonism which I take to be constitutive of human societies; while by politics, I refer to the set of practices and institutions through which an order is created, organizing human coexistence in the context of confliction provided by the political." Consequently, it is only when we recognize the political in relation to its agonistic dimension—the potential benefits of certain forms of conflict—that we can begin to address the central question for democratic politics.[12]

This also implies that we have to pay greater attention to the role of the urban as the provider of spaces of difference and disagreement. Disagreement, though, is not about arguing, but what is being argued—the presence or absence of a common object or idea between the participants. According to this point of view, it is rather naïve, overly optimistic, and ultimately confining to expect a society of total consensus and agreement. The satisfactions of urban life are in part the pleasures of participation in the diversity of the spaces of the other. And it is physical space that provides the necessary infrastructure for alternative and democratic forms of social interaction. As Mouffe insists, "Instead of trying to design institutions which, through supposedly impartial procedures, would reconcile all interests and values, the aim of all who are interested in defending and radicalizing democracy should be to contribute to the creation of vibrant, agonistic public spaces where different hegemonic political projects could be confronted." [13]

Similarly, the intention behind engaging new subjectivities and collectives through the frameworks of ecological urbanism is to engender greater opportunities for social and spatial democracy. While recognizing the significance of agonistic pluralism, the urban will also need to go beyond the purely political by acknowledging the ethical and the just. For Slavoj Žižek, "In this precise sense, ethics is a *supplement* of the political: there is no political 'taking sides' without minimal reference to some ethical normativity which transcends the sphere of the purely Political." [14] Still others have warned us about the consequences of undue emphasis on the ethical over law and politics. Jacques Rancière has argued this in the case of Guantanamo—another example of a contemporary camp—as "the paradoxical constitution of an individual's absolute right whose rights have, in fact, been absolutely negated." [15]

Guattari's conception of an ethics of the ecological is an inherently political project with a commitment to countering the global dominance of capitalism. The recent financial crisis, with all its ramifications, suggests the ongoing need for a methodological reconceptualization of our contemporary cosmopolitan condition. [16] In this context, it is now up to us to develop the aesthetic means— the projects—that propose alternative, inspiring, and ductile sensibilities for our ethico-political interactions with the environment.[17] These projects will also provide the stage for the messiness, the unpredictability, and the instability of the urban, and, in turn, for more just as well as more pleasurable futures. This is both the challenge and the promise of ecological urbanism.

NOTES

A version of this text originally appeared as the introduction to *Ecological Urbanism*, M. Mostafavi with G. Doherty (eds) (Cambridge, Mass.): Harvard University Graduate School of Design (Baden, Switzerland): Lars Müller Publishers, 2010.

1 *The Guardian*, June 1, 2007.

2 G. Bateson, *Steps to an Ecology of Mind* (New York: Ballantine, 1972; reprint Chicago: University of Chicago Press, 2000), p. 491. Bateson goes on to say, "Formerly we thought of a hierarchy of taxa—individual, family line, subspecies, species, etc.—as units of survival. We now see a different hierarchy of units—gene-in-organism, organism-in-environment, ecosystem, etc. Ecology, in the widest sense, turns out to be the study of the interaction and survival of ideas and programs (i.e. differences, complexes of differences, etc.) in circuits."

3 F. Guattari, *The Three Ecologies* (London and New Brunswick, NJ: Athlone Press, 2000), p. 28.

4 H. Lefebvre, *Writings on Cities*, "Transduction elaborates and constructs a theoretical object, a possible object from information related to reality and a problematic posed by this reality. Transduction assumes an incessant feedback between the conceptual framework used and empirical observations. Its theory (methodology) gives shape to certain spontaneous mental operations of the planner, the architect, the sociologist, the politician and the philosopher. It introduces rigor in invention and knowledge in utopia."

5 www.oma.eu/, Parc de la Villette, Paris, France, 1982.

6 Ibid. Furthermore, the competition "seemed to offer the ingredients for a complete investigation of the potential for a European Culture of Congestion. Here was the par excellence metropolitan condition of Europe: a terrain vague between the historical city—itself raped by the greedy needs of the 20th century—and the plankton of the banlieue ... what La Villette finally suggested was the pure exploitation of the metropolitan condition: density without architecture, a culture of 'invisible' congestion."

7 H. Frumpkin, Frank L., Jackson R., *Urban Sprawl and Public Health: Designing, Planning, and Building for Healthy Communities* (Washington, DC: Island Press, 2004), p. xi.

8 R. Banham, *Los Angeles: The Architecture of Four Ecologies*, 2nd edn (Berkeley: University of California Press, 2009; originally published in 1971).

9 The concept of "informality" is not limited to the cities of the developing world but is also at the heart of most industrial nations. This condition is often rendered more explicit through the impacts of urban migration. Film-makers the Dardenne brothers have recently dealt with this topic in *Lorna's Silence*, a film shot in the grim and gritty context of the Belgian city of Liège.

10 A. Simone, "The last shall be first: African urbanities and the larger urban world." In A. Huyssen, ed., *Other Cities, Other Worlds: Urban Imaginaries in a Globalizing Age* (Durham and London: Duke University Press, 2008), pp. 104–106.

11 Bateson, *Steps to an Ecology of Mind*, p. 505.

12 C. Mouffe, "Agonistic public spaces, democratic politics, and the dynamic of passions." In: J. Backstein, D. Birnbaum, S.O. Wallenstein, eds, *Thinking Worlds: The Moscow Conference on Philosophy, Politics, and Art* (Berlin and Moscow: Sternberg Press and Interros Publishing, 2008), pp. 95–96.

13 Mouffe, "Agonistic public spaces," p. 104. In this context, it is interesting to consider the work of the contemporary artist/designer Krzysztof Wodiczko, who through a series of interactive instruments and urban projections has given voice to the other.

14 S. Žižek, *The Indivisible Remainder: An Essay on Schelling and Related Matters* (London and New York: Verso, 1996), p. 213.

15 J. Rancière, "Guantanamo, justice, and Bushspeak: Prisoners of the infinite," *CounterPunch*, April 30, 2002.

16 In contrast to multiculturalism that is a form of "plural monoculturalism," cosmopolitanism "makes the inclusion of others a reality and/or its maxim." See U. Beck, *World at Risk* (Cambridge: Polity Press, 2007), p. 56.

17 According to Jacques Rancière, in its broadest sense aesthetics "refers to the distribution of the sensible that determines a mode of articulation between forms of action, production, perception, and thought. This general definition extends aesthetics beyond the strict realm of art to include the conceptual coordinates and modes of visibility operative in the political domain." *The Politics of Aesthetics*, p. 82.

Contributors

Gregory H. Albjerg is HNTB's national director of airspace planning. He is a registered professional engineer and an active licensed pilot with instrument rating. He also has three years' experience as an air traffic controller with the FAA. Greg has been directly involved in a wide variety of airport engineering, planning, and environmental projects ranging from small general aviation airports to major air carrier airports. He is recognized industry-wide for his airspace and air traffic expertise. Greg combines his strong understanding of airfield planning, design, and operational aspects into plans that get designed and built.

Jill Allen recently earned her Master in Urban Planning, with concentrations in Urban Design and Ecological Planning, from the Harvard Graduate School of Design (2010). She also holds a BA in Architecture (2008) and a BA in Economics (2008) from Clemson University. She has been involved with the Zofnass Program since 2009, when she joined the program as a research assistant. She is interested in applying landscape ecology principles to design and planning decisions at multiple spatial scales—from neighborhoods to cities to urban regions.

Annissa Alusi is an undergraduate at Harvard College, concentrating in Environmental Sciences and Engineering. She is currently a research assistant for Professors Amy Edmondson and Robert Eccles at Harvard Business School, focusing on the development of eco-cities. Annissa is interested in business and technology, particularly as related to sustainable urbanization and alternative energy sources.

Julie Bartels Smith is an Accredited Business Communicator and President of JBSmith Communications. The firm specializes in strategic communications planning and writing for local and international clients in the fields of engineering, healthcare, financial services, human resources, insurance, and retail operations. Julie holds a degree in journalism from the University of Missouri—Columbia. She has received numerous local and national awards, including the 2003 Arthur E. Lowell Award for Excellence in Organizational Communications and the 2010 Entrepreneur of the Year Award from the local chapter of the International Association of Business Communicators.

Pierre Bélanger is Associate Professor and Landscape Architect at the Harvard University Graduate School of Design. His public work and research focus on the convergence of urbanism, landscape, and ecology in the interrelated fields of planning, design, and engineering. Pierre is editor of the *Landscape Infrastructures* DVD (Canadian National Research Council, 2009) and his most recent publications include *Regionalization* (JOLA, 2010), *Redefining Infrastructure* (Ecological Urbanism, 2010), and *Landscape as Infrastructure* (Landscape Journal, 2009). Pierre is a government-appointed member of the Ontario Food Terminal Board and recipient of the Professional Prix de Rome awarded by the Canada Council for the Arts.

Christopher Benosky joined the AECOM Design + Planning New York City office two years ago as the firm's Regional Director of Environmental and Ecological Planning Services. Christopher has over 24 years of experience in the fields of wetland and stream restoration design and construction, hydrologic and hydraulic analyses, stormwater management system design, Low-Impact Development, Water-Sensitive Urban Design, dam engineering, geotechnical engineering, construction cost estimation, and construction management. As Regional Director of AECOM's Environmental and Ecological Planning Services, he is focusing on developing the firm's water and environmental services to provide clients with more comprehensive design approaches and innovative, sustainable design solutions. Christopher earned his Bachelor's and Master's Degrees in Civil Engineering from the Ohio State University. He is currently a licensed Professional Engineer in New York, New Jersey, Pennsylvania, Connecticut, Delaware, North Carolina, and Florida. He is also a member of the American Society of Civil Engineers and he is a nationally certified Floodplain Manager.

Lidia Berger is Vice President and National Sustainable Director for the Federal Program, HDR Architecture. She has 17 years of professional experience in the nation's capital and is noted for her leadership roles in several industry organizations. Lidia is a founding member of the USGBC National Capital Region Chapter and was involved in the development of the LEED-CI rating system, serving also on the LEED-EB Core Committee. She has managed teams performing SROI studies for clients such as Johns Hopkins University and the US Army Corps of Engineers. She received her Master of Environmental Management—Leadership in Environmental Policy Degree from Duke University. Lidia is on the editorial advisory board of *Eco-Structure* magazine and is a nationally known speaker, giving SROI presentations for the USGBC Webinar Series, Practice Greenhealth, USGBC Federal Summit, EcoBuild and EcoBuild Federal, and Tradeline Conference.

Joe Bryan is Vice President for the surface freight transportation practice of Halcrow in Boston, MA, with over 25 years' experience in the field. He possesses broad practical experience in freight carrier management in multiple modes and has been a substantial contributor to the development of public and public–private freight planning in the USA. Bryan has given guidance to the US Department of Transportation on the benefits of road pricing for the trucking industry, advised a major inter-regional truck line on market expansion and network development, and provided strategic direction for a variety of public and public–private freight corridor studies. At the urban level, he has aided MPOs in large and medium size cities to understand the distribution systems, operating requirements, and future needs of goods and services movement in their regions, and to prepare responsive strategies. Bryan is an author of the original AASHTO Freight Rail Bottom Line Report, a contributor to the subsequent AASHTO Bottom Line series on logistics and multimodal freight, and a developer and instructor for the National Highway Institute's Advanced Freight Planning Course. His rail work includes co-authorship of an NCHRP guidebook on the use of rail freight solutions to relieve highway congestion, and multiple verified statements for the Surface Transportation Board in support of railroad merger applications. Bryan is Chairman of the Committee on Urban Freight Transportation at the Transportation Research Board, National Academy of Sciences. He holds an MBA from the Tuck School at Dartmouth College, and a BA from Princeton University.

Margaret Cederoth is an urban planner at Parsons Brinckerhoff with over a decade of experience working in the areas of transportation and sustainability planning, land use, and international planning.

She has developed sustainability strategies and policies for major infrastructure projects, as well as the first planned carbon-neutral city in the UAE, Masdar. She has a Masters of Urban and Regional Planning from the University of Illinois, Urbana—Champaign.

Brian R. Cox is Senior Public Relations Manager for HNTB Corporation, providing strategic communications counsel to the aviation market sector and Department of Transportation market sector. A graduate of the University of Kansas, he has more than 20 years' experience in marketing and communications, with additional time spent in safety management and law enforcement. Brian specializes in external communications and twice has been recognized nationally for his public relations expertise by the Public Relations Society of America.

Robert G. Eccles is Professor of Management Practice at the Harvard Business School. His research interests are sustainable urbanization, integrated reporting, and professional service firms. Recent publications include *One Report: Integrated Reporting for a Sustainable Strategy* (with Michael P. Krzus) (John Wiley & Sons, 2010) and "Integrated Reporting in the Cloud" (with Kyle Armbrester) for *IESE Insight* (2011; 8: 13–20). He is a member of the board of directors of Living PlanIT. Robert received his AM and PhD in Sociology from Harvard University and an SB in Mathematics and SB in Humanities and Social Science from the Massachusetts Institute of Technology.

Amy C. Edmondson is the Novartis Professor of Leadership and Management at Harvard Business School. Her research examines leadership, learning, and innovation in industries where multidisciplinary collaboration is essential. Before her academic career, Amy was Chief Engineer for Buckminster Fuller and is the author of *A Fuller Explanation: The Synergetic Geometry of R. Buckminster Fuller* (Birkhäuser Boston, 1987). She received her PhD in Organizational Behavior, AM in Psychology, and AB in Engineering and Design from Harvard University

Michael D. Feldman has been involved in airport development and management for 30 years. A consistent focus during Michael's career has been on impact reduction and mitigation of large industrial-scale facilities. He returned to Los Angeles World Airports in July 2009 to assume the position of Deputy Executive Director over Facilities Management. In this position, he is responsible for the activities of the Facilities Planning, Facilities Engineering, Environmental Services, Inspection Services, and Construction and Maintenance divisions.

Richard T.T. Forman is the PAES Professor of Landscape Ecology at Harvard University, where he teaches ecological courses in the Graduate School of Design and in Harvard College. His primary scholarly interest is linking science with spatial pattern to interweave nature and people on the land. Often considered to be a "father" of landscape ecology and also of road ecology, he helps catalyze the emergence of urban-region ecology and planning. Other research interests include changing land mosaics, conservation and land use planning, built-and-greenspace urban forms, and the patch–corridor–matrix model. He formerly taught at Rutgers University and the University of Wisconsin, and received the Lindback Foundation Award for Excellence in Teaching. He has served as president or vice president of three professional societies, and has received awards and honors in France, Colombia, the UK, Italy, China, the Czech Republic, Australia, and the USA. Richard has authored numerous articles, and his books include *Landscape Ecology* (1986), the award-winning *Land Mosaics* (1995), *Landscape Ecology Principles in Landscape Architecture and Land-Use Planning* (1996), *Road Ecology* (2003), *Mosaico territorial para la region metropolitana de Barcelona* (2004), and *Urban Regions: Ecology and Planning beyond the City* (2008). He received a Haverford College BS, University of Pennsylvania PhD, honorary Doctor of Humane Letters from Miami University, and honorary Doctor of Science from Florida International University.

Andreas Georgoulias is a Lecturer in Architecture at the Harvard Graduate School of Design, and a founding member and core group researcher at the Zofnass Program for Sustainable Infrastructure. Andreas is a registered architect and has worked in design with Obermeyer, in construction management with Hochtief and GSA, and in project financing with UniCredit transportation and public–private partnerships group. His research focuses on multidisciplinary

collaborative design, innovation, and delivery of large-scale sustainable developments and infrastructures. Georgoulias holds a professional degree in Architecture Engineering from the National Technical University of Athens, a Master in Design Studies, and a Doctor of Design from the Harvard Graduate School of Design.

James S. Grant has over 27 years' experience and currently serves as Director for the Energy and Fueling Services Group in HNTB's Bellevue, Washington, office. He has expertise as a mechanical engineer, working primarily in the areas of central utility plants, renewable-energy systems, energy conservation, and aviation fueling systems for both commercial and industrial facilities. His responsibilities frequently encompass project management, scope definition, planning, design, scheduling, and supervision of a design group and maintaining client relationships. His expertise in sustainability has earned him leadership roles on green projects at many of the country's leading airports. At his home airport of Seattle–Tacoma International, he was responsible for a $100 million mechanical infrastructure program. While working with the Clark County Department of Aviation in Las Vegas, Nevada, Grant prepared an energy alternatives evaluation in support of the proposed new Ivanpah Valley Airport. For the Santa Barbara Airport, he successfully completed a greenhouse gas inventory and carbon footprint reduction plan. At Los Angeles International Airport, he oversaw the replacement concept for the central terminal area central utility plant, and authored LAX's utilities master plan. As lead engineer on the Terminal 2 West Expansion at San Diego International Airport, he was responsible for the central utility plant, which included renewable energy sources and a reduction in energy costs.

Katherine Henderson is a versatile professional with expertise in sustainable planning and development, sustainability reporting, organizational development, technical writing, and environmental services. Katherine consults on a variety of strategic and technical issues, covering topical areas such as organizational sustainability planning, city and regional planning, green infrastructure, and green building. As a leading member of the Americas Sustainability Task Force, Katherine helps set goals, coordinate efforts, and implement sustainability initiatives across the division. She also serves as editor of Parsons Brinckerhoff's annual sustainability report for the Americas, published for the first time in 2009.

Erin Hyland is Halcrow's Coordinator of Sustainability Initiatives for North America. As part of her remit, she supports corporate initiatives and information exchange across business groups and markets. She also coordinates development, implementation, and reporting of key performance indicators to benchmark and monitor Halcrow's sustainability targets and operations nationally as part of the organization's Corporate Social Responsibility. She works on strategic planning, market studies, operations and process reviews, demographic and land use analyses, and economic development studies. She also has an interest in sustainability planning, specifically policy and financing mechanisms for carbon and other emissions reduction within the goods movement sector. Erin has been involved with a number of transportation greenhouse gas emissions studies for freight and passenger movement for Transport Canada and the Ministry of Transportation and Infrastructure in British Columbia, as well as the Port Strategic Business Assessment for the Port Authority of New York and New Jersey. Hyland was a co-author of *Powering Forward*, a collaborative project between Columbia University and the New York City Economic Development Corporation, published in June 2006. This study provided a comprehensive analysis of renewable energy potential for the City of New York, outlining the existing energy structure, policy limitations and opportunities, potential financing tools, and actual resource potential. Hyland has a BS in Biology from Cornell University and an MS in Urban Planning from Columbia University.

Richard John is Chief Operating Officer at the National Energy Foundation (NEF), where his work on energy and carbon management is predominantly focused on providing policy and practical implementation advice to government. Richard is also responsible for teams providing consultancy advice on carbon management, energy efficiency, and small-scale renewable-energy sources, including provision of support to the Carbon Trust Standard Company—the leading independent verification approach to carbon emissions in the UK. Prior to NEF, Richard was Head of Sustainability

at AECOM Europe. Richard has presented extensively on climate change globally.

Anthony Kane is a Research Associate at the Harvard Graduate School of Design and has been a contributor to the Zofnass Program for Sustainable Infrastructure since 2010. His work focuses primarily on sustainability in the built environment and advanced fabrication methods. He has collaborated on research projects for the GSA, EPA, Sitra (the Finnish Innovation Fund), and ASCER (the Spanish Tile Manufacturers' Association). Anthony holds a Bachelor of Architecture from Virginia Tech and a Master in Design Studies from the Harvard Graduate School of Design.

George C. Kendrick is a Senior Principal at international design firm Stantec Consulting, where he coordinates strategic planning and design for large-scale renewable-energy projects. With over 30 years' experience in industry, academia, and environmental consulting, George has coordinated environmental assessments and technical support for a wide range of development projects, including work on more than 80 wind farms, regional studies related to hydropower licensing, mine site restoration, and critical issues analysis for client renewable energy portfolios. A certified professional geologist, George holds an MS from the University of Montana and an AB in Earth Sciences from Dartmouth College.

Susannah Kerr Adler is a Vice President with Parsons Brinckerhoff (PB), leading the development of the company's vertical infrastructure practice and is responsible for staff oversight, financial performance, business generation, and client relationship management. She has direct day-to-day responsibility for the Architecture and Buildings Technical Excellence Center. Susannah also serves as PB America's Director of Sustainability Services across both company operations and project work. In this position, she leads a core team of specialists in defining, measuring, and continually improving PB's commitment to sustainability. Focus areas for the group are climate change, green design, power generation, and water. She is also active with the American Public Transportation Association's task force on sustainability.

Stephane Larocque is the Practice Group Leader for HDR's Sustainable Return on Investment (SROI) process, which emphasizes environmental and social benefits such as reduced emissions and improved health and safety. He has well over a decade of experience in applied finance and economics in both the private and public sectors, complemented with an MBA—Finance. Throughout his career he has excelled in a wide variety of disciplines, most notably: cost–benefit analysis, business case analysis, cost–risk analysis, and regulatory filings. As the lead developer for SROI, Larocque has successfully managed teams performing studies for clients throughout North America including: the US Army, Johns Hopkins University, BSNF and UP Railroads, the City of Boston, and the State of California. He is also a seasoned public presenter, presenting SROI at conferences for groups such as the Green Building Council, Practice Green Health, New Partners for Smart Growth, and the American Planning Association, as well as guest lecturing at Columbia University.

Lisa K. McDaniel is a Project Manager with SCS Engineers, based in the firm's Overland Park, Kansas, office. She has managed or directed solid waste management planning assignments throughout the USA. She received her BS in Biology from Illinois State University in 1983 and her MEn in Environmental Science from Miami University of Ohio in 1986.

Michael W. McLaughlin is a Senior Vice President with SCS Engineers, based in the firm's Reston, Virginia, office. He is a co-leader of SCS's practice in sustainability and greenhouse gas services, is a licensed professional engineer, and is an active member of the Virginia State Bar. SCS is recognized by *Engineering News Record* as the largest solid waste engineering firm in the USA. He received his BS in Civil (Environmental) Engineering from Virginia Tech in 1976, and his JD from Washington and Lee University School of Law in 1979.

Alexios Monopolis, a native of Corfu, Greece, and Baltimore, Maryland, is the Program Manager and Coach for "Harvard on the Move," a community initiative created to promote physical and psychological wellness, and also serves as Harvard's Resident Sustainability Tutor, based at Kirkland House. Alexios holds six degrees, from Dartmouth, Oxford, Harvard, and the University of California, including a PhD in Environmental Science and Management. His research examines the psychological dimensions of sustainability. Professionally, he has worked for the White House, the National Geographic Society, and as an international search and rescuer, photojournalist, and wilderness guide. Alexios, a former President of the Dartmouth Outing Club, focuses his spare time on outdoor adventure sports.

Mohsen Mostafavi, an architect and educator, is the Alexander and Victoria Wiley Professor of Design and Dean at the Harvard Graduate School of Design. He was formerly the Gale and Ira Drukier Dean of the College of Architecture, Art, and Planning at Cornell University. Previously, he was the Chairman of the Architectural Association School of Architecture in London. Mohsen serves on the steering committee of the Aga Khan Award for Architecture, the board of the Van Alen Institute, and on numerous university committees including the Harvard University Committee on the Arts, as well as the Committee on Common Spaces. He has served on the design committee of the London Development Agency (LDA), the RIBA Gold Medal, and is currently involved as a consultant on a number of international architectural and urban projects. Mohsen received a Diploma in Architecture from the AA in 1976 and undertook research on counter-reformation urban history at the Universities of Essex and Cambridge. Previously, he was Director of the Master of Architecture I Program at Harvard University's Graduate School of Design. He has also taught at the University of Pennsylvania, the University of Cambridge, and the Frankfurt Academy of Fine Arts (Städelschule). His research and design projects have been published in many journals, including *The Architectural Review*, *AAFiles*, *Arquitectura*, *Bauwelt*, *Casabella*, *Centre*, and *Daidalos*. Some of his publications include: *On Weathering: The Life of Buildings in Time* (with David Leatherbarrow) (MIT, 1993), which received the American Institute of Architects prize for writing on architectural theory; *Approximations* (AA/MIT, 2002); *Surface Architecture* (MIT, 2002), which received the CICA Bruno Zevi Book Award; *Logique Visuelle* (Idea Books, 2003); *Landscape Urbanism: A Manual for the Machinic Landscape* (AA Publications, 2004); *Structure as Space*, (AA Publications, 2006); and *Ecological Urbanism* (Lars Müller Publishers, 2010).

Gregory Norris founded and directs Sylvatica, an international Life Cycle Assessment institute that consults on Life Cycle Assessment to the UN, governments in the USA and abroad, a variety of Fortune 500 companies, industrial associations, smaller companies, and the non-profit sector. He is Visiting Professor with the Applied Sustainability Center (ASC) at the University of Arkansas, where he helps the ASC advance the availability of valid and transparent life cycle inventory data, and its application to spur innovation for sustainability. Gregory has led the development of the methods, modeling, and software to implement Life Cycle Assessment within the US Green Building Council's LEED rating system. He founded Earthster, an open-source sustainable information platform, and New Earth, a global fund for community-driven sustainable development. Gregory teaches Life Cycle Assessment and is Adjunct Lecturer at the Harvard School of Public Health. He is an editor for the *International Journal of Life Cycle Assessment* and the *Journal of Industrial Ecology*.

John Norton Jr. is MWH's North American Renewable Energy Practice Lead and an Adjunct Professor of Chemical Engineering at the University of Michigan, where he developed the graduate course "Sustainable Engineering Systems." He is also the editor of the IWA's *Journal of Water and Climate Change*. He helps lead and facilitate MWH's corporate initiatives to integrate sustainable approaches into the planning and design of infrastructure systems. He co-authored the chapter on "Sustainability and energy management" in the Water Environment Federation's (WEF) *Design of Municipal Wastewater Treatment Plants* (MOP-8), is sole author of the WEF review article on distributed/decentralized water treatment systems, and is co-author on the review article of the Water-Energy Nexus. Norton helped write the UK Water Industry Research Carbon Accounting Standards and was a technical lead on the project integrating these standards into the Thames Water utility business management system. He is also the technical and financial lead for the team delivering the Strategic Energy Study and Implementation Plan for the Metropolitan Water District of Southern California, the largest water utility in the world. Norton has authored more than 45 papers and reports focusing on the financial and technical assessment of urban water systems, alternative waste and potable water technologies, and efficiency/

benchmarking assessment. His work on water systems was cited in two reports to the United States Congress. In the past year he has been an invited speaker at over a dozen universities, including Columbia, UCLA, Rutgers, and the University of Michigan. He has been featured in a number of publications for issues such as carbon accounting within complex organizations, financing renewable-energy projects, and electrical grid stability.

Shaun O'Rourke is a Landscape and Ecological Designer at AECOM in New York City with specialization in sustainable urban land planning. His focus at AECOM is how design and ecology can be optimized to increase the overall health and productivity of a region. Shaun has worked with numerous US and international cities to develop performance-based sustainability guidelines for proposed development. Prior to joining AECOM, he worked on projects with the United States Forest Service focused on community participation and developing tools for defining and understanding ecological processes within dense urban environments. He has presented at numerous conferences and universities across the country including EcoBuild, Accelerate, Harvard University, Yale University, and SUNY ESF.

Dimitris Papanikolaou is a graduate student and researcher in the Smart Cities group at the MIT Media Lab where he guides the fleet management and sustainability directions of the Mobility on Demand project. Dimitris has worked with Prof. William J. Mitchell and is currently working with Kent Larson. His research focuses on innovative ways of using technology, policy, and design to create sustainable, distributed, and responsive infrastructure ecosystems that utilize collective intelligence through incentive mechanisms. Dimitris holds a SMArchS degree in Design and Computation from MIT, where he studied as a Fulbright Scholar, and a Professional Diploma in Architectural Engineering from the National Technical University of Athens in Greece.

Tom A. Pedersen is Senior Vice President and Director of Sustainability at CDM, where he is responsible for driving continual sustainability performance improvement in CDM projects and global operations encompassing over 4000 employees in 100 offices worldwide. He leads the development and implementation of CDM's Sustainability Management System, Sustainability Performance Report, internal Sustainability and CDM website and blog, Sustainability Representatives Team and portal, and Sustainapedia. With over 32 years of environmental consulting experience, he has provided consultation on strategy, sustainability, organizational development, business process improvement, and management system development and implementation to a wide array of clients including Royal Caribbean Cruises Ltd, Lucent Technologies, T3 Energy Services, PetroChina, Camden County Municipal Utilities Authority, Los Angeles World Airports, Harvard University, Massachusetts Institute of Technology, US Agency for International Development and currently for Lambert—St Louis International Airport and US Customs and Border Protection. Tom has served on the ISO 14001 Environmental Management System (EMS) US Technical Advisory Group (TAG) and the ISO 26000 Social Responsibility TAG. He is Vice Chair of the Water Environment Federation (WEF) Sustainability Community of Practice and Chair of the WEF EMS Committee. He received his BS from Cornell University and his MS from the Pennsylvania State University.

Spiro Pollalis is Professor of Design, Technology, and Management at the Harvard Graduate School of Design, where he teaches design and development. His current research focuses on sustainability and quality of life in large-scale projects. He has taught as a visiting professor at Uni-Stuttgart, Germany; TU-Delft, Holland; ETH-Z, Switzerland; and the UPatras, Greece, and offers joint courses with the Harvard Business School. Currently, Spiro is founder of and directs the two largest research projects at the Graduate School of Design: the Zofnass Program and the RMJM Program. The Zofnass Program develops industry guidelines for the sustainability of infrastructure and aims to initiate policy changes in the USA. The Zofnass Program engages the Harvard-wide faculty in its advisory committee and among the largest engineering firms in its industry liaison committee. The industry guidelines are developed by Harvard researchers, based on the most advanced projects of today. The RMJM Program researches the role of design in the implementation of policy in large-scale projects and the organization of the private sector to address the new mega-projects. In 1997, Spiro founded the Center

for Design Informatics (CDI) at Harvard, dedicated to the exploration of information technology in enhancing the physical space, which he directed until the completion of its mission in 2004. CDI was a major player during the period when information technology and the Internet had an emerging impact on the design, real-estate, and construction fields. Spiro is among the originators of the concept of the ubiquitous city anchored on Doxiadis's theories. He is a consultant to the General Services Administration (GSA) and an adviser to the new economic city of Incheon, Korea. Leading a team of SK Telecom, he won the design of the information technology infrastructure of the new administrative city in Korea for the Korean Land Corporation. He also leads the developer's team for planning the new economic city in the eastern province of Saudi Arabia and a new city in Pakistan. During his sabbatical in 2001–2, he advised the President's office at the Swiss Federal Institute in Zurich (ETH-Z) on the use of information technology for research and teaching. He received his first degree from the University in Athens (EMP) and his Master's Degree and PhD from MIT. His MBA in High Technology is from Northeastern University. He has an honorary Master's Degree in Architecture from Harvard.

Stephen Ramos received his doctorate from the Harvard University Graduate School of Design. His book, *Dubai Amplified: The Engineering of a Port Geography* is published with Ashgate Press. Stephen is a founding editor of the journal *New Geographies*, which focuses on contemporary issues of urbanism and architecture. He has published in various journals, including *Volume*, *Harvard Design Magazine*, and *Neutra*. His professional practice includes work with the Fundación Metrópoli in Madrid, the International Society of City and Regional Planners in The Hague, and development work in Central America.

Daniel Schodek is the Kumagai Research Professor of Architectural Technology in the Department of Architecture at the Harvard University Graduate School of Design (GSD), where he taught from 1969 until 2008. He was also Director of the Master in Design Studies Program at the GSD. His recent technical research interests lie within a broad architectural design context that emphasizes recent developments in computer-aided design and computer-aided manufacturing (CAD/CAM), design for assembly, smart materials, and automation. As reflected in his books *Structures* (now in its 5th edition, Prentice-Hall, Inc.) and *Structure in Sculpture* (MIT Press, 1993), he has also had a long involvement with the design of contemporary structures in an architectural context. He also has interests in the history of building technology, as is reflected by his book *Landmarks in American Civil Engineering* (MIT Press, 1987). A co-authored book that reflects his interest in CAD/CAM techniques in architecture *Digital Design and Manufacturing: Applications in Architecture and Design* (John Wiley & Sons) was published in 2004. Another that deals with smart materials and systems, *Smart Materials in Architecture and Design* (The Architectural Press), was also released in 2004. Daniel has published numerous articles and research reports, including several in the GSD Technology Report Series that deal with CAD/CAM applications in architecture and proceedings of symposia held at the GSD on the topic. These include: *New Technologies in Architecture: Digital Design and Manufacturing Techniques, New Technologies in Architecture II & III: Digital Design and Manufacturing Technique, Patient Transport Module: Stroke PTM Feasibility Study Report*, and *Re-Visions: Recording Architecture I.* Others are on diverse topics that include articles and encyclopedia entries on materials, housing technologies, discussions of the seismic behavior of existing housing, medical environments, and a host of other subjects. His research work has been sponsored by the Defense Advanced Research Products Agency (DARPA), the National Science Foundation (NSF), the Joint Center for Housing Studies, the Historic American Engineering Record, and other organizations. Daniel holds a PhD in Civil Engineering from MIT, and MS and BS degrees in Architectural Engineering from the University of Texas at Austin and an honorary MA from Harvard University.

Ronald C. Siecke is HNTB's Chair of Aviation Services, leading a nationwide network of dedicated aviation engineers, architects, and planners. He has 20-plus years of experience in planning, design, and management of civil engineering projects. His responsibilities have included multi-discipline technical supervision, overall project planning and team organization, subconsultant oversight, budget and schedule control. Ronald has successfully completed work on a broad range of aviation projects ranging from operational improvements to large-scale developments with complex transportation issues. He also brings extensive experience in the area of airport landside circulation systems, including the design of curbside loading areas, parking facilities, and multi-level terminal roadways.

Scott Snelling, of Parsons Brinckerhoff, has ten years' experience in the design, construction management, and inspection of bridges and tunnels, with a specialty in movable bridges. Scott has written and been interviewed on the subject of rating bridge projects for sustainability by several trade magazines, including: *Engineering News Record, Bridge Design and Engineering, Greensource, Aspire,* and *Rebuilding America's Infrastructure.* Scott is the Vice Chair of the American Society of Civil Engineers' sustainable infrastructure project rating committee.

Bill Valentine is Chairman and Design Principal of HOK, a global architectural design and services firm. A 49-year veteran of HOK, Valentine serves as a vocal advocate for sustainability with employees and clients, as well as leading the design of several projects each year. Within the design and construction industry, Bill actively promotes his definition of "good design" as a simple idea, elegantly executed and inspiring, with social significance and in harmony with the environment. Valentine's diverse, award-winning design portfolio includes the Wellmark Blue Cross/Blue Shield Corporate Headquarters Building in Des Moines, Iowa; Phoenix Automated Train Project at Phoenix International Airport; the Biogen Idec Research and Development Campus in San Diego; Natural Sciences 1 and Natural Sciences 2 at the University of California—Irvine; Nortel Campus in Ottawa, Canada; Adobe Systems Inc. World Headquarters in San Jose; Levi's Plaza in San Francisco; Microsoft Augusta Campus in Redmond, Washington; Moscone Convention Center in San Francisco; Phoenix Municipal Courthouse; and King Khaled International Airport in Riyadh, Saudi Arabia. His recent awards include being named "Corporate Real Estate Executive of the Year" by CoreNet Global's Northern California Chapter and being honored with the "Outstanding Business Executive" award by the American Public Transportation Association. Bill earned a Bachelor of Architecture Degree from North Carolina State University and a Master of Architecture Degree from the Harvard Graduate School of Design. A Fellow of the American Institute of Architects, he is a frequent speaker and author on sustainable design topics.

Susan Warner-Dooley is Vice President and National Director of Aviation Strategic, Business, and Financial Planning at HNTB. She is an experienced senior airport executive, having served on several senior management teams guiding five large-hub and one medium-hub airports, including international gateways and fortress hubs, with interface throughout all functional areas of airport management. Her expertise includes a comprehensive understanding of airport strategic positioning, finances, operations, and capital development; extensive experience in structuring and negotiating airline and commercial business arrangements while enhancing airline and tenant relations; strong proficiency in working with policymakers and stakeholders; and a passion for exploring new approaches and promoting best-management practices.

John Williams is a Senior Vice President and National Director of Sustainable Development for HDR, Inc. and a faculty member at Columbia University. Three years ago Williams set out to work with a team of HDR economists as well as two research teams from Columbia to develop a means of measuring and assigning monetary value to the attributes of "Green." The effort resulted in the creation of the Sustainable Return on Investment (SROI) framework that quantifies and provides a transparent means of articulating the direct cash as well as non-cash and external costs and benefits for a given product, project, program, or initiative across the triple bottom line. At a time when there is tremendous interest in producing "Green" results, but a lack of will until a business case can be made, SROI is a solution that has been applied on behalf of nearly $7 billion in investment decisions. The framework, which HDR introduced into the public domain during the 2009 Clinton Global Initiative annual meeting, has been well received.

Paul A. Yarossi is President of HNTB Holdings Ltd, serves on the company's board of directors, and is responsible for overseeing and directing the firm's governance, capitalization strategy, compliance, and audit functions, as well as its external and government relations. He also participates in a number of high-level roles on behalf of the

industry, which gives him a broad perspective on current issues and trends. He serves as Senior Vice Chairman of the American Road and Transportation Builders Association, the US transportation construction industry's representative in Washington, DC. Paul also has presented testimony to the US House Transportation and Infrastructure Subcommittee on Highways and Transit.

Paul Zofnass is President of the Environmental Financial Consulting Group (EFCG), a firm he founded in 1990 to provide financial, strategic, and investment banking services initially to the environmental engineering and consulting firms, and now to the overall engineering/consulting ("e/c") industry. The EFCG is headquartered in New York City, and serves as a retained adviser to many of the major global e/c firms. The EFCG has hosted for 20 years the annual Engineering/Consulting CEO Conference, which brings together the leaders of over 200 major engineering firms throughout the world. The EFCG is also the leading merger and acquisition adviser to the e/c industry. Paul is a Magna Cum Laude graduate of Harvard College, and an alumnus of both the Harvard Business School and the Harvard Law School. His wife is an attorney in New York, and both his daughters have graduated from Harvard College. In addition to funding this Infrastructure Sustainability Initiative, he is also funding the New England Forests Exhibit at the Harvard Museum of Natural History, and is responsible for creating and funding a 250-acre nature preserve near his weekend home in Pound Ridge, NY, just north of New York City, on which he has built a 10-mile hiking/nature trail known as the Westchester Wilderness Walk/Zofnass Family Preserve.

Tiona Zuzul is a doctoral candidate in the strategy department at Harvard Business School. Her research examines the goals, strategies, and business models of organizations involved in sustainable urbanization. She is particularly interested in the way that different individuals and organizations collaborate to arrive at innovative solutions in this emerging context. Previously, Zuzul worked in strategy consulting, and received her AB from Harvard College and her MSc from the London School of Economics.

Index